MEDIA, CULTURE AND SOCIETY

A Critical Reader

edited by
Richard Collins, James Curran,
Nicholas Garnham, Paddy Scannell,
Philip Schlesinger and Colin Sparks

⑤ SAGE Publications
London · Thousand Oaks · New Delhi

SAGE Publications Ltd
6 Bonhill Street
London EC2A 4PU

SAGE Publications Inc
2455 Teller Road
Newbury Park, California 91320

SAGE Publications India Pvt Ltd
32, M-Block Market
Greater Kailash – 1
New Delhi 110 048

British Library Cataloguing in Publication Data

Media, culture and society: a critical reader.
　1. Mass media—Social aspects
　I. Collins, Richard
　302.2′34　　　HM258

ISBN 0-8039-9748-5
ISBN 0-8039-9749-3 (pbk)

Library of Congress Catalog Card Number 86-060923

Phototypeset by Sunrise Setting, Torquay, Devon
Printed in Great Britain by J. W. Arrowsmith Ltd, Bristol

First printing 1986
Reprinted 1987
Reprinted 1990
Reprinted 1992
Reprinted 1993
Reprinted 1996

Contents

Introduction

The articles published in this reader represent a selection of some of the best work published in *Media, Culture and Society* between 1979, the year of its foundation, and 1985. The articles have been selected and grouped to illustrate the major intellectual themes and concerns that distinguish the approach of *Media, Culture and Society* to the analysis of the mass media from other approaches — for example, the classical tradition of empirical 'effects' studies, with which many, especially non-British, readers, may be more familiar.

We start with 'Approaches to Cultural Theory' in order to place the analysis of the mass media in the broadest possible cultural and social context. Indeed, all the chapters in this reader serve to make two fundamental points. First, the mass media are always contingent and specific historical examples of a range of institutional means by which, in any society, symbolic forms, and the meanings they create and carry, are produced, distributed and consumed. These institutions will differ from society to society and from one historical period to another with differing, but crucial, effects on social structure and action in general. Second, it follows that any analysis of the mass media must be based, if only implicitly, upon general theories as to the nature of social and cultural structures and, in particular, as to the effectiveness of symbolic forms in the maintenance or change of those structures.

The development of the social division of labour has endowed a specific social group — intellectuals or cultural producers — with the task of running these specialized institutions of cultural production and distribution. In 'Intellectuals and Cultural Production', therefore, we go on to examine the constitution and social role of this group and to analyse its relationship both to cultural consumers and to other centres of social power.

Finally, in 'British Broadcasting and the Public Sphere' we have collected articles which give, in a specific national and historical context, concrete examples of those more general theoretical positions. At first glance, this section may appear to non-British readers as of only marginal and parochial interest. It serves, however, not only as a case study for replication in other socio-cultural contexts, but also illustrates our conviction that the mass media and the cultural apparatus of which they are a part can be analysed and interpreted only *within* their concrete, historical specificity, and, second, that such an analysis can never be separated from questions and debates concerning the balance of social power and the nature and future of the polity within which that analysis takes place. Thus contemporary policy analysis is firmly and intimately linked in this work to the widest theoretical and historical concerns. In this sense, all the articles collected here are consciously part of a critical tradition.

Readers may prefer to sample some of the articles before returning to the rest of this introduction which serves to explain in more detail, particularly to readers unfamiliar with the development of British media and cultural studies, the genesis and development of the intellectual concerns outlined above. It will place this collection of articles in their specific historical and socio-cultural context and expand upon the brief introduction to each section.

Media, Culture and Society has always been international in scope and has, in particular, aimed to make available work from non-Anglo-Saxon research traditions to an English-speaking readership. None the less, its intellectual concerns and analytical approach strongly reflect the special nature of British media studies. It is important therefore to outline for readers unfamiliar with that field those distinctive characteristics which distinguish British media studies from other national traditions.

When *Media, Culture and Society* came into being, British media studies were divided broadly into two antagonistic schools: on the one hand, the 'empirical', which largely derived from the US tradition of positivist sociology; and on the other, the 'theoretical', dominated by various versions of Marxism. The 'empirical' school focused upon a narrow set of institutions and cultural practices, namely mass communication, studied in isolation from other social and cultural practices and institutions. In its general intellectual approach it remained deeply marked by that tradition which used the mass society/industrial society model. Its work emphasized 'effects' studies, which were considered in terms of the isolated short-term effects upon atomized individuals, and upon organizational studies of media institutions which were considered once again in isolation from broader socio-economic trends. This school, however, was never dominant in Britain, where in contrast to the US, media studies developed not out of sociology but out of literary studies. From the start, British media studies were concerned with the mass media as just one, historically specific, aspect of the cultural field as a whole. In the 1970s this school became dominated by various versions of Western Marxism, particularly French Marxism. It was concerned not with mass communication as such, but with the role of ideology within Western capitalist societies. It was 'theoretical' in the sense that it believed that the correct formulation of general social theories must precede and determine research at the micro-level.

When *Media, Culture and Society* was launched it refused to take sides with either of these two traditions. As we wrote in the original editorial, 'We do not propose ourselves as the apostles of sweetness and light attempting to reconcile these two positions from some intermediate stance. Nor do we favour one orthodoxy to the exclusion of the other. But we do intend to encourage research and debate within and between these two traditions . . .' However, this did not involve an uncritical stance towards the existing work of either tradition, but rather a selective reading of the strengths and weaknesses of each.

The empirical school of media studies is well established internationally and has developed a strong record of enquiry into the study of the effects of the media and the sociology of media organizations. *Media, Culture and Society* cannot claim to have made any substantial contribution to publication in the first of these areas, partly because it has been traditionally located within a model of 'mass communications' abstracted from their more general social determinants which we felt was unhelpful and partly because this research tradition is well represented elsewhere.

But the journal has published a number of empirical studies of media organizations and, more unusually, of media and cultural history. Debates over the interpretation of history have, within a wide range of periods and topics, proved to be the meeting point of theoretical reflection upon the relationship between society and media organizations and the symbolic content they transmit. Issues of social change, class structure, state formation and cultural development have all been argued in articles that have transcended the apparent separation between the theoretical and the empirical.

This general convergence found a strong reflection in two key areas of interest. The study of press history, which has a long tradition of concerning itself with the relationship between press freedom and the state machine, had, by the late 1970s, reached a point at which its concerns were focused upon the economic determinants of press publishing, the ways in which they related to state policy, and the complex interconnections between these factors and the cultural and political life of a highly class-stratified audience. At the same time, the historians of broadcasting in Britain had always been forced to confront such questions. The particular structure of British broadcasting, with the right to broadcast initially restricted to the state-funded BBC and then shared between that institution and a number of profit-oriented commercial companies, has meant that the material underpinnings of broadcasting practice have always been in the foreground of historical attention. The role, too, of the BBC as a purveyor of what is usually termed the 'national culture' has always been an object of study. Both the intentions of the founders and subsequent arguments about the structure of broadcasting have involved disputes over the definitions of cultural life, its relation to state policy and commercial profit, and its relationship to the experiences of audiences.

From the historical branch of the empirical tradition it was therefore possible to identify a cluster of concerns and concepts which the journal took up. Among the themes that have been extensively debated are the material basis of the production of media artefacts, the relationship between the media and social change, social stratification as a key element both in media consumption and in audience formation, and the role of the state in determining the structure of media systems.

The other, theoretical, current also contributed selectively to *Media, Culture and Society*, but in a very different way. The first and most obvious way in which the journal was indebted to this current was in its adoption of a critical stance towards the world's existing media systems. In Britain, the dominant view among media practitioners and the bulk of scholars within the empirical tradition has been that, while there might be room for improvement here and there, the fundamental patterns of the media and of culture are natural and inevitable, and not properly subject to any fundamental questioning.

The theoretical current, and in particular that large part of it which might be termed Marxist, placed the existing media structures and practices as contingent instances within more general social determinations. These same general considerations also helped to define the scope of the journal more widely as it concerned itself with the 'media' in the broadest possible sense. The rejection of the term 'mass communication' was a conscious one, designed to prevent an unnecessary narrowing. Our intention was to consider the mass media as aspects of cultural systems and of social life, without assuming any a priori hierarchy of importance over other forms.

But although *Media, Culture and Society* was heavily influenced by an explicitly 'Marxist' tradition, it distanced itself from what was then widely recognized as the dominant element within Marxism—that derived from the particular interpretation of Marx given by the French philosopher, Louis Althusser. His work had, it is true, been especially important in rendering the question of 'ideology' central to social thought, but the manner in which Althusser presented this issue seemed to us to conceal more than it revealed.

Marxism has always been concerned with the relationship between the production of material life and the ideas that people hold about society and their place in it. The relationship between 'base' and 'superstructure', and the way in which the former may be said to 'determine' the latter, has been a central aspect of the Marxist study of ideology and of culture in general. Indeed, it has often been supposed that this determinate relationship constituted the sum total of the Marxist theory of ideology. In the past much of the work in this field was what is usually termed 'reductivist' in that it attempted to demonstrate the exact way in which ideas were derived from material life.

The Althusserian interpretation of Marxism represented a sharp break with reductivism. Heavily influenced by that version of structuralism which derived from Saussurean linguistics, Althusserian Marxism was from the start suspicious of the reductivist notion that one set of human activities or 'practices' could be collapsed into, or even related to, another. At the same time, as a consequence of its intellectual heritage, it was concerned with analysing the internal organization of discrete practices. Clearly, the linguistics-inspired attention to inherent structure and the Marxist-inspired concern with determination form uneasy intellectual bedfellows, and Althusser proposed a number of formulations to attempt to reconcile the two. Perhaps his major achievement was to be able to convince so many people for so long that he had in fact managed the feat.

The version of the Althusserian solution which found greatest currency in Britain was that which argued that determination could only be said to operate 'in the last instance'. In effect, that meant the rejection of any rigorous notion that determination is a result of a causal connection between base and superstructure. Rather, the internal articulations of practices, and in particular ideology, were studied *within* the framework provided by other practices, especially economic life. A powerful and influential example of this current of thought was the work produced by Stuart Hall and his collaborators at the Centre for Contemporary Cultural Studies at the University of Birmingham in the 1970s.

The other major result of the influence of Althusser in Britain developed as a critique of his work. The obvious and logical criticism, as advanced by Hirst and others, was to reject the notion of any economic determination whatsoever and to concentrate all intellectual efforts upon the immanent analysis of discourses. The most important representative of this current of thought in the study of the media was the journal of film theory, *Screen*, in which the analysis of the discourse of the 'classic Hollywood text' was extensively developed.

It should be noted that Althusser had argued that the condition for the effectiveness of ideology was a particular mental structure resulting from the mechanisms of psychic formation analysed by Freud and his problematic follower Lacan. Althusserian accounts of ideology thus tend to give substantial weight to those aspects of ideological structures which can be said to reproduce mental structures, and to the development of psychoanalytic theory to account for their effectiveness. In the case of *Screen*, it could be argued that the determination of ideology by material life was replaced by the determination of ideology by mental life.

Media, Culture and Society was in large measure conceived as a counter-argument to those two ways of thinking about the problem of ideology. One unintended consequence of those developments was that in the emphasis placed on the autonomy of the cultural— that is, on the media and on textual readings of their 'ideological effect'—a central tenet of Marxist thought disappeared, namely the attempt to grasp and analyse 'the totality', the whole social formation. The journal is not tied to a Marxist perspective, but it does accept the legacy of that critical problem bequeathed by Marx as quite central to its concerns. Thus, though we do not have one favoured line on how to think about the social whole, we have, from the beginning, maintained a number of overlapping approaches which address that problem. Some are well represented in this collection, notably our insistence (in line with classic Marxism) on the importance of analysing the economic determinants of the media industry and the communications infrastructure, as reflected in the chapters by Curran and Garnham.

At the same time, we have stressed the importance of the *production* of culture. Rather than taking the cultural product (text) as a privileged object for analysis, we try to explore all those processes that produce the product with *this* particular form and content for *that* particular consumer. In this respect the work of the French sociologist, Pierre Bourdieu, is exemplary, for it examines the economic and class determinism both of the production of symbolic goods and of the differentiated taste-publics for those goods. Paul DiMaggio, drawing on Bourdieu, shares these concerns and his chapter is a good example of empirical historical enquiry into the material basis of high culture in nineteenth-century America. Bourdieu's work is dense and compressed. The introduction to his writings by Garnham and Williams expresses our desire to make available in English translation significant European work, and to interpret it adequately for Anglo-American readers. Other contributions confirm the complexity of the manifold social pressures that shape actual media production and their relations of consumption: Scannell, in an historical context, examines the political determinants of British broadcasting and Mattelart, in a global context, studies the construction of feminine identities by the culture industries. The overall range of these contributions indicates our attention to the social whole in national and international contexts.

We have also been concerned with media and communication policy, which is usually thought of in two ways: as an administrative issue concerned with rational, efficient planning, or as a public issue concerned with open debate on the social and political effects of policy. The former is the work of a technical intelligentsia that serves the apparatus of the state and private corporations; the latter is the concern of a critical intelligentsia that serves a democratic public interest. We see ourselves, and the journal, as serving the interests of the latter. This is reflected in the concerns of the last two sections of this reader, namely the role of intellectuals and the public sphere.

As Schlesinger shows, intellectuals cannot be thought of as a distinct social stratum with an identifiable set of concerns. Nor does the cultural capital at their disposal have, as Bourdieu argues, the same purchase or power as real capital. We do not want to make over-inflated claims on behalf of a critical intelligentsia (echoing the rhetoric of professional communications). Philip Elliott's chapter indeed points to the impoverishment of the public sphere and the marginalization of intellectuals by current technological, economic and political trends. Elliott's tragically early death at the age of 40 was a grievous loss for he embodies, as his contributions to this reader make plain, that concern to uphold a 'culture of critical discourse' in which intellectual criticism and rational public debate address themselves to matters of general contemporary interest.

Elliott ties the role of intellectuals to the maintenance of a critical 'public sphere'. This term, derived from the writings of Jurgen Habermas, may be considered in two ways. First, as an historical concept, it refers to opinion-publics that develop outside the state to defend the general interest and to advocate, through open discussion, progressive changes in state policy. The second use of the term is normative, and it raises two related questions: what are the necessary preconditions for an *autonomous* public sphere, and can there be such a thing as a *general* public interest? The first question throws into sharp relief the difficulties of guaranteeing conditions of public discussion which are free from management, manipulation or constraint either by external agents or by participants in the discourse. The second question asks whether interests (class or gender, say) are *necessarily* partial and sectional—and therefore against the interests of others—or whether agreement can, in principle, be reached on what might be general human interests.

Such questions are particularly relevant to broadcasting and the British media system, which are grounded in the concept of public service. They underlie the role of radio and television as a new kind of public forum, their relations to the state and to the general public, and their search for appropriate formats, styles and voices with which to address their audiences. These issues, with different emphases, are common to the contributions of Cardiff, Chaney and Scannell, and that of Elliott, Murdock and Schlesinger. Threaded through them all is a recognition of an ethos that, however contradictory, claims broadcasting as a public sphere operating in the general social interest.

Many of the contributions selected for this reader are historical. We do not think of history merely as 'the past'. An historical society is characterized by change, and the differences between 'then' and 'now' are the measure of that process. The modern media of mass communication are themselves the medium and the outcome of change. It is not a paradox, then, to claim that an historical sense enables us to recognize and respond to new social pressures as they become salient. One that we scarcely foresaw in 1979 was the remarkably rapid growth of innovations in telecommunications and information technology. These transformations are changing the very basis of what we recognize as the mass media, with profound implications for public policy at national and transnational levels. The contribution by Collins on cabling policy in the UK thus represents a growing area of concern, which will undoubtedly be a major force of future selection from *Media, Culture and Society*.

PART ONE

Approaches to cultural theory

The soil from which *Media, Culture and Society* sprang was that of British media studies in the mid-1970s, the dominant concepts and concerns of which were defined, not by sociology, but by cultural studies. Much of the work published in the journal continues to be marked by this influence, in the way it places the study of the mass media within the context of an always historically specific cultural totality and dynamic, in its interest in theories of culture and modes of cultural analysis, in its concern to analyse the relation between cultural form and material life and its broad, if critical, allegiance to a Marxist problematic.

Stuart Hall's 'Cultural Studies: Two Paradigms' reviews the major theoretical roots of that cultural studies tradition. He sees the dominant tradition as that derived from the work of Raymond Williams, Richard Hoggart and E.P. Thompson, with its stress on lived experience and concrete cultural practices. This tradition then intermingles with, and in many cases is superseded by, the structuralist tradition stemming from Levi-Strauss and, crucially, Althusser, with its stress upon ideology and signifying practices. In defining the core of cultural studies Hall rejects positions derived from Lacanian psychoanalysis because they operate with a trans-historical view of the subject and an asocial view of contradictions. He also attacks the positions derived from Foucault's discourse theory on the grounds of its radical indeterminacy.

In general, *Media, Culture and Society* has shared those rejections. But Hall also rejects classical 'political economy' as too abstract and epochal in its analysis of the commodity form to give a grip on concrete cultural formations. It was disagreement on this issue which, from the start, differentiated the work of *Media, Culture and Society* from that developed at the Centre for Contemporary Cultural Studies, of which Stuart Hall was at the time director. Nicholas Garnham's 'Contribution to a Political Economy of Mass Communication' maps out the terms of this disagreement and the grounds for a revaluation of the contribution of political economy to the study of mass communications and culture. In part, this is done in the form of a critique of the work of Williams and Hall. Garnham argues that the concrete cultural formations of capitalism can only be understood as part of the analysis of the capitalist mode of production, if only because so much of our culture is produced and consumed in the form of commodities by profit-seeking institutions. He goes on to outline some of the major analytical implications of such a view.

John Corner's 'Codes and Cultural Analysis' offers an alternative critique of work produced at the Centre for Contemporary Cultural Studies. He takes to task much of the work in cultural and media studies which has been influenced by the structuralist model of language because of the slack and obfuscatory use of the concept of code. In his words, 'many instances of its present use do not deliver what is promised and sometimes obscure what is a prime intent of any cultural research to make clear—that is, how social meaning gets made.'

Finally, Michèle Mattelart's 'Women and the Cultural Industries' links the traditions of 'political economy' and discourse analysis. In her analysis of those forms of TV and radio programming which particularly appeal to female audiences, she argues that on one level these melodramatic serials—soap operas—are the result of producing commodities for an audience already segmented by capitalism's division of labour, especially that division between work outside the home and the domestic sphere. On another level, however, she argues that the only explanation for the pleasure women derive from such programmes must lie in the context of the relationship between their form and the deep structure of group unconsciousness.

Contribution to a political economy of mass-communication

NICHOLAS GARNHAM*

Introduction

'The major modern communication systems are now so evidently key institutions in advanced capitalist societies that they require the same kind of attention, at least initially, that is given to the institutions of industrial production and distribution. Studies of the ownership and control of the capitalist press, the capitalist cinema, and capitalist and state capitalist radio and television interlock, historically and theoretically, with wider analysis of capitalist society, capitalist economy and the neo-capitalist state. Further, many of the same institutions require analysis in the context of modern imperialism and neo-colonialism, to which they are crucially relevant.

Over and above their empirical results, these analyses force theoretical revision of the formula of base and superstructure and of the definition of productive forces, in a social area in which large scale capitalist economic activity and cultural production are now inseparable. Unless this theoretical revision is made, even the best work of the radical and anti-capitalist empiricists is in the end overlaid or absorbed by the specific theoretical structures of bourgeois cultural sociology' (R. Williams, 1977: 136).

The purpose of this article is to support this call for a major revision within cultural theory, to explain why such a revision is necessary and to begin to explore some of its consequences.

The fact that Williams's own call for this theoretical revision is hidden, gnomically, in a book of literary theory, and has thus not received the attention it deserves within mass-media research, is itself symptomatic of the existing ideological resistances to such a revision, not only within 'bourgeois cultural theory', but also within what pass for Marxist alternatives. Indeed, I will go on to argue that in his effort to break with this all pervasive idealism, Williams, in formulating his own 'cultural materialism', has reacted by taking too materialist a stance.

What this article calls for, therefore, is the elaboration of a political economy of culture with a political economy of mass-communication taking its subsidiary place within that wider framework as the analysis of an important, but historically specific mode of the wider process of cultural production and reproduction. The need to elaborate such a political economy is intensely practical. It stems from actual changes in the structure of contemporary capitalism as they effect what has been dubbed 'The Culture Industry' and the relationship of that industry to the State. Symptoms

* School of Communication, Polytechnic of Central London, UK.

of the urgent political problems raised by these changes can be observed throughout the developed, capitalist world. They can be seen in a whole range of Government Reports and interventions of which, in Britain, the most obvious recent examples are the Royal Commission on the Press, the Annan Committee Report and the subsequent White Paper on Broadcasting, the Prime Minister's Working Party on the Film Industry and its proposals for a British Film Authority. They can be seen underlying the present dispute at Times Newspapers, the debate over the allocation of the fourth TV channel and the present financial problems of the BBC. Parallels to these reports, problems and debates can be found in all the member countries of OECD. At an international level, recent debates in UNESCO and the continuing diplomatic activity surrounding the concept of a New World Information Order can only be properly understood in this context. In the face of such developments most current mass-media research and theorizing is demonstrably inadequate.

Before moving on to examine some of the theoretical problems raised by this shift in research emphasis, let me give just one concrete example of the kind of information to which it gives privileged attention and why. During the last few weeks in Britain we have witnessed the failure of the Government to provide the BBC with adequate finance, a matter of great and ill-understood strategic significance in the whole development of British broadcasting and a subject that will repay substantive analysis from the perspective I am here outlining in a future edition of this journal. We have also witnessed the reactivation of the debate on TV and Violence by the publication of Dr Belson's study, a matter of undoubted importance to anyone concerned with mass-media research in Britain. Nonetheless, in my view the most significant development of the period was hidden away on the financial pages, namely the take-over of British Relay Wireless by the Electronic Rental Group, making ERG the second largest TV rental group in the UK. The significance of this take-over is that it was financed by a £10 million loan from ERG's controlling share-holder Philips Electronic. Now Philips is one of the firms involved in the audio-visual sector of the culture industry, in terms of total sales the world's third largest after General Electric and ITT and in terms of the proportion of its business related to electronic audio-visual manufacture and production it is the world leader by some way. The next phase of development of the culture industry will involve the attempt to develop and exploit the domestic entertainment market, particularly through video. Control of a rental network will be one of the keys to success in the competitive struggle for this market for two reasons: firstly, as has been true for domestic TV receivers, because the necessary hardware can only be sold in sufficient quantity on credit, but secondly, and here we have a crucial distinction between the new developments and the rental of TV receivers, because there is no internationally agreed technical standard for video recorders and players (whether of cassettes or discs) with the result that the decision on the choice of hardware limits the consumers subsequent choice of software. Now since, of all the world's major electronic companies, only Philips is already in a position to develop co-ordinated software production (through such subsidiaries as Polygram and Phonogram) control of tied rental outlets for their hardware would give them a vertically integrated international cultural monopoly of a scale and type not yet seen in this sector and with cultural consequences over the medium term (10 to 20 years) that make our petty domestic disputes over the allocation of the fourth channel pale into insignificance (see *Financial Times*, 19 December 1978).

A necessary return to fundamentals

Before returning to further concrete examples of the problems a political economy of mass-communication tries to analyse, it is necessary, precisely because of the dominance of idealism within the analysis of culture and of the mass-media, to make an unavoidable theoretical digression in order to base subsequent discussion firmly within the necessary historical materialist perspective. In asking for a shift within mass-media research towards historical materialism, one is asserting an order of priorities which is both a hierarchy of concrete historical and material determinants in the real world as well as an order of research priorities. That is to say, we are faced with the problem of understanding an actual historical process which itself concretely exhibits structurally ordered determinants within which material production is ultimately determinant, which is what makes our theory materialist, while at the same time there are a limited number of researchers with limited material resources among which I include time, who must thus choose, from within the complex totality of the historical social process, to examine those aspects of the process which are likely to lead to the clearest understanding of the dynamics of that process and through that understanding to its human control. It is this question of choice which underlies Marx's own mode of abstraction. Thus, in opposition to that post-Althusserian/ Lacanian current which has been dangerously dominant within recent British Marxist research in the area of mass-media, a current of which *Screen* is a representative example, one asserts, not that the problem of subjectivity for instance is of no interest, but that it is of less interest than that of class or capital accumulation. Moreover, one is not asserting that such a hierarchy of historical determinants of research concerns is universal, that there is A theory of mass-media, but that they correspond to the actual historically specific hierarchy of a particular social formation. Or as Marx himself put it,

my analytical method . . . does not start out from man, but from the analytically given social period.[1]

That is to say the economic is determinant under capitalism, because capitalism is a mode of social organization characterized by the domination of an abstract system of exchange relations. Further the particular relationship between the abstract and the concrete or between 'phenomenal forms' and 'real relations' or between ideas and matter, which is appropriate to historical materialism as a mode of analysis of capitalism, stems from the real relation between the abstract (exchange relations) and the concrete (individual lived experience, real labour etc.) within the social formation itself. In a social formation in which social relations were not abstracted into a relation of exchange a different theoretical relationship between the abstract and the concrete would hold.

Moreover, the abstract should not be opposed to the concrete, just as the phenomenal forms should not be opposed to the real relations. One is precisely a form of the other. That is to say, the exchange relation has a concrete material reality in the form of money, bills of exchange, credit cards, banks etc., but its mode of operation and with it the reproduction of the capitalist social formation depends upon its abstraction, the fact that it works 'behind men's backs' and thus 'can be determined with the

---

[1] See Marx, 'Notes on Adolph Wagner' in Marx (1975). Quoted in Corrigan and Singer (1978). Here Corrigan and Singer present an extended version of this methodological argument. See also Sayer (forthcoming).

precision of natural science'. It can only be determined with such precision so long as it is a supra-individual social process. This is both a methodological and historical postulate. That is to say, the necessary condition for a capitalist social formation is the existence of a more or less universal domination of social relations by the exchange relation, i.e. a market economy. Wherever such domination is challenged (and we do not and never have seen, in this sense, an 'ideal' capitalist social formation) by explicit political action, by human will and reason, the logic of capital is challenged. It is for this reason that the State is a necessarily contradictory form.

This leads us to the concept of ideology which so dominates our field of study and to the central problem within cultural theory, namely the base/superstructure relationship. The central postulate of historical materialism is that man as a biological organism must undertake a constant material exchange with nature and it is this exchange that is named labour. Within history the labour/nature relationship has become increasingly mediated through specific modes of production, thus making the links more difficult to analyse. Because of this difficulty the possibility of error and thus of ideology enters. But it remains a material fact that, ultimately, material production in this direct sense is determinate in that it is only the surplus produced by this labour that enables other forms of human activity to be pursued. Thus the superstructure remains dependent upon and determined by the base of material production in that very fundamental sense.

Clearly the greater the surplus to immediate physical reproductive needs the greater the autonomy of the superstructure and indeed the greater the possible variation and diversity within superstructural organization, always providing of course that the mode of material production is such as to guarantee the necessary surplus. In this important sense the superstructure/culture is and remains subordinate and secondary and the crucial questions are the relationship between, on the one hand, the mode of extraction and distribution of the material surplus, e.g. class relations and, on the other, the allocation of this material surplus within the superstructure, for instance, the problem of public expenditure among others. But while, historically, the superstructure has become more autonomous, there still remain direct, narrow material constraints upon individuals even within developed, industrial societies. Everyone has to eat and sleep and be maintained at a given body temperature in determinate temporal cycles. Thus, as Marx himself noted, every economy is an economy of time (Marx, 1973), which is why labour-time is so crucial an analytical concept. Cultural reproduction is still directly governed by these material determinants in the sense that the time and resources available to those who have to sell their labour power to capital, within labour-time constraints largely imposed by capital, remain limited and they still use the most significant proportion of their available time and material resources in order to ensure material, biological reproduction.

It is at this primary level both theoretically and actually that social being determines social consciousness. Thus economism, the concern for immediate physical survival and reproduction within the dominant relations of exchange is an immediate and rational response to the determinants of social being. What E. P. Thompson has recently dubbed 'lumped bourgeois intellectuals' (Thompson, 1978) too easily forget this, both because their material conditions of existence are often less immediately determinate and also because of a guilty conscience concerning the subjective relationship of exploitation in which they stand *vis-à-vis* productive material labour.

The material, the economic and the ideological

No political economy of culture can avoid discussion of the base/superstructure relationship, but in so doing it needs to avoid the twin traps of economic reductionism and of the idealist autonomization of the ideological level. The central problem with the base/superstructure metaphor as with the related culture/society dichotomy is that being a metaphor of polarity, essentially binary in form, it is unable adequately to deal with the number of distinctions that are necessary, in this instance between the material, the economic and the ideological. These should be seen not as three levels, but as analytically distinct, but coterminous moments both of concrete social practices and of concrete analysis. Furthermore, any political economy needs to hold constantly to the historicity of the specific articulations between these moments. There is a sense in which the base/superstructure metaphor always does imply a notion of expressive totality, a totality in which either the superstructure is expressive of an economic base (under capitalism of a capitalist economic base) or, on the other hand, a tautological sense of expressive totality by which all phenomena of a social formation are expressive of that social formation. That is to say, the notion of expressive totality can be used either deterministically or relationally. For me at least it is clear that the analysis in *Capital* is of the latter type. That is to say what is being analysed is not, as Mandel (1975) has stressed, a social formation in equilibrium but in disequilibrium; an uncompleted at the time Marx wrote, and still incomplete, process of capitalist development, a development which was marked not by the total domination and determinacy of capitalist economic forms, an expressive totality in that sense, but on the contrary by a series of shifting relationships between the economic and other instances each interacting with the other in a process of uneven and contradictory development, so that the totality of the social formation at any historic moment was only expressive of the actual state of those shifting interrelationships.

Thus the pertinence or meaning of any analytical category, such as base and superstructure, expressing as it does a relationship, will shift as the historical reality it is used to explain shifts. Similarly, we could say that the purpose of a political economy of culture is to elucidate what Marx and Engels meant in the German Ideology by 'control of the means of mental production', while stressing that the meaning that they gave to the term was quite clearly historical and therefore shifting and was never meant to be frozen into some simple dichotomy as it has so often been in subsequent Marxist writing. Further the political economy of mass-media is the analysis of a specific historical phase of this general development linked to historically distinct modalities of cultural production and reproduction.

In his discussion of base and superstructure in *Marxism and Literature*, Williams points out that, although, in stressing the determinacy of the base against bourgeois idealism, one version of Marxist cultural theory has been accused, both by bourgeois and Marxist critics, of 'vulgar materialism', 'the truth is that it was never materialist enough'. And he continues:

What any notion of a 'self-subsistent order' suppresses is the material character of the productive forces which produce such a version of production. Indeed it is often a way of suppressing full consciousness of the very nature of such a society. If 'production', in capitalist society, is the production of commodities for a market, then different but misleading terms are found for every other kind of production and productive force. What is most often suppressed is the direct material production of 'politics'. Yet any ruling class devotes a significant part of material production to establishing a political order. The social and political order which maintains a capitalist market, like the social and political struggle that created it, is necessarily a material production. From castles and palaces and churches to prisons and workhouses and schools; from weapons of war to a controlled press: any ruling class, in variable ways though always materially, produces a social and political order. These are never superstructural activities. They are the necessary material production within which an apparently self-subsistent mode of production can alone be carried on. The complexity of the process is especially remarkable in advanced capitalist societies, where it is wholly beside the point to isolate 'production' and 'industry' from the comparable material production of 'defence', 'law and order', 'welfare', 'entertainment' and 'public opinion'. In failing to grasp the material character of the production of a social and political order, this specialised (and bourgeois) materialism failed also, but even more conspicuously, to understand the material character of the production of a cultural order. The concept of the superstructure was then not a reduction but an evasion (Williams, 1977: 92–93).

Williams's stress here on the materiality of the cultural process is a necessary correction to both bourgeois idealism and its post-Althusserian Marxist variants. But this formulation also suffers from a misleading reductionism by failing to distinguish between the material and the economic. It is in fact a materialist rather than a historical materialist formulation. The absence of this necessary distinction is contained in the apparently insignificant but crucial phrase 'in variable ways though always materially', for it is precisely the specific articulations of these variable ways that characterize various stages of pre-capitalist and capitalist development, that characterize the shifting meaning of what Marx and Engels called 'control of the means of mental production', shifts which it is the central purpose of a political economy of mass-communication to map and analyse. Certainly a licensed press and a commercial, 'free' press are both material, but the economic differences between these two forms of 'political' control are precisely what differentiates a capitalist from a pre-capitalist form. Similarly, the difference between the economic structure of private and public education constitutes within the same materiality, the substance of 'political' struggle. While the materiality of politics, i.e. its maintenance out of the total social surplus of material production, is a general, universal phenomenon, the ways in which that surplus is extracted and distributed and the relation of that economic form to the political are historically distinct and specific, so that, at present, the matter of subsidies to political parties or to the Press becomes an object of 'political' struggle to change economic forms and by so doing to change 'political' structures.

Similarly, while Williams is correct to stress the materiality of all social practices it cannot be said, from an economic perspective, that it is wholly beside the point to isolate 'production' and 'industry' from the material production of 'defence', etc., when what is often in question when considering the relation between these various social practices is not their shared materiality, but on the contrary their significantly different economic articulation, for instance the variance between those practices carried on by private capital for profit, the publication of a newspaper for instance, and those practices carried on by the State outside direct commodity production, e.g. the BBC or the State education system. To collapse all this into a general category of 'material' production is precisely an 'evasion', both of the differing and developing economic articulations between various forms of material production and also of the amount of cultural production and reproduction that takes place within the industrial sphere as narrowly defined, in the organizations of the labour process with its industrial psychologists, its labour relations experts, its time and motion study experts, its production engineers and its personnel managers, in the structures of employer paternalism, in the organization of the market itself, etc. To take one example of such an articulation one might hypothesize that the relationship between the male predominance in newspaper readership compared with TV was not unconnected with the contrast between the culture of work as against the culture of home and has important political consequences.

This confusion between the material and the economic is common and it is worth dwelling briefly on the nature of the distinction. Insofar as historical materialism is materialist, it is based upon the postulates that Williams outlines. But insofar as it is historical, it is concerned to analyse the specific and shifting modes of this fundamental material relation, all of which are forms of that relation. In particular, it is postulated that any form of extended social relationship depends upon the extraction and distribution of material surplus and the means by which this is achieved is thus the central determining characteristic of any social formation. Such modes of social production and exchange are cultural, hence the very real problem of making a society/culture differentiation without narrowing the definition of culture to include only those elements of social interaction which involve a secondary level of abstraction, namely the representation of concrete, material relations in *symbolic* forms. Thus we must distinguish two types of form, a social form which is a series of material relations that, insofar as they operate unconsciously, can be abstractly analysed and determined with the precision of natural science, and a cultural form which, while it entails a material support, is not itself material and which has an essentially mediated relationship with the material reality it represents. Indeed, there is an essential divide between these distinct formal realms, the existence of which allows ideology to enter, because it allows denial and the lie, both of which depend upon a relationship which is not determinant. However, this autonomy is bought at the cost of a loss of real or material effectivity. Cultural forms only become effective when they are translated into social forms which do have material effectivity. Thus there is a constant dialectic at the cultural level between autonomy and effectivity and it is at the level of social effectivity that material production is ultimately determinant.

However, to return to the level of social forms, the economic is a specific historical form of the social relations of production and distribution. It is the form these relations take in a social formation within which commodity exchange is dominant. Thus, it is possible to argue that the economic is superstructural in relation to the material base or structure, that it could in fact be seen as the dominant level of the superstructure. For what Marx argues in *Capital* is that the real historical transition to capitalism involves a move from a system of social relations and domination based upon the direct physical control of landed property and people to one based upon the increasingly indirect control through commodity exchange and, in particular, through the exchange of the commodity of labour power, and that this real historical process is a real process of social abstraction which thus requires appropriate theoretical abstraction for its analysis. It is because the economic is the most abstract and fundamental form of the social relation within capitalism that it is primary both theoretically and actually, but as a historically specific representation of a predeterminate material relationship.

It is the real existence of this abstract economic level of extended commodity production that allows for the development of an increasing division of labour and thus for the development of the specific superstructural forms of capitalism. Thus the relative autonomy of the superstructure is a real and increasingly central characteristic of capitalism, but it is itself determined at the level of the economic and ultimately it is a form, at two levels of mediation, of a material relation which also remains determinant in and through the economic.

The inadequacies of existing Marxist theory

From this perspective available historical materialist theories are inadequate to deal with the real practical challenges they face largely because they offer reductionist explanations which favour either a simple economic determinism or an ideological autonomy, thus failing to analyse and explain precisely that which makes the object of analysis centrally significant, namely the relationship between the economic and the ideological. Thus we are offered the following.

(a) An unproblematic acceptance of the base/superstructure model drawn from a partial reading of the German Ideology which, unargued, simply states that the mass-media are ideological tools of ruling-class domination either through direct ownership or, as in the case of broadcasting, via ruling class control of the State. Such a position neglects both the specific effects of subordinating cultural production and reproduction to the general logic of capitalist commodity production and the specificities of the varying and shifting relationships between economic, ideological and political levels within actual concrete historical moments. Miliband in *Marxism and Politics* expresses a classic version of this theory:

Whatever else the immense output of the mass media is intended to achieve, it is *also* intended to help prevent the development of class-consciousness in the working class and to reduce as much as possible any hankering it might have for a radical alternative to capitalism. The ways in which this is attempted are endlessly different; and the degree of success achieved varies considerably from country to country and from one period to another—there are other influences at work. But the fact remains that 'the class which has the means of material production at its disposal' does have, 'control at the same time of the means of mental production': and that it does seek to use them for the weakening of opposition to the established order. Nor is the point much affected by the fact that the state in almost all capitalist countries 'owns' the radio and television—its purpose is identical (Miliband, 1977: 50).

It should be noted here that for all its philosophical sophistication the Althusserian position on ISA represents little if any advance on this position, as indeed Simon Clarke (1977) has correctly noted with respect to the Milliband/Poulantzas controversy.

(b) Secondly, and in partial reaction against this classic Marxist explanation of the role of the mass-media, we are offered an elaboration of the relative autonomy of the superstructure and within the superstructure of the ideological and political levels. All such theories in their effort to reject economism or, as Althusser puts it, 'the idea of a "pure and simple" non-overdetermined contradiction', to a greater or lesser extent have also removed economic determinacy, i.e. as Althusser again puts it, in such theories 'the lonely hour of the "last instance" never comes' (Althusser, 1969: 113). This general position has rightly developed the insights of the Frankfurt School into the importance of the superstructure and of mediation, while damagingly neglecting a crucial component of the Frankfurt School's original position, namely the fact that under monopoly capitalism the superstructure becomes precisely industrialized; it is invaded by the base and the base/superstructure distinction breaks down but via a collapse into the base rather than, as is the tendency with the post-Althusserian position, via the transformation of the base into another autonomous superstructural discourse.

In our age the objective social tendency is incarnate in the hidden subjective purpose of company directors, the foremost among whom are in the most powerful sectors of industry—

steel, petroleum, electricity and chemicals. Culture monopolies are weak and dependant in comparison. They cannot afford to neglect their appeasement of the real holders of power if their sphere of activity in mass-society is not to undergo a series of purges (Adorno and Hork-heimer, 1977: 351).

The truth of this original insight is demonstrated monthly as firms in the cultural sector are absorbed into large industrial conglomerates and brought under the sway of their business logic. Indeed, the real weakness of the Frankfurt School's original position was not their failure to realize the importance of the base or the economic, but insufficiently to take account of the economically contradictory nature of the process they observed and thus to see the industrialization of culture as unproblematic and irresistible. Those who have come after, while rightly criticizing the Frankfurt School for its absence of concrete class analysis, an absence stemming precisely from their insufficiently nuanced analysis of the economic level, in developing their theories of the effectivity of the superstructure have, ironically, massively compounded the original error.

The most distinguished exponent of the post-Althusserian position in Britain, Stuart Hall, in his essay 'Culture, the Media and the Ideological Effect' (Curran et al., 1977), recognizes that there is a decisive relationship between the growth of the mass-media and 'everything that we now understand as characterizing "monopoly capitalism" ', but at the same time refuses an analysis of this decisive relationship claiming that 'these aspects of the growth and expansion of the media historically have to be left to one side by the exclusive attention given here to media as "ideo-logical apparatuses".' Murdoch and Golding (1979) rightly criticize Hall and claim that 'on the contrary the ways in which the mass-media function as "ideological apparatuses" can only be adequately understood when they are systematically related to their position as large scale commercial enterprises in a capitalist economic system and if these relations are examined historically'. Hall's failure to do this leads him to explain the ideological effect in terms of pre-existent and ideologically predetermined communicators or encoders choosing from a pre-existent and ideologically pre-determined set of codes so that there is a systematic tendency of the media to re-produce the ideological field of society in such a way as to reproduce also its structure of domination. That is to say he offers the description of an ideological process, but not an explanation of why or how it takes place, except in tautological terms.

Moreover, he is led by his mode of analysis, as again Murdoch and Golding rightly point out, to favour a specific and atypical instance of media practice, namely public service broadcasting and indeed within that, an atypical form, namely informational broadcasting. While stressing that the production of the ideological effect requires work and struggle, his mode of analysis does not allow him to deal, for instance, with an important and developing moment in that struggle within the Press caused by a contradiction between the crucial underpinning idea of a 'free press' and the economic pressures towards monopoly or the relationship precisely between the ideological effect of broadcasting and the fact that it is perceived by its audience to be under State control as opposed to the biased privately owned press.

(c) A further elaboration of the post-Althusserian position, popular within film studies leads in its elaboration of a theory of autonomous discourses effectively to an evacuation of the field of historical materialism, whatever its materialistic rhetoric, placing its determinacy in the last instance on the unconscious as theorized within an essentially idealist, indeed Platonist, problematic. Such idiocies need detain us no further.[2]

(d) Finally, Dallas Smythe, identifying the excessive stress on the autonomy of the ideological level within Western Marxism as its 'Blind-spot', rightly redirects our attention away from the mass-media as ideological apparatuses and back to their economic function within capitalism. But in so doing, he proposes an extreme reductionist theory. For Smythe, any political economy of mass-media must be based upon an analysis of its commodity form and for him the commodity form specific to the mass-media is the Audience, that is to say, for Smythe, the crucial function of the mass-media is not to sell packages of ideology to consumers, but audiences to advertisers. Now it is undoubtedly important to focus attention upon the ways in which the mass-media manufacture and sell audiences as one moment in the complex circuit of capital that structures the operation of the mass-media economically. Moreover, to stress this moment as the crucial one and to concentrate on the mass-media's directly functional role for capital as advertising vehicles is undoubtedly a more plausible reflection of reality in the North American context than it would be in Europe. However, Smythe's theory misunderstands the function of the commodity form as an abstraction within Marxist economic theory and thus neglects the relationship between specific forms of the commodity, in this case the audience, and the commodity form in general. As a result, his theory lacks any sense of contradiction, failing to account for the function of those cultural commodities directly exchanged, failing to account for the role of the State, failing sufficiently to elaborate the function for capital of advertising itself and, perhaps most crucially of all, failing to relate the process of audience production by the mass-media to determinants of class and to class-struggle.[3]

The ideological level

What problems is it, then, that a political economy of mass-communication attempts to analyse. The research perspective, whose theoretical and historical basis I have briefly outlined, attempts to shift attention away from the conception of the mass-media as ISAs and sees them first as economic entities with both a direct economic role as creators of surplus value through commodity production and exchange and an indirect role, through advertising, in the creation of surplus value within other sectors of commodity production. Indeed, a political economy of mass-communication in part chooses its object of study precisely because it offers a challenge to the Althusser/Poulantzas theorization of the social formation as structured into the relatively autonomous levels of the economic, the ideological and the political. For the major institutions of mass-communication, the press and broadcasting, although, as will be analysed later, displaying notable differences of articulation, both at the same time display the close inter-weaving within concrete institutions and within their specific commodity forms of the economic, the ideological and the political. When we buy a newspaper we participate simultaneously in an economic exchange, in subjection to or reaction against an ideological formation and often in a quite specific act of political identification or at least involvement. We also know from historical

[2] We intend to publish a detailed critique of this position in a forthcoming issue. In the meantime, see Thompson (1978), Williams (1977) and Corrigan and Singer (1978) [Eds].

[3] See Smythe (1977), Murdoch (1978), Smythe (1978) and Levant (1978).

analysis of the development of the press that the nature of the political involvement is quite specifically economically conditioned. Similarly, TV news is economically determined within commodity production in general, performs an ideological function and explicitly operates within politics, in terms of balance, etc.

While accepting that the mass media can be and are politically and ideologically over-determined within many specific conjunctures, a political economy, as I understand it, rests upon ultimate determination by the economic (a level that itself always remains problematic and to be defined in the process of analysis).

Indeed, one of the key features of the mass media within monopoly capitalism has been the exercise of political, and ideological domination through the economic.[4] What concerns us in fact is firstly to stress, from the analytical perspective, the validity of the base/superstructure model while at the same time pointing to and analysing the ways in which the development of monopoly capitalism has industrialized the superstructure. Indeed Marx's own central insight into the capitalist mode of production stressed its generalizing, abstracting drive; the pressure to reduce everything to the equivalence of exchange value.

Before going on to examine the economic level and its specific articulations within the cultural sphere, let us look at the relationship between the material conditions of production (not, as we have seen, to be confused with the economic far less the capitalist modes of such production, which are specific forms) on the one hand and ideological forms on the other. That is to say how do we relate Williams's correct stress, within the limits indicated, upon the materiality of cultural production, to Marx's famous distinction 'between the material transformations of the economic conditions of production, which can be determined with the precision of natural science, and the legal, political, aesthetic or philosophic—in short—ideological—forms in which men become conscious of this conflict and fight it out' (Marx, 1859).

What the quotation from Marx underlines is the importance of the distinction between the two levels, a distinction focused upon the difference between the *unconscious* forces governing material production 'beyond our will', etc. and the conscious form of ideology. If we follow the Althusserians and make ideology an unconscious process this crucial distinction is lost.

As far as the mass-media specifically are concerned this distinction points to the need to distinguish between the media as processes of material production (whether capitalist or not is precisely a question for analysis) on the one hand, and as sites of ideological struggle on the other and the relationship between those two levels or instances.

There are here two distinctions to be made. I think we can liken ideological practice to what Marx called the 'real labour process'.

Looking at the process of production from its real side, i.e. as a process which creates new use-values by performing useful labour with existing use values, we find it to be a *real labour process*. As such its element, its conceptually specific components, are those of the labour process itself, of any labour process, irrespective of the mode of production or the stage of economic development in which they find themselves (Marx, 1976).

That is to say the process of consciousness and of representation, for instance, language, are real processes by which human beings socially appropriate their environment (nature) which pre-exist and continue to exist within specifically

[4] See J. Curran, 'Capitalism and Control of the Press 1800–1979', in Curran *et al.* (1977).

capitalist modes of ideological production and indeed upon which these capitalist modes rest.

The materiality of such ideological production *qua* ideology rests upon the fact that consciousness is a human transformation of 'real' experience, it is in that sense 'practical knowledge'. Clearly therefore, the relationship of any particular instance of ideological production to the totality of social experience will depend upon an analysis of the experiential position of the human consciousness in question, e.g. the conventional and simple definition of class consciousness as based upon the direct experience of a given position within the capital/labour relationship. Of course in any complex society such direct experience becomes highly mediated both diachronically and synchronically. But its translation into forms of representation is nonetheless a process of consciousness which is different from and in its forms has no necessary correspondence with, the economic processes to which it relates or of which it is a representation. Indeed as a representation it is precisely by definition distinct from those processes which it represents.

Moreover ideological forms can never be simply collapsed into a system of exchange values, i.e. the specifically capitalist mode of production, precisely because ideological forms, forms of consciousness, are concerned with difference, with distinction; they are by definition heterogeneous (as Marx himself remarked when discussing the limited possibilities for the subsumption of ideological production under capitalism, 'I want the doctor and not his errand boy'). Whereas exchange value is precisely the realm of equivalence.[5]

Material and mental production

In order to study the connection between intellectual and material production it is above all essential to conceive the latter in its determined historical form and not as a general category. For example, there corresponds to the capitalist mode of production a type of intellectual production quite different from that which corresponded to the mediaeval mode of production. Unless material production itself is understood in its specific historical form, it is impossible to grasp the characteristics of the intellectual production which corresponds to it or the reciprocal action between the two (Marx, 1963: 96–97).

We need to lay stress on and distinguish two distinct but related moments in a historical materialist analysis of intellectual production.

(a) Culture as a superstructural phenomenon in relation to non-cultural modes of material production, i.e. on the one hand, the dominant or hegemonic cultural production paid for out of capitalist *revenue* and, on the other, a subordinate working class or oppositional culture paid for out of wages. Cultural production in this sense and its articulations with the sphere of material production involves one specific interpretation of the meaning in The German Ideology of 'control of the means of mental production', i.e. through the direct payment of ideologists and the necessary maintenance of the physical instruments of their ideological production. It is within that analytical perspective that we need to analyse the historical development of the 'historically specific needs' of the working class and their sustenance of 'organic intellectuals' and of specific instruments of cultural production such as trade-unions.

(b) Culture as part of material production itself, directly subordinate to or at least in a closely determined articulation with the laws of development of capital. This is both a latter historical phase, part of developing monopoly capitalism, the pheno-

[5] For a detailed discussion of this problem see Baudrillard (1972, 1975).

menon dubbed 'the industrialization of culture', but it also lives alongside the other moment and in specific instances we need to analyse the interrelationship between these two distinct modes of intellectual production within intellectual production (Culture in its narrow sense) in general.

What, in general, has been lost in Marxist studies of the mass media is the precise historical elaboration of what Marx and Engels meant in The German Ideology by 'control of the means of mental production'.

In general it is clear, I think, in The German Ideology that, reflecting the contemporary stage of capitalist development, Marx and Engels were concerned with the payment of ideologists, of intellectuals, out of capitalist revenue. It is this perspective that Raymond Williams picks up in the passage already cited. That is to say they rightly saw that superstructural activities require a cohort of mental workers who were not directly economically or materially productive and thus whose price of reproduction must be borne by the sphere of material production. Since under capitalism it was capitalists who were extracting this surplus, it was they who could redistribute this surplus into superstructural activities of their choosing and by so doing exert direct economic pressures on the ideologists who were their hired servants.

The creation of surplus labour on the one side corresponds to the creation of minus labour, relative idleness (or non-productive labour at best) on the other. This goes without saying as regards capital itself; but holds then also for the classes with which it shares; hence of paupers, flunkeys, lick-spittles, etc. living from the surplus product, in short, the whole train of retainers; the part of the *servant* class which lives not from capital but from revenue (Marx, 1973: 401).

This direct relationship remains important and should not be forgotten. That is to say the working class also developed, out of its wages, a subordinate or counter culture with its own 'organic intellectuals' such as paid trade-union officials, co-operative organizers, journalists, etc., but the surplus available for this purpose was exiguous both really and comparatively, so that this direct ideological power was decisively weighted in favour of capital and remains so. Compare a small organisation like Counter Information Services with the public relations and research investment of a major company. Look at the way in which large companies manipulate the legal system by their ability to sustain expensive, long drawn out actions (e.g. the Thalidomide case). Look at the way media research itself has been and is significantly influenced by the flow of funds from vested commercial interests.

There now exists of course, as the division of labour has developed further, a more mediated version of this employment of ideologists out of revenue, namely, as Bourdieu has analysed, the creation of a subordinate fraction of the capitalist class who possess cultural capital (Bourdieu and Passeron, 1977). Just as younger sons of the aristocracy went into Church and army, so now a section of the capitalist class occupies key positions in the cultural sector. The class origins of ideological workers remains an important but neglected aspect of media analysis. This does not of course mean that such people necessarily reproduce ruling class ideology (see Engels and William Morris for obvious counter examples). It does mean that there is a structural tendency so to do.

Neglect of this aspect of direct economic control of ideologists is reflected in current discussion of the ideological role of the media where there is much sophisticated discussion of professionalization, of heirarchies of discourse, of hegemonic and subordinate codes, etc. discussions which often serve to mask a reality which is ever present to those actually working in the media, namely the possibility of losing one's job. This economic reality is of course often internalized by both employee and employer in the form of the ideologies of professionalism or managerialism but it remains nonetheless potent for that, indeed is the underpinning which professionalism requires. Once again, this was a fact that Adorno and Horkheimer did not make the mistake of forgetting:

> Under the private culture monopoly it is a fact that 'tyranny leaves the body free and directs its attack at the soul'. The ruler no longer says, 'You must think as I do, or die'. He says, 'You are free not to think as I do, your life, your property, everything shall remain yours, but from this day on you are a stranger among us'. Not to conform means to be rendered powerless, economically and therefore, spiritually—to be 'self-employed'. When the outsider is excluded from the concern, he can only too easily be accused of incompetence. Whereas today in material production the mechanism of supply and demand is disintegrating in the superstructure it still operates as a check in the ruler's favour.[6]

The second moment, upon which of course increasingly in the actual historical development the former moment has come to depend, is the actual control by capital within the process of commodity production of the means of cultural production. This moment was clearly under-developed at the time when The German Ideology was written but, while not entirely superceding the other moment as I have indicated, it is this moment that has become crucial for an analysis of cultural reproduction under monopoly capitalism.[7] Within the sphere of cultural production the development of specifically economic, industrial forms was in part possible precisely because of the effect of the other moment, i.e. working class powers of cultural resistance were weakened. A good example of this is R. Williams' suggestion that the popular success of ITV and of the general invasion of American commercialized cultural forms was a reaction on the part of the working class to the liberating overthrow of a particular hegemonic cultural formation represented by the BBC. It is in particular on the implications of this second moment that I wish to concentrate, i.e. the effects of the imposition of capital logic upon cultural production.

As I have indicated there has been a tendency to see such an imposition as ideologically non-contradictory. One must stress at the outset that this is not so. Because capital controls the means of cultural production in the sense that the production and exchange of cultural commodities becomes the dominant forms of cultural relationship, it does not follow that these cultural commodities will necessarily support, either in their explicit content or in their mode of cultural appropriation, the dominant ideology. Indeed as Terry Lovell has recently stressed and as, once again, Adorno and Horkheimer made clear, the cultural commodity possesses an inherent contradiction, a contradiction which, as with the other contradictions within the capitalist mode of production, may be profoundly subversive.[8] Whether

---

[6] Adorno and Horkheimer, 'The Dialectic of Enlightenment', in Curran et al. (1977: 133, 358–359).

[7] But note Marx's own comments in the Grundrisse, p. 532:

The highest development of capital exists when the general conditions of the process of social production are not paid out of deduction from the social revenue, the state's taxes—where revenue and not capital appears as the labour fund, and where the worker, although he is a free wage worker like any other, nevertheless stands economically in a different relation—but rather out of capital as capital. This shows the degree to which capital has subjugated all conditions of social production to itself, on the one side; and, on the other side, hence, the extent to which social reproduction wealth has been capitalised and all needs are satisfied through the exchange form (Marx's italics).

[8] See T. Lovell (1979) and Adorno and Horkheimer:

Nevertheless the culture industry remains the entertainment business. Its influence over the consumer is established by entertainment; that will ultimately be broken not by an outright decree, but by the hostility inherent in the principle of entertainment to what is greater than itself (in Curran et al., 1977: 361).

it is or not depends upon a concrete analysis of a specific conjuncture. Before turning to the general implications of the proposition that one definition of the control of the means of mental production is the take-over of large areas of cultural production and reproduction by capitalist commodity production, what the proposition leads one to question is that stress on intentionality which we find in theories such as that of Milliband. It is quite clear in Marx's analysis of *Capital* that he wished to distinguish firmly between the logic of capital and the intention of individual capitalists, even at the economic, let alone the ideological, level:

The fact that baking, shoemaking, etc. are only just being put on a capitalist basis in England is entirely due to the circumstances that English capital cherished feudal preconceptions of 'respectability'. It was 'respectable' to sell Negroes into slavery, but it was not respectable to make sausages, shoes or bread (Marx, 1976: 1014, footnote).

It is perhaps worth noting in passing that this characteristic of British capital still operates with respect to the media, which still carry a certain bohemian, mountebank and marginal reputation. Hence the characteristics of the particular capitals who started ITV for instance or who developed the British film industry in the 1930s or the role of colonial capital via Beaverbrook and Murdoch in the British Press. Such attitudes still affect the Tory party in its ambivalent relation to commercial broadcasting.

The function fulfilled by the capitalist is no more than the function of capital—viz. the valorization of value by absorbing living labour—executed *consciously* and *willingly*. The capitalist functions only as personified capital, capital as a person, just as the worker is no more than *labour* personified (Marx, 1976: 989).

What this quotation points to is the importance of not viewing capitalists, for analytical purposes, as unified subjects. That is to say a given person or group can only be described as capitalist in those moments when s/he or they are acting in conscious and willed accord with the logic of capital accumulation. Thus there may well be many such conscious, willed actions, never mind unconscious actions, that are contradictory to the logic of capital, of course always within determinate limits. There may be therefore a clear divergence between the functions of capital within the material process of mental production and the conscious, willed intentions of the capitalist or of their ideologues. We cannot predict *a priori* which at any time will be predominant, e.g. how long a Harmsworth, a Beaverbrook or a Thomson will keep a loss-making newspaper going for reasons of social prestige or political power, although clearly the outer limits of such possibilities of deviation by the individual capitalist will be determined by the norms of capital's logic.

There is then, and this cannot be sufficiently stressed, no necessary coincidence between the effects of the capitalist process proper and the ideological needs of the dominant class. On the contrary the entire thesis of capital points to the opposite conclusion.

This, for instance, effects assumptions concerning the relationship between capital and the State. To take one example, the proportion of the budget of the COI that has to be devoted to paid access to the media, i.e. the use of paid advertising for Government propaganda or information, has risen in the last decade from 20% to 50%. Such evidence can be interpreted in two ways. Either there is an observable conflict between the ideological needs of the State and the accumulation process within the media sector (leaving aside the question of whether the State is in fact the representative of capital or of the dominant class and therefore whether such a conflict would represent a contradiction between the economic and ideological needs of that class in general or whether it represents a contradiction between the ideological needs of capital in general versus the economic needs of a class fraction who control the media sector). Alternatively, this evidence can be interpreted to show the increasing sway of capitalist logic over the political and ideological level, i.e. forcing it to work increasingly through direct exchange relations within the economic.

This question of intentionality within ideological production is, of course, central to the media debate, within both the bourgeois and Marxist problematic. That is to say one argument runs, for instance the Frankfurt School tradition, that the mass media are important because monopoly capitalism has moved from direct coercion of the working class, for instance within the labour process, to ideological coercion as its preferred method of domination and the mass-media or ISA's are crucial in this process.

But do we in fact require this shift onto the terrain of ideology in order to explain the absence of direct coercion. Marx himself on the contrary saw the avoidance of such coercion as central to the economic mechanism of capitalism. That is to say the abstraction of exchange value, the wage-form, etc. were in themselves quite powerful enough to explain the dominance of capital and indeed that this non-coercive dominance was both historically necessary and progressive. Bourdieu has developed this general proposition.[9]

Thus at the level of material production, of the life process in the realm of the social—for that is what the process of production is—we find the *same* situation that we find in *religion* at the ideological level, namely the inversion of subject into object and vice-versa. Viewed *historically* this inversion is the indispensable transition without which wealth as such, i.e. the relentless productive forces of social labour, which alone can form the material base of a free human society, could not possibly be created by force at the expense of the majority (Marx, 1976: 990).

Mental production and capitalist commodity production

Let us now turn back to look at mental production, of which the mass media are an example, as processes of capitalist production and at the implications for our modes of social communication of the subsumption by capital of the real forms of ideological production.

This needs to be looked at historically, i.e. unlike the capital logic or capital derivation school we must not see capitalism as a mode of production which arrives *sui generis* and then sprouts a social formation like dragon's teeth. It is rather a specific form which grew within a pre-existing social formation and is involved in a process of expansion and conquest of non-capitalist sectors, a process which is incomplete and contradictory. This process of expansion involves both the subsumption of other areas of material production and pre-capitalist forms of economic organisation and also of non-economic activity under the sway of the economic in its capitalist form.

[9] See Bourdieu (1971: 183–197):

It is in the degree of objectification of the accumulated social capital that one finds the basis of all pertinent differences between the modes of domination . . . Objectification guarantees the permanence and cumulativity of material and symbolic acquisition which can thus subsist without agents having to recreate them continuously and in their entirety by deliberate action; but, because the profits of their institutions are the object of differential appropriation, objectification also and inseparably ensures the reproduction of the structure of distribution of the capital which, in its various forms, is the precondition for such appropriation, and in so doing, reproduces the structure of the relation of dominance and dependence (p. 184).

When examining mass communication within predominantly capitalist social formations we must not make the mistake of assuming that they are therefore necessarily capitalist, i.e. we cannot make the easy elision Miliband makes between those sectors controlled by private capital and those controlled by the State. Nor can we assume that all non-State sectors are in fact capitalist. Indeed the relationship between pre-capitalist and capitalist forms within the media sector is a significant feature both economically and ideologically, i.e. the relationship between notions of creative freedom, freedom of the Press, the Fourth Channel debate, community communication, etc. This relationship significantly determines the forms of the struggle within the media over the labour process.

Thus artisanal modes of labour organization ranging from individual craft production, i.e. the authorship of a book, to the small group, i.e. the independent film company or record producer, remain common and important within the cultural sphere. Such residues have been the focus for struggle against the logic of capital and have produced a powerful anti-economic cultural ideology (see the whole culture/society tradition). Nonetheless in certain instances such artisanal organization may be functional for capital so long as capital controls the means of mass reproduction of the authorial product and of the means of mass distribution, because it ensures the necessary production of a range of heterogeneous cultural artefacts from which capital can choose for further exploitation without capital having to bear the risks and overheads for this production which are born directly by labour. Indeed, the ideology of creative freedom can be used by capital to keep their labour force divided and weak and with no control over the strategic moments of the total labour process. Thus, for instance, while the Open Broadcasting Authority will be fought for by cultural workers under the banner of creative freedom and against the apparent interests of capital in the form of ITV, such a structure of small-scale freelance production, if it were to be realized, would be more functional for capital in general than an extension of the present structure, because it would open British broadcasting more fully both to advertising and to the pressures of the international market.[10]

Nor must we make the mistake of assuming an easy equation between private ownership and capitalism.

Where capital still appears only in its elementary forms such as commodities . . . or money, the capitalist manifests himself in the already familiar character of the owner of money or commodities. But such a person is no more a capitalist in himself than money or commodities are capital in themselves. They become translated into capital only in certain specific circumstances and their owners likewise become capitalist only when these circumstances obtain (Marx, 1976: 976).

What then are these circumstances? The central characteristic of capital is growth or accumulation.

In itself the sum of money may only be defined as capital if it is employed, spent, with the aim of increasing it, if it is spent expressly in order to increase it. In the case of the sum of value or money this phenomenon is its destiny, its inner law, its tendency, while to the capitalist, i.e. the owner of the sum of money, in whose hands it shall acquire its function, it appears as intention, purpose (Marx, 1976: 976).

Thus to examine the specifically capitalist mode of media production we need to see the ways in which capital uses the real process of media production in order to increase its value, in order to grow, and the barriers which are placed in the way of

[10] For a fuller elaboration of the modes of labour organization within capitalist cultural industries, see Huet et al. (1978).

this process either by the inherent contradictions of the process itself or by external forces.

At a minimum in order to accumulate capital must bring living labour into the production process by exchanging in the sphere of circulation through the wage bargain. It must combine this living labour in a determinate manner with objectified labour as means of production (raw materials and instruments) in the production of a commodity in the exchange of which surplus value will be realized.

In a fully constituted capitalist mode based upon relative surplus value and competition between capitals this process of growth requires ever increased productivity and ever widening markets.

Historically the sphere of mental production or non-material production presented and continues to present important barriers to this process and the forms and dynamics of the mass media can in part be understood as resulting from a continuous attempt to surmount those barriers and from the concretely various successes and failures of this attempt.

We thus start from the historical materialist assumption that the development of capitalism or the capitalist mode of production is:

(a) a contradictory process;
(b) not yet complete.

The contradictory nature of the process is in part intrinsic, i.e. the conflict between capital and labour, the conflict between capital accumulation and the socialization of the forces and relations of production, the conflict between the drive to accumulate through the extraction of relative surplus value and labour power as the creator of surplus value, a contradiction expressed in the tendency of the rate of profit to fall.

In part the contradictions are extrinsic, that is to say related precisely to the relationship between developing capitalism and the non-capitalist areas of the social formation. The necessary expansion of the valorization process is not a process of automatic expansion; it comes up against social and political barriers; it needs to conquer physical barriers, e.g. communication and transport; it requires the necessary accumulation of capital, etc.

We see these contradictions in the field of mass-media:

(a) in resistances both actual and ideological to the industrialization of the artisanal modes of cultural production;
(b) in the conflicts between national and international capitals, sometimes mediated through the State and sometimes direct, e.g. the split in the Tory party over the original introduction of commercial broadcasting—or the developing struggle over national versus supra-national control of European satellite broadcasting—or the existence of quotas on the importation of foreign film and TV material;
(c) growing Third World demand for a New World Information Order.

The problem with cultural and informational goods is that, because their use value is almost limitless, i.e. cannot be destroyed or consumed by use, it is extremely difficult to attach an exchange value to them. They are in fact, in general, classic public goods. What we are considering is what Marx called 'non-material production'. Marx discusses such production in the context of a discussion of the distinction between productive and non-productive labour (whether such a distinction can be maintained and, if so, its analytical significance, is a matter of general importance within the field of the political economy of culture which we cannot pursue further here). In brief, Marx clearly foresaw difficulties in subsuming non-material production under capitalism. He identified two possible forms of such production:

(1) It results in commodities which exist separately from the producer, i.e. they can circulate in the interval between production and consumption as commodities, e.g. books, paintings and all products of art as distinct from the artistic achievement of the practising artist. Here capitalist production is possible only within very narrow limits. Apart from such cases as, say, sculptors who employ assistants, these people (where they are not independent) mainly work for merchants capital, e.g. booksellers, a pattern that is only transitional in itself and can only lead to a capitalist mode of production in the formal sense. Nor is the position altered by the fact that exploitation is at its greatest precisely in these transitional forms.

(2) The product is not separable from the act of producing. Here too the capitalist mode of production occurs only on a limited scale and in the nature of the case it can only operate in certain areas (I want the doctor not his errand boy). For example, in teaching institutions the teacher can be no more than wage-labour for the entrepreneur of the learning factory. Such peripheral phenomena can be ignored when considering capitalist production as a whole.

(Marx, 1976: 1047–1048).

This passage would be worth lengthy analysis. At this stage I would only like to point to the following.

(a) The relevance of example (1) for the debate between Marcuse and Benjamin concerning the role of the aura of a work of art and the effect on that aura of the attempt to subject culture production to at least the forces of capitalist production.[11]

(b) The need to look, with reference to the observation concerning the degree of exploitation in this field, at the evidence of the persistent low pay of cultural workers and the extent to which even the most advanced sectors of capitalist cultural production depend upon drawing relative surplus value from sectors which still operate a pre-capitalist artisanal mode of economic organization.[12]

(c) The above relates to the need to examine the relationship between Marx's belief that capitalist production of cultural goods was possible only within very narrow limits, the phenomenon of Baumol's disease (Baumol and Bouran, 1976) and the ever increasing pressure on the State to intervene in the cultural sector.

(d) Similar considerations are raised by Marx's second example where the product is not separable from the act of producing, thus raising strict limits to productivity and thus raising relative costs.

The economic contradictions that arise from the nature of cultural commodities takes different forms within different sectors of the media and at different historical moments.

Five main ways have been adopted in an attempt to circumvent the problem.

(a) Copyright. This is in effect an attempt to commoditize information via the uniqueness of authorship or by turning the author into a commodity. But this only works if you either then make the commodity scarce, i.e. stress its uniqueness. We see this in the economics of the art market. Or if you control supply, i.e. control access to the means of reproduction such as printing presses and film laboratories. However, if such control is used to over-price it will encourage the development of pirating alternatives. This is now a major problem internationally for the cultural industries in records, books, films and even TV programmes.

(b) Control of access to consumption through a box-office mechanism at the point of sale and/or through economic control of the channels of distribution, i.e. newspapers and cinema.

The problem here is that such control is resistant to economies of scale and as the

[11] See Benjamin (1977) for the positive view and Marcuse (1972) for the negative view.
[12] See Huet et al. (1978) for theoretical elaboration and Krust (1977) for data. See also discussion in Owen, Beebe and Manning (1974), which shows, from a neo-classical perspective that the so-called economic efficiency of US TV depends upon high unemployment in Hollywood.

theatre found when faced by the cinema and the cinema when faced by broadcasting, is highly susceptible to competition from more efficient technologies of reproduction and distribution. However, as broadcasting demonstrates, the massive economies of scale produced by these more efficient means of distribution by destroying the box office, i.e. by making access open, create major problems of creating the necessary moment of exchange.

(c) Built-in obsolescence through the manipulation of time. This was the great achievement of the newspaper which, by creating rapidly decaying information, created thereby a constant need to re-consume. But this manipulation of time has its limits since consumption time is physically limited. (The central importance of time within the economics of the mass-media is a subject to which I intend to give substantive treatment in a subsequent article.)

(d) The creation, packaging and sale, not of cultural and informational goods to direct consumers, but of audiences to advertisers (Smythe, 1977).

(e) State patronage.

The inherent tendency towards the socialization of cultural and informational goods has always given the State an important role in this field from the days of direct patronage of cultural workers by King, Aristocracy and Church via the early subsidy of newspapers by governments and political parties, through public libraries and public education, to the key contemporary example of broadcasting.

In brief therefore, the specific nature of the commodity form within cultural production leads to a constant problem of realization and thus to a two-way pressure either towards advertising finance or towards State finance. We find these pressures quite clearly at the moment in the growing controversy over sponsorship in sport and the arts.[13]

The questions these pressures raise is in what ways (a) advertising and (b) State intervention in this sphere is functional or disfunctional for capitalism in general on the one hand and on the other the effect of such pressures upon cultural production itself.

The modes of extraction and distribution of the cultural surplus

Since all cultural forms are material in the sense that they take time which will only be available after the needs of physical reproduction are satisfied, the material requirements of the cultural process must be extracted as surplus from direct material production. As we have seen this can be done by paying for cultural production directly out of revenue. But as Marx remarked of capitalism in general, it has found it more efficient as a means of control to extract surpluses directly by means of economic processes. Thus the developments of the capitalist mode of production and its associated division of mental and manual labour has lead to the development of the extraction of the necessary surplus for the maintenance of cultural production and reproduction directly via the commodity and exchange form. But this process will only take place to the extent that:

(a) there is surplus capital searching for opportunities for valorization;

(b) the anticipated rate of profit in the chosen sphere of cultural production is at least as high as that available elsewhere.

[13] See, for instance, P. Harland (1978) and recent correspondence in the *Times* concerning the Arts Council's expression of disapproval of its grant recipients giving too large a billing to commercial sponsors at the expense of itself.

Where these conditions do not exist cultural processes will have to continue to be undertaken by the direct transfer of resources, i.e. by the expenditure of surplus. This may take place under the following conditions.

(a) By capitalist as individuals or groups funding such activities, e.g. the classic model of arts patronage. Such a form may be sustained within the contemporary capitalist social formation by means of tax concessions. It may be channelled through charitable foundations, etc.

Such funding leads to direct ideological control, legitimated as the cultural extension of private property, namely personal taste. This sphere can give rise to significant political battles, e.g. the wealth tax/national heritage debate.

But examples within the media field are the direct subsidy of newspapers by political parties or by politically ambitious individuals, e.g. Beaverbrook, Goldsmith and possibly now Broakes and Matthews, the new owners of the *Express* Group and Morgan-Grampian.

(b) Via the State. Here electronic communication is the key case. The exact mix in the field of both telephonic and broadcast communication between the State and capital needs examination state by state. As any superficial examination will show, key differences between Western Europe and the United States give the lie to any simple capital logic explanation of how the particular economic and institutional forms, within which electronic communication has developed, have arisen.

The explanation of such differences and the present conjunctural relations between national capitals and the State, between states and between international capital and states in this area would have to take account of the following.

(1) The structures of national capitals.

(2) The existing State structure, i.e. federal structure of US and Germany as opposed to centralized structure of Britain and even more, France.

(3) The strategic requirements of the State, e.g. the State-inspired creation of RCA as the first step in a long history of the US government's explicit geo–political involvement in communication, the clearest case of which is satellites, such a policy requiring intervention to restructure national capitals.

(4) The balance of forces between sections of capital and the relations of that balance of force to the State's assessment of both economic and strategic requirements, e.g. the foundation of the BBC in which we see an interaction between the needs of the nascent British electronic industry, which the State wished to foster both for strategic and economic reasons, but which was only interested in the sales of hardware and was able to shift the expense and ideological problems of programme production onto the State, because the State needed also to take account both of the economically and politically powerful British press, which was opposed to competition for advertising and of a culturally conservative and elitist ruling class fraction.[14]

To sum up, historically the development of the material process known as the superstructure depended upon the availability of a surplus in the sphere of direct material production, i.e. the sphere of the extraction, shaping and consumption of nature. Historically the shape of that superstructure is determined by the social relations of production, because it is these social relations that determine the distribution of that surplus. For example, Athenian democracy as a form of political practice depends directly materially upon the slave economy that supported it by making time

[14] For a discussion of the relationship between the French State and private capital in the development of the electronic audio-visual field in general, see Flichy (1978) and Huet *et al.* (1978).

available for political activity to a non-productive class. Such directly material considerations remain important, i.e. in a planned economy like the Soviet Union direct choices have to be made between for instance producing more shoes or the paper for more newspapers. Such considerations may be acute in the planning of media systems in Third World countries and indeed it is the influencing of such decisions in the interest not of the indigenous economy or social formation but of a foreign high surplus economy that is one of the matters at issue in the media imperialism debate. It is a less obvious form of the starvation caused in some countries by the development of industrialized agriculture serving a world market. Under developing capitalism the means of cultural production may be provided either in commodity form as part of the accumulation process, e.g. records or as part of the realization process of other sectors of the capitalist economy, e.g. advertising or directly out of capitalist revenue, e.g. arts patronage or the Thomson family and *The Times* or through the State.

Each of the above means of surplus distribution to the cultural sphere will differentially affect the ways in which the dominant class controls the means of cultural production. Different contradictions will come into play, contradictions which need to be specifically analysed in each conjunctural case. Not only are these contradictions intrinsic to each subsidiary mode of cultural production but there are also contradictions which arise because of conflicts between them, e.g. between broadcasting whether state or private and the press, a conflict in its turn differentially mediated through competition for readers/viewers and through competition for advertising.

The industrialization of culture

While drawing different conclusions as to the significance of the phenomenon both bourgeois and Marxist economists agree that the current phase of capitalist development is characterized by the following.

(a) Unprecedented capital concentration in all the key traditional manufacturing sectors accompanied in general by a rising surplus.

(b) A resulting problem of valorization which drives surplus capital in search of other areas of investment.

(c) An associated development of the so-called service sector characterized by the industrialization of sectors which were either more primitively organised or, as in the sphere of domestic labour, altogether outside the market.

These tendencies are now rapidly affecting the whole cultural, mass-media sector. This has been extensively documented by A. Mattelart in his recent 'Multi-nationales et systeme de communication' and, for France, by A. Huet *et al.* in their 'Capitalisme et industries culturelles'. So all I wish to do here, is point out certain key aspects and examples of this tendency.

This absorption of the sphere of reproduction into full-scale commodity production is characterized by the following.

(a) Increased international competition and the resulting take-over of domestic, national publishing companies, advertising agencies, private broadcasting stations etc. by multinational companies. See, for instance, the example of Phillips given at the start of this piece. This competition also leads to increasing penetration by international media products, particularly Anglo-Saxon.[15]

[15] It should be noted that from this point of view the UK is in a privileged position since it is second only to the USA as a media exporter.

(b) A sharpening struggle within cultural production over the labour process in an attempt by capital to increase productivity in a sector which is notoriously resistant to such increases. This struggle has been most marked recently in the newspaper industry with the present dispute at Times Newspapers being the most notorious and current example in Britain.

(c) Increasingly persistent attempts to open up new markets in order to absorb excess capital. The most obvious example of this is the increasing pressure throughout Western Europe to privatize public broadcasting. See, for instance, the case of Italy, but the current crisis in the financing of the BBC and Annan's proposals for an advertising financed O.B.A. must be seen in this light.

(d) Attempts to open up new markets for both cultural hard-ware and soft-ware by introducing new communication technologies, such as cable TV, satellites, Teletext, etc. Because of the huge infrastructural investments involved and the comparatively low rate of return on such investments these moves involve close alliances between capital and the State in an attempt to get the tax-payer to carry the cost of the distribution system, while private capital takes the profits from the sale of hardware and from the subsequent development of a consumer durable market in such items as teletex decoders and of a software market, e.g. Pay TV. The full development of this push into new technologies has undoubtedly been slowed down significantly by the current recession in the Western economies, but the long-term implications for national cultures, for class cultures and for freedom of expression of all these trends, not only in the Third World where the problem is dramatized as media imperialism, but in the capitalist heartlands, are profoundly significant.

Thus I return to where I started by reiterating that the development of political economy in the cultural sphere is not a mere matter of theoretical interest but of urgent practical political priority. So long as Marxist analysis concentrates on the ideological content of the mass media it will be difficult to develop coherent political strategies for resisting the underlying dynamics of development in the cultural sphere in general which rest firmly and increasingly upon the logic of generalized commodity production. In order to understand the structure of our culture, its production, consumption and reproduction and of the role of the mass media in that process, we increasingly need to confront some of the central questions of political economy in general, the problem of productive and non-productive labour, the relation between the private and public sectors and the role of the State in capitalist accumulation, the role of advertising within late capitalism, etc.

As long ago as 1960, Asa Briggs wrote in his Fisher Memorial Lecture:

The provision of entertainment has never been a subject of great interest either to economists or to economic historians—at least in their working hours. Yet in 20th century conditions it is proper to talk of a highly organized entertainment industry, to distinguish within it between production and distribution, to examine forces making for competition, integration, concentration and control and to relate such study to the statistics of national income and output, the development of advertising, international economic relations and—not least—to the central economic concept of the market which, in the 20th century, is as much concerned with leisure as it is with work (Briggs, 1960).

Nearly two decades later that research gap remains and there has been little coherent effort to understand the process known as 'the industrialization of culture', a process by which, as Briggs put it, 'Massive market interests have come to dominate an area of life which, until recently, was dominated by individuals themselves' (Briggs, 1960).

Bibliography

ADORNO, T. and HORKHEIMER, M. (1977). The culture industry (abridged), in J. Curran *et al.*, (eds), *Mass Communication and Society*, Edward Arnold, London

ALTHUSSER, L. (1969). *Contradiction and Over-determination*, Allen Lane, London

BAUDRILLARD, J. (1972). *Pour une Critique de l'Economic Politique du Signe*, Gallimard, Paris

BAUDRILLARD, J. (1975). *The Mirror of Production*, Tela Press, St. Louis

BAUMOL, W. J. and BOURAN, W. G. (1976). On the performing arts: the anatomy of their economic problems, in M. Blang, (ed.), *The Economics of the Arts*, Martin Robertson, London

BENJAMIN, W. (1977). The work of art in the age of mechanical reproduction, in Curran *et al.*, op. cit.

BOTTOMORE, T. and RUBEL, M. (1963). Theories of surplus value, in *K. Marx on Sociology and Social Philosophy*, pp. 96, 97, Pelican

BOURDIEU, P. (1971). *Outline of a Theory of Practice*, CUP

BOURDIEU, P. and PASSERON, J. L. (1977). *Reproduction*, Sage, London

BRIGGS, A. (1960). Fisher Memorial Lecture, University of Adelaide

CLARKE, S. (1977). Marxism, sociology and Poulantzas's theory of the state, *Capital and Class*, no. 2, Summer

CORRIGAN, P. and SINGER, D. (1978). Hindess and Hirst: a critical review, *Socialist Register*, Merlin, London

CURRAN, J. *et al.*, (eds) (1977). *Mass-Communication and Society*, Edward Arnold, London

Financial Times (1978). Electronic Rentals ups its ratings, 19 December

FLICHY, P. (1978). *Contribution à une Étude du Industries de l'Audiovisual*, Institut National de l'Audiovisual

HARLAND, P. (1978). Enter the money men, stage right, *Sunday Times*, 11 June

HUET, A. *et al.* (1978). *Capitalisme et Industries Culturelles*, University of Grenoble Press

KRUST, M. (1977). *Droit au Travail et Problems d'Emploi du Travailleur Culturels du Spectacle et de l'Interpretation Musicale dans la Communante Economique Europeene*, CCE

LEVANT, P. (1978). The audience commodity: on the blindspot debate, *Canadian Journal of Political and Social Theory*

LOVELL, T. (1979). *Realism, Ideology and Film*, British Film Institute, London (forthcoming)

MANDEL, E. (1975). *Late Capitalism*, ch. 1, NLB, London

MARCUSE, H. (1972). Art as a form of reality, *New Left Review* 74

MARX, K. (1859). Preface to a contribution to a critique of political economy, in Marx, K. and Engels, F., (eds), *Selected Works*, vol. 1, p. 364, Lawrence and Wishart, London (1962)

MARX, K. (1973). *Grundrisse*, Pelican, London

MARX, K. (1975). Notes on Adolph Wagner, in T. Carver, (ed.), *Texts on Method*, p. 201, Blackwell, Oxford

MARX, K. (1976). Results of the immediate process of production, in *Capital*, vol. 1, Pelican

MILLIBAND, R. R. (1977). *Marxism and Politics*, p. 50, OUP

MURDOCH, G. (1978). Blindspots about Western Marxism: a reply to Dallas Smythe, *Canadian Journal of Political and Social Theory*, vol. 2, no. 2

MURDOCH, G. and GOLDING, P. (1979). Ideology and the mass media: the question of determination, in M. Barrett *et al.* (eds) *Ideology and Cultural Production*, Croom-Helm, London

OWEN, B., BEEBE, J. and MANNING, W. (1974). *TV Economics*, D. C. Heath, London

SAYER, D. (1979). *Marx's Method*, Harvester Press, forthcoming

SMYTHE, D. (1977). Communication: blindspot of Western Marxism, *Canadian Journal of Political and Social Theory*, vol. 1, no. 3

SMYTHE, D. (1978). Rejoinder to Graham Murdoch, *Canadian Journal of Political and Social Theory*, vol. 2, no. 2

THOMPSON, E. P. (1978). *The Poverty of Theory*, Merlin, London

WILLIAMS, R. (1977). *Marxism and Literature*, OUP

Cultural studies: two paradigms

STUART HALL*

In serious, critical intellectual work, there are no 'absolute beginnings' and few un-broken continuities. Neither the endless unwinding of 'tradition', so beloved of the History of Ideas, nor the absolutism of the 'epistemological rupture', punctuating Thought into its 'false' and 'correct' parts, once favoured by the Althussereans, will do. What we find, instead, is an untidy but characteristic unevenness of development. What is important are the significant *breaks*—where old lines of thought are disrupted, older constellations displaced, and elements, old and new, are regrouped around a different set of premises and themes. Changes in a problematic do significantly transform the nature of the questions asked, the forms in which they are proposed, and the manner in which they can be adequately answered. Such shifts in perspective reflect, not only the results of an internal intellectual labour, but the manner in which real historical developments and transformations are appropriated in thought, and provide Thought, not with its guarantee of 'correctness' but with its fundamental orientations, its conditions of existence. It is because of this complex articulation between thinking and historical reality, reflected in the social categories of thought, and the continuous dialectic between 'knowledge' and 'power', that the breaks are worth recording.

Cultural Studies, as a distinctive problematic, emerges from one such moment, in the mid-1950s. It was certainly not the first time that its characteristic questions had been put on the table. Quite the contrary. The two books which helped to stake out the new terrain—Hoggart's *Uses of Literacy* and Williams's *Culture And Society*—were both, in different ways, works (in part) of recovery. Hoggart's book took its reference from the 'cultural debate', long sustained in the arguments around 'mass society' and in the tradition of work identified with Leavis and *Scrutiny*. *Culture And Society* reconstructed a long tradition which Williams defined as consisting, in sum, of 'a record of a number of important and continuing reactions to . . . changes in our social, economic and political life' and offering 'a special kind of map by means of which the nature of the changes can be explored' (p. 16). The books looked, at first, simply like updating of these earlier concerns, with reference to the post-war world. Retrospectively, their 'breaks' with the traditions of thinking in which they were situated seem as important, if not more so, than their continuity with them. The *Uses of Literacy* did set out—much in the spirit of 'practical criticism'—to 'read' working class culture for the values and meanings embodied in its patterns and arrangements: as if they were certain kinds of 'texts'. But the application of this method to a living culture, and the rejection of the terms of the 'cultural debate' (polarized around the high/low culture distinction) was a thorough-going departure. *Culture and Society*—

* The Open University.

in one and the same movement—constituted a tradition (*the* 'culture-and-society' tradition), defined its 'unity' (not in terms of common positions but in its characteristic concerns and the idiom of its inquiry), itself made a distinctive modern contribution to it—*and* wrote its epitaph. The Williams book which succeeded it—*The Long Revolution*—clearly indicated that the 'culture-and-society' mode of reflection could only be completed and developed by moving somewhere else—to a significantly different kind of analysis. The very difficulty of some of the writing in *The Long Revolution*—with its attempt to 'theorize' on the back of a tradition resolutely empirical and particularist in its idiom of thought, the experiential 'thickness' of its concepts, and the generalizing movement of argument in it—stems, in part, from this determination to *move on* (Williams's work, right through to the most recent *Politics And Letters*, is exemplary precisely in its sustained developmentalism). The 'good' and the 'bad' parts of *The Long Revolution* both arise from its status as a work 'of the break'. The same could be said of E. P. Thompson's *Making Of The English Working Class*, which belongs decisively to this 'moment', even though, chronologically it appeared somewhat later. It, too, had been 'thought' within certain distinctive historical traditions: English marxist historiography, Economic and 'Labour' History. But in its foregrounding of the questions of culture, consciousness and experience, and its accent on agency, it also made a decisive break: with a certain kind of techno-logical evolutionism, with a reductive economism and an organizational determinism. Between them, these three books constituted the *caesura* out of which—among other things—'Cultural Studies' emerged.

They were, of course, seminal and formative texts. They were not, in any sense, 'text-books' for the founding of a new academic sub-discipline: nothing could have been farther from their intrinsic impulse. Whether historical or contemporary in focus, they were, themselves, focused *by*, organized through and constituted responses to, the immediate pressures of the time and society in which they were written. They not only took 'culture' seriously—as a dimension without which historical trans-formations, past and present, simply could not adequately be thought. They were, themselves, 'cultural' in the *Culture And Society* sense. They forced on their readers' attention the proposition that 'concentrated in the word *culture* are questions directly raised by the great historical changes which the changes in industry, democracy and class, in their own way, represent, and to which the changes in art are a closely related response' (p. 16). This was a question for the 1960s and 70s, as well as the 1860s and 70s. And this is perhaps the point to note that this line of thinking was roughly coterminous with what has been called the 'agenda' of the early New Left, to which these writers, in one sense or another, belonged, and whose texts these were. This connection placed the 'politics of intellectual work' squarely at the centre of Cultural Studies from the beginning—a concern from which, fortunately, it has never been, and can never be, freed. In a deep sense, the 'settling of accounts' in *Culture And Society*, the first part of *The Long Revolution*, Hoggart's densely particular, concrete study of some aspects of working-class culture and Thompson's historical recon-struction of the formation of a class culture and popular traditions in the 1790–1830 period formed, between them, the break, and defined the space from which a new area of study and practice opened. In terms of intellectual bearings and emphases, this was—if ever such a thing can be found—Cultural Studies moment of 're-founding'. The institutionalization of Cultural Studies—first, in the Centre at Birmingham, and then in courses and publications from a variety of sources and places—with its characteristic gains and losses, belongs to the 1960s and later.

'Culture' was the site of the convergence. But what definitions of this core concept emerged from this body of work? And, since this line of thinking has decisively shaped Cultural Studies, and represents the most formative *indigenous* or 'native' tradition, around what space was its concerns and concepts unified? The fact is that no single, unproblematic definition of 'culture' is to be found here. The concept remains a complex one—a site of convergent interests, rather than a logically or conceptually clarified idea. This 'richness' is an area of continuing tension and difficulty in the field. It might be useful, therefore, briefly to resume the characteristic stresses and emphases through which the concept has arrived at its present state of (in)-determinacy. (The characterizations which follow are, necessarily crude and over-simplified, synthesizing rather than carefully analytic). Two main problematics only are discussed.

Two rather different ways of conceptualizing 'culture' can be drawn out of the many suggestive formulations in Raymond Williams's *Long Revolution*. The first relates 'culture' to the sum of the available descriptions through which societies make sense of and reflect their common experiences. This definition takes up the earlier stress on 'ideas', but subjects it to a thorough reworking. The conception of 'culture' is itself democratized and socialized. It no longer consists of the sum of the 'best that has been thought and said', regarded as the summits of an achieved civilization— that ideal of perfection to which, in earlier usage, all aspired. Even 'art'—assigned in the earlier framework a privileged position, as touchstone of the highest values of civilization—is now redefined as only one, special, form of a general social process: the giving and taking of meanings, and the slow development of 'common' meanings— a common culture: 'culture', in this special sense, 'is ordinary' (to borrow the title of one of Williams's earliest attempts to make his general position more widely accessible). If even the highest, most refined of descriptions offered in works of literature are also 'part of the general process which creates conventions and institutions, through which the meanings that are valued by the community are shared and made active' (p. 55), then there is no way in which this process can be hived off or distinguished or set apart from the other practices of the historical process: 'Since our way of seeing things is literally our way of living, the process of communication is in fact the process of community: the sharing of common meanings, and thence common activities and purposes; the offering, reception and comparison of new meanings, leading to tensions and achievements of growth and change' (p. 55). Accordingly, there is no way in which the communication of descriptions, understood in this way, can be set aside and compared externally with other things. 'If the art is part of society, there is no solid whole, outside it, to which, by the form of our question, we concede priority. The art is there, as an activity, with the production, the trading, the politics, the raising of families. To study the relations adequately we must study them actively, seeing all activities as particular and contemporary forms of human energy'.

If this first emphasis takes up and re-works the connotation of the term 'culture' with the domain of 'ideas', the second emphasis is more deliberately anthropological, and emphasizes that aspect of 'culture' which refers to social *practices*. It is from this second emphasis that the somewhat simplified definition—'culture is a whole way of life'—has been rather too neatly abstracted. Williams did relate this aspect of the concept to the more 'documentary'—that is, descriptive, even ethnographic—usage of the term. But the earlier definition seems to me the more central one, into which 'way of life' is integrated. The important point in the argument rests on the active and indissoluble relationships between elements or social practices normally separated out. It is in *this* context that the 'theory of culture' is defined as 'the study of relation-ships between elements in a whole way of life'. 'Culture' is not *a* practice; nor is it simply the descriptive sum of the 'mores and folkways' of societies—as it tended to become in certain kinds of anthropology. It is threaded through *all* social practices, and is the sum of their inter-relationship. The question of what, then, is studied, and how, resolves itself. The 'culture' is those patterns of organization, those characteristic forms of human energy which can be discovered as revealing themselves—in 'un-expected identities and correspondences' as well as in 'discontinuities of an un-expected kind' (p. 63)—within or underlying *all* social practices. The analysis of culture is, then, 'the attempt to discover the nature of the organization which is the complex of these relationships'. It begins with 'the discovery of patterns of a character-istic kind'. One will discover them, not in the art, production, trading, politics, the raising of families, treated as separate activities, but through 'studying a general organization in a particular example' (p. 61). Analytically, one must study 'the relation-ships between these patterns'. The purpose of the analysis is to grasp how the inter-actions between all these practices and patterns are lived and experienced as a whole, in any particular period. This is its 'structure of feeling'.

It is easier to see what Williams was getting at, and why he was pushed along this path, if we understand what were the problems he addressed, and what pitfalls he was trying to avoid. This is particularly necessary because *The Long Revolution* (like many of Williams's work) carries on a submerged, almost 'silent' dialogue with alternative positions, which are not always as clearly identified as one would wish. There is a clear engagement with the 'idealist' and 'civilizing' definitions of culture— both the equation of 'culture' with *ideas*, in the idealist tradition; and the assimilation of culture to an *ideal*, prevalent in the elitist terms of the 'cultural debate'. But there is also a more extended engagement with certain kinds of Marxism, against which Williams's definitions are consciously pitched. He is arguing against the literal operations of the base/superstructure metaphor, which in classical Marxism ascribed the domain of ideas and of meanings to the 'superstructures', themselves conceived as merely reflective of and determined in some simple fashion by 'the base'; without a social effectivity of their own. That is to say, his argument is constructed against a vulgar materialism and an economic determinism. He offers, instead, a radical inter-actionism: in effect, the interaction of all practices in and with one another, skirting the problem of determinacy. The distinctions between practices is overcome by seeing them all as variant forms of *praxis*—of a general human activity and energy. The underlying patterns which distinguish the complex of practices in any specific society at any specific time are the characteristic 'forms of its organization' which underlie them all, and which can therefore be traced in each.

There have been several, radical revisions of this early position: and each has contributed much to the redefinition of what Cultural Studies is and should be. We have acknowledged already the exemplary nature of Williams's project, in constantly rethinking and revising older arguments—in going on thinking. Nevertheless, one is struck by a marked line of continuity through these seminal revisions. One such moment is the occasion of his recognition of Lucien Goldmann's work, and through him, of the array of marxist thinkers who had given particular attention to super-structural forms and whose work began, for the first time, to appear in English translation in the mid-1960s. The contrast between the alternative marxist traditions which sustained writers like Goldman and Lukacs, as compared with Williams's isolated position and the impoverished Marxist tradition he had to draw on, is sharply delineated. But the points of convergence—both what they are against, and what they are about—are identified in ways which are not altogether out of line with his earlier arguments. Here is the negative, which he sees as linking his work to Goldmann's: 'I came to believe that I had to give up, or at least to leave aside, what I knew as the Marxist tradition: to attempt to develop a theory of social totality; to see the study of culture as the study of relations between elements in a whole way of life; to find ways of studying structure . . . which could stay in touch with and illuminate particular art works and forms, but also forms and relations of more general social life; to replace the formula of base and superstructure with the more active idea of a field of mutually if also unevenly determining forces' (*NLR* 67, May–June 1971). And here is the positive—the point where the convergence is marked between Williams's 'structure of feeling' and Goldmann's 'genetic structuralism': 'I found in my own work that I had to develop the idea of a structure of feeling . . . But then I found Goldmann beginning . . . from a concept of structure which contained, in itself, a relation between social and literary facts. This relation, he insisted, was not a matter of content, but of mental structures: "categories which simultaneously organize the empirical consciousness of a particular social group, and the imaginative world created by the writer". By definition, these structures are not individually but collectively created'. The stress there on the interactivity of practices and on the underlying totalities, and the homologies between them, is characteristic and significant. 'A correspondence of content between a writer and his world is less significant than this correspondence of organization, of structure'.

A second such 'moment' is the point where Williams really takes on board E. P. Thompson's critique of *The Long Revolution* (cf. the review in *NLR* 9 and 10)—that no 'whole way of life' is without its dimension of struggle and confrontation between opposed *ways* of life—and attempts to rethink the key issues of determination and domination via Gramsci's concept of 'hegemony'. This essay ('Base and Superstructure', *NLR* 82, 1973) is a seminal one, especially in its elaboration of dominant, residual and emergent cultural practices, and its return to the problematic of determinacy as 'limits and pressures'. None the less, the earlier emphases recur, with force: 'we cannot separate literature and art from other kinds of social practice, in such a way as to make them subject to quite special and distinct laws'. And, 'no mode of production, and therefore no dominant society or order of society, and therefore no dominant culture, in reality exhausts human practice, human energy, human intention'. And this note is carried forward—indeed, it is radically accented—in Williams's most sustained and succinct recent statement of his position: the masterly condensations of *Marxism And Literature*. Against the structuralist emphasis on the specificity and 'autonomy' of practices, and their analytic separation of societies into their discrete instances, Williams's stress is on 'constitutive activity' in general, on 'sensuous human activity, as practice', from Marx's first 'thesis' on Feuerbach; on different practices conceived as a 'whole indissoluble practice'; on totality. 'Thus, contrary to one development in Marxism, it is not "the base" and "the superstructure" that need to be studied, but specific and indissoluble real processes, within which the decisive relationship, from a Marxist point of view, is that expressed by the complex idea of "determination" ' (*M & L*, pp. 30–31, 82).

At one level, Williams's and Thompson's work can only be said to converge around the terms of the same problematic through the operation of a violent and schematically dichotomous theorization. The organizing terrain of Thompson's work—classes as relations, popular struggle, and historical forms of consciousness, class cultures in their historical particularity—is foreign to the more reflective and 'generalizing' mode in which Williams typically works. And the dialogue between them begins with a very sharp encounter. The review of *The Long Revolution*, which Thompson undertook, took Williams sharply to task for the evolutionary way in which culture as a 'whole way of life' had been conceptualized; for his tendency to absorb conflicts between class cultures into the terms of an extended 'conversation'; for his impersonal tone— above the contending classes, as it were; and for the imperializing sweep of his concept of 'culture' (which, heterogeneously, swept everything into its orbit because it was the study of the interrelationships between the forms of energy and organization underlying *all* practices. But wasn't this—Thompson asked—where History came in?) Progressively, we can see how Williams has persistently rethought the terms of his original paradigm to take these criticisms into account—though this is accomplished (as it so frequently is in Williams) obliquely: via a particular appropriation of Gramsci, rather than in a more direct modification.

Thompson also operates with a more 'classical' distinction than Williams, between 'social being' and 'social consciousness' (the terms he infinitely prefers, from Marx, to the more fashionable 'base and superstructure'). Thus, where Williams insists on the absorption of all practices into the totality of 'real, indissoluble practice', Thompson does deploy an older distinction between what is 'culture' and what is 'not culture'. 'Any theory of culture must include the concept of the dialectical interaction between culture and something that is *not* culture.' Yet the definition of culture is not, after all, so far removed from Williams's: 'We must suppose the raw material of life experience to be at one pole, and all the infinitely complex human disciplines and systems, articulate and inarticulate, formalised in institutions or dispersed in the least formal ways, which "handle", transmit or distort this raw material to be at the other'. Similarly, with respect to the commonality of 'practice' which underlies all the distinct practices: 'It is the active process—which is at the same time the process through which men make their history—that I am insisting upon' (*NLR* 9, p. 33, 1961). And the two positions come close together around—again—certain distinctive negatives and positives. Negatively, against the 'base/superstructure' metaphor, and a reductionist or 'economistic' definition of determinacy. On the first: 'The dialectical intercourse between social being and social consciousness—or between "culture" and "*not* culture"—is at the heart of any comprehension of the historical process within the Marxist tradition . . . The tradition inherits a dialectic that is right, but the particular mechanical metaphor through which it is expressed is wrong. This metaphor from constructional engineering . . . must in any case be inadequate to describe the flux of conflict, the dialectic of a changing social process . . . All the metaphors which are commonly offered have a tendency to lead the mind into schematic modes and away from the interaction of being-consciousness'. And on 'reductionism': 'Reductionism is a lapse in historical logic by which political or cultural events are "explained" in terms of the class affiliations of the actors . . . But the mediation between "interest" and "belief" was not through Nairn's "complex of superstructures" but through the people themselves' ('Peculiarities of the English', *Socialist Register*, 1965, pp. 351–352). And, more positively—a simple statement which may be taken as defining virtually the whole of Thompson's historical work, from *The Making* to *Whigs And Hunters*, *The Poverty of Theory* and beyond—'capitalist society was founded upon forms of exploitation which are simultaneously economic, moral and cultural. Take up the essential defining productive relationship . . . and turn it round, and it reveals itself now in one aspect (wage–labour), now in another (an acquisitive ethos), and now in another (the alienation of such intellectual faculties as are not required by the worker in his productive role)' (ibid., p. 356).

Here, then, despite the many significant differences, is the outline of one significant line of thinking in Cultural Studies—some would say, *the* dominant paradigm. It stands opposed to the residual and merely-reflective rôle assigned to 'the cultural'. In its different ways, it conceptualizes culture as interwoven with all social practices; and those practices, in turn, as a common form of human activity: sensuous human praxis, the activity through which men and women make history. It is opposed to the base-superstructure way of formulating the relationship between ideal and material forces, especially where the 'base' is defined as the determination by 'the economic' in any simple sense. It prefers the wider formulation—the dialectic between social being and social consciousness: neither separable into its distinct poles (in some alternative formulations, the dialectic between 'culture' and 'non-culture'). It defines 'culture' as *both* the meanings and values which arise amongst distinctive social groups and classes, on the basis of their given historical conditions and relationships, through which they 'handle' and respond to the conditions of existence; *and* as the lived traditions and practices through which those 'understandings' are expressed and in which they are embodied. Williams brings together these two aspects—definitions and ways of life—around the concept of 'culture' itself. Thompson brings the two elements—consciousness and conditions—around the concept of 'experience'. Both positions entail certain difficult fluctuations around these key terms. Williams so totally absorbs 'definitions of experience' into our 'ways of living', and both into an indissoluble real material practice-in-general, as to obviate any distinction between 'culture' and 'not-culture'. Thompson sometimes uses 'experience' in the more usual sense of consciousness, as the collective ways in which men 'handle, transmit or distort' their given conditions, the raw materials of life; sometimes as the domain of the 'lived', the mid-term *between* 'conditions' and 'culture'; and sometimes as the objective conditions themselves—against which particular modes of consciousness are counterposed. But, whatever the terms, both positions tend to read structures of relations in terms of how they are 'lived' and 'experienced'. Williams's 'structure of feeling'—with its deliberate condensation of apparently incompatible elements—is characteristic. But the same is true of Thompson, despite his far fuller historical grasp of the 'given-ness' or structuredness of the relations and conditions into which men and women necessarily and involuntarily enter, and his clearer attention to the determinacy of productive and exploitative relations under capitalism. This is a consequence of giving culture-consciousness and experience so pivotal a place in the analysis. The *experiential pull* in this paradigm, and the emphasis on the creative and on historical agency, constitutes the two key elements in the *humanism* of the position outlined. Each, consequently accords 'experience' an authenticating position in any cultural analysis. It is, ultimately, where and how people experience their conditions of life, define them and respond to them, which, for Thompson defines why every mode of production is also a culture, and every struggle between classes is always also a struggle between cultural modalities; and which, for Williams, is what a 'cultural analysis', in the final instance, should deliver. In 'experience', all the different practices intersect; within 'culture' the different practices interact—even if on an uneven and mutually determining basis. This sense of cultural totality—of *the whole* historical process—over-rides any effort to keep the instances and elements distinct. Their real interconnection, under given historical conditions, must be matched by a totalizing movement 'in thought', in the analysis. It establishes for both the strongest protocols against any form of analytic abstraction which distinguishes practices, or which sets out to test the 'actual historical movement' in all its intertwined complexity and particularity by any more sustained logical or analytical operation. These positions, especially in their more concrete historical rendering (*The Making*, *The Country And The City*) are the very opposite of a Hegelian search for underlying Essences. Yet, in their tendency to reduce practices to *praxis* and to find common and homologous 'forms' underlying the most apparently differentiated areas, their movement is 'essentialising'. They have a particular way of understanding the totality— though it is with a small 't', concrete and historically determinate, uneven in its correspondences. They understand it 'expressively'. And since they constantly inflect the more traditional analysis towards the experiential level, or read the other structures and relations downwards from the vantage point of how they are 'lived', they are properly (even if not adequately or fully) characterized as 'culturalist' in their emphasis: even when all the caveats and qualifications against a too rapid 'dichotomous theorizing' have been entered. (Cf. for 'culturalism', Richard Johnson's two seminal articles on the operation of the paradigm: in 'Histories of Culture/ Theories of Ideology', *Ideology And Cultural Production*, eds M. Barrett, P. Corrigan *et al.*, Croom Helm, 1979; and 'Three Problematics' in *Working Class Culture*: Clarke, Critcher and Johnson, Hutchinsons and CCCS, 1979. For the dangers in 'dichotomous theorizing', cf. the Introduction, 'Representation and Cultural Production', to Barrett, Corrigan *et al.*)

The 'culturalist' strand in Cultural Studies was interrupted by the arrival on the intellectual scene of the 'structuralisms'. These, possibly more varied than the 'culturalisms', nevertheless shared certain positions and orientations in common which makes their designation under a single title not altogether misleading. It has been remarked that whereas the 'culturalist' paradigm can be defined without requiring a conceptual reference to the term 'ideology' (the *word*, of course, does appear: but it is not a key concept), the 'structuralist' interventions have been largely articulated around the concept of 'ideology': in keeping with its more impeccably Marxist lineage, 'culture' does not figure so prominently. Whilst this may be true of the Marxist structuralists, it is at best less than half the truth about the structuralist enterprise as such. But it is now a common error to condense the latter exclusively around the impact of Althusser and all that has followed in the wake of his interventions—where 'ideology' has played a seminal, but modulated rôle: and to omit the significance of Levi–Strauss. Yet, in strict historical terms, it was Levi–Strauss, and the early semiotics, which made the first break. And though the Marxist structuralisms have superseded the latter, they owed, and continue to owe, an immense theoretical debt (often fended off or down-graded into footnotes, in the search for a retrospective orthodoxy) to his work. It was Levi–Strauss's structuralism which, in its appropriation of the linguistic paradigm, after Saussure, offered the promise to the 'human sciences of culture' of a paradigm capable of rendering them scientific and rigorous in a thoroughly new way. And when, in Althusser's work, the more classical Marxist themes were recovered, it remained the case that Marx was 'read'—and reconstituted—through the terms of the linguistic paradigm. In *Reading Capital*, for example, the case is made that the mode of production—to coin a phrase—could best be understood as if "structured like a language" (through the selective combination of invariant elements). The a-historical and synchronic stress, against the historical emphases of 'culturalism', derived from a similar source. So did a preoccupation with 'the social, *sui generis*'—used not adjectivally but substantively: a usage Levi–Strauss derived, not from Marx, but from Durkheim (the Durkheim who analysed the social categories of thought—e.g. in *Primitive Classification*—rather than the Durkheim of *The Division Of Labour*, who became the founding father of American structural-functionalism).

Levi–Strauss did, on occasion, toy with certain Marxist formulations. Thus, 'Marxism, if not Marx himself, has too commonly reasoned as though practices followed directly from praxis. Without questioning the undoubted primacy of infra-structures, I believe that there is always a mediator between praxis and practices, namely, the conceptual scheme by the operation of which matter and form, neither with any independent existence, are realized as structures, that is as entities which are both empirical and intelligible'. But this—to coin another phrase—was largely 'gestural'. This structuralism shared with culturalism a radical break with the terms of the base/superstructure metaphor, as derived from the simpler parts of the *German Ideology*. And, though "It is to this theory of the superstructures, scarcely touched on by Marx" to which Levi–Strauss aspired to contribute, his contribution was such as to break in a radical way with its whole terms of reference, as finally and irrevocably as the 'culturalists' did. Here—and we must include Althusser in this characterization—culturalists and structuralists alike ascribed to the domains hitherto defined as 'super-structural' a specificity and effectivity, a constitutive primacy, which pushed them beyond the terms of reference of 'base' and 'superstructure'. Levi–Strauss and Althusser, too, were anti-reductionist and anti-economist in their very cast of thought, and critically attacked that transitive causality which, for so long, had passed itself off as 'classical Marxism'.

Levi–Strauss worked consistently with the term 'culture'. He regarded 'ideologies' as of much lesser importance: mere 'secondary rationalizations'. Like Williams and Goldmann, he worked, not at the level of correspondences between the *content* of a practice, but at the level of their forms and structures. But the manner in which these were conceptualized were altogether at variance with either the 'culturalism' of Williams or Goldmann's 'genetic structuralism'. This divergence can be identified in three distinct ways. First, he conceptualized 'culture' as the categories and frame-works in thought and language through which different societies classified out their conditions of existence—above all (since Levi–Strauss was an anthropologist), the relations between the human and the natural worlds. Second, he thought of the manner and practice through which these categories and mental frameworks were produced and transformed, largely on an analogy with the ways in which language itself—the principal medium of 'culture'—operated. He identified what was specific to them and their operation as the 'production of meaning': they were, above all, *signifying* practices. Third, after some early flirtations with Durkheim and Mauss's social categories of thought, he largely gave up the question of the relation *between* signifying and non-signifying practices—between 'culture' and 'not-culture', to use other terms—for the sake of concentrating on the *internal* relations within signifying practices by means of which the categories of meaning were produced. This left the question of determinacy, of totality, largely in abeyance. The causal logic of deter-minacy was abandoned in favour of a structuralist causality—a logic of *arrangement*, of internal relations, of articulation of parts within a structure. Each of these aspects is also positively present in Althusser's work and that of the Marxist structuralists, even when the terms of reference had been regrounded in Marx's 'immense theoretical revolution'. In one of Althusser's seminal formulations about ideology—defined as the themes, concepts and representations through which men and women 'live', in an imaginary relation, their relation to their real conditions of existence—we can see the skeleton outline of Levi–Strauss's 'conceptual schemes between praxis and practices'. 'Ideologies' are here being conceptualized, not as the contents and surface forms of ideas, but as the unconscious categories through which conditions are represented and lived. We have already commented on the active presence in Althusser's thinking of the linguistic paradigm—the second element identified above. And though, in the concept of 'over-determination'—one of his most seminal and fruitful contributions—Althusser did return to the problems of the relations *between* practices and the question of determinacy (proposing, incidentally, a thoroughly novel and highly suggestive reformulation, which has received far too little subsequent attention), he did tend to reinforce the 'relative autonomy' of different practices, and their internal specificities, conditions and effects at the expense of an 'expressive' conception of the totality, with its typical homologies and correspondences.

Aside from the wholly distinct intellectual and conceptual universes within which these alternative paradigms developed, there were certain points where, despite their apparent overlaps, culturalism and structuralism were starkly counterposed. We can identify this counterposition at one of its sharpest points precisely around the concept of 'experience', and the rôle the term played in each perspective. Whereas, in 'culturalism', experience was the ground—the terrain of 'the lived'—where consciousness and conditions intersected, structuralism insisted that 'experience' could not, by definition, be the ground of anything, since one could only 'live' and experience one's conditions *in and through* the categories, classifications and frameworks of the culture. These categories, however, did not arise from or in experience: rather, experience was their 'effect'. The culturalists had defined the forms of consciousness and culture as collective. But they had stopped far short of the radical proposition that, in culture and in language, the subject was 'spoken by' the categories of culture in which he/she thought, rather than 'speaking them'. These categories were, however, not merely collective rather than individual productions: they were *unconscious* structures. That is why, though Levi–Strauss spoke only of 'Culture', his concept provided the basis for an easy translation, by Althusser, into the conceptual framework of ideology: 'Ideology is indeed a system of "representations", but in the majority of cases these representations have nothing to do with "consciousness": . . . it is above all as structures that they impose on the vast majority of men, not via their "consciousness" . . . it is within this ideological unconsciousness that men succeed in altering the "lived" relation between them and the world and acquiring that new form of specific unconsciousness called "consciousness"'(*For Marx*, p. 233). It was, in this sense, that 'experience' was conceived, not as an authenticating source but as an effect: not as a reflection of the real but as an 'imaginary relation'. It was only a short step—the one which separates *For Marx* from the 'Ideological State Apparatuses' essay—to the development of an account of how this 'imaginary relation' served, not simply the dominance of a ruling class over a dominated one, but (through the reproduction of the relations of production, and the constitution of labour-power in a form fit for capitalist exploitation) the expanded reproduction of the mode of production itself. Many of the other lines of divergence between the two paradigms flow from this point: the conception of 'men' as bearers of the structures that speak and place them, rather than as active agents in the making of their own history; the emphasis on a structural rather than a historical 'logic'; the preoccupation with the constitution—in 'theory'—of a non-ideological, scientific discourse; and hence the privileging of conceptual work and of Theory as guaranteed; the recasting of history as a march of the structures (cf. passim, *The Poverty of Theory*): the structuralist 'machine'. . .

There is no space in which to follow through the many ramifications which have followed from the development of one or other of these 'master paradigms' in Cultural Studies. Though they by no means account for all, or even nearly all, of the many strategies adopted, it is fair to say that, between them, they have defined the principal lines of development in the field. The seminal debates have been polarized around their thematics; some of the best concrete work has flowed from the efforts to set one or other of these paradigms to work on particular problems and materials. Characteristically—the sectarian and self-righteous climate of critical intellectual work in England being what it is, and its dependency being so marked—the arguments and debates have most frequently been over-polarized into their extremes. At these extremities, they frequently appear only as mirror-reflections or inversions of one another. Here, the broad typologies we have been working with—for the sake of convenient exposition—become the prison-house of thought.

Without suggesting that there can be any easy synthesis between them, it might usefully be said at this point that neither 'culturalism' nor 'structuralism' is, in its present manifestation, adequate to the task of constructing the study of culture as a conceptually clarified and theoretically informed domain of study. Nevertheless, something fundamental to it emerges from a rough comparison of their respective strengths and limitations.

The great strength of the structuralisms is their stress on 'determinate conditions'. They remind us that, unless the dialectic really can be held, in any particular analysis, between both halves of the proposition—that 'men make history . . . on the basis of conditions which are not of their making'—the result will inevitably be a naïve humanism, with its necessary consequence: a voluntarist and populist political practice. The fact that 'men' can become conscious of their conditions, organize to struggle against them and in fact transform them—without which no active politics can even be conceived, let alone practised—must not be allowed to override the awareness of the fact that, in capitalist relations, men and women are placed and positioned in relations which constitute them as agents. 'Pessimism of the intellect, optimism of the will' is a better starting point than a simple heroic affirmation. Structuralism does enable us to begin to think—as Marx insisted—of the *relations* of a structure on the basis of something other than their reduction to relationships between 'people'. This was Marx's privileged level of abstraction: that which enabled him to break with the obvious but incorrect starting point of 'political economy'—bare individuals.

But this connects with a second strength: the recognition by structuralism not only of the necessity of abstraction as the instrument of thought through which 'real relations' are appropriated, but also of the presence, in Marx's work, of a continuous and complex movement *between different levels of abstraction*. It is, of course, the case—as 'culturalism' argues—that, in historical reality, practices do not appear neatly distinguished out into their respective instances. However, to think about or to analyse the complexity of the real, the act of practice of thinking is required; and this necessitates the use of the power of abstraction and analysis, the formation of concepts with which to cut into the complexity of the real, in order precisely to reveal and bring to light relationships and structures which cannot be visible to the naïve naked eye, and which can neither present nor authenticate themselves: 'In the analysis of economic forms, neither microscopes nor chemical reagents are of assistance. The power of abstraction must replace both'. Of course, structuralism has frequently taken this proposition to its extreme. Because thought is impossible without 'the power of abstraction', it has confused this with giving an absolute primacy to the level of the formation of concepts—and at the highest, most abstract level of abstraction only: Theory with a capital 'T' then becomes judge and jury. But this is precisely to lose the insight just won from Marx's own practice. For it is clear in, for example, *Capital*, that the *method*—whilst, of course, taking place 'in thought' (as Marx asked in the 1857 Introduction, where else?)—rests, not on the simple exercise of abstraction but on the movement and relations which the argument is constantly establishing between *different levels* of abstraction: at each, the premises in play must be distinguished from those which—for the sake of the argument—have to be held constant. The movement to another level of magnification (to deploy the microscope metaphor) requires the specifying of further conditions of existence not supplied at a previous, more abstract level: in this way, by successive abstractions of different magnitudes, to *move towards* the constitution, the *reproduction*, of 'the concrete in thought' as an effect of a certain kind of thinking. This method is adequately represented in *neither* the absolutism of Theoretical Practice, in structuralism, nor in the anti-abstraction 'Poverty Of Theory' position into which, in reaction, culturalism appears to have been driven or driven itself. Nevertheless it is intrinsically *theoretical*, and must be. Here, structuralism's insistence that thought does not reflect reality, but is articulated on and appropriates it, is a necessary starting point. An adequate *working through* of the consequences of this argument might begin to produce a method which takes us outside the permanent oscillations between abstraction/anti-abstraction and the false dichotomies of Theoreticism *vs.* Empiricism which have both marked and disfigured the structuralism/culturalism encounter to date.

Structuralism has another strength, in its conception of 'the whole'. There is a sense in which, though culturalism constantly insists on the radical particularity of its practices, its mode of conceptualizing the 'totality' has something of the complex simplicity of an expressive totality behind it. Its complexity is constituted by the fluidity with which practices move into and out of one another: but this complexity is reducible, conceptually, to the 'simplicity' of praxis—human activity, as such—in which the same contradictions constantly appear, homologously reflected in each. Structuralism goes too far in erecting the machine of a 'Structure', with its self-generating propensities (a 'Spinozean eternity', whose function is only the sum of its effects: a truly structural*ist* deviation), equipped with its distinctive instances. Yet it represents an advance over culturalism in the conception it has of the necessary *complexity* of the unity of a structure (over-determination being a more successful way of thinking this complexity than the combinatory invariance of structuralist causality). Moreover, it has the conceptual ability to think of a unity which is constructed through the *differences* between, rather than the homology of, practices. Here, again, it has won a critical insight about Marx's method: one thinks of the complex passages of the 1857 Introduction to the *Grundrisse* where Marx demonstrates how it is possible to think of the 'unity' of a social formation as constructed, not out of identity but out of *difference*. Of course, the stress on difference can—and has—led the structuralisms into a fundamental conceptual heterogeneity, in which all sense of structure and totality is lost. Foucault and other post-Althusshereans have taken this devious path into the absolute, not the relative, autonomy of practices, via their necessary heterogeneity and 'necessary non-correspondence'. But the emphasis on unity-in-difference, on complex unity—Marx's concrete as the 'unity of many determinations'—can be worked in another, and ultimately more fruitful direction: towards the problematic of relative autonomy and 'over-determination', and the study of *articulation*. Again, articulation contains the danger of a high formalism. But it also has the considerable advantage of enabling us to think of how specific practices (articulated around contradictions which do not all arise in the same way, at the same point, in the same moment), can nevertheless be thought *together*. The structuralist paradigm thus does—if properly developed—enable us to begin really to *conceptualize* the specificity of different practices (analytically distinguished, abstracted out), without losing its grip on the ensemble which they constitute. Culturalism constantly affirms the specificity of different practices—'culture' must not be absorbed into 'the economic': but it lacks an adequate way of establishing this specificity theoretically.

The third strength which structuralism exhibits lies in its decentering of 'experience' and its seminal work in elaborating the neglected category of 'ideology'. It is difficult to conceive of a Cultural Studies thought within a Marxist paradigm which is innocent of the category of 'ideology'. Of course, culturalism constantly make reference to this concept: but it does not in fact lie at the centre of its conceptual universe. The authenticating power and reference of 'experience' imposes a barrier between culturalism and a proper conception of 'ideology'. Yet, without it, the effectivity of 'culture' for the reproduction of a particular mode of production cannot be grasped. It is true that there is a marked tendency in the more recent structuralist conceptualisations of 'ideology' to give it a functionalist reading—as the necessary cement of the social formation. From this position, it is indeed impossible—as culturalism would correctly argue—to conceive either of ideologies which are not, by definition, 'dominant': or of the concept of struggle (the latter's appearance in Althusser's famous ISA's article being—to coin yet another phrase—largely 'gestural'). Nevertheless, work is already being done which suggests ways in which the field of ideology may be adequately conceptualized as a terrain of struggle (through the work of Gramsci, and more recently, of Laclau), and these have structuralist rather than culturalist bearings.

Culturalism's strengths can almost be derived from the weaknesses of the structuralist position already noted, and from the latter's strategic absences and silences. It has insisted, correctly, on the affirmative moment of the development of conscious struggle and organization as a necessary element in the analysis of history, ideology and consciousness: against its persistent down-grading in the structuralist paradigm. Here, again, it is largely Gramsci who has provided us with a set of more refined terms through which to link the largely 'unconscious' and given cultural categories of 'common sense' with the formation of more active and organic ideologies, which have the capacity to intervene in the ground of common sense and popular traditions and, through such interventions, to organize masses of men and women. In this sense, culturalism *properly* restores the dialectic between the unconsciousness of cultural categories and the moment of conscious organization: even if, in its characteristic movement, it has tended to match structuralism's over-emphasis on 'conditions' with an altogether too-inclusive emphasis on 'consciousness'. It therefore not only recovers—as the necessary moment of any analysis—the process by means of which classes-in-themselves, defined primarily by the way in which economic relations position 'men' as agents—become active historical and political forces—for-themselves: it also—against its own anti-theoretical good sense—*requires* that, when properly developed, each moment must be understood in terms of the level of abstraction at which the analysis is operating. Again, Gramsci has begun to point a way through this false polarization in his discussion of 'the passage between the structure and the sphere of the complex superstructures', and its distinct forms and moments.

We have concentrated in this argument largely on a characterization of what seem to us to be the two seminal paradigms at work in Cultural Studies. Of course, they are by no means the only active ones. New developments and lines of thinking are by no means adequately netted with reference to them. Nevertheless, these paradigms can, in a sense, be deployed to measure what appear to us to be the radical weaknesses or inadequacies of those which offer themselves as alternative rallying-points. Here, briefly, we identify three.

The first is that which follows on from Levi–Strauss, early semiotics and the terms of the linguistic paradigm, and the centering on 'signifying practices', moving by way of psychoanalytic concepts and Lacan to a radical recentering of virtually the whole terrain of Cultural Studies around the terms 'discourse' and 'the subject'. One way of understanding this line of thinking is to see it as an attempt to fill that empty space in early structuralism (of both the Marxist and non-Marxist varieties) where, in earlier discourses, 'the subject' and subjectivity might have been expected to appear but did not. This is, of course, precisely one of the key points where culturalism brings its pointed criticisms to bear on structuralism's 'process without a subject'. The difference is that, whereas culturalism would correct for the hyper-structuralism of earlier models by restoring the unified subject (collective or individual) of consciousness at the centre of 'the Structure', discourse theory, by way of the Freudian concepts of the unconscious and the Lacanian concepts of how subjects are constituted in language (through the entry into the Symbolic and the Law of Culture), restores the *decentered* subject, the contradictory subject, as a set of positions in language and knowledge, from which culture can appear to be enunciated. This approach clearly identifies a gap, not only in structuralism but in Marxism itself. The problem is that the manner in which this 'subject' of culture is conceptualized is of a trans-historical and 'universal' character: it addresses the subject-in-general, not historically-determinate social subjects, or socially determinate particular languages. Thus it is incapable, so far, of moving its in-general propositions to the level of concrete historical analysis. The second difficulty is that the processes of contradiction and struggle—lodged by early structuralism wholly at the level of 'the structure'—are now, by one of those persistent mirror-inversions, lodged exclusively at the level of the unconscious processes of the subject. It may be, as culturalism often argues, that the 'subjective' is a necessary moment of any such analysis. But this is a very different proposition from dismantling the whole of the social processes of particular modes of production and social formations, and reconstituting them exclusively at the level of unconscious psychoanalytic processes. Though important work has been done, both within this paradigm and to define and develop it, its claims to have replaced *all* the terms of the earlier paradigms with a more adequate set of concepts seems wildly over-ambitious. Its claims to have integrated Marxism into a more adequate materialism is, largely, a semantic rather than a conceptual claim.

A second development is the attempt to return to the terms of a more classical 'political economy' of culture. This position argues that the concentration on the cultural and ideological aspects has been wildly over-done. It would restore the older terms of 'base/superstructure', finding, in the last-instance determination of the cultural-ideological by the economic, that hierarchy of determinations which both alternatives appear to lack. This position insists that the economic processes and structures of cultural production are more significant than their cultural-ideological aspect: and that these are quite adequately caught in the more classical terminology of profit, exploitation, surplus-value and the analysis of culture as commodity. It retains a notion of ideology as 'false consciousness'.

There is, of course, some strength to the claim that both structuralism and culturalism, in their different ways, have neglected the economic analysis of cultural and ideological production. All the same, with the return to this more 'classical' terrain, many of the problems which originally beset it also reappear. The specificity of the effect of the cultural and ideological dimension once more tends to disappear. It tends to conceive the economic level as not only a 'necessary' but a 'sufficient' explanation of cultural and ideological effects. Its focus on the analysis of the commodity form, similarly, blurs all the carefully established distinctions between different practices, since it is the most *generic* aspects of the commodity-form which attract attention. Its deductions are therefore, largely, confined to an epochal level of abstraction: the generalizations about the commodity-form hold true throughout the capitalist epoch as a whole. Very little by way of concrete and conjunctural analysis can be derived at this high-level 'logic of capital' form of abstraction. It also tends to its own kind of functionalism—a functionalism of 'logic' rather than of 'structure' or history. This approach, too, has insights which are well worth following through. But it sacrifices too much of what has been painfully secured, without a compensating gain in explanatory power.

The third position is closely related to the structuralist enterprise, but has followed the path of 'difference' through into a radical heterogeneity. Foucault's work currently enjoying another of those uncritical periods of discipleship through which British intellectuals reproduce today their dependency on yesterday's French ideas— has had an exceedingly positive effect: above all because—in suspending the nearly-insoluble problems of determination Foucault has made possible a welcome return to the concrete analysis of particular ideological and discursive formations, and the sites of their elaboration. Foucault and Gramsci between them account for much of the most productive work on *concrete analysis* now being undertaken in the field: thereby reinforcing and—paradoxically—supporting the sense of the concrete historical instance which has always been one of culturalism's principal strengths. But, again, Foucault's example is positive only if his general epistemological position is not swallowed whole. For in fact Foucault so resolutely suspends judgment, and adopts so thoroughgoing a scepticism about any determinacy or relationship between practices, other than the largely contingent, that we are entitled to see him, not as an agnostic on these questions, but as deeply committed to the necessary non-correspondence of all practices to one another. From such a position neither a social formation, nor the State, can be adequately thought. And indeed Foucault is constantly falling into the pit which he has dug for himself. For when—against his well-defended epistemological positions—he stumbles across certain 'correspondences' (for example, the simple fact that all the major moments of transition he has traced in each of his studies—on the prison, sexuality, medicine, the asylum, language and political economy—all appear to converge around exactly that point where industrial capitalism and the bourgeoisie make their fateful, historical rendezvous), he lapses into a vulgar reductionism, which thoroughly belies the sophisticated positions he has elsewhere advanced.[1]

[1] He is quite capable of wheeling in through the back door the classes he recently expelled from the front.

I have said enough to indicate that, in my view, the line in Cultural Studies which has attempted to *think forwards* from the best elements in the structuralist and culturalist enterprises, by way of some of the concepts elaborated in Gramsci's work, comes closest to meeting the requirements of the field of study. And the reason for that should by now also be obvious. Though neither structuralism nor culturalism will do, as self-sufficient paradigms of study, they have a centrality to the field which all the other contenders lack because, between them (in their divergences as well as their convergences) they address what must be the *core problem* of Cultural Studies. They constantly return us to the terrain marked out by those strongly coupled but not mutually exclusive concepts culture/ideology. They pose, together, the problems consequent on trying to think *both* the specificity of different practices and the forms of the articulated unity they constitute. They make a constant, if flawed, return to the base/superstructure metaphor. They are correct in insisting that this question— which resumes all the problems of a non-reductive determinacy—is the heart of the matter: and that, on the solution of this problem will turn the capacity of Cultural Studies to supercede the endless oscillations between idealism and reductionism. They confront—even if in radically opposed ways—the dialectic between conditions and consciousness. At another level, they pose the question of the relation between the logic of thinking and the 'logic' of historical process. They continue to hold out the promise of a properly materialist theory of culture. In their sustained and mutually reinforcing antagonisms they hold out no promise of an easy synthesis. But, between them, they define where, if at all, is the space, and what are the limits, within which such a synthesis might be constituted. In Cultural Studies, theirs are the 'names of the game'.

Codes and cultural analysis

JOHN CORNER*

> 'We mean by code, for instance, a verbal language such as English, Italian or German; visual systems, such as traffic signals, road signals, card games, etc; and so on.'
>
> Umberto Eco.

Introduction

One of the most ambitious projects to be undertaken in the still disputed academic area of 'cultural studies' has been the connecting of the study of linguistic forms with the study of social structure, processes and behaviour.[1] The relationship between society and language or, more broadly, symbolic structures, has long been an important element of social and anthropological research, but the new emphasis is one which seeks to obtain a precision of socio-cultural analysis in keeping both with the 'scientific' levels of systematic investigation achieved by modern linguistics and, quite often, the 'scientific' ambitions of much radical social theory. The system of a particular language and the system of the particular society which uses it are seen to be in an important, mutually determining relationship—such that linguistic study of a certain kind offers inroads into an understanding of a society and its characteristic processes. Linguistic paradigms have also been used in the study of a whole range of cultural phenomena, including those not previously thought of as having directly linguistic dimensions, such as photography, dress and aspects of social behaviour and organisation. A widened meaning of 'language' has emerged.

Many of the researchers who have addressed themselves to this broadly socio-linguistic enterprise (as well as work in sociolinguistics from a social science base there has been a range of structuralist, semiotic and literary critical influences) have had resort at some point or other to the notion of 'code', which they have used with varying degrees of emphasis and according to a number of definitions. In this article I propose to examine some of the problems of these usages, concentrating on dominant tendencies within the area of cultural studies/communication studies.

Codes

Although 'code' is widely used in general speech and writing to indicate levels of rule-system ranging from the closure of the morse-code (a tight set of correlations) to the relative openness and generality of a code of norms or of conduct (which might at times be describable as the unspoken and implicitly organised tendencies of behavioural propriety) in the area of linguistic social research something close to the idea of a set of rule-governed operations is usually indicated by the term. That is to say, the usage points towards something closer to the morse-code than to the normal

---

* Centre for Communication Studies, Liverpool University.

[1] Many examples could be given of the centrality of the approach but perhaps Hall (1973) is most illustrative:

> 'My purpose is to suggest that, in the analysis of culture, the inter-connection between societal structures and processes and formal or symbolic structures is absolutely pivotal.'

uses of code of manners, where an altogether more loosely-arranged set of guiding conventions, a lower level of determinations, is suggested.

It is worth noting here that as well as different levels of *systemic organisation* being involved, there is also a matter of *transformation* to be considered. The morse-code allows one, by precise equivalents, to transmit language in the form of a broken audio tone or light beam; a code of manners, whilst it certainly exerts some systematic pressure on behavioural choice, does not strictly speaking *encode* anything at all. It may give a socially determined coherence and a regulated means of expression to areas of social experience but expression is not synonymous with *transformation across systems*. On this count, many contemporary uses of code in cultural analysis appear to be closer to code of manners than to morse code, though there is frequently assumed to be a high level of systemic inter-connection at work, as I shall discuss later.

A number of introductory texts in the area slide around this issue rather confidently, as if code suggested a spectrum of relatively unproblematic systemic states and that the shift from semaphore to social behaviour was purely one of degree. It is true that matters of degree enter into the question of how the production of human and social meanings is variously organised and controlled but that is not to say that they are 'mere' matters of degree or that they do not require careful differentiation. In fact, most confusions in cultural code theory seem to be due less to the researchers artfully abusing the term as to their falling victims to its general imprecision when on its own and its wide range of meanings in specialised contexts.

The concept 'code' has entered communications and cultural studies in Britain through three rather distinct lines of research:

(1) The technological paradigms of much early work on 'communication theory', paradigms in which the terms 'encoding' and 'decoding' are borrowed from information theory and telecommunications and indicate the conversion of 'message' into 'signal' and the reverse (Shannon and Weaver, 1949). This usage is still operative in many models and perspectives seeking a unified (and therefore often highly abstract) general theory of communication. Combined with genetic and psychological perspectives, it is present also in the influential work of Bateson (1951) and Wilden (1972).

(2) The class-specific, sociolinguist theories of Basil Bernstein and his fellow researchers, notably those at the University of London Institute of Education. Here code is defined as 'frame of consistency' and 'social structuring of meanings' (Bernstein, 1971). In a development of the concept (Hasan, 1973), codes are seen to be related to the 'semantic structure of a message' both as this is determined by 'social relationships' and as it, in turn, determines those 'varieties of language' which are in fact the 'verbal realizations' of the codes, here described primarily as 'codes of behaviour'. The categories 'restricted' and 'elaborated' are, of course, the code forms most often referred to in this research tradition. Widely influential in education, the theory has been used elsewhere, including political sociology.

(3) The developing project of semiotics as a general approach to the study of social meaning linked to a structuralist cultural analysis. In this perspective, the location of individual meaning elements within rule-governed wholes—signifying systems—is a fundamental proposition, quite often extended to all social meaning. The particular level of closure indicated by the use of the term code is frequently clear if implicit in the various and detailed theoretical and analytic treatments, treatments which usually involve the identification of separate codes at work in a given text or piece of

social action. Here, Barthes (1971, 1972), Eco (1972, 1976) Burgelin (1968) and Hall (1973) have been key influential texts, whilst Levi-Strauss (1963) provided, quite early on, a structuralist, anthropological version of socio-textual analysis. (See also Geertz, 1973 and Leach, 1976.)

Although research in communication studies has produced what appears at times to be a conflation of these three broad uses of 'code', any points of convergence must be considered in the light of the rather different implications, both in terms of the notion 'systemic organisation' and that of 'transformation', which the approaches carry. We must also note the location of these approaches within differing social or political theories. Furthermore, although 'code' is most often used as a 'language-society' bridging concept, usage varies in the emphasis placed on social or linguistic characteristics—to the extent, that in some cases, the notion hardly seems to be 'bridging' at all but to be conceptualised as lying almost entirely within the distinctive territories of either the linguistician (language form, dialect, register) or the sociologist (socialisation, belief-system, social structure). Nevertheless, perspectives (2) and (3) above can be related (and both distinguished from perspective (1)) insofar as they both address themselves, if at times only implicitly, to one of the central issues in modern 'cultural studies' and, indeed, a central one in much political and social research—ideology, variously and problematically related to consciousness and language. Here, the relation of (3) above to media analysis is my prime concern.

It is the development of research in this area, stemming from a resurgence in Marxist work on social knowledge, which has helped to promote the use of linguistic paradigms in social research (in combination with other influences like the 'new' anthropology), although the emphasis on textual analysis and the 'reading' of ideological formulations has not gone unchallenged in Marxist media research.[2]

Bernstein's concern with 'the structures of cultural transmission' thus connects with Umberto Eco's more formalistically ambitious belief that 'Semiology shows us the universe of ideologies arranged in codes and sub-codes within the universe of signs' (Eco, 1972).

It has been claimed that, at one level, 'an ideology may be defined as a system of semantic rules to generate messages' (Eliseo Veron quoted in Camargo, 1974) so that the appropriateness of the concept code to ideological analysis is apparent. It offers the possibility of plotting 'cultural transmission' and its constitutive language-systems with a gratifying sense of precision. Though less important, it also seems to be the case that its connotation of covert dealings has won for the term an extra, if improper, allure in the eyes of some critical researchers investigating political and social knowledge as perpetrated 'myth'.

One final point I would make by way of preliminary observation is that the theoretical and definitional problem of the 'tightness' of internal correlations within a specific 'code' and also the problem of the precise character of the transformations (if any) being worked are often compounded by the notion of a plurality of codes or code systems at work in the same text, artefact or communicative behaviour. That is to say, the relationship of these systems, codes and subcodes (see Eco above) to one another—as alternative or jointly contributory factors in the production of social meaning (and the latter in ways involving varying degrees of overlap, superimposition

---

[2] Murdock and Golding (1977) are quite emphatic in opposing what they see as a dangerous bias towards 'readings' of media artifacts and their ideological structures which are insufficiently grounded in social and economic analysis. Semiotics and socio-literary approaches (including work in cultural studies) come in for particular criticism.

or what Barthes calls 'imbrication')—further troubles the theory of codes in cultural analysis.

Code and media texts

The 'Unity' of Current Affairs Television (Hall, 1976) illustrates some of the difficulties in using 'code' in an analysis of media texts and professional media practices. In a theoretical foreword to the case-study of an edition of *Panorama* which forms the centrepiece of the paper, it is argued that

Several different codes are required to construct the meaning of a message; it is the product of several meaning systems in combination.

Initially, these different 'meaning systems' appear to be identified as the sound and visual tracks of a television programme, tracks which operate both independently (horizontally) and in combination (vertically). Later in the piece, however, code is used in a broader, richer sense

Connotational and ideological codes are therefore at work, organising the elements of the message, as well as those codes which enable the broadcaster, literally to 'get a meaning across'.

The distinction indicated here, between denotational and connotational coding, suggests important differences within the range of relationships possible between codes and a primary language system, differences to which I shall return later.

Even further into the main *Panorama* study, which is concerned with, among other things, the strategic, rhetorical control over 'discussion' exerted by James Callaghan in a 1974 Election Special, code appears to signal a still more general and yet apparently more categorisable and discrete system of meaning. Referring to Callaghan's undermining of some previous comments made by William Whitelaw, the authors note

Callaghan accomplishes this by explicitly signalling, and then openly playing with, the fact that two codes are at work—the political code (hard opposition and attack) and the 'Parliamentary Debate' code (rudeness is a sort of polite game).

Callaghan is later said to block the intervention of the studio chairman by resorting to a gambit invoking the idea of the responsibilities of the politician—a ploy which the researchers see as an appeal 'in the name of a 'higher duty'—(a more powerful code)'.

It is clear, I think, from these examples alone that the linguistic levels, the degrees of systematicity and the kinds of organising influence of the 'codes' variously indicated in the paper are difficult to subsume within a single, unifying concept of codification. From the extract above, it is hard to judge the status of the parenthesized glosses—are they elements of, or summaries of, the respective codes? If the latter, just how useful is it to call 'hard opposition and attack' the 'political code'? If the former, what are the codic relationships involved and on what specific political set of generating principles do they systematically depend? Although initially the term seems to promise the mapping of highly structured and socially determined systems of linguistic behaviour it quite soon becomes used to denote the inflection of any utterance in the televised discussion towards this or that rhetorical strategy and to denote, too, the principles and policies which the strategies are used to articulate and uphold (the 'code' of the broadcaster consisting presumably of arguments adducing professional broadcasting values, the 'codes' of the politician being variously grounded in notions of public responsibility and representative authority as these are interpreted through party perspectives).

This inadequately theorised shift away from natural language equivalents ('getting meaning across') towards the social inflections and implications of specific utterances (where the notions of register and rhetoric would seem equally useful *given the levels of system evidenced*) is a slide observable in a number of cultural studies' analyses making central use of 'code'. The employment of the term to describe almost any discernible cultural convention or behavioural pattern, whether notions of transformation or of a discernible systemic invariance are appropriate or not offers an obstacle to clarity of analysis and I shall return to this aspect of the problem later.

In the case of *The 'Unity' of Current Affairs Television*, even if one allows the argument that there is a plurality of very different *kinds* of code at work at varying levels in the total discourse of the programme analysed, there is considerable difficulty in relating these codes to each other within a notion of the total discourse's *determination*. In the latter part of the analysis of the *Panorama* programme Callaghan is seen to 'break the rules' by taking over a chairmanship role, thus securing a sizeable 'win' in terms of the televised contest of arguments. Nevertheless, the authors of the paper go on to remark that 'we think it can be established that, within the rules and codes of the programme, a "Callaghan win" is the reading which this programme prefers.' The notion of the 'preferring' of one reading of a text rather than others by mechanisms *within the text* which weight possible interpretations in one direction is central to much of the research at the Birmingham Centre. It has led to subtle studies of the reading act as one involving the realization of meanings through the complex negotiation of differing interpretative frames with textual devices, some of which tend to close-off the apparent choice of interpretation in a number of ingeniously ingenuous ways—for instance, the variety of naturalistic techniques used in film and television programme construction. Such textual 'work' is identified by the cultural studies researcher and used as a sort of constellation of clues which permits a tracing-back to, and reconstruction of, the ideological formations ('fields of force' of meaning and value) within which the text was produced.

Yet to return to the *Panorama* example, it is unclear how this process of 'preferring', if it is to be theorised as a function of the 'codes of the programme', relates to those other codes mentioned earlier by the researchers—the codes contributing to the *transmission* of visual and verbal meanings; those involved in 'getting the meaning across'. What we apparently have is a situation in which Callaghan breaks a code only to have that breach registered as a 'win' within the 'codes of the programme' and transmitted as such through what were earlier called 'the several different codes required to construct the meaning of a message'. It is not made clear how these 'metacodes' of the programme somehow negate the codes at work in the debate which forms the programme's subject or how the various verbal and kinesic codes combine with the visual codes of television discourse to augment or lessen the 'dominance' achieved at other levels. One has the impression that code is being used quite frequently in lieu of 'inflection', 'register' or even 'principle' and is therefore giving to the analysis a far tighter sense of traced and inter-connected configurations of determined meaning than is actually evidenced. At the point in the paper where the authors develop their notion of 'preferred reading' they remark

However, *it is in the nature of all linguistic systems which employ codes,* that more than one reading can potentially be produced: that more than one message-structure can be constructed (my italics).

It would be useful to know, here, just what sort of linguistic systems do *not* employ codes and through that knowledge to find out what the conditions of employment are as understood by the researchers.

Codes and determinations

In an earlier, influential article on *The Determinations of Newsphotographs*, Hall (1972b) follows Barthes and Eco by setting out to show how various levels of coding operate to constitute the meaning (in its structured complexity) of a specific photograph. He theorises the notion of code level used in the '*Unity*' paper with the comment

Thus, whereas the codes which 'cover' the signifying function of the linguistic sign at the denotative level are relatively closed 'sets', from which quite tightly constructed rules of transformation can be generated: codes of connotation, constructed over and above the denoted sign, are necessarily cultural, conventionalised, historical.

Hall, again following Barthes (1972) refers to the latter area as one of 'second-order' meanings. A few pages later, he notes in a partial re-working of the same point, that

... denotative codes are relatively 'closed', connotative codes are relatively 'open'. Connotative codes are tight enough to generate meanings of their own, but these codes do not produce one invariant meaning—they tend to delimit meanings *within a preferred range or horizon*.

However, in a rather confusing way, Hall then goes on to see the preferred *range* of the connotational level, which he calls 'this polysemy', as the field *within which* a further preferring operation (operated by codes of preferencing within the text?) secures a narrower 'dominant reading among the variants'—a closure of the (apparent) openness or polysemy.

To what extent these further codes operate with an invariance of internal relationships Hall does not say, nor does he question the suitability of the term 'coding' to describe the variety of levels of meaning-producing activity which his paper details. He focuses on the question of what happens when a reader/viewer does not take the 'preferred reading' but either produces some modified version of this through 'negotiation' or else 'takes' a radically different meaning from that 'preferred'. The question is dealt with by Hall in terms of his theory of 'coding' and exposes, I think, some further problems in that theory.

The primary issue which Hall wants to address is that of differentiated readings of the same text; the way in which different meanings are constructed on the same 'site' and from the same textual system exerting its 'cueing' pressures. If the argument is that 'it is in the nature of all linguistic systems which employ a code, that more than one reading can potentially be produced' then Hall is intent here on giving that position a detailed theoretical grounding. To do this, he refers to a paper by Eco (1972) in which a typology of codification is developed in the context of a semiological argument and a detailed definition is offered of the concept 'code'.

By code we mean a system of communicative conventions paradigmatically coupling term to term, a series of sign vehicles to a series of semantic units (or 'meanings') and establishing the structural organisation of both systems, each of them being governed by combinatorial rules, establishing the way in which the elements (sign-vehicles and semantic units) are syntagmatically concatenated.

After giving a number of examples of different sorts of code Eco suggests, importantly it seems to me, that

After these definitions let us restrict the concept of code to the basic conventional systems, it is in fact with these elements that it is possible to then work out 'secondary codes'; or 'sub codes' more or less systematized, which furnish new lexical elements or give a different connotation to lexical elements contained in the basic code.

So it is argued that the 'more or less systematized' clusterings do not qualify for the term 'code'—a notion which is reserved for the 'basic conventional systems' from which the 'subcodes' operate as a sort of fine-tuning of meaning, related to social contexts and specific areas of discourse (Eco discusses, among other subcodes, the aesthetic subcode, the erotic subcode and the montage subcode). Nevertheless, Eco is still tempted to use 'code' in ways which seem to conflict with his earlier definition, suggesting at one point that 'the conventions at the basis of gastronomic choices . . . form a code' without specifying just how these satisfy the definitional criteria previously argued for. Moreover, it is clear that his offered distinction is not directly parallel to connotation/denotation nor to Hall's comments on 'second-order' (and, by implication) 'first-order' meaning.

In the course of his initial discussion, Eco also refers to what he terms 'aberrant decoding'. The example he offers of this process rather exotically involves the manner in which the Achean conquerors of Crete would interpret the stucco relief in the Palace of Knossos. The iconography of these paintings, their use of certain conventional correlations in artistic representation (e.g. stick—sceptre, brown face—youth) constituted a code which was culturally specific to the artist's community and therefore one which, it is argued, was not available as part of cultural experience to the new, invading culture. Insofar as the invaders understood or 'made sense' of the paintings, Eco continues, they did so in an *aberrant* way—one not in alignment with the moment of encoding.

It is this idea which Hall develops in his discussion of the 'preferred reading' of newsphotographs (although he is anxious to remove the pejorative idea of 'aberrance' from what he wants to see as the progressive possibilities of the differential reading—an approach actually advocated by Eco himself in a *post scriptum* comment to the English translation of his paper). Hall re-works the idea of 'aberrant decoding' in terms of political and class-related behaviour in contemporary society; in terms of a theory of ideological reproduction. Using a terminology taken from Frank Parkin's work on social meaning systems (Parkin, 1971), work which suggests how it is that differing versions of the same behaviour or communication can be 'read' as a result of differing interpretative frames generated by differing socio-economic locations, Hall suggests that

It is possible for the reader to decode the message of the photo in a wholly contrary way, either because he does not know the sender's code or because he recognises the code in use but *chooses to employ a different code* (italics in original).

In Eco's illustration there was a disjunction of geographical culture (and to some extent of historical time) between the encoding conventions and whatever interpretative frames interested Acheans chose to use on the Knossos reliefs. Moreover, the convention system itself was squarely founded upon one-for-one correlations—at its lowest level therefore (for there were presumably more nuanced levels of expressive convention) it was tightly systemic. One wonders how the modern 'oppositional' (aberrant) reader/decoder of a newsphotograph manages to achieve anything like the codic ignorance of someone from 'another culture' or the related degree of codic independence when he or she 'chooses to employ a different code'. In fact, this second case, the willed employment of a code *known to be different* from the one 'preferred', seems to be more a case of 'double decoding' than anything close to Eco's idea of aberrance, since a conscious, cognitive shift follows the recognition, by the reader, of 'preferred codes' at work and this shift involves a meta-level of interpretation—an active, aware reading *against* the rhetorical grain of the text as that grain is 'realized' at the lower level of reading. There are problems, in both cases, concerning the nature of meaning production/transmission and the levels of *consciousness* involved—and these problems are rather blurred over by the manner in which 'code' is used.

If, to use Hall's illustration, a newspaper reader chooses to interpret the photograph (of a policeman being kicked in the face by an anti-Vietnam-war demonstrator) within an interpretative framing developed from the belief, say, that 'the cause of anti-Vietnam war demonstrators is a just and legitimate one in our society; the forces of law and order are performing here a repressive political function', how does this interpretation get made? How does the general attitude (a political code?) determine or combine with the lower-level interpretative procedures by which such things as facial expressions, aggressive postures, the 'civic' resonances of the confrontation (regardless of the particular attitudinal versions of these) get 'read off'? What is critical here is the degree of variation and independence of specific interpretative processes, their reliance on common cultural ground at certain levels of operation, including much denotative work, and their differences—as interpretative procedures—at 'higher' levels of cultural connotation. One should not exclude the possibility that middle-range variations may in some cases be subsumed within the same higher level interpretative frame (thus, for instance, a general deploring of violence against the agency of civil 'law and order' could be mediated through a variety of different positions on, say, the role of the police in public demonstrations, the legitimacy of such demonstrations and the legitimacy of the United States's operations in Vietnam).

Hall's complex typology, a treatment of the successive levels of signification at which a cultural text is 'worked' or 'inscribed', perhaps commits him to an ambitiously wide range of reference for the idea of 'coding'. It refers at one level to the photograph as 'iconic sign', one employing 'formal-denotative codes' and moves through a number of levels of more or less technical/professional 'work' (news production, retouching, cropping, page composition etc.) until it makes contact with the culturally expressive meaning-systems at the 'ideological level'—the level at which Parkin's typology is taken up to aid the mapping of differentially realized ('taken') meaning.

This layering of the analysis upwards to the ideological level does not mean that culturally informed decisions are not taking place at the more fundamental levels of 'working the sign' however, as Hall reminds us. Nevertheless, the overall structuration which Hall suggests by his notion of determining 'codes' is not brought out in the analysis with the degree of systemic inter-relatedness which the theoretical preface to his article promises.

The photograph: code (or analogue? or analogic code?)

I have traced Hall's use of code in cultural analysis, both as a theory and as an analytic tool in specific research, in relation to the work of Eco. In choosing to discuss work on the photograph I hope to have provided a context in which the consideration of 'codes' can be pushed one stage further back to primary concepts, since the question of whether the photograph is a 'coded' form at all has been examined, with differing conclusions, both by Roland Barthes, perhaps the most influential of the continental semioticians, and, in a critical commentary on Barthes, by Hall.

One of the difficulties of talking about a 'visual language' in respect of photography is the lack of anything equivalent to the denotative vocabulary and regularised syntax of natural language. Before discussing the arguments of Barthes and Hall in this respect, it might be useful to offer an example of the sort of problems that can arise as a result of this difficulty. Such an example is afforded by Camargo (1974) in which there is developed an 'ideological analysis' of a *Daily Telegraph* magazine cover. The cover shows an expensively but conservatively dressed man and woman standing some distance apart with two identically dressed children, a child on the right-hand side of each adult. Moreover, symmetry is further emphasised in that each adult holds a child by the left hand. At the left 'heel' of the man sits a dog. Behind them is a terraced pathway and behind that, dominating the upper half of the frame, is a castle. Having earlier told us, as a general point, that 'denotative meanings are given by the code whilst the connotative meanings are given by subcodes' (here, following Eco) Camargo argues that 'The denotative meaning of this picture is: the couple, their children and their castle (home).' As many of my students have pointed out, there is some difficulty in finding 'denotative' evidence of the possessive ('their children', 'their home') in the photograph. Anyway, what would such evidence look like? What seems to have happened is that Camargo has 'read off' possession at the 'connotative level' (and I would certainly not wish to argue against this particular visual registering of the culturally 'obvious') and then incorporated (rendered back) these significations into her theorisation of the denotative. The use of denotative connotative differentiation in the cultural analysis of visual texts needs perhaps to retain some flexibility and sense of dialectical relation if it is to avoid problems such as this; problems which frequently follow from too rigid an attempt at applying a natural language model. This returns us to some of the more provocative theoretical considerations on photography of Barthes.

In a widely-cited though quite often misunderstood paper, *Rhetoric of The Image* (1971), Barthes refers to the 'absolutely analogic' nature of the photographic component of an advertisement for *Panzani* pasta. What he has to say about this has a general relation to much of my earlier discussion of codification

The photograph implies, without doubt, a certain arrangement of the scene (framing, reduction, flattening) but this event is not a *transformation* (as a coding might be). The equivalence appropriate to a true system of signs is lost and a quasi-identity is posed. In other words, the sign of this message is no longer drawn into an established reserve i.e. it is not coded, and we are dealing with the paradox (to which we will return) of a *message without code*.

Barthes' use of the ideas of rule-governed transformation and an 'established reserve' is here deployed against the notion of the coded photograph, although clearly he is aware of a certain level of intervention, of a 'worked' discontinuity between, in his terms, signifier and signified. Nevertheless, for him the photograph is 'analogic' since its relationship to what it represents is one of direct resemblance in contrast to the arbitrary ('digital') codings of, say, natural language.

Since Barthes' position has produced much comment it is worth quoting a later passage in the same paper where he develops the argument.

In the photo—at least at the level of the literal message, the relationship of signifieds to signifiers is not one of 'transformation' but of 'recording', and the absence of a code clearly reinforces the myth of the 'natural' photograph; the scene is there, captured mechanically, but not humanly (the mechanical is here the guarantee of objectivity). Man's intervention in the photograph (framing, distance, lighting, focus, filter etc.) all belong in effect to the plane of connotation; everything happens as if there was at the beginning (even Utopian) a brute photo (frontal and clear) on which man disposed, thanks to certain techniques, signs drawn from a cultural code.

So Barthes here distinguishes between cultural codes and the special case of the photograph's denotative method, which he earlier contrasts to the culturally constituted, transformative activity of drawing.

It is understandable that the passage has raised a few problems. The less than satisfactory remark, given the main thesis concerning 'objectivity', about the absence of the codes 'reinforcing the *myth*' of photographic naturalism (is Barthes arguing here that such naturalism is an illusion?) and the shift to flourishingly dramatic hyperbole at the end are characteristic of a style which frequently cultivates enigma at just those moments when the diligent reader is seeking to follow the argument between the insights. There is also the question—it may be one of translation—of the relationship of 'analogue' to 'analogic code', since Barthes talks of the latter at one stage in his paper and it would be difficult to argue that the photograph's 'message without a code' was, in fact, the product of an 'analogic code' without being perversely unhelpful even by the standards of Barthesian playfulness.

Just how 'natural' Barthes thinks photographic denotation to be, allowing for his decidedly whimsical phrasings, has worried some commentators on his paper. Trevor Millum, in an introduction to the Birmingham Centre translation of the piece, remarks:

surely the pictorial message is coded in the photograph no less than in the sketch? Does not the camera *itself* carry out the coding? Otherwise why is it that children, and members of cultures unfamiliar with photography, have to *learn* to interpret photos?

Millum goes on to comment that a refusal of the notion of the uncoded photograph allows 'the photo (to) be replaced within the mainstream of semiological thought.' However, he hardly engages with the argument (nor perhaps has space to do so) in the detail needed to refute Barthes' claims. The suggestion that the 'camera itself' carries out the coding is not sufficiently clear as a proposition to do more than its immediate function of rhetorical questioning—in fact, if anything it tends to suggest that 'mechanical' level of operations referred to by Barthes himself. Similarly, though the point about 'learning to interpret' photographs is clearly relevant, the central factors to be borne in mind here are, I imagine, precisely 'reduction', 'flattening' and 'framing' together with other, related qualities—characteristics which Barthes allows as interventionary moments in the production of the 'resemblance' but which he disallows as grounds for talking of 'codification'. Moreover Barthes himself, in the course of his paper, draws our attention to the child's learning to 'read' that something is a picture.

Stuart Hall, in an essay on documentary journalism, *The Social Eye of Picture Post* (1972*a*), takes issue at greater length with Barthes' line of argument (as well as Barthes, he cites Metz, Pasolini and Bazin as being at least half-supporters of 'indexical' theories). Like Millum, Hall stresses the importance of regarding the photograph as a product of codes, if unique and complex ones. Hall is concerned specifically with the components of the 'rhetoric of visual exposition' employed by the *Picture Post*, noting particularly layout, captioning and characteristic content. He contrasts the modern colour supplement (photographic romanticism) with the *Post's* use of 'realist' black and white and notes that we are not dealing 'with "natural" versus "conventional" photography but with *two different codes*' (italics in original). Yet apart from these remarks on the socially constructed connotations of photographic tones, Hall, again rather like Millum, does not actually introduce any more social factors into a theory of photographic production than did Barthes in the paper under criticism.

At times, it seems as if Barthes' mistake is seen to be that of placing the analysis of photography at least partially into some enclave of 'innocent denotation'. Phrases in Barthes' arguments like 'guarantee of objectivity' serve to cause anxiety in this respect, although such usages are nearly always specific and qualified, as well as often having more than a touch of stylish irony about them. Overall, it is hard to see Barthes' approach as one promoting a theory of pre-cultural signification; for Barthes the photograph is a thoroughly cultural form though he wishes to retain a recognition of its distinctive method of sign production. Although imperfectly argued, his comments still constitute a necessary object of address for those researchers who wish to develop a visual semiotics.

Throughout my discussion I have illustrated a central premise at work in the use of 'code' in cultural analysis—that cultural conventions and their variants operate with a degree of internal coherence and regularity comparable to that found in natural language. This premise, which is a very important structuralist thesis, usefully de-naturalises the operation of meaning-systems in society and allows an emphasis (though one not often developed in detail) on their historical and social origins and their rôle in constituting the configurations of social reality. In doing so, however, it often fails to monitor the implications of the linguistic paradigm at each level of application and in terms of each specific piece of analysis. When Hall, in '*Determinations*', remarks that 'in language, there is no message without a code' two questions are prompted—what is to count as 'language' and is the 'code' here synonymous with language or is it a secondary system acting upon it? It is worth noting, too, that the above quotation seems out of alignment with that reference made in the later '*Unity*' piece to 'linguistic systems which employ codes' as if to suggest that some such systems did *not* employ them.

Many studies informed by semiotics consider natural language to be, as it were, the 'primary code', though the extent to which it is its levels of systemic determinacy or its 'transformative' work within perception and experience (experience as a codification of reality) that gain it this title is often unclear. Hawkes (1977) summarises the underlying postulates of much work in social semiotics thus

In short, a culture comes to terms with nature by means of 'encoding', through language. And it requires only a slight extension of this view to produce the implication that perhaps the entire field of social behaviour which constitutes the culture might in fact also represent an act of 'encoding' on the model of language. In fact, it might itself be a language.

This is perhaps a more qualified position on the issue of 'society as discourse' than many researchers in the field would adopt—the shift from 'on the model of' to 'itself be' is crucial and is not always signalled quite so clearly.

Conclusions

I have suggested throughout this paper that many researchers have been unclear in their use of the term 'code' in studies of human communication and that, whether deriving from a positivistic technological model or from the hypotheses of semiology (sometimes less hypotheses than presumptions), the term often seems to offer more than is actually rendered in the aiding of our understanding of human signification and of the social construction of meaning. Paramount here is its taking-for-granted, without adequate research, of high levels of systemic organisation among cultural phenomena, levels often involving a fixity of relationships. This is theorised in forms often derived from structuralist linguistics and leads too often to a rigidity of analysis similar to many functionalist explanations in social science; systems being inferred from 'typical' transformations and correlates which in fact only constitute a very small number of actually observed and plotted relationships.

A further problem is that of the relations within and between cultural codes and subcodes, since in many cases the choice of system-title used in a piece of research (the journalistic code, the code of the programme, the erotic subcode etc.) seems quite abitrary and does not facilitate either referral 'downwards' to primary signification nor 'upwards' into a theory of ideological reproduction (how the 'structures' are put 'in dominance').

The precise *nature* of the inter-relationships proposed between different levels of signifying practice is often only minimally suggested, even where some notion of 'levels' informs a classificatory system. The problem of codetermining and conflicting codes frequently remains unaddressed.

A recent piece of published research (Brunsdon and Morley, 1978) stemming from Birmingham Centre work evinces these continuing difficulties whilst offering detailed analysis of the BBC's *Nationwide*. In discussion of the use of personal pronouns in the programme, reference is made to certain characteristics which become, it is argued, 'at the level of the code, the site of complex ideological work'. However, this 'level', its relation to other linguistic or cultural levels and its possible internal differentiation are not issues taken up further in the research, although there are two or three subsequent references to various moments of encoding and decoding which do *suggest* a degree of differentiation.

Researchers have continued to tackle the problems of a general theory of codes in a number of ways, attempting to distinguish between code as system (s-code) and code as correlation (code) (Eco, 1976); between code as 'system of explicit social conventions' and hermeneutics as 'system of implicit, latent and purely contingent signs' (Guiraud, 1975) and endeavouring to redefine code in 'tighter' or 'looser' terms.[3] Guiraud suggests a process by which 'looser' sign patterns acquire a consensual legitimacy and directness of reference to the point where they have 'the status of a technical code'.

Many uses of the term are almost metaphorical in that, rather than positing configurations at some linguistic level of organisation with attendant and important ideas of *predictability*, they suggest a conventional ordering 'of some sort' and serve to emphasise the fact that cultural meanings are achieved in relation to other cultural

---

[3] One recent move towards a 'loosening' can be discerned in Eco (1979). In an argument concerning the educational use of television, Eco notes that

One is led to assume that under the umbrella term of codes and sub-codes, one is not only gathering something similar to the verbal, lexical or grammatical competence but also something more akin to rhetorical competence (p. 19).

He goes on to argue that 'rhetorical competence'

cannot be made explicit in the format of a set of grammatical rules but resides rather in the format of a storage of previous texts (p. 19).

From the context, it is clear that this is more an argument about the *acquisition* of competence than one about the possibilities for its *analysis* and I refer the reader to the article as a whole for an understanding of Eco's notion of the 'textual' as distinct from the 'grammatical'.

meanings as well as in relation to that which they express or refer to (a difficult area of theory, this) and therefore are not self-contained pairings of signifier and signified. Such a useful emphasis is, however, some way from the tenor of many research conclusions in semiotics, which do not show the hesitancy stemming from a sense of the limitations of the notion but instead imply regularised, plottable and predictable operations occurring with a considerable precision. In contrast to this, certain work exploring a general cultural semantics has made only guarded or limited use of the concept 'code'. In his early work, Barthes himself develops the idea of 'rhetoric' far more centrally and this, I think, permits him greater subtlety if also denying him the neat 'scientific' accuracies sought by others.

Goffman's *Frame Analysis* (1974) has an interesting footnote in which he refers to some diverse uses and connotations of 'code' in the course of discussing his choice of the not quite synonymous 'key'—on the whole, I believe, a more successful concept, if avowedly metaphoric in that it is a conscious *approximation* by reference to another, more fully known and grasped, condition or phenomenon. Work developing from Voloshinov's (1973) recently rediscovered notion of 'multi-accentuality' (the intersection, in signs, of differently oriented semantic inflections stemming from different social positions of use) also seems to offer a valuable theorisation of differential social meaning, linking to some extent the problematics of semiology to those of one kind of sociolinguistics.

It is not, finally, the intention of this discussion paper to advocate the rejection of 'code' as a concept in cultural studies. It cannot be denied that the term has been used most frequently in some of the most exciting and suggestive work to be carried out in that broad area of inquiry. Here, Hall's papers over the past ten years constitute an outstanding example. What I think can be concluded is that many instances of its present use do not deliver what is promised and sometimes obscure what it is a prime intention of any cultural research to make clear—that is, how social meanings get made.

Bibliography

BARTHES, R. (1971). The rhetoric of the image, *Working Papers in Cultural Studies*, no. 1, C.C.C.S., University of Birmingham. Translated by Brian Trench

BARTHES, R. (1972). *Mythologies*, Jonathan Cape, London. Translated by Annette Lavers

BATESON, G. (1951). *Communication: the Social Matrix of Psychiatry*, The Norton Library, New York

BERNSTEIN, B. (1971). Social class, language and socialisation, *Current Trends in Linguistics*, vol. 12, Mouton, The Hague

BRUNSDON, C. and MORLEY, D. (1978) *Everyday Television: Nationwide*, B.F.I. monograph no. 10, London

BURGELIN, O. (1972). Structural analysis and mass communications, in D. McQuail (ed.), *Sociology of Mass Communications*, Penguin, London

CAMARGO, M. DE (1974). *The Ideological Dimension of Media Messages*, Stencilled occasional paper, C.C.C.S., University of Birmingham

ECO, U. (1972). Towards a semiotic inquiry into the television message, *Working Papers in Cultural Studies*, no. 6, C.C.C.S., University of Birmingham

ECO, U. (1976). *A Theory of Semiotics*, Indiana University Press, Indiana, USA

ECO, U. (1979). Can television teach? *Screen Education* no. 31, B.F.I., London

GOFFMAN, E. (1974). *Frame Analysis*, Harper and Row, New York

GUIRAUD, P. (1975). *Semiology*, Routledge and Kegan Paul, London

HALL, S. (1972a). The social eye of *Picture Post*, *Working Papers in Cultural Studies*, no. 2, C.C.C.S., University of Birmingham

HALL, S. (1972*b*). The determinations of newsphotographs, *Working Papers in Cultural Studies*, no. 3, C.C.C.S., University of Birmingham

HALL, S. (1973). Encoding and decoding in the television discourse, Stencilled occasional paper, C.C.C.S., University of Birmingham

HALL, S. (1976). The 'unity' of current affairs television, *Working Papers in Cultural Studies*, no. 9, C.C.C.S., University of Birmingham (with I. Connell and L. Curti)

HASAN, R. (1973). Code, register and social dialect, in B. Bernstein (ed.), *Class, Codes and Control*, vol. 2, Routledge and Kegan Paul, London

HAWKES, T. (1977). *Structuralism and Semiotics*, Methuen, London

LEACH, E. (1976). *Culture and Communication*, Cambridge University Press

MURDOCK, G. and GOLDING, P. (1977). Capitalism, Communication and Class Relations, in (J. Curran *et al.*, eds), *Mass Communication and Society*, Edward Arnold, London

PARKIN, F. (1971). *Class Inequality and Political Order*, MacGibbon and Kee, London

SHANNON, C. and WEAVER, W. (1966). *Communication and Culture*, Holt, Rinehart and Winston, New York

VOLOSHINOV, V. N. (1973). *Marxism and the Philosophy of Language*, Seminar Press, New York

WILDEN, A. (1972). *System and Structure*, Tavistock, London

Correction

In the bibliography, after Shannon, C. and Weaver, W. delete reference and substitute: (1949) *The Mathematical Theory of Communication*, Illinois University Press, Illinois.

Additions

Add to bibliography:

GEERTZ, C. (1973). *The Interpretation of Cultures*, Basic Books, New York.

LEVI-STRAUSS, C. (1963). *Structural Anthropology*, translated by C. Jacobson and B. Schoepf, Basic Books, New York.

Women and the cultural industries

MICHELE MATTELART*

Translation by Keith Reader

This article forms part of a still unpublished study (Mattelart, 1982) carried out for the Cultural Development Division of UNESCO in May 1981. In its complete version, the study deals with several themes. This article deals with the very first theme. The study itself follows with a development around the notions of modernity and permanence in 'modern' branches of the cultural industry. Another section, 'The crisis and restructuring of ethical values', asks questions about the way in which cultural industries approach the remodelling of feminine rôles and values in periods of crisis.

Everyday Life, the media and women's reality

An episode that occurs in the 1920s—in other words, right at the beginning of that important technological medium that radio was to become—provides a good illustration of the close link between symbolic mass-production and the production of material goods in the nascent industrial society of the United States. At the same time, it shows us how woman was straightaway singled out, from this commercial point of view, to become the favourite target for mass-media messages, an essential factor in the organization of their programmes.

Mr Glen Sample worked at the time for a small advertising agency (which was to become in the 1960s 'Dancer Fitzgerald and Sample'). He was the first person to adapt for radio a serial that had appeared in a newspaper—'The married life of Helen and Warren'. On the air this became 'Betty and Bob' and was sponsored by the well known make of flour Gold Medal, which at the time was produced by the firm Washburn Grosby and Co., later to become General Mills.

Shortly afterwards, Mr Sample won over Oxydol washing-powder when the firm which launched it, Procter and Gamble, was on the point of going to the wall under the attack of the English firm Unilever, which had successfully launched the make Rinso. Massively plugged by Mr Sample's radio serials and the advertising that interrupted them, Oxydol triumphed over Rinso. The serial 'Ma Perkins', whose career on the air went on and on for almost 30 years, gave Oxydol the decisive impetus (David and Costa, 1976). 'Soap-opera', the radio and subsequently television version of the 'lonely-hearts' press, was born.

The name given to the new genre is as interesting as it is unusual. Is it not unprecedented for a cultural product to indicate so crudely its material origin (here linked to the sale of soap and detergent) and its inscription as a factor in the battle

---

* Université de Paris VIII.

63

between the different commercial brands? At the same time, a whole *household* definition of a broadcast literature (or sub-literature) reveals itself plainly, making unambiguously clear a twofold function that is in fact unified: to promote the sale of household products, and to integrate the housewife into her function and task by offering her romantic gratification.

Only much later did the feminine factor come to be determinant in the programming of European radio-stations, notably in France. In fact, French radio did not start as a public service. There were State stations before the war, but they co-existed with private ones. Advertising certainly existed there, but not (as in the same period in the United States) as the norm around which programming was structured.[1] It usually intervened only as a subsidy for cultural programmes (often concerts), which were also supported by groups of listeners. We can observe a certain continuity between the classic forms of cultural life (concerts, plays, shows put on by local associations etc.) and the programming of these radio stations, which does not create any specificity of radio as such. The history of television was likewise marked by the same preponderance of classic culture. Nor did a specifically televisual genre come into being straight away; rather, plays, films and concerts were transmitted by television.

These programmes included, in the morning, 'Women's Hour' (the day's menu, recipes etc.), but, we repeat, their programming, whose highspot was undoubtedly the news, was made up essentially of rebroadcast concerts, cultural and scientific broadcasts, radio plays and entertainment programmes (quiz games etc.)—all types of programme which do not immediately segregate their audience by sex.

Only after World War II, when so-called 'peripheral' radio stations made their appearance, escaping the previous State monopoly of broadcasting, did the commercial model become dominant. And this model was progressively to acknowledge the tremendous importance of the mass female public.

Radio Luxembourg came into existence in 1933 with the lofty aim of 'acquainting listeners in different countries with the artistic and cultural master-pieces of the whole world'. In 1935, it introduced 'L'heure des dames et des demoiselles' (= 'Women's Hour'), which became a feminine byword and continued right through to 1966. In 1935, the introduction of radio serials coincided with the beginnings of a wider development of programming: as with all private radio stations, entertainment began to nibble away the air-time hitherto reserved for classical music. Regularly, radio games, weekly radio plays, and the 'hurly-burly of the music-hall' (sponsored by Cadoricin Lotion) made their appearance. From 1955, Europe-1 and Radio Luxembourg (now RTL—Radio Television Luxembourg) competed vigorously through radio serials. To Europe's serial, RTL riposted with 'Nicole et l'amour' (Nicole and Love). It was also in competition with RTL that Europe-1 introduced Ménie Grégorie's well known programmes of advice on sexuality and family psychology (information from Duval, 1979).

RTL rapidly multiplied its claims to be the leading commercial radio station. The first multinational radio station in Europe, it was also the first to broadcast throughout the day. In 1977, this same station calmly admitted that advertising could take up to 20 per cent of its air-time, that most of its public was female, and that these considerations laid down certain lines for it to follow. 'Women's attitude towards radio is significant: what they fundamentally want is somebody there . . . RTL will therefore fill this space and accompany our listener with its voice, in her home, *in her everyday life'* (author's italics) (from an RTL publicity handout).

Everyday life. Day-to-day life. These represent a specific idea of time within which woman's social and economic rôle is carried out. It is in the everyday time of domestic life that the fundamental discrimination of sex rôles is expressed, the separation between public and private, production and reproduction. The sphere of public interests and production is assigned to man, that of private life and reproduction to woman. The hierarchy of values finds expression through the positive value attached to masculine time (defined by action, change and history) and the negative value attached to feminine time which, for all its potential richness, is implicitly discriminated against in our society, interiorized and lived through as the time of banal everyday life, repetition and monotony.

Invisible work

For a few years now, the international feminist movement, with the aid of analytical work by specialists in social science (male and female), has been vigorously denouncing the negative value attached to women's household work, which becomes transparently obvious when we think that it has been regarded as self-evident that this work should be unpaid. Now, 'as a rule, once manual work is paid, it takes on economic value, so that any unpaid work (such as women's housework) becomes economically, and thus also socially and culturally, devalued' (Stavenhagen, 1980).[2]

The part played by this *invisible work* in the functioning of economies has been amply demonstrated. Everywhere, in developed and developing countries alike, women form the mainstay of the *support economy* which makes it possible for all the other activities to be carried on. A woman at home performs a fundamental rôle in any economy: she restores the labour force each day. This economic activity, carried on by most layers of the female population, is of great importance; but the indicators by which the socio-economic situation of each country is defined, and its development measured, conceal the economic value of household work.

The arrival of capitalism, which introduced the factory and institutionalized the sale of labour-power, undoubtedly represented a decisive moment in the segregation of sex rôles in the productive process, by depriving the family of its old function as a productive unit. But we should beware of a nostalgic attitude, and of the tendency to idealize the situation that traditional society gave women in productive activities. It has been shown (with reference to Africa, for example) that this often went hand in hand with forms of slavery. Capitalism merely continued and deepened a hierarchical division of labour which had come into being well before as modes of production developed, reserving for males the most prestigious and best-rewarded work and restricting women to the lowest kind. This sex rôle discrimination is fundamental to the maintenance of the capitalist economy, and it has been shown that 'but for this vast female underpinning, the women who provide food and clothing for the proletariat in a world where the necessary facilities for a collective restoration of labour energy simply do not exist, the hours of surplus value extorted from the worker by capital would be fewer. We can even say that women's work in the home is expressed through men's work outside by the creation of surplus value' (Larguia and Dumoulin, 1975).

Gradually separated from the world of production, through the long process of consolidation of the monogamous family which brings about a close link between the system of relations within the family unit and that of private property, woman, by virtue of the kind of tasks she carries out at home and her dependence on man, is the cement of class society. This division of labour finds expression in a definition of masculine and feminine qualities transmitted, reinforced and rearticulated by the different institutions of society (the Church, schools, the media). Girls will be docile, submissive, clean, chaste, prudish; they will play quiet games and enjoy indoor activities. Conversely, boys will be sexually aggressive, prone to show off their physical strength, to develop their 'innate' sense of leadership and so forth.

The invisibility of women's work and the concealment of the productive value of their household tasks are of decisive importance in determining the image of them projected by the media and the media's relationship with them. The media have made a point of following the traditional household timetable. Radio and television programming is very revealing in this respect. It punctuates the day with moments that make women's condition 'all worth while' and helps to compensate for being shut up at home all day. It makes women's work legitimate, not as work but as a duty that forms part of their natural function.

The genre of these women's broadcasts may differ (afternoon magazines, television serials, radio serials); the values around which their themes are structured can correspond to different points in women's relation to capital, and to the more or less modern and free-thinking character of the sections of the bourgeoisie that produce them. But they still have in common the rôle of integrating women into their everyday life.

The exception confirms the rule—adventure consecrates routine

In this process of integration, the melodramatic serial on radio or television has traditionally played a supremely important part. The serial can take several different forms and has several different tendencies, which it is not our job to analyse here. We shall simply say that most serials take as their target the family audience. On the other hand, the melodramatic serial, which carries on in radio and television where 'lonely-hearts' columns leave off, addresses primarily the working-class female public. Because of the immense impact of this genre in Latin America and other Catholic countries, there is a tendency to think of it as a Latin genre. But we can see that it exists, with variations (as might be expected), on the screens and the air waves of every country in the world, at least the capitalist part of it. It is all too well known that the more a channel declares itself to be fulfilling a cultural function and/or that of a public service, the fewer serials it will broadcast; and this is even truer of melodramatic serials, which on the other hand are everywhere on commercial channels. The profile of their audience, and their very regularity, make them excellent terrain for advertisers (in one hour of these serials in Venezuela for example, there are 20 minutes of advertising. It has also been noted that there is a close link between the kind of products advertised and the subject of the day's episode.)

In Latin America, undoubtedly the supreme territory for this genre (known as *Telenovela*) and more and more a major centre of diffusion, the State channels (insignificant compared with the commercial ones—they attract only 10 per cent of the public on average) display a tendency to win over the large public audience of this genre by making it more 'up-market'. Major authors of contemporary Latin American literature (Salvador Garmendia in Venezuela, Gabriel Garcia Marquez in Colombia, Jorge Amado in Brazil) have been invited to contribute to this strategy of renewal, which opposes to the commercial model of the dominant channels the cultural alternative ('cultural television'). There is no doubt that the works that stem from this collaboration offer female audiences (and others) the chance to encounter cultural products which show a much richer and more complex approach to human experience and emotion. But can we here still speak of melodramatic serials or 'telenovelas'?

The conditions of production currently prevalent in commercial Latin American broadcasting companies encourage directors. In order to keep costs down and profits up, to adhere to rules of serialization that lead to stereotyped banalities, shooting-time is minimal; the script of the following day's episode is improvised from one day to the next within the context of the time-honoured formulae of these mass-produced artifacts. The stereotyped structure of these productions annuls the possibility of openness to public reaction and criticism which this 'on-the-spot' shooting would otherwise make possible, in obvious contrast to the mode of production in other sectors of the cultural industry. The rule of commercialism, which has as its first principle to mine the same vein to exhaustion, means that these stories go on and on interminably. The Venezuelan government had to limit the number of episodes by decree.

There is no denying that the interplay in this or that country between cultural channels (even in a minority) and commercial ones can lead the latter to modify their programming, and particularly the raise their level, especially when they realize that the new 'cultural serials' attract large audiences. Even so, in the current circumstances, these serials, like the 'lonely-hearts' press, remain dominated by a principle of obscurantism, one of segregation of audiences. That is the key to the matter. This genre conforms to the principles of division of the market that govern the culture industry. In the press, to refer to socially distinct targets (from the standpoint of both purchasing power and cultural power), publishers and publicists alike speak of 'upmarket' and 'downmarket'. In the field of television, the melodramatic serial indisputably belongs in the second category. As we said when talking about the duality of the female market, a duality which increasingly pervades the whole mass-cultural apparatus (one of market democratization and segregation at the same time):

These two products of modern capitalism, women's magazines on one hand and photo-novels on the other, belong to specific moments and represent different mechanisms of bourgeois domination. They are complementary. Photo-novel magazines may tend to develop more in the context of the obscurantism caused by fascism or other present-day authoritarian régimes. But they are still there amid the everyday normality of liberal democracy. Furthermore, women's magazines correspond to the enlightened dimension of the most up-to-date section of the ruling class. The two genres express the different alliances that the bourgeoisie tries to conclude with women from different strata of society. And the variations that may, depending on the historical moment, indicate the dominance of one genre over another are indissolubly linked to the type of consensus the State may be able to produce and the model of development it favours (Mattelart, 1979a).

This segregation of female audiences is so marked that the international distribution of photo-novels (for example) is carried out by firms which can certainly be described as multinational, but whose position nonetheless remains marginal compared to the largest multinational publishers. This market is dominated by Italian and Spanish firms, and to a lesser extent French firms with Italian contacts,[3] along with firms based in Miami but actually the inheritors of exiled businesses that were already flourishing in Batista's Cuba. One example is the De Armas group, which is at the head of a real 'lonely-hearts' empire, and at the same time transmits multinational power in Latin America and acts as the distributor there for the Spanish versions of magazines such as *Good Housekeeping* and *Cosmopolitan,* while itself publishing an international women's magazine for the Latin American market, *Vanidades.*[4] (It is worth noting that Cuba was among the pioneers of the radio serial, right from the 1930s, and exported it to other Latin American countries). Only in June 1978, under the titles *Kiss* and *Darling*, did the so-called 'photo-novel magazines' make their appearance in the United States in supermarkets and drugstores. As *Advertising Age* proclaimed in its handout of 26 June 1978, '. . . *Kiss* and *Darling* mark the first American attempt at photo-novels, a form exceedingly popular in Europe. Photo-novel magazines are similar to comic books, except that, instead of drawings, the panels contain photos of people with dialogue balloons inserted above their heads.' Establishing continuity between this genre and 'Mills and Boon'-style literature, these magazines are aimed at the women who read the 'Harlequin' collection, a large multinational publisher of sentimental literature, whose parent company is based in Canada. Its French offshoot, which has operated from Paris since 1978, sold in 1980 between 17,000,000 and 25,000,000 copies of this collection, 'which carries you off into a wonderful world whose one and only dazzling heroine will be *YOU*'. It publishes 18 titles per month, 140 per year. These figures certainly carry us off into a fabulous dream-world.

Today, the international distribution of television serials is the province of autonomous Latin American firms, who are greatly helped by the existence of a large Spanish-speaking market in the United States. This international distribution is sometimes reflected in international production, or at least script-writing. Spanish-speaking inhabitants of Miami are thus persuaded to lend a hand. This expansion has up to now taken place primarily in the United States, Central and South America and the Caribbean. It has now got as far as the Arab countries (notably Saudi Arabia) and, via Brazil, those African countries which were once Portuguese possessions. European countries such as Spain and Portugal are also fertile territory. In 1979, according to the figures of Televisa (the monopoly Mexican commercial-television station), Mexico exported 24,000 programme-hours per year of these serials, to the United States, Central and South America, the Caribbean and now Arab countries as well. It is easier to grasp the size of this figure if we bear in mind that (according to a classic UNESCO study of 1972—Varis and Nordenstreng, 1972) neither French nor British television exported more than 20,000 programme-hours in that year. North American television at the same period was exporting anything from 100,000 to 200,000 programme-hours and, at the time, Mexico exported only 6000 hours at the most. Its expansion is now in full flight. The infiltration of the United States by Mexican televison has caused friction between the two countries. The firm Univision, controlled by Televisa, had made it possible, thanks to the satellite Westar, to receive Televisa programmes directly in New York and Los Angeles, whence they are channelled to the rest of the United States. This meant that by the end of 1976 more than 13 million households watched Televisa in the United States as against only 5 million in Mexico. While nowhere near so large as the Mexican industry, Venezuela is also launching an attack on the international market. Between 1975 and 1977, 23 'oil serials', as they are known, were exported to North and South America, Spain, Portugal and Saudi Arabia.

It remains true that the melodramatic serial on radio or television is the fictional genre most clearly addressed to a mass female public. These productions usually bear a woman's name as their title—*Natacha, Simplemente María, Rafaela* or whatever. It has been shown that this is a condition of their success. The serials whose titles included men's names had less of an impact. In Latin American countries, these productions continue to exist side-by-side with imported series (generally North American), or more up-to-date programmes fully involved with the symbolic universe of the industrialized world and reflecting the relative emancipation of women participating in professional life on an equal footing with men. But the traditional productions still enjoy more success. It is through these serials that the principal audience-battle between the different stations is fought out.

There have been enough content analyses and ideological readings of melodramatic serials and linked genres (such as photo-novels) for us to feel able to give a highly condensed summary here (cf. Mattelart, 1977; Dardigna, 1978; Butler Flora and Flora, 1978). The plot generally revolves round the ups and downs of a love-affair which brings together people separated by social class (or age, or previous ties, or a combination of all three). The family context tends to be riddled in rather higgledy-piggledy fashion with social pathology and individual problems— unhappy homes, incurable diseases, illegitimate children, alcoholism, incestuous or quasi-incestuous cohabitation and so on. The variations run the whole gamut from romantic adventures to social dramas. In Latin America, the serials are very much marked by sex and violence, obsessively present (though always shrouded in implication and innuendo) in the form of blackmail or rape (at least, that is what one deduces must have happened). The unrolling of the story through all kinds of ambiguities, avowals, mistaken identities and interventions of a *deus ex machina* reveals a highly normative message whose structure is Manichean: the good and the virtuous are rewarded. Love sanctioned by the legitimate union of marriage is better than passion, which is always punished by fate. The female characters ennoble the values of purity and virginity for girls, who often become heroic martyrs to men who in fact get away with abusing their masculine authority and class-power; but, after putting her through great suffering and temptation, they confirm the happiness of the girl from a modest background by offering her a ring and married life. The sacrifice, courage, and self-denial of wives and mothers are other attitudes reinforced by these messages, crowned as they are by the return of the husband, the renewed gratitude of the son, or the simple satisfaction that comes from doing one's duty.

Monotony also has its exceptions. The serial makes possible a symbolic revenge on the triviality of everyday life, whose monotonous repetitiveness is countered by the day-by-day episodes of the heroine's exceptional adventure. Household work, experienced as unproductive and of low socio-economic standing, is countered by programmes which give value to the realm of private life and a female world dominated by 'love' and 'emotion'.

Even before 1917, Alexandra Kollontaï, writing about the social basis of the female question, observed how very far from innocent love stories were, and how the realm of private life had been sedulously infiltrated by bourgeois standards:

'Even that bourgeoisie that proclaimed love to be a "private matter" knew how to use its moral guidelines to channel love in the direction that best suited its class-interests' (Kollontaï, French edition, 1973).

The greatest of the repressions carried out by what we have elsewhere called 'the order of the heart'—the order that governs the organization of melodramatic discourses—is that it invalidates any form of struggle against social inequalities (the existence of which is admitted) by means of this diffuse explanation: only love can cross class barriers. Not only is the solution individual—never collective—it is also linked to the miracle of love. Love comes to be a universal explanation which can resolve social contradictions through denying them, for the order of society, like love, is founded on Fate. The repressive order of the heart has two helpmates: Nature and Fate.

But we can notice that from the 'content' point of view a tendency to increase the realism of these discourses brings them closer to the real situations of working people. These new serials, at any rate in Venezuela, show an increasing concern to stick to real life. Let us look at one such example, and observe the unchanged manner in which it smooths over points of conflict. The serial 'Dona Juana' explicitly refers to a problem that affects all social strata, but principally the working people, and implacably brings out the sexist character of society—that of irresponsible paternity, of illegitimate children brought up by their mother alone, not recognized by the father who abandons the mother after making her pregnant. 'Dona Juana' portrays these women, and their brave struggle against male hostility and fecklessness. But this woman, of humble background, does not learn to define herself as an independent individual, even though her struggle shows the strength and energy she can display as head of the family. The *dénouement* still follows a conservative and conventional pattern: thanks to an almost miraculous stroke of luck, the father finds his daughter and recognizes her. He thereby satisfies simultaneously the mother's dream and that of the daughter—that the child can bear its father's name and thus escape the stigma of illegitimacy.

It is no secret that the ideological function of these narrative discourses resides primarily in the fact that they are given as representations of reality, and therefore cleave to certain features of the reality of social and class conflict, which they implicitly explain (through the mechanisms of the story) from a certain point of view, itself likewise linked to the objective reality of class struggle. The serial's twin task—of representing reality and explaining it—defines its rôle of reproducing the conditions of production of the social formation, predisposing women to accept the 'natural' explanation of their domination.

On the consumer process

A tendency—also a necessity—that has recently emerged in media studies is that which rejects the inevitably passive character often imputed to the way in which people receive the messages addressed to them. What is questioned, in other words, is the act of consumption itself, the process of reception by which a subject annexes the message addressed to it. This means that the monolithic nature of the ideological effect of domination is likewise questioned. For that is the key problem. The media transmit a set of values corresponding to the interests of a particular power system. Can we infer that the recipients, reacting to these signals like Pavlov's dogs, interiorize these structures of domination once and for all? The spotlight is turned, in other words, on the act of looking and consuming: what is the relationship between the message and the subject that receives it within an individual history, or the history of a group or class? Oddly enough, there are a great many studies of media power structures, national and international, and a great many too of the content of media messages, but very few on the manner in which the 'dominated' groups and individuals read and respond to them, or oppose to them a specific manner of, precisely, *appropriation*, and resist them (if need be through a diversion of the original intention, implicit or explicit) in the name of some project of their own.

Our study of the Popular Unity régime in Chile brought us to try to ascertain if that historical moment, characterized by intensified social confrontations and a mobilization of popular consciousness, led to a critical attitude towards such messages as the melodramatic serials which appeared on television just as in the past. In the most active strata of working-class womanhood, we discovered that these messages were not necessarily read as their senders intended, and that the way in which they were received denied their internal logic, leading to a roundabout process of consumption. These demystifications, particularly of the illusory social mobility often presented in the serials, emerged in comments, such as the following:[5]

The lovers in these serials are always from a wealthy family, or a well-heeled profession, never workmen. The working-class always appear as servants, or else in the character of a girl who, thanks to some miraculous encounter, becomes a great lady overnight.

Perhaps episodes can occur in real life like those depicted in these serials, but at what cost? In real life one cannot become rich without exploiting somebody else, and the serials show that the road to riches is an easy one. At whose expense do these young men and women make their wealth? It all goes to give the working-class false hopes (Mattelart, 1979*b*).

Where pleasure poses a problem

What is disturbing is the exhilaration that these tales continue to give spectators who are critically aware of how alienating they are and who have located the mechanisms through which their nefarious work is carried on. We cannot simply ignore the question of taste, of the pleasure (albeit a bitter one when it goes hand in hand with a developed consciousness) produced by these fictional products of the cultural industry. There *is* a problem here, and one hitherto scarcely tackled. As an initial approach to it, we shall merely put forward some hypotheses about female expectations and exhilaration.

We have spoken of the female sense of time. In *Notes on Modernity*, we wrote in 1971:

The mythical hostility between the notion of woman and that of change must go back to the association—common to all cultures—between the image of femininity and that of the vital elements, water and earth, elements of permanence and fertility. The image of woman is linked with the idea of continuation, perpetuation, duration. To the time-scale of rupture, crisis, and chaos—corresponding to the concept and representation of change—can be contrasted the *female time-scale*, a cycle drawing concentric lines that always return to the point from which they set out, uniting past, present, and future. It is a fluid perception of time, inhabited by eternal functions: home-making, marriage, motherhood. The figure of female evolution both justifies (by contrast) and compensates for that of male evolution, which fits into the double reality of struggle and world domination (M. Mattelart, in Spanish, 1971; English translation, 1979*a*).[6]

This specific inflection given by femininity to time can be defined at once as *repetition* and as *eternity*: the return of the same, eternal recurrence, the return of the cycle that links it into cosmic time, the occasion for unparalleled ecstasy in unison with the rhythm of nature, and along with that the infinite, womb-like dimension, the myth of permanence and duration.

It was this notion of a specifically female idea of time that led us to formulate the hypothesis that, above and beyond their themes and images, their signifying chains forever retracing the dominant ideology, these lengthy tales unrolling over protracted periods by means of regular daily consignments might have much in common with this experience of repetition and eternity. These tales could well correspond to the psychic structures of women not caught up in a forward-looking idea of time, a time of change. These vast stories, delivered in small daily instalments and daily repeated, would then serve, through their stereotyped rhythms, to satisfy the expectations of female subjective time. By cultivating the enjoyment of this non-forward-looking sense of time, these stories tend to hold up women's access to the time of history, the time of planned action.

We shall need to check this intuition in the light of recent scientific researches in the field of subjectivity and the unconscious structures of personality. Hitherto we have been too satisfied with looking for the alienating quality of the products of the culture industry merely in the discursive unities of image and word. But what continues to pose a problem, as we said earlier, is the fascination these products still exercise over spectators (of either sex) who are perfectly capable of giving an acute analysis of the serials' alienating characteristics. What collective masochism, what suicidal group-attitude can explain this fascination? Is the power of the culture industry not also to be found outside the subjects with which it deals, the anecdotes it transmits, which are but epiphenomena of its real message? What is not said would then count for more than what is said. Does the culture industry not reinvest the alienated psychic patterns of the mass of people, patterns which are elements of nature as well as of culture? Could its ideological function not also be fulfilled in this constant restimulation of the deep structures of a socially created unconscious? The crucial importance of the question in terms of formal or informal strategies of resistance should be plain. The complement to the basic need of development of self-awareness should surely be the need to sound out the 'group unconscious'.

We cannot leave the problem here. We have to see what these questions can contribute to the construction of an alternative, and how we can give a *non-alienated* answer to these deep unconscious structures. African film makers such as the Ethiopian Haile Gerima, director of *Harvest: 3000 Years*,[7] have clearly understood the importance of adopting these structures of perception and modelling their narratives on a psychic demand which (and the paradox is only an apparent one) can perfectly well be satisfied in a completely different manner from the old Indian melodramas which enjoy such great popularity in Africa.[8] Shot very slowly, these old films, whose rhythm is linked to a specific measure of time, largely satisfy the demands that Tanzanian peasants have made on groups of film makers who want to get them to participate in the production of their own image.[9] The misguided identification of technological with human progress has often led to the error of colonizing the production of a national image through the stereotyped techniques of the modern image-industry. This blocks the contribution to culture that could be made by groups who have remained deeply connected with the rhythm of country life, close to the cycle of nature, and still uncontaminated by a system of production which (on the symbolic level at least) is increasingly dominated by sensationalism and omission. At a time when the ideas of development and growth are being called into question by the very countries which do not want to repeat the mistakes of core countries, is it not also necessary to take account of the contribution these countries can make to the relation between images and filmic time?

The question of women brings us face to face with the same problem. The notion women, *qua* dominated group, have of time can be viewed in two ways: on the one hand as alienated, on the other as a positive alternative to the dominant idea of time as geared to production. The female sense of time is viewed in a more and more positive light as models of development are questioned and the limitations of a society governed by the rule of the highest possible GNP become plain. Increasingly influential social movements tell us that work and career are not everything. This new sensibility gives a heightened value to women's work and the gestures of their everyday life. The division of work between 'male' and 'female' qualities has reduced the emotional and intellectual capacity of women as much as that of men. And it is now plain that, however urgent it is to increase awareness of the productive value of household tasks, it is also vital to restore value to areas that are not directly productive.

When, in *Jeanne Dielman,* the Belgian director Chantal Ackerman films the everyday banalities of a woman's existence at their full length, she does two things at once: she attempts to endow with its own language her subjective experience as a woman, silenced by culture up to now, and at the same time she gives us a creative shock which makes it possible to understand by contrast what the customary norm of film-time is.

This feminine time is, along with increased awareness of the body, at the heart of the effort being made by women today to give cultural expression to what they as women feel. Beyond the supposedly equal status they may have acquired in the world of production, women are trying to get across what makes them unique and different on the level of subjective experience and symbolic representation. This diffuse attempt is leading them to delve into their age-old memory linked to the space and time of reproduction, in which today part of their specific sensitivity is still shaped. A specific, and unalterably different, sensitivity because it is linked with psychological, biological and sexual differences which have traditionally been used to subordinate them, and one which today needs to be expressed as an alternative world of symbols and meaning.

It is stimulating to observe that this research seems to be paralleled by the exploration of the time-sense of dominated and marginal races and continents being carried out in, for example, Latin American narrative fiction. This allows us to think that it will really be possible to give a non-alienated answer to the female interiorization of the twofold dimension of time—repetition and eternity. Novels such as Gabriel Garcia Marquez's *One Hundred Years of Solitude,* or José Donoso's *The Dark Bird of Night,* are vast tales based on cyclic progress and monumental stretches of time, majestic replies to unconscious demand which provide democratic and liberating outlets, rather than the feeble and imitative products that merely conform to the commercial precepts of market democracy.

The balance between fiction and information

Various studies have clearly brought out the split that can exist within one television channel between *informative* programmes intended for women and *fictional* ones (drama series, serials etc.). This split can even be seen as distinguishing the informative programmes intended for women, and hence conveying a particular image of them, from the rest of the programmes, which convey another.

Let us first of all look at '*The influence of audio-visual media upon the social and cultural behaviour of women in Japan*' (Nuita, 1980). The author shows how, immediately after the end of World War II, the Japanese state broadcasting authority (NHK) helped women to free themselves from their virtual confinement within the family; this was achieved through the programme 'Woman's Hour' and even more by group listening to radio, especially to educational programmes. These programmes were entirely in accord with the policy of modernization in Japan, started by the occupying forces and taking the form for women of a policy of emancipation. The programme was then reinforced by another series—*NHK Female Classes*—which dealt with a variety of themes, from problems of family consumption to political, economic and social questions, first on radio, then on television. Around these broadcasts—and this initiative is emblematic of the break that had been made with traditional conceptions of women in the media—were set up women's study groups to fight the tendency to isolation and domestic imprisonment which could have been perpetuated, or even made worse, by solitary listening to broadcasts. Thus, the whole enterprise of civic education for women was served by these NHK programmes, which came to a stop in 1969, partly because Japan's rapid economic development between 1965 and 1969 meant that more and more women took outside jobs, which made it difficult to organize daytime group meetings. It is interesting to note that, by starting to bring women together, the media had in a way played a rôle analogous to work, until economic expansion brought paid work back onto the agenda. Nowadays, there are a certain number of strictly educational programmes which still serve as a focus for female study groups. But we have to interpret this use of the media to promote the development of society in the light of the overall characteristics of media programming in Japan, and particularly of the dominant image of woman transmitted by the media. Nuita says that both drama serials and television plays purvey a stereotyped image of woman. These occupy an enormous amount of programme-time, so that traditional social norms are reinforced. 'Traditionally the Japanese woman has been brought up to fulfil her role as daughter, wife, and mother'; hence, the characters of the 'tender mother' or the 'good little wife' are dominant. There are a few television plays that show pioneering or resistant female characters, but as a rule 'these plays present woman as always willing to conform to the dominant attitude, and go to reinforce traditional female ways of thinking'.

This duality can also be observed in some magazines, especially those which are reluctant to adopt a squarely modernist approach and would rather remain within the confines of a part-traditional, part-modern attitude.[10] The editorials may evince some kind of 'progressive' intention, conforming to a mildly liberal image of woman in their treatment of permissive morality. But, in the same issue, the fiction (a novel serialized over several numbers) will portray woman in the most conventional light imaginable: passive, dependent, prone to a sugary-sweet view of life.

This leads us to deepen our analysis to the media as they operate in liberal democracies. Their political function is to reproduce the co-existence of different social classes and groups. Thus they constitute a place where social tensions are reduced; everbody has a part to play. But at the same time society has to reassert its cohesiveness by reproducing the legitimacy of public opinion (defined as that of an 'average citizen'.[11] This 'average citizen'—in fact an abstract entity in the service of social inertic—becomes the basic norm to mediate change and ensure the continuance of tradition. It is in the interests of this basic norm that the balance between information and fiction is established.

This is what the author of the Japanese study says in her remarks on dramatic and other kinds of fiction: 'Overall, society demands that women correspond to the type of the good wife and good mother. This is why the main characteristic of the female characters in family plays is not a sense of independence, but conformity with existing social standards.' Information programmes, on the other hand, meet the demands of other groups, which the media are under an obligation to satisfy if they are to fulfil their task of communication and satisfy divergent interests while mediating their contradictions.

But there is more than one element to take into account. To the crucial question, 'What is the relationship between information and fiction?', we have offered two kinds of answer, that given by the Japanese broadcasting system and that given by certain magazines. We could find similar examples in other developing and developed countries. As the terrain on which social negotiation takes place, the media make possible—indeed necessary—the co-existence of may varied points of view. The diversity of genres within television and radio, like that of sections within a magazine, expresses (in however trite a way) this necessity, which relates to a rather more complex aspect of the media's answer to the problem of 'diversity'. We should here point out a fundamental difference which stems from the different places the media occupy in the social formation. Some are under a statutory obligation to favour variety and diversity, others to go further and respect *pluralism*. This distinction is an important one, for it determines the different kinds of answers different media give to a single problem, and thus highlights their specific institutional functions.

A magazine, especially a women's magazine, addresses a fairly consistent and equally defined public. The magazines that interest us—those which circulate in accordance with market laws (i.e. not those produced by government organizations or political groups)—are usually controlled by a press group, answerable only to itself and its public. Its task is to take its public through the different stages of a development whose success is gauged by the volume of sales. Within a press group which aims at the female market, a division of labour generally occurs: some magazines cater for the demand of one sector of the population, others for a different kind. (The same holds good for the daily press.) So the same group, as we have already seen, will publish photo-novel magazines and modern, not to say *avant-garde*, ones—a distinction known as 'down-market' *versus* 'up-market', both turning out equally professional products. This division of labour, we have suggested, can also arise within one particular magazine. This division and variety bring into play a complex but logical array of elements governed by commercial as much as ideological factors. The ideology professed by a magazine is invariably the result of its commercial situation (except—cf. Mattelart, 1976—in a period of crisis).

On the other hand, a medium such as television, especially when it is controlled by criteria of public service, has to give air-time to identifiable public groups whose opinions and ideologies are different, or even incompatible—the very groups that mark the pluralism of a liberal society. The definition of a public service enjoins upon it, in different ways depending on the situation, a rôle of information and social leadership, and of development of democratic life. It has to favour the development of citizens' abilities so that they may be better aware of their rights and better placed to defend them. It also has to show all the major currents of opinion and act as the platform on which society can express itself. *But* it cannot turn itself into an *avant-garde* medium. Its task of ensuring the maintenance of the social order implies a rigorous codification of its pluralism, so that it can cultivate a certain conservatism in the service of the *status quo*. The natural interplay between the informative broadcasts which boost women's rôle and image and the bulk of the fictional ones thus appears as a basic mechanism of this conservatism. The limits of pluralism have been judiciously assessed:

Pluralism admits several ideologies, opinions and moralities. From this liberality it derives a system, banishing dogmatism and opposing repressive systematisation. Quite right too. Yet liberal pluralism itself is systematic and dogmatic in its own way. The number of accepted opinions is few; the liberal accepts several moral codes, but demands some kind of morality. He accepts several religions, but demands some kind of religious sentiment. Old or new, liberalism tends to institutionalize accepted opinions, acceptable moralities or ideologies . . . . This leads to a tendency to hallow establishment opinions and values (Lefebvre, 1970)[12]

The monograph written by a Quebec political scientist (Légaré, 1980) about the Canadian national television programme 'Today's Woman' helps us to define what 'pluralism' means and the limits it imposes, on itself and others, on the treatment of the female question in liberal society. She stresses that this programme is what it is because of the enterprise of its producer and the intelligence and combativity of her and her team through the past 15 years (the producer since 1966 has been Michelle Lasnier). At the same time, she points out the inescapable link between this programme and the part played by Radio Canada in the evolution of Canadian society, 'a part connected with the support it gives to the multiplicity of groups concerned with social development'. The programme's chances of helping social development are connected with the criteria that govern a public service, at a time characterized by the 'radical remodelling of all our social, economic and political structures'. It was only through tenacious efforts that 'Today's Woman' won its nowadays indispensable place on the screen. Through its different phases, this programme contributed decisively, first to helping women fulfil more satisfactorily their rôles as housewives and mothers, through giving credit to their knowledge and articulacy, giving them the necessary tools better to carry out their task in society, and democratizing practical knowledge and competence.

Later it helped women to realize who they were, where they were and how changes were affecting them, by describing the development in women's situation (in a couple, in a family or in childhood), by keeping them abreast of social change in Quebec, and by informing them of artistic and literary developments. The fact that the programme nowadays deals less and less with fashion and cooking and more and more with sociology, psychology and education indicates how it has evolved and helped to open out new kinds of position stemming from the women's movement (whether organized or not).

Ms Légaré goes on to show that the image of women constructed in this programme is distinct from that constructed by the other programmes on the same channel, whose serials, comedies and advertisements combine to reconfirm the natural dominance of the male[13] As the producer of the programme herself admits, 'Today's Woman' is the programme that best corresponds to the requirements of a public service—'and not by broadcasting songs, either'.

But the history of the programme will enable us to catch the mechanisms of the *status quo* at work. In the conflicts between the programme's team and audience and the management of the channel, we can (albeit very succinctly) detect the limits of pluralism. 'Today's Woman' is currently being affected by a crisis of growth, due as much to its 15-year-long success with its audience as to the specific manner in which its production team conceives female themes. This crisis of growth should take the form of expansion, or even of a multiplication of programmes to cater for the multiplicity of popular demand and the different aspects from which female themes can be viewed. This lays bare the limits imposed upon 'women's programmes' as normally understood in the media, even though these limits can be very markedly extended if the programmes are not conventionally understood by the team in charge of them.[14]

It is significant that, when demands were made for this programme to be broadcast at a peak hour, for the benefit of the general public as well as of working women, they were given the thumbs-down. The reason for this refusal—needless to say, never acknowledged openly—was surely that a programme called 'Today's Woman' cannot depart from its allocated afternoon slot without calling into question the very standards that govern the channel's programming. If diversity and pluralism require the co-existence of several types of programme, each type is distinguished from the other among other things by the time at which it is broadcast, which corresponds to the conventional division of time in accordance with sex rôles. To adapt Henri Lefebvre's statement, could we not say that liberal media accept several different ways of conceiving of woman's rôle and image, but demand some kind of feminine specificity?

One important question still remains. Of the two areas information and fiction, which has the greater public impact, from the nebulous point of view of its 'effects'—i.e. the attitudes, ambitions and models it transmits? To answer this, we should need an extensive study of audiences, in an interdisciplinary perspective combining the approaches of sociology, anthropology, psychoanalysis and semiology. This may be highly controversial. We should begin by pointing out that it has long been recognized by cultural critics that mass-culture brings together a variety of different areas: the 'real' and the 'imaginary' [in their Lacanian sense—trans.], the effect of fictional conventions upon the field of information, the sensationalist tendency of that field and so forth. The boundary between reality and fiction becomes progressively vaguer. In this sense, 'Today's Woman' seems to be an exception to the rule. Let us add that for us it clearly belongs in the field of information, even though its channel is an 'entertainment' one—yet further confirmation of the ideology implicit in the definition of a woman's programme! The effect of fictional standards upon the field of information, conversely, can be seen in most women's radio or television broadcasts.

Rather than trying to give a hard and fast answer to the question, we shall simply identify where the conflict is, drawing attention to the importance of fiction for reasons other than the amount of air-time it takes up. We are inclined on balance to think that fiction has a greater impact upon the majority of people than informative programmes. A life-style is more easily transmitted fictionally than non-fictionally. Fictional programmes—serials, series, family comedies—are the places where the feelings and ideas of the 'silent majority' are confirmed, where accepted wisdom on the hierarchy of rôles and values is reiterated and repermuted in such a way as to reinforce the beliefs and practices of the greatest number. They are also the place where disruptive elements are digested, and non-conformist ideas absorbed. This zone of mass-culture is the privileged space where authority does not need to speak politically in order to act politically.

Fiction and information do not refer to the same things. However affected by fictional values they may be, information programmes still refer to *reality*. Fictional programmes refer to the other text, the already-said, the already-written. Reality manifests tension, effort, history, and an openness to the future, the developing, the unknown. The already-said reiterates the past, renews the sense of security which in spite of everything it gives.

Notes

1. Advertising revenue rapidly became important for American commercial radio, and the sponsors would take responsibility for part of the programme, organizing it as they chose. This made ambitious programmes possible from the start. Certain opinion-groups soon became anxious about the increasing impact of radio advertising, and a motion was put before the Senate in 1936 to reduce it (Miquel, 1972).

2. A great many women and women's groups have studied this problem (viz. Baxandall *et al.*, 1976; *IDS Bulletin*, 1979; Dalla Costa, 1972).

3. Mexico, an essential outlet for international publishers in Latin America, also produces a great many photo-novels and 'lonely-hearts' journals, like Argentina and Brazil. In all these countries, production is professional and industrial, whereas in Colombia it is still predominantly artisanal.

4. In 1979, Harlequin Enterprises, king of the 'romance novel', announced its intention of building up a publishing empire in the USA. It began by buying the Laufer Company, which publishers *Tiger Beat,* a number of teenage magazines, and Rona Barrett gossip magazines (cf. Compaine, 1979).

5. Countries on the road to socialism show how difficult it is to remove from the screens these highly popular serials. In Allende's Chile, television Channel 9 used the serial *Simplemente Maria* as a 'hook' to win audiences for the television news that followed it. In Nicaragua, the government reinstated the serials because of popular reaction. The same problem crops up with Indian melodramas in Mozambique.

6. Cf. the following quote from Julia Kristeva: 'Feminine subjectivity seems to give its own measure to time, emphasising repetition and eternity. On the one hand: cycles, gestation, the eternal recurrence of a biological rhythm in harmony with that of nature, . . . an extra-subjective, cosmic time that can give rise to nameless ecstasies. On the other, and perhaps as a result, a monumental kind of time, seamless and flawless, so little connected with linear time that the very word "time" is hardly appropriate to it' (Kristeva, 1979).

7. The critic Robert Grelier spoke of this film thus: 'Structured around three axes—the exploitative landowner, the 'madman', and the peasants—*Harvest: 3000 Years* is inspired by a song which is heard three times in the film and which says: "Our bride, our new bride, your 3000-year-old wedding-dress is still untorn." This song inspires the dream of the young peasant who helps his father at the plough, and will punctuate the film like a leitmotif. This poor country, still feudal, is portrayed uncondescendingly, pitilessly, but with great nobility. Tiredness and sweat appear on the peasant's faces like stigmata of exploitation.

'Here words do not invade everything, and the image is free to go its own way. Speech occurs only where necessary. Sound—or rather noise—regains its rightful place in daily life. Oral tradition, dreams, allegories, symbols are used as active documents in this documentary vision, but never become excuses for aestheticism or for the prettifying of a form whose main quality is the sobriety of its images. Time and technology pass through the landscape without stopping, like a convoy of lorries in a cloud of dust. Omnipresent tradition maintains privileges which are perhaps changing, but at a price—the destruction of the class-relationships that govern this society. These relationships are hinted at by the ''madman'', but are not obvious to most of the actors' (Grelier, 1977).

8. Melodrama is the dominant genre in the Indian commercial cinema. In India today, the cinema is the main mass communication medium; it is the world's leading film-making country. Much of its commercial production (a mixture of songs, myths, violence, laughter, dancing, tears and suffering, involving stars idolized by the masses) is exported to Africa, both black and northern. Mozambique, for example, is having to contend with its population's attraction for these films. A very high proportion of films imported there are Indian, and this still reflects their previous dominance (shared with Hong Kong karate films). Egypt is another major centre of melo-dramatic film making, most of whose products go to the Middle East.

9. Cf. Leveri et al. (1978). The villagers showed a preference for a linear montage, a shooting-rhythm that for instance showed the process of manufacture or cultivation at its full length. They also showed a clear desire to link the theme of work in with those of social, family and everyday life.

10. This happens with a number of French magazines, some of which have lost out through too sudden a change of direction. *Bonne Soirée* decided after 1968 to react against its traditional format by including rather more 'contemporary material', and proceeded to lose 300,000 readers in six months. These women's magazines are read primarily in the provinces.

11. Pierre Bourdieu has shown that 'public opinion' is in fact a mystification (Bourdieu, 1979).

12. It is worth pointing out that commercial stations, less under the thumb of public interest and morality, can show themselves more tolerant than State channels. This is suggested by the Japanese author when he says that (several private programmes at one time were criticized for depicting adultery or other non-legitimate types of sexual relation).

13. We have no desire to interrupt our study of Canadian television with an example drawn from French society. But this is the point to look at our analysis of the loathsome appropriation of feminist themes in a recent French TV serial. Here, what was at stake was not the traditional rôle and image of woman, but an overt commitment to pouring scorn on the women's movement and its ideas and symbols. The viciousness of this appalled us, as you will see from the analysis in the Appendix.

14. Calling the genre into question destabilizes the whole order of communication. Any communications policy that tries to redefine media–public relations will come up against this 'divide-and-rule' pigeon-holing (cf. Mattelart, 1980).

Bibliography

BAXANDALL, R., EWEN, E. and GORDON, L. (1976). The working class has two sexes, *Monthly Review*, Vol. 28, no. 3

BOURDIEU, P. (1979). Public opinion does not exist, in Mattelart, A. and Siegelaub, S. (eds), *Communication and Class Struggle, an Anthology*, New York, International General

BUTLER FLORA, C. and FLORA, J. L. (1978). The fotonovela as a tool for class and cultural domination, *Latin American Perspectives*, issue 16, vol. V, no. 1

COMPAINE, B. M. (1979). *Who owns the Media?*, New York, Harmony Books

DALLA COSTA, M. (1972). Women and the subversion of the community, *The Power of Women and the Subversion of the Community*, Bristol, Falling Wall Press

DARDIGNA, A. M. (1978). *La Presse Féminine, Fonction Idéologique*, Paris, Maspero

DAVID, M. and COSTA, C. (1976). Since 1895, radio finds its niche in media world, *Advertising Age*, 19 April

DUVAL, R. (1979). *Histoire de la Radio en France*, Paris, Alain Moreau

FRIEDAN, B. (1963). *The Feminine Mystique*, New York, Dell

GRELIER, R. (1977). Le récoite de 3.000 ans, *Le Revue du Cinéma*, no. 320–321, October

INSTITUTE OF DEVELOPMENT STUDIES, UNIVERSITY OF SUSSEX (1979). Special issue on the continuing subordination of women in the development process, *IDS Bulletin*, April

KOLLONTAÏ, A. (1973). *Marxisme et Révolution Sexuelle*, Paris, Maspero

KRISTEVA, J. (1979). Le Temps des Femmes, *34/44*, Revue du Département de Sciences des Textes, Université de Paris VII, Paris

LARGUIA, I. and DUMOULIN, J. (1975). Towards a science of women's liberation, *Latin America and Empire Report*, North American Congress on Latin America, no. 6, New York

LEFEBVRE, H. (1970). *Le Manifeste Différentialiste*, Paris Gallimard

LÉGARÉ, A. (1980). Le cas de l'émission 'Femme d'aujourd'hui' (Canada), *L'influence des medias audiovisuels sur le comportement socio-culturel des femmes. 2 exemples: le Japon et le Canada, Dossier Documentaire, no 17*, Section Développement Culturel, UNESCO, Paris.

LEVERI, M., MAGONGO, P., MBUNGIRA, S. and SICELOFF, J. (1978). *Understanding and Use of Educational Films in Villages in Tanzania*, Dar es Salaam, Audiovisual Institute

MATTELART, A. (1980). *Mass Media, Ideologies and the Revolutionary Movement*, Brighton, Harvester

MATTELART, M. (1976). Chile: the feminine version of the Coup d'Etat, in Nash, J. and Safa, H. (eds.), *Sex and Class in Latin America*, New York, Praeger

MATTELART, M. (1977). *La Cultura de la Opresión Femenina*, Mexico, Editorial Era

MATTELART, M. (1979*a*). Notes on modernity: a way of reading women's magazines, in Mattelart, A. and Siegelaub, S. (eds), *Communication and Class Struggle, an Anthology*, New York, International General

MATTELART, M. (1979*b*). Chili: Formation politique et lecture critique de la télévision, *Revue Tiers-Monde*, vol. XX, no. 79

MATTELART, M. (1982). *Femmes et Industries Culturelles*, Dossier Documentaire, Paris, Section Développement Culturel, UNESCO (English translation in press)

MIQUEL, P. (1972). *Histoire de la Radio et de la Télévision*, Paris, Richelieu

NUITA, Y. (1980). L'influence des medias audiovisuels sur le comportement socioculturel des femmes au Japon, in *L'Influence des Medias Audiovisuels sur le Comportement Socioculturel des Femmes. 2 Exemples: le Japon et le Canada*, Dossier Documentaire, no. 17, Paris, Section Développement culturel, UNESCO

STAVENHAGEN, R. (1980). La femme invisible, *Courrier de l'UNESCO*, July

VARIS, T. and NORDENSTRENG, K. (1974). *La Télévision Circule-t-elle à Sens Unique?*, Paris, UNESCO

Appendix

This is an annotated summary of the serial *Les Amours des Années Folles* (= *Those Years of Crazy, Gay Love*), by Marion Sarrault, broadcast on the French channel Antenne 2 between 12.29 and 12.45 each day except Saturday and Sunday. The synopsis is taken from *Le Matin* (2–13 February 1981).

Monday, 2 February (N.B. This serial is sub-titled 'The Working Woman')
Tony Royère, after brilliant studies as an engineer, is about to leave her mother (a war widow) and her two younger sisters, Étiennette (secretary to a Parisian newspaper) and Pernette (a salesgirl in a fashionable boutique).

N.B. Tony's 'androgynous' Christian name, compared to the 'good old French' names of her two sisters. Also her 'masculine' profession, contrasted with two typically feminine ones.

Tuesday, 3 February
Catherine Groux, who also has to work to support herself, meets the Royère family and Maurice Olivier, who, in love with Tony, reveals his distress through a careless gesture.

Wednesday, 4 February
Maurice Olivier seeks consolation in spending his spare time with Pernette, while Catherine Groux gets a job and Tony and Arnaud (her husband) arrive in Isora, Bernardine Lavraux d'Avral falls head-over-heels in love with Tony.

Thursday, 5 February
Catherine's husband, Philippe Groux, is suffering from an incurable illness. In Isora, Tony has her first talk with her husband about her invention and the rôle of Maurice Olivier, of whom Arnaud is insanely jealous.

N.B. This serial respects one fundamental rule of melodrama: that of extreme family situations and psychological turmoil altering the characters' emotional states (as here with the incurable husband). This situation also justifies Catherine Groux's search for work, whereas Tony's desire to work is connected with a 'feminist' definition of her character. Also note the connotations of scientific work and invention, both traditionally masculine spheres.

Friday, 6 February
In Isora, Bernardine and Tony feel more and more drawn to each other, to Arnaud's disquiet.

N.B. The connection between female emancipation and lesbianism.

Monday, 9 February
Still in Isora, Bernardine has decided to set up Tony and Arnaud, along with an experimental laboratory for Tony, in her château, rather than seeing her go off to the factory in Avrel.

N.B. Homosexual tendencies begin to become plainer. Much of the suspense will be connected with this situation. At the same time the imbalance becomes clear between the importance of 'scientific research' and that of her husband in Tony's life. This has to be judged by implicit reference to the other idea of women's work embodied in Catherine Broux, who has to work because of her husband's illness. She is the positive pole of reference whereby to judge the deviant behaviour of other 'working women'.

Tuesday, 10 February
In Isora, Bernardine behaves as though she were in love with Tony right under her husband's nose and in the presence of several friends: Father Ferdinand, her former favourite Thérèse de Preuil, and Étiennette, whom Bernardine has brought along as her private secretary.

N.B. The long-standing homosexual tendencies of one of the characters. Note also the stifling closeness of the relationships, another standby of the melodramatic serial. The people involved in these imbroglios are linked by close family relationships.

Wednesday, 11 February
Catherine's husband has committed suicide. In Isora, things are going from bad to worse between Bernardine and her husband, who is jealous of his wife's obvious attentions to Tony.

Thursday, 12 February
Bernardine returns to Isora with Maurice Olivier, whom Tony needs for her work. Arnaud, whom Tony has compelled to depart for the factory in Avral, has gone, uttering various threats.

Friday, 13 February
Arnaud puts his threats into practice by making Étiennette his mistress. But, realizing that he has wrecked his marriage, he tries to kill Bernardine, whom he blames for his problems. Thérèse de Preuil, who has tried to step between them, is wounded. . . .

PART TWO

Intellectuals and cultural production

In this section we present articles which take up one of *Media, Culture and Society*'s central preoccupations: the role of intellectuals in the production of culture. Discussions of academic theories, journalism, aspects of broadcasting and film-making, the work of artists and novelists have all concerned those occupational categories which are widely considered to be 'intellectual'. It is hardly surprising, therefore, that many of our contributors should have dealt with the analysis of the intellectuals' social position in various social formations. A central question here—one which obviously preoccupies intellectuals themselves—is the measure of autonomy available for intellectual work in a given society.

In his critical survey of recent social theory, Philip Schlesinger argues that the sociology of intellectuals may best proceed by taking the question of relative autonomy as a seminal starting-point. He criticizes Alvin Gouldner's over-optimistic projection of the future rise to class power of the intellectuals, and also evaluates some recent East European dissident writings. One of the central points which emerges from his survey is the difficulty of defining the boundaries between the 'intellectuals' and the 'intelligentsia' as social categories. Indeed, social theories about intellectuals seem almost invariably to be founded in normative assumptions which assign to intellectuals an historic mission. Schlesinger concludes that much recent theory, while mistrustful of the intellectuals as an ally of the working class, is at the same time generally defensive of their special interests.

Philip Elliott's contribution moves from the more formal level of theoretical criticism to a substantive argument. He is sceptical of theories which proclaim the intellectuals' rise to power and he argues that the prophecies of an 'information rich' society are misleading. What we may expect, in his grim scenario for the near future, is a pattern of media development based on the proliferation of highly commercialized distribution technologies and the growth of the 'strong state'. These two tendencies will erode what remains of the 'public sphere', causing irretrievable damage to conceptions of public service broadcasting and the gradual demise of critical intellectual work and political debate. Far from being the advance party of a new order, the intellectuals are in retreat. The prophets of the information society, in this view, are peddling a fairy-tale: so-called media abundance actually shrinks democratic opportunities rather than enlarging them.

The question of the intellectuals also appears in the work of Pierre Bourdieu, whose sociology lays bare the underlying logic of the strategies of cultural producers and the forms of distinction present in cultural consumption. Bourdieu's work is highly complex and defies easy summary. Its presence in these pages testifies to *Media, Culture and Society*'s determination to present significant continental European work to Anglo-American readers, irrespective of its difficulty or unfamiliarity.

Nicholas Garnham and Raymond Williams offer an extensive introduction to Bourdieu's work which situates it in the context of contemporary France. As they explain, at the centre of Bourdieu's work is a concern with the relative autonomy of intellectual practice and of symbolic power. However, Bourdieu's work is at the same time an analysis and critique of how notions of autonomy function as part of a defensive strategy for those who exercise symbolic power: in his terms, they are subject to the structuring logic of their fields of operation.

In the first of his two essays, Bourdieu sets out to demonstrate the social basis of aesthetic tastes. He argues that cultural preferences in consumption are structured by one's social origin and by the educational capital at one's disposal. These combine to mould the set of discriminations applied in judgements of artistic value, whether these are seen as 'legitimate' high art, or as middle-brow and popular art. By dismissing the idea of a 'natural' aesthetic disposition, Bourdieu is also offering a critique of those who represent the intellectual faculty as something neutral and distant from material reality. This is, he argues, a bourgeois perception rooted in the space afforded by economic advantage.

In his second study, Bourdieu attacks the ideology of the 'creator' of cultural products. To concentrate on authorship as an explanation for artistic work is to conceal the economic basis of artistic production, and to fail to understand the structuring of artistic markets. For Bourdieu, the trade in culture works through its denial of the economic character of cultural goods and by investing them with what he calls 'symbolic capital'. The fields in which cultural goods are produced are highly structured locations in which continual struggles for recognition take place, particularly around the poles of 'bourgeois' and avant-garde art.

Paul DiMaggio's study deals with the ways in which urban elites in late nineteenth-century Boston consciously forged distinctions between high culture and popular culture. A strongly classified high culture, he contends, emerged with new organizational models of cultural practice in the 1870s, namely the Museum of Fine Arts and the Boston Symphony Orchestra. These, DiMaggio demonstrates, were private initiatives taken by the Boston brahmins which were to have far-reaching consequences for the social organization of cultural consumption. As their direct political power waned, the social elite sought exclusivity and cultural legitimation through the creation of new vehicles for the distribution of culture—those which enhanced the social differentiation between middle-class and working-class audiences.

In search of the intellectuals: some comments on recent theory

PHILIP SCHLESINGER*

Introduction

What should we expect of a theory of the intellectuals? How should it define its object, and what should be its scope? Are the intellectuals a class, one which is marching inexorably to power on the backs of the proletariats of East and West? Are the intellectuals locked in a class struggle with the bourgeoisies of advanced capitalism and the party bureaucracies of state socialism? Will the intellectuals be the crucial organizers of a transition to socialism after which they will deny their own separate interests and work for the emancipation of all?

In the present revival of concern with the question of the intellectuals these have been some of the major preoccupations of a number of Marxist and post-Marxist writers. This essay will examine a body of recent literature on the intellectuals. After reviewing quite briefly a number of the key themes in this field I shall subject several writers to a more detailed scrutiny. The second section will concentrate upon Gouldner's attempt to develop a 'general theory' of the intellectuals and intelligentsia, whereas in the third part the focus will be the work of a number of East European dissident writers, Rakovski, Bahro, Konrád and Szelényi, all of whom have considered the rôle of intellectuals in the reform of state socialism. I will conclude with a few thoughts on the implications of these theories.

Some current concerns

Let us consider some of the issues presently in debate as these provide an entry point for the later discussion. Without attempting to be exhaustive[1] we can single out the following: intellectuals and socialist political strategies, intellectuals and the production of ideology and culture, and the question of comparing intellectual strata in different social formations.

For some years intellectual strata have been seen as of key importance in the transformation of the political systems of both East and West. In part, certainly on the left, this perception reflects the widely acknowledged 'crisis of Marxism', belatedly announced in the late 1970s by the contemporary 'pope of theory', Louis Althusser (1979).[2] On a practical level there has been the failure to achieve anything resembling a socialist democracy, East or West. This goes hand in hand with a theoretical crisis, which, in the West, is centred upon the failure of the

* School of Social Sciences, Thames Polytechnic.

working class to act according to the scenario of revolution. As Eric Hobsbawm has noted, this entails a changed 'view of the actual forces which will bring about the transition from capitalism to socialism and the strategy and tactics for doing so' (Hobsbawm, 1979: 218). At the centre of Marxist debate have been the 'intermediate strata' and the question of their class alignment, especially in relation to student radicals, the technical intellectuals, the expansion of the welfare state bureaucracy and the growth of science and 'information' (cf. Ross, 1978; Hobsbawm, 1979; Brym, 1980; Rootes, 1980). These have also been at the heart of contemporary non-Marxist discussions of class structure.

In the East, current thinking about the intellectuals has been spurred on by the perennial difficulties of reforming the state-socialist system from within, particularly in terms of decentralizing economic decision-making, modifying the leading rôle of the party, and liberalizing the culture. Reformers have looked for the agency which might transform the party and state. One answer, of course, is the working class, and events in Poland of late have given some renewed credibility to this view (Ascherson, 1981). Another answer, the one which we will consider here, is that the only hope lies, ultimately, in change brought about at the instigation of the intelligentsia.

Debates in the East are of major concern in the West, for socialist strategies here also have to confront the post-Stalinist legacy of repression and inefficiency. While this is especially true for Communist parties, 'existing socialism' is also a negative instance waved in the faces of socialists and social democrats.

One might illustrate contemporary concerns by reference to discussions which arise out of the problematic originally developed by Antonio Gramsci. A modern watered-down version of the Gramscian theory of hegemony has been the present 'Eurocommunist' strategy of fusing a new social bloc comprising the 'forces of labour and the forces of culture' (Carrillo, 1977). In this conception, the various middle strata, including those highly educated and professional sectors of the population generally considered to be the intellectuals, are seen as having a common objective interest in the struggles of the proletariat against monopoly capital. This analysis reflects Gramsci's 'expanded' conception of the intellectuals, one which focused upon the rôle of mental labour in the organization of production generally, not just upon intellectuals as producers of ideologies. In the 'Eurocommunist' versions, the leadership rôle assigned to the 'organic intellectuals' of the proletariat has been replaced. All those capable of management, administration and of the provision of ideological leadership, who are not clearly aligned with monopoly capital, are seen as functional elements in the transition to, and the running of, a socialist society.

It is precisely this broad alliance strategy which has aroused criticisms of the definition of the middle strata. In perhaps the best known theoretical critique, Nicos Poulantzas argued that an undiscriminating approach towards the 'new petite bourgeoisie' was likely to be politically unsound, as only certain fractions of it could be seen as potentially aligned with the interests of the proletariat (Poulantzas, 1975). Intellectuals are seen as members of the petite bourgeoisie and as engaged in a process of mental labour which necessitates the ideological domination of the working class. Erik Olin Wright has substantially modified this blanket argument, suggesting that the intellectuals occupy 'contradictory class locations', economically between the working class and the petite bourgeoisie, and ideologically between the working class and the bourgeoisie (Wright, 1979).

Whatever the differences in such analyses of the 'boundary problem' in Western class structure, they are animated by the quest for a sound alliance strategy for socialist transformations, one in which intellectual strata are invariably seen as playing a significant part.

A more limited focus, but one which has enjoyed considerable attention, has been the rôle played by various types of intellectuals in the production of ideology. Naturally, this question has been at the heart of debates about the relations between media, culture and society with which this journal is concerned. So it is hardly surprising that much recent work on cultural production (notably in the area of news) has also been about the question of ideological power.

The 'dominant ideology thesis' holds that the hegemonic ideology in capitalism works to conceal the real nature of social relations and to produce the political quiescence of the subordinate classes. Although there are dangers in overstating the case, it would be equally mistaken to assume, as some have, that ideological questions are relatively unimportant (cf. Abercrombie, Hill and Turner, 1980). Few now argue the crudely reductionist view that the dominant ideology is a direct expression of capitalist economic interests. In sophisticated versions, such as Bourdieu's, 'symbolic power' is analysed in a non-reductionist manner. For instance, it is acknowledged that while specialized forms of intellectual production are constrained by capitalist class relations, the 'intellectual field' nevertheless obeys its own logic. Thus professional cultural producers, even conservative ideologists, 'always threaten to divert to their own advantage the power of defining the social world which they hold by delegation. The dominated fraction always tends to set cultural capital—to which it owes its position—at the top of the hierarchy of the principles of hierarchisation' (Bourdieu, 1979: 81). In such analyses, therefore, the intellectuals are seen as the dominated fraction of the dominant class. The possibility of autonomy is afforded by the way in which the 'intellectual field' is structured, in particular that it is not purely subject to the vagaries of market forces.

The stress upon the effects of a dominant ideology upon social relations is linked to the view that 'instruments of communication and knowledge are, as such, instruments of power' (ibid.: 81). Critics of the 'dominant ideology thesis' do have a point when they take issue with overstatements of ideological effects. Régis Debray's recent work merits such strictures. In his contemporary chronicle of the rise of the 'mediocracy', Debray has argued that during the past century 'intellectual power' in France has been subject to a series of displacements, from the university to publishing to the mass media, and that the latter 'ensure the maximum socialisation of private stupidity' (Debray, 1981: 242). This is a particularly disabling cultural pessimism which is the more suspect since the electoral victories of the French socialists would seem to suggest that socialization of private stupidity is less than complete.

In the course of his analysis, Debray raises the question of a comparative approach to the intellectuals. He observes that 'the sociology of real socialism integrates the intelligentsia into its official framework in order to neutralise it as a political force; the sociology of real capitalism ignores (or marginalises) it in order to conceal it as an active political force and to perpetuate the illusion that it does not exist' (ibid.: 29).[3] While one might assent to the first proposition, the second is entirely without foundation. Although the 'intelligentsia' does not exist as an official category in the West, the work of Daniel Bell and John Kenneth Galbraith, to name but two, testifies amply to 'real capitalist sociology's' concern with the intellectuals. Moreover, whereas Debray's focus is exclusively upon limited categories of cultural producers, the work of Bell and Galbraith, with its strong emphasis upon the growth of science and technology as productive forces ranges very widely indeed. 'Knowledge-bearing' strata, located in the educational system, the cultural industries, administrative organizations, scientific enterprises, the military and so forth are seen as playing an increasingly significant rôle not just in the production process, but also in the centres of decision-making (Galbraith, 1967; Bell, 1973, 1980a.)

These comments on Debray's work merely exemplify what Raymond Williams has called 'the general difficulty of the initial definition of "intellectuals"' (Williams, 1981: 215). A pre-eminent or exclusive focus upon intellectuals as ideologists or as cultural producers seems far too narrow. This constricted definition certainly accords with popular conceptions, but as is clear, both Marxist and non-Marxist sociologies have found it necessary to go beyond it.

Indeed, the very concepts with which the debate proceeds have undergone significant shifts in meaning (Huszar, 1976). The term 'intelligentsia', as Aleksander Gella has noted, arose first in Eastern and Central Europe around the middle of the nineteenth century. It then referred to a 'culturally homogeneous stratum' in Russia and Poland which was 'set apart from other educated elements of European society by a specific combination of psychological characteristics, manners, style of life, social status, and above all, value systems' (Gella, 1976: 13). In Poland 'the defence of the national culture against the occupying powers was the mission of the intelligentsia', and in the case of Russia it 'espoused the cause of economic modernization and social emancipation' (Vaughan, 1978: 191). From the start in Europe, the formation of the intellectuals was closely tied to nationalist movements and the rise of the nation state. Within contemporary state socialism, this 'classical' notion of the intelligentsia has been redefined and the old stratum has been destroyed. It has been replaced, as Debray rightly says, by an official sociological conception of the 'working intelligentsia', a stratum whose membership consists of all those possessing tertiary education (Churchward, 1973). As we shall see, critical analyses of state socialism eschew this category.

There is a certain overlapping between the classical concept of the intelligentsia and those conceptions of the intellectual which stress social and cultural criticism and progressive politics. The term 'intellectual', although current before the late nineteenth century (Williams, 1976: 140–141) acquired its broader social significance only then, with the publication of the *Manifeste des Intellectuels*, issued in 1898 by scholars, artists and scientists concerned about the implications of the Dreyfus affair.[4]

The formation of intellectual strata in the West had its own peculiarities. Habermas (1974) has pointed out links between the market economy, the constitutional state and the emergence of the bourgeois 'public sphere' in the second half of the eighteenth century. The 'public sphere', in which space existed for the relatively autonomous organization of political action and debate, and in which the emergent mass media assumed increasing importance, was the locus *par excellence* for the development of critical intellectuals. The classical bourgeois public sphere no longer exists, and the modern equivalent space, as Philip Elliott argues in this issue, is likely to shrink even further.

In a somewhat similar vein, Bourdieu has noted how, during the nineteenth century, notions of artistic independence from the public and the 'emancipation of the creative intention' were consequent upon the formation of an 'intellectual field'. The creation of literary and artistic markets provided conditions for 'the establishment of properly intellectual professions', which, freed from the constraints of direct patronage, could lay claim to 'independence'. As Bourdieu argues, the very concepts and values defining the vocation of the intellectual coincided with the emergence of the new rôle (Bourdieu, 1971: 163–164).

Such cursory observations make it plain enough that any approach to the intellectuals needs to take account of conceptual shifts and of those very changes in social formations to which the concepts refer. In this connection, it seems appropriate to endorse Gramsci's argument that the starting-point should be 'the system of relations in which [intellectual] activities (and therefore the intellectual groups who personify them) have their place within the general complex of social relations' (Gramsci, 1971: 8). This position obviously entails rejecting what Huszar has called the myth of the 'eternal intellectual': the idea that there is some essential, timeless intellectuality or some ideal social posture adopted by intellectuals throughout the ages.

What follows from this is a concern with the ways in which the 'relative autonomy' of intellectual practices relates to the forms of social integration of the society in question. In the case of state socialism intellectual autonomy is conditioned by the extent to which centralized bureaucratic controls are used to direct politics, the culture and the economy. Our Polish contribution makes this plain enough, with its trenchant observations on the ways in which tactics of divide and rule have been used against both the intelligentsia and the working class in the interest of monopolizing power for the party-state.

In the case of contemporary capitalism, the focus is much more upon the operations of various markets. In a variety of ways, all of the Western contributors to this issue have addressed the question of the relative autonomy of the intellectuals with respect to different markets for culture. Elliott sees the growth of the mass entertainment markets of the 'information society' as squeezing out critical intellectual work as the public sphere comes under more pressure. Herman argues that the 'science' of economics is substantially subject to market pressures and casts doubt upon the professional autonomy of US economists. Kadushin suggests that the decline of intellectual circles in the US has had a deleterious effect on the cultural markets for 'serious' books. Finally, Reader has outlined aspects of the markets for intellectual products in Britain and France and has examined the profound contrasts in the diffusion of ideas.

The further development of a cultural sociology focused on forms of intellectual production plainly needs to explore the crucial question of modes of autonomy and integration on a comparative and systematic basis. The better we grasp these variations, the sounder our appraisal of the rôle of intellectuals in social change is likely to be. In the next two sections we will consider in some detail how several theorists have aligned themselves on this question. The basic alternatives have been well expressed by Brym and Gella. Brym argues that intellectuals, as members of the middle strata, are politically subordinate to one or another of a society's 'fundamental classes' as these have 'a greater capacity to create occupational and political opportunities for members of the middle strata, and through these linkages influence them ideologically' (Brym, 1980: 71). For his part, Gella suggests that 'the entire body of the new intelligentsia will soon go beyond the stage of an amorphous agglomerate into the position of a dominating class . . . in both socialist and capitalist societies' (Gella, 1976: 31–32). This is the position advocated by Alvin Gouldner, to whose work we now turn.

Intellectuals as a 'flawed universal class'

The interest of Alvin Gouldner's 'theses' on the intellectuals lies in the extremes to which he takes his argument. For him, the intellectuals are not dependent groupings in various societies enjoying varying degrees of autonomy according to what each system permits, but rather they are a globally ascendant 'New Class'. Gouldner's is the most recent sustained attempt within Western sociology to offer a general view on intellectuals. That in itself is sufficient to make his position noteworthy, although, rather surprisingly, it does not seem to have been particularly widely discussed.[5] Gouldner's standpoint on intellectuals reached its final formulation in a book entitled *The Future of Intellectuals and the Rise of the New Class* (1979). Several years earlier, he had published a very focused essay on 'revolutionary intellectuals' (Gouldner, 1975–76) and subsequently he developed his more general 'theses' under the title of the 'New Class Project' in the journal *Theory and Society* in 1978; these eventually became the book.

To put it in context, Gouldner's theory of the intellectuals is entirely of a piece with his position on the nature and rôle of sociology. By the beginning of the 1970s, Gouldner had come to be seen as the outstanding contemporary spokesman for a 'reflexive' sociology, one aware of its own assumptions and conditions of existence. Such self-consciousness was taken to be the prerequisite for the sociologist to make his or her contribution to social change, in the first instance within the praxis of sociology and of academic life themselves and thus ultimately, it was supposed, to the wider social order (Gouldner, 1971: 488 ff.). Although Gouldner's criticisms of a technocratized and managerial sociology serving the welfare state were much to the point, his desire to create a new 'work ethic' for the sociologist constituted an inflated concern with the likely results of the transformation of sociological practice. Today, as the welfare state decays before the monetarist offensive one might wryly reflect that the 'liberal technologue' of Gouldner's denunciations is much to be preferred to the neo-conservative ideologue now in the ascendancy.

By the end of the 1970s, the concern with the intellectual practice of social theorists and researchers had substantially broadened out into a consideration of the intellectuals and the intelligentsia as a whole. Gouldner had moved on from 'reflexive sociology' to what he termed 'left-Hegelianism' by the time *The Future of Intellectuals* was written, a view which 'sees our knowledge systems as historically shaped forces that embody limits and, indeed, pathologies' (1979: 5). On the way to this destination he had briefly been a 'Marxist outlaw', that is, one who 'holds that even Marxism must be subject to critique' (1976: xiv). Apart from the undoubted amusement value of such labels, Gouldner was making a point which is central to his theory of the intellectuals: namely, that Marxism had failed to be reflexive and, especially, that the 'Marxist scenario of class struggle was never able to account for itself, for those who produced the scenario, for Marx and Engels themselves' (1979: 9).[6] Thus Gouldner changed his hats and he changed his idiom, but the voice is undoubtedly the same, and so is the theme song. Whereas the reflexive sociologist stripped away the false consciousness of academic sociology, the

Left Hegelian of a decade later had an even more significant task: to tell the New Class what it is really doing. Aspirations to leadership and professed egalitarianism are uneasy bed-fellows, hence the *mauvaise foi* of the intellectuals. Consequently, it 'is the special task of critical theory and critical theorists to block the repression of the New Class's revolutionary rôle, and help this surface to public visibility' (1979: 11.).

Gouldner's project is 'to formulate a frame of reference within which the New Class can be situated. . . to understand [it] as a world historical phenomenon. Rather than viewing the New Class as if it were composed just of technicians and engineers, the effort that follows moves toward a *general* theory of the New Class as encompassing *both* technical intelligentsia *and* intellectuals. . . my interest is in the New Class in *both* late capitalism and in the authoritarian state socialism of the USSR, without arguing or implying any more general "convergence" thesis . . . the two most important theoretical foundations needed for a general theory of the New Class will be, first, a theory of its distinctive language behaviour, its distinctive culture of discourse and, secondly, a general theory of capital within which the New Class's "human capital" or the old class's moneyed capital will be special cases' (1979: 5).

We need not be surprised that such a grand design over-reaches itself; indeed, we may well suspect that some of the overstatement is for effect. In fact, Gouldner's claims to have discovered a new class with its own distinctive base in 'cultural capital' will not withstand scrutiny. His theory is subject to conceptual slippage, is inconsistent in its analysis of class and of capital, has a questionable view of class agency, and uses a notion of 'speech community' so broad as to explain nothing. The difficulties are such that they raise the question of whether a 'general theory' of the intellectuals is even possible.

The New Class and class struggles

Gouldner sees the New Class as 'mass produced' by an educational system which has assumed a steadily increasing importance during this century. He views this class as internally differentiated into the intelligentsia and the intellectuals. 'The New Class is elitist and self-seeking and uses its special knowledge to advance its own interests and power to control its work situation . . . . In my own left Hegelian sociology, the New Class bearers of knowledge are seen as an embryonic new "universal class"—as the prefigured embodiment of such future as the working class still has' (1979: 7–8). Gouldner claims that his conception of the New Class is Marxian in that 'there are certain commonalities in the New Class's relationship to the means of production, and in particular, to what I shall later call cultural or human capital' (1979: 8). The power of the New Class is seen as residing in its 'considerable *de facto* control over the mode of production' and in its knowledge of the means of administration. Gouldner, therefore, endorses a version of the managerialist thesis which asserts the importance of the separation of ownership from control in the capitalist enterprise. The occupational categories comprising the New Class are extensive: in one list those working in the media, education, welfare and medical services and technical specialists in the military are included; another, largely overlapping, list specifies engineers, managers, social workers, academics, government officials, editors and reporters.

In the advanced capitalist states the axis of class struggle is between the class with legal ownership of the means of production and that with effective possession of those means. If one accepts the managerialist thesis, as Gouldner is inclined to, this contest has the effect of putting 'the old moneyed class on the historical shelf' (1979: 12, 13). This seems a curiously perverse point of view at a time of monetarist revival. Moreover, as so many of Gouldner's New Class work within state bureaucracies which are precisely the target of neo-conservative ideology and practice, one must doubt whether it is as blessed by the process of historical development as is alleged.

In state socialism the main conflict is held to be between the New Class and the Vanguard Party and the State. 'Each strives to maintain its relative autonomy vis-à-vis the other two . . . . The requisites for the autonomy of the New Class are undermined by the Vanguard and the latter's autonomy is subverted by the State' (1979: 80). The distinctions between these are not developed, with ensuing difficulties, as we shall see.

Gouldner sees the New Class, apparently both under socialism and under capitalism as a 'cultural bourgeoisie' which 'appropriates privately the advantages of an historically and collectively produced cultural capital'. It is, he says, a genuine capital in its own right 'that generates a stock of income' (1979: 19). The ideology of the New Class everywhere is that of socialism, understood as an extension of the power of the state in the interests of 'cultural capital': an 'egalitarianism' directed against existing forms of privilege, but not in order to emancipate the working class. While the idea that intellectuals may preach socialism and thereby seek personal or group advantages is hardly shockingly novel, the view that the New Class *tout court* is statist makes one pause. Gouldner confronts us with a curious proposition. It is hardly empirically true that *all* intellectuals are committed to the expansion of the state as the present revival of minimalist argument testifies. However, Gouldner has engaged in a telling sleight of hand, for to have acknowledged basic ideological cleavages amongst members of the New Class would have raised serious questions about its unity.

It is especially important for Gouldner to have a satisfactory answer here as he has chosen to define his New Class as consisting of two fractions, the intellectuals and the intelligentsia.[7] These fractions differ substantially in orientation: the intellectuals are Habermasians whose interests 'are primarily critical, emancipatory, hermeneutic and hence often political', whereas the intelligentsia are Kuhnians who 'concentrate their efforts on solving the "puzzles" or "paradigms" on which normal science centres' (1979: 48). What then ensures the unity of the class?

The unity of the class

Gouldner supports his claim that the New Class is indeed a class by developing a 'general theory' of capital in which cultural capital is seen as one form and money capital as another. The nub of the argument is contained in the following passages:

An investment in education is not simply a consumable. Something is left over, which produces a subsequent flow of income. It is *cultural capital*, the economic basis of the New Class. . . . It is not capital because it increases productivity, but simply because it provides incomes, because these incomes are enforceable, *and* because they are legitimated intrinsically, depending on the continued availability or withholding of their services and activities (1979: 27, 23).

What this view entails is an important shift from the initial definition of class as involving a common relation to the means of production. That, indeed, is the position of Marxism. However, what Gouldner ends up with seems rather different. Capital is seen pre-eminently as something which produces socially enforceable claims to *income*. Cultural capital in this conception, therefore, pertains to the selling-power of those possessing specific skills and forms of knowledge. There has evidently been a shift from the characteristically Marxian concern with relations of production to an undoubtedly Weberian focus upon matters of *distribution* in the market.[8]

Apart from the thoroughgoing inconsistency of this standpoint, it is hard to see how cultural capital as Gouldner conceives of it could provide the basis for a class. As Ivan Szelényi has pointed out (1980: 192–193), 'everyone who can sell his or her labour power on the market will have at least a little of his so-called ''cultural capital'' '. Even a little knowledge is a marketable thing.

Gouldner's argument, however, does not rest upon marketability along. The possession of cultural capital, he says, makes the New Class into a 'speech community', one which makes use of a 'culture of critical discourse' (CCD).[9] Such critical discourse justifies its assertions without invoking authorities and aims to convince by rational argument. Of particular importance for Gouldner's position is the argument that the 'shared ideology of the intellectuals and intelligentsia' is an ideology about discourse (1979: 28).

A shared ideology about the formal nature of argument, therefore, is invoked as the condition of class unity. This is the necessary counterweight to what Gouldner acknowledges is a likely divergence between radically minded intellectuals and the conservatively inclined intelligentsia. Their common class interest is a consequence of the supremacy of language in any critical discourse. Therefore both fractions need 'to prevent or oppose all forms of censorship of their speech variety and to install it as the standard of good speech' (1979: 29).

An immediate problem springs to mind, and that is just where does the potential unity stop? Logically, the argument should lead to a new internation-alism—cultural capitalists of the world unite!—but it is quite evident from Gouldner's text that the New Class is principally engaged in its struggles at a national level, and in terms of the different obstacles which are faced inside different social systems. Moreover the conditions for its rise to international power remain unaddressed.

This is because Gouldner solves the problem with a technological determinist argument. Writing in slightly better times, he argued that 'East and West, *détente* is a project of the New Class' and that the 'worldwide technological development and competition' in which it results will in the long run enhance its rise to power (1979: 92). The vagaries of international relations hardly support this optimistic vision. Besides, the profits on the expansion of trade seem more likely to accrue to the allegedly dying moneyed capital, particularly in the guise of transnational corporations. These organizations, moreover, are staffed by the legions of the technical intelligentsia and backed up by intellectual apologists besides.

These difficulties remain unconsidered, such, apparently, is Gouldner's extraordinary faith in an ultimately rational—intellectual-borne—resolution to all our problems. As he observes elsewhere, 'The larger speech repertoire available to men, the greater the likelihood that all men will become brothers' (1975–76: 36). Such an all-embracing notion of a speech community is ultimately vacuous, and projects a return to those palmy days before the Tower of Babel was built.

The primary condition of New Class unity is, therefore, plainly idealist: the possession of CCD. But as rational argument does not of itself provide sufficient grounds for the unity of a class, nor a new rock upon which to found harmonious international relations, Gouldner offers some further factors in explanation. In effect, these are a mixture of the ideal and the material. Of considerable importance is the blockage of opportunities for the New Class, both East and West. This is faced alongside status deprivation, and, two divergent orientations: the intelligentsia's, who find their technical interest blocked, and that of the intellectuals, who have a commitment to the social totality (1979: 58). It is difficult to see how these, taken in combination, *need* lead to a unified class consciousness. Gouldner does recognize this difficulty, and likens his position on this question to that of Daniel Bell, one of 'non-doctrinaire open-mindedness' (1979: 95).[10] This collapse into agnosticism runs counter to the futuristic thrust of his theses.

The problem of class agency

Aside from this ambivalent quality to his argument, Gouldner encounters some fundamental difficulties in his conception of class action. So far, we have treated his theory as though it possessed a degree of coherence which it in fact does not. The difficulty has to do with the way in which the New Class's formation and historical continuity is conceptualized. Throughout his text Gouldner gives instances of the New Class's actions. It was present at the Bolshevik revolution and has led the revolutions in China, Cambodia, Cuba and Vietnam. The New Class has entered history in the turn of century US socialist movement, is now ensconced in the Democratic Party and was active in the anti-Vietnam war movement. It also is present in Third World military and nationalist leaderships. The present 'Eurocommunist' strategy is another manifestation of New Class politics as is contemporary terrorism. The list could be expanded considerably: it is a 'world historical phenomenon' indeed.

The central difficulty, which such a list of events and political strategies raises, is that it imputes an historical identity to the New Class and a consciousness of its interests which runs counter to Gouldner's scepticism as to whether it can in fact acquire unity, for it is treated as an *already constituted* social agent. For instance, he talks of the international ecology movement as 'only the most recent strategy in the New Class's guerilla [sic] war against the old class' (1979: 17). There is also a considerable uncertainty as to when the formation of the New Class actually began, as at one point Gouldner writes of 'tensions between the emerging New Class and bourgeoisie' at the beginnings of bourgeois society. Then, over the page, he observes that the 'bourgeois revolution was based on an alliance between the propertied and educated section of the middle class—the bourgeoisie and the intelligentsia' (1979: 64, 65). A similar conceptual slippage pervades what he has to say about state socialist regimes. On the one hand, Gouldner insists upon the major rôle played by intellectuals in the revolutionary process. Thus, members of the New Class are evidently present at the inception of socialism. On the other hand, his model of socialist state organization suggests that the New Class is entirely *outside* the system of rule. The Leninist party whose practice is codified in *What is to be done?* was invented to secure the interests of intellectuals and has been an 'organizational mediation' of the political practice of the New Class. Yet, democratic centralism requires a discipline which curbs CCD, limiting the cultural capitalists' freedom. But does this mean that the party hacks and bureaucrats who do now rule have ceased to be intellectuals or that they are merely compromised ones? They would seem to be members of the intelligentsia *already in power*. The concepts of the 'intelligentsia' and of the 'bureaucracy' are, therefore, hardly distinct.

Ultimately, one must conclude, the problems with Gouldner's analysis lie in his failure to address systematically a number of related issues. First of all, the wide historical canvas is used in a way which effaces the particularity of given periods of development and which conflates the distinctive positions of the intellectuals under capitalism and under socialism. The difficulties of comparison are not explicitly addressed but are made to disappear definitionally through the symmetrical application of the concepts of 'intellectual' and 'intelligentsia'. Consider, for instance, the differences in the 'public sphere' in state-socialist and liberal-democratic regimes and their implications for the organization of intellectual activity. Gouldner is aware of this as his book *The Dialectic of Ideology and Technology* shows. There, he argues for the crucial importance of a 'media-critical politics' which recognizes the central rôle played by the media, however constrained, in bourgeois societies: 'It is through the mass media and through them alone that there is today any possibility at all of a truly mass public enlightenment that might go beyond what universities elicit, i.e. beyond small elites and educated elitism. It is through the media that the system may be made to "dance to its own melody", or to expose itself' (1976: 160). He also draws a distinction between bureaucratic dictatorship and 'this floundering thing . . . parliamentary democracy', a system which permits a 'public' of sorts to exist without total integration into the state.[11] In the much more schematic organization of his 'theses' on the intellectuals, these insights disappear.

Secondly, Gouldner says virtually nothing about the organization of the state in each form of society.[12] The absence of a specific analysis of the workings of the state apparatuses, and the consequent silence about the political processes involved in their capture, means that the modes of accession to power of the New Class are left vague. We are told that it is likely to occur, but never how. Moreover, not only is state organization neglected but so is the supra-state level.

Finally, the emphasis upon the specific language of the cultural bourgeoisie leads to all other linguistic forms being lumped into a residual category. This carries an implicit message: the thought of the intellectuals is in effect identified with rationality itself, or, at least, the most rational thought currently available. Could one not therefore judge that Gouldner, despite his desire to debunk the particular interests of the intellectuals has ended up by celebrating their superiority?

East European views

It would be surprising if some of Gouldner's preoccupations and formulations did not find their echo in recent writings from Eastern Europe on the intellectuals. The condition of such theorizing has been the obviously 'blocked' nature of state-socialism and the disillusioning experience of efforts to reform the ruling party from within. The Czech experiment of 1968 and the ensuing 'normalization' have constituted the focal point of recent thinking. It is perhaps too early to say how the lessons of Poland from August 1980 will be assimilated in terms of theorizing about the respective rôles of sections of the intelligentsia and of the working class in seeking to achieve reforms of the system, although the importance of their *collaboration* in challenging the party has been noted (Brus, 1980: 9–10).

The critical rôle played by the classical intelligentsia in pre-Soviet days is now associated with the various forms of intellectual dissidence in state-socialist societies. Antonin Liehm, the Czech reformer in exile, has characterized the post-Stalinist arrangements as a 'new social contract' under which 'the citizens hand over to the state all of their individual and collective rights, and the state assures them in return stable employment at an average wage for a minimum contribution of labour and personal initiative' (Liehm, 1975: 158). He goes on to suggest, excessively perhaps, that in the general spiritual void which is the condition and the consequence of the contract' the voice of the intellectuals 'constitutes the only real and authentic testimony of the situation created by the contract' (ibid.: 162).

At all events, there can be little doubt that social theory produced as *samizdat* has an especial poignancy and interest. In the cases considered all those concerned have suffered more or less severe difficulties. György Bence and János Kis, who wrote *Towards an East European Marxism* (1977) under the *nom de plume* of Marc Rakovski were dismissed from their academic positions in the early 1970s (Bence and Kis, 1980: 293–294). George Konrád and Ivan Szelényi were briefly jailed, prosecuted for 'counterrevolutionary' writing, and encouraged to emigrate, which Szelényi did. Their book *The Intellectuals on the Road to Class Power* (1979) was finally published in the West several years after these events. Rudolf Bahro, author of *The Alternative in Eastern Europe* (1978) was imprisoned for 'espionage' before being released into exile in the West.

All of these writers, and especially Konrád and Szelényi, are preoccupied with the rôle of the intelligentsia in present-day state socialism, and, in particular, the extent to which it might be an agent of social, economic and political reform. There are two main lines of argument. Whereas Rakovski and Konrád and Szelényi see the intelligentsia as playing a crucial rôle in more or less radical change, Bahro, for his part, has a much more fundamental concern: he postulates the need to dissolve the division of labour and sees the intelligentsia as an instrument to that end, but one which is dangerously likely to substitute its own rule for that of the displaced party-state bureaucracy.

Rakovski: the limits of reform

Rakovski's analysis begins with a general reformulation of the kind of Marxism needed when approaching state socialist societies. Soviet-type regimes are class societies, but 'a different kind of class society existing alongside capitalism' (1977: 15). He argues that the ideology of 'market socialism' is the ideology of the reformers. Bureaucratic planning results in a struggle over power and control, where the 'political elite of the ruling class' resists the incursions of the reformers who are 'that segment of the ruling class which extends from the decision-makers at enterprise level to those who, although they are decision-makers at the national economic level, nevertheless remain outside the political elite' (ibid.: 21). The struggle, in other words is limited to the ruling class which consists of those who play a rôle 'in making and/or preparing decisions within the state administrative hierarchy' (ibid.: 86). And, argues Rakovski, the desire for reform does not shake the essentials of the system: it merely reflects the efforts of various already quite privileged groups to secure more leverage within it. The economic inefficiencies of the existing system and the brakes placed upon the exercise of technical expertise form the central points of criticism. However, a crucial limit on the advance of the managers and experts is the working class's perception that these groups are pursuing their own limited interest rather than contributing to a general rise in living standards. After the invasion of Czechoslovakia in 1968 the ex-reformist strata realized the limitations and came largely to accept the dominance of the political elite. The managers and experts are not seen as part of a new class, a position which obviously runs directly counter to Gouldner's thesis.

After this rather bleak account of the limited possibilities of change issuing from the managers and experts—one quite at variance with Gouldner's view of their revolutionary potential—Rakovski attempts to specify more exactly who are the intelligentsia. He—like other East European writers—rejects the official Soviet sociological definition as inadequate, especially if we want to grasp the nature of dissidence. To understand dissent, we should focus upon 'the social group which is capable of forming an autonomous ideology (which is) the sub-group of intellectual workers whose members are in regular contact with the process of cultural and scientific creation' (ibid.: 43). Despite pressures to conform, and the disappearance both in the East and West of the conditions which permitted a free intelligentsia to flourish, there is none the less a degree of freedom possessed by intellectual strata which is not shared by the working class. In spite of strict controls on intellectual production there are still certain features of 'post-Stalinist' societies which permit the intellectuals to develop room for manoeuvre. In other words, something of a 'public sphere' exists. Non-conformism is to be explained by the experience of various groups pushing at the margins of the permissible in the 'post-Stalinist equilibrium' of the later 1960s. Non-conformism is also part of the internal structure of intellectual production, reinforced by international contacts which apply pressure for change. Outside of the internal dynamics of intellectual work itself (which seems here to be identified with that of academics and of scientists) there are structural factors. The rise of factory-type scientific and cultural production produces the need for auxiliaries, what Rakovski terms a 'sub-intelligentsia', where those who are marginalized can eke out a living: 'the non-conformist counter-culture forms in the sphere of communication between intellectuals; it is an irreducible epiphenomenon of intellectual work, and inevitably establishes a connection between all those who conform to the intelligentsia's subculture and way of life' (ibid.: 65). Hence the need to pay attention to the communicative possibilities afforded by the counter-public sphere and to extend these. Rakovski's analysis of the intellectuals therefore encompasses cultural creators and economic and political groups, and locates them as fractions of the ruling class which are struggling for more power. In the last analysis, however, the vast majority of intellectuals will side with the political elite against the working class to maintain their common privileges.

Like Gouldner, Rakovski argues that intellectual production is inherently antipathetic to the constraints of censorship. The 'counter-public sphere' permits the possibility of communication, however limited, and is obviously a precondition for the dissemination of criticism and for the expansion of democratic rights. But whereas Gouldner stresses the growing strength of 'cultural capital', Rakovski is all too aware of its weaknesses. This conceptualization of the 'counter-public sphere' and its fragilities suggests a fruitful basis for comparison with the debates over the 'relative autonomy' of culture in capitalist democracies.

Konrád and Szelényi: intellectuals as ruling class

In their lengthy work on the intelligentsia in Eastern Europe, Konrád and Szelényi begin by making a most valuable theoretical distinction. It is essential, they argue, to reject the 'generic' concept of the intellectuals, one which defines them 'quite independently of historical ages and modes of production'. This approach leads to a view of their social mission as 'fundamentally teleological', 'for culture is society's effort to give purpose to a world which is itself purposeless' (1979: 12). What Konrád and Szelényi advocate as an alternative is an examination of 'the actual position which the intellectuals occupy in a variety of concrete social structures' by employing a 'genetic' concept, one 'which entails a description of the functions their cultural mission serves and the interests it articulates in specific social contexts' (ibid.: 12). This is formally very close to the Gramscian position noted at the beginning of this essay.

It is a great pity that Konrád and Szelényi do not stick to their methodological dictum. While there is much that is illuminating in their work, it is vitiated by that very teleological vision of the intelligentsia which they deplore. Their work shares a fatal ambiguity with that of Gouldner, one which consists in the identification of the intelligentsia as a class currently *in statu nascendi* while at the same time treating it practically as though it were *already constituted*.

Part of the difficulty here arises, as Alec Nove has pointed out, from the confusing use of the single term 'intelligentsia' for several distinctive formations: first, the revolutionary intellectuals prior to October 1917, then for the Stalinist apparatus, and finally for the bureaucrats of the present day: 'The word "bureaucrat" may be much more applicable to the present generation of leading cadres. In spirit and in educational and social bacground, they are as different from Stalin's henchmen of the thirties as these in their turn were from the revolutionary intelligentsia they destroyed' (Nove, 1980: 229).

This conflation reproduces, albeit on a more limited scale, the difficulties associated with Gouldner's effort to develop a general theory. Furthermore, underlying the whole account is an exceedingly idealistic attribution to the intellectuals of perpetual power-hunger throughout the ages, one which is now finally about to achieve its satisfaction—or perhaps actualization would be a better term—within the framework of the state-socialist mode of redistribution. This contradicts the commitment to a 'genetic approach'.

Konrád and Szelényi argue that Marxism's focus upon the question of ownership of property is singularly inapposite for the analysis of a state-socialism where private ownership has largely disappeared. What is needed is to take account of systems of authority and rule, and of the ways in which they are legitimized, a position which forms the starting-point of the Weberian sociology of domination. State-socialism is characterized by 'the institutions of expropriation of surplus' (Szelényi, 1978–79: 61) which are oddly designated as 'rationally redistributive'. The focus, therefore, is quite plainly upon distribution rather than upon relations of production, which throughout their analysis remain rather enigmatic. State-socialist regimes are dichotomous, with an intelligentsia facing a working class. Szelényi sets out this view most clearly in an article published shortly before the book:

All those who have a vested interest in the maximisation of redistributive power are members of a new dominating class, since their interests are antagonistic to those of the direct producers. If we define the new class this way, it obviously includes more than just the bureaucracy or even the techno-bureaucracy. It potentially comprises the whole intelligentsia (Szelényi, 1978–79: 52).

The power to redistribute the social product is therefore the bone of contention, and the 'direct producers', the working class, have quite a bone to pick. But on the whole they are passive actors, stand-bys, in the drama of struggle within rational redistributive regimes. The redistributors (coterminous with the rather elastic category of the intellectuals) are legitimized in their exercise of power 'on the basis of an alleged monopoly of the teleological knowledge necessary for a rational, socially just and economically efficient allocation of surplus' (Szelényi, 1978–79: 62). The emphasis upon the possession of knowledge as both a strategic resource and as a legitimized entitlement to decide on others' behalf recalls features of Gouldner's position.

The Weberian distinction between formal and substantive rationality so relevant in the case of Western technocratic theorists also operates in the work of Konrád and Szelényi. Whereas, they say, bureaucracies in bourgeois societies operate according to the dictates of formal rationality, those in state socialism are governed by substantive rationality: or, *telos* dominates *techné*. The redistributive bureaucrats are 'people not only with executive skills, but with moral commitment and historical vision' (1978–79: 65). And that historical vision meant that the East European intelligentsia welcomed Bolshevism as the best legitimation for 'their long march to power'. By comparison, intellectuals in the West have been professionals working according to the dictates of the market, and have had a technocratic orientation.

The working class, as observed, are bystanders in the class struggles of state-socialism. One reason is that, according to Konrád and Szelényi, they do not produce their own 'organic intellectuals' for these are immediately absorbed into the intelligentsia. However, in the 1970s there were signs of working-class self-assertion, but more important were the marginal intellectuals who were espousing the cause of socialist self-management—a doctrine directly challenging the redistributive ethos and the institutions of centralized control.

For Konrád and Szelényi, like Rakovski, the important struggles take place *within* the dominant class. Their characterization of this class is not entirely systematic. On the one hand, they talk of the intellectuals as a class in the process of formation, on the other as though it has existed ever since the October Revolution. They distinguish three key sets of functionaries within the class: the ideologues, the technocrats and the police. The function of central redistribution, at the top of the bureaucratic pyramid, is carried out by the state and party bureaucracy, which is also termed the ruling or governing elite, and which is described as a segment of the intellectual class. This makes it pretty clear that the intellectual class in part *has* arrived.

What, therefore, is involved in talking of its rise to class power? In fact, this is a completely misleading formulation as is made clear from a chapter entitled 'The struggle for power within the intelligentsia'. The Stalinization of the Bolshevik Party, argue Konrád and Szelényi, involved the creation of a new elite which was 'elevated above the intellectual class and the party as a whole' (1979: 185). Stalinism 'is characterised by the power monopoly of the ruling elite', whereas post-Stalinism involves 'a joint exercise of power on the part of the ruling elite and the intellectual class, within which the hegemony still lies with the former' (ibid.: 201). Since the ruling elite is *of* the intellectual class, what is plainly being talked about is a re-adjustment of political dominance *within* the ruling class—although at times the loose formulations make this somewhat difficult to perceive. Eventually, Konrád and Szelényi make this quite clear: 'The stability of the post-Stalin era is founded on an alliance between the technocracy and the ruling elite' and 'by vindicating professional knowledge and achievement as principles which legitimate power, [the technocracy] has called into question the power monopoly of the ruling elite' (ibid.: 207, 209). Thus, the portentous march of the intellectuals comes down to a bid for power by technocrats frustrated by the restrictions of the party bureaucracy. The technocrats are in loose alliance with the humanistic intelligentsia who serve the useful function of pushing at the limits. Konrád and Szelényi counsel that the technocracy must espouse the rights of the working class, even though they are potential opponents, in order to forge an alliance which can make the decisive step of breaking the power of the political elite. The third phase of socialism will see the domination of the technocrats, but certainly not the emancipation of the working class from its subordination to the rule of a different fraction of the intelligentsia. This final scenario once more recalls Gouldner's views.

The analyses of Rakovski and of Konrád and Szelényi are, therefore, convergent in many respects. While they differ in their theoretical basis, the former employing a variant of Marxist class analysis, and the latter a neo-Weberian one, their characterizations of the intellectuals and of internal struggles within the dominant class are very similar. In particular, there is a great stress upon the likely marginality of the working class in change in Eastern Europe. It must be recalled, though, that these analyses antedate the Polish Summer of 1980. Rakovski's analysis of the intellectuals is more guarded possibly because it is subordinate to a broader theoretical project. For Konrád and Szelényi, however, the rise of the intelligentsia is the *Leitmotiv* of their study and so, while in reality similarly arguing that there will be significant re-adjustments in the dominant class, they tend to present their argument with more than a touch of *Sturm und Drang*. Both analyses are largely agnostic concerning the forms of political organization which might be consequent upon change, which is surely a serious weakness.

Bahro: auto-destruction of the intellectuals

Such agnosticism could not be said to obtain in the case of Rudolf Bahro's Marxist critique of 'actually existing socialism'. In particular, whereas Rakovski offers no plan for the transformation of Eastern European states, Bahro does, in the form of a cultural revolution against the 'politbureaucratic dictatorship' which involves far-reaching changes in social relations. It would scarcely be possible to enter into the details of Bahro's views here given the range of his concerns. However, there is one central theme in his thinking which bears closely upon the present discussion, namely his analysis of the division of labour.

An examination of the division of labour in both advanced capitalism and in 'proto-socialism', Bahro argues, discloses an hierarchical structure of levels of knowledge which are brought into play in the process of production. At the base of the pyramid are those performing functions of a 'simple and schematic' kind who possess a 'particularized experimental knowledge'. Those at the top, who are engaged in the 'analysis and synthesis of the natural and social totality' operate on the level of finished ideologies and produce political strategies (1978: 164). These different levels of knowledge and function are linked to the educational system and the qualifications it confers. This is, again, an argument about 'cultural capital' and its place in social reproduction. But Bahro, unlike Gouldner, makes a clear-cut theoretical connection between *productive* activity within the division of labour and the possession of given cultural attributes which are used to ensure *distributive* advantages.

For Bahro, the road to a genuine socialist democracy involves overthrowing the 'subalternity' induced by the division of labour. Such a 'subaltern' mentality, he considers, necessarily inhibits the development amongst the working class of a consciousness which would give them 'access to the social synthesis' (ibid.: 178). If this problem were to be seriously addressed, says Bahro, *inter alia* we would need to consider the enrichment of the personal economy of time: in particular, the opportunities for the development of abstraction and reflection in the process of socialization at home and at work. Bahro advocates a redivision of labour as part of a planned process of transition involving other changes in social relations such as a revolution in the content of education, the encouragement of intensified intra-group communication and the socialization of the 'process of social knowledge' involving the use of mass communications and forms of political representation (ibid.: 302–303).

Bahro's arguments about the intelligentsia have several dimensions. First of all, rather than stress the confrontation between intelligentsia and working class (as do Konrád and Szelényi), he starts from the view that 'it is impossible to separate *the* intelligentsia from the collective worker' (ibid.: 200). The contemporary socialist intelligentsia is, he argues, very diverse, and quite discontinuous with the traditional intelligentsia since it is recruited largely from the working class.

Second, Bahro quite explicitly argues that the challenge to the centralist control of the 'politbureaucracy' does *not* mean 'replacing the alleged "leading role of the working class" by a factual "leading role of the intelligentsia". The interests of the managerial, scientific and ideological intelligentsia, who are competent in their own eyes, bear as little a universal character as those of the immediate producers. The whole problem of general emancipation must be placed on a new basis, as far as its practical political form is concerned' (ibid.: 202). This is not a question countenanced by the other theorists we have considered, and is self-evidently integral to Bahro's Utopianism.

Bahro's view of the rôle of the intellectuals emerges with especial clarity in his appraisal of the 1968 Czech experiment. He argues that the demands for political democracy which issued from the intellectuals meant restricting the more fundamental changes in political, economic and social relations which were necessary. However, Ralph Miliband has made the pertinent observation that this position fails to recognize that 'the battle for democratic freedoms everywhere is not simply a prelude to the battle for socialism, but an intrinsic part of it' (Miliband, 1979: 280).

Despite his concern for general emancipation Bahro recognizes that in the exemplary case of Czechoslovakia 'the turn began among the ideologists, and *that mobilization for the reform ran like a chain reaction through the structure of education, from top to bottom*' (Bahro, 1978: 312). The explanation given for the emancipatory movement beginning precisely there acknowledges the implications of the division of labour and stratification of knowledge for the power of intellectuals:

Since the apparatus is the most prominent object of transformation it is only natural that the potential bloc of its antagonists should appear first of all with the head. The intellectual life of society in general, with its centre of gravity in the process of information and decision over reproduction and its goals, is the battlefield of the cultural revolution (ibid.: 317).

Moreover, the bureaucracy itself is not immune to the process of erosion from within, as more and more of its members are recruited from the intelligentsia, and inside it, and the party itself, there is increasing disillusionment with the workings of the system. Where Bahro's analysis coincides with that of Rakovski and Konrád and Szelényi is in the recognition that the impetus for change *must* come from strata near the top. Where he differs is in his emphasis upon the dangers this carries and in the demand that they should not act only in their own interest (ibid.: 328).

It is at this point that Bahro's third position on the intellectuals assumes major importance. A general transformation of state socialism involves a dismantling of the party apparatus and its replacement with a 'League of Communists'. This renovated structure is characterized, in the terms of Gramsci's famous formulation, as a 'collective intellectual'. As such it is to be the bearer of the general interest and to secure that interest against the special interests of the experts and of the technical intelligentsia who are to replace the 'politbureaucracy'.

One should remain duly alert to the lacunae in Bahro's contribution, while at the same time recognizing its far-reaching vision. In particular, the conception of *the* party as a 'collective intellectual' is hardly adequate to the great difficulties posed by the search for a democratic socialism. Gramsci's conception with its stress upon the dialectic between leaders and led remains an unrealized ideal, not least because of its lack of institutional specificity. Moreover, one must doubt whether in the conditions of advanced industrialism *the* party could ever be equal to the task demanded of giving expression to all the 'emancipatory interests' in society. Moreover, Bahro is rather dogmatically wedded to the notion that a socialist society requires only one party, on the doubtful grounds that a multi-party system is required only in a society with distinct class interests. Besides this, there are further difficulties in his concept of the state, from which the party, as a 'collective intellectual', is to be separated. Critics as diverse as Miliband and Ernest Mandel (1978: ch. 7) have noted that Bahro's proposals would leave the state's centralizing tendencies and monopoly of decision-making intact. As opposed to a multiplicity of parties and other social organizations and movements exercising corrective forms of accountability and control, Bahro's single 'collective intellectual' would seem powerless against a continuing bureaucratic domination which had merely shifted into new hands. There is an hubristic worm in the bud of Bahro's new design: how is he to avert the assertion of the interests of the specialists and technical intelligentsia which he so greatly fears?

While Bahro has hardly solved the problem of political organization in Eastern Europe, it is true, nevertheless, that he has firmly looked in the face the consequences for the intelligentsia of the dissolution of mental and manual labour. It is this which distinguishes his theory from those of the rest; for whereas Rakovski and Konrád and Szelényi see in the reformist rule of the intelligentsia a *solution* (however partial or temporary) to the problems of state-socialism, Bahro sees only yet another *problem*.

Concluding remarks

This essay has demonstrated that the effort to define and characterize the intellectuals is more than liberally provided with false turnings and nasty snares, not to speak of the odd pitfall or two. The difficulties of the search have not discouraged speculation amongst social theorists for whom the analysis of the forms and conditions of intellectual practice is quite unavoidable.

To address the question posed at the beginning, there is no simple answer to what should be expected from a theory of the intellectuals. It is easier to say what we should not expect. For one, this critique indicates that the perils of over-generalization are legion: Gouldner's work is exemplary in this regard. Moreover, both Gouldner's approach and that of Konrád and Szelényi strongly suggest the considerable dangers of succumbing to the discreet charms of an implicit teleology. Once the intellectuals are endowed with a single corporate identity their quest for power or their commitment to some universal mission become spontaneous attributes. Such teleological visions are sustained by conceptual imprecision: the less discriminating the analysis the more we seem to be talking about a single formation with a continuous life, a New Class, say, on the ascendant.

As an antidote one might stress the need for careful comparison between intellectual formations within different social systems or between different social formations of the same type. This is a proper and desirable objective which may contribute greatly to our sociological understanding. It has been suggested that a productive orientation for such work is the 'relative autonomy' available for intellectual production in different types of society.

On the question of class alliances, the various writers display a uniform conviction: the intellectuals will serve their own interests first while usually attempting to disguise their collective *amour propre* behind fine phrases. So, although Gouldner ends, in effect, by celebrating the superiority of intellectuals' discourse, his study was conceived as both prophecy and warning: as their rise is proclaimed so does the whistle need to be blown on the flawed universality of the New Class. For his part, Rakovski gloomily sees the East European intelligentsias deserting the working class in hard times, leaving them amidst the battered ruins of a failed reformism. Konrád and Szelényi anticipate the installation of the technocracy, who, while things may improve, will still exercise domination over the proletariat. Bahro, most disenchanted of all, finds a solution to the problem only by urging the abolition of any distinction between mental and manual labour, in effect advising the intellectuals to auto-destruct.

This last view is unlikely to produce much loud applause from those whose claims to power and privilege derive from 'cultural capital', 'teleological knowledge' or 'socially consecrated expertise'. Perhaps this is why theories of the intellectuals so often read like theories for the intellectuals.

Acknowledgements

I am most grateful to the following for their helpful comments: Philip Elliott, Nira Yuval-Davis, Mark Cousins, Chris Rootes, Yannis Kitromilides, Colin Sparks and Nicholas Garnham. It would be unfair to hold them guilty by association.

Notes

1. These questions are to be pursued in considerably greater depth in a full-length study currently in preparation.
2. Certainly belated by comparison with Lucio Colletti and Noberto Bobbio, for instance, who had much earlier noted the difficulties surrounding the Marxist theory of the state.
3. I have modified the English translation. The original (1979: 40) has the phrase 'la sociologie du socialisme réel' which is rendered 'the sociology of socialist regimes'. This fails to capture the claim made by the phrase 'real' or 'actually existing' socialism.

4. The brief text reads: 'We the undersigned, protesting against the breaches of secrecy which have surrounded the Esterhazy affair, persist in demanding a new hearing' (Bon and Burnier, 1971: 58).

5. Szelényi's (1980) review seems to be the most serious attempt to evaluate his book although he finds more coherence there than I do. Disco (1979: 160) has applied Gouldner's analysis to Habermas who is interpreted as articulating the New Class ideology of 'that sector . . . most concerned with normative critique'. He does not consider the obscurities of Gouldner's own views, however.

6. As Karabel (1976) points out, Gramsci's work is a substantial challenge to this view. However, Gouldner does not address himself in detail to Gramsci's views on 'organic intellectuals' which precisely *do* try to account for the scenarists, at least post-first-generation ones. How successfully is another question.

7. To put it thus simply is to make his position seem clearer than it is. Sometimes (e.g. 1979: 48) he refers to 'elites' within the New Class, but without specifying their boundaries.

8. As Frank Parkin has pointed out in the most cogent recent statement of a neo-Weberian position 'Cultural capital and credentialism . . . are notions that do not readily fit into the vocabulary of modes of production, other than as mere epiphenomena. Indeed they have the suspicious appearance of concepts relating to the distributive system, with all that implies in the way of Weberian contamination' (Parkin, 1979: 59). So far as Gouldner is concerned this is correct. However, Parkin does, I think, overstate the case. Bourdieu for instance has made out a case for using a conception of 'cultural capital' within a framework which remains broadly historical materialist.

9. Ultimately, this view does not differ that greatly from Karl Mannheim's (1936) view that the 'sociological bond' uniting the intelligentsia and giving them their potentiality for social detachment is the common experience of education. The *mission* differs, but the main enabling condition is broadly the same.

10. Bell's open-mindedness is rather less open these days as, positively disenchanted by the New Class, he has latterly sought 'to regain a sense of the sacred point to the direction in which our culture . . . will move' (1980b: 353).

11. This rather uncritically reproduces the totalitarianism/democracy distinction of totalitarian theory. However, as Rakovski (1977) indicates, there *is*, under some circumstances, space for a 'counter-public sphere'.

12. Nor, indeed, is this lacuna properly dealt with in his other work, unfortunately, where he either provides some further Weberian insights on bureaucracy in general (Gouldner, 1976) or an incisive account of classical Marxism's difficulties in squaring up to the consequences of its theory of the state, in particular, why it should wither away (Gouldner, 1980).

Bibliography

ABERCROMBIE, N., HILL, S. and TURNER, B., (1980). *The Dominant Ideology Thesis*, London, Allen and Unwin

ALTHUSSER, L. (1979). The crisis of Marxism, *Power and Opposition in Post-revolutionary Societies*, London, Ink Links

ASCHERSON, N. (1981). *The Polish August: the Self-limiting Revolution*, Harmondsworth, Penguin

BAHRO, R. (1978). *The Alternative in Eastern Europe*, London, New Left Books

BELL, D. (1973). *The Coming of the Post-Industrial Society: A Venture in Social Forecasting*, Harmondsworth, Penguin

BELL, D. (1980a). The New Class: a muddled concept, in *Sociological Journeys: Essays 1960–1980*, London, Heinemann

BELL, D. (1980b). The return of the sacred?, *Sociological Journeys*

BENCE, G. and KIS, J. (1980). On being a Marxist: a Hungarian View, *The Socialist Register*

BON, F. and BURNIER, M.-A. (1971). *Les Nouveaux Intellectuels*, Paris, Seuil

BOURDIEU, P. (1971). Intellectual field and creative project, in Young, M. F. D. (ed.), *Knowledge and Control*, London, Collier-MacMillan

BOURDIEU, P. (1979). Symbolic power, *Critique of Anthropology*, vol. 4, nos. 13 and 14, Summer

BRUS, W. (1980). Lessons of the Polish Summer, *Marxism Today*, November.

BRYM, R. J. (1980). *Intellectuals and Politics*, London, George Allen and Unwin

CARRILLO, S. (1977). *'Eurocommunism' and the State*, London, Lawrence and Wishart

CHURCHWARD, L. G. (1973). *The Soviet Intelligentsia*, London, Routledge and Kegan Paul

DEBRAY, R. (1981). *Teachers, Writers, Celebrities; The Intellectuals of Modern France*, London, New Left Books, Translation of *Le Pouvoir Intellectuel*, Paris, Ramsay, 1979

DISCO, C. (1979). Critical theory as ideology of the New Class, *Theory and Society*, vol. 8

GALBRAITH, J. K. (1967). *The New Industrial State*, Harmondsworth, Penguin

GELLA, A. (1976). An introduction to the sociology of the intelligentsia, in Gella A. (ed.), *The Intelligentsia and the Intellectuals: Theory, Method, and Case Study*, Beverly Hills, Sage

GOULDNER, A. (1971). *The Coming Crisis of Western Sociology*, London, Heinemann Educational Books

GOULDNER, A. (1975–76). Prologue to a theory of revolutionary intellectuals, *Telos*, no. 26, Winter

GOULDNER, A. (1976). *The Dialectic of Ideology and Technology*, London, MacMillan

GOULDNER, A. (1978). The New Class Project, *Theory and Society*, vol. 6

GOULDNER, A. (1979). *The Future of Intellectuals and the Rise of the New Class*, London, MacMillan

GOULDNER, A. (1980). *The Two Marxisms*, London, MacMillan

GRAMSCI, A. (1971). *Selections from the Prison Notebooks*, London, Lawrence and Wishart

HABERMAS, J. (1974). The public sphere, *New German Critique*, vol. 3

HOBSBAWM, E. (1979). Intellectuals and the labour movement, *Marxism Today*, July

HUSZAR, T. (1976). Changes in the concept of intellectuals, in Gella, A. (ed.), *The Intelligentsia and the Intellectuals: Theory, Method, and Case Study*, Beverly Hills, Sage

KARABEL, J. (1976). Revolutionary contradictions: Antonio Gramsci and the problem of intellectuals, *Politics and Society*, vol. 6

KONRÁD, G. and SZELÉNYI, I. (1979). *The Intellectuals on the Road to Class Power*, Brighton, Harvester Press

LIEHM, A. J. (1975). The intellectuals on the new social contract, *Telos*, no. 28, Spring

MANDEL, E. (1978). *From Stalinism to Eurocommunism*, London, New Left Books

MANNHEIM, K. (1936). *Ideology and Utopia*, London, Routledge and Kegan Paul

MILIBAND, R. (1979). A commentary on Rudolf Bahro's alternative, *The Socialist Register*.

NOVE, A. (1980). Review of Konrád and Szelényi, *Telos*, no. 44, Summer

PARKIN, F. (1979). *Marxism and Class Theory: A Bourgeois Critique*, London, Tavistock Publications

POULANTZAS, N. (1975). *Classes in Contemporary Capitalism*, London, New Left Books

RAKOVSKI, M. (1977). *Towards an East European Marxism*, London, Allison and Busby

ROOTES, C. A. (1980). Student radicalism, *Theory and Society*, no. 3

ROSS, G. (1978). Marxism and the new middle classes: French critiques, *Theory and Society*, no. 2

SZELÉNYI, I. (1978–79). The position of the intelligentsia in the class structure of state socialism, *Critique*, nos. 10–11, Winter–Spring

SZELÉNYI, I. (1980). Book review of Gouldner (1979), *Telos*, no. 45, Fall

VAUGHAN, M. (1978). The intellectuals in contemporary Europe, in Giner, S. and Archer, M. S. (eds.), *Contemporary Europe: Social Structures and Cultural Patterns*, London, Routledge and Kegan Paul

WILLIAMS, R. (1976). *Keywords: A vocabulary of Culture and Society*, London, Fontana

WILLIAMS, R. (1981). *Culture*, London, Fontana

WRIGHT, E. O. (1979). Intellectuals and the class structure of capitalist society in Walker, P. (ed.), *Between Labour and Capital*, Brighton, Harvester Press

Intellectuals, the 'information society' and the disappearance of the public sphere

PHILIP ELLIOTT*

This paper attempts to raise a series of questions about intellectuals, the mass media, the current course of technical and economic developments in society and their consequences for the culture.[1] It deals not only with the current situation but also with longer-term trends. Society is at the point when there is about to be another shift in the distributive forms of the mass media. This re-opens many of the questions which have already been discussed about centralized broadcasting, both radio and television, as well as other earlier mass media. It also raises questions about the future of the intellectuals in the sphere of cultural production.

The thesis I wish to advance is in marked contrast to that of Alvin Gouldner (1979), outlined by Philip Schlesinger in the opening paper. My argument is that the shift in the location of power from the nation state to the international economic system is graphically illustrated by current developments in the mass media and so too are the implications of this shift for the intellectual fraction of Gouldner's 'New Class'. It is not just that the 'new class' is destined not to come to power. The intellectuals are about to be robbed of those public forums in which they could engage in their 'culture of critical discourse'. Their toe-hold on power is crumbling under their feet.

The new distributive technologies have already re-opened some of the more enthralling controversies of the past. To take a trivial example, space invader games have already been criticized for taking too much of the time and attention of the young, for introducing them to violence and warfare and even leading them into delinquency to get the money to play the games. Such criticisms are very reminiscent of the worries that have greeted each new type of entertainment which was particularly attractive to youth and/or the lower classes.

More seriously, the battle lines are already being drawn between the cultural optimists and pessimists. There are those who see no reason to expect anything from technological developments than an acceleration of trends they already deplore. As an example we may take the following observation from Joe Weizenbaum, Professor of Computer Science at MIT, in an exchange with Daniel Bell:

We may recall the euphoric dreams articulated by then Secretary of Commerce, Herbert Hoover at the dawn of the commercial radio broadcasting and again by others when mass TV broadcasting was about to become a reality. It was foreseen that these media would exert an enormously beneficial influence on the shaping of American culture . . . . The technological dream was more than realised.

---

* Centre for Mass Communication Research, University of Leicester.

. . . But the cultural dream was cruelly mocked in its realisation. This magnificent technology, more than Wagnerian in its proportions. . . . What does it deliver to the masses? An occasional gem buried in immense avalanches of the ordure of everything that is most banal and insipid or pathological in our civilisation (Weizenbaum, 1980: 553–554).

Weizenbaum goes on to illustrate his argument by taking the home computer as another example of a product for which there is no demand until it exists and computer games as a trivialized, sensationalized version of the great ideal showing how intellectual potential can be transformed into a toy to kill, maim and destroy.[2]

On the other side Daniel Bell (1976, 1980), though he has his moments of general pessimism when considering topics like religion, speaks for the optimists who see the new technology as bringing about a quantum shift in the organization of society, a shift which will increase the scope for individual choice and rational decision. Bell is fond of drawing an analogy between the new computer technology with its communication adjuncts and the Alexandrian Library. This treasure house of knowledge in the ancient world contained all human knowledge as it was then available. The library made it freely available for the general benefit of mankind at that time. Computer science, cable technology and data banks are about to realize this dream on a much grander scale.

As always, it is important to set such technological changes in their social context. In this case the aim is supported by the fact that communication changes have vast implications for the organization of work, the economy, the rôles which people are able to play in society, their relationship to that society and to the polity. The corollary of this is that it is important to look not just at the technology but also at the political economy in which it is being developed, to consider what type of organizations and corporations are associated with the present range of media provision and which with the new technologies that are likely to be introduced, what interests they are likely to pursue, consciously and unconsciously, and the type of social and political structures that they are likely to both promote and reflect. These structural changes are bound to have a profound effect on the organization and content of forms of intellectual work.

The thesis I wish to advance is that what we are seeing and what we face is a continuation of the shift away from involving people in society as political citizens of nation states towards involving them as consumption units in a corporate world. The consequence of this for the culture is a continuation of the erosion of what Habermas called the public sphere or C. Wright Mills the community of publics. The hallmark of both these types of polity were contests between politically expressed demands based on knowledge, information and association in democratic, nation states—a type of society which Habermas sees as typical of the bourgeois moment of capitalism. Instead a mass society develops founded on an acceptable level of comfort, pleasure and control in which people participate as members of the market.

The consequence of relying on the market, as Nora and Minc (1978) argue, is to set very real limits on what people can hope to achieve. The market provides not for participation but for consumption. In other words, there is a sleight of hand in the arguments of Daniel Bell and others who look forward to an explosion of information and communication such as will create an information-based society with a more rational form of culture than we now enjoy. The sleight of hand lies in the assumption that new technologies will increase general access to information and open up new possibilities of two-way communication.

The first problem is one of access; the second, what we mean by information and communication. Access is not just a matter of physical means. It also involves having the rights and resources to make use of them. The analogy of a library is appealing because it suggests an open store of knowledge simply waiting for us to bumble around in. Moreover, the public library system is another of those services, like public education, established in the nineteenth and twentieth centuries, in recognition of a general right to knowledge. However poorly the ideal has been realized in practice, the library system has been inspired by the aim of an informed citizenry.

The weakness of the analogy between the old and the new becomes apparent however as soon as we consider the aims of the new controllers of information. What is in prospect, as Herbert Schiller (1981) has pointed out, is the privatization of information. The new information producers are commercial corporations who have a primary interest in keeping information secret to protect their commercial secrets. Their secondary interest is to produce a commodity for sale in the market. In the pursuit of this end, the American information industry is already putting pressure on the sources of public information, of which the main one is the government, to commercialize its operations. Information which was once available to the public as of right will, in future, be available at a price. As Schiller argues, there is likely to be a knock-on effect. Information for which there is not a market will not be produced. In Britain there is a neat illustration of the coincidence between political convenience and market forces in the gradual disappearance of the poverty statistics.[3]

There are other problems with the library analogy. Even libraries have catalogues—catalogues designed to make it easy to answer some questions and so inevitably more difficult to answer others. Who will be writing the catalogues? Who will be setting the questions and the range of possible answers? Indeed, who will have accumulated the stock of knowledge? Not, I submit, the myriad of individual subscribers at their computer terminals and yet, another characteristic of the technological Utopia will be a further domestication of living functions and privatization of social life.

Privatization in this sense is one of the key processes associated with the Frankfurt School's analysis of the media and their effect on social relationships, not through the messages they carry but the type of interaction they encourage. By concentrating activities within the home, the broadcast media of radio and television set up a type of human group which has no other connection with each other than their common use of the same service. The strong version of the Frankfurt school argument is that this opens up the possibility of manipulation, an argument which has been severely questioned by 'effects' research. A weak version of the argument is that this process of privatization deprives people of the possibility of answering back because it deprives them of the opportunities for association in which common needs might be recognized and demands formulated. Instead, to take a flippant but tragic example of someone who is, as they say, at the sharp end of this process, the modern housewife 'goes rushing for the shelter of a mother's little helper', in the words of the old Rolling Stones' lyric and seeks an individual solution to her problems. The example is not so flippant when you consider that the housewife is the supposed epitome of the isolated individual able to exercise free choice in the cornucopia of the consumer society.

The second problem of Bell's vision of a rational, information-rich society is that much of what we now take as information and as an informative process of communication based on a rational model are anything but, having a high level of symbolic, mythical content and passive, entertainment value. The importance attached to the concept of information owes much to the resilience of the ideal of society as a rational, democratic polity and to the success of intellectuals in promoting the equation information plus rational choice equals social progress. It is an equation which has been much disputed by conservative intellectuals. 'Hayek's law' for example claims that attempts at legislative reform always have opposite effects from those intended. It is only recently, however, that such arguments have begun to carry weight against the interventionist intellectuals of Gouldner's 'New Class' who had insinuated themselves into the machinery of national government as the providers and processors of the information on which the government should act. While the Labour Party and the SDP dispute their right to Tawney's name for a new interventionist, intellectual society, the intellectual initiative has passed to various right-wing societies and institutes.[4] These are able to attract private funds whereas the financial and occupational base of interventionist intellectualism in public sector research and educational institutions is being put under increasing pressure.

Nevertheless, the persistence of the Fabianesque concept of information as a necessary social resource can also be seen in discussions of the mass media. The growth of the press was based on two processes, the provision of useful information, mainly commercial and financial intelligence to interested parties, and political controversy. Print was the medium which underpinned the concept of the public sphere by providing an arena for political debate. Over time, both these functions have been transformed. From its original base in elite information, the commercial function has expanded beyond all recognition and with the transformation of news into a commodity, the political function has been eclipsed. Nevertheless, debates about the press are still carried on in terms of the argument for a free press able to supply the information and reflect the opinions necessary to foster decision-making in a democracy. The recent introduction of a new daily newspaper in Britain, the *Daily Star*, shows clearly that the mass market daily papers are a very different sort of animal. The lead features in the three tabloids on the day on which the *Daily Star* started in publication showed a quite explicit concern with irrationality, magic, extra-scientific potential and play on the sacred and profane dimensions. One featured a round-the-world-yachtswoman and a sex-change witch, the second organized an experiment among its readers to show that metal could be bent by mental power and the third discovered a vicar who painted nudes *à la* Gaugin.

A similar distinction was drawn by William Randolph Hearst, the American newspaper magnate, when he contrasted 'interesting' with 'merely important' news. 'Important news' was concerned with institutions, organizations and decision-making in society. 'Interesting' was that which appealed to individuals *qua* individuals, as individual members of the human race. This human interest aspect of news is part of the basis for a populist form of culture, one which exaggerates the commonalities between people and plays down structural divisions of interest. Those commonalities are exaggerated which revolve around consumption and the pursuit of pleasure. Consider the shift in meaning of 'us' and 'them'. As described by Richard Hoggart in *The Uses of Literacy*, 'them and us' was a common part of the working-class view of the world in the inter-war period he was describing. He defines 'them' as follows:

'Them' is a composite dramatic figure, the chief character in modern urban forms of the rural peasant-big house relationships. The world of 'them' is the world of the bosses whether those bosses are private individuals or as is increasingly the case today, public officials (Hoggart, 1958: 72).

Compare this with the idea of 'them' contained in a *Sun* editorial on the Notting Hill Carnival of 1977:

What Notting Hill has shown yet again is that violence on the streets is not a case of black against white or rich against poor. It is the yobs against the rest of us. That is true not only in Notting Hill but in Lewisham, Ladywood and in the turmoil that engulfed the Grunwick dispute. The same goes for the louts who disrupt soccer matches and smash up railway trains. It is not society which is on trial in any of these cases but the effectiveness of justice to defend the ordinary peaceful man.

Populist culture cannot magic away the evidence of social division and conflict. Instead it turns it into a question of membership or non-membership of society or even the human race. Non-members 'disrupt' entertainment and 'smash up' property. It is, as the *Sun* so elegantly puts it, a matter of 'the yobs against the rest of us'.

Information and communication are also the catch words used to describe the new type of society which will be ushered in by technological change and developments in electronics, data systems and the new distributive media. The new society, it is argued, will involve changes in the power relations within the mode of production. Those who control the information, intellectuals in one form or another, will have control of one of the means of production and so have a base for class power. The fallacy of this argument becomes apparent if we consider how much power the working class have been able to exercise through their control of another means of production, labour. The point is not who is allowed to contribute to the process of production but who extracts the surplus value from it and so has the resources to control the course of its development. Obituaries for the old class of money and capital to be found in the work of Gouldner *inter alia* seem a little premature. This leopard has changed its spots. The supra-national species has become more important, if less immediately visible, than the more familiar national species which is being extinguished.

National capital and national enterprises are increasingly vulnerable as the economic system becomes more and more internationalized. As Raymond Vernon has emphasized, this process of internationalization involves a complex and intricate network of commercial and financial ties and dependencies, a complexity which makes any attempt to identify a single class of institutions like the multi-national corporations or, more popularly, the 'gnomes of Zurich' liable to gross over-simplification. The complexity provides the old class with a new and effective camouflage in its changed form. Nevertheless, Vernon concludes that while greater economic interdependence is 'indispensable for continued economic growth . . . it seems at times to threaten some of the national goals for which the growth was intended, including national stability, egalitarianism, participation and protection' (Vernon, 1977: 193).

These national goals are ones which have been promoted, if not realized, by intellectuals. Indeed, as Schlesinger points out in his paper in this issue, the history of the intellectuals is that of a group which came to prominence through the promotion of nationalism in this century and the last. The nation state and its political system have given some intellectuals a mechanism through which to promote social policies which intervened in the operation of economic forces and attempted to alter some of their effects. The resurgence of monetarism is only a particularly topical reminder that many intellectuals have actively opposed such interventionism. As Eric Gabus of Nestlés put it in a conference defending the rôle of the multi-national corporations, 'the businessman depends on intellectuals to update the trend of public opinion'. But in so far as intellectuals had an independent hold on power to promote different goals, it was through the medium of the nation state and the attempt to use its political power. The process of technological change in the mass media provides us with a useful case to examine the implications of the shift in power away from the nation state and into the international economic system and the effects this is likely to have on culture, the rôle of the intellectuals and the future of the public sphere in which intellectuality was exercised.

To start with developments in the culture, we have already noted the growth of consumer populism, a development which Daniel Bell is quite pessimistic about for fear that shameless hedonism may overtake the Protestant ethic. One of the common interests which can be promoted on behalf of all 'the ordinary, peaceful citizens' of the *Sun* editorial, quoted above, is 'law and order'. This couplet has acquired a special significance in British culture as a way of turning consumer populism into a repressive form of culture which justifies strengthening the agents of the state, their exercise of power over the citizenry and the erosion of democratic, political control over that power.[5] Thus, in a period of general wage restraint, the police and the army have been consistently privileged, police powers are about to be further increased and the Chief Constable of Greater Manchester, James Anderton, has explicitly called for an end to 'political' scrutiny of the police. The use of 'political' in this and similar contexts has important negative overtones compared, for example, to 'democratic'. It illustrates the process of ghettoizing politics and politicians to which I shall return in discussing the effects of broadcasting on politics below. Another example of the increasing rôle of the repressive forces of the state is the use of military forces in a domestic operation, the Iranian Embassy siege.[6]

Three processes are especially noteworthy as contributions to this repressive culture.

(1) An exaggeration of crime, criminality and violence, as for example, the repeated claim that we live in a particularly violent age.

(2) The process of turning political, industrial and social dissent into a form of criminal activity and identifying such action with violence.

(3) The resurgence of that long-established form of ideological management, the Cold War, or its more recent variant, the War against Terrorism, so that dissent becomes identified with an alien threat to the nation, the Western World or our way of life.[7]

This last process is a timely reminder that these cultural developments are to a large extent international. In most parts of the world repression has gone far beyond the culture. The interests of the international economic order are such that the residual rôle assigned to national governments is to be the keeper of national order. To quote Vernon again, 'Foreign investors have demonstrated an unsurprising preference for a stable and friendly economic environment. In a number of developing countries that preference has meant that multinational enterprises have expanded their activities sharply immediately after a Rightist government has taken power or have reduced their activities immediately after a Leftist regime has taken control' (Vernon, 1977: 144).

These twin features of the contemporary culture—consumptive hedonism and anti-political repression—have a special significance given the implications which the new technology has for structural unemployment and the international reorganization of work and production.[8] People deprived of their only means of being involved in the capitalist system by right—that is by selling their labour power—will have to be involved from the other end by a right to consume. In the eyes of some protagonists of the new international system, this right is already established as the new basis for legitimating the distribution of power. Thus Gabus claims 'in a democratically, decentralised society the Multinational Company . . . can retain its economic power only through the goodwill of consumers who by the daily selection of the products they purchase, judge the usefulness of the Multinational Company and put a value on the services it supplies. The survival of this goodwill depends entirely on profitable dealings with a clientele whose needs the Multinational Company appreciates across national boundaries' (Gabus, 1977: 133). But if the right is established, capitalism is a long way from providing everyone with the means to exercise their rights. As we can see from the current international depression the $64,000 question with which the capitalist system seems unable to cope is how to ensure that supply reaches demand.

The preference, demonstrated by the current monetarist and deflationary policies adopted by most governments, is for a strategy which reduces supply to meet effective demand. Thereby large sections of the national and international population are effectively disenfranchised by their exclusion from the market. This brings the repressive aspect of the culture into play to restrict the scope for dissent of those unable to participate in the consumer society and to support repressive action by state forces against them.

The signs are that the market will be the main mechanism for allowing access to the new media services, either directly through the purchase of discs, tapes or subscription services, such as even the BBC is planning for its satellite transmissions, or indirectly through the sale of international advertising space. Direct sale will disadvantage a growing proportion of the population given that unemployment will prevent them from acquiring adequate means. Indirect sale gives another twist to the international spiral by putting yet more emphasis on cross-border consumerism.

The results of relying on these forms of the market are already apparent in the press where the only viable form of journalism is that founded on definable markets as in the leisure interest magazine field. In the case of the British provincial press monopoly control over a sectionalized market is an added bonus. By contrast the political journal and political content is being squeezed out and with it one locus for the operations of critical intellectuals, one forum through which they have contributed to the formulation of policy within the nation state. In so far as politics is not a consumable product, there is no advertising revenue on which political journalism can rely for the support of its services.

These developments in the press are suggestive of the type of content which is likely to survive in new forms of distributive media dependent on sale of item or sale of audience. The BBC's initial catalogue of video cassettes, for example, covers cooking, gardening and other leisure interests, already familiar topics in the magazine field. Plans to include drama and entertainment packages are held up by negotiations on the rights of performers and producers, but such material is expected to predominate once agreements have been reached. The possibility of political or current affairs cassettes has not been mooted.

Broadcasting in its traditional forms has already had a considerable impact on the political culture. The system of control under which it has operated has left little room for political partisanship. Instead the media of radio and television have given considerable support to generalized notions of public and community. Since its inception broadcasting has treated politics with considerable circumspection. Partisan politics was at first excluded completely and then confined to limited ghettoes and subject to stringent rules of balance. Election broadcasts and party politicals are both special cases in the general run of output. Such programmes are heavily signposted and the editorial control of the broadcasters is relinquished or disputed. In the place of partisan politics, general broadcasting has been particularly influential in developing a general notion of public and community as a way of meeting the requirements of balance and objectivity. Formulae were devised for the discussion of public affairs in, for example, BBC Radio's *Any Questions?* which gave pride of place to prominent citizens who were 'non-political'. One of their main qualifications for taking part was independence of party. In a sense broadcasting was only developing a standard practice of British administration to use those who have achieved prominence in one field to superintend developments in another by appointing them to various boards, committees and commissions. Recent work on the history of broadcasting has shown how the BBC was colonized by intellectuals of the professional middle class.[9] They were attracted by the opportunity to discuss public affairs in talks and feature programmes in terms of a general notion of the public interest. It was this same public interest to which intellectuals appealed to support their interventions in policy making and social engineering. The concept of the public good allowed intellectuals to step outside a straightforward technical rationality of judging the efficacy of means to take on questions of ends as well. Public service broadcasting enshrines such an idea in its very title.

Even such generalized notions are likely to be set aside as the new media limit the scope for political discourse even further. The pressure will be felt in two ways. First, the new distributive forms will simply leave out political discussion and criticism. Actuality programming, topical and with limited appeal, is the type of content most at risk. Second, the development of new distributive systems puts public service broadcasting under severe threat.

At least two conditions were necessary to enable public service broadcasting to develop. The first was the framework of government regulation which required a non-partisan approach. Successive governments have had continued misgivings about the progressivism of the community approach when it raised embarassing questions about current policies. The second was the national basis of distribution so that community was co-terminous with the citizenry of the nation state. To make the connections quite explicit, public service broadcasting can be said to have been a political medium of both the intellectuals and the nation state.

The current threat to public service broadcasting provide us with a very clear illustration of how weak is the intellectuals' hold over power and influence. Public service broadcasting has pursued a number of characteristically intellectual goals such as the preservation of the national culture by promoting broadcast versions of national classics and maintaining domestic production, the guardianship of cultural values by sponsoring non-commercial culture and programming for cultural values, and promoting national debate on public issues through a service of news, current affairs and documentaries. This last goal was pursued against consistent political suspicion and opposition, as Grace Wyndham Goldie (1977) makes clear in her account of the development of political television. As a result the debate has taken on the form outlined above.

Much media sociology has been particularly critical of the form as embodied in television news and emphasized the limited contribution that has made to awareness.[10] But on the other hand factual television in its various forms has been influential in putting issues on the public agenda. It has attracted accusations of left-wing bias and more generally that broadcasting has usurped the role of parliament. The documentary has been an effective way of raising questions about the public good and the documentary and current affairs departments of broadcasting have been successful in recruiting the type of educated elite which has traditionally gone into other intellectual and professional positions. News, as well as longer forms of presentation, has shown people suffering through no fault of their own by, for example, war and other disasters, natural and man-made. More important, there is the implicit or explicit suggestion that someone, national governments or international agencies, should do something about it. Disaster reports, for example, are routinely followed by enquiries into cause, prevention and what is and can be done to provide effective relief.

There is a sense in which such information necessarily has interventionist implications. This is what has led to a critique of the media from the Right. Coverage puts pressure on the authorities to act and it may be pressure to act in directions different from those they wish to take. Suffering stories in particular may make it more difficult for the authorities to maintain the support for the policies which produce the suffering such as going to war, pursuing a deflationary economic strategy or not preparing or providing for natural disasters.

So far this system has kept running on an uneasy combination of control and concession. Control by government ownership and economic influence on the broadcasting authorities to contain the liberal perspective in the public sphere of broadcasting and the acceptance by democratic governments of a responsibility to try to mitigate and contain the effects of various disasters for the comfort and well-being of their subjects. It is hard not to draw the conclusion that both the liberal aspect of the media and the ability and willingness of governments to accept such responsibilities are under threat in the developing crisis.

Of these two the public sphere in the media is clearly the most vulnerable. To a large extent the intellectual space there rests on notions of public service and journalistic responsibility. Public service is no longer financially viable. Broadcasting has exhausted non-advertising revenue as the licence fee becomes an increasingly unacceptable poll tax. Even without advertising revenue, public service broadcasting has had to compete with commercial systems and become less able to pursue different goals and to preserve its own distinct identity. The process is illustrated by the co-production movement or, more recently, by the BBC's agreement with the Rockefeller Centre Inc. to become a cable service supplier in the USA. Overseas the BBC is becoming another commercial media producer and distributor. In the United Kingdom, it is fighting a rear-guard action against moves to cable the country for entertainment, moves which appear to be unstoppable as they are led by the prospect of profit rather than public demand. In the press responsible journalism depends on the willingness of owners to pursue non-commercial goals. Conglomeration has made this less likely. Owners and managers are unable to allow the commercial slack in which journalistic space can develop.

Apart from finance, a second problem is the lack of regulatory will to continue to put national communication policy into regulatory form. The coalition of paternalist interests, to use Graham Murdock's phrase, that set up public service broadcasting—intellectual and cultural elites, politicians anxious to lay down rules of debate and new professionals skilled in the techniques of the new media—has been put on the defensive. While it can rally support against the government on an issue like the BBC external services, it is powerless against commercial interests campaigning in terms of variety and independence. Hence, in the United Kingdom cable franchises have been given to companies with no requirements for access or public service programming and in the United States such commitments are being written out of the Federal Communication Act.

Even given the political will however, a third problem is that national power is no longer adequate to regulate supra-national bodies. This problem is raised most dramatically by satellites but already pirate radio and the difficulties the Dutch and Italians have experienced in keeping control of land-based transmissions and cable systems show the dimensions of the problem. An exhibition of the new technology, organized by Philips, the Dutch electrical company, cites as a virtue of the new system of satellite communication that 'there is no need for the countries covered to give their permission'. A special problem for the democracies will be the difficulty of enforcing any rules of political debate. In so far as it survives it will depend on the ability of the wealthy to buy time, a prospect which clearly underlines the way in which the course of history favours an old, familiar class and not some aspiring newcomer, however well-intentioned.

In other fields it is possible to show separately how the nation state is under threat from internationalization and the intellectual hopelessly insecure in the face of the intelligentsia. The inability to control capital flows provides an illustration of the first and the demand for 'relevance' in education one of the second. Dealing with the media and cultural processes has the advantage, however, of demonstrating how these processes are intertwined. In this paper I have tried to do no more than outline a scenario but the argument should be sufficient to suggest that in this field of the media, which Hall (1977) has identified as the current site of the class struggle, the conflict is likely to be resolved by material rather than ideological processes.

Notes

1. I am indebted to my colleagues at the Centre for Mass Communication Research, Leicester University for discussions on the topics raised in this paper and to Philip Schlesinger, whose paper in this issue provided the final impetus to put pessimism to paper.
2. *The Daily Mirror* (10 April 1982) reported that British Telecom had designed a game of sink the Argentine navy for its Prestel service after the British task force had sailed for the Falkland Isles. Following protests this game was withdrawn.
3. Thus, for example, figures on the take-up rate of means-tested benefits are no longer available and the number below the 'poverty line' is now calculated biennially instead of annually.
4. On the dispute over Tawney's inheritance see Raphael Samuel's Socialist Society pamphlet, published by *The Guardian* (29 March and 5 April 1982). Examples of bodies which have begun to make more of the ideological running are the Institute for the Study of Conflict, the Institute for Economic Affairs, which now includes within it a Unit for Social Affairs, the Freedom Association, the Adam Smith Institute and the Centre for Policy Studies.
5. The work of Stuart Hall has been particularly influential in drawing attention to this process. See, for example, his Cobden Lecture, published in *The Guardian* (5 January 1980) and Hall *et al.* (1978). Other studies include Chibnall (1977) and Taylor (1981).

6. On the siege, see Philip Schlesinger (1980/81).
7. Chomsky and Herman (1979) make some pertinent observations on both these phenomena.
8. On unemployment see Jordan (1982) and Showler and Sinfield (1981).
9. In addition to Brigg's official history of the BBC there is the growing body of work by Scannell (1980) and Cardiff (1980).
10. For a general review see Golding and Elliott (1979). The most publicized critique is that of the Glasgow University Media Group (1976, 1980).

Bibliography

BELL, D. (1976). *The Cultural Contradictions of Capitalism*, London, Heinemann

BELL, D. (1980). The social framework of the information society, in Forrester, T. (ed.), *The Microelectronics Revolution*, Oxford, Blackwell

CARDIFF, D. (1980). The serious and the popular, *Media, Culture and Society*, vol. 2, no. 1

CHIBNALL, S. (1977). *Law-and-Order News*, London, Tavistock

CHOMSKY, N. and HERMAN, E. S. (1979). *The Political Economy of Human Rights*, 2 vol., Nottingham, Spokesman Books

GABUS, E. (1977). The external relations of multinational companies, in Curzon, G. and V., (eds), *The Multinational Enterprise in a Hostile World*, London, Macmillan

GLASGOW UNIVERSITY MEDIA GROUP (1976). *Bad News*, London, Routledge and Kegan Paul

GLASGOW UNIVERSITY MEDIA GROUP (1980). *More Bad News*, London, Routledge and Kegan Paul

GOLDIE, G. W. (1977) *Facing the Nation: Television and Politics, 1936–1976*, London, Bodley Head

GOLDING, P. and ELLIOTT, P. (1979). *Making the News*, London, Longman

GOULDNER, A. (1979). *The Future of the Intellectuals and the Rise of the New Class*, London, Macmillan

HALL, S. (1977). Culture, the media and the 'ideological effect', in Curran, J. *et al.*, (eds), *Mass Communication and Society*, London, Arnold

HALL, S. (1978). *Policing the Crisis*, London, Macmillan

HOGGART, R. (1958). *The Uses of Literacy*, Harmondsworth, Penguin

JORDAN, B. (1982). *Mass Unemployment and the Future of Britain*, Oxford, Blackwell

NORA, S. and MINC, A. (1978). *L'Informatisation de la Société*, Paris, La Documentation Française

SCANNELL, P. (1980). Broadcasting and the politics of unemployment, 1930–1935, *Media, Culture and Society*, vol. 2, no. 1

SCHILLER, H. (1981). *Who Knows: Information in the Age of the Fortune 500*. Norwood, NJ, Ablex

SCHLESINGER, P. (1980/81). Princes' Gate, 1980: the media politics of siege management, *Screen Education*, no. 37

SHOWLER, B. and SINFIELD, A. (eds) (1981). *The Workless State*, London, Martin Robertson

TAYLOR, I. (1981). *Law and Order*, London, Macmillan

VERNON, R. (1977). *Storm over the Multinationals*, London, Macmillan

WEIZENBAUM, J. (1980). Once more, the computer revolution, in Forrester, T. (ed.), *The Microelectronics Revolution*, Oxford, Blackwell

Pierre Bourdieu and the sociology of culture: an introduction

NICHOLAS GARNHAM* AND RAYMOND WILLIAMS†

The influence of Pierre Bourdieu upon Anglo-Saxon thought and research has been to date extremely fragmentary, restricted to the discipline of anthropology and to the sub-discipline of the sociology of education. These influences are marked by the publication in English of *Outlines of a Theory of Practice* and *Reproduction*, respectively.

Other aspects however of what has been recently described as 'a theoretical system that may be the most elegant and comprehensive since Talcott Parson's' (DiMaggio, 1979) have been largely ignored. This is especially true of the work in the history and sociology of culture carried out by Bourdieu and his colleagues at the Centre de Sociologie Européenne in Paris and published in that Centre's journal *Actes de la Recherche en Science Sociale*. Neglect of this aspect of Bourdieu's work is not only damaging in its own right within cultural studies, but this fragmentary and partial absorption of what is a rich and unified body of theory and related empirical work across a range of fields from the ethnography of Algeria to art, science, religion, language, political science and education to the epistemology and methodology of the social sciences in general can lead to a danger of seriously misreading the theory. A notable example of this danger can be found in the recent attempt by Halsey and his colleagues to refute Bourdieu's theory of cultural capital (Halsey, 1979).

Thus this introductory article takes the opportunity offered by the recent appearance in France of *La Distinction*, a book that sums up work, spanning over a decade and a half, in the sociology of French culture, to present a necessarily sketchy outline of the structure of Bourdieu's thought. Such an outline is intended both to serve as a contextualizing background to the readings from Bourdieu's theoretical and empirical work that follow, reading whose necessarily restricted scope could lead to just those misreadings and misunderstandings to which we have pointed, and to indicate what in particular Bourdieu's work has to offer us at this moment in what he would call the field of British media and cultural studies, for as his own theory would predict the entry of this particular symbolic production into a different field from that in which it was produced will necessarily give it a specifically different function.

The development of British media and cultural studies over the last decade or so has been characterized by two successive stages of development, stages that Bourdieu's own theory helps us to explain. The first saw the rise out of literary studies of a culturalist Marxism in opposition to both the subjectivism of Leavisite literary criticism and to that empirical, ahistorical sociology of mass-communication and popular culture whose intellectual and ideological roots lay in American sociology. The early work of the Birmingham Centre for Contemporary Cultural Studies marks that development. The second stage saw the development (and here the work of Screen is exemplary) under the influence first of Althusser and then of Lacan of a theoreticist

* School of Communication, Polytechnic of Central London.
† Jesus College, Cambridge.

Marxism which directed consideration of the problem of ideology away from economic and class determinants, seen as vulgarly economistic or sociologistic, and towards the 'text' as the privileged site for a relatively autonomous signifying practice and for the deciphering by means of symptomatic readings of the ideological effectivity of those practices. In the last couple of years this Althusserian current has been challenged by those reasserting from within an older Marxist tradition the value of empirical work in both sociology and history as against theoreticism and the need to restress the social efficacy and explanatory power of economic and class determinants.[1]

The potential value of Bourdieu's work at this specific moment within British media and cultural studies is that, in a movement of critique in the classic Marxist sense, he confronts and dialectically supersedes these partial and opposed positions. Thus he develops a theory of ideology (or rather of symbolic power since in general he reserves the term ideology for more explicit and coherent bodies of thought) based upon both concrete historical research and upon the use of the classical techniques of empirical sociology such as the statistical analysis of survey data. At the same time he develops his critique of theoreticism, in particular structuralist Marxism and its associated formalist tendencies, by specifying with accompanying empirical evidence the historical roots and economic and class determinants of the relative autonomy of intellectual practice, a relative autonomy that is in its turn the condition for the efficacy of intellectual practice as, in general, the practice of ideological domination.

'Ideologies owe their structure and their most specific functions to the social conditions of their production and circulation i.e. to the functions they fulfil, first for the specialists competing for the monopoly of the competences in question (religious, artistic, etc.) and secondarily and incidentally for the non-specialists. When we insist that ideologies are always *doubly determined*, that they owe their most specific characteristics not only to the interests of the classes and class fractions which they express (the sociodicy function) but also to the specific interests of those who produce them and to the specific logic of the field of production (usually transfigured into the ideology of 'creation' and the 'creator'), we obtain the means of escaping crude reduction of ideological products to the interests of the classes they serve (a short-circuit effect common in 'Marxist' critiques), without falling into the idealist illusion of treating ideological productions as self-sufficient and self-generating totalities amenable to pure, purely internal analysis (semiology)' (Bourdieu, 1977c*).

The work of which *La Distinction* is a summation is thus a frontal assault upon all essentialist theories of cultural appropriation (taste) and cultural production (creativity), upon all notions of absolute, universal cultural values and especially upon the intelligentsia and the ideologies of intellectual and cultural autonomy from economic and political determinants which that intelligentsia has constructed in defence of its material and symbolic interests as 'the dominated fraction of the dominant class'.

It can be argued that the central, indeed defining, problem of historical materialism is that of reproduction. This is a problem at both a material and symbolic level. That is to say it involves explaining not only how in social formations characterized by spatial extension and division of labour the actions of human agents are co-ordinated so as to ensure the inter-generational reproduction of the material conditions of existence (the problem of the mode of production) but also how the set of unequal class relations produced by that co-ordination is itself legitimized such that repro-

---

[1] See for instance Williams, 1977, Thompson, 1978, Golding and Murdoch, and Johnson in Barret *et al.* eds. 1979, Garnham, 1979.

* All references to Bourdieu are consolidated in a bibliography on pp. 295–296.

duction takes place relatively free from social conflict (the problem of the mode of domination). This of course also implies its converse, namely the problem of specifying the conditions under which reproduction does not take place leading to the more or less rapid transformation of the social formation (the problem of crisis and revolution).

It is to this general problem that Bourdieu's Theory of Practice is addressed. While Bourdieu has concentrated his attention upon the mode of domination, upon what he calls the exercise of Symbolic Power, his theory is cast in resolutely materialist terms and it is not just the terms borrowed from economics such as capital, profit, market and investment, which he uses to describe and analyse cultural practice, that links his theory to a properly economic analysis in the narrow sense of that term, that is to say to the analysis of the mode of production of material life, which for Bourdieu is always ultimately and not so ultimately determinate.

The second important link between Bourdieu's work and the central tradition of historical materialism is that it is caste in the form a 'critique' in the classical sense practiced by Marx himself. That is to say one must not make the mistake of appropriating Bourdieu's theoretical and empirical analysis of symbolic power to some marginal sub-discipline such as cultural studies or the sociology of culture and knowledge. This analysis lies at the very heart of his wider general theory, just as theories of fetishization and ideology do in Marx's work, because it provides the very conditions of its own potential scientificity. Bourdieu sees sociology as by definition the science of the social conditions determining human practices and thus the sociology of symbolic power is the science of the social conditions determining intellectual practice, conditions that are always concretely and specifically historical and the exposure of which are, in the movement of critique, the conditions for achieving an always partial because always socially conditioned escape from ideology into scientific practice and in that movement revealing the historically defined limits of available truth. This is further always a political act because it is the misrecognition of these conditions and limits that is the condition for the exercise of symbolic power to reinforce the tendency to reproduce the existing structure of class relations.[2]

The theory of knowledge is a dimension of political theory because the specifically symbolic power to improve the principles of the construction of reality—in particular, social reality—in a major dimension of political power (Bourdieu 1977a, p. 166).

Bourdieu describes clearly in the preface to his most recent book (Bourdieu, 1980b) how his own thought has grown out of and in reaction to those successively dominant influences in French thought Sartre and Levi-Strauss. (In particular he conducts a continual, ambiguous dance of intellectual repulsion and attraction with Sartre. Hence his choice of Flaubert as an exemplary case in his study of French cultural production.)

It is by no means easy to recall the social effects produced in the French intellectual field by the work of Claude Levi-Strauss and the concrete mediations through which a new conception of intellectual activity imposed itself upon a whole generation, a conception which was opposed in an entirely dialectical fashion to that figure of the 'total' intellectual, decisively turned towards the political, of which Jean Paul Sartre was the incarnation. This exemplary confrontation undoubtedly contributed not a little to encouraging in many of those who were at that time turning to the social sciences, an ambition to reconcile theoretical and practical aims, scientific and ethical or political vocations, which are so often split, to fulfil their task as researchers, a sort of militant craft, as far from pure science as it is from the prophetic, in a humbler and more responsible way (pp. 7–8).

[2] See Bourdieu, 1975a, 1979d.

Within Bourdieu's theoretical discourse the terms Subjectivism and Objectivism point to these two poles of post-war French intellectual life. His work in sociology has developed as a specific critique of these two schools of thought which he sees as two successive dialectical moments in the development of a truly scientific theory of practice which in its turn is the condition for an escape from the unconscious cycle of reproduction. Subjectivism, or as he calls it 'the phenomenal form of knowledge', by which he refers to such tendencies as social psychology, ethnomethodology as well as existentialism and phenomenology, focuses upon the individual actor and upon the experiential reality of social action. It is, according to Bourdieu, a characteristic tendency of sociology which studies its own society and within which therefore the observer is himself or herself also a participant. Objectivism on the other hand, by which in particular Bourdieu refers to all types of structuralism and functionalism, but especially to Levi-Strauss and Althusser, goes beyond the immediate experience of the individual actor to identify the 'social facts', the observable regularities of social action, but in so doing has a tendency to fetishize the structures, making the agents mere performers of preordained scores or bearers of the structure. This Bourdieu sees as a tendency to which anthropologists are especially prone as observers of societies of which they are not a part. While Subjectivism cannot recognize the social determinants of human action, the Objectivists have a tendency to succumb to that blindness to which intellectuals are particularly prone, indeed it is the ideology specific to wielders of symbolic power, namely the failure to recognize in the idealization of the structure and its logic an expression of their failure to recognize the social conditions of their own practice by failing to recognize the socially and historically specific conditions determining all human practice.

Inextricably intertwined in Bourdieu's work are the discourses of sociology and history. That is to say in developing his Theory of Practice or 'science of the economy of human practices', he sets himself the task of overcoming the opposition between Subjectivism and Objectivism by explaining the relationship between on the one hand the observed regularities of social action, the structure, and on the other the experiential reality of free, purposeful, reasoning human actors. However, in addition, his theory requires that any solution to this sociological problem must at the same time provide a properly historical explanation by specifying the social conditions under which the structure will be reproduced or conversely will be more or less rapidly transformed. Nor are these seen as two separate problems for one of Bourdieu's main criticisms of traditional sociology, whether Subjectivist or Objectivist, is what he calls its 'Genesis Amnesia',[3] for as with Keynes in economics Bourdieu is concerned to stress that any satisfactory explanation of human action must take full account of the fact that all human action, unlike its reconstruction in science, takes place irreversibly in time.[4] Thus for Bourdieu all human actors are involved in strategies in situations of which the outcome is uncertain because these strategies are opposed by the strategies of other actors. The problem therefore is to specify the mechanism by which unbeknownst in principle to the actors (for if they knew they would alter their strategy to take account of this knowledge) these strategies of improvization are objectively co-ordinated.[5]

The regulating mechanism Bourdieu proposes is the habitus.[6] This he describes as 'the strategy-generating principle enabling agents to cope with unforeseen and ever-

---

[3] See Bourdieu, 1977a, p. 79.
[4] See Bourdieu, 1977a, pp. 5-6.
[5] See Bourdieu, 1977a, ch. 1 pp. 1-30.
[6] See Bourdieu, 1977a, ch. 2, pp. 72-95.

changing situations . . . a system of lasting, transposable dispositions which, integrating past experiences, functions at every moment as a matrix of perceptions, appreciations and actions and makes possible the achievement of infinitely diversified tasks, thanks to the analogical transfer of schemes permitting the solution of similarly shaped problems'. The habitus is not just a random series of dispositions but operates according to a relatively coherent logic, what Bourdieu calls the logic of practice.

This logic is shaped primarily in early childhood within the family by the internalization of a given set of determinate objective conditions both directly material and material as mediated through the habitus and thus the practices of surrounding adults especially the parents. While later experience will alter the structure of the habitus's logic of practice, these alterations from school or work will be appropriated according to the structural logic of the existing habitus.[7]

This logic of practice since it must be operated unconsciously and since it cannot be explicitly inculcated must be both an impoverished logic in the sense of working with simple categorical distinctions and also flexible so that it can be applied as the structuring principle of practice across a wide range of situations. Thus the logic of practice operates with such simple dichotomous distinctions as high/low, inside/outside, near/far, male/female, good/bad, black/white, rare/common, distinguished/vulgar, etc., principles of categorization that develop in the immediate environment of the young child but can be subsequently applied across a wide range of fields and situations as unconscious regulating principles.[8]

Moreover the habitus is a unified phenomenon. It produces an ethos that relates all the practices produced by a habitus to a unifying set of principles. The habitus is also by definition not an individual phenomenon. That is to say it is internalized and operationalized by individuals but not to regulate solitary acts but precisely interaction. Thus the habitus is a family, group and especially class phenomenon, a logic derived from a common set of material conditions of existence to regulate the practice of a set of individuals in common response to those conditions. Indeed Bourdieu's definition of class is based on the habitus.[9]

Thus individual practice as regulated by the logic of practice is always a structural variant of group and especially class practice. However since the habitus regulates practice according to what Bourdieu calls a probabilistic logic, that is to say practice in a given present situation is conditioned by expectation of the outcome of a given course of action which in its turn is based, through the habitus, on the experience of past outcomes, while class origin is overdetermining of the structure of the habitus, practice is also determined by trajectory. Broadly by this Bourdieu refers to upward or downward social mobility of either the family, the class fraction or the class in a hierarchy of determinations from class to family. Crudely upward mobility will give an optimistic view of possible outcomes and downward mobility a pessimistic view each of which will determine a different set of practical orientations towards the various fields of social struggle. Bourdieu's classic example of the effect of expectations on practice is that of working-class attitudes to involvement in formal education. The point about these expectations is that like other aspects of the logic of practice they reflect not

---

[7] See Bourdieu, 1977a, pp. 77–8. The primacy and relative inertia of early-childhood influence on the habitus leads to what Bourdieu calls the hysteresis effect and explains his concern with inter-generational as well as inter-class differences and struggles (see The Production of Belief in this issue). In particular he uses it to explain the conservative and nostalgic tendencies in much progressive politics as well as its reactionary alternatives.

[8] See Bourdieu, 1977a, ch. 3, pp. 96–158.

[9] See Bourdieu, 1977a, pp. 81–7.

just random individual reactions to the social environment but on the contrary they are realistic assessments in terms of the habitus of the objective probabilities offered by a given state of the social field to an actor in a given class position.[10]

So when Bourdieu turns to the specific field of cultural consumption, or rather appropriation, the regularities his survey data reveals in taste patterns across a wide range of fields from food, clothing, interior decor and make-up to sport and popular and high art are markers or indices of the habitus of classes and class fractions and what Bourdieu is concerned to reveal is not a particular pattern of consumption or appropriation, since in a different state of the field other markers could be used for the same relational positions, but the logic which explains this particular relationship between a range of cultural goods and practices and a range of class habitus. Bourdieu's analysis of the concrete specificities of contemporary French cultural practice are thus part of his wider theory of symbolic power, its empirical validation and refinement and at the same time a political intervention in symbolic class struggle.

'Art is the site par excellence of the denial of the social world. But the same unconscious intention of denial is the underlying principle of a number of discourses whose overt purpose is to talk of the social world and which as a consequence can be written and read with a double meaning. (How many philosophers, sociologists, philologists came to philosophy, sociology or philology as places which because they are not properly fitted into social space allow one to escape definition? All those in effect utopians who do not wish to know where they are, are not the best placed to know about the social space in which they are placed. Would we have otherwise so many readings and 'lectores', materialists without material, thoughts without instruments of thought, thus without an object, and so few observations and as a consequence 'auctores'). We cannot advance and expand the science of the social world unless we force a turn of the tide by neutralizing this neutralization and by denying denial in all its forms of which the denial of reality inherent in the exaggerated radicalism of certain revolutionary discourses is by no means the least significant. Against a discourse that is neither true nor false, neither verifiable nor falsifiable, neither theoretical nor empirical which like Racine speaks not of cows but of lowing, cannot speak of Daz or of the singlets of the working class but only of mode of production and of proletariat or of the rôles and attitudes of the 'lower middle class', it is not enough to criticize it is necessary to show, objects and even people, to touch things with one's fingers—which does not mean pointing a finger at them—and to make people who are used to speaking what they think they think and so no longer think about what they say to make such people enter a popular bistro or a rugby ground, a golf course or a private club.' (Bourdieu, 1979d, pp. 596–597).

Bourdieu in the Durkheimian tradition sees symbolic systems, as such, as arbitrary, undetermined taxonomies, structuring structures in the sense that they do not reflect or represent a reality, but themselves structure that reality. Moreover, as in the Saussurean model of language, such systems are based upon 'difference' or 'distinction'. However he criticizes the idealism of the Durkheimian/Saussurean tradition by stressing that these systems, although arbitrary in themselves, are not arbitrary in their social function which is to represent, but in a misrecognized form, the structure of class relations and indeed it is their very arbitrariness that allows them to do this since if they were not arbitrary they could not be the object of class struggle. They represent class relations and in the same movement disguise that representation because their logic is that of 'distinction'. In English as in French the double meaning of that word, both a categorical and a social term, precisely mirrors the function of symbolic power.

Thus symbolic systems serve to reinforce class relations as internalized in the habitus since in the internalizing movement of appropriation their specific logic confirms the

10 See Bourdieu, 1974a and 1979d, ch. 2.

general logic of class determined practice. The internalization of the specific logic of symbolic systems or rather, since it is unified, the symbolic system, confirms a hierarchically organized range of distinctions such as rare/common, distinguished/vulgar, disinterested/interested, freedom from necessity/necessity, etc.

For Bourdieu all societies are characterized by a struggle between groups and/or classes and class fractions to maximize their interests in order to ensure their reproduction. The social formation is seen as a hierarchically organized series of fields within which human agents are engaged in specific struggles to maximize their control over the social resources specific to that field, the intellectual field, the educational field, the economic field etc. and within which the position of a social agent is relational, that is to say a shifting position determined by the totality of the lines of force specific to that field. The fields are hierarchically organized in a structure overdetermined by the field of class struggle over the production and distribution of material resources and each subordinate field reproduces within its own structural logic, the logic of the field of class struggle.

'the field which cannot be reduced to a single aggregate of isolated agents or to the sum of elements merely juxtaposed is, like a magnetic field, made up of a system of power lines. In other words the constituting agents or system of agents may be described as so many forces which, by their existence, opposition or combination, determine its specific structure at a given moment of time. In return each of these is defined by its particular position within this field from which it derives positional properties which cannot be assimilated to intrinsic properties' (Bourdieu, 1971c, p. 161).

Social groups and classes enter in each generation a historically given structured state of these fields and they develop and deploy their strategies of struggle on the basis of a historically given level of material, social and cultural endowment which may, in a given historical state of the field, be transformed into capital. Although the symbolic field like all fields is a field of class struggle and what is at stake is legitimizing or delegitimizing power, there is a tendency for the symbolic field to legitimize a given state of material class relations by means of the specific mechanism of misrecognition by which symbolic systems represent in a transformed, 'euphemized', 'disinterested' form the balance of forces and hierarchical structure of the field of material class relations.[11]

Bourdieu is also working with a model of historical development. He argues, based upon his anthropological field work with the Kabyle in Algeria, that in pre-industrial, so-called primitive social formations characterized by limited spatial extension, limited division of labour and simple reproduction, the material and symbolic, the mode of production and the mode of domination, cannot be separated. In such societies, with a low level of material resources, symbolic power has a direct economic function (e.g. in labour mobilization) and symbolic violence is the preferred mode for the exercise of power because overt differences in wealth could not be tolerated in such societies. Moreover, since, lacking the objectification of power in institutions such as a market or a church, and associated instruments of objectification such as writing, power relations have constantly to be reasserted in direct human interaction, the overt direct exercise of material force would be too expensive in material resources to allow for simple reproduction. Such societies exist in a state of Doxa, where the symbolic system is both common to all and taken-for-granted because existing at an implicit level as a logic of practice rather than as an explicit discourse.[12]

[11] See Bourdieu, 1977a, ch. 4, pp. 159–97 and 1979d.
[12] See Bourdieu, 1977a, pp. 171–83.

In the next stage of historical development, Bourdieu argues, economic development leads to the growth of an autonomous economic sphere related to the development of exchange relations and in the same movement breaks the thralldom of the
Doxa and creates a relatively autonomous symbolic sphere which, by making the symbolic system more explicit, creates class struggle in the symbolic sphere between
Orthodoxy and its necessary corollary Heterodoxy. At the same time there is created
both a specialized group of symbolic producers with an interest in securing a monopoly of the objectified instruments of symbolic struggle, especially written language,
an interest that pits them against the dominant economic class in a struggle over what
Bourdieu describes as 'the hierarchization of the principles of hierarchization'. At the
same time this specialized group shares a mutual interest with the dominant economic
class in maintaining the overall set of material class relations both because cultural
capital must ultimately be transformable into economic capital or material resources
and because the dominant economic class now require the services of the producers
of symbolic goods in the imposition and maintenance of orthodoxy. Because of this
mutual interest the symbolic system tends to reproduce the given state of class
relations. However once Heterodoxy has been created both political consciousness
and science become possible and class struggle and its relation to science can never
be totally exorcised from the symbolic field.

However in a transitional stage historically, Bourdieu argues, the creation of a
market economy and of competitive capitalism did lead to the more open exercise of
material class power. However this in its turn lead to more overt revolutionary and
reformist opposition such that the dominant class was forced in order to maintain its
dominance to progressively shift back to the use of symbolic power as the preferred
mode of domination.[13] It is with the specific modalities of this third contemporary
phase and with its historical roots in the nineteenth century that Bourdieu is now
principally concerned. Human agents enter the field of struggle that is the social
formation with historically given endowments, either in an incorporated state within
the habitus as dispositions and competences, or in an objectified state, as material
goods. It is these endowments that Bourdieu refers to as capital, for the purposes of
this exposition divided into economic and cultural capital. Each agent enters the
struggle with the aim of reproducing the capital of his or her group and if possible
augmenting it. To this end he or she pursues strategies of investment which involve
choosing the sub-fields and the modes of intervention in those sub-fields likely to
yield the highest profit on a given investment, one of the objects of struggle being the
relative returns to a given investment in a given field *vis-à-vis* investments in other
fields.[14] As Bourdieu puts it, he treats 'all practices, including those purporting to be
disinterested or gratuitous, and hence non-economic, as economic practices directed
towards the maximizing of material or symbolic profit' (Bourdieu, 1977a, p. 183).

This general struggle is ultimately determined by economic struggle in the field of
class relations because while there is convertibility between economic and cultural
capital in both directions (at differing rates of exchange according to a given state of
the struggle in each field and in the social field as a whole) it is the convertibility of
cultural into economic capital that ultimately defines it as capital and determines not
only the overall structure of the social field but also, in a transformed form, that of the
sub-fields, because economic capital being more easily transferable from generation
to generation is a more efficient reproductive mechanism. This is why the educational

[13] For this model of historical development see Bourdieu, 1977a, pp. 183–9.
[14] See Bourdieu, 1977a, pp. 171–97, 1975b and The Production of Belief in this issue.

system plays such an important rôle within Bourdieu's theory, because historically the development of such a system, as a system of certification, created a market in cultural capital within which certificates acted as money both in terms of a common, abstract socially guaranteed medium of exchange between cultural capitals and, crucially, between cultural capital and the labour market and thus access to economic capital.[15]

Cultural practice, as with all practices in general, involves appropriation rather than mere consumption. If one can use the analogy of food, the act of ingestion is merely the necessary condition for the process of digestion which enables the organism to extract those ingredients it requires for physical reproduction and reject the rest. In certain conditions digestion will not take place at all. Thus while it remains important that cultural stratification is in part determined directly by the unequal distribution of economic capital and thus of cultural goods (i.e., the working class cannot afford picture collections, large personal libraries, frequent visits to the theatre and opera, etc.) in terms of the legitimation function of cultural practice the ways in which these objective class distinctions are internalized within the habitus as differing dispositions, differing attitudes towards culture and differing abilities to utilize cultural objects and practices, and thus result in a different logic of cultural practice, are more important. This is why Bourdieu has been particularly concerned to analyse the class determinants of the use of and attitudes towards relatively widely available cultural practices such as museums and photography.[16]

The cultural field serves as a marker and thus a reinforcer of class relations for two reasons. First because a field occupied by objects and practices with minimal use-value, indeed in the sub-field of art with a positive rejection of use value, is a field in which *par excellence* the struggle is governed by a pure logic of difference or distinction, a pure logic of positionality. Secondly because the specifically historical creation of art as a special category of social object and social practice defined by its difference from and distance from everyday material reality and indeed its superiority to it, together with its matching ideology, namely the post-Kantian aesthetics of 'pure' form and 'disinterestedness', are an expression of and objectively actually depend upon the relative distance from economic necessity provided by the bourgeois possession of economic capital. Works of art, Bourdieu argues, require for their appropriation first an aesthetic disposition, that is to say an internalized willingness to play the game of art, to see the world from a distance, to bracket off a range of objects and practices from the immediate urgency of the struggle for social reproduction and that this disposition is the determinate expression in an incorporated form in the habitus of the material conditions of existence of the dominant class, the bourgeoisie.[17] Secondly specific competences are required, that is to say a knowledge of the codes specific to a given art form, competences that are not innate but can only be acquired either through inculcation in the setting of the family through experience of a range of artistic objects and practices and/or through formal inculcation in school. Bourdieu argues that distinct patterns of cultural consumption are associated with these different modes of acquisition of cultural competence, modes of acquisition that oppose culturally but also in a social hierarchy related to the age of the family's economic capital, the old bourgeoisie who acquire their cultural competence in the

---

[15] See Bourdieu, 1977a, pp. 183–97.

[16] See Bourdieu, 1965b, 1966, 1979d, pp. 301–21, 1968a. For the relationship between the notion of cultural competence and the ploitical rôle of opinion polls see Bourdieu 1979c and 1979d, pp. 463–42.

[17] See The Aristocracy of Culture in this issue.

family so that it appears to be second nature, a natural gift for discrimination, and those who acquire their cultural competence through school and are exposed to all the cultural scorn and insecurity directed at the autodidact, an insecurity that leads them to stick closely to the hierarchies of cultural legitimacy while the children of the old bourgeoisie can express the assurance of their natural taste in a contempt for such hierarchies and by legitimizing new forms of cultural practice such as cinema and jazz.

One of the main ways in which the convertibility of economic and cultural capital is assured is via control over that scarce resource time. This control takes two forms. First the ability to invest economically in educational time whether in the family, for instance by an educated mother not working and devoting her time to the cultural development of her children, or in school, in order to pass on or acquire cultural capital in the form of dispositions and competences. It is this relation between economic and cultural capital that is reflected in differential class access to different levels of education and to the certification that accompanies it, which in its turn legitimates the stratification of cultural practice linked to achieved level of education, for instance newspaper readership. But secondly and more originally Bourdieu argues that it has been characteristic of the development of cultural practice in the narrowly artistic sense to maximize the complexity of coding (expressed in common parlance as the level of 'difficulty') both textually and inter-textually (thus requiring a wider and wider range of cultural reference, art being increasingly about other works of art) and this development has meant that art necessarily requires for its appropriation high levels of consumption time (for instance in order to see films from the point of view of auteur theory one has to see all the films by that auteur). Since cultural consumption time is differentially available between classes and between fractions of the dominant class, this development steadily reinforces class divisions while legitimizing these divisions by labelling those excluded from the cultural discourse as stupid, philistine, etc.

But the investment of consumption time is not an absolute governed simply by its availability. Since time is always a scarce resource the decision to invest time in a given mode of cultural appropriation will depend upon the relations of force within a given field or set of fields which in their turn will determine the returns that can be expected from a given investment. Those expectations will in their turn, as in all fields of practice, be determined by the habitus. Thus for instance whether a given agent chooses to cultivate literary, musical or artistic competences in general as opposed to sporting or technical competences will depend upon the market objectively open for the investment of his capital and the relative valuation within these markets of these competences. Thus whether someone chooses to acquire and mobilize in social intercourse knowledge of the field of football or of Western European art, of train spotting or avant-garde cinema, competences between which it is crucial to restress no hierarchical valuations are being or can be made, will depend upon the cultural and economic endowments with which he or she enters the social field, the fields objectively and realistically open for investment given the position of class origin from which he or she starts and the relative weight of various fields.[18] Thus it may be possible to acquire relatively rapidly and mobilize against weak opposition a competence in film criticism whereas if one entered the field of fine art scholarship with weak cultural capital one would be doomed to marginality and failure. In this context, for example, the recent much discussed differences between Britain and some of her industrial competitors in terms of the differential social and therefore economic profit

[18] See Bourdieu, 1975a, b, 1979d.

resulting from investment by an individual and by a class in cultural rather than technical competences is very relevant.[19]

Thus the logic of the cultural field operates in such a way as to create, reproduce and legitimate (reproduce because legitimate) a set of class relations structured around two great divides, those between the dominant and dominated classes and within the dominant class between the dominant and dominated fractions. The dominant class, roughly equivalent to what the Oxford Social mobility study calls the service class (Halsey, 1979), is those possessing high amounts of economic and cultural capital and the dominated class those possessing exiguous amounts of both (Bourdieu sometimes refers to them as working-class (classe ouvrière) and sometimes as les classes populaires (i.e. including the peasantry as a distinct class). The primary distinction operated by the dominant culture and the cultural practices it legitimates (and by so doing those practices it delegitimates) is of culture as all that which is different from, distanced from the experiences and practices of the dominated class, from all that is 'common', 'vulgar', 'popular'. In response, at the deepest level of the class ethos the dominated class reject the dominant culture in a movement of pure negation. However in opposition they construct, at an implicit level, as what Bourdieu calls the aesthetic of the culture of necessity, an aesthetic that relegates form at the expense of subject and function, that refuses to judge works of art or cultural practices on their own terms but judges them according to the social and ethical values of the class ethos, that values participation and immediate semi-sensual gratification at the expense of disinterested and distanced contemplation.[20] Bourdieu clearly sees his work as part of an essentially political effort to legitimize this implicit aesthetic against all current formalisms whether of the right or left, against both what he calls the racism of class which dismisses working class taste as beyond redemption by culture and against a naive populism that tries to assimilate that taste to the norms of legitimate culture, seeing miners banners as works of art. He is particularly severe upon the left 'deconstructionists' whose theories and practices he sees as the latest and most effective of the ideologies of those monopolizers of cultural capital, the dominated fraction of the dominant class, ideologies that always serve to reinforce through misrecognition the dominance of the dominant class.[21]

Brechtian 'distanciation' can be seen as the movement of withdrawal by which the intellectual affirms, at the very heart of popular art, his distance from popular art, a distance that renders popular art intellectually acceptable, that is to say acceptable to intellectuals and, more profoundly, his distance from the people, a distance that this bracketing of the people by intellectuals presupposes (Bourdieu 1979d, p. 568).

The two fractions into which the dominant class is divided are defined in terms of the relative weight in their patrimony of economic and cultural capital. Broadly Bourdieu sees a historical development whereby the dominant class has divided into two specialized groups, the dominant one concerned with material reproduction in the sphere of production, the dominated concerned with the legitimation of material reproduction through the exercise of symbolic power. While for reasons already given the specialized producers of symbolic goods will ultimately always remain subordinate to economic capital they nonetheless are involved in a struggle with the dominant fraction over the relative legitimacy and therefore value of cultural as opposed to economic capital. Thus intellectuals in the widest sense of that term will always

[19] See Bourdieu, 1979d, pp. 68–101.
[20] See The Aristocracy of Culture in this issue.
[21] See Bourdieu, 1979d, pp. 543–64.

struggle to maximize the autonomy of the cultural field and to raise the social value of the specific competences involved in part by constantly trying to raise the scarcity of those competences. It is for this reason that while intellectuals may mobilize wider concepts of political democracy or economic equality in their struggle against economic capital they will always resist as a body moves towards cultural democracy. It is the specificities of this contradiction in particular that requires analysis in any given historical conjuncture if one is to understand the political position and rôle of intellectuals.[22]

It is precisely by stressing their 'disinterestedness' in the sense of their distance from crude material values that they maximize their interest in terms of the value at which they can ultimately convert their cultural capital into economic capital or alternatively ensure the reproduction of their cultural capital, in particular through their control of the education system and increasingly of the state bureaucracy in general. For the problem that Bourdieu is concerned with is not merely that of establishing a determinate relationship between class and cultural appropriation in a given state of the field of cultural consumption nor between cultural production and class in a given state of the field of cultural production. The problem is more difficult and complex than that for what his general theory of practice as well as his specific theory of symbolic power require him to explain is how the free, apparently autonomous practices of the agents involved in the two different fields and thus whose actions are governed by a different specific logic of practice, how they so interact as to not just produce but reproduce the class patterns of cultural practice in general and by so doing tend to reproduce the given set of class relations in general.

Bourdieu argues on the basis of detailed studies of the class origins, cultural practices and associated ideologies (i.e. critical theories) of French intellectuals in the nineteenth and twentieth centuries and of the corresponding consumption patterns among the dominant class as a whole that the struggle between the fractions takes the form of a struggle between intellectuals for dominance within their specific subfield i.e. painting, literature, social science, the academic world etc. and for the dominance of their subfield within the intellectual field as a whole. It is this constant struggle that explains sociologically and historically that process of constant renewal, or at least change, that the Russian Formalists identified as the dynamic principle of art itself. The notion of 'making new'.[23]

Thus a new entrant, especially a new generation of potential symbolic producers, a potentiality already heavily class determined, faces a field in which the dominant positions are already occupied. This hierarchy of dominance is ultimately determined by the economic market for symbolic goods provided by the dominant fraction and thus by the rate at which different forms of cultural capital can be transferred into economic capital. The field is thus arranged along two axis. One axis relates to the direct transfer of cultural capital into economic capital via an immediate transfer in the cultural market i.e. by painting pictures for rich buyers, writing novels or plays which appeal to the dominant fraction or by entering sub-disciplines which the dominant fraction values highly and to which it thus gives high salaries, research grants, consultancies, etc. (i.e. medicine and the natural sciences rather than the social sciences or humanities and within medicine heart surgery rather than geriatrics). However too obvious a success in the market or what is worse too obvious a desire for such success leads to cultural delegitimization because of the overall struggle between

[22] See Bourdieu, 1975*b* and The Production of Belief *op. cit.*
[23] See Bourdieu, 1975*a, b.*

cultural and economic capital. Thus the other axis relates to the maximization of cultural capital which translates the principle which structures the economic class field, namely wealth and the distance from necessity that wealth both allows and represents, into rarity and cultural purity. Thus along this axis the avant-garde is more highly valued than mainstream, so-called 'bourgeois' art, pure science than applied science, fine art than graphic art, until recently at least left-wing rather than right-wing politics and so on.[24]

Facing this specifically structured field, which presents a variety of investment possibilities, are a cohort of potential producers themselves structured according to the laws of the formation of the habitus by the same objective set of class relations that structure the field of symbolic production. Firstly entry to the field at all is structured on class lines by the range of dispositions resulting from the objective assessment of the likelihood of success from any given class starting point. Thus a working-class agent is simply less likely to see him or herself as a painter or novelist (or at least as a professional painter or novelist) than a member of the bourgeoisie because such a career requires a high investment of cultural capital which implies for a member of the working class a high investment of time in education to acquire the necessary competences. However since economic success also requires the ability to fit the disposition for cultural appropriation of the bourgeoisie (e.g., surgeons or conductors or successful novelists and playwrights require objectively bourgeois social attributes) a working-class entrant will be forced in the direction of attempting to maximize the return on acquired cultural capital, which is indeed the point of entry into the dominant class for members of the dominated class, by choosing to enter fields which maximize the possible return while minimizing the possible risks. However in general the strategy of maximizing cultural capital is both economically risky and expensive since it requires in the early years of practice an ostentatious refusal of direct economic interest and is directed against those who are occupying the culturally most powerful positions within the symbolic field. Thus Bourdieu argues, particularly in relation to Flaubert and the art-for-arts sake movement, that the strategy of maximizing cultural capital although it often takes on necessarily, as part of the strategy, the lineaments of political radicalism, of opposition to the bourgeoisie, requires existing membership of the dominant fraction of the dominant class to be a viable strategy. Thus Bourdieu argues specifically against Sartre's psychological analysis of Flaubert's artistic development, arguing that this cannot explain the properly sociological fact that all the leading practitioners and theorists of 'art for arts sake' came from the provincial bourgeoisie, thus disposing them to challenge the dominant cultural forms of the Parisian bourgeoisie, while at the same time they all had private means to sustain an uneconomic cultural strategy. He also argues that Flaubert's position as a younger son was typical and that there is a consistent class strategy of using the symbolic field much as the church and the army were used by the aristocracy to ensure a comfortable, high status career for younger sons and increasingly daughters without dissipating the family's economic capital.[25] As a new twist to this strategy he sees the growth of new media related professions and marginal service industries such as restaurants, craft shops, health clinics, etc., as related to the need, because of the relative democratization of education, to create jobs for members of the old bourgeoisie where inherited as opposed to acquired cultural capital can be put to most profitable use.[26]

[24] See Bourdieu, 1971c, 1975a, b, 1979d, pp. 68–101.
[25] See Bourdieu, 1975b.
[26] See Bourdieu, 1979d, p. 415.

Thus both direct economic pressures and the cultural investment required for successful competition for cultural dominance ensure a tendency for the class structure of the dominant class to reproduce itself and its control over symbolic production since those entering the field will possess a habitus which either predisposes them to support the dominant ideology i.e. members of the dominant fraction directly entering dominant positions or upward mobile members of the petty bourgeoisie forced to invest their small amount of hard-earned cultural capital in the lower echelons of economically favoured positions ensuring a relatively risk free but low return on their investment. On the other hand, what opposition there is is transmuted into the terms of the practical logic of cultural struggle which values rarity and cultural distinction with its associated modes of cultural appropriation, requiring high levels of cultural competence and capital, and thus excluding objectively the dominated class from consumption while legitimizing class distinction as cultural distinction.

Bourdieu's work raises a number of questions for us. First and most obvious is the need, within the terms of the theory, for comparative work to analyse the similarities and differences inscribed in different histories of the strategies of domination and resistance employed by the dominant and dominated classes and between fractions of the dominant class in Britain as opposed to France. The recent work by Mulhern on 'The Moment of Scrutiny', is exemplary in this regard.

Another research problem is that raised by Murdoch and Golding, Garnham and Miege *et al.*, namely the effect on the operation of symbolic power of the increased intervention of economic capital directly into the field of the production of symbolic goods via the so-called culture industries and the ways this might effect the field of force in the struggle between the fractions of the dominant class in a situation in which the economic interests of the dominant fraction directly threaten the cultural interests of the dominated fraction.

Then there is the question of Bourdieu's politics. DiMaggio recently described his position as that of a Durkheimian anthropologist rather than a Marxist revolutionary and the French Marxists, who are so often the target of his attacks, have in return accused him of a relativistic pessimism. If to be as objective as possible about the possibilities of a major and immediate transformation of the social formation of advanced capitalism is to be pessimistic, then Bourdieu is, rightly in our view, pessimistic. However it has to be stated that unlike many who would criticize this position he is (a) resolutely committed to a materialist theory of class struggle and of the position of symbolic struggle within that wider struggle (b) especially in *La Distinction* he exhibits a very rare attribute on the left, namely a positive and unpatronizing valuation of the cultural values and aspirations of the working class which at the same time never lapses into naive populism or workerism (c) that his theory, while focused on the problem of Symbolic power, allows fully for the concrete analysis of the specific contradictions between the objective social conditions determined by the mode of production and the consciousness and practices of classes and class fractions, contradictions that might offer the concrete possibility of revolutionary mobilization and action. However it has to be said that there seems to us (and this is very much a question of tone, nuance and attitude) to be a functionalist/determinist residue in Bourdieu's concept of reproduction which leads him to place less emphasis on the possibilities of real change and innovation than either his theory or his empirical research makes necessary. In our view it is necessary to distinguish within the process of reproduction between 'replication' and 'reformation'.[27] Reformation points us towards the spaces that are opened up in conjunc-

27 See Williams, 1980 (in press).

tural situations in which the dominant class is objectively weakened and which thus offers opportunities for real innovation in the social structure, for shifts in the structure of power in the field of class relations which, while falling short of 'revolution' in the classical sense, are nonetheless of real and substantial historical importance and are objectively 'revolutionary' within a longer historical rhythm. For instance it seems to us that Bourdieu points to just such a potential for 'reformation' in his analysis of the contradictions produced by the current state of class relations in the field of education and employment in France. Here he argues that the dominant class, as part of the wider historical movement towards the use of symbolic power as the preferred mode of domination, has increasingly shifted from economic to cultural capital as its preferred mode of accumulation (for instance gaining privileged access to economic power via control of the higher reaches of the state and state-economic bureaucracy which in its turn is controlled by means of privileged access to the dominant institutions of higher education—the so-called Grandes Ecoles). This shift however because of the relative inefficiency of cultural capital for reproduction purposes unless it can be translated back into economic capital, presents the dominant class with a major problem. As a result of the increased 'democratization' of education in response to reformist pressures, pressures which had in part to be met in order to retain the legitimizing power of schooling as a reproduction mechanism, the working class's educational expectations have been raised and at the same time because of the necessary linkage between school and the job market its expectations of the better job associated with that attained educational level. These expectations are not being and cannot be met because in order to retain schooling as an operation of hierarchization through which they retain control of the new centres of economic power and thus legitimate that control, the dominant class are forced objectively to devalue educational qualifications, while at the same time the objective developments in the field of material production is yielding to massive de-skilling and the proletarianization of sectors of traditional mental labour. This is a problem, some would argue, that is already calling forth a strategy of domination increasingly reliant on direct rather than symbolic violence. What is not clear is the extent to which Bourdieu himself would draw these conclusions from his own concrete analysis.[28]

Finally there is the epistemological problem of the social conditions of Bourdieu's own intellectual practice. This of course relates to the problem of social change, of 'reformation'. If Bourdieu's is a progressive political intervention, as he clearly believes and with which we agree, does the structure of the symbolic field according to his own theory doom the intervention to recuperation and futility or on the other hand are there conditions under which the logic proper to the symbolic field can produce contradictions at the symbolic level such that they no longer tend to reproduce the given set of class relations.

Bibliography

BARRET, M. *et al.* (eds.) (1979). *Ideology and Cultural Production*, Croom Helm.

GARNHAM, N. (1979). Subjectivity, ideology, class and historical materialism, *Screen* Vol. 20 No. 1 Spring

THOMPSON, E. P. (1978). *The Poverty of Theory*, Merlin, London

WILLIAMS, R. (1977). *Marxism and Literature*, Oxford University Press, London

WILLIAMS, R. (1980). *Culture*, Fontana New Sociology, London (in press)

[28] See Bourdieu, 1979d, pp. 145–85.

The production of belief: contribution to an economy of symbolic goods*

PIERRE BOURDIEU
Translation by Richard Nice

> 'Once again, I don't like this word "entrepreneur" '
>> Sven Nielsen, Chairman and Managing
>> Director of Presses de la Cité

> 'In another area, I had the honour, if not the pleasure, of losing money by com-
> missioning the two monumental volumes of Carlos Baker's translation of
> Hemingway'
>> Robert Laffont

The art business, a trade in things that have no price, belongs to the class of practices in which the logic of the pre-capitalist economy lives on (as it does, in another sphere, in the economy of exchanges between the generations). These practices, functioning as practical *negations*,† can only work by pretending not to be doing what they are doing. Defying ordinary logic, they lend themselves to two opposed readings, both equally false, which each undo their essential duality and duplicity by reducing them either to the disavowal or to what is disavowed—to disinterestedness or self-interest. The challenge which economies based on disavowal of the 'economic' present to all forms of economism lies precisely in the fact that they function, and can function, in practice—and not merely in the agents' representations—only by virtue of a constant, collective repression of narrowly 'economic' interest and of the real nature of the practices revealed by 'economic' analysis.[1]

The disavowal of the 'economy'

In this economic universe, whose very functioning is defined by a 'refusal' of the 'commercial' which is in fact a collective disavowal of commercial interests and profits, the most 'anti-economic' and most visibly 'disinterested' behaviours, which in an 'economic' universe would be those most ruthlessly condemned, contain a form of economic rationality (even in the restricted sense) and in no way exclude their authors from even the 'economic' profits awaiting those who conform to the law of this universe. In other words, alongside the pursuit of 'economic' profit, which treats the cultural goods business as a business like any other, and not the most profitable, 'economically' speaking (as the best-informed, i.e. the most 'disinterested', art dealers

---

* Extract from *Actes de la Recherche en Science Sociale* (1977), Vol. 13, pp. 3–43.

† The terms *negation, denial* and *disavowal* are used to render the French *dénégation*, which itself is used in a sense akin to that of Freud's *Verneinung*. See J. Laplanche and J. B. Pontalis, *The Language of Psycho-analysis* (Hogarth Press, London: 1973), entry 'Negation', pp. 261–263 (translator's note).

[1] From now on, the inverted commas will indicate when the 'economy' is to be understood in the narrow sense in which economism understands it.

point out) and merely adapts itself to the demand of an already converted clientele, there is also room for the *accumulation of symbolic capital*. 'Symbolic capital' is to be understood as economic or political capital that is disavowed, mis-recognized and thereby recognized, hence legitimate, a 'credit' which, under certain conditions, and always in the long run, guarantees 'economic' profits. Producers and vendors of cultural goods who 'go commercial' condemn themselves, and not only from an ethical or aesthetic point of view, because they deprive themselves of the opportunities open to those who can *recognize* the specific demands of this universe and who, by concealing from themselves and others the interests at stake in their practice, obtain the means of deriving profits from disinterestedness. In short, when the only usable, effective capital is the (mis)recognized, legitimate capital called 'prestige' or 'authority', the economic capital that cultural undertakings generally require cannot secure the specific profits produced by the field—nor the 'economic' profits they always imply— unless it is reconverted into symbolic capital. For the author, the critic, the art dealer, the publisher or the theatre manager, the only legitimate accumulation consists in making a name for oneself, a known, recognized name, a capital of consecration implying a power to consecrate objects (with a trademark or signature) or persons (through publication, exhibition, etc.) and therefore to give value, and to appropriate the profits from this operation.

The disavowal (*dénégation*) is neither a real negation of the 'economic' interest which always haunts the most 'disinterested' practices, nor a simple 'dissimulation' of the mercenary aspects of the practice, as even the most attentive observers have supposed. The disavowed economic enterprise of the art dealer or publisher, 'cultural bankers' in whom art and business meet in practice—which predisposes them for the rôle of scapegoat—cannot succeed, even in 'economic' terms, unless it is guided by a practical mastery of the laws of the functioning of the field in which cultural goods are produced and circulate, i.e. by an entirely improbable, and in any case rarely achieved, combination of the realism required for minor concessions to 'economic' necessities that are disavowed but not denied and of the conviction which excludes them.[2] The fact that the disavowal of the 'economy' is neither a simple ideological

---

[2] The 'great' publisher, like the 'great' art-dealer, combines 'economic' prudence (people often poke fun at him for his 'housekeeping' ways) with intellectual daring. He thus sets himself apart from those who condemn themselves, 'economically' at least, because they apply the same daring or the same casualness both in their commercial business and in their intellectual venture (not to mention those who combine economic imprudence with artistic prudence: 'A mistake over the cost-prices or the print runs can lead to disaster, even if the sales are excellent. When Jean-Jacques Pauvert embarked on reprinting the Littré (multi-volume dictionary) it looked like a promising venture because of the unexpectedly large number of subscribers. But when it was about to be published, they found there had been a mistake in estimating the cost-price, and they would be losing fifteen francs on each set. Pauvert had to abandon the deal to another publisher'—B. Demory, 'Le livre à l'âge de l'industrie', *L'Expansion*, October 1970, p. 110).
    It becomes clearer why Jérôme Lindon commands the admiration both of the big 'commercial' publisher and the small avant-garde publisher: 'A publisher with a very small team and low overheads can make a good living and express his own personality. This requires very strict financial discipline on his part, since he is caught between the need to maintain financial equilibrium and the temptation to expand. I have great admiration for Jérôme Lindon, the director of Les Editions de Minuit, who has been able to maintain that difficult balance throughout his publishing life. He has been able to promote the things he liked, and nothing else, without being blown off course. Publishers like him are needed to give birth to the nouveau roman, and publishers like me are needed to reflect the varied facets of life and creation' (R. Laffont, *Editeur*, Paris, Laffont, 1974, pp. 291–292).
    'It was during the Algerian war, and I can say that for three years I lived like an FLN militant, at the same time as I was becoming a publisher. At Editions de Minuit, Jérôme Lindon, who has always been an example for me, was denouncing torture' (F. Maspero, 'Maspero entre tous les feux', *Nouvel Observateur*, 17 September 1973).

mask nor a complete repudiation of economic interest, explains why on the one hand, new producers whose only capital is their conviction can establish themselves in the market by appealing to the values whereby the dominant figures accumulated their symbolic capital, and why, on the other hand, only those who can come to terms with the 'economic' constraints inscribed in this bad-faith economy can reap the full 'economic' profits of their symbolic capital.

Who creates the 'creator'?

The 'charisma' ideology which is the ultimate basis of belief in the value of a work of art and which is therefore the basis of functioning of the field of production and circulation of cultural commodities, is undoubtedly the main obstacle to a rigorous science of the production of the value of cultural goods. It is this ideology which directs attention to the *apparent producer*, the painter, writer or composer, in short, the 'author', suppressing the question of what authorizes the author. If it is all too obvious that the price of a picture is not determined by the sum of the production costs—the raw material and the painter's labour time—and if works of art provide a golden example for those who seek to refute Marx's labour theory of value (which anyway gives a special status to artistic production), this is perhaps because people wrongly define the unit of production or, which amounts to the same thing, the process of production.

The question can be asked in its most concrete form (which it sometimes assumes in the eyes of the agents): who is the true producer of the value of the work—the painter or the dealer, the writer or the publisher, the playwright or the theatre manager? The ideology of creation, which makes the author the first and last source of the value of his work, conceals the fact that the cultural businessman (art dealer, publisher, etc.) is at one and the same time the person who exploits the labour of the 'creator' by trading in the 'sacred' and the person who, by putting it on the market, by exhibiting, publishing or staging it, *consecrates* a product which he has 'discovered' and which would otherwise remain a mere natural resource; and the more consecrated he personally is, the more strongly he consecrates the work.[3] The art trader is not just the agent who gives the work a commercial value by bringing it into a market; he is not just the representative, the impresario, who 'defends the authors he loves'. He is the person who can proclaim the value of the author he defends (cf. the fiction of the catalogue or blurb) and above all 'invests his prestige' in the author's cause, acting as a 'symbolic banker' who offers as security all the symbolic capital he has accumulated (which he is liable to forfeit if he backs a 'loser').[4] This investment, of which the accompanying 'economic' investments are themselves only a guarantee, is what brings the producer into the cycle of consecration. Entering the field of literature is not so much like going into religion as getting into a select club: the publisher is one of those prestigious sponsors (together with preface-writers and critics) who effusively recommend their candidate. Even clearer is the rôle of the art dealer who

---

[3] This analysis, which applies in the first instance to new works by unknown authors, is equally valid for 'under-rated' or 'dated' and even 'classic' works, which can always be treated to 'rediscoveries', 'revivals' and 're-readings' (hence so many unclassifiable philosophical, literary and theatrical productions, of which the paradigm is the avant-garde staging of traditional texts).

[4] It is no accident that the art-trader's *guarantor* rôle is particularly visible in the field of painting where the purchaser's (the collector's) 'economic' investment is incomparably greater than in literature or even the theatre. Raymonde Moulin observes that 'a contract signed with a major gallery has a commercial value and that, in the eyes of the amateurs, the dealer is 'the guarantor of the quality of the works' (R. Moulin, *Le Marché de la peinture en France*, Paris, Les Editions de Minuit, 1967, p. 329).

literally has to 'introduce' the artist and his work into ever more select company (group exhibitions, one-man shows, prestigious collections, museums) and ever more sought-after places. But the law of this universe, whereby the less visible the investment, the more productive it is symbolically, means that promotion exercises, which in the business world take the overt form of publicity, must here be euphemized. The art trader cannot serve his 'discovery' unless he applies all his conviction, which rules out 'sordidly commercial' manoeuvres, manipulation and the 'hard sell', in favour of the softer, more discreet forms of 'public relations' (which are themselves a highly euphemized form of publicity)—receptions, society gatherings, and judiciously placed confidences.[5]

The circle of belief

But in moving back from the 'creator' to the 'discoverer' or 'creator of the creator', we have only displaced the initial question and we still have to determine the source of the art-businessman's acknowledged power to consecrate. The charisma ideology has a ready-made answer: the 'great' dealers, the 'great' publishers, are inspired talent-spotters who, guided by their disinterested, unreasoning passion for a work of art, have 'made' the painter or writer, or have helped him make himself, by encouraging him in difficult moments with the faith they had in him, guiding him with their advice and freeing him from material worries.[6] To avoid an endless regress in the chain of causes, perhaps it is necessary to cease thinking in the logic, which a whole tradition encourages, of the 'first beginning', which inevitably leads to faith in the 'creator'. It is not sufficient to indicate, as people often do, that the 'discoverer' never discovers anything that is not already discovered, at least by a few—painters already known to a small number of painters or connoisseurs, authors 'introduced' by other authors (it is well known, for example, that the manuscripts that will be published hardly ever arrive directly, but almost always through recognized go-betweens). His 'authority' is itself a credit-based value, which only exists in the relationship with the field of production as a whole, i.e. with the artists or writers who belong to his 'stable'—'a publisher', said one of them, 'is his catalogue'—and with those who do not and would or would not like to; in the relationship with the other dealers or publishers who do or do not envy him his painters or writers and are or are not capable of taking them from him; in the relationship with the critics, who do or do not believe in his judgment, and speak of his 'products' with varying degrees of respect; in the relationship with his clients and customers, who perceive his 'trademark' with greater or lesser clarity and do or do not place their trust in it. This

---

[5] It goes without saying that, depending on the position in the field of production, promotion activities range from overt use of publicity techniques (press advertisements, catalogues etc.) and economic and symbolic pressure (e.g. on the juries who award the prizes or on the critics) to the haughty and rather ostentatious refusal to make any concessions to 'the world', which can, in the long run, be the supreme form of value imposition (only available to a few).

[6] The ideology transfigures real functions. Only the publisher or dealer, who devotes most of his time to it, can organize and rationalize the marketing of the work, which, especially in the case of painting, is a considerable undertaking, presupposing information (as to the 'worthwhile' places in which to exhibit, especially abroad) and material means. But, above all, he alone, acting as a go-between and a screen, can enable the producer to maintain a charismatic, i.e. inspired and 'disinterested', image of himself and his activity, by sparing him the tasks associated with the valorizing of his work, which are both ridiculous, demoralizing and ineffective (symbolically at least). (The writer's or painter's craft, and the corresponding images of them, would probably be totally different if the producers had to market their products personally and if they depended directly, for their conditions of existence, on the sanctions of the market or on agencies which know and recognize no other sanctions, like 'commercial' publishing firms.)

'authority' is nothing other than 'credit' with a set of agents who constitute 'connections' whose value is proportionate to the credit they themselves command. It is all too obvious that critics also collaborate with the art trader in the effort of consecration which makes the reputation and, at least in the long term, the monetary value of works. 'Discovering' the 'new talents', they guide buyers' and sellers' choices by their writings or advice (they are often manuscript readers or series editors in publishing houses or accredited preface-writers for galleries) and by their verdicts, which though offered as purely aesthetic, entail significant economic effects (juries for literary prizes). Among the makers of the work of art, we must finally include the public which helps to make its value by appropriating it materially (collectors) or symbolically (audiences, readers), and by objectively or subjectively identifying part of its own value with these appropriations. In short, what 'makes reputations' is not, as provincial Rastignacs naïvely think, this or that 'influential' person, this or that institution, review, magazine, academy, coterie, dealer or publisher; it is not even the whole set of what are sometimes called 'personalities of the world of arts and letters'; it is the field of production, understood as the system of objective relations between these agents or institutions and as the site of the struggles for the monopoly of the power to consecrate, in which the value of works of art and belief in that value are continuously generated.[7]

Faith and bad faith

The source of the efficacy of all acts of consecration is the field itself, the locus of the accumulated social energy which the agents and institutions help to reproduce through the struggles in which they try to appropriate it and into which they put what they have acquired from it in previous struggles. The value of works of art in general—the basis of the value of each particular work—and the belief which underlies it, are generated in the incessant, innumerable struggles to establish the value of this or that particular work, i.e. not only in the competition between agents (authors, actors, writers, critics, directors, publishers, dealers, etc.) whose interests (in the broadest sense) are linked to different cultural goods, 'middle-brow' theatre (théâtre 'bourgeois') or 'high-brow' theatre (théâtre 'intellectuel'), 'established' painting or avant-garde painting, 'mainstream' literature or 'advanced' literature, but also in the conflicts between agents occupying different positions in the production of products of the same type, painters and dealers, authors and publishers, writers and critics, etc. Even if these struggles never clearly set the 'commercial' against the 'non-commercial', 'disinterestedness' against 'cynicism', they almost always involve recognition of the ultimate values of 'disinterestedness' through the denunciation of the mercenary compromises or calculating manoeuvres of the adversary, so that disavowal of the 'economy' is placed at the very heart of the field, as the principle governing its functioning and transformation.

This is why the dual reality of the ambivalent painter–dealer or writer–publisher relationship is most clearly revealed in moments of crisis, when the objective reality of each of the positions and their relationship is unveiled and the values which do the

[7] In reply to those who might seek to refute these arguments by invoking a cosy picture of solidarity between 'fellow producers' or 'colleagues', one would have to point to all the forms of 'unfair competition', of which *plagiarism* (more or less skilfully disguised) is only the best known and the most visible, or the violence—purely symbolic, of course—of the aggressions with which producers endeavour to discredit their rivals (c.f. the recent history of painting, which offers countless examples, one of the most typical, to cite only the dead, being the relationship between Yves Klein and Piero Manzoni).

veiling are reaffirmed. No one is better placed than the art-trader to know the interests of the makers of works and the strategies they use to defend their interests or to conceal their strategies. Although he forms a protective screen between the artist and the market, he is also what links him to the market and so provokes, by his very existence, cruel unmaskings of the truth of artistic practice. To impose his own interests, he only has to take the artist at his word when he professes 'disinterestedness'. One soon learns from conversations with these middle-men that, with a few illustrious exceptions, seemingly designed to recall the ideal, painters and writers are deeply self-interested, calculating, obsessed with money and ready to do anything to succeed. As for the artists, who cannot even denounce the exploitation they suffer without confessing their self-interested motives, they are the ones best placed to see the middle-men's strategies and the eye for an (economically) profitable investment which guides their actual aesthetic investments. The makers and marketers of works of art are adversaries in collusion, who each abide by the same law which demands the repression of direct manifestations of personal interest, at least in its overtly 'economic' form, and which has every appearance of transcendence although it is only the product of the cross-censorship weighing more or less equally on each of those who impose it on all the others.

A similar mechanism operates when an unknown artist, without credit or credibility, is turned into a known and recognized artist. The struggle to impose the dominant definition of art, i.e. to impose a style, embodied in a particular producer or group of producers, gives the work of art a value by putting it at stake, inside and outside the field of production. Everyone can challenge his adversaries' claim to distinguish art from non-art without ever calling into question this fundamental claim. Precisely because of the conviction that good and bad painting exist, competitors can exclude each other from the field of painting, thereby giving it the stakes and the motor without which it could not function. And nothing better conceals the objective collusion which is the matrix of specifically artistic value than the conflicts through which it operates.

Ritual sacrilege

This argument might be countered by pointing to the attempts made with increasing frequency in the 1960s, especially in the world of painting, to break the circle of belief. But it is all too obvious that these ritual acts of sacrilege, profanations which only ever scandalize the believers, are bound to become sacred in their turn and provide the basis for a new belief. One thinks of Manzoni, with his tins of 'artist's shit', his magic pedestals which could turn any object placed on them into a work of art, or his signatures on living people which made them *objets d'art*; or Ben, with his many 'gestures' of provocation or derision such as exhibiting a piece of cardboard labelled 'unique copy' or a canvas bearing the words 'canvas 45 cm long'. Paradoxically, nothing more clearly reveals the logic of the functioning of the artistic field than the fate of these apparently radical attempts at subversion. Because they expose the art of artistic creation to a mockery already annexed to the artistic tradition by Duchamp, they are immediately converted into artistic 'acts', recorded as such and thus consecrated and celebrated by the makers of taste. Art cannot reveal the truth about art without snatching it away again by turning the revelation into an artistic event. And it is significant, *a contrario*, that all attempts to call into question the field of artistic production, the logic of its functioning and the functions it performs, through the highly sublimated and ambiguous means of discourse or artistic 'acts' (e.g. Maciunas or Flynt) are no less necessarily bound to be condemned even by the most heterodox guardians of artistic orthodoxy, because in refusing to play the game, to challenge in accordance with the rules, i.e. artistically, their authors call into question not a way of playing the game, but the game itself and the belief which supports it. This is the one unforgivable transgression.

Collective mis-recognition

The quasi-magical potency of the signature is nothing other than the power, bestowed on certain individuals, to mobilize the symbolic energy produced by the functioning of the whole field, i.e. the faith in the game and its stakes that is produced by the game itself. As Marcel Mauss observed, the problem with magic is not so much to know what are the specific properties of the magician, or even of the magical operations and representations, but rather to discover the bases of the collective belief or, more precisely, the *collective misrecognition*, collectively produced and maintained, which is the source of the power the magician appropriates. If it is 'impossible to understand magic without the magic group', this is because the magician's power, of which the miracle of the signature or personal trademark is merely an outstanding example, is a *valid imposture*, a legitimate abuse of power, collectively misrecognized and so recognized. The artist who puts his name on a ready-made article and produces an object whose market price is incommensurate with its cost of production is collectively mandated to perform a magic act which would be nothing without the whole tradition leading up to his gesture, and without the universe of celebrants and believers who give it meaning and value in terms of that tradition. The source of 'creative' power, the ineffable *mana* or charisma celebrated by the tradition, need not be sought anywhere other than in the field, i.e. in the system of objective relations which constitute it, in the struggles of which it is the site and in the specific form of energy or capital which is generated there.

So it is both true and untrue to say that the commercial value of a work of art is incommensurate with its cost of production. It is true if one only takes account of the manufacture of the material object; it is not true if one is referring to the production of the work of art as a sacred, consecrated object, the product of a vast operation of *social alchemy* jointly conducted, with equal conviction and very unequal profits, by all the agents involved in the field of production, i.e. obscure artists and writers as well as 'consecrated' masters, critics and publishers as well as authors, enthusiastic clients as well as convinced vendors. These are contributions, including the most obscure, which the partial materialism of economism ignores, and which only have to be taken into account in order to see that the production of the work of art, i.e. of the artist, is no exception to the law of the conservation of social energy.[8]

[8] These arguments take further and specify those which I have put forward with reference to *haute couture*, in which the economic stakes and the disavowal strategies are much more evident (see Bourdieu and Delsaut, 1975*d*), and philosophy; in the latter case the emphasis was placed on the contribution of interpreters and commentators to the miscognition-recognition of the work (see Bourdieu, 1975*e*). The present text does not aim to *apply* knowledge of the general properties of fields that have been established elsewhere, to new fields. Rather, it seeks to *bring the invariant laws of the functioning and transformation of fields of struggle to a higher level of explicitness and generality*, by comparing several fields (painting, theatre, literature, and journalism) in which the different laws do not appear with the same degree of clarity, for reasons which have to do either with the nature of the data available or with specific properties. This procedure contrasts both with theoreticist formalism, which is its own object, and with idiographic empiricism, which can never move beyond the scholastic accumulation of falsifiable propositions.

The establishment and the challengers

Because the fields of cultural goods production are universes of belief which can only function insofar as they succeed in simultaneously producing products and the need for those products through practices which are the denial of the ordinary practices of the 'economy', the struggles which take place within them are ultimate conflicts involving the whole relation to the 'economy'. The 'zealots', whose only capital is their belief in the principles of the bad-faith economy and who preach a return to the sources, the absolute and intransigent renunciation of the early days, condemn in the same breath the merchants in the temple who bring 'commercial' practices and interests into the area of the sacred, and the pharisees who derive temporal profits from their accumulated capital of consecration by means of an exemplary submission to the demands of the field. Thus the fundamental law of the field is constantly reasserted by 'newcomers', who have most interest in repudiating self-interest.

The opposition between the 'commercial' and the 'non-commercial' reappears everywhere. It is the generative principle of most of the judgments which, in the theatre, cinema, painting or literature, claim to establish the frontier between what is and what is not art, i.e. in practice, between 'bourgeois' art and 'intellectual' art, between 'traditional' and 'avant-garde' art, or, in Parisian terms, between the 'right bank' and the 'left bank'.[9] While this opposition can change its substantive content and designate very different realities in different fields, it remains structurally invariant in different fields and in the same field at different moments. It is always an opposition between small-scale and large-scale ('commercial') production, i.e. between the primacy of production and the field of producers or even the sub-field of producers for producers, and the primacy of marketing, audience, sales, and success measured quantitatively; between the deferred, lasting success of 'classics' and the immediate, temporary success of best-sellers; between a production based on denial of the 'economy' and of profit (sales targets, etc.) which ignores or challenges the expectations of the established audience and serves no other demand than the one it itself produces, but in the long term, and a production which secures success and the corresponding profits by adjusting to a pre-existing demand. The characteristics of the commercial enterprise and the characteristics of the cultural enterprise, understood as a more or less disavowed relation to the commercial enterprise, are inseparable. The differences in the relationship to 'economic' considerations and to the audience coincide with the differences officially recognized and identified by the taxonomies prevailing in the field. Thus the opposition between 'genuine' art and 'commercial' art corresponds to the opposition between ordinary entrepreneurs seeking immediate economic profit and cultural entrepreneurs struggling to accumulate specifically cultural capital, albeit at the cost of temporarily renouncing economic profit. As for the opposition which is made within the latter group between consecrated art and avant-garde art, or between orthodoxy and heresy, it distinguishes between, on the one hand, those who dominate the field of production and the market through the economic and symbolic capital they have been able to accumulate in earlier struggles by virtue of a particu-

[9] A couple of examples, chosen from among hundreds: 'I know a painter who has real quality as regards skill, material, etc., but for me the stuff he turns out is totally commercial; he manufactures it, like bars of soap . . . When artists become very well-known, they often tend to go in for mass production' (gallery director, interview). Avant-gardism has often nothing to offer to guarantee its conviction beyond its indifference to money and its spirit of protest: 'Money doesn't count for him; even beyond the notion of public service, he sees culture as a vehicle for social protest' (de Baecque 1968).

larly successful combination of the contradictory capacities specifically demanded by the law of the field, and, on the other hand, the newcomers, who have and want no other audience than their competitors—established producers whom their practice tends to discredit by imposing new products—or other newcomers with whom they vie in novelty.

Their position in the structure of simultaneously economic and symbolic power relations which defines the field of production, i.e. in the structure of the distribution of the specific capital (and of the corresponding economic capital), governs the characteristics and strategies of the agents or institutions, through the intermediary of a practical or conscious evaluation of the objective chances of profit. Those in dominant positions operate essentially defensive strategies, designed to perpetuate the status quo by maintaining themselves and the principles on which their dominance is based. The world is as it should be, since they are on top and clearly deserve to be there; excellence therefore consists in being what one is, with reserve and under-statement, urbanely hinting at the immensity of one's means by the economy of one's means, refusing the assertive, attention-seeking strategies which expose the pretensions of the young pretenders. The dominant are drawn towards silence, discretion and secrecy, and their orthodox discourse, which is only ever wrung from them by the need to rectify the heresies of the newcomers, is never more than the explicit affir-mation of self-evident principles which go without saying and would go better unsaid. 'Social problems' are social relations: they emerge from confrontation between two groups, two systems of antagonistic interests and theses. In the relationship which constitutes them, the choice of the moment and sites of battle is left to the initiative of the challengers, who break the silence of the *doxa* and call into question the un-problematic, taken-for-granted world of the dominant groups. The dominated pro-ducers, for their part, in order to gain a foothold in the market, have to resort to subversive strategies which will eventually bring them the disavowed profits only if they succeed in overturning the hierarchy of the field without disturbing the principles on which the field is based. Thus their revolutions are only ever partial ones, which displace the censorships and transgress the conventions but do so in the name of the same underlying principles. This is why the strategy par excellence is the 'return to the sources' which is the basis of all heretical subversion and all aesthetic revolutions, because it enables the insurgents to turn against the establishment the arms which they use to justify their domination, in particular asceticism, daring, ardour, rigour and disinterestedness. The strategy of beating the dominant groups at their own game by demanding that they respect the fundamental law of the field, refusal of the 'economy', can only work if it manifests exemplary sincerity in its own refusal.

Because they are based on a relation to culture which is necessarily also a relation to the 'economy' and the market, institutions producing and marketing cultural goods, whether in painting, literature, theatre or cinema, tend to be organised into struc-turally and functionally homologous systems which also stand in a relation of struc-tural homology with the field of the fractions of the dominant class (from which the greater part of their clientele is drawn). This homology is most evident in the case of the theatre. The opposition between 'bourgeois theatre' and 'avant-garde theatre', the equivalent of which can be found in painting and in literature, and which functions as a principle of division whereby authors, works, styles and subjects can be classified practically, is rooted in reality. It is found both in the social characteristics of the audiences of the different Paris theatres (age, occupation, place of residence, frequency of attendance, prices they are prepared to pay, etc.) and in the—perfectly congruent—

Table 1. *The over-lap of audiences between theatres (the 1963–4 season)*

	TEP	TNP	Théâtre de France (Odéon)	Athénée	Vieux Colombier	Montparnasse G. Baty	Comédie Française	Atelier	Ambigu	Michodière	Théâtre de Paris	Comédie Champs Elysées	Ambassadeurs	Moderne	Antoine	Gymnase	Variétés
TEP	X	57	48	35	35												
TNP		X	48		32		36										
Théâtre de France (Odéon)	56		X				48	36									
Athénée	50	45		X	36												
Vieux Colombier	49	47			X		43										
Montparnasse G. Baty		49				X	48				47						
Comédie Française	40	48					X	35									
Atelier		39					38	X			41						
Ambigu		48					49		X		46						
Michodière		38			41		47			X							
Théâtre de Paris							37	49		38	X						
Comédie Champs Elysées							49	55			49	X					
Ambassadeurs								58		39	46		X				
Moderne								57			56		40	X			
Antoine								43			40			42	X		
Gymnase							36	40			37					X	
Variétés							38	42			46						X

We have shown for each theatre as a percentage, the three theatres that the audiences for each theatre had been to most frequently (from SEMA. La situation du théâtre en France, Tome II, Annexe, Données statistiques, Tableau 42).

characteristics of the authors performed (age, social origin, place of residence, life-style, etc.), the works, and the theatrical businesses themselves.

'Highbrow' theatre in fact contrasts with 'middle-brow' theatre ('*théâtre de boulevard*') in all these respects at once. On one side, there are the big subsidized theatres (Odéon, Théâtre de l'Est parisien, Théâtre national populaire) and the few small left-bank theatres (Vieux Colombier, Montparnasse, Gaston Baty, etc.),[10] which are risky undertakings both economically and culturally, always on the verge of bankruptcy, offering unconventional shows (as regards content and/or *mise en scène*) at relatively low prices to a young, 'intellectual' audience (students, intellectuals, teachers). On the other side, the 'bourgeois'[11] theatres (in order of intensity of the pertinent properties: Gymnase, Théâtre de Paris, Antoine, Ambassadeurs, Ambigu, Michodière, Variétés), ordinary commercial businesses whose concern for economic

[10] To remain within the limits of the information available (that provided by Pierre Guetta's excellent survey, *Le théâtre et son public*, roneo, Paris, Ministere des Affaires Culturelles, 1966, 2 vol.), I have only cited the theatres mentioned in this study. Out of 43 Parisian theatres listed in 1975 in the specialized press (excluding the subsidised theatres), 29 (two-thirds) offer entertainments which clearly belong to the 'boulevard' category; 8 present classical or neutral ('unmarked') works; and 6 present works which can be regarded as belonging to intellectual theatre.

[11] Here, and throughout this text, 'bourgeois' is shorthand for 'dominant fractions of the dominant class' when used as a noun, and, when used as an adjective, for 'structurally linked to these fractions'. 'Intellectual' functions in the same way for 'dominated fractions of the dominant class'.

profitability forces them into extremely prudent cultural strategies, which take no risks and create none for their audiences, and offer shows that have already succeeded (adaptations of British and American plays, revivals of middlebrow 'classics') or have been newly written in accordance with tried and tested formulae. Their audience tends to be older, more 'bourgeois' (executives, the professions, businessmen), and is prepared to pay high prices for shows of pure entertainment whose conventions and staging correspond to an aesthetic that has not changed for a century. Between the 'poor theatre' which caters for the dominant-class fractions richest in cultural capital and poorest in economic capital, and the 'rich theatre', which caters for the fractions richest in economic capital and poorest (in relative terms) in cultural capital, stand the classic theatres (Comédie Française, Atelier), which are neutral ground, since they draw their audience more or less equally from all fractions of the dominant class and share parts of their constituency with all types of theatre.[12] Their programmes too are neutral or eclectic: 'avant-garde boulevard' (as the drama critic of La Croix put it), represented by Anouilh, or the consecrated avant-garde.[13]

Games with mirrors

This structure is no new phenomenon. When Françoise Dorin, in Le Tournant, one of the great boulevard successes, places an avant-garde author in typical vaudeville situations, she is simply rediscovering (and for the same reasons) the same strategies which Scribe used in La Camaraderie, against Delacroix, Hugo and Berlioz: in 1836, to reassure a worthy public alarmed by the outrages and excesses of the Romantics, Scribe gave them Oscar Rigaut, a poet famed for his funeral odes but exposed as a hedonist, in short, a man like others, ill-placed to call the bourgeois 'grocers'.[14]

[12] Analysis of the overlaps between the constituencies of the various theatres confirms these analyses. At one extreme, the TEP, which draws almost half its audience from the dominated fractions of the dominant class, shares its clientele with the other 'intellectual' theatres (TNP, Odéon, Vieux Colombier and Athénée); at the other extreme, the boulevard theatres (Antoine, Variétés) almost half of whose audience consists of employers, senior executives and their wives; between the two, the Comédie Française and the Atelier share their audience with all the theatres.

[13] A more detailed analysis would reveal a whole set of oppositions (in the different respects considered above) within avant-garde theatre and even boulevard theatre. Thus, a careful reading of the statistics on attendance suggests that a 'smart' bourgeois theatre (Théâtre de Paris, Ambassadeurs, which present works—Comment réussir en affaires and Photo-finish by Peter Ustinov—praised by Le Figaro—12 February 1964 and 6 January 1964—and even, in the first case, by the Nouvel Observateur—5 March 1964), attended by an audience of cultivated bourgeois, tending to live in Paris and to be regular theatre-goers, can be contrasted with a more 'low-brow' bourgeois theatre, offering 'Parisian' entertainments (Michodière—La preuve par quatre, by Félicien Marceau; Antoine—Mary, Mary; Variétés—Un homme comblé, by J. Deval), which received very hostile reviews, the first from the Nouvel Observateur—12 February 1964—and the other two from Le Figaro— 26 September 1963 and 28 December 1964. Their audience is more provincial, less familiar with the theatre, and more petty-bourgeois, containing a higher proportion of junior executives and, in particular, craftsmen and shop-keepers. Although it is not possible to verify this statistically (as I have endeavoured to do in the case of painting and literature), everything suggests that the authors and actors of these different categories of theatres are also opposed in accordance with the same principles. Thus, the big stars in successful boulevard plays (generally also receiving a percentage of the box-office receipts) could earn up to 2,000 francs an evening in 1972, and 'known' actors 300–500 francs per performance; actors belonging to the Comédie Française, who receive less per performance than leading private-theatre actors, are paid a basic monthly rate with bonuses for each performance and, in the case of share-holding members of the company, a proportion of the annual profits, according to length of service; while the actors in the small left-bank theatres suffer precarious employment and extremely low incomes.

[14] Descotes, 1964, p. 298. This sort of caricature would not occur so often in theatrical works themselves (e.g. the parody of the nouveau roman in Michel Perrin's Haute fidélité, 1963) and, even more often, in the writings of the critics, if 'bourgeois' authors were not assured of the complicity of their 'bourgeois' audience when they settle their scores with avant-garde authors and bring 'intellectual comfort' to the 'bourgeois' who feel threatened by 'intellectual' theatre.

Françoise Dorin's play, which dramatizes a middlebrow playwright's attempts to convert himself into an avant-garde playwright, can be regarded as a sort of socio-logical test which demonstrates how the opposition which structures the whole space of cultural production operates simultaneously in people's minds, in the form of systems of classification and categories of perception, and in objective reality, through the mechanisms which produce the complementary oppositions between playwrights and their theatres, critics and their newspapers. The play itself offers the contrasting portraits of two theatres: on the one hand, technical clarity (p. 47) and skill (p. 158), gaiety, lightness (pp. 79, 101) and frivolity (p. 101), 'typically French' qualities (p. 101); on the other, 'pretentiousness camouflaged under ostentatious starkness' (p. 67), 'a confidence-trick of presentation' (p. 68), humourlessness, portentousness and pretentiousness (pp. 80, 85), gloomy speeches and décors ("a black curtain and a scaffold certainly help . . .", pp. 27, 67). In short, dramatists, plays, speeches, epi-grams, that are 'courageously light', joyous, lively, uncomplicated, true-to-life, as opposed to 'thinking', i.e. miserable, tedious, problematic and obscure. 'We had a bounce in our backsides. They think with theirs' (p. 36). There is no overcoming this opposition, because it separates 'intellectuals' and 'bourgeois' even in the interests they have most manifestly in common. All the contrasts which Françoise Dorin and the 'bourgeois' critics mobilize in their judgments on the theatre (in the form of oppo-sitions between the 'black curtain' and the 'beautiful set', 'the wall well lit, well decorated' 'the actors well washed, well dressed'), and, indeed, in their whole world view, are summed up in the opposition between 'la vie en noir' and 'la vie en rose'—dark thoughts and rose-coloured spectacles—which, as we shall see, ultimately stems from two very different ways of *denying the social world*.[15]

Faced with an object so clearly organized in accordance with the canonical oppo-sition, the critics, themselves distributed within the space of the press in accordance with the structure which underlies the object classified and the classificatory system they apply to it, reproduce, in the space of the judgments whereby they classify it and themselves, the space within which they are themselves classified (a perfect circle from which there is no escape except by objectifying it). In other words, the different judgments expressed on *Le Tournant* vary, in their form and content, according to the publication in which they appear, i.e. from the greatest distance of the critic and his readership *vis-à-vis* the 'intellectual' world to the greatest distance *vis-à-vis* the play and its 'bourgeois' audience and the smallest distance *vis-à-vis* the 'intellectual' world.[16]

What the papers say: the play of homology

The subtle shifts in meaning and style which, from *L'Aurore* to *Le Figaro* and from *Le Figaro* to *L'Express*, lead to the neutral discourse of *Le Monde* and thence to the

[15] To given an idea of the power and pregnancy of these taxonomies, one example will suffice: statistical study of class tastes shows that 'intellectual' and 'bourgeois' preferences can be organised around the opposition between Goya and Renoir; to describe the contrasting fortunes of two con-cierge's daughters, one of whom 'marries into the servants' quarters' and the other becomes owner of a 'seventh floor flat with a terrace', Françoise Dorin compares the first to a Goya, the second to a Renoir (Dorin, 1973, p. 115).

[16] What is bought is not just a newspaper but also a generative principle producing opinions, atti-tudes, 'positions', defined by a distinctive position in a field of institutionalized position-generators. And we may postulate that a reader will feel more completely and adequately expressed, the more perfect the homology between his paper's position in the field of the press and the position he occupies in the field of the classes (or class fractions), the basis of his opinion-generating principle.

(eloquent) silence of *Le Nouvel Observateur* can only be fully understood when one knows that they accompany a steady rise in the educational level of the readership (which, here as elsewhere, is a reliable indicator of the level of transmission or supply of the corresponding messages), and a rise in the proportion of those class fractions—public-sector executives and teachers—who not only read most in general but also differ from all other groups by a particularly high rate of readership of the papers with the highest level of transmission (*Le Monde* and *Le Nouvel Observateur*); and, conversely, a decline in the proportion of those fractions—big commercial and industrial employers—who not only read least in general but also differ from other groups by a particularly high rate of readership of the papers with the lowest level of transmission (*France-Soir*, *L'Aurore*). To put it more simply, the structured space of discourses reproduces, in its own terms, the structured space of the newspapers and of the readerships for whom they are produced, with, at one end of the field, big commercial and industrial employers, *France-Soir* and *L'Aurore*, and, at the other end, public sector executives and teachers, *Le Monde* and *Le Nouvel Observateur*,[17] the central positions being occupied by private-sector executives, engineers and the professions and, as regards the press, *Le Figaro* and especially *L'Express*, which is read more or less equally by all the dominant-class fractions (except the commercial employers) and constitutes the neutral point in this universe.[18] Thus the space of judgments on the theatre is homologous with the space of the newspapers for which they are produced and which make them known; and also with the space of the theatres and plays about which they are formulated—these homologies and all the games they allow being made possible by the homology between each of these spaces and the space of the dominant class.

Let us now run through the space of the judgments aroused by the experimental stimulus of Françoise Dorin's play, moving from 'right' to 'left' and from 'right-bank' to 'left-bank'. First, *L'Aurore*: 'Cheeky Françoise Dorin is going to be in hot water with our *snooty*, *Marxist* intelligentsia (the two go together). The author of 'Un sale égoïste' shows no respect for the solemn *boredom*, profound emptiness and vertiginous nullity which characterize so many so-called 'avant-garde' theatrical productions. She dares to profane with sacrilegious laughter the notorious 'incommunicability of beings' which is the alpha and omega of the contemporary stage. And this perverse *reactionary*, who flatters the lowest appetites of consumer society, far from acknowledging the error of her ways and wearing her boulevard playwright's reputation with humility, has the impudence to prefer the jollity of Sacha Guitry, or Feydeau's bedroom farces, to the darkness visible of Marguerite Duras or Arrabal. This is a crime it will be difficult to forgive. Especially since she commits it with cheerfulness and gaiety, using all the dreadful devices which make lasting successes' (Gilbert Guilleminaud, *L'Aurore*, 12 January 1973).

Situated at the fringe of the intellectual field, at a point where he almost has to speak as an outsider ('our intelligentsia'), the *L'Aurore* critic does not mince his words

[17] Analysis of the overlaps in readership confirms that *France-Soir* is very close to *L'Aurore*; that *Le Figaro* and *L'Express* are more or less equidistant from all the others (*Le Figaro* inclining rather towards *France-Soir* whereas *L'Express* inclines towards the *Nouvel Observateur*); and that *Le Monde* and the *Nouvel Observateur* constitute a final cluster.

[18] Private-sector executives, engineers and the professions are characterized by a medium overall rate of readership and a distinctly higher rate of readership of *Le Monde* than businessmen and industrialists. (The private-sector executives remain closer to the industrialists by virtue of their quantity of low-level reading—*France-Soir*, *L'Aurore*—and also their high rate of readership of financial and business journals—*Les Echos*, *Information*, *Entreprise*—whereas the members of the professions are closer to the teachers by virtue of their rate of readership of the *Nouvel Observateur*.)

Table 2. *Degree of penetration of newspapers and weeklies in relation to fractions of the dominant class (no. of readers at the time of this survey among 1,000 heads of families in the relevant category)*

	France-Soir	L'Aurore	La Croix	Le Figaro	L'Express	Le Monde	Le Nouvel Observateur	Total
Commercial entrepreneurs	**170**	70	—	102	190	77	44	463
Industrialists	111	75	—	152	309	78	28	449
Private sector executives	**139**	**111**	51	197	368	221	82	750
Engineers	99	23	70	**218**	374	270	71	681
The professions	87	37	**54**	167	371	163	**131**	585
Civil servants Teachers	121	**100**	22	**234**	**375**	**385**	103	943
Literary and scientific professions	64	62	29	173	**398**	**329**	**217**	845
Total	118	72	31	178	335	231	99	

Bold figures indicate the two highest values in each column.

* This number, the sum of all readers in the given category, is obviously an approximation since it doesn't take account of double readership.

Source: CESP, study of press readership among top management and higher civil service, Paris, 1970.

(he calls a reactionary a reactionary) and does not hide his strategies. The rhetorical effect of putting words into the opponent's mouth, in conditions in which his discourse, functioning as an ironic antiphrasis, objectively says the opposite of what it means, presupposes and brings into play the very structure of the field of criticism and his relationship of immediate connivance with his public, based on homology of position.

From *L'Aurore* we move to *Le Figaro*. In perfect harmony with the author of *Le Tournant*—the harmony of orchestrated habitus—the *Figaro* critic cannot but experience absolute delight at a play which so perfectly corresponds to his categories of perception and appreciation, his view of the theatre and his view of the world:

How grateful we should be to Mme Françoise Dorin for being a *courageously light* author, which means to say that she is *wittily* dramatic, and *smilingly serious*, irreverent without fragility, pushing the comedy into outright vaudeville, *but* in the subtlest way imaginable; an author who wields satire *with elegance*, an author who at all times demonstrates astounding virtuosity. . . . Françoise Dorin knows *more than any of us* about the *tricks of the dramatist's art, the springs of comedy*, the *potential of a situation*, the comic or biting force of the *mot juste*. . . . Yes, what skill in taking things apart, what irony in the deliberate side-stepping, what mastery in the way she lets you see her pulling the strings! *Le Tournant* gives every sort of enjoyment without an ounce of self-indulgence or vulgarity. And without ever being facile either, since it is quite clear that right now, *conformism lies with the avant-garde*, absurdity lies in gravity and imposture in tedium. Mme Françoise Dorin will *relieve a well-balanced audience* by bringing them back into *balance* with healthy laughter. . . . Hurry and see for yourselves and I think you will *laugh so heartily* that you will forget to think how anguishing it can be for a writer to wonder if she is still in tune with the times in which she lives. . . . In the end it is a question everyone asks themselves and only humour and *incurable optimism* can free them from it! (Jean-Jacques Gautier, *Le Figaro*, 12 January 1973).

From *Le Figaro* one moves naturally to *L'Express*, which remains poised between endorsement and distance, thereby attaining a distinctly higher degree of euphemization:

It's bound to be a runaway success. . . . A witty and amusing play. A character. An actor who puts the part on like a glove: Jean Piat. With an *unfailing virtuosity that is only occasionally drawn out too long*, with a *sly cunning, a perfect mastery of the tricks of the trade*, Françoise Dorin has written a play on the 'turning point' in the Boulevard which is, ironically, the most traditional of Boulevard plays. *Only morose pedants will probe too far into the contrast between two conceptions of political life and the underlying private life.* The brilliant dialogue, full of *witticisms and epigrams*, is often viciously sarcastic. But Romain is not a caricature, he is much less stupid than the run-of-the-mill avant-garde writer. Philippe has *the plum role*, because he is on his own ground. What the author of 'Comme au théâtre' gently wants to suggest is that the Boulevard is where people speak and behave 'as in real life', and this is true, but it is only a partial truth, and not just because it is a class truth (Robert Kanters, *L'Express*, 15–21 January 1973).

Here the approval, which is still total, already begins to be qualified by systematic use of formulations that are ambiguous even as regards the oppositions involved: 'It's likely to be a runaway success', 'a sly cunning, a perfect mastery of the tricks of the trade', 'Philippe has the plum rôle', all formulae which could also be taken pejoratively. And we even find, surfacing through its negation, a glimmer of the other truth ('Only morose pedants will probe too far . . .') or even of the truth *tout court*, but doubly neutralized, by ambiguity and negation ('and not just because it is a class truth').

Le Monde offers a perfect example of ostentatiously neutral discourse, even-handedly dismissing both sides, both the overtly political discourse of *L'Aurore* and the disdainful silence of *Le Nouvel Observateur*:

The simple or simplistic argument is complicated by a very subtle 'two-tier' structure, as if there were two plays overlapping. One by Françoise Dorin, a conventional author, the other invented by Philippe Roussel, who tries to take 'the turning' towards modern theatre. This game performs a circular movement, like a boomerang. Françoise Dorin deliberately exposes the Boulevard clichés which Philippe attacks and, through his voice, utters a violent denunci-ation of the bourgeosie. On the second tier, she contrasts this language with that of a young author whom she assails with equal vigour. Finally, the trajectory brings the weapon back onto the Boulevard stage, and the futilities of the mechanism are unmasked by the devices of the traditional theatre, which have therefore lost nothing of their value. Philippe is able to declare himself a 'courageously light' playwright, inventing 'characters who talk like everybody'; he can claim that his art is 'without frontiers' and therefore non-political. However, the demon-stration is entirely distorted by the model avant-garde author chosen by Françoise Dorin. Vankovitz is an epigone of Marguerite Duras, a belated existentialist with militant leanings. He is caricatural in the extreme, as is the theatre that is denounced here ('A black curtain and a scaffold certainly help!' or the title of a play: 'Do take a little infinity in your coffee, Mr Karsov'). The audience gloats at this derisive picture of the modern theatre; the denunciation of the bourgeoisie is an amusing provocation inasmuch as it rebounds onto a detested victim and finishes him off. . . . To the extent that it reflects the state of bourgeois theatre and reveals its systems of defence, *Le Tournant* can be regarded as an *important work*. Few plays let through so much anxiety about an 'external' threat and *recuperate* it with so much unconscious fury (Louis Dandrel, *Le Monde*, 13 January 1973).

The ambiguity which Robert Kanters was already cultivating here reaches its peaks. The argument is 'simple *or* simplistic', take your pick; the play is split in two, offering two works for the reader to choose, a 'violent' but 'recuperatory' critique of the 'bourgeoisie' and a defence of non-political art. For anyone naïve enough to ask whether the critic is 'for or against', whether he finds the play 'good or bad', there are two answers: first, an 'objective informant's' dutiful report that the avant-garde author portrayed is 'caricatural in the extreme' and that 'the audience gloats (*jubile*)' (but without our knowing where the critic stands in relation to this audience, and therefore what the significance of this gloating is); then, after a series of judgments that are kept ambiguous by many reservations, nuances and academic attenuations ('Insofar as . . .', 'can be regarded as . . .'), the assertion that *Le Tournant* is 'an important work', but, be it noted, as a document illustrating the crisis of modern civilization, as they would say at *Sciences Po*.[19]

Although the silence of *Le Nouvel Observateur* no doubt signifies something in itself, we can form an approximate idea of what its position might have been by reading its review of Félicien Marceau's play *La preuve par quatre* or the review of *Le Tournant* by Philippe Tesson, then editor of *Combat*, published in *Le Canard Enchaîné*:

Theatre seems to me the wrong term to apply to these *society gatherings of tradesmen and businesswomen* in the course of which a famous and much loved actor recites the laboriously witty text of an equally famous author in the middle of an elaborate stage set, even a revolving one decorated with Folon's measured humour. . . . No 'ceremony' here, no 'catharsis' or 'revelation' either, still less improvisation. Just a warmed-up dish of plain cooking (*cuisine bourgeoise*) for stomachs that have seen it all before. . . . The audience, like all boulevard audiences in Paris, bursts out laughing, at the right time, in the most conformist places, wherever this spirit of easy-going rationalism comes into play. The connivance is perfect and the actors are all in on it. This play could have been written ten, twenty or thirty years ago (M Pierret, *Le Nouvel Observateur*, 12 February 1964, reviewing Felicien Marceau's *La preuve par quatre*).

Françoise Dorin *really knows a thing or two*. She's a first-rate *recuperator* and terribly *well-bred*. Her *Le Tournant* is an excellent Boulevard comedy, which works mainly on bad faith and demagogy. The lady wants to prove that avant-garde theatre is tripe. To do so, she takes a *big bag of tricks* and need I say that as soon as she pulls one out the *audience* rolls in the aisles and shouts for more. Our author, who was just waiting for that, does it again. She gives us a young lefty playwright called Vankovitz—get it?—and puts him in various ridiculous, uncomfortable and rather shady situations, to show that this young gentleman is no more disinterested, no less bourgeois, than you and I. What common sense, Mme Dorin, what lucidity and what honesty! You at least have the courage to stand by your opinions, and very healthy, red-white-and-blue ones they are too (Philippe Tesson, *Le Canard enchaîné*, 17 March 1973).

Presuppositions and misplaced remarks

Because the field is objectively polarized, critics on either side can pick out the same properties and use the same concepts to designate them ('crafty', 'tricks', 'common sense', 'healthy', etc.) but these concepts take on an ironic value ('common sense . . .') and thus function in reverse when addressed to a public which does not share the same relationship of connivance which is moreover strongly denounced ("as soon as she pulls one out, the audience rolls in the aisles" . . . "the author was just waiting for that". . . . Nothing more clearly shows than does the theatre, which can only work on the basis of total connivance between the author and the audience (this is why the correspondence between the categories of theatres and the divisions of the dominant class is so close and so visible), that the meaning and value of words (and especially

---

[19] This art of conciliation and compromise achieves the virtuosity of art for art's sake with the critic of *La Croix*, who laces his unconditional approval with such subtly articulated justifications, with understatements through double-negation, nuances, reservations and self-corrections, that the final *conciliatio oppositorum*, so naïvely jesuitical 'in form and substance', as he would say, almost seems to go without saying: '*Le Tournant*, as I have said, seems to me an admirable work, in both form and substance. This is not to say it will not put many people's teeth on edge. I happened to be sitting next to an unconditional supporter of the avant-garde and throughout the evening I was aware of his suppressed anger. However, I by no means conclude that Françoise Dorin is unfair to certain very respectable—albeit often tedious—experiments in the contemporary theatre. . . . And if she concludes—her preference is delicately hinted—with the triumph of the 'Boulevard'—but a boulevard that is itself avant-garde—that is precisely because for many years a master like Anouilh has placed himself as a guide at the crossroads of these two paths' (Jean Vigneron, *La Croix*, 21 January 1973).

jokes) depends on the market on which they are uttered; that the same sentences can take on opposite meanings when addressed to groups with opposite presuppositions. Françoise Dorin simply exploits the structural logic of the field of the dominant class when, presenting the misadventures of an avant-garde author to a boulevard audience, she turns against avant-garde theatre the weapon it likes to use against 'bourgeois' conversation and against the 'bourgeois theatre' which reproduces its truisms and clichés (one thinks of Ionesco, describing *The Bald Prima-Donna* or *Jacques* as 'a sort of parody or caricature of boulevard theatre, a boulevard theatre decomposing and becoming insane'). Breaking the relation of ethical and aesthetic symbiosis which links 'intellectual' discourse with its audience, she turns it into a series of *'misplaced' remarks* which shock or provoke laughter because they are not uttered in the appropriate place and before the appropriate audience. They become, in the literal sense, a *parody*, a discourse which establishes with its audience the immediate complicity of laughter only because it has persuaded them to reject the presuppositions of the parodied discourse, if indeed they ever accepted those presuppositions.

The foundations of connivance

It would be a mistake to regard the term-for-term relationship between the critics' discourse and the properties of their readerships as a sufficient explanation. If the polemical image each camp has of its opponents leaves so much room for this type of explanation, that is because it makes it possible to disqualify aesthetic or ethical choices by reference to the fundamental law of the field, by exposing cynical calculation as their source, e.g. the pursuit of success at all costs, even through provocation and scandal (more of a right-bank argument) or self-interested servility, with the theme (favoured on the left bank) of the 'lackey of the bourgeoisie'. In fact, the *partial objectifications* of self-interested polemics (which is what almost all studies of the 'intellectuals' amount to) miss the essential point by describing as the product of a conscious calculation what is, in fact, the almost miraculous encounter of two systems of interests (which may coexist in the person of the 'bourgeois' writer) or, more precisely, of the structural and functional homology between any given writer's or artist's position in the field of production and the position of his audience in the field of the classes and class fractions. The so-called *'écrivains de service'*, whose opponents accuse them of being the servants of the bourgeoisie, are justified in protesting that strictly speaking they serve no one: they serve objectively only because, with total sincerity, in full unawareness of what they are doing, they serve their own interests, i.e. specific interests, highly sublimated and euphemized, such as the 'interest' in a particular form of theatre or philosophy which is logically associated with a certain position in a certain field and which (except in periods of crisis) has every likelihood of masking its own political implications, even in the eyes of its protagonists. Through the logic of homologies, the practices and works of the agents in a specialized, relatively autonomous field of production are necessarily *overdetermined*; the functions they fulfil in the internal struggles are inevitably accompanied by external functions, which are conferred on them in the symbolic struggles among the fractions of the dominant class and, in the long run at least, among the classes.[20] Critics serve their reader-

---

[20] The logic of the functioning of the fields of cultural goods production as fields of struggle favouring strategies aimed at distinction means that the products of their functioning, whether *haute couture* 'creations' or novels, are predisposed to function *differentially*, as instruments of distinction, first between the class fractions and then between the classes.

ships so well only because the homology between their position in the intellectual field and their readership's position within the dominant-class field is the basis of an objective connivance (based on the same principles as that required by the theatre, especially for comedy) which means that they most sincerely, and therefore most effectively, defend the ideological interests of their clientele when defending their own interests as intellectuals against their specific adversaries, the occupants of opposing positions in the field of production.[21]

The power to convince

'Sincerity' (which is one of the preconditions of symbolic efficacy) is only possible— and only achieved—when there is a perfect and immediate harmony between the expectations inscribed in the position occupied (in a less consecrated universe, one would say 'the job description') and the dispositions of the occupant. It is impossible to understand how dispositions come to be adjusted to positions (so that the journalist is adjusted to his newspaper and consequently to that paper's readership, and the readers are adjusted to the paper and so to the journalist) unless one is aware that the objective structures of the field of production give rise to categories of perception which structure the perception and appreciation of its products. This explains how antithetical couples—of persons (all the '*maîtres à penser*') or institutions, newspapers (*Figaro/Nouvel Observateur*, or in a different practical context, *Nouvel Observateur/ Humanité*), theatres (right-bank/left-bank, private/subsidized, etc.) galleries pub- lishers, reviews, couturiers, etc.—can function as classificatory schemes, which exist and signify only in their mutual relations, and serve as landmarks or beacons. As is seen more clearly in avant-garde painting than anywhere else, a practical mastery of these markers, a sort of sense of social direction, is indispensable in order to be able to navigate in a hierarchically structured space in which movement is always fraught with the danger of losing class, in which *places*—galleries, theatres, publishing-houses—make all the difference (e.g. between 'commercial porn' and 'quality eroticism') because these sites designate an audience which, on the basis of the homology between the field of production and the field of consumption, qualifies the product consumed, helping to give it rarity or vulgarity. This practical mastery gives its possessors a 'nose' and a 'feeling', without any need for cynical calculation, for 'what needs to be done', where to do it, how, and with whom, in view of all that has been done and is being done, all those who are doing it, and where.[22] Choosing the right place of publication, the right publisher, journal, gallery or magazine is vitally important because for each author, each form of production and product, there is a corresponding *natural site* in the field of production, and producers or pro- ducts that are not in their right place are more or less bound to fail. All the homologies which guarantee a receptive audience and sympathetic critics for the producer who has found his place in the structure work in the opposite way for those who have strayed from their natural site. Avant-garde publishers and the producers of best-

[21] We can believe those critics most noted for their conformity to their expectations of their reader- ship when they insist that they never espouse their readers' opinions and often fight against them. Thus, Jean-Jacques Gautier (1972, pp. 25–26) rightly says that the effectiveness of his critiques stems not from a demagogic adjustment to the audience but from an objective agreement, which permits a perfect sincerity between critic and audience that is also essential in order to be *believed* and therefore efficacious.

[22] 'You're not informed like that, they're just things you feel . . . I didn't know exactly what I was doing. There are people who sent things in, I didn't know. . . . Information means having a vague sense, wanting to say things and coming across the right way. . . . It's lots of little things, it's feelings, not information' (painter, interview).

sellers both agree that they would inevitably come to grief if they took it into their heads to publish works objectively assigned to the opposite pole in the publishing universe: Minuit best-sellers and Laffont nouveaux romans. Similarly, in accordance with the law that one only ever preaches to the converted, a critic can only 'influence' his readers insofar as they extend him this power because they are structurally attuned to him in their view of the social world, their tastes and their whole habitus. Jean-Jacques Gautier gives a good description of this elective affinity between the journalist, his paper and his readers: a good *Figaro* editor, who has chosen himself and been chosen through the same mechanisms, chooses a *Figaro* literary critic because 'he has the right tone for speaking to the readers of the paper', because, without having deliberately tried, 'he naturally speaks the language of *Le Figaro*' and is the paper's 'ideal reader'. 'If tomorrow I started speaking the language of *Les Temps Modernes*, for example, or *Saintes Chapelles des Lettres*, people would no longer read me or understand me, so they would not listen to me, because I would be assuming a certain number of ideas or arguments which our readers don't give a damn about'.[23] To each position there correspond presuppositions, a doxa, and the homology between the producers' positions and their clients' is the precondition for this complicity, which is that much more strongly required when fundamental values are involved, as they are in the theatre. The fact that the choices whereby individuals join groups or groups co-opt individuals are oriented by a practical mastery of the laws of the field explains the frequent occurrence of the miraculous agreement between objective structures and internalized structures which enables the producers of cultural goods to produce objectively necessary and overdetermined discourses in full freedom and sincerity.

The sincerity in duplicity and euphemization which gives ideological discourse its particular symbolic force derives, firstly, from the fact that the specific interests—relatively autonomous with respect to class interests—attached to a position in a specialized field cannot be satisfied legitimately, and therefore efficiently, except at the cost of perfect submission to the laws of the field, i.e. in this particular case, disavowal of the usual form of interest; and, secondly, from the fact that the homology which exists between all fields of struggle organized on the basis of an unequal distribution of a particular kind of capital means that the highly censored and euphemized discourses and practices which are thus produced by reference to 'pure', purely 'internal' ends, are always predisposed to perform additional, external functions. They do so the more effectively the less aware they are aware of doing so, and when their adjustment to demand is not the product of conscious design but the result of a structural correspondence.

The long run and the short run

The fundamental principle of the differences between 'commercial' businesses and 'cultural' businesses is once again to be found in the characteristics of cultural goods

---

[23] Gautier, 1972, p. 26. Publishers are also perfectly aware that a book's success depends on where it is published. They know what is 'made for them' and what is not and observe that a certain book which was 'right for them' (e.g. Gallimard) has done badly with another publisher (e.g. Laffont). The adjustment between author and publisher and then between book and readership is thus the result of a series of choices which all involve the publisher's brand image. Authors choose their publisher in terms of this image, and he chooses them in terms of his own idea of his firm; readers are also influenced by their image of the publisher (e.g. 'Minuit is highbrow') which no doubt helps to explain the failure of 'misplaced' books. It is this mechanism which leads a publisher to say, quite correctly: 'Each publisher is the best in his category'.

Figure 1. Comparative growth in the sales of three books published by Editions de Minuit. Source: Editions de Minuit.

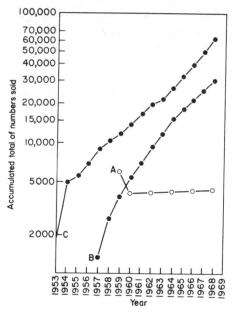

and of the market on which they are offered. A firm is that much closer to the 'commercial' pole (and, conversely, that much further from the 'cultural' pole), the more directly and completely the products it offers correspond to a pre-existent demand, i.e. to pre-existent interests, and in pre-established forms. This gives, on the one hand, a short production cycle, based on the concern to minimize risks by adjusting in advance to the identifiable demand and provided with marketing circuits and presentational devices (eye-catching dust-jackets, advertising, public relations, etc.) intended to ensure a rapid return of profits through rapid circulation of products with built-in obsolescence. On the other hand, there is a long production cycle, based on acceptance of the risk inherent in cultural investments[24] and above all on submission to the specific laws of the art trade. Having no market in the present, this entirely future-oriented production presupposes high-risk investments tending to build up stocks of products which may either relapse into the status of material objects (valued as such, by the weight of paper) or rise to the status of cultural objects endowed with an econ-

---

[24] It is said that Jean-Jacques Nathan (Fernand Nathan), who is regarded as being first and foremost a 'manager', defines publishing as 'a highly speculative trade'. The risks are indeed high and the chances of making a profit when publishing a young writer are minute. A novel which does not succeed may have a (short-term) life-span of less than three weeks; then there are the lost or damaged copies or those too soiled to be returned, and those that do come back reduced to the state of worthless paper. In the case of moderate short-term success, once the production costs, royalties and distribution costs are deducted, about 20% of the retail price is left for the publisher who has to offset the unsold copies, finance his stocks, and pay his overheads and taxes. But when a book extends its career beyond the first year and enters the back-list, it constitutes a financial 'flywheel' which provides the basis for forecasting and for a long-term investment policy. When the first edition has amortized the overheads, the book can be reprinted at a considerably lower cost-price and will guarantee a regular income (direct income and also supplementary royalties, translations, paperback editions, TV or film adaptations) which helps to finance further more or less risky investments that may also eventually build up the back-list.

omic value incommensurate with the value of the material components which go into producing them.[25]

The uncertainty and randomness characterizing the production of cultural goods can be seen in the sales curves of three works published by Editions de Minuit.[26] In Figure 1, curve A represents the sales of a prize-winning novel which, after a strong initial demand (of 6,143 copies distributed in 1959, 4,298 were sold by 1960, after deduction of unsold copies), achieves low annual sales (70 or so a year on average). Robbe Grillet's *La Jalousie* (curve B), published in 1957, sold only 746 copies in its first year and took four years to catch up with the initial sales of the prize-winning novel (in 1960), but, thanks to a steady annual rate of growth in sales (29% a year average from 1960 to 1964, 19% from 1964 to 1968), had achieved a total of 29,462 in 1968. Beckett's *En attendant Godot* (curve C) published in 1952, took five years to reach 10,000, but grew at a fairly steady 20% every year except 1963. From this point the curve begins to take on an exponential form and by 1968 (with an annual figure of 14,298) total sales had reached 64,897.

Time and money

Thus the various publishing houses can be characterized according to the distribution of their commitments between risky, long-term investments (*Godot*) and safe, short-term investments,[27] and, by the same token, according to the proportion of their authors, who are long-term or short-term writers. The latter include journalists extending their usual activity into 'current-affairs' books, 'personalities' presenting their 'personal testimony' in essays or memoirs and professional writers who stick to the rules of a tried and tested aesthetic (award-winning literature, best-selling novels, etc.).[28]

[25] Because of the unequal lengths of the cycle of production it is rarely meaningful to compare annual statements from different publishing houses. The annual statement gives an increasingly incomplete picture of the firm's real position, as one moves away from firms with rapid turn-over, i.e. as the proportion of long-cycle products in the firm's activity increases. For example, to assess the value of the stocks, one can consider the *production cost*, the *wholesale price*, which is unpredictable, or the *price of the paper*. These different methods of valuation very are unequally appropriate, depending on whether one is dealing with 'commercial' firms whose stock returns very rapidly to the state of printed paper or firms for which it constitutes a capital which constantly tends to appreciate.

[26] A further case, which cannot appear on the diagram, ought to be added—that of simple failure, i.e. a *Godot* whose career was over by the end of 1952 leaving a balance sheet badly in the red.

[27] Among the guaranteed short-term investments, we must also include all the publishing strategies designed to *exploit a backlist*: new editions, naturally, but also paperback editions (for Gallimard, this is the *Folio* series).

[28] Although one must never ignore the 'moiré' effect produced in every field by the fact that the different possible structurations (here, for example, according to age, size, degree of political and/or aesthetic avant-gardism) never coincide perfectly, the fact remains that the relative weight of long-term and short-term firms can probably be regarded as the dominant structuring principle of the field. In this respect, we find an opposition between the small avant-garde firms, Pauvert, Maspero and Minuit (to which one could add Bourgois, if it did not occupy a culturally and economically ambiguous position, because of its link with Les Presses de la Cité), and the 'big' publishers, Laffont, Presses de la Cité and Hachette, the intermediate positions being occupied by firms like Flammarion (where experimental series coexist with specially commissioned collective works) Albin Michel and Calmann-Lévy, old, 'traditional' publishing houses, run by 'heirs' whose heritage is both a strength and a brake, and above all Grasset, once a 'great' publishing house, now absorbed by the Hachette empire, and Gallimard, a former avant-garde firm that has now attained the peak of consecration and combines back-list exploitation with long-term undertakings (which are only possible on the basis of accumulated cultural capital—le Chemin, Bibliothèque des sciences humaines). The sub-field of firms mainly oriented towards long-term production and towards an 'intellectual' readership is polarized around the opposition between Maspero and Minuit (which represents the avant-garde moving towards conse-

Footnote continued overleaf

An examination of two publishing houses that are characteristic of the two poles of the publishing field, Robert Laffont and Editions de Minuit, will enable us to grasp the numerous aspects of the oppositions between the two sectors of the field. Robert Laffont is a large firm (700 employees) publishing a considerable number of new titles each year (about 200), overtly success-oriented (in 1976 it had seven prints of over 100,000 copies, fourteen of over 50,000 and fifty of over 20,000). This entails a large sales department, considerable expenditure on advertising and public relations (especially directed towards booksellers), and also a systematic policy of choices guided by a sense of the safe investment (until 1975, almost half the Laffont list consisted of translations of works already successful abroad) and the hunt for best-sellers (the list of 'famous names' with which Robert Laffont refutes those who 'refuse to recognize us as serious literary publishers' includes Bernard Clavel, Max Gallo, Françoise Dorin, Georges Emmanual Clancier and Pierre Rey). By contrast, Editions de Minuit, a small firm employing a dozen people, publishing fewer than twenty titles a year (by no more than about forty novelists or dramatists in twenty-five years), devoting a minute proportion of its turnover to publicity (and even deriving a strategic advantage from its refusal to use the lower forms of public relations), is quite used to sales under 500 ('P's first book, which sold more than 500 copies, was only our ninth') and print-runs under 3,000 (in 1975, it was stated that out of 17 new titles published in the three years since 1971, 14 had sold less than 3,000 copies and the other three had not gone beyond 5,000). The firm is always loss-making, if only its new publications are considered, but lives on its past investments, i.e. the profits regularly accruing from those of its publications which have become famous (e.g. *Godot*, which sold fewer than 200 copies in 1952 and 25 years later had sold more than 500,000 copies).

These two temporal structures correspond to two very different economic structures. Like all the other public companies (e.g. Hachette or Presses de la Cité) Laffont has an obligation to its shareholders (Time-Life in this case) to make profits, despite very substantial overheads, and so it must 'turn over' very rapidly what is essentially an economic capital (without taking the time required to convert it into cultural capital). Editions de Minuit does not have to worry about profits (which are partly redistributed to the personnel) and can plough back the income from its ever-growing assets into long-term undertakings. The scale of the firm and the volume of production not only influence cultural policy through the size of the overheads and the concern with getting a return on the capital; they also directly affect the behaviour of those responsible for selecting manuscripts. The small publisher, with the aid of a few advisors who are themselves 'house' authors, is able to have personal knowledge of all the books published. In short, everything combines to discourage the manager of a big publishing house from going in for high-risk, long term investments: the financial structure of his firm, the economic constraints which force him to seek a return on the capital, and therefore to think primarily in terms of sales, and the conditions in which he works, which make it practically impossible to have direct contact with manuscripts

Footnote continued

cration) on one side, and Gallimard, situated in the dominant position, with Le Seuil representing the neutral point in the field, (just as Gallimard whose authors feature both in the best-seller list and in the list of intellectual best-sellers, constitutes the neutral point of the whole field). The practical mastery of this structure, which also guides, for example, the founders of a newspaper when they 'feel there is an opening' or 'aim to fill a gap' left by the existing media, is seen at work in the rigorously topographical vision of a young publisher, Delorme, founder of Galilée, who was trying to fit in 'between Minuit, Maspero and Seuil' (quoted by J. Jossin, *L'Express*, 30 August 1976).

and authors.[29] By contrast, the avant-garde publisher is able to confront the financial risks he faces (which are, in any case, objectively smaller) by investing (in both senses) in undertakings which can, at best, bring only symbolically profits, but only on condition that he fully recognizes the specific stakes of the field of production and, like the writers or 'intellectuals' whom he publishes, pursues the sole specific profit awarded by the field, at least in the short term, i.e. 'renown' and the corresponding 'intellectual authority'.[30] The strategies which he applies in his relations with the press are perfectly adapted (without necessarily having been so conceived) to the objective demands of the most advanced fraction of the field, i.e. to the 'intellectual' ideal of negation, which demands refusal of temporal compromises and tends to establish a negative correlation between success and, true artistic value. Whereas short-cycle production, like *haute couture*, is heavily dependent on a whole set of agents and institutions specializing in 'promotion' (newspaper, magazine, TV and radio critics) which must be constantly maintained and periodically mobilized (with the annual literary prizes performing a function analogous to that of fashion 'collections'),[31] long-cycle production, which derives practically no benefit from the free publicity of press articles about the prize competitions and the prizes themselves, depends entirely on the activity of a few 'talent-spotters', i.e. avant-garde authors and critics who 'make' the publishing-house by giving it credit (by publishing with it, taking manuscripts there and speaking well of authors published by it) and expect it to merit their confidence by refraining from discrediting itself with excessively brilliant worldly successes ('Minuit would be devalued in the eyes of the hundred people around Saint-Germain who really count if it won the *Prix Goncourt*') and thereby discrediting those who are published by it or praise its publications ('intellectuals think less of writers who win prizes'; 'the ideal career for a young writer is a slow one').[32] It also depends on the educational system, which alone can provide those who preach in the desert with devotees and followers capable of recognizing their virtues.

The total opposition between *best-sellers*, here today and gone tomorrow, and *classics*, best-sellers over the long run, which owe their consecration, and therefore their widespread durable market, to the educational system,[33] is the basis not only of two completely different ways of organizing production and marketing, but also

[29] It is well-known in the 'trade' that the head of one of the largest French publishing houses reads hardly any of the manuscripts he publishes and that his working day is devoted to purely managerial tasks (production committee meetings, meetings with lawyers, heads of subsidiaries, etc.).

[30] In fact most of his professional actions are 'intellectual acts', analogous to the signature of literary or political manifestos or petitions (with some risks, as well—consider the publication of *La Question*) which earn him the usual gratifications of 'intellectuals' (intellectual prestige, interviews, radio discussions, etc.).

[31] Robert Laffont recognizes this dependence when, in order to explain the declining ratio of translations to original works, he invokes, in addition to the increased advances payable for translation rights, 'the decisive influence of the media, especially television and radio, in promoting a book': 'The author's personality and eloquence are an important factor in these media's choices and consequently in access to the public. In this respect, foreign authors, with the exception of a few international celebrities, are naturally at a disadvantage' (*Vient de paraître*—Robert Laffont's monthly publicity bulletin—January 1977).

[32] Here too, cultural logic and 'economic' logic converge. As the fate of Les Éditions du Pavois shows, a literary prize can be disastrous, from a strictly 'economic' point of view, for a young publishing house suddenly faced with the enormous investments required to reprint and distribute a prize-winning book.

[33] This is seen particularly clearly in the theatre, where the classics market (the 'classical matinées' at the Comédie Française) obeys quite specific rules because of its dependence on the educational system.

of two contrasting images of the activity of the writer and even the publisher, a simple businessman or a bold 'talent-spotter' who will succeed only if he is able to sense the *specific laws* of a market yet to come, i.e. espouse the interests and demands of those who will make those laws, the writers he publishes.[34] There are also two opposing images of the criteria of success. For 'bourgeois' writers and their readers, success is intrinsically a guarantee of value. That is why, in this market, the successful get more successful. Publishers help to make best-sellers by printing further impressions; the best thing a critic can do for a book or play is to predict 'success' for it ('It's bound to be a runaway success'—R. Kanters, *L'Express*, 15–21 January 1973; 'I put my money on success for *Le Tournant* with my eyes closed'—Pierre Marcabru, *France-Soir*, 12 January 1973). Failure, of course, is an irrevocable condemnation; a writer without a public is a writer without talent (the same Robert Kanters refers to 'playwrights without talent and without an audience, such as Arrabal').

As for the opposing camp's vision, in which success is suspect[35] and asceticism in this world is the precondition for salvation in the next, its basis lies in the economy of cultural production itself, according to which, investments are recompensed only if they are in a sense thrown away, like a gift, which can only achieve the most precious return gift, gratitude (*reconaissance*—recognition), so long as it is experienced as a one-way transaction; and, as with the gift, which it converts into pure generosity by masking the expected return-gift which the synchronization of barter reveals, it is the *intervening time* which provides a screen and disguises the profit awaiting the most disinterested investors.

Orthodoxy and heresy

The eschatological vision structuring the opposition between avant-garde and 'bourgeois' art, between the material ascesis which guarantees spiritual consecration, and worldly success, which is marked, *inter alia*, by institutional recognition (prizes, academies, etc.) and by financial rewards, helps to disguise the true relationship between the field of cultural production and the field of power, by reproducing the opposition (which does not rule out complementarity) between the dominated and dominant fractions of the dominant class, i.e. between cultural power (associated with less economic wealth) and economic and political power (associated with less cultural wealth), in the specific logic of the intellectual field, i.e. in the transfigured form of the conflict between two aesthetics. Specifically aesthetic conflicts about the legitimate vision of the world, i.e. in the last resort, about what deserves to be represented and the right way to represent it, are political conflicts (appearing in their most euphemized form) for the power to impose the dominant definition of reality, and social

---

[34] The same opposition is found in all fields. André de Baecque describes the opposition he sees as characterizing the theatrical field, between the 'businessmen' and the 'militants': 'Theatre managers are people of all sorts. They have one thing in common; with each new show, they put an investment of money and talent at risk on an unpredictable market. But the similarity stops there. Their motivations spring from very different ideologies. For some, the theatre is a financial speculation like any other, more picturesque perhaps, but giving rise to the same cold-blooded strategy made up of the taking of options, calculated risks, liquidity problems, exclusive rights, sometimes negotiated internationally. For others, it is the vehicle of a message, or the tool of a mission. Sometimes a militant even does good business . . .' (de Baecque, 1968).

[35] Without going so far as to make failure a guarantee of quality, as the 'bourgeois' writer's polemical vision would have it: 'Nowadays, if you want to succeed, you need failures. Failure inspires confidence. Success is suspect' (Dorin, 1973, p. 46).

reality in particular. On the right, reproductive art[36] constructed in accordance with the generative schemes of 'straight', 'straight-forward' representation of reality, and social reality in particular, i.e. orthodoxy (e.g. par excellence, 'bourgeois theatre') is likely to give those who perceive it in accordance with these schemes the reassuring experience of the immediate self-evidence of the representation, i.e. of the necessity of the mode of representation and of the world represented. This orthodox art would be timeless if it were not continuously pushed into the past by the movement brought into the field of production by the dominated fractions' insistence on using the powers they are granted to change the world-view and overturn the temporal and *temporary* hierarchies to which 'bourgeois' taste clings. As holders of an (always partial) delegated legitimacy in cultural matters, cultural producers—especially those who produce solely for other producers—always tend to divert their authority to their own advantage and therefore to impose their own variant of the dominant world-view as the only legitimate one. But the challenging of the established artistic hierarchies and the heretical displacement of the socially accepted limit between what does and does not deserve to be preserved, admired and transmitted cannot achieve its specifically artistic effect of subversion unless it tacitly recognizes the fact and the legitimacy of such delimitation by making the shifting of that limit an artistic act and thereby claiming for the artist a monopoly in legitimate transgression of the boundary between the sacred and the profane, and therefore a monopoly in revolutions in artistic taxonomies.

The field of cultural production is the area par excellence of clashes between the dominant fractions of the dominant class, who sometimes fight there in person but more often through producers oriented towards defending their 'ideas' and satisfying their 'tastes', and the dominated fractions who are totally involved in this struggle.[37] This conflict brings about the integration in a single field of the various socially specialized sub-fields, particular markets which are completely separate in social and even geographical space, in which the different fractions of the dominant class can find products adjusted to their tastes, whether in the theatre, in painting, fashion or decoration.

The 'polemical' view which makes a sweeping condemnation of all economically powerful firms ignores the distinction between those which are only rich in economic capital, and treat cultural goods—books, plays or pictures—as ordinary products, i.e. as sources of immediate profit, and those which derive a sometimes very substantial economic profit from the cultural capital which they originally accumulated through strategies based on denial of the 'economy'. The differences in the scale of the businesses, measured by turnover or staff, are matched by equally decisive differences in their relation to the 'economy' which, among recently established smaller firms, separate the small 'commercial' publishers, often heading for rapid growth, such as

---

36 'Oh dear! All I do is reproduce what I see and hear, just arranging it and adapting it. Just my luck! What I see is always attractive, what I hear is often funny. I live in luxury and champagne bubbles' (Dorin, 1973, p. 27). There is no need to evoke reproductive painting, nowadays incarnated by the 'impressionists' who are known to supply the publishers specialising in reproductions of works of art with all their best-sellers (apart from the *Mona Lisa*): Renoir (*Girl with Flowers, Le Moulin de la Galette*), Van Gogh (*L'eglise d'Auvers*), Monet (*Les coquelicots*), Degas (*Ballet Rehearsal*) Gauguin (*Peasant Women*) (information supplied by the Louvre, 1973). In the literary field, there is the vast output of biographies, memoirs, diaries and testimonies, which, from Laffont to Lattès, from Nielsen to Orban, provide 'bourgeois' readers with alternative 'real-life' experiences.

37 In literature, as elsewhere, full-time producers (and, *a fortiori*, producers for producers) are far from having a monopoly of production. Out of 100 people in *Who's Who* who have produced literary works, more than a third are non-professionals (industrialists, 14%; senior civil servants, 11%; doctors, 7% etc.) and the proportion of part-time producers is even greater in the areas of political writing (45%) and general writing (48%).

Lattès, Laffont (as distinct from Robert Laffont), Orban, Authier or Mengès[38] and the small avant-garde publishers, which are often short-lived (Galilée, France Adèle, Entente, Phébus), just as, at the other extreme, they separate the 'great publisher' from the 'big publisher', a great consecrated publisher like Gallimard from a big 'book merchant' like Nielsen.

Without entering into a systematic analysis of the field of the galleries, which, owing to the homology with the field of publishing, would lead to repetitions, we may simply observe that, here too, the differences which separate the galleries according to their seniority (and their celebrity), and therefore according to the degree of consecration and the market value of the works they own, are replicated by differences in their relation to the 'economy'. The 'sales galleries', having no 'stable' of their own (e.g. Beaubourg) exhibit, in relatively eclectic fashion, painters of very different periods, schools and ages, (abstracts as well as post-surrealists, a few European hyper-realists, some new realists), i.e. whose greater 'accessibility' (owing to their more classic status or their 'decorative' potential) can find purchasers outside the circle of professional and semi-professional collectors (among the 'jet-set executives' and 'trendy industrialists' as an informant put it). This enables them to pick out and attract a fraction of the avant-garde painters who have already been 'noticed' by offering them a slightly compromising form of consecration, i.e. a market in which the prices are much higher than in the avant-garde galleries.[39] By contrast, galleries like Sonnabend, Denise René or Durand-Ruel, which mark dates in the history of painting because they have been able in their time to assemble a 'school', are characterized by a *systematic slant*.[40] Thus in the succession of painters presented by the Sonnabend gallery one can see the logic of an artistic development which leads from the 'new American painting' and Pop Art, with painters such as Rauschenberg, Jaspers Johns, Jim Dine, to Oldenburg, Lichtenstein, Wesselman, Rosenquist, Warhol, sometimes classified under the label Minimal Art, and to the most recent innovations of *art pauvre*, conceptual art and art by correspondence. Likewise, there is a clear connection between the geometric abstraction which made the name of the Denise René gallery (founded in 1945 and inaugurated with a Vasarely exhibition) and kinetic art, with artists such as Max Bill and Vasareley forming a sort of link between the visual experiments of the inter-war years (especially the Bauhaus) and the optical and technological experiments of the new generation.

Ways of growing old

The opposition between the two economies, i.e. between two relationships to the 'economy', can thus be seen as an opposition between two life-cycles of the cultural-

[38] Among the latter, one could also distinguish between those who have come into publishing with explicitly commercial aims, such as Jean-Claude Lattès, who started as a press attaché with Laffont and originally saw his project as a Laffont series (Edition spéciale), or Olivier Orban (both of whom went straight for commissioned stories), and those who have fallen back on 'pot-boilers' after various abortive projects such as Guy Authier or Jean-Paul Mengès.

[39] By the same logic, the discoverer-publisher is always liable to see his 'discoveries' seduced by richer or more consecrated publishers, who offer their name, their reputation, their influence on prize juries, and also publicity and better royalties.

[40] As opposed to the Sonnabend gallery, which brings together young (the oldest is 50) but already relatively recognized painters, and to the Durand-Ruel gallery, whose painters are almost all dead and famous, the Denise René gallery, which stands in that particular point in the space-time of the artistic field in which the normally incompatible profits of the avant-garde and of consecration are momentarily superimposed, combines a group of already strongly consecrated painters (abstract) with an avant-garde or rear avant-garde group (kinetic art) as if it had momentarily managed to escape the dialectic of distinction which sweeps schools away into the past.

production business, two different ways in which firms, producers and products *grow old*.[41] The trajectory leading from the avant-garde to consecration and the trajectory leading from the small firm to the 'big' firm are mutually exclusive. The small commercial firm has no more chance of becoming a great consecrated firm than the big 'commercial' writer (e.g. Guy des Cars or Cécil Saint-Laurent) has of occupying a recognized position in the consecrated avant-garde. In the case of 'commercial' firms, whose sole target is the accumulation of 'economic' capital and which can only get bigger or disappear (through bankruptcy or take-over), the only pertinent distinction concerns the size of the firm, which tends to grow with time; in the case of firms characterized by a high degree of disavowal of the 'economy' and submission to the specific logic of the cultural goods economy, the chronological opposition between the newcomers and the old-established, the challengers and the veterans, the avant-garde and the 'classic' tends to merge with the 'economic' opposition between the poor and the rich (who are *also* the big), the 'cheap' and the 'dear', and ageing is almost inevitably accompanied by an 'economic' transformation of the relation to the 'economy', i.e. a moderating of the denial of the 'economy' which is in dialectical relation with the scale of business and the size of the firm. The only defence against 'getting old' is a refusal to 'get fat' through profits and for profit, a refusal to enter the dialectic of profit which, by increasing the size of the firm and consequently the overheads, imposes a pursuit of profit through larger markets, leading to the devaluation entailed in a 'mass appeal'.[42]

A firm which enters the phase of exploiting accumulated cultural capital runs two different economies simultaneously, one oriented towards production, authors and innovation (in the case of Gallimard, this is the series edited by Georges Lambrichs) the other towards exploiting its resources and marketing its consecrated products (with series such as the Pléiade editions and especially *Folio* or Idées). It is easy to imagine the contradictions which result from the incompatibility of the two economies. The organization appropriate for producing, marketing and promoting one category of products is totally unsuited for the other. Moreover, the weight of the constraints which management and marketing bring to bear on the institution and on ways of thinking tends to rule out high-risk investments, when, that is, the authors who might give rise to them are not already turned towards other publishers by the firm's prestige. (They may equally be discouraged by the fact that the 'intellectual' series tend to pass unnotice when they appear in lists in which they are 'out of place' or even 'incongruous' e.g. as an extreme case, Laffont's '*Ecarts*' and '*Change*' series.) It goes without saying that though the disappearance of the firm's founder may accelerate

[41] The analytical opposition between the two economies implies no value judgment, although in the ordinary struggles of artistic life it is only ever expressed in the form of value judgments and although despite all the efforts to distance and objectify, it is liable to be read in polemical terms. As I have shown elsewhere, the categories of perception and appreciation (e.g. obscure/clear or easy, deep/light, original/banal, etc.) which function in the world of art are oppositions that are almost universally applicable and are based, in the last analysis, through the opposition between rarity and divulgation or vulgarization, uniqueness and multiplicity, quality and quantity, on the social opposition between the 'elite' and the 'masses', between 'elite' (or 'quality') products and 'mass' products.

[42] This effect is perfectly visible in haute couture or perfumery, where the consecrated establishments are able to keep going for several generations (e.g. Caron, Chanel and especially Guerlain) only by means of a policy aimed at artificially perpetuating the rarity of the product (e.g. the 'Exclusive concessions' which limit sales outlets to a few places which are themselves chosen for their rarity—the great couturiers' own shops, perfume shops in the smartest districts, airports). Since ageing is here synonymous with vulgarization, the oldest brands (Coty, Lancôme, Worth, Molyneux, Bourjois, etc.) have a second career, down-market.

the process, it is not sufficient to explain a process which is inscribed in the logic of the development of cultural businesses.

The differences which separate the small avant-garde firms from the 'big firms' and 'great publishers' have their equivalents in the differences that can be found, among the products, between the 'new' product, temporarily without 'economic' value, the 'old' product, irretrievably devalued, and the 'ancient' or 'classic' product, which has a constant or constantly growing 'economic' value. One also finds similar differences among the producers, between the avant-garde, recruited mainly among the (biologically) young, without being limited to a generation, 'finished' or 'outdated' authors or artists (who may be biologically young), and the consecrated avant-garde, the 'classics'.

The classical and the old-fashioned

It is clear that the primacy the field of cultural production gives to youth can, once again, be traced back to the basis of the field in the rejection of power and of the 'economy'. The reason why 'intellectuals' and artists always tend to align themselves with 'youth' in their manner of dress and in their whole bodily *hexis* is that, in representations as in reality, the opposition between the 'old' and the 'young' is homologous with the opposition between power and 'bourgeois' seriousness on the one hand, and indifference to power or money and the 'intellectual' refusal of the 'spirit of seriousness', on the other hand. The 'bourgeois' world-view, which measures age by power or by the corresponding relation to power, endorses this opposition when it identifies the 'intellectual' with the young 'bourgeois' by virtue of their common status as dominated fractions of the dominant group, from whom money and power are temporarily withheld.[43]

But the priority given to 'youth' and to the associated values of change and originality cannot be understood solely in terms of the relationship between 'artists' and 'bourgeois'. It also expresses the specific law of change in the field of production, i.e. the dialectic of distinction whereby institutions, schools, artists and works which are inevitably associated with a moment in the history of art, which have 'marked a date' or which 'become dated', are condemned to fall into the past and to become *classic* or *out-dated*, to drop into the 'dustbin' of history or become part of history, in the eternal present of *culture*, where schools and tendencies that were totally incompatible 'in their time' can peacefully coexist because they have been canonized, academicized and neutralized.

---

[43] We may therefore formulate the hypothesis that acquisition of the social indices of maturity, which is both the condition and the effect of accession to positions of power, and abandonment of the practices associated with adolescent irresponsibility (to which cultural and even political 'avant-gardist' practices belong) have to be more and more precocious as one moves from the artists to the teachers, from the teachers to the members of the professions, and from the professions to the employers; or to put it another way, that the members of the same biological age-group, e.g. all the students in the *grandes écoles*, have different social ages, marked by different symbolic attributes and conducts, according to the objective future they are heading for. The Beaux-Arts student has to be *younger* than the *normalien*, and the *normalien* has to be *younger* than the *Polytechnicien* or the student at ENA. One would have to apply the same logic in analysing the relationship between the sexes within the dominant fraction of the dominant class and more specifically the effects on the division of labour (especially in culture and art) of the dominated-dominant position assigned to women in the 'bourgeoisie' which brings them relatively closer to the young 'bourgeois' and the 'intellectuals', predisposing them to the rôle of *mediator between the dominant and dominated fractions* (which they have always played, particularly through the 'salons').

Being different

It is not sufficient to say that the history of the field is the history of the struggle for the monopolistic power to impose the legitimate categories of perception and appreciation. The *struggle itself* creates the history of the field; through the struggle the field is given a temporal dimension. The ageing of authors, works or schools is something quite different from the product of a mechanical slippage into the past. It is the continuous creation of the battle between those who have made their names (*fait date*) and are struggling to stay in view and those who cannot make their own names without relegating to the past the established figures, whose interest lies in freezing the movement of time, fixing the present state of the field for ever. On one side are the dominant figures, who want continuity, identity, reproduction; on the other, the newcomers, who seek discontinuity, difference, revolution. To 'make one's name' (*faire date*) means making one's *mark*, achieving recognition (in both senses) of one's *difference* from other producers, especially the most consecrated of them; at the same time, it means *creating a new position* beyond the positions presently occupied, *ahead* of them, in the *avant-garde*. To introduce difference is to produce time. Hence the importance, in this struggle for life and survival, of the *distinctive marks* which, at best, aim to identify what are often the most superficial and most visible properties of a set of works or producers. Words—the names of schools or groups, proper names— are so important only because they make things. These distinctive signs produce existence in a world in which the only way to *be* is to be *different*, to 'make one's name', either personally or as a group. The names of schools or groups which have proliferated in recent painting (pop art, minimal art, process art, land art, body art, conceptive art, *arte povera*, Fluxus, new realism, *nouvelle figuration*, *support-surface*, *art pauvre*, op art, kinetic art, etc.) are pseudo-concepts, *practical* classifying tools which create resemblances and differences by naming them; they are produced in the *struggle for recognition* by the artists themselves or their accredited critics and function as *emblems* which distinguish galleries, groups and artists and therefore the products they make or sell.[44]

As the newcomers come into existence, i.e. accede to legitimate difference, or even, for a certain time, exclusive legitimacy, they necessarily push back into the past the consecrated producers with whom they are compared, 'dating' their products and the taste of those who remain attached to them. Thus the various galleries or publishing houses, like the various artists or writers, are distributed at every moment according to their artistic age, i.e. according to the age of their mode of artistic production and the degree to which this generative scheme, which is also a scheme of perception and appreciation, has been canonized and secularized. The field of the galleries reproduces *in synchrony* the history of artistic movements since the late nineteenth century. Each major gallery was an avant-garde gallery at some time or other, and it is that much more famous and that much more capable of consecrating (or, which amounts to the same thing, sells that much more dearly), the more distant

---

44 Academic criticism is condemned to interminable arguments about the definition and scope of these pseudo-concepts, which are generally no more than names which identify practical groupings such as the painters assembled in an outstanding exhibition or a consecrated gallery or the authors on the list of the same publisher (and which are worth neither more nor less than convenient associations such as 'Denise René is geometric abstract', 'Alexandre Iolas is Max Ernst', or, among the painters, 'Arman is dustbins' or 'Christo is packages') and many concepts in literary or artistic criticism are no more than a 'learned' designation of similar practical groupings (e.g. 'littérature objectale' for 'nouveau roman', itself standing for 'all the novelists published by Editions de Minuit').

its *floruit*, the more widely known and recognized its 'brand' ('geometrical abstract' or 'American pop') but also the more it is encapsulated in that 'brand' ('Durand-Ruel, the Impressionist dealer'), in a pseudo-concept which is also a destiny.

At every moment, in whichever field (the field of class struggles, the field of the dominant class, the field of cultural production), the agents and institutions involved in the game are at once contemporaries and out of phase. The *field of the present* is just another name for the field of struggles (as shown by the fact that an author of the past is present exactly insofar as he is at stake) and contemporaneity in the sense of presence in the same present, in the present and presence of others, exists, in practice, only in the struggle which synchronizes discordant times (so that, as I hope to show elsewhere, one of the major effects of great historical crises, of the events which *make history* (*font date*), is that they synchronize the times of fields defined by specific structural durations). But the struggle which *produces* contemporaneity in the form of the confrontation of different times can only take place because the agents and groups it brings together are not present in the same present. One only has to think of a particular field (painting, literature or the theatre) to see that the agents and institutions who clash, objectively at least, through competition and conflict, are separated in time and in terms of time. One group, situated at the vanguard, have no contemporaries with whom they exchange recognition (apart from other avant-garde producers), and therefore no audience, except in the future. The other group, commonly called the 'conservatives', only recognize their contemporaries in the past. The temporal movement resulting from the appearance of a group capable of 'making history' by establishing an advanced position induces a displacement of the structure of the field of the present, i.e. of the chronological hierarchy of the opposing positions in a given field (e.g. pop art, kinetic art and figurative art). Each position is moved down one rung in the chronological hierarchy which is at the same time a social hierarchy. The avant-garde is at every moment separated by an artistic generation (i.e. the gap between two modes of artistic production) from the consecrated avant-garde, which is itself separated by another artistic generation from the avant-garde that was already consecrated at the moment it entered the field. This is why, in the space of the artistic field as in social space, distances between styles or life-styles are never better measured than in terms of time.[45]

The consecrated authors who dominate the field of production also dominate the market; they are not only the most expensive or the most profitable but also the most readable and the most acceptable because they have become part of 'general culture' through a process of familiarization which may or may not have been accompanied by specific teaching. This means that through them, the strategies directed against their domination always additionally hit the distinguished consumers of their distinctive products. To bring a new producer, a new product and a new system of tastes onto the market at a given moment, is to push the whole set of producers, products and systems of tastes into the past. The process whereby the field of production becomes a temporal structure also defines the temporal status of taste. Because the different positions in the hierarchical space of the field of production (which can be equally well

[45] Tastes can be 'dated', by reference to what was avant-garde taste in different periods: 'Photography is outdated'. 'Why?' 'Because it's gone out of fashion; because it's linked to the conceptual art of two or three years ago' .'Who would say this: "When I look at a picture, I'm not interested in what it represents"?' 'Nowadays, people who don't know much about art. Its typical of someone who has no idea about art to say that. *Twenty years ago*, I don't even know if twenty years ago the abstract painters would have said that, I don't think so. It's the sort of person who doesn't know anything and who says, "You can't fool me, what counts is whether it's pretty" ' (Avant-garde painter, age 35).

identified by the names of institutions, galleries, publishers and theatres or by the names of artists or schools) are at the same time tastes in a social hierarchy, every transformation of the structure of the field leads to a displacement of the structure of tastes, i.e. of the system of symbolic distinctions between groups. Oppositions homologous with those existing today between the taste of avant-garde artists, the taste of 'intellectuals', advanced 'bourgeois' taste and provincial 'bourgeois' taste, which find their means of expression on markets symbolized by the Sonnabend, Denise René or Durand-Ruel galleries, would have been able to express themselves equally effectively in 1945, when Denise René represented the avant-garde, or in 1875, when Durand-Ruel was in that position.

This model is particularly relevant nowadays, because owing to the near-perfect unification of the artistic field and its history, each artistic act which 'makes history' by introducing a new position into the field 'displaces' the whole series of previous artistic acts. Because the whole series of pertinent events is practically present in the latest, in the same way that the six digits already dialled on the telephone are contained in the seventh, an aesthetic act is irreducible to any other act in a different place in the series and the series itself tends towards uniqueness and irreversibility. As Marcel Duchamp points out, this explains why *returns* to past styles have never been more frequent than in these times of frenetic pursuit of originality:

The characteristic of the century now coming to an end is that it is like a double-barrelled gun. Kandinsky and Kupka invented abstraction. Then abstraction died. No one was going to talk about it any more. It came back thirty-five years later with the American abstract expressionists. You could say that cubism reappeared in an impoverished form in the post-war Paris school. Dada came back in the same way. A second shot, second wind. It's a phenomenon typical of this century. You didn't find that in the 18th or 19th centuries. After the Romantics, came Courbet. And Romanticism never came back. Even the pre-Raphaelites aren't a rehash of the Romantics.[46]

In fact, these are always *apparent* returns, since they are separated from what they rediscover by a negative reference to something which was itself the negation (of the negation of the negation, etc.) of what they rediscover (when, that is, the intention is not simply of pastiche, a parody which presupposes all the intervening history).[47] In the present stage of the artistic field, there is no room for naïvety, and every act, every gesture, every event, is, as a painter nicely put 'a sort of nudge or wink between accomplices'.[48] In and through the games of distinction, these winks and nudges, silent, hidden references to other artists, past or present, confirm a complicity which excludes the layman, who is always bound to miss what is essential, namely the inter-relations and interactions of which the work is only the silent trace. Never has the very structure of the field been present so practically in every act of production.

Never too has the irreducibility of the work of cultural production to the artist's

[46] Interview published in VH 101, 3, Autumn 1970, pp. 55–61.

[47] That is why it would be naïve to think that the relationship between the age and the degree of accessibility of works of art disappears when the logic of distinction leads to a (second-degree) return to an old mode of expression (e.g. at present, 'neo-dadaism', 'new realism', or 'hyperrealism').

[48] This game of nudges and winks, which has to be played very fast and very 'naturally', even more mercilessly excludes the 'failure', who makes the same kind of moves as everybody else, but out of phase, usually too late, who falls into all the traps, a clumsy buffoon who ends up serving as a foil for those who make him their unwilling or unwitting accomplice; unless, finally understanding the rule of the game, he turns his status into a choice and makes systematic failure his artistic speciality. (Apropos of a painter who perfectly illustrates this trajectory, another painter said admirably: 'Once he was just a bad painter who wanted to succeed, now he's doing work on a bad painter who wants to succeed. It's excellent'.)

own labour appeared so clearly. The primary reason is that the new definition of the artist and of artistic work brings the artist's work closer to that of the 'intellectual' and makes it more dependent than ever on 'intellectual' commentaries. Whether as a critic but also the leader of a school (e.g. Restany and the new realists), or as a fellow-traveller contributing his reflexive discourse to the production of a work which is always in part its own commentary or to reflection on an art which often itself incorporates a reflection on art, the intellectual has never before so directly participated, through his work on art and the artist, in an artistic work which always consists partly of *working on himself* as an artist. Accompanied by historians writing the chronicles of their discoveries, by philosophers who comment on their 'acts' and who interpret and over-interpret their works, artists can constantly invent the distinguishing strategies on which their artistic survival depends, only by putting into their practice the practical mastery of the objective truth of their practice, thanks to the combination of knowingness and naïvety, calculation and innocence, faith and bad faith that is required by *mandarin games*, cultivated games with the inherited culture, whose common feature is that they identify 'creation' with the introduction of *deviations* (*écarts*), which only the initiated can perceive, with respect to forms and formulae that are known to all. The emergence of this new definition of the artist and his craft cannot be understood independently of the transformations of the artistic field. The constitution of an unprecedented array of institutions for recording, preserving and analysing works (reproductions, catalogues, art journals, museums acquiring the most modern works, etc.), the growth in the personnel employed, full-time or part-time, in the *celebration* of works of art, the increased circulation of works and artists, with great international exhibitions and the increasing number of chains of galleries with branches in many countries—all combine to favour the establishment of an unprecedented relationship between the body of interpreters and the work of art, analogous to that found in the great esoteric traditions. To such an extent that one has to be blind not to see that discourse about a work is not a mere accompaniment, intended to assist its perception and appreciation, but a stage in the production of the work, of its meaning and value. But once again it is sufficient to quote Marcel Duchamp:

Q.   But to come back to your ready-mades, I thought that R. Mutt, the signature on The Fountain, was the manufacturer's name. But in an article by Rosalind Krauss, I read: 'R. Mutt, a pun on the German, Armut, or poverty'. 'Poverty' would entirely change the meaning of The Fountain.

M.D. Rosalind Krauss? The redhead? It isn't that at all. You can deny it. Mutt comes from Mott Works, the name of a big firm that makes sanitary equipment. But Mott was too close, so I made it Mutt, because there was a strip cartoon in the papers in those days, Mutt and Jef, everybody knew it. So right from the start there was a resonance. Mutt was a fat little guy, and Jef was tall and thin . . . I wanted a different name. And I added Richard . . . Richard is a good name for a loo! You see, it's the opposite of poverty. . . . But not even that, just R.—R. Mutt.

Q.   What possible interpretation is there of the Bicycle Wheel? Should one see it as the integration of movement into the work of art? Or as a fundamental point of departure, like the Chinese who invented the wheel?

M.D. That machine has no intention, except to get rid of the appearance of a work of art. It was a whim. I didn't call it a work of art. I wanted to throw off the desire to create works of art. Why do works have to be static? The thing—the bicycle wheel—came before the idea. Without any intention of making a song and dance about it, not at all so as to say: '*I* did that, and nobody has ever done it before me'. Besides, the originals have never been sold.

Q.   What about the geometry book left out in the weather? Can one say that it's the idea of integrating time and space? With a pun on 'géometrie dans l'espace' (solid geometry) and 'temps', the rain and sun that transforms the book?

M.D.   No, no more than the idea of integrating movement and sculpture. It was just a joke. A pure joke. To denigrate the solemnity of a book of principles.

Here we see, directly exposed, the injection of meaning and value by commentary and commentary on commentary—to which the naïve but knowing exposure of the falsity of the commentary contributes in its turn. The ideology of the inexhaustible work of art, or of 'reading' as re-creation masks—through the quasi-exposure which is often seen in matters of faith—the fact that the work is indeed made not twice, but a hundred times, by all those who are interested in it, who find a material or symbolic profit in reading it, classifying it, deciphering it, commenting on it, combating it, knowing it, possessing it. Enrichment accompanies ageing when the work manages to enter the game, when it becomes a stake in the game and so incorporates some of the energy produced in the struggle of which it is the object. The struggle, which sends the work into the past, is also what ensures it a form of survival; lifting it from the state of a dead letter, a mere thing subject to the ordinary laws of ageing, the struggle at least ensures it the sad eternity of academic debate.[49]

Bibliography

DE BAECQUE, A. (1968). Faillite au théâtre, *L'Expansion*, December 1968
DESCOTES, M. (1964). *Le Public de théâtre et son histoire*, P.U.F., Paris
DORIN, F. (1973). *Le Tournant*, Julliard, Paris
DUTOURD, J. (1971). *Le paradoxe du critique*, Flammarion, Paris
GAUTIER, J. J. (1972). *Théâtre d'aujourd'hui*, Julliard, Paris

[49] The next task would be to show the contribution the economy of works of art, as a limiting case in which the mechanisms of negation and their effects are more clearly seen (and not as an exception to the laws of economy), makes to the understanding of ordinary economic practices, in which the need to veil the naked truth of the transaction is also present to varying degrees (as is shown by the use made of a whole apparatus of symbolic agents).

The aristocracy of culture*

PIERRE BOURDIEU

Translation by Richard Nice

Rarely does sociology more resemble social psychoanalysis than when it confronts an object like *taste*, one of the most vital stakes in the struggles fought in the field of the dominant class and the field of cultural production. This is not only because the judgment of taste is the supreme manifestation of the *discernment* which, by reconciling reason and sensibility, the pedant who understands without feeling and the man of the world who enjoys without understanding, defines the accomplished individual. Nor is it solely because every rule of propriety designates in advance the project of defining this indefinable essence as a clear manifestation of philistinism—whether it be the academic propriety which, from Riegl and Wölfflin to Elie Faure and Henri Focillon, and from the most scholastic commentators on the classics to the avant-garde semiologists, imposes a formalist reading of the work of art, or the upper-class propriety which treats taste as one of the surest signs of true nobility and cannot conceive of referring taste to anything other than itself.

Here the sociologist finds himself in the area *par excellence* of the denial of the social. It is not sufficient to overcome the initial self-evident appearances, in other words to relate taste, the uncreated source of all 'creation', to the social conditions of which it is the product, knowing full well that the very same people who strive to repress the clear relation between taste and education, between culture as that which is cultivated and culture as the process of cultivating, will be amazed that anyone should expend so much effort in scientifically proving that self-evident fact. He must also question that relationship, which is only apparently self-explanatory, and unravel the paradox whereby the relationship with educational capital is just as strong in areas which the educational system does not teach. And he must do this without ever being able to appeal unconditionally to the positivistic arbitration of what are called facts. Hidden behind the statistical relationships between educational capital or social origin and this or that type of knowledge or way of applying it, there are relationships between groups maintaining different, and even antagonistic, relations to culture, depending on the conditions in which they acquired their cultural capital and the markets in which they can derive most profit from it. But we have not yet finished with the self-evident. The question itself has to be questioned—in other words, the relation to culture which it *tacitly* privileges—in order to establish whether a change in the content and form of the question would not be sufficient to transform the relationships observed. There is no way out of the game of culture; and one's only chance of objectifying the true nature of the game is to objectify as fully as possible the very operations which one is obliged to use in order to achieve that objectification. *De te fabula narratur*. The reminder is meant for the reader as well as the sociologist. Paradoxically, the games of culture are protected against objectification by all the

* Extract from *La Distinction*, pp. 9–61, Paris: Les Editions de Minuit.

Reprinted in *Distinction*, pp. 11–57, London: Routledge and Kegan Paul, 1984 (translated by Richard Nice).

partial objectifications which the actors involved in the game perform on each other: scholarly critics cannot grasp the objective reality of society aesthetes without abandoning their grasp of the true nature of their own activity; and the same is true of the opponents. The same law of mutual lucidity and reflexive blindness governs the antagonism between 'intellectuals' and 'bourgeois' (or their spokespersons in the field of production). And even when bearing in mind the function which legitimate culture performs in class relations, one is still liable to be led into accepting one or the other of the self-interested representations of culture which 'intellectuals' and 'bourgeois' endlessly fling at each other. Up to now the sociology of the production and producers of culture has never escaped from the play of opposing images, in which 'right-wing intellectuals' and 'left-wing intellectuals' (as the current taxonomy puts it) subject their opponents and their strategies to an objectivist reduction which vested interests make that much easier. The objectification is always bound to remain *partial*, and therefore false, so long as it fails to include the point of view from which it speaks and so fails to construct the *game as a whole*. Only at the level of the field of positions is it possible to grasp both the generic interests associated with the fact of taking part in the game and the specific interests attached to the different positions, and, through this, the form and content of the self-positionings in which these interests are expressed. Despite the aura of objectivity they like to assume, neither the 'sociology of the intellectuals', which is traditionally the business of 'right-wing intellectuals', nor the critique of 'right-wing thought', the traditional speciality of 'left-wing intellectuals', is anything more than a series of symbolic aggressions which take on additional force when they dress themselves up in the impeccable neutrality of science. They tacitly agree in leaving hidden what is essential, namely the structure of objective positions which is the source, *inter alia*, of the view which the occupants of each position can have of the occupants of the other positions and which determines the specific form and force of each group's propensity to present and receive a group's partial truth as if it were a full account of the objective relations between the groups.

* * *

Our inquiry sought to determine how the cultivated disposition and cultural competence that are revealed in the nature of the cultural goods consumed and in the way they are consumed vary according to the category of agents and the area to which they applied, from the most legitimate areas such as painting or music to the most 'personal' ones such as clothing, furniture or cookery, and, within the legitimate domains, according to the markets—'academic' and 'non-academic'—on which they may be placed. This led us to establish two basic facts: on the one hand, the very close relationship linking cultural practices (or the corresponding opinions) to educational capital (measured by qualifications) and, secondarily, to social origin (measured by father's occupation) and, on the other hand, the fact that, at equivalent levels of educational capital, the weight of social origin in the practice- and preference-explaining system increases as one moves away from the most legitimate areas of culture.[1]

The more the competences measured are recognized by the school system and the more 'academic' the techniques used to measure them, the stronger is the relation

[1] The analyses presented here are based on a survey by questionnaire, carried out in 1963 and 1967–68, on a sample of 1,217 people. Appendix I (pp. 587–605 of the French text) gives full information concerning the composition of the sample, the questionnaire, and the main procedures used to analyse it.

between performance and educational qualification. The latter, as a more or less adequate indicator of the number of years of scholastic inculcation, guarantees cultural capital more or less completely depending on whether it is inherited from the family or acquired at school and so it is an unequally adequate indicator of this capital. The strongest correlation between performance and educational capital *qua* cultural capital recognized and guaranteed by the educational system (which is very unequally responsible for its acquisition) is observed when, with the question on the composers of a series of musical works, the survey takes the form of a very 'scholastic' exercise[2] on knowledge very close to the knowledge taught by the educational system and strongly recognized on the academic market.

Sixty-seven per cent of people with a CEP* or a CAP cannot identify more than two composers (from sixteen works), compared to 45% of those with a BEPC, 19% of those who went to a technical college (*petite école*) or started higher education and only 7% of those having a qualification equal or superior to a *licence*. Whereas none of the manual or clerical workers questioned was capable of naming twelve or more of the composers of the sixteen works, 52% of the artistic producers and teachers (and 78% of the teachers in higher education) achieve this score.

The level of non-response to the question on favourite painters or pieces of music is also closely correlated with level of education, with a strong opposition between the dominant class and the working classes, craftsmen and small tradesmen. (However, since in this case whether or not people answer the question doubtless depends as much on their dispositions as on their pure competence, the cultural aspirations of the new petty-bourgeoisie—middle-rank business executives, the medical and social services, secretaries, cultural intermediaries—find an outlet here.) Similarly, listening to the most 'highbrow' radio stations, France-Musique and France-Culture, and to musical or cultural broadcasts, owning a record-player, listening to records (without specifying the type, which minimizes the differences), visiting art-galleries, and the corresponding knowledge of painting—features which are strongly correlated with one another—obey the same logic and, being strongly linked to educational capital, set the classes and class fractions in a clear hierarchy (with a reverse distribution for listening to variety programmes). In the case of activities like practising a plastic art or playing a musical instrument, which presuppose a cultural capital generally acquired outside the educational system and (relatively) independent of the level of academic certification, the correlation with social class, which is again strong, is established via social trajectory (which explains the special position of the new petty-bourgeoisie).

The closer one moves towards the most legitimate areas, such as music or painting, and, within these areas, which can be set in a hierarchy according to their modal degree of legitimacy, towards certain genres or certain works, the more the differences in educational capital are associated with major differences both in knowledge and in preferences. The differences between classical music and modern songs are reproduced within each of these areas by differences (produced in accordance with the same principles) between genres, such as opera and operetta, or quartets and symphonies,

---

[2] The researcher read out a list of sixteen musical works and asked the interviewee to name the composer of each work.

* *Scholastic terms and abbreviations*: CEP: Certificat d'études primaires, formerly marking completion of primary education; CAP: Certificat d'aptitude professionnelle, the lowest trade certificate; BEPC: Brevet d'études du premier degré, marking completion of first part of secondary schooling; baccalauréat: examination at end of secondary schooling; petite école: minor tertiary technical college; licence: university degree (3-year course); agrégation: competitive examination to recruit top category of secondary teachers; grande ecole: one of the set of highly selective colleges including Polytechnique, Ecole Normale Supérieure, and a number of engineering and business schools.

periods, such as contemporary and classical, between composers, and between works. Thus, among works of music, the Well-Tempered Clavier and the Concerto for the Left Hand (which, as we shall see, are distinguished by the modes of acquisition and consumption which they presuppose), are opposed to the Strauss waltzes and the Sabre Dance, pieces which are devalued either by belonging to a lower genre ('light music') or by their popularization (since the dialectic of distinction and pretension designates as devalued 'middle-brow' art those legitimate works which become 'popularized')[3] just as in the world of song, Brassens and Ferré are opposed to Guétary and Petula Clark, these differences corresponding in each case to differences in educational capital[4] (see Table 1).

Table 1. *Preference for songs and music*

Class position	Educational qualification	Guétary	P. Clark	Brassens	Ferré	Blue Danube	Sabre Dance	Well-tempered Clavier	Concerto for the Left Hand
Working class	without diploma, CEP, CAP	33	31	38	20	65	28	1	—
	BECP and further	17	17	61	22	62.5	12.5	—	—
Middle class	without diploma, CEP, CAP	23	29	41	21	64	26	1.5	1.5
	BECP and further of which	12.5	19	47.5	39	27	16	8	4
	BECP, bac	12	21	46.5	39	31	17.5	5	4
	études supérieures	17	9	54	39	3	5	21	4
Upper class	without diploma, CEP, CAP	16	44	36	12	17	21	8	8
	BECP and further of which	5	17	74	35	16	8	15	13
	BECP, bac	8.5	24	65	29	14	11	3	6
	higher education of which	4	14.5	77	39	16.5	7	19	15
	petite école	5	20	73.5	32	19.5	5.5	10	18
	licence	4.5	17	73	34.5	17	9.5	29.5	12
	agrég., grande école	—	3	90	49.5	11.5	3	29.5	12

How to read the table: out of 100 individuals belonging to the working class, possessing a CEP, a CAP or no diploma, 33 mention Guétary, 31 Petula Clark among their three favourite singers (from a list of 12 singers), 65 mention the Blue Danube and 28 the Sabre Dance among their three favourite pieces of music (from a list of 16).

Thus, of all the objects offered for consumers' choice, there are none more *classifying* than legitimate works of art, which, while distinctive in general, enable the production of distinctions ad infinitum by playing on divisions and sub-divisions into genres, periods, styles, authors, etc. Within the universe of particular tastes which can be recreated by successive divisions, it is thus possible, still keeping to the major oppositions, to distinguish three zones of taste which roughly correspond to educational

[3] The most perfect manifestation of this effect in the world of legitimate music is the fate of Albinoni's 'famous Adagio' (as the record-sleeves call it), or of so many works of Vivaldi which in less than 20 years have fallen from the prestigious status of musicologists' discoveries to the status of jingles on popular radio stations and petty-bourgeois record-players.

[4] In fact, the weight of the secondary factors—composition of the capital, volume of the inherited cultural capital (or social trajectory) age, place of residence—varies with the works. Thus, as one moves towards the works that are least legitimate (at the moment in question) factors such as age become increasingly important; in the case of *Rhapsody in Blue* or the *Hungarian Rhapsody*, there is a closer correlation with age than with education, father's occupational category, sex, or place of residence.

Figure 2. Distribution of preferences for three musical works in relation to class position.

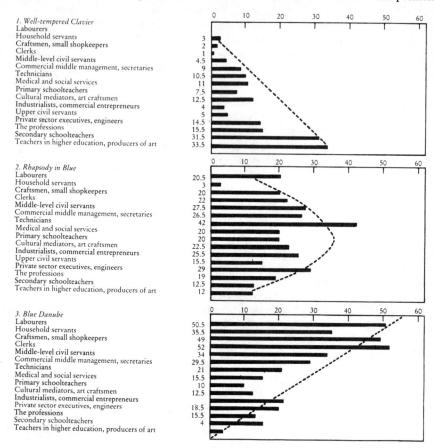

1. Well-tempered Clavier
Labourers
Household servants   3
Craftsmen, small shopkeepers   2
Clerks   1
Middle-level civil servants   4.5
Commercial middle management, secretaries   9
Technicians   10.5
Medical and social services   11
Primary schoolteachers   7.5
Cultural mediators, art craftsmen   12.5
Industrialists, commercial entrepreneurs   4
Upper civil servants   5
Private sector executives, engineers   14.5
The professions   15.5
Secondary schoolteachers   31.5
Teachers in higher education, producers of art   33.5

2. Rhapsody in Blue
Labourers   20.5
Household servants   3
Craftsmen, small shopkeepers   20
Clerks   22
Middle-level civil servants   27.5
Commercial middle management, secretaries   26.5
Technicians   42
Medical and social services   20
Primary schoolteachers   20
Cultural mediators, art craftsmen   22.5
Industrialists, commercial entrepreneurs   25.5
Upper civil servants   15.5
Private sector executives, engineers   29
The professions   19
Secondary schoolteachers   12.5
Teachers in higher education, producers of art   12

3. Blue Danube
Labourers   50.5
Household servants   35.5
Craftsmen, small shopkeepers   49
Clerks   52
Middle-level civil servants   34
Commercial middle management, secretaries   29.5
Technicians   21
Medical and social services   15.5
Primary schoolteachers   10
Cultural mediators, art craftsmen   12.5
Industrialists, commercial entrepreneurs
Private sector executives, engineers   18.5
The professions   15.5
Secondary schoolteachers   4
Teachers in higher education, producers of art

levels and social classes (1) *Legitimate taste*, i.e. the taste for legitimate works, here represented by the Well-Tempered Clavier (histogram no. 1), the Art of Fugue or the Concerto for the Left Hand, or, in painting, Brueghel or Goya, which the most self-assured aesthetes can combine with the most legitimate of the arts in the process of legitimation—cinema, jazz or even the song (here, for example, Léo Ferré, Jacques Douai)—increases with educational level and is highest in those fractions of the dominant class that are richest in educational capital. (2) *'Middle-brow' taste* which brings together the minor works of the major arts, in this case Rhapsody in Blue (histogram no. 2), the Hungarian Rhapsody, or, in painting, Utrillo, Buffet or even Renoir, and the major works of the minor arts, such as Jacques Brel and Gilbert Bécaud in the art of song, is more common in the lower-middle classes (*classes moyennes*) than in the working classes (*classes populaires*) or in the 'intellectual' fractions of the dominant class. (3) Finally, *'popular' taste*, represented here by the choice of works of so-called 'light' music or classical music devalued by popularization, such as the Blue Danube (histogram no. 3), La Traviata or l'Arlésienne, and especially songs totally devoid of artistic ambition or pretension such as those of Mariano, Guétary or Petula Clark, is most frequent among the working classes and varies in inverse ratio to educational capital (which explains why it is rather more common among industrial and commercial employers or even senior executives than among primary teachers and cultural intermediaries).[5]

En-titlement

Knowing the relationship which exists between cultural capital inherited from the family and academic capital, by virtue of the logic of the transmission of cultural capital and the functioning of the educational system, we are unable to impute the strong correlation observed between competence in music or painting (and the practice it presupposes and makes possible) and academic capital solely to the operation of the educational system (still less to the specifically artistic education it is supposed to give, which is clearly almost non-existent). Academic capital is in fact the guaranteed product of the combined effects of cultural transmission by the family and cultural transmission by the school (the efficiency of which depends on the amount of cultural capital directly inherited from the family). Through its value-inculcating and value-imposing operations, the school also helps (to a greater or lesser extent, depending on the initial disposition, i.e. class of origin) to form a general transposable disposition towards legitimate culture which is first acquired with respect to scholastically recognized knowledge and practices but tends to be applied beyond the bounds of the curriculum, taking the form of a 'disinterested' propensity to accumulate experience and knowledge which may not be directly profitable on the academic market.[6]

So there is nothing paradoxical in the fact that in its ends and means the educational system defines the enterprise of *legitimate self-teaching* which the acquisition of 'general culture' presupposes, an enterprise that is ever more strongly demanded as one rises in the educational hierarchy (between sections, disciplines and specialities, etc., or between levels). The essentially contradictory phrase 'legitimate self-teaching' is intended to indicate the difference in kind between the highly valued 'extra-curricular' culture of the holder of academic qualifications and the illegitimate extra-curricular culture of the autodidact. The reader of *Science et Vie* who talks about the genetic code or the incest taboo exposes himself to ridicule as soon as he ventures outside the circle of his peers, whereas Lévi-Strauss or Monod can only derive additional prestige from his excursions into the field of music or philosophy. Illegitimate extra-curricular culture, whether it be the knowledge accumulated by the self-taught or 'experience' acquired in and through practice, outside the control of the institution specifically mandated to inculcate it and officially sanction its acquisition, like the art of cooking or herbal medicine, craftsmen's skills or the stand-in's irreplaceable knowledge, is only valorized to the strict extent of its technical efficiency,

[5] The three profiles presented here are perfectly typical of those that are found when one draws a graph of the distribution of a whole set of choices characteristic of different class fractions (arranged in a hierarchy, within each class, according to educational capital). The first one (*The Well-tempered Clavier*) reappears in the case of all the authors or works named above, and also for 'reading philosophical essays' and 'visiting museums', etc.; the second (*Rhapsody in Blue*) characterizes, in addition to all the works and authors mentioned in the text (plus *The Twilight of the Gods*), 'photography', 'comfortable, cosy home', etc.; and the third (*Blue Danube*) is equally valid for 'romantic stories' and 'neat, clean home', etc.

[6] The educational system defines non-curricular general culture (la culture 'libre'), negatively at least, by delimiting within the dominant culture the area of what it puts into its syllabuses and controls by its examinations. It has been shown that the most 'scholastic' cultural objects are those taught and required at the lowest levels of schooling (the extreme form of the 'scholastic' being the 'elementary') and that the educational system sets an increasingly high value on 'general' culture and increasingly refuses 'scholastic' measurements of culture (such as direct, closed questions on authors, dates and events) as one moves towards the highest levels of the system.

without any social added-value, and is exposed to legal sanctions (like the illegal practice of medicine) whenever it emerges from the domestic universe to compete with authorized competences.

Thus, it is written into the tacit definition of the academic qualification *formally* guaranteeing a specific competence (e.g. an engineering diploma) that it *really* guarantees possession of a 'general culture' whose breadth is proportionate to the prestige of the qualification;[7] and, conversely, that no real guarantee may be sought of what it guarantees formally and really or, to put it another way, of the extent to which it guarantees what it guarantees. This effect of symbolic imposition is most intense in the case of the diplomas consecrating the cultural élite. The qualifications awarded by the French *grandes écoles* guarantee, without any other guarantee, a competence extending far beyond what they are supposed to guarantee. This is by virtue of a clause which, though tacit, is firstly binding on the qualification-holders themselves, who are called upon really to procure the attributes assigned to them by status.[8]

This process occurs at all stages of schooling, through the manipulation of aspirations and demands—in other words, of self-image and self-esteem—which the educational system carries out by channelling pupils towards prestigious or devalued positions implying or excluding legitimate practice. The effect of 'allocation' i.e. assignment to a section, a discipline (philosophy or geography, mathematics or geology, to take the extremes), or an institution (a *grande école* that is more or less *grande*, or a faculty), mainly operates through the social image of the position in question and the prospects objectively inscribed in it, among the foremost of which are a certain type of cultural accumulation and a certain image of cultural accomplishment.[9] The official differences produced by academic classifications tend to produce (or reinforce) real differences by inducing in the classified individuals a collectively recognized and supported belief in the differences, thus producing behaviours that are intended to bring real being into line with official being. Activities as alien to the explicit demands of the institution as keeping a diary, wearing heavy make-up, theatre-going or going dancing, writing poems or playing rugby can thus find themselves inscribed in the position allotted within the institution as a *tacit demand* constantly underlined by various mediations. Among the most important of these are teachers' conscious or unconscious expectations and peer-group pressure, whose ethical orientation is itself defined by the class values brought into and reinforced by the institution. This allocation effect, and the status assignment it entails, doubtless play a major rôle in the fact that the educational institution succeeds in imposing cultural practices that it does not teach and does not even explicitly demand but which belong to the attributes statutorily attached to the position it assigns, the qualifications it awards and the social positions to which the latter give access.

This logic doubtless helps to explain how the legitimate disposition that is acquired by frequenting a particular class of works, namely the literary and philosophical

[7] This legitimate or soon-to-be legitimate culture, in the form of practical and conscious mastery of the means of symbolic appropriation of legitimate or soon-to-be legitimate works, which characterizes the 'cultivated man' (according to the dominant definition at a given moment), is what the questionnaire sought to measure.

[8] This effect of status ascription is also largely responsible for the differences observed between the sexes (especially in the working and lower-middle classes) in all the areas which are statutorily assigned to men, such as the legitimate culture (especially the most typically masculine regions of that culture, such as history or science) and, above all, politics.

[9] One of the most obvious 'advantages' which strong educational capital gives in intellectual or scientific competition is high self-esteem and high ambition, which may be manifested in the breadth of the problems tackled (more 'theoretical', for example), elevation of style, etc. (see Bourdieu, 1975a).

propensity — natural inclination disposition tendency [handwritten annotation]

works recognized by the academic canon, comes to be extended to other, less legitimate works, such as avant-garde literature, or to areas enjoying less academic recognition, such as the cinema. The generalizing tendency is inscribed in the very principle of the disposition to *recognize* legitimate works, a propensity and capacity to recognize their legitimacy and perceive them as worthy of admiration in themselves which is inseparable from the capacity to recognize in them something already known, i.e. the stylistic traits appropriate to characterize them in their singularity ('it's a Rembrandt' or even 'it's the Helmeted Man') or as belonging to a class of works ('it's Impressionist'). This explains why the propensity and capacity to accumulate 'gratuitous' knowledge such as the names of film directors are more closely and exclusively linked to educational capital than is mere cinema-going, which is more dependent on income, place of residence and age.

Cinema-going, measured by the number of films seen among the twenty films mentioned, is lower among the less-educated than the more highly educated, but also lower among provincials (in Lille) than among Parisians, among low-income than among high-income groups, and among old than among young people. And the same relationships are found in the surveys by the Centre d'études des supports de publicité. The proportion who say they have been to the cinema at least once in the previous week (a more reliable indicator of behaviour than a question on cinema-going in the course of the year, for which the tendency to overstate is particularly strong) is rather greater among men than women (7.8% compared to 5.3%), greater in the Paris area (10.9%) than in towns of over 100,000 people (7.7%) or in rural areas (3.6%), greater among senior executives and members of the professions (11.1%) than among junior executives (9.5%), white-collar workers (9.7%), skilled blue-collar workers and foremen (7.3%), semi-skilled workers (6.3%), small employers (5.2%) and farmers (2.6%). But the greatest contrasts are between the youngest (22.4% of the 21–24 year olds had been to the cinema at least once in the previous week) and the oldest (only 3.2% of the 35 to 49 year olds, 1.7% of the 50 to 64 year olds and 1.1% of the over-65s) and between the most and least highly educated (18.2% of those who had been through higher education, 9.5% of those who had had secondary education, and 2.2% of those who had had only primary education or none at all had been to the cinema in the previous week) (cf. Centre d'études des supports de publicité, *Etude sur l'audience du cinéma*, Paris, 1975, XVI).

Knowledge of directors is much more closely linked to cultural capital than is mere cinema-going. Only 5% of the interviewees who had an elementary school diploma could name at least four directors (from a list of twenty films) compared to 10% of holders of the BEPC or the *baccalauréat* and 22% of those who had had higher education, whereas the proportion in each category who had seen at least four of the twenty films was 22, 33 and 40% respectively. Thus, although film viewing also varies with educational capital (less so, however, than visits to museums and concerts), it seems that differences in consumption are not sufficient to explain the differences in knowledge of directors between holders of different qualifications. This conclusion would probably also hold good for jazz, strip cartoons, detective stories or science fiction, now that these genres have begun to achieve cultural consecration.[10] An

10 At equal levels, knowledge of film directors is considerably stronger in Paris than in Lille, and the further one moves from the most scholastic and most legitimate areas, the greater the gap between the Parisians and the provincials. In order to explain this, it is no doubt necessary to invoke the constant reinforcements the cultivated disposition derives from all that is called the 'cultural atmosphere', i.e. all the incitements provided by a peer group whose social composition and cultural level is defined by its place of residence and also, inextricably associated with this, from the range of cultural goods on offer.

additional proof: while increasing slightly with level of education (from 13% for the least educated to 18% for those with secondary education and 23% for the most qualified), *knowledge of actors* varies mainly—and considerably—with the number of films seen. This awareness, like knowledge of the slightest events in the lives of TV personalities, presupposes a disposition closer to that required by the acquisition of ordinary knowledge about everyday things and people than to the legitimate disposition. And indeed, these least-educated regular cinema-goers know as many actors' names as the most highly-educated.[11] By contrast, although, at equivalent levels of education, knowledge of directors increases with number of films seen, in this area assiduous cinema-going does not compensate for absence of educational capital. Forty-five per cent of the CEP-holders who had seen at least four of the films mentioned could not name a single director compared to 27.5% of those with a BEPC or the baccalauréat and 13% of those who had been through higher education.

Such competence is not necessarily acquired by means of the 'scholastic' labours in which some 'cinephiles' or 'jazzophiles' indulge (e.g. transcribing film credits onto catalogue cards).[12] Most often it results from the unintentional learning made possible by a disposition acquired through domestic or scholastic acquisition of legitimate culture. This transposable disposition, armed with a set of perceptual and evaluative schemes that are available for general application, inclines its owner towards other cultural experiences and enables him or her to perceive, classify and memorize them differently. Where some only see 'a Western starring Burt Lancaster,' others 'discover an early John Sturges' or 'the latest Peckinpah'. In identifying what is worthy of being seen and the right way to see it they are aided by their whole social group (which guides and reminds them with its 'have you seen . . .?' and 'you must see . . .') and by the whole corporation of critics mandated by the group to produce legitimate classifications and the discourse necessarily accompanying any artistic enjoyment worthy of the name.

It is possible to explain in such terms why cultural practices which schools do not teach and never explicitly demand vary in such close relation to educational qualifications (it being understood, of course, that we are provisionally suspending the distinction between the school's rôle in the correlation observed and that of the other socializing agencies, in particular the family). But the fact that educational qualifications function as a condition of entry to the universe of legitimate culture cannot be fully explained without taking into account another, still more hidden, effect which

[11] Among those who have seen at least four of the films mentioned, 45% of those who have had only primary education are able to name four actors, as against 35% of those who have had secondary education and 47% of those who have had some higher education. Interest in actors is greatest among office workers: on average they name 2.8 actors and one director, whereas the craftsmen and small shopkeepers, skilled workers and foremen name, on average, only 0.8 actors and 0.3 directors. (The secretaries and junior commercial executives, who also know a large number of actors—average 2.4— are more interested in directors—average 1.4—and those in the social and medical services even name more directors—1.7—than actors—1.4). The reading of sensational weeklies (e.g. *Ici Paris*) which give information about the lives of stars is a product of a similar disposition to interest in actors; it is more frequent among women than men (10.8% have read *Ici Paris* in the last week, compared to 9.3% of the men), among skilled workers and foremen (14.5%), semi-skilled workers (13.6%), or office-workers (10.3%) than among junior executives (8.6%) and especially senior executives and members of the professions (3.8%) (*CESP* 1975, Part I, p. 242).

[12] It is among the petty-bourgeoisie endowed with cultural capital that one finds most of the devoted 'cinephiles' whose knowledge of directors and actors extends beyond their direct experience of the corresponding films. Thirty-one per cent of the office workers name actors in films they have not seen and 32% of those working in the medical and social services name the directors of films they have not seen. (No craftsman or small shopkeeper is able to do this and only 7% of the skilled workers and foremen name actors in films they have not seen.)

the educational system, again reinforcing the work of the bourgeois family, exerts through the very conditions within which it inculcates. The educational qualification designates certain conditions of existence, those which constitute the precondition for obtaining the qualification and also for the aesthetic disposition, the most rigorously demanded of all the terms of entry which the world of legitimate culture (always tacitly) imposes. Anticipating what will be demonstrated later, we may posit, in broad terms, that it is because they are linked either to a bourgeois origin or to the quasi-bourgeois mode of existence presupposed by prolonged schooling, or (most often) to both of these combined, that educational qualifications come to be seen as a guarantee of the capacity to adopt the aesthetic disposition.

The aesthetic disposition

Any legitimate work tends *in fact* to impose the norms of its own perception and tacitly defines as the only legitimate mode of perception the one which brings into play a certain disposition and a certain competence. Recognizing this fact does not mean that we are constituting a particular mode of perception as an essence, thereby falling into the illusion which is the basis of recognition of artistic legitimacy. It does mean that we take note of the fact that all agents, whether they like it or not, whether or not they have the means of conforming to them, find themselves objectively measured by those norms. At the same time it becomes possible to establish whether these dispositions and competences are gifts of nature, as the charismatic ideology of the relation to the work of art would have it, or products of learning, and to bring to light the hidden conditions of the miracle of the unequal class distribution of the capacity for inspired encounters with works of art and high culture in general.

Every essentialist analysis of the aesthetic disposition, the only socially accepted 'right' way of approaching the objects socially designated as works of art, i.e. as both demanding and deserving to be approached with a specifically aesthetic intention capable of recognizing and constituting them as works of art, is bound to fail. Refusing to take account of the collective and individual genesis of this product of history which must be endlessly re-produced by education, it is unable to reconstruct its sole *raison d'être*, i.e. the historical reason which underlies the arbitrary necessity of the institution. If the work of art is indeed, as Panofsky says, that which 'demands to be experienced aesthetically', and if any object, natural or artificial, can be perceived aesthetically, how can one escape the conclusion that it is the aesthetic intention which 'makes' the work of art, or, to transpose a formula of Saussure's, that it is the aesthetic point of view that creates the aesthetic object? To get out of this vicious circle, Panofsky has to endow the work of art with an 'intention', in the Scholastic sense. A purely 'practical' perception contradicts this objective intention, just as an aesthetic perception would in a sense be a practical negation of the objective intention of a signal, a red light for example, which requires a 'practical' response, braking. Thus, within the class of worked-upon objects, themselves defined in opposition to natural objects, the class of art objects would be defined by the fact that it demands to be perceived aesthetically, i.e. in terms of *form* rather than *function*. But how can such a definition be made operational? Panofsky himself observes that it is virtually impossible to determine scientifically at what moment a worked-upon object becomes an art object, i.e. at what moment form takes over from function:

If I write to a friend to invite him to dinner, my letter is primarily a communication. But the more I shift the emphasis to the form of my script, the more nearly does it become a work of calligraphy; and the more I emphasize the form of my language . . . the more nearly does it become a work of literature or poetry (Panofsky 1955, p. 12).

Does this mean that the demarcation line between the world of technical objects and the world of aesthetic objects depends on the 'intention' of the producer of those objects? In fact, this 'intention' is itself the product of the social norms and conventions which combine to define the always uncertain and historically changing frontier between simple technical objects and *objets d'art*:

'Classical taste,' Panofsky observes, 'demanded that private letters, legal speeches and the shields of heroes should be "artistic" . . . while modern taste demands that architecture and ash trays should be "functional" ' (Panofsky 1955, p. 13).

But the apprehension and appreciation of the work also depend on the beholder's intention, which is itself a function of the conventional norms governing the relation to the work of art in a certain historical and social situation and also of the beholder's capacity to conform to those norms, i.e. his or her artistic training. To break out of this circle one only has to observe that the ideal of 'pure' perception of a work of art *qua* work of art is the product of the enunciation and systematization of the principles of specifically aesthetic legitimacy which accompany the constituting of a relatively autonomous artistic field. The aesthetic mode of perception in the 'pure' form which it has now assumed corresponds to a particular state of the mode of artistic production. An art which, like all post-impressionist painting for example, is the product of an artistic intention which asserts the *absolute primacy of form over function*, of the mode of representation over the object represented, *categorically* demands a purely aesthetic disposition which earlier art demanded only conditionally. The demiurgic ambition of the artist, capable of applying to *any* object the pure intention of artistic research which is an end in itself, calls for unlimited receptiveness on the part of an aesthete capable of applying the specifically aesthetic intention to any object, whether or not it has been produced with aesthetic intention.

This demand is objectified in the art museum; there the aesthetic disposition becomes an institution. Nothing more totally manifests and achieves the autonomizing of aesthetic activity *vis-à-vis* extra-aesthetic interests or functions than the art museum's juxtaposition of works. Though originally subordinated to quite different or even incompatible functions (crucifix and fetish, Pietà and still life), they tacitly demand attention to form rather than function, technique rather than theme, and, being constructed in styles that are mutually exclusive but all equally necessary, they are a practical challenge to the expectation of realistic representation as defined by the arbitrary canons of a familiar aesthetic, and so lead naturally from stylistic relativism to the neutralization of the very function of representation. Objects previously treated as collectors' curios or historical and ethnographic documents have acceded to the status of works of art, thereby materializing the omnipotence of the aesthetic gaze and making it difficult to ignore the fact that—if it is not to be merely an arbitrary and therefore suspect affirmation of this absolute power—artistic contemplation now has to include a degree of erudition which is liable to damage the illusion of immediate illumination which is an essential element of pure pleasure.

Pure taste and 'barbarous' taste

In short, never has more been demanded of the spectator, who is now required to reproduce the original operation whereby the artist (with the complicity of his whole intellectual field) produced this new fetish.[13] But never perhaps has he been given so much in return. The naïve exhibitionism of 'conspicuous consumption', which seeks distinction in the crude display of ill-mastered luxury, is nothing compared to the unique capacity of the pure gaze, a quasi-creative power which sets the aesthete from the common herd by a radical difference which seems to be inscribed in 'persons'. One only has to read Ortega y Gasset to see the reinforcement the charismatic ideology derives from modern art, which is 'essentially unpopular, indeed, anti-popular' and from the 'curious sociological effect' it produces by dividing the public into two 'antagonistic castes' 'those who understand and those who do not'. 'This implies', Ortega goes on, 'that some possess an organ of understanding which others have been denied; that these are two distinct varieties of the human species. The new art is not for everyone, like Romantic art, but destined for an especially gifted minority.' And he ascribes to the 'humiliation' and 'obscure sense of inferiority' inspired by 'this art of privilege, sensuous nobility, instinctive aristocracy', the irri-tation it arouses in the mass, 'unworthy of artistic sacraments':

For a century and a half, the 'people', the mass, claimed to be the whole of society. The music of Stravinsky or the plays of Pirandello have the sociological power of obliging them to see themselves as they are, as the 'common people', a mere ingredient among others in the social structure, the inert material of the historical process, a secondary factor in the spiritual cosmos. By contrast, the young art helps the 'best' to know and recognize one another in the greyness of the multitude and to learn their mission, which is to be few in number and to have to fight against the multitude (Ortega y Gasset, 1976, pp. 15–17).

And to show that the self-legitimating imagination of the 'happy few' has no limits, one only has to quote a recent text by Suzanne Langer, who is presented as 'one of the world's most influential philosophers':

In the past, the masses did not have access to art; music, painting, and even books, were pleasures reserved for the rich. It might have been supposed that the poor, the 'common people', would have enjoyed them equally, if they had had the chance. But now that everyone can read, go to museums, listen to great music, at least on the radio, the judgement of the masses about these things has become a reality and through this it has become clear that great art is not a direct sensuous pleasure. Otherwise, like cookies or cocktails, it would flatter uneducated taste as much as cultured taste (Langer, 1968, p. 183).

It should not be thought that the relationship of distinction (which may or may not imply the conscious intention of distinguishing oneself from common people) is only an incidental component in the aesthetic disposition. The pure gaze implies a break with the ordinary attitude towards the world which, as such, is a social break. We can agree with Ortega y Gasset when he attributes to modern art—which merely takes to its extreme conclusions an intention implicit in art since the Renaissance—a systematic refusal of all that is 'human', by which he means the passions, emotions and feelings which *ordinary* people put into their *ordinary* existence and consequently all the themes and objects capable of evoking them:

'People like a play when they are able to take an interest in the human destinies put before them', in which 'they participate as if they were real-life events' (Ortega y Gasset, 1975, pp. 18–19).

Rejecting the 'human' clearly means rejecting what is generic, i.e. *common*, 'easy', and immediately accessible, starting with everything that reduces the aesthetic animal to

[13] For a more extensive analysis of the opposition between the specifically aesthetic disposition and the 'practical' disposition, and of the collective and individual genesis of the 'pure' disposition which genesis-amnesia tends to constitute as 'natural', see Bourdieu 1971b and 1975b. For an analysis of the aesthetic *illusio* and of the *collusio* which produces it, see 'The Production of Belief'.

pure and simple animality, to palpable pleasure or sensual desire. The interest in the content of the representation which leads people to call 'beautiful' the representation of beautiful things, especially those which speak most immediately to the senses and the sensibility, is rejected in favour of the indifference and distance which refuse to subordinate judgment of the representation to the nature of the object represented.[14] It can be seen that it is not so easy to describe the 'pure' gaze without also describing the naïve gaze which it defines itself against, and vice versa; and that there is no *neutral*, impartial, 'pure' description of either of these opposing visions (which does not mean that one has to subscribe to aesthetic relativism, when it is so obvious that the 'popular aesthetic' is defined in relation to 'high' aesthetics and that reference to legitimate art and its negative judgment on 'popular' taste never ceases to haunt popular experience of beauty). Refusal or privation? It is as dangerous to attribute the coherence of a systematic aesthetic to the objectively aesthetic commitments of ordinary people as it is to adopt, albeit unconsciously, the strictly negative conception of ordinary vision which is the basis of every 'high' aesthetic.

The popular 'aesthetic'

Everything takes place as if the popular 'aesthetic' were based on the affirmation of continuity between art and life, which implies the subordination of form to function, or, one might say, on refusing the refusal which is the starting point of the high aesthetic, i.e. the clear-cut separation of ordinary dispositions from the specifically aesthetic disposition. The hostility of the working class and of the middle-class fractions least rich in cultural capital towards every kind of formal experimentation asserts itself both in the theatre and in painting, or, still more clearly because they have less legitimacy, in photography and the cinema. In the theatre as in the cinema, the popular audience delights in plots that proceed logically and chronologically towards a happy end, and 'identifies' better with simply drawn situations and characters than with ambiguous and symbolic figures and actions or the enigmatic problems of the theatre of cruelty, not to mention the suspended animation of Beckettian heroes or the bland absurdities of Pinteresque dialogue. Their reluctance and refusal springs not just from lack of familiarity but from a deep-rooted demand for participation, which formal experiment systematically disappoints, especially when, refusing to offer the 'vulgar' attractions of an art of illusion, the theatrical fiction denounces itself, as in all forms of 'theatre within the theatre'. Pirandello supplies the paradigm here, in plays in which the actors are actors unable to act—*Six Characters in Search of an Author, Comme ci (ou comme ça)* or *Ce soir on improvise*—and Genet supplies the formula in the Prologue to *The Blacks*:

We shall have the politeness, which you have taught us, to make communication impossible. The distance initially between us we shall increase, by our splendid gestures, our manners and our insolence, for we are also actors.

The desire to enter into the game, identifying with the characters' joys and sufferings, worrying about their fate, espousing their hopes and ideals, living their life, is based on a form of *investment*, a sort of deliberate 'naïvety', ingenuousness, good-natured

---

[14] The 'cultivated' spectator's concern with distinction is paralleled by the artist's concern (which grows with the autonomy of the field of production) to assert his autonomy *vis-a-vis* external demands (of which commissions are the most visible form) and to give priority to *form*, over which he has full control, rather than function, which leads him, through art for art's sake, i.e. art for artists, to an art of pure form.

credulity ('we're here to enjoy ourselves') which tends to accept formal experiments and specifically artistic effects only to the extent that they can be forgotten and do not get in the way of the substance of the work.

The cultural gulf which associates each class of works with its public means that it is not easy to obtain working-class people's first-hand judgments on formalist innovations in modern art. However, television, which brings certain performances of 'high' art into the home, or certain cultural institutions (such as the Beaubourg Centre or the Maisons de la Culture) which briefly bring a working-class public into contact with high art and sometimes avant-garde works, create what are virtually experimental situations, neither more nor less artificial or unreal than those produced by any survey on legitimate culture in a working-class milieu. One then observes the confusion, sometimes almost a sort of panic mingled with revolt, that is induced by some exhibits—I am thinking of Ben's heap of coal, on view in Beaubourg shortly after it opened—whose parodic intention, entirely defined in terms of an artistic field and its relatively autonomous history, is seen as a sort of aggression, an affront to common sense and sensible people. Likewise, when formal experimentation insinuates itself into their familiar entertainments (e.g. TV variety shows with special effects, à la Averty), working-class viewers protest, not only because they do not feel the need for these fancy games, but because they sometimes understand that they derive their necessity from the logic of a field of production which excludes them precisely by these games: 'I don't like those cut-up things at all, where you see a head, then a nose, then a leg. . . . First you see a singer all drawn out, three metres tall, then the next minute he's got arms two metres long. Do you find that funny? Oh, I just don't like it, it's stupid, I don't see the point of distorting things' (baker, Grenoble).

Formal experiment—which, in literature or the theatre, leads to *obscurity*—is, in the eyes of the working-class public, one sign of what is sometimes felt to be a desire to keep the uninitiated at arm's length, or, as one respondent said about certain cultural programmes on TV, to speak to other initiates 'over the heads of the audience'.[15] It is part of the paraphernalia which always announces the sacred character, separate and separating, of high culture—the icy solemnity of the great museums, the grandiose luxury of the opera-houses and major theatres, the décors and decorum of concert-halls.[16] Everything takes place as if the working-class audience vaguely grasped what is implied in conspicuous formality, both in art and in life, i.e. a sort of censorship of the expressive content, which explodes in the expressiveness of popular language, and, by the same token, a distancing, inherent in the calculated coldness of all formal exploration, a refusal to communicate concealed in the heart of the communication itself, both in an art which takes back and refuses what it seems to deliver, and in

---

15 A number of surveys confirm this hostility towards any kind of formal experiment. One study found a large number of viewers disconcerted by *Les Perses*, a stylized production which was difficult to follow because of the absence of dialogue and of a visible plot (*Les Téléspectateurs en 1967*, Rapport des études de marché de l'ORTF, I, pp. 69 ff.). Another, which compares reactions to the 'UNICEF gala', classical in style, and the less traditional 'Allegro', establishes that the working-class audience regard unusual camera angles and stylized decor as an impoverishment of reality and often perceive over-exposed shots as technical failures; they applaud what they call 'atmosphere', i.e. a certain quality of the relationship between the audience and the performers, and deplore the absence of a compere as a lack of 'warmth' (ibid., p. 78).

16 The department store is, in a sense, the poor-man's gallery: not only because it presents objects which belong to the familiar world, whose use is known, which could be inserted into the everyday decor, which can be named and judged with everyday words (warm/cold; plain/fancy; gaudy/dull; comfortable/austere, etc.); but more especially because, there, people do not feel themselves measured against transcendent norms, i.e. the principles of the life-style of a supposedly higher class, but feel free to judge freely, in the name of the legitimate arbitrariness of tastes and colours.

bourgeois politeness, whose impeccable formalism is a permanent warning against the temptation of familiarity. Conversely, popular entertainment secures the spectator's participation in the show and collective participation in a festivity. If circus or melodrama (which are recreated by some sporting spectacles such as wrestling and, to a lesser extent, boxing and all forms of team games, such as those which have been televised) are more 'popular' than entertainments like dancing or theatre, this is not merely because, being less formalized (as is seen, for example, by comparing acrobatics with dancing) and less euphemized, they offer more direct, more immediate satisfactions. It is also because, through the collective gatherings they give rise to and the array of spectacular delights they offer (I am thinking also of the music-hall, the operetta or the big feature film)—fabulous décors, glittering costumes, exciting music, lively action, enthusiastic actors—like all forms of the comic and especially those working through satire or parody of the 'great' (mimics, *chansonniers*, etc.), they satisfy the taste for and sense of revelry, the free speaking and hearty laughter which liberate by setting the social world head over heels, overturning conventions and proprieties.

Aesthetic distanciation

This is the very opposite of the detachment of the aesthete, who, as is seen when he appropriates one of the objects of popular taste (e.g. westerns or strip cartoons), introduces a distance, a gap—the measure of his distant distinction—*vis-à-vis* 'first-degree' perception, by displacing the interest from the 'content', characters, plot, etc., to the form, to the specifically artistic effects which are only appreciated *relationally*, through a comparison with other works which is incompatible with immersion in the singularity of the work immediately given. Detachment, disinterestedness, indifference, which aesthetic theory has so often presented as the only way to recognize the work of art for what it is, autonomous, *selbständig*, that one ends up forgetting that they really mean disinvestment, detachment, indifference, in other words the refusal to invest oneself and take things seriously. Worldly-wise readers of Rousseau's *Lettre sur les spectacles*,[17] who have long been aware that there is nothing more naïve and vulgar than to invest too much passion in the things of the mind or to expect too much seriousness of them, tending to assume that intellectual creativity is opposed to moral integrity or political consistency, have no answer to Virginia Woolf when she criticizes the novels of Wells, Galsworthy and Bennett because 'they leave a strange feeling of incompleteness and dissatisfaction' and give the feeling that it is essential to 'do something, join an association, or, still more desperate, sign a cheque', in contrast to works like *Tristram Shandy* or *Pride and Prejudice*, which, being perfectly 'self-contained', 'in no way inspire the desire to do something, except, of course, to read the book again and understand it better (Woolf, 1948, p. 70).

But the refusal of any sort of involvement through a 'vulgar' surrender to easy seduction and collective enthusiasm, which is, indirectly at least, the origin of the taste for formal experiments and object-less representations, is perhaps most clearly seen in reactions to paintings. Thus we find that the higher the *level of education*,[18]

---

[17] Garat, in his *Mémoire sur M. Suard*, tells us that Rousseau's *Discours sur le rétablissement des lettres et des arts* provoked 'a sort of terror' in a readership accustomed to take nothing seriously.

[18] The capacity to designate unremarkable objects as suitable for being transfigured by the act of artistic promotion performed by photography, the most accessible of the means of artistic production, varies in exactly the same way as knowledge of directors. This is understandable since in both cases we have a relatively scholastic measurement applied to a competence more remote from formal education than the competence implied in the expression of preference in music or painting.

the greater is the proportion of the interviewees who, when asked whether a series of objects would make beautiful photographs, refuse the ordinary objects of popular admiration—a first communion, a sunset or a landscape—as 'vulgar' or 'ugly', or reject them as 'trivial', silly, a bit 'wet', or, in Ortega y Gasset's terms, naïvely 'human'; and the greater is the proportion who assert the autonomy of the representation with respect to the thing represented by declaring that a beautiful photograph, and *a fortiori* a beautiful painting, can be made from objects socially designated as meaningless—a metal frame, the bark of a tree, and especially cabbages, a trivial object *par excellence*—or ugly and repulsive—such as a car crash, a butcher's stall (chosen for the Rembrandt allusion) or a snake (for the Boileau reference)—or misplaced—e.g. a pregnant woman (see Tables 2 and 3).

Since it was not possible to set up a genuine experimental situation, we collected the interviewees' statements about the things they consider 'photographable' and which therefore seem to them capable of being looked at aesthetically (as opposed to things excluded on account of their triviality or ugliness, or for ethical reasons). The capacity to adopt the aesthetic attitude is thus measured by the gap (which, in a field of production which evolves through the dialectic of distinction, is also a time-lag, a *backwardness*) between what is constituted as an aesthetic object by the individual or group concerned and what is constituted aesthetically in a given state of the field of production by the holders of aesthetic legitimacy.

The following question was put to the interviewees: 'Given the following subjects, is a photographer more likely to make a beautiful, interesting, trivial or ugly photo: a landscape, a car crash, etc.?' In the preliminary survey, the interviewees were shown actual photographs, mostly famous ones, of the objects which were merely named in the full-scale survey—pebbles, a pregnant woman, etc. The reactions evoked by the mere idea of the image were entirely consistent with those produced by the image itself (evidence that the value attributed to the image tends to correspond to the value attributed to the thing). Photographs were used partly to avoid the legitimacy-imposing effects of paintings and partly because photography is perceived as a more accessible practice, so that the judgments expressed were likely to be less unreal.

Although the test employed was designed to collect statements of artistic intention rather than to measure the ability to put the intention into practice in doing painting or photography or even in the perception of works of art, it makes it possible to identify the factors which determine the capacity to adopt the posture socially designated as specifically aesthetic.[19] The statistics reveal the relationship between cultural capital and the negative and positive indices (refusal of 'wetness'; the capacity to valorize the trivial) of the aesthetic disposition (or, at least, the capacity to operate the arbitrary classification which, within the universe of worked-upon objects, distinguishes the objects socially designated as deserving and demanding an aesthetic approach which can recognize and constitute them as works of art). In addition, they show that the preferred objects of photography with aesthetic ambitions, e.g. the folk dance, the weaver, or the little girl with her cat—are in an intermediate position. The proportion

[19] Factor analysis of judgments on 'photographable' objects reveals an opposition within each class between the fractions richest in cultural capital and poorest in economic capital and the fractions richest in economic capital and poorest in cultural capital. In the case of the dominant class, higher-education teachers and artistic producers (and, secondarily, secondary teachers and the professions) are opposed to industrial and commercial employers; private-sector executives and engineers are in an intermediate position. In the petty-bourgeoisie, the cultural intermediaries, distinctly separated from the closest fractions, the primary teachers, medical services and artistic craftsmen, are opposed to the small shopkeepers or craftsmen and the office workers.

Table 2. *Aesthetic disposition in relation to academic capital*

	No reply or inco- herent	Ugly	Trivial	Inter- esting	Beautiful	Total
First communion						
Without diploma, CEP $n = 314$	2	5	19	23	51	100
CAP $n = 97$	4	1	26	38	31	100
BEPC $n = 197$	2.5	7	27	31	32.5	100
Baccalauréat $n = 217$	2	12	43	24	19	100
Some higher edn.						
$n = 118$	4	13	45	23	15	100
Licence $n = 182$	1	11	53	28	7	100
Agrégation, grande école						
$n = 71$	4	15.5	49	6	25.5	100
Folk dancing						
Without diploma, CEP $n=314$	1	0.5	3	41	54.5	100
CAP $n = 97$	4	—	3	33	60	100
BEPC $n = 197$	3.5	—	7	33.5	56	100
Baccalauréat $n = 217$	2	0.5	13	47.5	37	100
Some higher edn.						
$n = 118$	6	2.5	13	37	41.5	100
Licence $n = 182$	2	1	11	49.5	36.5	100
Agrégation, grande école						
$n = 71$	4	6	22.5	28	39.5	100
Tree bark						
Without diploma, CEP $n=314$	2	14.5	46.5	21.5	15.5	100
CAP $n = 97$	5	1	20	37	37	100
BEPC $n = 197$	2.5	8.5	31.5	30	27.5	100
Baccalauréat $n = 217$	2	3	21	32	42	100
Some higher edn.						
$n = 118$	6	1	23	25	45	100
Licence $n = 182$	—	3	18	23	56	100
Agrégation, grande école						
$n = 71$	4	3	8.5	24	60.5	100
Butcher's shop						
Without diploma, CEP $n=314$	1.5	31	46	16.5	5	100
CAP $n = 97$	6	15.5	48.5	24	6	100
BEPC $n = 197$	3	28	47	17	5	100
Baccalauréat $n = 217$	3	29.5	32	25	10.5	100
Some higher edn.						
$n = 118$	4	30.5	29	18.5	18	100
Licence $n = 182$	4.5	29.5	22.5	24	19.5	100
Agrégation, grandee école						
$n = 71$	4	23.5	23	18	25.5	100
Cabbages						
Without diploma, CEP $n=314$	2	28	56	10	4	100
CAP $n = 97$	5	16.5	63	7	8.5	100
BEPC $n = 197$	2	17	55	13	13	100
Baccalauréat $n = 217$	2	17.5	48.5	19	13	100
Some higher edn.						
$n = 118$	6	9	47.5	19.5	18	100
Licence $n = 182$	2	16	51.5	8	22.5	100
Agrégation, grande école						
$n = 71$	3	11	38	21	27	100

The respondents had to answer this question: 'Given the following subjects, is a photographer more likely to make a beautiful, interesting, trivial, or ugly photo: a landscape, a car crash, a little girl playing with a cat, a pregnant woman, a still life, a woman suckling a child, a metal frame, tramps quarrelling, cabbages, a sunset over the sea, a weaver at his loom, a folk-dance, a rope, a butcher's stall, a famous monument, a scrap-yard, a first communion, a wounded man, a snake, an "old master"?'

Table 3. *Aesthetic disposition in relation to class position and educational qualification*

Top block — **Pregnant woman** and **Cabbages**

Class	Qualification	Pregnant woman						Cabbages					
		No reply or incoherent	Ugly	Trivial	Interesting	Beautiful	Total	No reply or incoherent	Ugly	Trivial	Interesting	Beautiful	Total
Working class	without diploma CEP, CAP (n=143)	1.5	40	36.5	14	8	100	1.5	28	57	8.5	5	100
	BEPC and further (n=18)		39	22	11	28	100		5.5	72.5	16.5	5.5	100
Middle class	without diploma CEP, CAP (n=243)	1	46	27.5	15	10.5	100	2	22.5	61.5	10	4	100
	BEPC and further (n=335) of which:	3.5	34	30	13.5	19	100	2.5	17.5	49.5	14.5	16	100
	BEPC (n=149)	3.5	39	35	9	13.5	100		21	56	8.5	12.5	100
	bac. (n=140)	3.5	37	21	17.5	21	100	3	15.5	45	19.5	17	100
	higher edn. (n=46)	4	8.5	42	13	32.5	100	3	13	41	20	22	100
Upper class	without diploma CEP, CAP (n=143)	20	36	24	12	8	100	20	36	28	12	4	100
	BEPC and further (n=432) of which:	3	36	22	19	20	100	3	14.5	48	15.5	19	100
	BEPC (n=31)	6.5	48.5	38.5		6.5	100	6.5	6.5	38.5	32.5	16	100
	bac. (n=76)		60.5	16	5	18.5	100		21	55.5	17	6.5	100
	higher edn. (n=325) of which:	3	30	22.5	23	21.5	100	3	14	47.5	13.5	22	100
	petite école (n=80)	7.5	17.5	30.0	32.5	12.5	100	6.5	6.5	52	20	15	100
	licence (n=174)	0.5	36	21.5	19.5	22.5	100	2	18.5	49	7.5	23	100
	agrég., grande école (n=71)	4	29.5	17	20	29.5	100	3	11	38	21	27	100

Bottom block — **Snake** and **Sunset over sea**

Class	Qualification	Snake						Sunset over sea					
		No reply or incoherent	Ugly	Trivial	Interesting	Beautiful	Total	No reply or incoherent	Ugly	Trivial	Interesting	Beautiful	Total
Working class	without diploma CEP, CAP (n=143)	1	35	16	38	10	100	1		1	10	8.5	100
	BEPC and further (n=18)		28	22	39	11	100			6	6	8.5	100
Middle class	without diploma CEP, CAP (n=243)	1	25	23	35	16	100	1		2.5	6	90	100
	BEPC and further (n=335) of which:	3	28.5	14	30.5	24	100	1.5	0.5	9	8.5	78	100
	BEPC (n=149)	3	38	8.5	43	16.5	100		1.5	4.5	6.5	86	100
	bac. (n=140)	4	21	17	34	24	100	1.5	1.5	10	9	75	100
	higher edn. (n=46)	2	19.5	24	9	45.5	100	4	2	20	13	63	100
Upper class	without diploma CEP, CAP (n=143)	20	36	4	24	16	100	20	2	8	8	64	100
	BEPC and further (n=432) of which:	3	18	13	38	28	100	2		15	17	63	100
	BEPC (n=31)	6.5	19.5	16	29	29	100		3	22.5		77.5	100
	bac. (n=76)		22.5	8	50	19.5	100			14.5	8	77.5	100
	higher edn. (n=325) of which:	4	16.5	14.5	35.5	29.5	100	3		14	21	58	100
	petite école (n=80)	5	14	20	36	25	100	6	5	10	26.5	52.5	100
	licence (n=174)	2.5	20	14.5	35	28	100		5	13	24	58	100
	agrég., grande école (n=71)	5.5	11.5	8.5	36.5	38	100	5.5	1.5	19.5	8.5	65	100

It is immediately clear that the category 'BEPC and above' (created for the sake of formal comparability) does not have the same content in the different social classes: the proportion of high qualifications within this category rises with social class. (This essentially explains why the rarest choices—'beautiful' for the cabbages or the snake, 'ugly', 'trivial' or 'interesting' for the sunset—become more numerous as one moves up the social scale. The apparent exception in the case of the pregnant woman is due to the absence of women, who are known to be more likely to accept this subject, in this category.)

of respondents who consider that these things can make a beautiful photograph is highest at the levels of the CAP and BEPC, whereas at higher levels they tend to be judged uninteresting or trivial.[20]

The statistics also show that women are much more likely than men to manifest their repugnance at repugnant, horrible or distasteful objects. Forty-four and a half per cent of them, as against 35% of the men, consider that there can only be an ugly photograph of a wounded man, and there are similar differences for the butcher's stall (33.5 and 27%), the snake (30.5 and 21.5%) or the pregnant woman (45 and 33.5%) whereas the gap disappears with the still life (6 and 6.5%) and the cabbages (20.5 and 19%). The traditional division of labour between the sexes assigns 'human' or 'humanitarian' tasks and feelings to women and more readily allows them effusions and tears, in the name of the opposition between reason and sensibility; men are, *ex officio*, on the side of culture whereas women (like the working class) are cast on the side of nature. Women are therefore less imperatively required to censor and repress 'natural' feelings, as the aesthetic disposition demands (which indicates, incidentally, that, as will be shown subsequently, the refusal of nature, or rather the refusal to surrender to nature, which is the mark of dominant groups—who start with *self*-control—is the basis of the aesthetic disposition).[21]

Thus, nothing more rigorously distinguishes the different classes than the disposition objectively demanded by the legitimate consumption of legitimate works, the aptitude for taking a specifically aesthetic point of view on objects already constituted aesthetically—and therefore put forward for the admiration of those who have learned to recognize the signs of the admirable—and the even rarer capacity to constitute aesthetically objects that are ordinary or even 'common' (because they are appropriated, aesthetically or otherwise, by the 'common people') or to apply the principles of a 'pure' aesthetic in the most everyday choices of everyday life, in cooking, dress or decoration, for example.

Statistical enquiry is indispensable in order to establish beyond dispute the social conditions of possibility (which will have to be made more explicit) of the 'pure' disposition. However, because it inevitably looks like a scholastic test intended to measure the respondents against a norm tacitly regarded as absolute, it may fail to capture the meanings which this disposition and the whole attitude to the world expressed in it have for the different social classes. What the logic of the test would lead one to describe as an incapacity (and that is what it is, from the standpoint of the norms defining legitimate perception of works of art) is *also* a refusal which stems

[20] The proportion of respondents who say a first communion can make a beautiful photo declines up to the level of the *licence* (basic university degree) and then rises up to the highest level. This is because a relatively large proportion of the highest-qualified subjects assert their aesthetic disposition by declaring that *any* object can be perceived aesthetically. Thus, in the dominant class, the proportion who declare that a sunset can make a beautiful photo is greatest at the lowest educational level, declines at intermediate levels (some higher education, a minor engineering school), and grows strongly again among those who have completed several years of higher education and who tend to consider that anything is suitable for beautiful photography.

[21] Women's revulsion is expressed more overtly, at the expense of aesthetic neutralization, the more completely they are subject to the traditional model of the sexual division of labour, and, in other words, the weaker their cultural capital and the lower their position in the social hierarchy. Women in the new petty-bourgeoisie who, in general, make much greater concessions to affective considerations than the men in the same category (although they are equally likely to say that there can be a beautiful photograph of cabbages), much more rarely accept that a photograph of a pregnant woman can only be ugly than women in any other category (31.5% of them, as against 70% of the wives of industrial and commercial employers, 69.5% of the wives of craftsmen and shopkeepers, 47.5% of the wives of manual workers, office workers and junior executives). In doing so, they manifest simultaneously their aesthetic pretensions and their desire to be seen as 'liberated' from the ethical taboos imposed on their sex.

from a denunciation of the arbitrary or ostentations gratuitousness of stylistic exercises or purely formalistic experiments. A certain 'aesthetic', which maintains that a photograph is justified by the object photographed or by the possible use of the photographic image, is being brought into play when manual workers almost invariably reject photography for photography's sake (e.g. the photo of pebbles) as useless, perverse or bourgeois: 'A waste of film', 'They must have film to throw away', 'I tell you, there are some people who don't know what to do with their time', 'Haven't they got anything better to do with their time than photograph things like that?' 'That's middle-class photography'.[22]

An anti-Kantian 'aesthetic'

It is no accident that, when one sets about reconstructing its logic, the popular 'aesthetic' appears as the negative opposite of the Kantian aesthetic and that the popular ethos implicitly answers each proposition of the Analytic of the Beautiful with a thesis contradicting it. In order to apprehend what makes the specificity of aesthetic judgment, Kant ingeniously distinguished 'that which pleases' from 'that which gives pleasure', and, more generally, strove to separate 'disinterestedness', the sole guarantee of the specifically aesthetic quality of contemplation, from 'the interest of the senses', which defines 'the agreeable', and from 'the interest of Reason', which defines 'the Good'. By contrast, working-class people, who expect every image to fulfil a *function*, if only that of a sign, refer, often explicitly, to norms of morality or agreeableness, in all their judgments. Thus the photograph of a dead soldier provokes judgments which, whether positive or negative, are always responses to the reality of the thing represented or to the functions the representation could serve, the horror of war or the denunciation of the horrors of war which the photograph is supposed to produce simply by showing that horror.[23] Similarly, popular naturalism recognizes beauty in the image of a beautiful thing or, more rarely, in a beautiful image of a beautiful thing: 'Now, that's good, it's almost symmetrical. Besides, she's a beautiful woman. A beautiful woman always looks good in a photo.' The Parisian manual worker echoes the plain-speaking of Hippias the Sophist:

I'll tell him what beauty is and I'm not likely to be refuted by him! The fact is, Socrates, to be frank, a beautiful woman, that's what beauty is!

This 'aesthetic', which subordinates the form and the very existence of the image to its function, is necessarily pluralistic and conditional. The insistence with which the respondents point out the limits and conditions of validity of their judgments, distinguishing, for each photograph, the possible uses or audiences, or, more precisely, the possible use for each audience ('as a news photo, it's not bad', 'all right, if it's for

[22] It must never be forgotten that the working-class 'aesthetic' is a *dominated* 'aesthetic' which is constantly obliged to define itself in terms of the dominant aesthetics. The members of the working class, who can neither ignore the high-art aesthetic which denounces their own 'aesthetic', nor abandon their socially conditioned inclinations, but still less proclaim them and legitimate them, often experience their relationship to the aesthetic norms in a twofold and contradictory way. This is seen when some manual workers grant 'pure' photographs a purely verbal recognition (this is also the case with many petty-bourgeois and even some bourgeois, who as regards paintings, for example, differ from the working class mainly by what they know is the right thing to say or do or, still better, *not* to say): 'It's beautiful but it would never occur to me to take a thing like that', 'Yes, it's very beautiful, but you have to like it, it's not my style'.
[23] The documents on which these analyses are based will be found in Bourdieu *et al.* (1965*b*) pp. 113–114.

showing to kids') shows that they reject the idea that a photograph can please 'universally'. 'A photo of a pregnant woman is all right for me, not for other people', said a white-collar worker, who has to use his concern for propriety as a way of expressing anxiety about what is 'showable' and therefore entitled to demand admiration. Because the image is always judged by reference to the function it fulfils for the person who looks at it or which he thinks it could fulfil for other classes of beholders, aesthetic judgment naturally takes the form of a hypothetical judgment implicitly based on recognition of 'genres', the perfection and scope of which are defined by a *concept*. Almost three-quarters of the judgments expressed begin with an 'if', and the effort to recognize culminates in classification into a genre, or, which amounts to the same thing, in the attribution of a social use, the different genres being defined in terms of their use and their users ('it's a publicity photo', 'it's a pure document', 'it's a laboratory photo', 'it's a competition photo', 'it's an educational photo', etc.). And photographs of nudes are almost always received with comments that reduce them to the stereotype of their social function: 'All right in Pigalle', 'it's the sort of photos they keep under the counter'. It is not surprising that this 'aesthetic', which bases appreciation on informative, tangible or moral interest, can only refuse images of the trivial, or, which amounts to the same thing in terms of this logic, the triviality of the image: judgment never gives the image of the object autonomy with respect to the object of the image. Of all the characteristics proper to the image, only colour (which Kant regarded as less pure than form) can prevent rejection of photographs of trivial things. Nothing is more alien to popular consciousness than the idea of an aesthetic pleasure that, to put it in Kantian terms, is independent of the charming of the senses. Thus judgments on the photographs most strongly rejected on grounds of futility (pebbles, bark, wave) almost always end with the reservation that 'in colour, it might be pretty'; and some respondents even manage to formulate the maxim governing their attitude, when they declare that 'if the colours are good, a colour photograph is always beautiful'. In short, Kant is indeed referring to popular taste when he writes:

Taste that requires an added element of charm and emotion for its delight, not to speak of adopting this as the measure of its approval, has not yet emerged from barbarism (Kant, 1952, p. 65).

Refusal of the trivial (*insignifiant*) image, which has neither meaning nor interest, or the ambiguous image, means refusing to treat it as finality without purpose, as an image signifying itself, and therefore having no other referent than itself. The value of a photograph is measured by the interest of the information it conveys, and by the clarity with which it fulfils this informative function, in short, its *legibility*, which itself varies with the legibility of its intention or function, the judgment it provokes being more or less favourable depending on the expressive adequacy of the signifier to the signified. It therefore contains the expectation of the title or caption which, by declaring the signifying intention, makes it possible to judge whether the realization signifies or illustrates it adequately. If formal explorations, in avant-garde theatre or non-figurative painting, or simply in classical music, are disconcerting to working-class people, this is partly because they feel incapable of *understanding* what these things *must* signify, insofar as they are signs. Hence the initiated may experience as inadequate and unworthy a satisfaction that cannot be grounded in a meaning transcendent to the object. Not knowing what the 'intention' is, they feel incapable of distinguishing a *tour de force* from clumsiness, telling a 'sincere' formal device from cynical imposture.[24] But formal refinement is also that which, by putting form, i.e. the artist, in the foreground, with his own interests, his technical problems, his effects, his play of references, throws the thing itself into the background and precludes direct communion with the beauty of the world—a beautiful child, a beautiful girl, a beautiful animal or a beautiful landscape. The representation is expected to be a feast for the eyes and, like still life, to 'stir up memories and anticipations of feasts enjoyed and feasts to come'.[25] Nothing is more opposed to celebration of the beauty and joy of the world that is looked for in the work of art, 'a choice which praises', than the devices of cubist or abstract painting, which are perceived and unanimously denounced as aggressions against the thing represented, against the natural order and especially the human form. In short, however perfectly it performs its representative function, the work is only seen as fully justified if the thing represented is worthy of being represented, if the representative function is subordinated to a higher function, such as that of capturing and exalting a reality that is worthy of being made eternal. Such is the basis of the 'barbarous taste' to which the most antithetical forms of the dominant aesthetic always refer negatively and which only recognizes realist representation, in other words a respectful, humble, submissive representation of objects designated by their beauty or their social importance.

Aesthetics, ethics and aestheticism

When confronted with legitimate works of art, people most lacking the specific competence apply to them the perceptual schemes of their own ethos, which structure their everyday perception of everyday existence. These schemes, giving rise to products of an unwilled, unselfconscious systematicity, are opposed to the more or less fully explicit principles of an aesthetic.[26] The result is a systematic 'reduction' of the things of art to the things of life, a bracketing of form in favour of 'human' content, which is barbarism *par excellence* from the standpoint of the pure aesthetic. Everything takes place as if the emphasis on form could only be achieved by means of a neutralization of any kind of affective or ethical interest in the object of representation which accompanies (without any necessary cause-effect relation) mastery of the means of grasping the distinctive properties which this particular form takes on in its relations with other forms (i.e. through reference to the universe of works of art and its history).

The aestheticism which makes the artistic intention the basis of the 'art of living' implies a sort of moral agnosticism, the perfect antithesis of the ethical disposition which subordinates art to the values of the art of living. The aesthetic intention can only contradict the dispositions of the ethos or the norms of the ethic which, at each moment, define the *legitimate objects and modes of representation* for the different social classes, excluding from the universe of the 'representable' certain realities and certain ways of representing them. Thus the easiest, and so the most frequent and most spectacular way to '*épater le bourgeois*' by proving the extent of one's power to confer aesthetic status is to transgress ever more radically the ethical censorships

24 The confessions with which workers faced with modern pictures betray their exclusion ('I don't understand what it means' or: 'I like it but I don't understand it') contrast with the knowing silence of the bourgeois, who, though equally disconcerted, at least know that they have to refuse—or, at least, conceal—the naive expectation of expressiveness that is betrayed by the concern to 'understand' ('programme music' and the titles foisted on so many sonatas, concertos and symphonies are sufficient indication that this expectation is not exclusively popular).

25 Gombrich (1963) p. 104.

26 The populist image of the proletariat as an opaque, dense, hard 'in-itself' the perfect antithesis of the intellectual or aesthete, a self-transparent, insubstantial 'in-itself', has a certain basis here.

(e.g. in matters of sex) which the other classes accept even within the area which the dominant disposition defines as aesthetic. Or, more subtly, it is done by conferring aesthetic status on objects or ways of representing them which are excluded by the dominant aesthetic of the time, or on objects that are given aesthetic status by dominated aesthetics.

One only has to read the index of contents recently published by *Art vivant* (1974), a 'vaguely modern review run by a clique of academics who are vaguely art historians' (as an avant-garde painter nicely put it), which occupies a sort of neutral point in the field of avant-garde art criticism between *Flashart* or *Art press* and *Artitude* or *Opus*. In the list of features and titles one finds: *Africa* (one title: 'Art must be for all'), *Architecture* (two titles, including 'Architecture without an architect') *Comic Strips* (five titles, nine pages out of the forty-six in the whole index), *Kids' Art*, *Kitsch* (three titles, five pages), *Photography* (two titles, three pages), *Street Art* (fifteen titles, twenty-three pages, including 'Art in the Street?', 'Art in the Street First Episode', 'Beauty in the Back-streets. You just have to know how to look.' 'A Suburb sets the Pace'), *Science-Fiction-Utopia* (two titles, three pages), *Underground* (one title) *Writing–Ideograms–Graffiti* (two titles, four pages). The aim of inverting or *transgressing* which is clearly manifested by this list is necessarily contained within the limits assigned to it *a contrario* by the aesthetic conventions it denounces and by the need to secure recognition of the aesthetic nature of the transgression of the limits (i.e. recognition of its conformity to the norms of the transgressing group). Hence the almost Markovian logic of the choices, with, for the cinema, Antonioni, Chaplin, cinémathèque, Eisenstein, eroticism-pornography, Fellini, Godard, Klein, Monroe, underground, Warhol.

This commitment to *symbolic transgression*, which is often combined with political neutrality or revolutionary aestheticism, is the almost perfect antithesis of petit-bourgeois moralism or of what Sartre used to call the revolutionary's 'seriousness'.[27] The ethical indifference which the aesthetic disposition implies when it becomes the basis of the art of living is in fact the root of the ethical aversion to artists (or intellectuals) which manifests itself particularly vehemently among the declining and threatened fractions of the petty-bourgeoisie (especially independent craftsmen and shopkeepers) who tend to express their regressive and repressive dispositions in all areas of practice (especially in educational matters and *vis-à-vis* students and student demonstrations), but also among the rising fractions of that class whose striving for virtue and deep insecurity renders them very receptive to the phantasm of 'pornocracy'.

The pure disposition is so universally recognized as legitimate that no voice is heard pointing out that the definition of art, and through it the art of living, is an object of struggle among the classes. Dominated life-styles (*arts de vivre*), which have practically never received systematic expression, are almost always perceived, even by their defenders, from the destructive or reductive viewpoint of the dominant aesthetic, so that their own only options are degradation or self-destructive rehabilitation ('popular culture'). This is why we must look to Proudhon[28] for a naïvely systematic expression of the *petty-bourgeois aesthetic*, which subordinates art to the core values of the art of living and identifies the cynical perversion of the artist's life-style as the source of the absolute primacy given to form:

Under the influence of property, the artist, *depraved* in his reason, *dissolute in his morals*, *venal*

---

[27] This is seen clearly in literature and in the theatre (e.g. the American 'new wave' of the 1960s).
[28] Dickens could also have been cited.

and without dignity, is the impure image of egoism. The idea of *justice* and *honesty* slides over his heart without taking root, and of all the classes of society, the artist class is the poorest in strong souls and noble characters (Proudhon, 1939*a*, p. 226—my italics).

Art for art's sake, as it has been called, not having its legitimacy within itself, being based on nothing, is nothing. It is *debauchery* of the heart and *dissolution* of the mind. Separated from right and duty, cultivated and pursued as the highest thought of the soul and the supreme manifestation of humanity, art or the ideal, stripped of the greater part of itself, reduced to being nothing more than an *excitement of fantasy and the senses*, is the source of *sin*, the origin of all servitude, the poisoned spring from which, according to the Bible, flow all the *fornications* and abominations of the earth. . . . Art for art's sake, I say, verse for verse's sake, style for style's sake, form for form's sake, fantasy for fantasy's sake, all the diseases which like a plague of lice are gnawing away at our epoch, are *vice* in all its refinement, the quintessence of evil (Proudhon, 1939*a*, p. 71—my italics).

What is condemned is the autonomy of form and the artist's right to the formal experiments by which he claims mastery of what ought to be merely a matter of 'execution':

I do not wish to argue about nobility, or elegance, or pose, or style, or gesture, or any aspect of what constitutes the execution of a work of art and is the usual object of traditional criticism (Proudhon, 1939*a*, p. 166).

Dependent on demand in the choice of their objects, artists take their revenge in the execution:

There are church painters, history painters, genre painters (in other words painters of anecdotes or farces), portrait painters, landscape painters, animal painters, seascape painters, painters of Venus, painters of fantasy. One specializes in nudes, another in drapery. Then each one endeavours to distinguish himself by one of the means which contribute to the execution. One goes in for sketching, another for colour; this one attends to composition, that one to perspective, a third to costume or local colour; one shines through sentiment, another through his idealized or realistic figures; yet another redeems the futility of his subject by the fineness of his detail. Each strives to have his own trick, his own *je ne sais quoi*, a personal manner, and so, with the help of fashion, reputations are made and unmade (Proudhon, 1939*b*, p. 271).

In contrast to this decadent art cut off from social life, respecting neither God nor man, an art worthy of the name must be subordinate to science, morality and justice. It must aim to arouse the moral sense, to inspire feelings of dignity and delicacy, to idealize reality, to substitute for the thing the ideal of the thing, by painting the true and not the real. In a word, it must educate. To do so, it must transmit not personal impressions (like David in *The Tennis-Court Oath*, or Delacroix) but, like Courbet in *Les Paysans de Flagey*, reconstitute the social and historical truth which *all* may judge. ('Each of us only has to consult himself to be able, after brief consideration, to state a judgment on any work of art'.)[29] And it would be a pity to conclude without quoting a eulogy of the small detached house which would surely be massively endorsed by the lower-middle and working classes:

I would give the Louvre, the Tuileries, Notre-Dame—and the Vendôme column into the bargain—to live in my own home, in a *little house of my own design*, where I would live alone, in the middle of a little plot of ground, a quarter of an acre or so, where I'd have water, shade, a lawn, and silence. And if I thought of putting a statue in it, it wouldn't be a Jupiter or an Apollo—those gentlemen are nothing to me—nor view of London, Rome, Constantinople or Venice. God preserve me from such places! I'd put there what I lack—mountains, vineyards, meadows, goats, cows, sheep, reapers and shepherds (Proudhon, 1939*a*, p. 256).[30]

[29] Proudhon (1939*b*) p. 49.

[30] It is impossible completely to understand the acceptance of the theses of Zdanov, who is very close to Proudhon in several respects, without taking into account the correspondences between his 'aesthetic' and the working-class or petit-bourgeois ethos of a number of the leaders of the French Communist Party.

Neutralization and the universe of possibilities

Unlike non-specific perception, the specifically aesthetic perception of a work of art (in which there are of course degrees of accomplishment) is armed with a _pertinence principle_ which is socially constituted and acquired. This principle of selection enables it to pick out and retain, from among the elements offered to the eye (e.g. leaves or clouds considered merely as indices or signals invested with a denotative function—'it's a poplar', 'there's going to be a storm'), all the stylistic traits—and only those—which, when relocated in the universe of stylistic possibilities, distinguish a particular manner of treating the elements selected, whether clouds or leaves, i.e. a style as a mode of representation expressing the mode of perception and thought that is proper to a period, a class or class fraction, a group of artists or a particular artist. No stylistic characterization of a work of art is possible without presupposing at least implicit reference to the compossible alternatives, whether simultaneous—to distinguish it from its contemporaries—or successive—to contrast it with earlier or later works by the same or a different artist. Exhibitions devoted to an artist's whole _oeuvre_ or to a genre (e.g. the still-life exhibition in Bordeaux in 1978) are the objective realization of the field of _interchangeable_ stylistic possibilities which is brought into play when one 'recognizes' the singularities of the characteristic style of a work of art. As Gombrich demonstrates, Mondrian's _Broadway Boogie-Woogie_ only takes on its 'full meaning' in terms of a previous idea of Mondrian's work and of the expectations it favours. The 'impression of gay abandon' given by the play of bright, strongly contrasting patches of colour can only arise in a mind familiar with 'an art of straight lines and a few primary colours in carefully balanced rectangles' and capable of perceiving the 'relaxed style of popular music' in the distance from the 'severity' which is expected. And as soon as one imagines this painting attributed to Severini, who tries to express in some of his paintings 'the rhythm of dance music in works of brilliant chaos,' it is clear that, measured by this stylistic yardstick, Mondrian's picture would rather suggest the First Brandenburg Concerto (Gombrich, 1960, p. 313).

The aesthetic disposition, understood as the aptitude for perceiving and deciphering specifically stylistic characteristics, is thus inseparable from specifically artistic competence. The latter may be acquired by explicit learning or simply by regular contact with works of art, especially those assembled in museums and galleries, where the diversity of their original functions is neutralized by their being displayed in a place consecrated to art, so that they invite pure interest in form. This practical mastery enables its possessor to situate each element of a universe of artistic representations in a class defined in relation to the class composed of all the artistic representations consciously or unconsciously excluded. Thus, an awareness of the stylistic features which make up the stylistic _originality_ of all the works of a period relative to those of another period, or, within this class, of the works of one school relative to another, or of the works of one artist relative to the works of his school or period, or even of an artist's particular period or work relative to his whole _oeuvre_, is inseparable from an awareness of the stylistic _redundancies_, i.e. the typical treatments of the pictorial matter which define a style. In short, a grasp of the resemblances presupposes implicit or explicit reference to the differences, and vice versa. Attribution is always implicitly based on reference to 'typical works' consciously or unconsciously selected because they present to a particularly high degree the qualities more or less explicitly recognized as pertinent in a given system of classification. Everything suggests that, even among specialists, the criteria of pertinence which define the stylistic properties of key works generally remain implicit and that the aesthetic taxonomies implicitly mobilized to distinguish, classify and order works of art never have the rigour which aesthetic theories sometimes try to lend them.

In fact, the simple *placing* which the amateur or specialist performs when he undertakes attribution has nothing in common with the genuinely scientific intention of grasping the work's immanent reason and *raison d'être* by reconstructing the perceived situation, the subjectively experienced problematic, which is nothing other than the space of the positions and self-positionings constituting the field, and within which the artistic intention of the artist in question has defined itself, generally *by opposition*. The references which this reconstructing operation deploys have nothing to do with the kinds of semantic echo or affective correspondence which adorn celebratory discourse; they are the indispensable means of constructing the field of thematic or stylistic possibilities in relation to which, objectively and to some extent subjectively, the possibility selected by the artist presented itself. Thus, to understand why the early Romantic painters returned to primitive art, one would have to reconstitute the whole universe of reference of the pupils of David, with their long beards and Greek costumes, who 'outdoing their master's cult of antiquity, wanted to go back to Homer, the Bible and Ossian, and condemned the style of classical antiquity itself as "rococo", "Van Loo" or "Pompadour" ' (Benichou, 1973, p. 212). This would lead one back to the inextricably ethical and aesthetic alternatives—such as the identification of the naïve with the pure and the natural—in terms of which their choices were made and which have nothing in common with the transhistorical oppositions beloved of formalist aesthetics.[31]

But the celebrant's or devotee's intention is not that of understanding and, in the ordinary routine of the cult of the work of art, the play of academic or urbane references has no other function than to bring the work into an interminable circuit of inter-legitimation, so that a reference to Jan Brueghel's *Bouquet of Flowers* lends dignity to Jean-Michel Picart's *Bouquet of Flowers with Parrot* just as, in another context, reference to the latter can, being less common, serve to enhance the former. This play of cultured allusions and analogies endlessly pointing to other analogies, which, like the cardinal oppositions in mythical or ritual systems, never have to justify themselves by stating the basis of the relating which they perform, weaves around the works a complex web of factitious experiences, each answering and reinforcing all the others, which *creates* the enchantment of artistic contemplation. It is the source of the 'idolatry' to which Proust refers, which leads one to find

an actress's robe or a society woman's dress beautiful . . . not because the cloth is beautiful but because it is the cloth painted by Moreau or described by Balzac (Proust, 1947, p. 173).[32]

31 For a similar critique of the application of an empty opposition (between 'soft focus' and 'hard focus') to the German Romantic painters, see Gombrich (1969), p. 33.

32 Analogy, functioning as a circular mode of thought, makes it possible to tour the whole area of art and luxury *without ever leaving it*. Thus Château Margaux wine can be described with the same words used to describe the Château, just as others will evoke Proust apropos of Monet or Franck, which is a good way of talking about neither: 'The house is in the image of the vintage. Noble, austere, even a little solemn. Château Margaux has the air of an ancient temple devoted to the cult of wine. . . . Vineyard or dwelling, Margaux refuses all embellishments. But just as the wine has to be served before it unfolds all its charms, so the residence waits for the visitor to enter before it reveals its own. In each case the same words spring to one's lips: elegance, distinction, delicacy, and that subtle satisfaction given from something which has received the most attentive and indeed loving care for generations. A wine long matured, a house long inhabited: Margaux the vintage and Margaux the château are the product of two equally rare things: *rigour and time*' (Schlumberger, *Connaissance du Arts*, November 1973, pp. 101–105).

Distance from necessity

To explain the correlation between educational capital and the propensity or at least the aspiration to appreciate a work 'independently of its content', as the culturally most ambitious respondents put it, and more generally the propensity to make the 'gratuitous' and 'disinterested' investments demanded by legitimate works, it is not sufficient to point to the fact that schooling provides the linguistic tools and the references which enable aesthetic experience to be expressed and to be constituted by being expressed. What is in fact affirmed in this relationship is the dependence of the aesthetic disposition on the past and present material conditions of existence which are the precondition of both its constitution and its application and also of the accumulation of a cultural capital (whether or not educationally sanctioned) which can only be acquired by means of a sort of withdrawal from economic necessity. The aesthetic disposition which tends to bracket off the nature and function of the object represented and to exclude any 'naïve' reaction—horror at the horrible, desire for the desirable, pious reverence for the sacred—along with all purely ethical responses, in order to concentrate solely upon the mode of representation, the style, perceived and appreciated by comparison with other styles, is one dimension of a total relation to the world and to others, a life-style, in which the effects of particular conditions of existence are expressed in a mis-recognizable form. These conditions of existence, which are the precondition for all learning of legitimate culture, whether implicit and diffuse, as domestic cultural training generally is, or explicit and specific, as in scholastic training, are characterized by the suspension and removal of economic necessity and by objective and subjective distance from practical urgencies, which is the basis of objective and subjective distance from groups subjected to those determinisms.

To be able to play the games of culture with the playful seriousness which Plato demanded, a seriousness without the 'spirit of seriousness', one has to belong to the ranks of those who have been able, not necessarily to make their whole existence a sort of children's game, as artists do, but at least to maintain for a long time, sometimes a whole life-time, a child's relation to the world. (All children start life as baby bourgeois, in a relation of magical power over others and, through them, over the world, but they grow out of it sooner or later). This is clearly seen when, by an accident of social genetics, into the well-policed world of intellectual games there comes one of those people (one thinks of Rousseau or Chernyshevsky) who bring inappropriate stakes and interests into the games of culture; who get so involved in the game that they abandon the margin of neutralizing distance that the *illusio* demands; who treat intellectual struggles, the object of so many pathetic manifestos, as a simple question of right and wrong, life and death. This is why the logic of the game has already assigned them rôles—eccentric or boor—which they will *play* despite themselves in the eyes of those who know how to stay within the bounds of the intellectual illusion and who cannot see them any other way.

The aesthetic disposition, a generalized capacity to neutralize ordinary urgencies and to bracket off practical ends, a durable inclination and aptitude for practice without a practical function, can only be constituted within an experience of the world freed from urgency and through the practice of activities which are an end in themselves, such as scholastic exercises or the contemplation of works of art. In other words, it presupposes the distance from the world (of which the 'rôle distance' brought to light by Goffman is a particular case) which is the basis of the bourgeois experience of the world. Contrary to what certain mechanistic theories would suggest, even in its most specifically artistic dimension, the pedagogic action of the family and the school operates at least as much through the economic and social conditions which are the precondition of its operation as through the contents which it inculcates.[33] The scholastic world of regulated games and exercises for exercises' sake is, at least in this respect, less remote than it might appear from the 'bourgeois' world and the countless 'disinterested' and 'gratuitous' acts which go to make up its distinctive rarity, such as home maintenance and decoration, occasioning a daily squandering of care, time and labour (often through the intermediary of servants), walking and tourism, movements without any other aim than physical exercise and the symbolic appropriation of a world reduced to the status of a landscape, or ceremonies and receptions, pretexts for a display of ritual luxuries, décors, conversations and finery, not to mention, of course, artistic practices and enjoyments. It is not surprising that bourgeois adolescents, who are both economically privileged and (temporarily) excluded from the reality of economic power, sometimes express their distance from the bourgeois world which they cannot really appropriate by a refusal of complicity whose most refined expression is a propensity towards aesthetics and aestheticism. In this respect they share common ground with the women of the bourgeoisie, who, being partially excluded from economic activity, find fulfilment in stage-managing the décor of bourgeois existence, when they are not seeking refuge or revenge in aesthetics.

Economic power is first and foremost a power to keep economic necessity at arm's length. This is why it universally asserts itself by the destruction of riches, conspicuous consumption, squandering, and every form of *gratuitous* luxury. Thus, whereas the court aristocracy made the whole of life a continuous spectacle, the bourgeoisie has established the opposition between what is paid for and what is free, the interested and the disinterested, in the form of the opposition, which Weber saw as characterizing it, between place of work and place of residence, working days and holidays, the outside (male) and the inside (female), business and sentiment, industry and art, the world of economic necessity and the world of artistic freedom that is snatched, by economic power, from that necessity.

Material or symbolic consumption of works of art constitutes one of the supreme manifestations of *ease*, in the sense both of leisure and facility.[34] The detachment of the pure gaze cannot be separated from a general disposition towards the 'gratuitous' and the 'disinterested', the paradoxical product of a negative economic conditioning which, through facility and freedom, engenders distance *vis-à-vis* necessity. At the same time, the aesthetic disposition is defined, objectively and subjectively, in relation to other dispositions. Objective distance from necessity and from those trapped within it combines with a conscious distance which doubles freedom by exhibiting it. As the objective distance from necessity grows, life-style increasingly becomes the product of what Weber calls a 'stylization of life', a systematic commitment which orients and organizes the most diverse practices—the choice of a vintage or a cheese or the decoration of a holiday home in the country. This affirmation of power over a dominated necessity always implies a claim to a legitimate superiority over those who, because they cannot assert the same contempt for contingencies in gratuitous luxury and conspicuous consumption, remain dominated by ordinary interests and urgencies. The

[33] For an analysis of the relationship between the scholastic environment (a world apart, exercises which are an end in themselves) and the relation to language which is required in all 'official' situations (see Bourdieu, 1973d; Bourdieu and Boltanski, 1975e).

[34] Virtually every treatise written in the classical period explicitly makes the link between ease and elegance of style and elegance of life-style. Consider, for example, the doctrine of *sprezzatura*, the nonchalance which, according to Castiglione, distinguishes the perfect courtier and the perfect artist.

tastes of freedom can only assert themselves as such in relation to the tastes of necessity, which are thereby brought to the level of the aesthetic and so defined as vulgar. This claim to aristocracy is less likely to be contested than any other, because the relation of the 'pure', 'disinterested' disposition to the conditions which make it possible, i.e. the material conditions of existence which are rarest because most freed from economic necessity, has every chance of passing unnoticed. The most 'classifying' privilege thus has the privilege of appearing to be the most natural one.

The aesthetic sense as the sense of distinction

Thus, the aesthetic disposition is one dimension of a distant, self-assured relation to the world and to others which presupposes objective assurance and distance. It is one manifestation of the system of dispositions produced by the social conditionings associated with a particular class of conditions of existence when they take the paradoxical form of the greatest freedom conceivable, at a given moment, with respect to the constraints of economic necessity. But it is also a *distinctive expression* of a privileged position in social space whose distinctive value is *objectively* established in its relationship to expressions generated from different conditions. Like every sort of taste, it unites and separates. Being the product of the conditionings associated with a particular class of conditions of existence, it unites all those who are the product of similar conditions but only by distinguishing them from all others. And it distinguishes in an essential way, since taste is the basis of all that one has—people and things—and of all that one is for others, whereby one classifies oneself and is classified by others.

Tastes (i.e. manifested preferences) are the practical affirmation of an inevitable difference. It is no accident that, when they have to be justified, they are asserted purely negatively, by the refusal of other tastes.[35] In matters of taste, more than anywhere else, all determination is negation;[36] and tastes are perhaps first and foremost distastes, disgust provoked by horror or visceral intolerance ('sick-making') of the tastes of others. There is no accounting for tastes: not because '*tous les goûts sont dans la nature*', but because each taste feels itself to be natural—and so it almost is, being a habitus—which amounts to rejecting others as unnatural and therefore vicious. Aesthetic intolerance can be terribly violent. Aversion to different life styles is perhaps one of the strongest barriers between the classes: class endogamy is evidence of it. The most intolerable thing for those who regard themselves as the possessors of legitimate culture is the sacrilegious reuniting of tastes which taste dictates shall be sep-

---

[35] Two examples, chosen from among hundreds, but paradigmatic, of explicit use of the scheme 'something other than': '*La Fiancée du pirate* is one of those very rare French films that are *really* satirical, *really* funny, because it does not resort to the carefully defused, prudently inoffensive comedy one finds in *la Grande Vandrouille* and *le Petit Baigneur*. . . . In short, it is *something other than* the dreary hackwork of boulevard farce' (J. L. Bory, *Le Nouvel Observateur*, 8 December 1969, my italics). 'Through distance, or at least, though difference, to endeavour to present a text on pictorial modernity *other than* the hackneyed banalities of *a certain style of art criticism*. *Between* verbose aphasia, the textual transcription of pictures, exclamations of recognition, *and* the works of specialized aesthetics, perhaps *marking* some of the ways in which conceptual, theoretical work gets to grips with contemporary plastic production' (G. Gassiot–Talabot et al., *Figurations* 1960/1973, Paris, Union générale des éditions, 1973, p. 7).

[36] This essential negativity, which is part of the very logic of the constitution of taste and its change, explains why, as Gombrich points out, 'the terminology of art history was so largely built on words denoting some principle of exclusion. Most movements in art erect some new taboo, some new negative principle, such as the banishing from painting by the impressionists of all 'anecdotal' elements. The positive slogans and shibboleths which we read in artists' or critics' manifestos past or present are usually much less well defined' (Gombrich, 1966, p. 89).

arated. This means that the games of artists and aesthetes and their struggles for the monopoly of artistic legitimacy are less innocent than they seem. At stake in every struggle over art there is also the imposition of an art of living, i.e. the transmutation of an arbitrary way of living into the legitimate way of life which casts every other way of living into arbitrariness.[37] The artist's life-style is always a challenge thrown at the bourgeois life-style, which it seeks to condemn as unreal and even absurd, by a sort of practical demonstration of the emptiness of the values and powers it pursues. The neutralizing relation to the world which defines the aesthetic disposition potentially implies a subversion of the spirit of seriousness required by bourgeois investments. Like the visibly ethical judgments of those who lack the means to make art the basis of their art of living, to see the world and other people through literary reminiscences and pictorial references, the 'pure' and purely aesthetic judgments of the artist and the aesthete spring from the dispositions of an ethos; but because of the legitimacy which they command so long as their relationship to the dispositions and interests of a group defined by strong cultural capital and weak economic capital remains unrecognized, they provide a sort of absolute reference in the necessarily endless play of mutually self-relativizing tastes. By a paradoxical reversal, they thereby help to legitimate the bourgeois claim to 'natural distinction' as *difference made absolute*.[38]

Bibliography

BENICHOU, P. (1973). *Le Sacre de l'ecrivain* 1750–1830, Jose Corti

GOMBRICH, E. H. (1960). *Art and Illusion*, Phaidon Press, London

GOMBRICH, E. H. (1963). *Meditations on a Hobby Horse*, Phaidon, London

GOMBRICH, E. H. (1966). *Norm and Form: Studies in the Art of the Renaissance*, Phaidon, London

GOMBRICH, E. H. (1969). *In Search of Cultural History*, Clarendon Press, Oxford

KANT, I. (1952). *The Critique of Judgement* (1790), Trans. J. C. Meredith, Oxford University Press, London

LANGER, S. K. (1968). On significance in music, In *Aesthetics and the Arts* (L. A. Jacobus, ed.), McGraw-Hill, New York

ORTEGA Y GASSET, J. (1976). *La deshumanización del arte*, Revista de occidente, Madrid

PANOFSKY, E. (1955). *Meaning in the Visual Arts*, Penguin, Harmondsworth

PROUST, M. (1947). *Pastiches et Melanges*, Gallimard, Paris

WOOLF, V. (1948). Mr Bennet and Mrs Brown. In (M. Schorer *et al.* eds.) *Criticism, The Foundations of Modern Literary Judgement*, Harcourt Brace, New York

[37] This is seen clearly in the case of the theatre, which touches more directly and more overtly on the implicit or explicit principles of the art of living. Especially in the case of comedy, it presupposes common values or interests or, more precisely, a complicity and connivance based on immediate assent to the same self-evident propositions, those of the *doxa*, the totality of opinions accepted at the level of prereflexive belief. (This explains why the institutions supplying the products, and the products themselves, are more sharply differentiated in the theatre than in any other art.)

[38] For an analysis of 'art for art's sake' as the expression of the artistic life-style, see Bourdieu, 1975*b*.

Cultural entrepreneurship in nineteenth-century Boston: the creation of an organizational base for high culture in America

PAUL DIMAGGIO*

Sociological and political discussions of culture have been predicated on a strong dichotomy between high culture—what goes on in museums, opera houses, symphony halls and theatres—and popular culture, of both the folk and commercial varieties. Such culture critics as Dwight McDonald (1957) and Theodor Adorno (1941) have based on this dichotomy thorough-going critiques of popular culture and the mass media. Defenders of popular culture (Lowenthal, 1961; Gans, 1974) have questioned the normative aspect of the critique of popular culture, but have, for the most part, accepted the basic categories. The distinction between high and popular culture has been implicit, as well, in the discussion of public policy towards culture in both the United States and Great Britain (DiMaggio and Useem, 1978).

Yet high and popular culture can be defined neither by qualities inherent to the work of art, nor, as some have argued, by simple reference to the class character of their publics. The distinction between high and popular culture, in its American version, emerged in the period between 1850 and 1900 out of the efforts of urban elites to build organizational forms that, first, isolated high culture and, second, differentiated it from popular culture. Americans did not merely adopt available European models. Instead they groped their way to a workable distinction. Not until two distinct organizational forms—the private or semi-private, non-profit cultural institution and the commercial popular-culture industry—took shape did the high/popular-culture dichotomy emerge in its modern form. Once these organizational models developed, the first in the bosom of elite urban status communities, the second in the relative impersonality of emerging regional and national markets, they shaped the rôle that cultural institutions would play, the careers of artists, the nature of the works created and performed, and the purposes and publics that cultural organizations would serve.

In this paper I will address only one side of this process of classification, the institutionalization of high culture and the creation of distinctly high-cultural organizations. While high culture could be defined only in opposition to popular culture, it is the process by which urban elites forged an institutional system embodying their ideas about the high arts that will engage us here. In order to grasp the extent to which the creation of modern high-cultural institutions was a task that involved elites as an organic group, we will focus on that process in one American city. Boston in the nineteenth century was the most active center of

---

* Institution for Social and Policy Studies, Yale University.

American culture; and its elite—the Boston Brahmins—constituted the most well defined status group of any of the urban upper classes of this period. For this reason the processes with which I am concerned appear here in particularly clear relief.[1]

When we look at Boston before 1850 we see a culture defined by the pulpit, the lectern and a collection of artistic efforts, amateurish by modern standards, in which effort rarely was made to distinguish between art and entertainment, or between culture and commerce. The arts in Boston were not self-conscious; they drew few boundaries. While intellectuals and ministers distinguished culture that elevated the spirit from that which debased it, there was relatively little agreement on what works or genres constituted which (see Hatch, 1962; Harris, 1966). Harvard's Pierian Sodality mixed popular songs with student compositions and works by European fine-arts composers. The Philharmonic Society played classical concerts, but also backed visiting popular vocalists. Throughout this period, most of Boston music was in the hands of commercial entrepreneurs. Gottlieb Graupner, the city's leading impresario in the 1830s, sold sheet music and instruments, published songs and promoted concerts at which religious, classical and popular tunes mingled freely. (One typical performance included a bit of Italian opera, a devotional song by Mrs Graupner, a piece by Verdi, 'Bluebell of Scotland' and 'The Origin of Common Nails', recited by Mr Bernard, a comedian.) The two exceptions, the Handel and Haydn Society and the Harvard Musical Association, founded in the 1840s and 1850s respectively, were associations of amateurs and professionals that appealed only to a relatively narrow segment of the elite.

The visual arts were also organized on a largely commercial basis in this era. In the 1840s, the American Art Union sold paintings by national lottery (Lynnes, 1953). These lotteries were succeeded, in Boston, New York and Philadelphia, by private galleries. Museums were modelled on Barnum's (Barnum, 1879; Harris, 1973): fine art was interspersed among such curiosities as bearded women and mutant animals, and popular entertainments were offered for the price of admission to a clientele that included working people as well as the upper middle class. Founded as a commercial venture in 1841, Moses Kemball's Boston Museum exhibited works by such painters as Sully and Peale alongside Chinese curiosities, stuffed animals, mermaids and dwarves. For the entrance fee visitors could also attend the Boston Museum Theatre, which presented works by Dickens and Shakespeare as well as performances by gymnasts and contortionists, and brought to Boston the leading players of the American and British stage (McGlinchee, 1940). The promiscuous combination of genres that later would be considered incompatible was not uncommon. As late as the 1880s, American circuses employed Shakespearian clowns who recited the bard's lines in full clown make-up (Fellows and Freeman, 1936).

By 1910, high and popular culture were encountered far less frequently in the same settings. The distinction towards which Boston's clerics and critics had groped 50 years before had emerged in institutional form. The Boston Symphony Orchestra was a permanent aggregation, wresting the favor of Boston's upper class

---

[1] The process, in other American cities, was to a large extent influenced by the Boston model. A final, more mundane, consideration recommends Boston as the focus for this study. The work in this paper is still in an exploratory stage, at which I am plundering history rather than writing it; the prolixity of nineteenth-century Boston's men and women of letters and the dedication and quality of her local historians makes Boston an ideal site for such an enterprise.

decisively from the commercial and co-operative ensembles with which it first competed. The Museum of Fine Arts, founded in 1873, was at the center of the city's artistic life, its exhibitions complemented by those of Harvard and the eccentric Mrs Gardner. Music and art critics might disagree on the merits of individual conductors or painters; but they were united in an aesthetic ideology that distinguished sharply between the nobility of art and the vulgarity of mere entertainment. The distinction between true art, distributed by not-for-profit corporations managed by artistic professionals and governed closely by prosperous and influential trustees, and popular entertainment, sponsored by entrepreneurs and distributed via the market to whomever would buy it, had taken a form that has persisted to the present. So, too, had the social distinctions that would differentiate the publics for high and popular culture.

The sacralization of art, the definition of high culture and its opposite, popular culture and the institutionalization of this classification, was the work of men and women whom I refer to as *cultural capitalists*. I use the term in two senses to describe the capitalists (and the professionals whose wealth came from the participation of their families in the industrial ventures—textiles, railroads and mining—of the day) who founded the museums and the symphony orchestras that embodied and elaborated the high-cultural ideal. They were capitalists in the sense that their wealth came from the management of industrial enterprises from which they extracted a profit, and cultural capitalists in that they invested some of these profits in the foundation and maintenance of distinctly cultural enterprises. They also—and this is the second sense in which I use the term—were collectors of what Bourdieu has called 'cultural capital', knowledge and familiarity with styles and genres that are socially valued and that confer prestige upon those who have mastered them (Bourdieu and Passeron, 1977, 1979). It was the vision of the founders of the institutions that have become, in effect, the treasuries of cultural capital upon which their descendants have drawn that defined the nature of cultural capital in American society.[2]

To create an institutional high culture, Boston's upper class had to accomplish three concurrent, but analytically distinct, projects: entrepreneurship, classification and framing. By entrepreneurship, I mean the creation of an organizational form that members of the elite could control and govern. By classification, I refer to the erection of strong and clearly defined boundaries between art and entertainment, the definition of a high art that elites and segments of the middle class could appropriate as their own cultural property; and the acknowledgment of that classification's legitimacy by other classes and the state. Finally, I use the term framing to refer to the development of a new etiquette of appropriation, a new relationship between the audience and the work of art.[3] The focus of this paper will be on the first of these three processes.

The predecessors: organizational models before the Gilded Age

By the close of the Civil War, Boston was in many ways the hub of America's cultural life. But, as Martin Green (1966) has illustrated, the unity of the city's

---

[2] In a third sense, 'cultural capital' might refer to the entrepreneurs of popular culture—the Barnums, the Keiths, the Shuberts and others—who turned culture into profits. While we will not consider this group at any length, we must remember that it was in opposition to their activities that the former defined their own.

[3] My debt to Bernstein (1975*a*, *b*) and to Mary Douglas (1966) is evident here. My use of the terms 'classification' and 'framing' is similar to Bernstein's.

economic and cultural elite, the relative vibrancy of Harvard and the vitality of the communal cultural associations of the elite—the Handel and Haydn Society, the Athenaeum, the Dante Circle, the singing clubs—made Boston unique among America's cities. Godkin called Boston 'the one place in America where wealth and the knowledge of how to use it are apt to coincide' (ibid.: 41).

Yet at the close of the Civil War, Boston lacked the organizational arrangements that could sustain a public 'high culture' distinct and insulated from more popular forms. As we have seen, the boundaries between high art and mass art were poorly drawn; artists and performers had not yet segmented elite and popular markets. It is not that the wealthy were uninterested in art. Henry Lee Higginson, later head of the Lee, Higginson brokerage house and founder of the Boston Symphony Orchestra, could reminisce of his not atypical student days in Cambridge in the mid-1850s:

we had been to the Italian opera, getting there seats for twenty-five cents in the upper gallery enjoying it highly. I had an inborn taste for music, which was nourished by a few concerts in Boston and by the opera (Perry, 1921: 29).

His wife recollected

There were private theatricals, sometimes in German, there was a German class, and there were readings which finished with a delightful social gathering in the evening. He [Higginson] belonged to a private singing club in Boston, and often went to James Savage's room in Holworthy, where there was much informal singing and music (ibid.: 81).

Many young Brahmins, like Higginson, spent time in Europe, studying art or music (e.g. Adams, 1928). And many more learned and played music in or around Boston (Whipple, n.d.), or attended public lectures on the arts.

Nor was there a lack of theories about the nature of good art. Although aesthetic philosophies blossomed after the high-culture institutions were established, even the mid-1850s nurtured aesthetic philosophers like Brook Farmer John S. Dwight, editor of *Dwight's Journal of Music*. Some Bostonians were aware of the latest developments in European music and acquainted with classical standards in the visual arts.

High culture (and by this I mean a strongly classified, consensually defined body of art distinct from 'popular' fare) failed to develop in Boston prior to the 1870s because the organizational models through which art was distributed were not equipped to define and sustain such a body and a view of art. Each of the three major models for organizing the distribution of aesthetic experience before 1870—the for-profit firm, the co-operative enterprise and the communal association—was flawed in some important way.

The problems of the privately owned, for-profit firm are most obvious. As Weber (1968, vol. 2, sec. 9: 937) has argued, the market declassifies culture: presenters of cultural events mix genres and cross boundaries to reach out to larger audiences. The Boston Museum, founded in the 1840s, mixed fine art and sideshow oddities, Shakespeare and theatrical ephemerata. For-profit galleries exhibited art as spectacle: when James Jackson Jarves showed his fine collection of Italian primitives at Derby's Institute of Fine Arts in New York, 'the decor of this . . . dazzlingly ornate commercial emporium . . . caused much more favorable comment than Jarves' queer old pictures' (Burt, 1977: 57).

If anything, commerce was even less favorable to the insulation of high art in the performance media. Fine-art theatre in Boston never seems to have got off the ground. And the numerous commercial orchestras that either resided in or toured Boston during this period mixed fine-arts and light music indiscriminately. A memoir of the period recalls a concert of the Germania Society (one of the better orchestras of this type):

One of the numbers was the "Railway Gallop,"—composer forgotten—during the playing of which a little mock steam-engine kept scooting about the floor of the hall, with black cotton wool smoke coming out of the funnel.

The same writer describes the memorable

evening when a fantasia on themes from Wallace's "Maritana" was played as a duet for mouth harmonica and the Great Organ; a combination, as the program informed us, "never before attempted in the history of music!" (William F. Apthorp, quoted in Howe, 1914).

As with the visual arts, the commercial treatment of serious music tended to the extravagant rather than to the sacred. In 1869, an entrepreneur organized a Peace Jubilee to celebrate the end of the Civil War. A structure large enough to accommodate 30,000 people was built (at what would later be the first site of the Museum of Fine Arts) and 'star' instrumentalists and vocalists were contracted to perform along with an orchestra of 1000 and a chorus of 10,000. As a finale, the orchestra (which included 330 strings, 75 drums and 83 tubas) played the anvil chorus with accompaniment from a squadron of firemen beating anvils, and the firing of live canon (Fisher, 1918: 45–46).

An alternative form of organization, embraced by some musical societies, was the workers' co-operative, in which each member had a vote, shared in the profits of the enterprise and elected a conductor from among their number.[4] The co-operative was vulnerable to market incentives. Perhaps more important, however, it was (also like its privately owned counterpart) unable to secure the complete allegiance of its members, who supported themselves by playing many different kinds of music in a wide range of settings. The early New York Philharmonic, for example, performed as a group only monthly. Members anticipated the concert

as a pleasant relief from more remunerative occupational duties, and the rehearsal periods were cluttered up with routine business matters, from which members could absent themselves with relative impunity (Mueller, 1951: 41).

The lines dividing non-profit, co-operative, for-profit and public enterprise were not as strong in the nineteenth century as they would become in the twentieth. Civic-minded guarantors might hold stock in commercial ventures with no hope of gaining a profit (e.g. Symphony Hall at the end of the century). The goals of the charitable corporation were usually defined into its charter, but otherwise it legally resembled its for-profit counterpart. Even less clearly defined was what I call the voluntary association: closed associations of individuals (sometimes incorporated, sometimes not) to further the aims of the participating members, rather than of the community as a whole. For associations like the Handel and Haydn Society, which might give public concerts, or the Athenaeum, which took an active rôle in public affairs, privateness was relative. But, ultimately, each was a voluntary and exclusive instrument of its members.

Why were these communal associations ill-suited to serve as the organizational bases for high culture in Boston? Why could the Athenaeum, a private library, or the Boston Art Club, which sponsored contemporary art shows (Boston Art Club,

[4] See Couch (1976a, b) and Mueller (1951: 37ff.) for more detailed descriptions of this form.

1878), not have developed continuous programs of public exhibitions? Could not the Handel and Haydn Society, the Harvard Musical Association (formed by Harvard graduates who wished to pursue after graduation musical interests developed in the College's Pierian Sodality) or one of the numerous singing circles have developed into a permanent orchestra? They faced no commercial temptations to study, exhibit or perform any but the highest art. (Indeed, the Harvard Musical Association's performances were so austere as to give rise to the proverb 'dull as a symphony concert' (Howe, 1914: 8)).

None of them, however, could, by the late nineteenth century, claim to speak for the community as a whole, even if they chose to. Each represented only a fraction (although, in the case of Athenaeum, a very large and potent fraction) of the elite; and, in the case of the musical associations and the Art Club, members of the middle class and artistic professionals were active as well. The culture of an elite status group must be monopolized, it must be legitimate and it must be sacralized. Boston's cultural capitalists would have to find a form able to achieve all these aims: a single organizational base for each art form; institutions that could claim to serve the community, even as they defined the community to include only the elite and the upper-middle classes; and enough social distance between artist and audience, between performer and public, to permit the mystification necessary to define a body of artistic work as sacred.

This they did in the period between 1870 and 1900. By the end of the century, in art and music (but not in theatre (see Twentieth Century Club, 1919; Poggi, 1968)), the differences between high- and popular-culture artists and performers were becoming distinct, as were the physical settings in which high and popular art were presented.

The form that the distribution of high culture would take was the non-profit corporation, governed by a self-perpetuating board of trustees who, eventually, would delegate most artistic decisions to professional artists or art historians (Zolberg, 1974; 1981). The charitable corporation was not designed to define a high culture that elites could monopolize; nor are non-profit organizations by their nature exclusive. But the non-profit corporation had five virtues that enabled it to play a key rôle in this instance. First, the corporation was a familiar and successful tool by which nineteenth-century elites organized their affairs (see Frederickson, 1965; Story, 1980; Hall, forthcoming). In the economic realm it enabled them to raise capital for such profitable ventures as the Calumet and Hecla Mines, the western railroads and the telephone company. In the non-profit arena, it had been a useful instrument for elite communal governance at Harvard, the Massachusetts General Hospital and a host of charitable institutions (Story, 1980). Second, by entrusting governance decisions to trustees who were committed either to providing financial support or to soliciting it from their peers, the non-profit form effectively (if not completely) insulated museums and orchestras from the pressures of the market. Third, by vesting control in a well integrated social and financial elite, the charitable corporation enabled its governors to rule without interference from the state or from other social classes. Fourth, those organizations whose trustees were able to enlist the support of the greater part of the elite could provide the stability needed for a necessarily lengthy process of defining art and developing ancillary institutions to insulate high-cultural from popular-cultural work, performance and careers. Finally, and less obviously, the goals of the charitable corporation, unlike those of the profit-seeking firm, are diffuse and ambiguous enough to accommodate a range of conflicting purposes and changing ends. The broad charters of Boston's major cultural organizations permitted their missions to be redefined with time, and enabled their governors to claim (and to believe) that they pursued communitarian goals even as they institutionalized a view and vision of art that made elite culture less and less accessible to the vast majority of Boston's citizens.

The context of cultural capitalism

In almost every literate society, dominant status groups or classes eventually have developed their own styles of art and the institutional means of supporting them. It was predictable that this would happen in the United States, despite the absence of an hereditary aristocracy. It is more difficult, however, to explain the timing of this process. Dwight and others wished (but failed) to start a permanent professional symphony orchestra from at least the late 1840s. The Athenaeum's proprietors tried to raise a public subscription to purchase the Jarves collection in the late 1850s, but they failed. What had changed?

Consider, first, the simple increase in scale and wealth between 1800 and 1870. At the time of the revolution, Boston's population was under 10,000. By 1800 it had risen to 25,000; by 1846 it was 120,000. By 1870, over a quarter of a million people lived in Boston (Lane, 1975). The increase in the size of the local cultural market facilitated a boom in theatre building in the 1830s (Nye, 1960: 264), a rise in the number and stability of book and music stores (Fisher, 1918: 30) and the growth of markets for theatre, music, opera, dancing and equestrian shows (Nye, 1960: 143). The growth of population was accompanied by an increase in wealth. Boston's first fortunes were mercantile, the fruits of the China trade, large by local, but small by national standards. In 1840, Boston had but a handful of millionaires. By 1890, after post-Civil War booms in railroads, mining, banking and communications, there were 400 (Jaher, 1968, 1972; Story, 1980). Even the physical scale of the city changed during this period: beginning in 1856, developers began filling in the waters of the Back Bay, creating a huge track of publicly owned land, partially devoted to civic and cultural buildings. As wealthy outlanders from Lawrence, Lynn and Lexington migrated to Beacon Hill and Cambridge, streetcars reduced the cost and the difficulty of travel to Boston from its suburbs (Warner, 1970). In short, Boston was larger, wealthier and more compact in 1870 than it had been 50 years before.

With growth came challenges to the stability of the community and to the cultural authority (Starr, forthcoming) of elites. Irish immigrants flowed into Boston from the 1840s to work in the city's industrial enterprises (Handlin, 1972; Thernstrom, 1972); industrial employment rôles doubled between 1845 and 1855 (Handlin, 1972). With industry and immigration came disease, pauperism, alcoholism, rising infant mortality and vice. The Catholic Irish were, by provenance and religion, outside the consensus that the Brahmins had established. By 1900, 30% of Boston's residents were foreign-born and 70% were of foreign parentage (Green, 1966: 102). By the close of the Civil War, Boston's immigrants were organizing to challenge the native elite in the political arena (Solomon, 1956).

If immigration and industrialization wrought traumatic changes in the city's social fabric, the political assault on Brahmin institutions by native populists proved even more frightening. The Know-Nothings who captured state government in the 1850s attacked the social exclusivity of Harvard College frontally, amending its charter and threatening state control over its governance, hiring and admissions policies (Story, 1980). Scalded by these attacks, Boston's leadership retreated from the public sector to found a system of non-profit organizations that permitted them to maintain some control over the community even as they lost their command of its political institutions.[5]

Story (1980) argues persuasively that this political challenge, and the wave of institution-building that followed it, transformed the Brahmins from an elite into a social class.[6] As a social class, the Brahmins built institutions (schools, almshouses and charitable societies) aimed at securing control over the city's social life (Huggins, 1971; Vogel, 1981). As a status group, they constructed organizations (clubs, prep schools and cultural institutions) to seal themselves off from their increasingly unruly environment. Thus Vernon Parrington's only partially accurate observation that 'The Brahmins conceived the great business of life to be the erection of barriers against the intrusion of the unpleasant' (quoted in Shiverick, 1970: 129). The creation of a network of private institutions that could define and monopolize high art was an essential part of this process of building cultural boundaries.

The Brahmin class, however, was neither large enough to constitute a public for large-scale arts organizations, nor was it content to keep its cultural achievements solely to itself. Alongside of, and complicating, the Brahmins' drive towards exclusivity was a conflicting desire, as they saw it, to educate the community. The growth of the middle class during this period—a class that was economically and socially closer to the working class and thus in greater need of differentiating itself from it culturally—provided a natural clientele for Boston's inchoate high culture. While we have all too little information about the nature of the visitors to Boston's Museum or of the audiences for the Symphony, it seems certain from contemporary accounts (and sheer arithmetic) that many of them were middle class. The same impulse that created the markets for etiquette and instruction books in the mid-nineteenth century helped populate the galleries and concert halls of the century's last quarter (Nye, 1960; Douglas, 1978).

Cultural entrepreneurship: the Museum of Fine Arts and the Boston Symphony Orchestra

The first step in the creation of a high culture was the centralization of artistic activities within institutions controlled by Boston's cultural capitalists. This was accomplished with the foundings of the Museum of Fine Arts and the Boston Symphony Orchestra. These institutions were to provide a framework, in the visual arts and music, respectively, for the definition of high art, for its segregation from popular forms and for the elaboration of an etiquette of appropriation.

Bostonians had sought to found a museum for some time before 1870. In 1858, the state legislature, dominated by factions unfriendly to Boston's elite, refused to provide Back Bay land for a similar venture (Harris, 1962: 548). The immediate impetus for the Museum, however, was a bequest by Colonel Timothy Bigelow Lawrence of an armor collection too large for the Athenaeum's small gallery to

---

[5] Shiverick (1970) notes the contrast between the founding of the public library in the 1850s and that of the private art museum 20 years later, both enterprises in which Athenaeum members were central.

[6] I use the term 'class' to refer to a self-conscious elite united by bonds of economic interest, kinship and culture (see Thompson, 1966: 8; Story, 1980: xi).

accommodate. Three years earlier the Athenaeum's Fine Arts Committee had suggested that the galleries be expanded, but nothing had been done. With the Lawrence bequest, and his widow's offer to contribute a wing to a new gallery, the trustees voted that

the present is a proper time for making an appeal to the public and especially to the friends of the Fine Arts, to raise the sum required to make available Mrs. Lawrence's proposed donation, and, if possible, to provide even larger means to carry out so noble a design in the confident hope that it may be attended with success . . . (Whitehill, 1970: 6–8).

A new museum promised to solve problems for several of Boston's elite institutions: Harvard had a collection of prints for which it sought a fire-safe depository, and MIT and the American Social Science Association possessed collections of architectural casts too large for them to store conveniently. After a series of meetings between the Athenaeum trustees and other public and private decision makers, it was decided to raise money for a museum on a tract of land in the Back Bay. (The land, owned by the Boston Water Power Company, was made available through the intervention of Mathias Denman Ross, a local developer who was keenly aware of the effects of public and cultural buildings on the value of nearby real estate.) In 1870 the state legislature chartered the enterprise and, with the help of the Athenaeum, which sponsored exhibitions throughout this period, fund-raising began.[7]

The initial aspirations of the Museum founders were somewhat modest. The key figure in the founding was Charles Callahan Perkins, great-nephew of a China-trade magnate, kinsman of the chairman of the Athenaeum's Fine Arts Committee and himself President of the Boston Art Club. Perkins wrote two books on Italian sculpture in the 1860s, championed arts education in Boston's public schools and served as head of the American Social Science Association's arts-education panel in 1869. (He had studied painting and sculpture in Europe for almost 10 years, before concluding that he lacked the creativity to be a good artist.) Perkins, in a report to the ASSA had asserted 'the feasibility of establishing a regular Museum of Art at moderate expense', with primarily educational aims. Since Boston's collections had few originals, he recommended that the new collection consist of reproductions, primarily plaster casts of sculpture and architecture.

The breadth of response to the first appeal for funds for the museum is striking. Although the economy was not robust, $261,425 was collected for the building. Of this amount, the largest gift was $25,000, only two were larger than $5000 and all but $100,000 came from over 1000 gifts of less than $2000 from such sources as local newspapers, public-school teachers and workers at a piano factory. (By contrast, when the Museum sought to raise $400,000 for new galleries and an endowment 15 years later, $218,000 of the initial $240,000 in contributions came from a mere 58 donors (Whitehill, 1970: 42).)

One reason for the breadth of early support was that the Museum, although in private hands, was to be a professedly communitarian and educational venture. The Board of Trustees contained a large segment of the Brahmin class: All but one of the first 23 trustees were proprietors of the Athenaeum; 11 were members of the Saturday Club, while many others were members of the Somerset and St Botolph's clubs; most were graduates of Harvard and many were active in its affairs. The public nature of the Board was further emphasized by the inclusion on it of permanent and *ex-officio* appointments: from Harvard, MIT and the Athenaeum; the

[7] This section relies heavily upon Walter Muir Whitehill's classic two-volume history of the Museum (1970) and, to a lesser extent, on Neil Harris' fine paper (1962) for its facts, albeit not for their interpretation.

Mayor, the Chairman of the Boston Public Library's board, the trustee of the Lowell Institute, the Secretary of the State Board of Education and the Superintendent of Boston's schools. The trustees dedicated the institution to education; one hoped that the breadth of the board's membership would ensure that the Museum's managers would be 'prevented from squandering their funds upon the private fancies of would-be connoisseurs'. Indeed, the articles of incorporation required that the Museum be open free of charge at least four times a month. The public responded by flooding the Museum on free weekend days in the early years (Harris, 1962: 48–52).

The centralization of the visual arts around a museum required only the provision of a building and an institution controlled by a board of civic-minded members of the elite. The Museum functioned on a relatively small budget in its early years, under the direction of Charles Greely Loring, a Harvard graduate and Civil War general, who had studied Egyptology when his physician sent him to the banks of the Nile. The Museum's founders, facing the need to raise substantial funds, organized both private and public support carefully, mobilizing a consensus in favor of their project from the onset.

By contrast, the Boston Symphony Orchestra was, for its first years at least, a one-man operation, forced to wrest hegemony over Boston's musical life from several contenders, each with its own coterie of elite support. That Henry Lee Higginson, a partner in the brokerage firm of Lee, Higginson, was able to do so was a consequence of the soundness of his organizational vision, the firmness of his commitment, and, equally important, his centrality to Boston's economic and social elite.

In a sense, Higginson began as a relative outsider. Although his father, founder of the family firm, made a fortune in shipping, Henry was the first of his line to matriculate at Harvard; and soon he dropped out (claiming poor vision), visiting Europe and returning to private tutelage in Cambridge. Upon completing his education, he studied music in Europe for several years, ultimately against the wishes of his father, as their tense and sometimes acrimonious correspondence suggests (Perry, 1921: 121–135). After an accident lamed his arm, he returned to the United States for good, fought in the Civil War, married a daughter of the Harvard scientist Louis Agassiz and, following a disastrous venture in southern farming and a lucrative investment in the Calumet and Hecla copper mines, finally joined his father's State Street firm.[8]

Higginson was a knowledgeable student of music, and a follower of the aesthetic doctrines of John S. Dwight. As early as 1840, Dwight had called for the founding of a permanent orchestra in Boston. 'This promises something', he wrote of an amateur performance.

We could not but feel that the materials that evening collected might, if they could be kept together through the year, and induced to practice, form an orchestra worthy to execute the grand works of Haydn and Mozart. . . . To secure these ends might not a plan of this kind be realized? Let a few of our most accomplished and refined musicians institute a series of cheap instrumental concerts. . . . Let them engage to perform quartettes, etc., occasionally a symphony, by the best masters and no others. Let them repeat the best and most characteristic pieces enough to make them a study to the audiences (Howe, 1914: 4–5).

[8] In Henry Adams words, 'Higginson, after a desperate struggle, was forced into State Street' (Adams, 1928: 210). In later years, Higginson told a relative that 'he never walked into 44 State Street without wanting to sit down on the doorstep and cry' (Perry, 1921: 135).

As we have seen, a number of ensembles attempted to realize Dwight's ambitions. But it was Higginson's organizational skills (and his money) that gave Boston the nation's first permanent, philanthropically supported and governed, full-season symphony orchestra. In achieving the dream of a large permanent orchestra devoted to fine-arts music, Higginson faced and overcame two challenges: first, establishing control over fine-arts music in Boston as a whole; and, second, enforcing internal discipline over the orchestra's members. Against him were arrayed the supporters of Boston's existing ensembles, principally the Philharmonia and the Harvard Musical Association, and the city's musicians, jealous of their personal and professional autonomy.

Higginson published his plans for the orchestra in a column, headed 'In the Interest of Good Music', that appeared in several of Boston's newspapers:

Notwithstanding the development of musical taste in Boston, we have never yet possessed a full and permanent orchestra, offering the best music at low prices, such as may be found in all the large European cities. . . . The essential condition of such orchestras is their stability, whereas ours are necessarily shifting and uncertain, because we are dependent upon musicians whose work and time are largely pledged elsewhere. To obviate this difficulty the following plan is offered. It is an effort made simply in the interest of good music, and though individual in as much as it is independent of societies or clubs, it is in no way antagonistic to any previously existing musical organization (Howe, 1914: 41).

In this last sentence, Higginson treads on delicate ground. He goes on to praise, specifically, the Handel and Haydn Society and the Harvard Musical Association, the two musical societies with the closest Brahmin connections, while indicating implicitly that there will be no further need for the services of the latter. To launch this new enterprise, Higginson proposes to spend, annually, $20,000 of his own money until the orchestra becomes self-supporting.

Despite a measure of public incredulity, and some resentment at Higginson's choice of European conductor, George Henschel, over local candidates, the BSO opened in December 1881 to the enthusiastic response of the musical public. (The demand for tickets was great; lines formed outside the box office the evening before they went on sale.) The social complexion of the first night's audience is indicated by a report in a Boston newspaper that 'the spirit of the music so affected the audience that when the English national air was recognized in Weber's Festival Overture, the people arose en masse and remained standing until the close'. By employing local musicians and permitting them to play with the Philharmonic Society and the Harvard Musical Association (both of which, like the BSO, offered about 20 concerts that season), Higginson earned the gratitude of the city's music lovers.

The trouble began in February 1882, when the players received Higginson's terms for the following season. To continue to work for the Symphony, they would be required to make themselves available for rehearsals and performances from October through April, four days a week, and to play for no other conductor or musical association. (The Handel and Haydn Society, which had strong ties to the Athenaeum, was exempted from this prohibition.) The implications of the contract, which the players resisted unsuccessfully, were clear: Boston's other orchestras, lacking the salaries that Higginson's subsidies permitted, would be unable to compete for the services of Boston's musicians. (To make matters worse, a number of the city's journeymen musicians received no offers from Higginson at all.)

The response of the press, particularly of the Brahmin *Transcript,* suggests that loyalists of the other ensembles responded to Higginson's actions with outrage. The *Transcript* editorialized of Higginson

He thus "makes a corner" in orchestral players, and monopolizes these for his own concerts and those of the Handel and Haydn Society. . . . Mr. Higginson's gift becomes an imposition, it is something that we must receive, or else we look musical starvation in the face. It is as if a man should make a poor friend a present of several baskets of champagne and, at the same time, cut off his whole water supply.

A more populist newspaper complained that the 'monopoly of music' was 'an idea that could scarcely have emanated from any association except that of deluded wealth with arrant charlatanism'. Even *Music,* a New York publication originally friendly to Higginson's efforts, called his contract

a direct stab at the older organizations and rival conductors of Boston. It means that one or two organizations may make efforts to place their concerts on the off days which Mr. Henschel has been pleased to allow them, but some must be left in the cold, orchestraless and forlorn. . . . The manner in which the proposal was made was also one that forebodes tyranny. Some of the oldest members of the Orchestra, men whose services to music in Boston have entitled them to deference and respect, were omitted altogether, and will be left out of the new organization. It was intimated strongly that in case the offer was rejected by the men, their places would be filled from the ranks of European orchestras (Howe, 1914: 67–69).

Higginson and his orchestra weathered the storm. Attendance stayed up and, within a year, his was the only orchestral association in Boston, co-existing peacefully with the smaller Handel and Haydn Society. In order to achieve the kind of ensemble he desired, however, Higginson had to ensure that his musicians would commit their time and their attention to the BSO alone, and accept his (and his agent's, the conductor's) authority as inviolate. Since, in the past, all musicians, whatever their affiliations, were freelancers upon whom no single obligation weighed supreme, accomplishing these aspirations required a fundamental change in the relationship between musicians and their employers.

In part, effecting this internal monopolization of attention was simply a matter of gaining an external monopoly of classical-music performance. With the surrender of the Philharmonic Society and the Harvard Musical Association, two major competitors for the working time of Boston's musicians disappeared. Nonetheless, while his musicians were now more dependent upon the BSO for their livelihoods, and thus more amenable to his demands, his control over the work force was still challenged by the availability of light-music or dance engagements, teaching commitments and the tradition of lax discipline to which the players were accustomed.

Throughout his life, Higginson fought to maintain control over the Orchestra's employees, and the issue of discipline was foremost in his mind from the beginning. In an early plan for the Orchestra, he suggested engaging a conductor and eight to ten exceptionally good younger musicians from outside Boston at a fixed salary, 'who would be ready at my call to play anywhere', and then to draw around them the best of our Boston musicians, thus refreshing and renewing the present orchestra, and getting more nearly possession of it . . . (Howe, 1914: 28). At that time, exclusive employment contracts were so rare that the more timid Henschel, after agreeing to serve as conductor, tried to convince Higginson to abandon his insistence on total commitment. 'I assure you', he wrote as the first orchestra was being assembled, that is the best thing we can do, and if you have any confidence in my judgment, pray drop all conditions in the contract except those relating to our own welfare. I mean now the conditions of discipline, etc. (Perry, 1921: 299).

Despite his frequent assertions that he yielded in all cases to his conductors' advice on orchestral matters, Higginson, as we have seen, insisted on exclusive contracts in the orchestra's second year, threatening to break any strike with the importation of European players. Although he won that battle, he nonetheless replaced the locals gradually, over the course of the next decade, with new men with few Boston ties, mostly European, of greater technical accomplishment, upon whose loyalty he could count (Howe, 1914: 121–123).

In this, Higginson was not merely following a European model. 'My contracts', he wrote an associate in 1888, 'are very strong, indeed much stronger than European contracts usually are . . .' (Perry, 1921: 398). Characteristic of the orchestra contract was section 12:

If said musician fails to play to the satisfaction of said Higginson, said Higginson may dismiss said musician from the Orchestra, paying his salary to the time of dismissal, and shall not be liable to pay him any compensation or damages for such dismissal (Perry, 1921: 398).

Higginson was undeniably an autocrat. In later years he rejected the suggestions of friends to place the Orchestra under a board of trustees; and he used the threat of discontinuing his annual subventions as a bludgeon to forestall the unionization of the players. Yet Higginson accomplished what all orchestras would have to achieve if orchestral work was to be separated permanently from the playing of popular music and Dwight's dream of a permanent orchestra devoted to high-art music achieved: the creation of a permanent musical work force, under exclusive contract, willing to accept without question the authority of the conductor.

The Brahmins as an organization-forming class

The Museum of Fine Arts and the Boston Symphony Orchestra were both organizations embedded in a social class, formal organizations whose official structure was draped around the ongoing life of the group that governed, patronized, and staffed them.[9] They were not separate products of different segments of an elite; or of artists and critics who mobilized wealthy men to bankroll their causes. Rather they were the creations of a densely connected self-conscious social group intensely unified by multiple ties among its members based in kinship, commerce, club life and participation in a wide range of philanthropic associations. Indeed, if, as Stinchcombe (1965) has argued, there are 'organization-forming organizations'— organizations that spawn off other organizations in profusion—there are also organization-forming status groups, and the Brahmins were one of these. This they could be not just because of their cultural or religious convictions (to which Green (1966), Baltzell (1979) and Hall (forthcoming) have called attention), but because they were integrated by their families' marriages, their Harvard educations, their joint business ventures, their memberships in a web of social clubs and their trusteeships of charitable and cultural organizations. This integration is exemplified

[9] In James Thompson's terms, they were organizations whose resource dependencies all coincided. For their financial support, for their governance and for their clients, they looked to a class whose members were 'functionally interdependent and interact[ed] regularly with respect to religious, economic, recreational, and governmental matters' (Thompson, 1967: 27).

in the associations of Higginson, and in the ties between the Museum and the Orchestra during the last 20 years of the nineteenth century.

It is likely that Higginson's keen instinct for brokerage—and the obligations he accrued as principal in one of Boston's two major houses—served him well in his efforts to establish the Orchestra. At first glance, Higginson's achievement in creating America's first elite-governed permanent symphony orchestra in Boston appears to be the work of a rugged individualist. On closer inspection, we see that it was precisely Higginson's centrality to the Brahmin social structure that enabled him to succeed. Only a lone, centrally located entrepreneur could have done what Higginson did, because to do so ruffled so many feathers: a committee would have compromised with the supporters of other musical associations and with the patrons of the more established local musicians. Nonetheless, if Higginson's youthful marginality permitted the attempt, it was his eventual centrality that enabled him to succeed. His career illustrates the importance of kinship, commerce, clubs and philanthropy in Boston elite life. Ties in each of these areas reinforced those in the others; each facilitated the success of the Orchestra, and each brought him into close connection with the cultural capitalists active in the MFA and led, eventually, to his selection as a Museum trustee.

Higginson was born a cousin to some of the leading families in Boston: the Cabots, the Lowells, the Perkins, the Morses, the Jacksons, the Channings and the Paines, among others (Perry, 1921: 14). (The first four of these families produced trustees of the Museum of Fine Arts during Higginson's lifetime. His kinsman Frances W. Higginson was also a Museum trustee.) In Cambridge, he was close to Charles Lowell and, after his first European adventure, he studied with Samuel Eliot, a cousin of Harvard President Charles W. Eliot, and later a trustee of the Museum. During this period, he spent a great deal of time in the salon-like household of Louis Agassiz, befriending the scientist's son and marrying his daughter. So close did Henry remain to his Harvard classmates that, despite his withdrawal after freshman year, they permitted him to take part in their class's Commencement exercises.

When Henry went into business, he brought his family and college ties with him. A contemporary said of the Lee, Higginson firm, it 'owed in some measure to family alliances its well-advised connections with the best financial enterprises of the day' (Perry, 1921: 272). Indeed, Higginson's first successful speculation was his investment in the Calumet and Hecla mines, at the behest of his in-laws Agassiz and Shaw (the latter an early donor of paintings to the Museum). The family firm was instrumental in the development of the western railroads, through the efforts of cousin Charles Jackson Paine. In this enterprise, Higginson associated with John M. Forbes and with Charles H. Perkins (kinsman of the MFA founder). Higginson was so intimate with the latter that he invested Perkins' money without consultation. Lee, Higginson made a fortune in the telephone company, and Higginson, in later years, was a director of General Electric. In some of these ventures, the firm co-operated with other Boston financiers. Higginson was on close terms with his competitors Kidder of Kidder, Peabody (the Museum's first treasurer) and Endicott, President of the New England Trust and Suffolk Savings (and the Museum's second Treasurer). Gardiner Martin Lane was a partner in Lee, Higginson when he resigned his position to assume the Museum's presidency in 1907.

Higginson was also an active clubman, a member of the Tavern Club, (and its

President for twenty years), the Wednesday Evening Club, the Wintersnight, Friday Night and Officers Clubs, New York's Knickerbocker Club and, from 1893, the Saturday Club. Among his Tavern Club colleagues were Harvard's Charles Eliot Norton (spiritual godfather of the Museum's aesthetes), William Dean Howells and Henry Lee. At the Friday Club he consorted with Howells, William James and Henry Adams. At the Saturday Club, his clubmates included the MFA's Thomas Gold Appleton and Martin Brimmer.

In the 1890s, Higginson's career in Boston philanthropy blossomed. (By now he was on the MFA's Board. Earlier, when the Museum's first President, Martin Brimmer, asked Charles Eliot Norton if Higginson should be invited, Norton wrote back that 'Higginson would be excellent, but he never attends meetings' (Harris, 1962: 551).) He lavished most of his attention (beyond that devoted to the Orchestra) on Harvard, which elected him a Fellow in 1893. He gave Harvard Soldiers Field and a new student union, was Treasurer of Radcliffe College, played a key rôle in the founding of the Graduate School of Business, patronized the medical school and gave anonymous gifts to deserving faculties.[10] Higginson's position as Fellow of Harvard placed him at the summit of Boston's institutional life and undoubtedly reinforced his contacts with the Museum's trustees and friends. His personal art collection, which included Turners, Corots and Rodins, encouraged such interactions as well. (In 1893, he donated a valuable Dutch master to the MFA.)

Thus was the Orchestra's founder embedded in the Brahmin community. When Lee, Higginson furnished an emergency loan of $17,000 to the Museum of Fine Arts in 1889, with little prospect of repayment, was this because he was on the Board; was it a consequence of Higginson's kinship ties with the Cabots, Perkinses or Lowells; his business alliances with Kidder or Endicott; his club friendship with Norton; Harvard ties to the Eliots? The range of possibilities renders the question trivial and illustrates how closely knit was Higginson's world.

In 1893, when Higginson demanded that Boston build him a new and suitable Symphony Hall, lest he abandon the Orchestra to bankruptcy and dissolution, the initial appeal for funds was signed by a broad cross section of the city's elite: his friends and kinsmen Agassiz, Lodge, Lowell, Lee and John Lowell Gardner; Harvard's Eliot, Norton, Longfellow, Shattuck and Parkman; Peabody of Kidder Peabody, to name a few. Present on the list were at least four of Higginson's fellow MFA trustees: the President (Martin Brimmer), the Treasurer (by now, John L. Gardner), Eliot and Norton.[11] The group raised over $400,000, a substantial stake in that financially troubled year.

Conclusions

The Museum of Fine Arts and the Boston Symphony Orchestra were creations of the Brahmins, and the Brahmins alone. As such, their origins are easier to

[10] Higginson, whose vision extended beyond Boston, also gave generously to Princeton, Williams, the University of Virginia and Middlesex, and sent the Orchestra to play, at his expense, at Williams, Princeton and Yale.

[11] Higginson's relationship with Gardner and his mildly scandalous wife Isabella Stewart Gardner, is revealing. When Isabella, a New Yorker, entered Boston society in the 1880s, she was accorded a frosty reception. According to Morris Carter, her biographer and the first Director of her collection, she won social acceptance by employing the BSO to entertain at one of her parties (Carter, 1925), an action that would have required Higginson's approval. After her palace opened (more or less) to the public in 1909, Higginson presented her with a book compiled by her admirers (Green, 1966: 112).

understand than were British or Continental efforts in which aristocrats and bourgeoisie played complex and interrelated rôles (Wolff, 1982). The Brahmins were a status group, and as such they strove towards exclusivity, towards the definition of a prestigious culture that they could monopolize as their own. Yet they were also a social class, and they were concerned, as is any dominant social class, with establishing hegemony over those they dominated. Some Marxist students of culture have misinterpreted the cultural institutions as efforts to dictate taste or to inculcate the masses with the ideas of elites. Certainly, the cultural capitalists, consummate organizers and intelligent men and women, were wise enough to understand the impossibility of socializing the masses in institutions from which they effectively were barred. Their concern with education, however, was not simply window-dressing or an effort at public relations. Higginson, for example, devoted much of his fortune to American universities and secondary schools. He once wrote a kinsman, from whom he sought a donation of $100,000 for Harvard, 'Educate, and save ourselves and our families and our money from the mobs!' (Perry, 1921: 329). Moreover, a secret or thoroughly esoteric culture could not have served to legitimate the status of American elites; it would be necessary to share it, at least partially. The tension between monopolization and hegemony, between exclusivity and legitimation, was a constant counterpoint to the efforts at classification of American urban elites.

This explains, in part, the initial emphasis on education at the Museum of Fine Arts. Yet, from the first, the Museum managers sought to educate through distinguishing true from vulgar art—at first, cautiously, later with more confidence. In the years that followed they would place increased emphasis on the original art that became available to them, until they abandoned reproductions altogether and with them their emphasis on education. In a less dramatic way, the Orchestra, which began with an artistic mandate, would further classify the contents of its programs and frame the aesthetic experience in the years to come.

In structure, however, the Museum and the Orchestra were similar innovations. Each was private, controlled by members of the Brahmin class, and established on the corporate model, dependent on private philanthropy and relatively long-range financial planning; each was sparely staffed and relied for much of its management on elite volunteers; and each counted among its founders wealthy men with considerable scholarly or artistic credentials who were centrally located in Boston's elite social structure. The Museum was established under broad auspices for the education of the community as a whole; the Orchestra was created by one man in the service of art and of those in the community with the sophistication or motivation to appreciate it. Within 40 years, the logic of cultural capitalism would moderate sharply, if not eliminate, these historically grounded differences. The Symphony would come to resemble the Museum in charter and governance, and the Museum would abandon its broad social mission in favor of aestheticism and an elite clientele.

The creation of the MFA, the BSO and similar organizations throughout the United States created a base through which the ideal of high culture could be given institutional flesh. The alliance between class and culture that emerged was defined by, and thus inseparable from, its organizational mediation. As a consequence, the classification 'high culture/popular culture' is comprehensible only in its dual sense as characterizing both a ritual classification and the organizational systems that give that classification meaning.

Acknowledgments

For advice and encouragement I am indebted to Randall Collins, David Karen, Michael Schudson, Ann Swidler and to the members of Professor Mary Douglas's 'Mass Media and Mythology' seminar at the New York University Institute for the Humanities, of Theda Skocpol's graduate research seminar at Harvard University and of Paul Hirsch's production-of-culture session at the 1980 Sociology and the Arts conference in Chicago. Research and institutional support from the Andrew W. Mellon Foundation and from Yale University's Program on Non-Profit Organizations is gratefully acknowledged.

References

ADAMS, H. (1928). *The Education of Henry Adams: An Autobiography*, New York, Book League of America

ADORNO, T. W. (1941). On popular music, *Studies in Philosophy and Social Science*, vol. 9, no. 1

BALTZELL, E. D. (1979). *Puritan Boston and Quaker Philadelphia*, New York, Free Press

BARNUM, P. T. (1879). *Struggles and Triumphs; or Forty Years Recollections*, Buffalo, New York, The Courier Company

BERNSTEIN, B. (1975*a*). On the classification and framing of educational knowledge, in *Class, Codes and Control*, vol. 3, London, Routledge and Kegan Paul

BERNSTEIN, B. (1975*b*). Ritual in education, in *Class, Codes and Control*, vol. 3, London, Routledge and Kegan Paul

BOSTON ART CLUB (1878). *Constitution and By-Laws of the Boston Art Club, With a Sketch of its History*, Boston, E. H. Trulan

BOURDIEU, P. and PASSERON, J.-C. (1977). *Reproduction in Education, Society and Culture*, Beverly Hills, Sage

BOURDIEU, P. and PASSERON, J.-C. (1979). *The Inheritors: French Students and their Relation to Culture*, Chicago, University of Chicago Press

BURT, N. (1977). *Palaces for the People*, Boston, Little, Brown and Co.

CARTER, M. (1925). *Isabella Stewart Gardner and Fenway Court*, Boston, Houghton Mifflin

COUCH, S. R. (1976*a*). Class, politics and symphony orchestras. *Society*, vol. 14, no. 1

COUCH, S. R. (1976*b*). The symphony orchestra in London and New York: some political considerations, presented at the Third Annual Conference on Social Theory and the Arts, Albany, New York

DIMAGGIO, P. and USEEM, M. (1978). Cultural property and public policy: Emerging tensions in government support for the arts, *Social Research*, vol. 45, Summer

DOUGLAS, A. (1978). *The Feminization of American Culture*, New York, Avon

DOUGLAS, M. (1966). *Purity and Danger: An Analysis of Pollution and Taboo*, London, Routledge and Kegan Paul

FELLOWS, D. W. and FREEMAN, A. A., (1936). *This Way to the Big Show: The Life of Dexter Fellows*, New York, Viking Press

FISHER, W. A. (1918). *Notes on Music in Old Boston*, Boston, Oliver Ditson

FREDERICKSON, G. M. (1965). *The Inner Civil War: Northern Intellectuals and the Crisis of the Union*, New York, Harper and Row

GANS, H. J. (1974). *Popular Culture and High Culture*, New York, Basic Books

GREEN, M. (1966). *The Problem of Boston*, New York, Norton

HALL, P. D. (forthcoming). *Institutions and the Making of American Culture*, Westport Connecticut, Greenwood

HANDLIN, O. (1972). *Boston's Immigrants, 1790–1880*, New York, Atheneum

HARRIS, N. (1962). The Gilded Age revisited: Boston and the museum movement, *American Quarterly*, vol. 14, Winter

HARRIS, N. (1966). *The Artist in American Society: The Formative Years, 1790–1860*, New York, George Braziller

HARRIS, N. (1973). *Humbug: The Art of P. T. Barnum*, Boston, Little, Brown and Co.

HATCH, C. (1962). Music for America: A cultural controversy of the 1850s, *American Quarterly*, vol. 14, Winter

HOWE, M. A. D. (1914). *The Boston Symphony Orchestra: An Historical Sketch*, Boston, Houghton Mifflin,

HUGGINS, N. J. (1971). *Protestants against Poverty: Boston's Charities, 1870–1900*, Westport, Connecticut, Greenwood

JAHER, F. C. (1968). The Boston Brahmins in the age of industrial capitalism, in Jaher, F. C. (ed.), *The Age of Industrialism in America*, New York, Oxford University Press

JAHER, F. C. (1972). Nineteenth-century elites in Boston and New York, *Journal of Social History*, vol. 6, Spring

LANE, R. (1975). *Policing the City: Boston, 1822–85*, New York, Atheneum

LOWENTHAL, L. (1961). *Literature, Popular Culture, and Society*, Englewood Cliffs, Prentice-Hall

LYNNES, R. (1953). *The Tastemakers*, New York, Grosset and Dunlap

MCDONALD, D. (1957). A theory of mass culture, in Rosenberg, B. and White, D. M. (eds), *Mass Culture: The Popular Arts in America*, Glencoe, Illinois, Free Press

MCGLINCHEE, C. (1940). *The First Decade of the Boston Museum*, Boston, Bruce Humphries

MUELLER, J. H. (1951). *The American Symphony Orchestra: A Social History of Musical Taste*, Bloomington, Indiana University Press

NYE, R. B. (1960). *The Cultural Life of the New Nation, 1776–1830*, New York, Harper and Row

PERRY, B. (1921). *Life and Letters of Henry Lee Higginson*, Boston, Atlantic Monthly Press

POGGI, J. (1968). *Theater in America: The Impact of Economic Forces, 1870–1967*, Ithaca, Cornell University Press

RYAN, K. (1915). *Old Boston Museum Days*, Boston, Little, Brown and Co.

SHIVERICK, N. C. (1970). The social reorganization of Boston, in Williams A. W., *A Social History of the Greater Boston Clubs*, New York, Barre

SOLOMON, B. M. (1956). *Ancestors and Immigrants*, New York, John Wiley

STARR, P. (forthcoming). *The Social Transformation of American Medicine*, New York, Basic Books

STINCHCOMBE, A. L. (1965). Social structure and organizations, in March, J. G. (ed.), *Handbook of Organizations*, Chicago, Rand McNally

STORY, R. (1980). *The Forging of an Aristocracy: Harvard and the Boston Upper Class, 1800–1870*, Middletown, Connecticut, Wesleyan University Press

THERNSTROM, S. (1972). *Poverty and Progress: Social Mobility in a Nineteenth-Century City*, New York, Atheneum

THOMPSON, E. P. (1966). *The Making of the English Working Class*, New York, Random House

THOMPSON, J. D. (1967). *Organizations in Action*, New York, McGraw-Hill

TWENTIETH CENTURY CLUB (1910). *The Amusement Situation in Boston*, Boston

VOGEL, M. (1981). *The Invention of the Modern Hospital*, Chicago, University of Chicago Press

WARNER, S. B. (1970). *Streetcar Suburbs: The Process of Growth in Boston, 1870–1900*, New York, Atheneum

WEBER, M. (1968). *Economy and Society*, 3 volumes, New York, Bedminster Press

WHIPPLE, G. M. (n.d.). *A Sketch of Musical Societies of Salem*, Salem, Massachusetts, Essex Institute

WHITEHILL, W. M. (1970). *Museum of Fine Arts, Boston: A Centennial History*, Cambridge, Harvard University Press

WOLFF, J. (1982). The problem of ideology in the sociology of art: a case study of Manchester in the nineteenth century, *Media, Culture and Society*, vol. 4, no. 1

ZOLBERG, V. L. (1974). The art institute of Chicago: the sociology of a cultural institution, Ph.D. Dissertation, Department of Sociology, University of Chicago

ZOLBERG, V. L. (1981). Conflicting visions of American art museums. *Theory and Society*, vol. 10, January

PART THREE

British broadcasting and the public sphere

The development of broadcasting in its institutional forms has had major consequences for modern democratic politics. It has created audiences drawn from all sections of the population, and thus a new public composed of nearly the whole of society. It was a radically new means of circulating information to all parts of the territory it served with an unsurpassed immediacy. It became a forum for debate and discussion on current matters of general concern, and thus a new site for the formation of public opinion. From the very beginning, political broadcasting has been the scene of strife between governments and broadcasters in which the stake has been public opinion. Whose interest does broadcasting serve? The state or society?

All these issues are exemplified in the development of British broadcasting. From the beginning it was constituted as a monopoly (the BBC) subject to state control and regulation, with a mandate to operate as a public service in the national interest. The BBC began transmitting in 1922, four years after the Representation of the People Act (1918) which created nearly universal adult suffrage and hence the conditions of modern, mass democracy. It was in the context, then, of a new relationship between state and people, rulers and ruled, that broadcasting started up; one in which the state for the first time formally represented the interests of all members of society. This representative role was delegated to broadcasting and developed in a number of ways; perhaps foremost as a national institution that synthesized new versions of the national culture.

This is the theme of David Chaney's chapter which demonstrates how broadcasting constitutes new civic rituals, forms of mass participation in moments of celebration or mourning, that bind society together in a common national identity. In the United States the office of the presidency and in Britain the royal family are both key symbolic institutions which broadcasting makes accessible to the people as richly representative of the American or British way of life. In this process tradition is constantly renovated to maintain a sense of historic continuity that readjusts to the changing conditions of modern society. This binding effect, this work of 'social cement', may well be the key ideological role of national broadcasting systems.

The production and reproduction of social unity papers over the cracks in the social fabric produced by sharp inequalities of economic, political and cultural power. A key role of modern governments is 'crisis management', the containment of internal pressures that threaten to disrupt the smooth functioning of society, particularly its economic life. A classic international crisis of that kind was the great recession of 1929 which in Britain produced the fall of the Labour government in 1931, and three million unemployed by late 1932. It is this 'moment' and how broadcasting responded to it that Paddy Scannell charts in his article. Unemployment was the crucial political and social problem of that time, and it was the first to be tackled by the BBC after the ban on controversial broadcasting, imposed by the state, was lifted in early 1928. Scannell shows not only the pressures on the broadcasters from government and parties—difficulties to which broadcasting is always exposed—but also their attempt to awaken in their national audience an awareness of the social consequences of unemployment, what the government was doing about it and what they, as individuals, could do. In so doing the BBC aspired to a representative mediatory role between government and people.

There have always been limits to this role, and to the ways in which broadcasting represents political issues, and nowhere is this more clearly seen than in the treatment of 'terrorism'—the subject of the contribution from Philip Elliott, Graham Murdock and Philip Schlesinger. It might be predicted that their enquiry into television's handling of this topic would show that it tended to support the state's official definition of it; and had they restricted themselves to news and current affairs programmes this might well have been their conclusion. But by examining the different inflections of discourses on terrorism in the spaces *within* and *between* fictional as well as factual programmes, they open up a much wider perspective on this sensitive political issue as well as showing the variable and contradictory nature of television's handling of difficult political and social themes.

David Cardiff tackles the question of the representative role of broadcasting from a different perspective. He illuminates the difficulties of the broadcasters in finding appropriate voices with which to speak to their audiences. What were appropriate styles and modes of address to an unseen public listening in the privacy of their own homes? The older techniques of the pulpit, the lecture hall or the public platform were intrusive in the placid, cosy domesticity of the family fireside. Cardiff carefully traces the development of 'serious' and 'popular' styles in the BBC Talks Department in the 1930s. This stratification of speakers, topics and audiences acknowledged differences of education, knowledge and cultural capital in the national audience.

Richard Collins considers the policy of Mrs Thatcher's government and argues that its embrace of new technologies and new ideologies in the name of the 'information society' threatens to destroy the established national role of British broadcasting and its reputation for producing programme material that speaks to the interests and needs of its audiences. He suggests that free market ideology and the expansion of channel capacity by broadband cable and direct broadcast satellites will create in this country the economic conditions that eroded its film industry and the television industries of countries such as Belgium and Canada.

Finally, James Curran argues that the conventional narrow focus of the portrait of predatory advertisers extracting favours from media clients obscures the more important and significant ways in which advertising shapes the media. The British media, he suggests, have been fashioned by advertisers in an essentially impersonal fashion in response to the marketing needs of the economic system and class inequalities of power and income within society.

Broadcasting and the politics of unemployment 1930–1935

PADDY SCANNELL*

Introduction

Our received accounts of social conditions in Britain in the thirties have been largely drawn from the mass of social documentation in films, literature and journalism that characterised the period. Mass Observation, *Picture Post*, the Left Book Club, the writings of Priestley and Orwell, the films of Rotha, Cavalcanti, Anstey and Elton— these, not to mention the 'dole' novels and the activities of the poets (cf. Hynes (1976) for an interesting account of many of these areas), have all contributed to our 'reading' of the period. Radio is a significantly absent source in this shopping list of essential references. Writers on broadcasting who refer to the period tend to character- ise the BBC throughout the thirties as 'ridden on a tight rein, amounting to no more than mild incursions by commentators into foreign politics and genteel discussions between political figures' (Burns, 1977, p. 17; cf. Kumar, 1977, pp. 235–236). Jonathan Dimbleby has accused the BBC of turning a blind eye to the reality of that decade. 'In an age of economic crisis, of political uncertainty, and of unemployment— where the poor "have no possessions, but pawn tickets and debts" and their children "lack fortune, lack opportunity, lack joy"—the BBC was content to purvey the general goodwill of a country vicar at a vestry tea party' (Dimbleby, 1975, pp. 66–67). The truth is much more complex. Briggs has rightly pointed out that the BBC was far more anxious than many of its critics genuinely to probe the conditions of England in the divided 1930s; and that there was no dearth of social reporting, though it provoked far more vigorous protest then than now (Briggs, 1965, p. 42).

This article offers such an account of two major contributions by radio (by no means the only ones) to examining the central political and economic problem of the early thirties—unemployment.[1] Both programme series (*S.O.S.*, 1933; *Time to Spare*, 1934) came at the height of the crisis; both introduced new methods of presenting social problems through the medium of radio; and both drew sharp reactions from the press, from politicians and from the listening public. The intentions of both series were the same; they were appeals to the conscience of the nation, a call for voluntary effort to mitigate the worst consequences of unemployment. Yet they were appropriated as political ammunition in very different ways. Though not

* School of Communication, Polytechnic of Central London.

[1] It would take a substantial monograph fully to cover the BBC's treatment of unemployment in the 1930s. Broadly speaking it was handled in three ways. Initially through talks by experts (amongst whom Keynes and Beveridge were prominent) on the underlying economic causes of the problem. Then through the new styles of investigative reporting described in this article. Third, from 1934 onwards the unemployed were recognised as a special minority within the listening audience, and programmes providing for their special needs and interests were run in the mornings and afternoons through to the outbreak of war. This particular use of radio as a social service deserves a fuller examination, but is beyond the scope of the present article.

intended as political interventions the techniques they used undercut their professed neutrality. The first series was used by a section of the left as evidence of a ruling class conspiracy between the Prime Minister, the Prince of Wales and the BBC. The second was so effectively appropriated by the left (both in Parliament and in the national press) as a stick with which to beat the National Government that Ramsay MacDonald attempted to stop the series. The more general implications of these programmes—their place within the wider activities of programme makers at that time; the social and political significance of the techniques they used; their internal consequences within the BBC—are examined in the final part of this article.

S.O.S.

Unemployment had originally been defined in relation to a particular social stratum—the unemployable. Beveridge's early study (*Unemployment. A Problem of Industry*, 1908) had dealt with the problem of residual categories in the work force, those least fitted for normal employment because of physical, mental or moral deficiency (Stevenson, 1977, p. 226). But in the crisis years of the great recession the collapse of industry and trade was seen to have thrown on the scrap heap many fit and able workers, skilled craftsmen, black-coat workers, professional people. Unemployment could happen to anyone, to one's neighbours or friends, to perfectly respectable people. 'There is not a special class or kind of people who constitute the unemployed. They come from almost every calling and have as great a variety of interests and capacities as any other member of the community. They are ordinary decent people like ourselves to whom an extraordinary misfortune has happened.' Thus the Master of Balliol, Dr A. D. Lindsay assured the listening public in the summer of 1932 ('Helping the Unemployed to Help Themselves', *The Listener*, 13 July 1932, p. 37). Lindsay drew attention to the work of The National Council for Social Services in co-ordinating voluntary schemes for assisting the unemployed to deploy their enforced 'leisure time' to good purpose.[2] *The Listener* frequently carried information on these schemes, and in early December a leading article dwelt on the urgent need for a unified social service to co-ordinate and extend recreational, social and occupational facilities for the unemployed. At the same time it announced that the BBC would provide a series of talks given by Mr S. P. B. Mais[3] who would give a first hand account, based on his own travels and enquiries, of what was being done up and down the country in the way of voluntary relief for those out of work.

In the meantime MacDonald's government was beginning to offer piecemeal support to some of these voluntary activities and on 19 December, broadcasting from Lossiemouth, MacDonald announced the government's decision to ask the N.C.S.S. to strengthen and widen their organisation for the purposes of co-ordinating the work of all voluntary bodies engaged in this field. The government said MacDonald, was doing what it could, but was hampered—like the employers—by the recession in world trade. He called for personal service, a community of friendship, 'the human hand supplementing the state machine' (*The Listener*, 28 December 1932, pp. 917–918).

Two weeks later the Prince of Wales, already an active supporter of the voluntary

---

[2] For details of the various schemes, cf. Mowatt (1968, pp. 488–490) and Hannington (1937) for a very different interpretation.

[3] Mais was a public school master, a writer of travel books, and an occasional broadcaster. In 1931 he had given a series of talks, *The Unknown Island*, in which he described a walking tour he had made of the less well known beauty spots in this country. On the basis of that piece of investigative reporting he was appointed to his present investigation.

movement, came to the microphone to introduce the BBC's series of talks. Some might argue, the Prince declared, that we were not facing the problem the right way, that voluntary service was starting at the wrong end, but there was a need in times of national crisis for all to co-operate. The causes of unemployment were beyond our control, and we might differ in our estimate of them, but it was largely within our power to control the effects of unemployment. The unemployed were just our fellow men, the same as ourselves, only less fortunate; our aims in relation to them must be practical not theoretical (*The Listener*, 11 January 1933, p. 37).

Thus heralded, Mais began his series of 11 reports, in a dramatic fashion:

Here is an S.O.S. message, probably the most urgent you will ever hear, and it vitally concerns you. You are called upon to create an entirely new social order. The bottom has apparently fallen out of the old world in which everything was subordinated to the day's work. We are now faced with a world in which one of the major problems is how best to occupy the day's enforced leisure. Some millions of our neighbours, without any preparation for it, have now got this leisure enforced upon them and, not unnaturally, are unable to cope with it. They do not understand how it has come about any more than you or I . . . We are not dealing with unemployables, but with first rate workmen, at least as capable as ourselves . . . It is not charity but a practical expression of friendliness that is needed . . . There is plenty for you to do, and you must do it if you care at all for your fellow countrymen. What therefore can you do at once? Make yourself known to the Manager of your local Labour Exchange, or if you live in a village, to the Schoolmaster or Parson. With their help collect a small number of unemployed who show any interest; find a hut for them to work on, and remember once it is started the men must run it entirely by themselves . . . (*The Listener*, 25 January 1933, p. 118).

The construction of this discourse, its mode of address, its positioning of the audience as middle-class like itself, its exclusion of the unemployed, its concealments and evasions, its transformation of the problem into the politics of the parish pump, into an exercise in good neighbourliness, should all be noted. But before showing a little more of the style and content of the reports that followed this introduction, the series must be more adequately placed within the context of the politics of unemployment in the months that preceded them.

Although in conception and intention the series was avowedly uncontroversial (non-political, non-partisan, simply an appeal to the nation as community), objections were raised to the series at the very start by the National Unemployed Workers Movement (NUWM), who regarded the speeches of MacDonald, of 'Edward Windsor' and of Mais as part of a ruling class conspiracy, an attempt to deflect attention from their movement, and to neutralise the political threat of their demands (Hannington, 1937, pp. 195–200).

The NUWM had been founded in 1921 by Wal Hannington, a toolmaker and member of the British CP. The NUWM was widely regarded as a communist organisation. It had organised demonstrations and protests against unemployment since the early twenties, but in late 1932, as the numbers of unemployed rose to nearly three million, Hannington led a series of massive protests against the government, which climaxed in the National Hunger March in October to demand the abolition of the means test. There were more mass demonstrations in London in the weeks following, and frequent clashes with the police who baton charged the crowds.[4] Hannington and other leaders were jailed. While serving his time he was told by a friendly prison padre that his marches had not been altogether unproductive—they

---

[4] An eye-witness account of the police baton charging a crowd in Hyde Park was given after the news one day by Howard Marshall (of whom more below). See *The Listener*, 11 November 1932, p. 643.

had stirred the conscience of the other class to the need for providing some kind of social life for the unemployed. What this meant more specifically, Hannington inferred, was the government's launching of the national campaign for the provision of social centres for the unemployed, following hard on the departure of the hunger marchers from London. The radio speeches by MacDonald and the Prince of Wales he regarded as a subtle and astute change of tactics by the ruling class in order to hold the unemployed more securely in their grip (cf. Hannington, 1937, p. 197).

With such arguments in mind the NUWM wrote immediately after the Prince of Wales's broadcast, to J. H. Whitley, Chairman of the BBC Board of Governors asking for the right to broadcast in the talks series on unemployment (*Manchester Guardian*, 12 January 1933). The request was turned down. The BBC stated that the talks were based on the actual experience of those who had been in the unemployed areas, and that it wished to avoid controversy. 'In other words', wrote *The Daily Worker* (20 January 1933), 'they want only one point of view, a point of view acceptable to the capitalist class and directed against the mass organisation of the unemployed.' Unabashed a deputation from the NUWM went to Broadcasting House to press their claims. There they were met by two detectives on the doorstep, and a member of the BBC management who promised to pass on their request (*The Times*, 21 January 1933). They were invited to return for discussions by the Director of Talks (Charles Siepmann) who added that the presence of the two CID men was in no way connected with any action on the part of the Corporation (*Manchester Guardian*, 26 January 1933). When the deputation of four (including Hannington) returned, there was a full scale police guard surrounding the building; two uniformed police inspectors, a sergeant and plain clothes men in the lobby, and in the side street behind Broadcasting House, a number of uniformed constables. After a 90 minute discussion their request to broadcast was again turned down. In a subsequent press statement the deputation declared that by their decision the BBC had placed itself in politics as a strong supporter of die-hard starvation and the National Government, and that the NUWM would organise a strong protest from the workers movement (*Manchester Guardian*, 28 January 1933).[5]

Siepmann was however sufficiently struck by the force of their arguments to refer the series, the following week, to the BBC's Parliamentary Advisory Committee. This was a small inter-party consultative committee (though the Labour Party refused to co-operate) set up in September 1932 at MacDonald's suggestion, to advise the BBC on political talks. Largely ineffective (it dwindled out of existence in 1935) it was more significant as an index of the routine character of consultation between the BBC and the political parties on sensitive issues after the right to handle controversy had been granted by Parliament. Siepmann proposed to the committee that since the series might legitimately be seen as controversial, the talks by Mais should be reduced in number, and replaced by a number of speakers giving their differing views on what politically should be done about unemployment—he suggested Lloyd George, Harold Macmillan and Ernest Bevin for the three parties, plus I. M. Sieff, G. D. H. Cole and finally a government spokesman. If this list scarcely represented the NUWM's position it had something of a progressive tinge to it. Siepmann was anxious to know if it represented an equitable balance of interests (Siepmann to John Buchan M.P., 2 February 1933). Neither Reith nor the committee

[5] This may have amounted to no more than a strongly worded letter of protest about the series to *The Radio Times* (24 February 1933, p. 459), from the Stockport WEA complaining of 'the exclusion of the spokesmen of the unemployed from the microphone'.

liked the proposal, nor anything very much like it (Reith to Siepmann, 7 February 1933) and the matter was dropped. Mais continued his talks, all on the theme of voluntary relief.

To gather material for his talks Mais travelled all over the country. He visited the out of work clubs, the settlements and labour exchanges; he talked not only to the organisers of such schemes but extensively to the unemployed themselves. He dealt not only with the obvious aspects of the problem (the industrial workers in the cities) but with more hidden aspects; unemployment in the countryside, amongst women, amongst the black-coated workers and the professions. It would not be hard to present the whole series in such a way as to endorse Hannington's view of the project. Indeed a North Region play dealing with unemployment and blackleg labour a few years later, contained a succinct parody of Mais's manner:

Marshall: I just thought you chaps might like to know what I heard at the [Out of Work] club last night.

Jock: I'll tell you what you heard: the capitalist class is the poor man's friend. Teach the unemployed lace-making and keep them cheerful. (*He produces a free imitation of S.P.B. Mais on the wireless.*) What these fellahs need is occupation. Make 'em feel they're wanted. Stout fellahs when you get to know them. Really grateful for all that's done for them . . . (*Blackleg*, Mary Stocks and John Orchard, producer Olive Shapley, North Region, 1 February 1939).

Yet Mais listened attentively to what the unemployed said and thought, and reported it back to the audience, even if he did not understand or agree with what was said to him. His reports are shot through with statements from the objects of all this middle class concern and goodwill, which uncomfortably subvert their intentions. At Brynmawr Mais tried to get a message from an old miner to pass on to the listening public: 'The people are all longing to know what do I said. What do you want done? What can people do?' He seemed surprised by the question and then repeated several times, ' "more honesty". But he didn't hold out any chance of getting that without a revolution.' In the Rhondda he was told that the bosses looked at you 'as though you were a piece of sicked up fat' (*The Listener*, 1 February 1933, pp. 163–164). At Lincoln he attended a meeting to discuss the formation of more clubs for the unemployed, in the course of which 'a black haired very frail young man got up and asked how anyone could expect an unemployed man to do physical jerks on 15s. a week, or play ping-pong while his wife was sitting at home before a half empty grate with only margarine to eat. I was more interested in him than in anyone else, so when the meeting was over I talked with him. He wouldn't allow that these clubs were doing any good at all. 'They're only meant', he said, 'to keep us quiet by people who are afraid.' He was right of course in suggesting that ping-pong does not provide a final solution. But he was wrong in denying that the service does no good at all' (*The Listener*, 22 March 1933, p. 452). A true innocent abroad, Mais was struck, while watching a women's keep fit class at Byker (Tyneside) by the neatness of their clothes. 'It's perhaps as well', he was told, 'that you can't see what they've got on underneath' (*The Listener*, 1 March 1933, p. 326).

Time to Spare

In the following year the Talks Department launched another major series on unemployment, which relied not on an outside observer, but on the unemployed themselves to come to the microphone and describe the human consequences of unemployment, how they managed living on the dole.[6] The series was produced by Felix Greene who solved the initially difficult task of finding appropriate speakers by getting in touch with societies and individuals all over the country who were constantly in touch with the unemployed, asking them to suggest speakers. But Greene came to feel that he could not hope to organise the series while sitting at a desk in his London office. He could get the facts of unemployment, but not the *feeling*. So he toured the country. He talked to the unemployed, went into their homes and clubs, met them in discussion groups and talked with them into the night. He selected the speakers from the hundreds he met, not because they were the saddest stories, but because they were the most typical and representative. Some found it difficult to write their story down though they could tell it well. When Greene tried to copy down what they said he found they spoke less freely. So he invited them to Broadcasting House, took them into a studio and got them talking freely again; meanwhile, unknown to them, their words were transcribed by secretaries in another room listening to them over a loudspeaker. There was no censorship. The BBC, Greene declared, deleted or altered nothing that the speakers wished to say (*The Radio Times*, 25 May 1934).

Time to Spare started on the National Programme (11 April 1934) with an introduction by Mais who began with a quotation from J. B. Priestley's just published *English Journey*. Although things had improved since last year Mais said, there was no call for complacency. Reiterating the theme of his own series, he called upon the listening public to dedicate themselves anew to the unemployed by searching about in town or village for some unemployed family in need of friendship, and not resting until they had been found[7] (*The Listener*, 11 April 1934, p. 620). In the weeks that followed the unemployed themselves came to speak of the way they lived: John Bentley, a tramp; John Evans, a miner from the Rhondda; John Rankin from the Clyde; Mrs Pallis from Sunderland; John Evans from Birmingham. There were eleven all told, and each speaker's fifteen minute talk was followed by a shorter postscript given by a suitably official person to point the moral of their tale.

The series received considerable publicity in the newspapers, particularly from the left wing press. *The Daily Worker* (5 May 1934) headlined the talk by John Evans (Birmingham), 'Forced to Live on 3½d. a day', and after Mrs Pallis spoke both *The Herald* and *The Worker* had the same headline: '16s. a week to feed family of five'. It was doubtless this prominent attention to the series which led the Ministry of Labour to begin investigating the claims of the speakers before the exchange in the House of Commons which made the programmes notorious.

The series had begun shortly before the third and final reading in the Commons of the Unemployment Bill. In the course of the debate Labour back-benchers took the government to task for the meanness of the means test, and the way it was administered. George Daggar (Abertillery, Monmouthshire) attacked the Minister of

[6] In between these two series *The Listener* had commissioned and published a series of articles (not broadcast) in which representative types of unemployed were asked to describe the psychological effects of unemployment—what it did to their social life, their intellectual faculties, their interest in public affairs, and their expectations for the future. It was then published as a book (Beales and Lambert, 1934), and was subsequently used as documentary evidence by Beveridge of the human consequences of unemployment (Beveridge, 1944, pp. 244–245).

[7] The BBC received over 4500 letters from listeners asking to be put in touch with a distressed family, offering help in the form of a small weekly sum of money, or to pay the family milk bill, or to provide clothes for the children. Other offers included help in the form of holidays or provisions, or work in the clubs and occupational centres. About £1520 was received in small donations which Greene arranged to be distributed amongst the speakers, other families, and the clubs and occupational centres (Greene to Siepmann, 26 June 1934).

Labour's claim that the unemployed were better off at present in view of the fall in the cost of living over the last three years. He produced as supporting evidence extracts from the talks in the *Time to Spare* series (as re-printed in *The Listener*), whose testimony, he claimed, could be accepted as reliable because they were broadcast by the BBC and hence were free from political theory or bias. Daggar quoted verbatim from the talks by John Evans (Birmingham), and John Evans from the Rhondda. In both passages the speakers told how their families managed on the dole money, which worked out at 8s. a week to feed four in the first case, and 12s. 6d. a week for three in the second case. R. S. Hudson, Parliamentary Secretary to the Minister of Labour, replied that he had made enquiries, and could assure the Hon. Member that the whole story was not given. Pressed on this point Hudson insisted that in two cases—John Evans of Birmingham and Mrs Pallis of Sunderland—there was no need whatever for there to have been any tragedy at all; that if those speakers had told the whole story of their circumstances it would have put a very different complexion on the matter. In neither instance would it have been possible to say they were very hard cases. They were not living on the amount they claimed (*Hansard*, 5th series, vol. 289, vol. VII, 1933–4 session, cols. 1524–8, 14 May 1934).

That exchange was eagerly picked up by the press, and a war of words ensued between the BBC and the Ministry of Labour. After a hasty internal review, the BBC issued a public statement that not only were the claims in the talks as broadcast correct, but there was nothing omitted that could justify Hudson's assertions. His statements in the Commons were based on a misunderstanding (*The Times*, 19 May 1934). Hudson however refused that escape clause, and in a letter to Reith (printed in *The Times*, 1 June 1934) re-stated his case that the speakers were untypical and had not stated the full facts. The government by now was seriously alarmed by the series. In early June *The Daily Herald* carried a story that the cabinet was thinking of stopping the talks: '*Time to Spare* is shattering too many illusions. Millions are being turned against the Government' (5 June 1934). Reith in fact, though this did not emerge at the time, was summoned to Number Ten and told by MacDonald that the series must stop. Reith replied that it was within the power of the government to order the BBC to discontinue the series but that if it did, he would, at that time in the schedule when the talks should be given, order the announcer to declare that the next 20 minutes would be silent because the government had refused to allow the unemployed to express their views. Faced with this threat MacDonald backed down and the series continued.

But as a conciliatory gesture to the government, Reith and others were anxious that the series should be rounded off with a talk that balanced out the objections that had been raised against it, and which gave the government what credit was due to it. The Prime Minister's Office was asked to submit the kind of material it would wish to have incorporated into the final talk, and MacDonald's private secretary sent Siepmann a complete script which expanded on what the government had done already for the unemployed, and elaborated on the extra benefits of the new act. Siepmann was anxious that the final talk should make it clear that the series was *not* a reflection on the government of the day. Reith and the Board of Governors were eager to see the script, and Siepmann worked hard to get the manuscript in final shape well in advance of the day it was broadcast. It was given by a suitably public (but not political) person—the Master of Balliol, who as we have seen, had been a supporter of the voluntary movement since it began in 1932. Lindsay's talk, which he wrote himself, made little use of the Downing Street material, but covered in a general way the points that Siepmann wanted establishing. He summarised the series as 'an eloquent sermon addressed to each one of us, recalling us to our personal responsibilities'. He went on smoothly to explain the gap between what was, and what was intended; between the responses of the unemployed to their situation and especially to their treatment by authority, and the strains on the official machinery (designed mainly to handle seasonal, or short term unemployment) which resulted in people not always getting the help the administration was ready to give them (*The Listener*, 4 July 1934).

At the same time as this final talk was being carefully prepared, Siepmann was conducting his own exhaustive inquiry into the specific charges made by Hudson against some of the speakers, and in early July presented his report to Reith. Hudson had made three points against the BBC: that it took insufficient care to check the facts and figures mentioned by the speakers; that those selected were exceptional and in no way representative; and that certain essential facts were omitted giving a distorted picture of the particular case, and in consequence of the general lot of the unemployed. These general complaints were embodied in specific instances of whom two, Mrs Pallis and John Evans of South Wales, were the most significant.

Mrs Pallis's case was exceptional, Hudson asserted, in that her husband had been out of work for a much longer period than average, and he was moreover a left-handed rivetter and as such at a disadvantage when it came to getting jobs. As regards the first point Siepmann had established that Mr Pallis's term of unemployment was, for his trade and for the area quite typical; and as to the second, 'we have it from Mr W. Brown, the Chief Engineer of Palmers of Jarrow, that left-handed rivetters stand an equal chance with right-handed rivetters when seeking employment'. Descending to the details of Mrs Pallis's talk Hudson complained that she made capital out of the absence of facilities for advice on birth control; omitted to mention that her children received free school meals; mentioned that her husband shared an allotment at a cost of 22s. a year which he could have obtained at a cheaper rate through the Society of Friends; and did not avail herself of the maternity services of the district. On the first point Hudson had got his facts all wrong, said Siepmann. Mrs Pallis knew all about birth control; what she said was that poor people could not afford it, and only incidentally remarked that some people did not know about facilities for advice.[8] Hudson had flatly declared that Mrs Pallis could have obtained advice on the subject from her local birth control clinic. Siepmann had carefully checked this out and had found that there was no local authority clinic in Sunderland; that the nearest voluntary clinic was in Newcastle, and that the local medical officer was opposed to voluntary clinics and to advice on birth control being given on anything other than medical grounds. The second and third points he dismissed as being really too trivial, and the last was irrelevant since Mrs Pallis made no reference at all to the maternity service in her talk.

[8] 'I know I've cried when I knew I had to have another baby, not for myself, but for what they have to be brought into—no work, no means, no jobs for them. But it means expense to avoid them. I know all about the avoidance part, but I haven't the means to carry it out. It costs money. . . . I think we ought to have some information from somewhere given to us. It's ignorance on some people's part; or, for people like myself who know, we haven't got the money' (Mrs Pallis, *The Listener*, 16 May 1934, p. 812).

This reference to birth control brought sackfulls of letters to the BBC, as Felix Greene recalls, complaining that the subject was mentioned on the radio. There were pressures from some of the Governors for the subject to be broached in late 1935, but it was not allowed to be discussed at all until well into the fifties. Corporation policy was expressed in a letter to the National Council for Civil Liberties (November 1942): 'The subject of birth control . . . has never yet been discussed at the microphone in this country. Broadcasting is not, in the Corporation's view, a suitable medium for discussion of this subject.'

John Evans, Hudson claimed, had stated in his talk that his daughter was earning 7s. a week, but the PAC said she was earning 12s. a week. Both facts were wrong, at least as broadcast. The child was earning 13s. a week. Evans had referred to her wages in relation to the sum she contributed weekly to the running of the household. She paid 7s. to the home, keeping 6s. for her maintenance, clothing and other expenses. While Evans's statement was, in law, an error of fact, it conveyed the sense he intended and in any case was a trivial point in relation to the talk as a whole.

The two other cases that Hudson raised were obscure and trivial but Siepmann painstakingly sifted the evidence and concluded that he was satisfied, after very careful investigation, that no case could be made against the BBC either for careless or irresponsible action, or for a distortion of the truth (Siepmann to Reith, 2 July 1934). Reith wrote the following day to MacDonald's secretary stating that the BBC believed the talks had presented a substantially accurate and representative picture of the hardships of the unemployed, but admitted that the series might have created the impression that the talks represented the lot of the average unemployed, which impression the BBC had carefully asked the Master of Balliol to remove. Reith regretted that party capital had been made of the series, but felt it was unfair to blame the BBC for this. 'We should more than regret that anyone should imagine that either with malice aforethought or through negligence on our part, the Government had suffered a prejudice' (Reith to Barlow, 3 July 1934). And that, officially, closed the matter.

The politics of social documentation

These two series should be seen as part of a wider effort by programme makers to find new ways of re-presenting politics, news and current social problems to the listening public. Responsibility at that time for news rested with the Talks Department which introduced, for an experimental six month period in 1933, a weekly radio 'newsreel' (using eye-witness accounts, studio analysis and recorded 'sound pictures') with the intention of putting across the day's events more vividly and in greater depth. This search for greater immediacy and realism prompted experiments in combining documentary features with straight talks. *Crisis in Spain* (11 June 1931), written by A. E. Harding, was a bravura piece of radio intended to give dramatic colour to, and a factual context for, a talks discussion on the recent events in Spain—the abdication of the monarchy, the establishment of the republic. It was the first British example of the reporting in radio form of contemporary events. Similarly, though in a more distanced historical way, a talks series on the history of trades unionism, introduced by J. H. Hammond (April 1934) was supplemented by carefully documented dramatisations of the Tolpuddle Martyrs and the Sheffield riots of 1867. The kind of reportage inaugurated by the Mais series was not an isolated instance. There was a major series of talks by Professor John Hilton on *Industrial Britain* (January to May 1934), a series of investigations of modern industry not from the point of view of management, but from that of the worker. *S.O.S.* takes on a slightly less reactionary appearance when seen in conjunction with another big talks series, *Other People's Houses* (commenced January 1933), with which it ran in tandem. The series alternated between eye-witness reports by Howard Marshall on the slums of Tyneside, London and Glasgow, and debates or talks by accredited experts and authorities on the housing problem.

Underlying this activity was a common commitment among programme makers to the importance of radio as a new form of social communication, and a common interest in developing effective methods of communicating via the spoken word. At one extreme were the modernist techniques so brilliantly used by Harding in *Crisis in Spain*, which drew on the practices of the Russian and European documentary film makers. But the major development was along the lines of *S.O.S.*, *Other People's Houses* and *Time to Spare*—the introduction of eye-witness accounts, a combination of investigative reporting with social documentation. When Howard Marshall gave his first report on housing conditions in Tyneside, he introduced a quite new discourse to radio. He had been inside the houses of the slum dwellers, he had talked to them and listened to their feelings on the conditions in which they lived, and in a direct and straight forward way reported back on what he saw and heard:

The first door at which I knocked in Cornwallis Square, Gateshead, was opened by a woman who was wiping her hands—she had been washing something in a bucket of greasy, dirty water—and a bunch of under-nourished, ragged children stared at me open mouthed. The old grandfather was huddled by the fire, a very sick man, and the husband pointed to a lump of plaster a foot wide which had fallen from the ceiling onto the ricketty bed. Bare boards, with rat holes here and there, a wooden box or two, uncurtained windows with broken sash cords, permanently closed, a great patch of moisture where damp had soaked through several layers of wall paper by the baby's cot: this was the room I saw by the cheerless light of an unshaded gas mantle. And always it was the same story: no water, no conveniences . . . (*The Listener*, 18 January 1933, p. 74).

We have long since become over familiar with such testamentary evidence. The location shots of slum dwellers in *Housing Problems* (Anstey and Elton, 1935), and Orwell's accounts in *The Road to Wigan Pier* (cf. Williams's comments in Williams, 1979, p. 390) are received and distant images of the working classes as victims in the 1930s. In their own time they spoke only to small and self-selecting audiences. But the contexts in which *Other People's Houses* and *Time to Spare* both operated gave the programmes an inescapable radical edge and a hard political thrust. There had not been heard before on radio such a spelling out of the facts of living on the dole or in a rat infested slum, in a way which broke through statistics and abstract debate to the realities of how people lived those conditions. Nor had working people been heard to tell of the conditions they endured and their feelings about them. Access to the microphone for such speakers was a significant extension of radio's social range. Radio addressed not the particular publics of the daily newspapers, not the specialised readership of the Left Book Club, not the tiny audiences for the documentary films, but the general public, society at large. As such, its interventions—coming as they did, not after, but at the height of the crisis—had an immediacy and widespread impact, sharpened by the fact that the BBC had not yet learnt to time its programmes with discretion. The programmes on housing and unemployment all coincided with new moves by the government to deal with the issues they confronted.[9]

The conditions they described, much more than was foreseen, were a critical challenge to the prejudices and ignorance of the listening public, and the shortcomings and failures of official solutions to the problems. Marshall's descriptions of the slums were greeted with frank disbelief by some listeners. 'Either you are the world's biggest liar, or you are trying to play the funny man', wrote one anonymous correspondent of his description of the East End slums. And Sir Cecil Levita M.P.,

[9] *Other People's Houses* began shortly after a housing bill was put before the commons (18 December 1932) which abolished all subsidies for council building except those scheduled for slum clearance: i.e. all municipal housing designed to reduce the numerical shortage of working class houses was to be stopped (Branson and Heinemann, 1973, p. 204).

one of the expert speakers in the series, sharply criticised Marshall's methods: 'All old towns contain worn out and bad houses. It is an unhappy fact. Probably they always will, and eye-witnesses will always, as ever, be able to harrow your feelings about such properties' (*The Listener*, 15 February 1933, p. 234). Marshall defended himself against his critics in his third talk. For those who doubted, he offered to arrange a tour of the East End to prove the accuracy of his accounts.

The framework of *Time to Spare* was in conception not much different from *S.O.S.* which the left had interpreted as a ruling class conspiracy. But the simple and radical act of letting the unemployed speak for themselves while the Commons debated the unemployment bill was enough to give the left a field day against the government which responded with an astonishing display of threat and bluster, revealing the wretched and pusillanimous spirit in which it interpreted state relief for the unemployed. The most disgraceful aspect of the whole affair was the harassment by the Ministry of Labour of those speakers whose statements it had challenged. In his *Radio Times* article, written at the height of the row, Felix Greene had emphasised that it took courage to come to the microphone and describe the facts of one's existence, when that existence was a struggle for the bare necessities: 'There are neighbours who will gossip, and the Press who will worry one, and the Public Assistance Officers who will make enquiries.' The full glare of press publicity fell particularly on Mrs Pallis and John Evans of Birmingham; and the former was subjected to persistent badgering by social workers and ministry officials who even went so far as to question her children at school as to whether they were receiving free meals. Evans was brought back from Ireland to undergo elaborate investigations before a committee which included the area relief officer and the chairman of the PAC. And Greene himself was obliged to write to a contact in South Wales asking him to investigate, in confidence, how much the daughter of John Evans, the miner, actually earned.

The Talks Department at that time, though its outlook was certainly progressive, could scarcely be described as left wing. There were very few people in the BBC— Harding perhaps was one—committed to a left wing politics. Yet the effect on those directly involved in making such programmes as *Other People's Houses* and *Time to Spare* was to transform their social or political perspectives. Marshall was deeply moved by his encounters with the slums and the plight of the people who lived there. When the series finished he wrote a documentary book called simply *Slum* in which he declared, 'Once you have seen the slums you will find your values change. You will be haunted. The shadow of the slums will fall over everything you do.' To write the book, to get the proper *feel* of the subject, Marshall felt the need to cut himself off entirely from his normally comfortable life; so he hired a room in a cheap lodging house in Poplar and struggled to set pen to paper. 'Do you really care much? I dare say you do. I dare say it is foolish of me to be writing here at all. I should be sitting securely in my club in St James Street, surrounded by familiar things, looking down at Poplar with detached benevolence. That would give me the right perspective: I should see the East End as a statistical problem—houses to the acre, families to a room, the infant mortality rate, and the whole complex tale of suffering set out to three places of decimals' (Marshall, 1933, pp. 3–4). Greene's response to the unemployed was much the same. 'Statistics we can read and put aside unmoved. The story of unemployment in terms of bread and worn out boots, rent that cannot be paid and hands that daily lose a little of their skill, and 'unstretched intellects' that know they rust for want of use—such stories cannot be put aside' (*Radio Times*,

25 May 1934). His encounter at first hand with the way the poor lived was the source of Greene's awakening left wing sympathies. He came to feel that there was something very wrong in a society enormously rich at one end and abjectly poor at the other. For a time he lived among the poor as a down and out himself, sleeping in doss houses and beginning really to grasp the wretchedness of poverty.

In the meantime the BBC's organisation was hardening into a division between production and administration with a rigorous system of control, whereby an elite of policy making high officials—with little experience of programme making, or any specialised knowledge of programme areas—began to impose corporate definitions of BBC policy across the whole range of programme output. There was a series of disparate moves by Reith which amounted to a systematic effort to weed out or nullify the activities of those programme makers whose work in one way or another was troublesome. In 1933 Harding was 'banished' to Manchester, after making a programme that offended the Polish Ambassador (Bridson, 1971, pp. 21–22). In 1934 John Coatman was brought in by Reith to head the News section. He was handpicked as a 'right wing offset' to balance the direction of talks and news—the first sign of the disintegration of the Talks Department (Briggs, 1965, p. 147). Finally in 1935, at a time when the BBC was under scrutiny from the Ullswater Committee, came the wholesale dismantling of the department. Siepmann was sent to tour the provinces as Director of Regional Relations. Greene was transferred to New York, Lionel Fielden to India, and R. A. Rendall to Palestine. Hilda Matheson, who had resigned as Head of Talks in an atmosphere of intrigue and bitterness in 1932, called it 'a dispersal and disintegration unparalleled in any other department. This has not been without consequent loss to the common body of knowledge, experience, technique and tradition'. Writing in the autumn of that year she detected in talks output 'a widespread impression of arrested development' (Matheson, 1935, pp. 512, 514). As Lionel Fielden put it, one of the most imaginative talks producers, before his long trek to India: 'The programme was no longer the thing. It was wiser in the BBC of 1935 to be a good administrator than to have any original ideas; better to spend your time cutting down artists' fees than rehearsing the artist; more paying to use a blue pencil than your mind' (Fielden, 1960, p. 142).[10]

There was a space available to broadcasters in the early thirties to open up broadcasting, to make it more immediately engaged in contemporary social and political life. We have seen the extent to which they took that chance, and the extent to which their work entered into the very fabric of political life, becoming material evidence (appropriated in quite contradictory ways) for debate and controversy. I have shown elsewhere (Scannell, 1979) how the categories of the 'political subject' and the 'social subject' were split in the developing post-war television service; the former being the preserve of television talks, the latter of a small documentary department. I suggested that this separation was the result of countervailing forces (pressures from the state on the one hand, obligations to the audience on the other) that have tugged at those working in the BBC since the thirties. What this account shows more exactly is that initially there was no such split; that the social documentation of *S.O.S.*, *Other People's Houses* and *Time to Spare* were precisely political interventions. Hilda Matheson saw them as evidence of how broadcasting might help make the modern state work—a means of bridging the gulf between expert and citizen, and of reducing

---

[10] Perhaps the best account of the complex politics of the Talks Department at this time, of the personalities involved, of the stifling of its creative vitality, of the weeding out of 'left-wing elements', etc. is Lambert (1940, pp. 59–89).

the awkward time lag between perceiving a remedy and making it understood (Matheson, 1933, p. 97). What they more exactly did, through exposing the very urgency of the problems, was to point to the inadequacies of the remedies proposed by the national government which was far removed from Hilda Matheson's idealistic conception of 'the modern state' (she had, like a true progressive of that time, the model of Stalin's Russia in mind, cf. pp. 95–97).

The government's displeasure at these well-intentioned critiques and the amount of trouble they gave the rulers of the BBC contributed towards a long retreat, by those departments responsible for controversy (talks especially), from such penetrating forms of social investigation. Social documentary re-appeared a little later in the thirties, but largely displaced to the regions (Manchester especially, under Harding's régime) where the dead hand of policy control did not so effectively reach. It had passed from talks to features (or documentary) producers. Its social basis was quite different, being largely literary and historical, or more interestingly re-presentations of everyday life for regional audiences. Impressive though these programmes were, particularly those of D. G. Bridson and Olive Shapley, what was lost was the central relevance of re-presentations of social conditions to the national politics of the time.

That closure in broadcasting, whereby the BBC sought to achieve one voice, a unified policy to project 'the nation in its corporate collective character' (the phrase is Burke's who applied it to the state), was something that had materially to be engineered within the institution, imposed on—and right across—the level of production. The programme makers had to be brought in line. Divide and rule. Bring in new people to establish orthodoxy. Split up departments. Stop the progressives from making programmes by 'promoting' them or sending them elsewhere. That materially is one side of how the BBC worked to produce its corporate ideology. The other side to that process is the way in which producers learn the rules, 'what goes', the limits of the possible, and develop routines and strategies that smooth their way to a less troubled life within the corporation. The dismantling of talks signified the end of experiment, of *possibilities*, and the decisive arrival of corporate thinking, of rationalisation, of planning and policy. The system of distribution had already been reconstructed to that end. The original network of local stations (1923–28) had been replaced by the *National* channel (1930) with a subordinated Regional alternative. What yet remained to be achieved was to make the level of production fit that system as it was intended to be; the bearer, across the whole range of output of a defined and unified policy of programming in the national interest. After 1935 the way was clear.

In the early thirties the form and content of programmes had not yet been systematised and routinised, and neither had their producers. That process of adaptation was to become increasingly evident in London (less so in the regions) after 1935 within the different politics (fascism and the threat of war) of the late thirties. Lessons had been learnt and programme makers began as a matter of course to anticipate in advance where trouble might come from and took steps accordingly. In 1936, Talks planned an ambitious social survey of Britain (it got no further than the planning stage), and at the outset Rose-Troupe warned all those involved of the dangers in such a project: 'We do not want to get into the difficulties such as a couple of years ago when we were doing a series dealing with the actual conditions of the unemployed' (Memo to Regional Directors, 12 February 1936). It is within the opportunities available under continuing determining pressures that programmes are finally delivered to their audiences. What programme makers in Head Office could deliver in the early thirties—the kinds of accounts they could offer of society to the listening public—and what they could deliver subsequently were two very different things.

Note on sources

I have relied extensively, for this article, on the invaluable records of the BBC Written Archive Centre, Caversham, Reading. All the major talks series referred to were printed in *The Listener*. I am grateful to Felix Greene for providing me with some important details in relation to his programme, *Time to Spare*.

Bibliography

BEALES, H. L. and LAMBERT, R. S. (1934). *Memoirs of the Unemployed*, Gollancz

BEVERIDGE, W. H. (1944). *Full Employment in a Free Society*, Allen and Unwin

BRANSON, N. and HEINEMANN, M. (1973). *Britain in the Nineteen Thirties*, Panther

BRIDSON, D. G. (1971). *Prospero and Ariel*, Gollancz

BRIGGS, A. (1965). *The History of Broadcasting in the United Kingdom*, vol. II, *The Golden Age of Wireless*, O.U.P.

BURNS, T. (1977). *The BBC: Public Institution, Private World*, Macmillan

DIMBLEBY, J. (1975). *Richard Dimbleby*, Hodder & Stoughton

FIELDEN, L. (1960). *The Natural Bent*, André Deutsch

HANNINGTON, W. (1937). *The Problem of the Distressed Areas*, Gollancz, Left Book Club Edition

HYNES, S. (1976). *The Auden Generation. Literature and Politics in England in the 1930s*, Bodley Head

KUMAR, K. (1977). Holding the middle ground: The BBC, the public and the professional broadcaster, *Mass Communication and Society* (J. Curran *et al.*, eds), Edward Arnold

LAMBERT, R. S. (1940). *Ariel and all his Quality*, Gollancz

MARSHALL, H. (1933). *Slum*, Heinemann

MATHESON, H. (1933). *Broadcasting*, Butterworth

MATHESON, H. (1935). 'The Record of the BBC', *Political Quarterly*, vol. 6, no. 4, pp. 506–518

MOWATT, C. L. (1968). *Britain Between the Wars*. Methuen, University Paperback

SCANNELL, P. (1979). The social eye of television, 1946–1955, *Media, Culture and Society*, vol. 1, no. 1

STEVENSON, J. (1977). *Social Conditions in Britain Between the Wars*, Penguin

WILLIAMS, R. (1979). *Politics and Letters*, New Left Books

The serious and the popular: aspects of the evolution of style in the radio talk 1928-1939[1]

DAVID CARDIFF*

This paper traces the early evolution of a number of techniques which are still consistently employed in Britain, in both radio and television, particularly in news, current affairs, documentary and magazine programmes. These are the straight talk, the discussion, the interview, the debate and a range of programme formats in which they were inserted. Anyone who has been exposed to these forms knows that, within each category, there are variations in style which depend upon such factors as the prestige of the programme, its subject matter and the status of the contributors. There are significant differences between a studio interview with a cabinet minister about economic policy, in the context of a serious current affairs programme, and an interview with a man-in-the-street about the effects of that policy, in the context of a popular magazine programme. In particular, those styles which distinguish the status of contributors have developed into a hierarchy of presentational rules which, while they reflect the wider social hierarchy, are at the same time symptomatic of tensions within broadcasting itself. When looked at historically, the evidence of variations in technique can be analysed as a shifting register of broadcasting strategies. The conventions reflect both the broad social outlook of the broadcasters, which were by no means confined to the BBC, and a range of motivations which were specific to their occupation; the need to achieve success in their programmes, whether judged in terms of communicating coherently or in terms of maximising the audience, the need to produce material appropriate to specific sections of the audience, the need to preserve a precarious autonomy, both for broadcasting in relation to the state and for individual BBC departments in relation to the governing bodies of the corporation, and, finally, the need to maintain a working relationship with individual contributors and other sources. In practice, these motivations often came into conflict and producers were faced with dilemmas which they attempted to resolve through a diplomacy in which questions of technique played an important part.

During the period covered by this paper there was considerable development in techniques for handling politically controversial material and there was a steady drift towards populism in the presentation of information in general. Much recent criticism of news, current affairs and factual documentary has focused on populist tendencies which may lead producers to be more concerned with attracting and holding the audience's attention than with communicating a coherent and intelligible message. In relation to controversial broadcasting, it has been argued that an obsessive concern with maintaining balance and impartiality can lead to a distortion in the definition of issues and to the allocation of an increasingly powerful rôle to professional

[1] The major source for material in this article was the BBC Written Archive Centre at Caversham.
* School of Communication, Polytechnic of Central London.

'mediators'—presenters, interviewers and chairmen—who set the agenda for discussion and prevent direct communication between outside contributors and the audience. But it is generally agreed that these are recent developments; that the populism reflects the commercialisation of culture in general and, in particular, the arrival of commercial television in 1954; that the elaboration of techniques for handling controversy dates from the breakdown of a national consensus on social and political issues which is supposed to have existed in Britain until the late 1950s. Certainly it is assumed that no such tendencies were to be found in the broadcasting of the Reithian period or in that period, lasting into the 1950s, which is held to have been haunted by the 'Reithian Ethos'. This paper will argue that, with certain important qualifications, these tendencies were present from the inception of British broadcasting. This is not simply in order to set the record straight, although some refinement of received opinions about the 'Reithian Ethos' is long overdue. Criticism of the output of today's radio and television is related to a wider argument about the political and economic basis of the mass media in Britain, in which the contrast between pre-commercial and post-commercial broadcasting acts as a crucial pivot. It is to this argument that we must return in the concluding section. But British broadcasting between 1928 and 1939 was dedicated to the ideal of public service. The Talks Department, with whose work this paper is largely concerned, took a leading though often unpopular rôle in attempting to educate and inform the public. In this rôle it was obliged to take seriously the need to attract an audience, even if its notion of that audience was unrealistic. It was in relation to a particular image of the listening public that the department's earliest interest in style developed.

The art of the spoken word

Most broadcasting was directed towards the home and the 'art' of radio talk was developed by broadcasters who held constantly in mind the image of a family audience, seated around the fireside at home. This image was celebrated in numerous articles in the *Radio Times* and in its occasional 'Home' and 'Fireside' issues. It was argued that the wireless was reinforcing family life in the face of counter-attractions such as 'picture houses, thés dansants and cabarets'. But at the same time it was widening the domestic horizon and 'making the home-staying folk citizens of the world' (J. A. R. Cairns, *Radio Times*, 12 December 1924). This conceptualisation of the audience as composed of privatised families clustered around the hearth predominated until the War. The social differentiation of the listening public was rarely referred to, although the distinction between Regional and National listeners had important policy implications. The image of the audience was cosily middle-class; its setting the suburban home or rural cottage. It was in relation to this image that radio could be seen as a force for social integration; it was a medium capable of uniting the private sphere of life with the public.

At first, the BBC had confined itself to linking its listeners to the symbolic heartland of the nation, through outside broadcasts of ceremonial state occasions and, whenever possible, through broadcasts by members of the Royal Family. But in 1928, when the government lifted its ban on the broadcasting of controversial matter, the Talks Department, under its first two directors, Hilda Matheson and Charles Siepmann, embarked upon an ambitious programme of talks on social and political issues. Hilda Matheson regarded broadcasting as a process of 'projection' and admired the Soviet Union's use of radio to diffuse its social planning. 'It is difficult to see', she wrote, 'how any political school of thought can dispense with broadcasting, since those who look forward to a dictatorship of either left or right or neither, are faced with the imperative need of securing at least an acquiescent public' (Matheson, 1933: 87). In the Britain of the early 1930s, with its deep social divisions sharpened by widespread unemployment, remedies were at least being suggested on the air, even if they were unlikely to be implemented by a National Government widely recognised as bereft of policies. The talks programme was dominated by contributions from the 'middle-of-the-road' progressive intellectuals; a group of experts, often academics, technocrats or administrators who, in this period, were politically non-aligned but were committed to improvements in the efficiency of social administration and the promotion of a planned economy. Typical of this group were figures like William Beveridge and Maynard Keynes, although some speakers were well to the left of them. Although the majority of talks were intended to 'interpret that vast field of interest and knowledge which is happily beyond the frontiers of acute current partisanship' (*BBC Handbook*, 1929: 41) individual talks often provoked criticism from the higher reaches of the BBC, from Parliament and from other external interest groups. The talks were only loosely topical and could best be described as offering an education for citizenship. But in encouraging listeners to become 'citizens of the world', Hilda Matheson did not forget that they were also 'stay-at-home folk'. She fostered the art of the spoken word as a means of domesticating the public utterance, as an attempt to soften and naturalise the intrusion of national figures into the fireside world of the family.

In outline, the art of the radio talk as it was then defined, is easily summarised. Since it was received by family groups it should be conversational in tone rather than declamatory, intimate rather than intimidating. The personality of the speaker should shine through his words. But because all broadcasting was 'live', it was agreed that talks should be scripted. Otherwise what they gained in colloquialism and personal style, they would lose in succinctness. As Briggs puts it, 'what was natural had first to become artificial before it would sound natural again' (Briggs, 1965: 126). But the very care that was taken with the scripting of talks soon gave rise to doubts about the aims of the Talks Department's editorial policy.

The colloquial style of talk was perfected by Professor John Hilton, who in 1937, gave a talk about talk in which he simultaneously employed the technique of writing for the ear and revealed its secrets. Referring to newspaper critics who had praised him for simply talking rather than reading from a script, he continued, 'Oh yes, I like that. For, of course, I read every word. If only I could pull it off every time— but you have to be at the top of your form. Yes, of course, every word's on paper even now—this—what I'm saying to you now—it's all here'. It was thought that this studied informality in speech, with its personal mode of address and carefully placed hesitations and slips of the tongue, could, if effectively done, achieve a form which transcended both ordinary speech and the written word. Hilton argued that this idiom was 'perhaps not "true to life"—but something better—truer than life' (transcript of recording). Thus the technique of writing for the ear was elevated to the status of an art and there is no doubt that Hilton himself used it most effectively. It would be a mistake to agree too easily with those critics who dismissed the Talks Department's concern with style as a mystique. It is true that Hilda Matheson could adopt a messianic tone when she argued that 'broadcasting is clearly rediscovering the spoken language, the impermanent but living tongue, as distinct from the permanent but silent print' (Matheson, 1933: 74). But her basic aim was to reach people whose lack of literary education barred them from access to 'complicated, difficult and novel ideas' (ibid.: 75).

There were a variety of criticisms levelled at the BBC's attitude towards the spoken word. Some critics felt that, far from being a new art form, the style was simply an artificial compromise which interfered with the direct transmission of information; that there was a tendency for the aims of informing and attracting listeners to come into conflict. It was also alleged that powerful or prestigious speakers were allowed to deliver their scripts as they wished, while lesser fry were subjected to detailed criticism. The attention paid to the mode of expression could be seen as a veiled form of censorship. A style originally devised for the edification of listeners had, it was claimed, evolved into a means for exercising a subtle control over contributors. While some evidence can be found to support each of these criticisms, none of them reached to the heart of the matter. In the majority of cases, the careful attention paid to scripts signalled an anxiety about how different kinds of speaker and different categories of talk should be defined and legitimated for the public.

The tension between the need to inform and the need to attract the public presented producers with a dilemma. The style of talk perfected by Hilton was simply not a suitable medium for communicating the technical ideas which were the staple ingredients of many a talks 'syllabus'. One talks assistant amused himself by imaging how Einstein might deliver a talk on the stars in the approved idiom. 'Well, I suppose all of us at some time or other have—er um—looked up on a clear night and seen the stars overhead. Of course when I say "stars" I mean planets too. It would never do to leave out the planets!' It was a style which, as he pointed out, 'people of some importance can usually resist having forced upon them ...' (Bloomfield, 1941: 84). There was an increasing tendency to draw a distinction between serious and popular categories of talk and talker. The speaker who had perfected the intimate, informal style might find himself relegated from the league of experts to the league of radio personalities. John Hilton himself began in 1933 with a serious series devoted to his own subject, industrial relations, but by the end of the decade was responsible for a kind of agony column of the air, championing the cause of the little man against the predations of confidence tricksters.

A typical example of the way in which popular and serious speakers were differentiated is afforded by an incident in relation to one of the BBC *National Lectures*. These radio lectures were instituted in 1928 and were intended, according to Reith, 'to hold the blue ribbon of broadcasting and to provide, on two or three occasions in the year, for the discussion of issues of major importance and the interpretation of new knowledge by men of distinction in the world of scholarship and affairs' (Reith to De La Mare, 16 February 1933). In 1935 it was noticed that one of these lectures, given by Lord Macmillan on 'Law and the Citizen' was to be followed within a few weeks by a talk on 'The Rule of Law' to be given by an ordinary barrister, Maurice Healy. Healy was very much a popular speaker who had contributed to a series of imaginary court cases, *Consider Your Verdict*, and had read short stories on the air. There was a minor panic when it was realised that listeners might, even after a five week interval, suppose his contribution to be as authoritative as the *National Lecture*. His producer wrote, 'Lord Macmillan's talk will be very much a lecture and I think it would be a good thing if you were to keep in mind the fact that your short address is very much a talk, full of that touching on 'I' and 'you' which comes so easily from yourself ...' (McLaren to Healy, 6 April 1936). He wanted Healy to make it quite clear that he was talking on a subject that was near to his heart but on which he was not an expert. Healy objected that, as a barrister, he was an expert and also baulked at being labelled in the *Radio Times* as 'a layman'. In the end he was credited as a lawyer 'speaking on this occasion as a layman'. But, from the BBC's point of view, an appropriate contrast between the two performances had been achieved. Lord Macmillan discussed 'the reign of law' as follows. 'The conception of what it embodies is the conception of certainty as opposed to arbitrariness. To know what we can lawfully do and what we cannot lawfully do; to be subject to laws constitutionally enacted and enforced . . .', etc. Healy began, 'Well, freedom is a vague word and you may well ask what I mean by freedom. For nobody is free to do exactly as he would like. The baby stretches his hand out for every toy he fancies and cries if he does not get it' (*The Listener*, 1936, vol. 15: 701 and 911).

The personal approach, with its 'I' and 'you', was by now reserved for radio personalities who offered mild diversion or solace rather than information. These speakers attracted a personal following which was to be useful to the BBC. When war broke out both Hilton and Healy were employed to boost the morale of listeners. But in the case of serious or controversial talks, the approach was very different. There was a direct antithesis to the example of Healy's talk on law in the case of talks given in 1933 by Harold Laski on *What Is The State?* Laski had first been approached by the BBC in 1928 and it was agreed at the time that, as a prominent left-winger, he would need 'careful vetting'. In the 1933 series it was felt that he had not sufficiently stressed interpretations of the rôle of the state which were opposed to his own. He was asked to insert 'some sort of statement from the "authoritarian" point of view' but also to make stylistic changes which involved 'cutting out the "I thinks" and "my views" and rephrasing in such a way that your point of view is put over impersonally' (Rendall to Laski, 30 January 1933). In fact, the use of the impersonal style became the rule for expert speakers precisely because the BBC wished to avoid the accusation that it was allowing them to use radio to promote their personal opinions. Little attempt was made to alter an expert's script in the direction of colloquial informality unless he happened to give a talk in a more popular series. For instance, Sir William Beveridge, who broadcast frequently on social and economic topics, agreed in 1937 to contribute to a light historical series of eye-witness accounts called *I Saw The Start*. His subject was the origin of labour exchanges. The producer complained that his script was stilted and 'unsuitable for an audience that wants to be talked to rather than at'. But Beveridge was 'not very easy to deal with because apparently he's used to being treated casually and having things left to him'. The producer was advised by his superior to 'do nothing more' (Cox to Barnes, 27 August 1937 and 1 September 1937).

This differentiation of speakers and topics into the serious and the popular represented a significant shift away from the original project of the Talks Department, as defined by Hilda Matheson. There was no longer any attempt to use the informal style in order to make serious, difficult and controversial issues more accessible to the public. There were several reasons for this. First, most of the experts were busy men and were not prepared to spend a great deal of time adapting their scripts and rehearsing their performances. Second, it was felt that to personalise and popularise serious issues almost constituted a breach of decorum, that only a dispassionate, academic manner would legitimate and authenticate the content of a talk. Third, the use of the personal style came into conflict with the BBC's ethic of impartiality; impersonal speech *sounded* more neutral. The sometimes intricate diplomacy over the style of scripts was more often concerned with establishing the credentials of a speaker, with situating him in a particular relationship with the audience, than with veiled censorship. There were occasional cases when producers, rather than admit that the BBC was censoring a talk, would object to the style in which it was expressed. This is not surprising, since style was the one area in which the producer could lay claim to a greater expertise than the contributor. To question the content of a talk delivered by a leading expert was to go beyond his professional brief. Talks producers were in fact known as 'talks assistants'—a title that implied a minimum of interference. In order to maintain good relations with contributors, it was essential to maintain this image of the producer's rôle. But as the need to attract the audience became more imperative, broadcasters began to value those contributors who were amenable to influence, who could be 'produced' though not necessarily controlled, above those whose status placed them out of editorial reach. For example, the *National Lectures* were reduced in number in 1938 because the BBC no longer felt the need to borrow the prestige of the distinguished speakers. Although the content of talks remained largely serious and heavily informative, the manner of delivery became increasingly populist. But because the popular style in the *individual* talk did not lend itself to the communication of difficult or controversial material, the producers turned to a range of other techniques which were thought to be more stimulating. These were the discussion, the debate and the interview. They had the additional advantage, where controversial matter was concerned, of ensuring that a more perfect balance between opposing viewpoints was achieved and of allowing for greater control over speakers in the studio.

Before tracing the origins of these techniques, it is necessary to sketch the historical context in which they were adopted. The two key developments in the production of talks after 1935 were an increasing caution in the handling of controversial issues and a growing tendency to popularise the format of talks. Paddy Scannell, in this issue, has touched on the reorganisation of the Talks Department at the time of the Ullswater Committee. It was recognised that in appointing Sir Richard Maconachie as Director of Talks the BBC had made a conservative choice. The shift in public concern away from domestic towards international issues, such as the Spanish Civil War, the rise of Fascism in Europe and impending war was accompanied by unprecedented Foreign Office interference in broadcasting. This resulted in the cancellation of talks from Harry Pollitt, leader of the British Communist Party, and Sir Oswald Mosley of the British Union of Fascists. (For a recent account, see Briggs, 1979: 198–201.) There is also evidence of interference on the issues of Palestine, Spain and Pacifism. The inability of the Board of Governors to withstand this pressure led to an intensification of the BBC's efforts at internal self-regulation. This was a period in which the ethic of balance and impartiality could be applied with a rigidity that was at times repugnant in its outcome. Late in 1938 a suggestion from the Talks Department that a 'reasoned statement of the Jewish point of view in recent events might be broadcast' was turned down by the Programme Board on the grounds that this was being covered adequately by news bulletins and that a talk might cause a demand for the expression of the opposite point of view (Programme Board, 1938: minutes 231 and 235).

From 1936 to 1939, talks became more 'popular' in two senses. First there was a greater attempt to represent the opinions and experiences of 'ordinary people' and in particular of working class people. Second, the format for radio talk became lighter; greater use was made of the round table discussion, of the miscellany of short talks in a magazine format and of interviewers, chairmen and presenters chosen for their qualities as broadcasters rather than for their expertise in a subject. A new kind of professional broadcaster was emerging, who might turn his hand to a variety of jobs; for instance Howard Marshall, primarily a cricket commentator, might turn up as a reporter on social issues, an interviewer in the magazine programme *At the Black Dog* and presenter of the youth-oriented *Under Twenty Club*. These changes reflected a general lightening of BBC programmes which was brought about by a number of factors. Audience research, which started in 1936, forced producers to take the differentiation in listeners' needs and tastes more seriously. There was a growing awareness of competition from the commercial stations on the Continent. Reith's departure, early in 1938, appears to have facilitated the process of popularisation. The BBC began to respond to the reiterated public criticism, often supported by newspaper polls, that its attitude towards listeners was distant and patronising. One symptom of a change in attitude was the introduction of audience participation shows on the American model; quizzes, spelling bees and amateur 'discovery' shows. Reviewing the developments of the previous three years, the *BBC Handbook* for 1940 noted that 'rightly or wrongly, it was being urged a year or two ago that the BBC was aloof from its listening millions, offering programmes with a complacent air of "Take it or leave it". These various experiments in "Listener participation" with many others are evidence that the ice, if it ever existed, has rapidly melted. New and friendlier contacts have been established on the air' (*BBC Handbook*, 1940: 83).

The influence of entertainment values on talks can be demonstrated in the rise of the magazine programme. It was the Variety Department which first adopted this format in 1933 with *In Town Tonight*. This programme frankly appealed to 'human interest', presenting a mixture of items reflecting 'the simple, fascinating things that humble folk do, and the high points achieved by men and women of distinction' (Cannell, 1935: 8). In the selection of contributors, a contrast of personalities was aimed at—'the marquess and the chimney sweep, the hawker, the sewer-man, the fruit seller, the film star and the famous author . . .' (ibid.: 7). The magazine programme in its pure form was produced by North Region in 1934. *Owt About Owt* was presented as a 'broadcast magazine', each series was a 'volume' and each programme a 'number' complete with 'cover illustration' by the Northern Studio Orchestra. *At the Black Dog* (1937), with its pub setting and genial host, could be described as the original British chat show. In 1936, the Talks Department started its own magazine, *The World Goes By*. Although it was intended to be more seriously topical than *In Town Tonight*, it was often in competition for the same speakers and rapidly developed a similarly 'human' approach. It was presented by Freddie Grisewood, one of the new breed of professional all-rounders, whose personality soon became intrinsic to the programme.

A new awareness, in the Talks Department, of the stratified nature of the audience was revealed in a memorandum on 'Talks Standards' written by Norman Luker, a senior talks assistant, in 1938. This divided the listeners into three groups. Group 'A' were the 'intelligent and well-informed', an audience which should only occasionally be catered for. Group 'B' were the 'intelligent and not so well-informed', whom Luker identified as the most important target. Pointing to the increase in secondary, university and adult education, to the huge sales of *Pelican* and *Left Book Club* publications devoted to serious issues and to the success of the new *Picture Post*, he argued that there was now a 'considerable serious-minded public anxious for mental pabulum which we are well placed to give them'. Group 'C', the largest part of the potential audience, included the 'not-so-intelligent and mostly uninformed' who, because of their 'extreme simplicity' would only listen to 'adventure' or 'personality' talks and were well served by *In Town Tonight*, although the department should 'continue to educate unobtrusively through the personality of men like Hilton . . .' (Luker to Maconachie, 25 November 1938). It was towards the middle ground of Group 'B' that the new styles of talk were directed. Luker noted that these groups did not necessarily reflect social stratification. Group 'C' might contain customers from Harrods and Group 'B', artisans and farm labourers.

Finally, the contribution of the Regional Stations, and North Region in particular, must be mentioned. Because their brief was to reflect the life of the local community, they were often more successful than the metropolitan producers in discovering the right idiom in which to reflect the opinions and experiences of ordinary people. In documentary features and in discussion programmes like *Northern Cockpit*, *Midland Parliament* or *Public Enquiry*, the regions broke new ground. But because discussion was limited to local issues, 'dangerous' controversy was avoided.

The discussion

Before 1928 there had been experiments with both scripted and unscripted discussions. The intention of the producers was not to emphasise conflict in the dialogue but to capture the quality of good 'table talk'. After the lifting of the ban on controversy in 1928, these light conversations were distinguished from what Miss Matheson referred to as 'hammer and tongs' controversial discussions. These were originally unscripted but soon gave rise to the familiar problems of lack of clarity and concision. At first the solution was seen, not in scripting but in the introduction of a third party who could mediate between the speakers and the listeners. The rôle of the third party was originally to elucidate difficult points. In relation to a discussion on science and philosophy held in 1928 Hilda Matheson suggested the inclusion of 'a "plain man" asking severly practical questions' (Matheson, 10 October 1928). Soon after this, the Director of Programmes, criticising a discussion which had drifted and contained mutual interruptions, suggested a third party 'not necessarily named as taking part in discussions but merely a voice, who would have controlled the discussion to the point of keeping the speakers to their subjects—telling them perhaps, not to speak at the same time—steering them off dangerous ground—acting in point of fact as an umpire but not taking part in the discussion itself' (R. Eckersley, 24 July 1929). At that time, interest was aroused in the Talks Department by an article in the *Berliner Tageblatt* on 'The Broadcast Tertius' which cited classical authority for such an addition to the dialogue. 'The old Romans, the well known masters of intellectual battles of flowers, had a dictum, *Tres faciunt collegium*. Such a dictum must have an appeal to the unknown and distant listener'. In practice, the third party was rarely used at the time but was to re-emerge after 1935 in the rôle of interviewer or chairman. Discussions in dialogue form continued to be scripted throughout the decade, great emphasis being placed on presenting a stimulating clash of opinions. This could be achieved either by a laborious exchange of manuscripts between speakers or by allowing one contributor to devise both sides of the argument. William Beveridge prepared a discussion with a Professor Ginsberg on the subject of The Family in 1932. He assured his producer that 'it leads up to quite a good difference of opinion between me and Ginsberg as to whether one can or should equalise opportunity for every individual (. . .). Of course we've got to make Ginsberg take it, and drill him and rehearse till we're tired. But I'm sure we can' (Beveridge to Adams, 4 March 1932).

Meanwhile, the possible entertainment value of discussions was being recognised by the Talks Department. In 1931, Hilda Matheson suggested a series to be called *Conversations in the Train*. 'The plan is that these conversations, which will be given with appropriate sound effects, shall seem to arise out of casual encounters in a train, and shall be of various subject matter which may be of topical, general or purely entertainment value' (Matheson to Eckersley, 4 December 1931). She approached literary rather than expert speakers, among them Roger Fry, Aldous Huxley, E. M. Forster and Dorothy L. Sayers. The conversations were first put on in 1932 and new series were introduced up to 1938. They were intended to be witty and it was soon discovered that writers of amusing dialogue did not necessarily make good performers, so actors were employed in their place and the programmes were produced with the co-operation of the Features and Drama Department. By 1935, a talks producer was boasting that the programmes were competing with *Music Hall* on the alternative channel and that the Variety Department was nervous at their competing entertainment value. But the hybrid form of the the programme was causing administrative problems and in 1938 it was taken over entirely by a drama producer, who announced that 'the series will in our hands deal with private and human problems rather than ones as cosmic as "Fixed Easter" or the metric system.' He planned to start with a conversation on 'Dogs' (Felton, 9 June 1938).

The 'human' treatment of issues was not to be purely the province of other departments. Early in 1937 Talks produced a number of unrehearsed and unscripted discussions under the title of *Men Talking*. They were modelled on an American series *The Chicago Round Table*. The producer hoped that 'these discussions will reveal the way people *feel* about subjects rather than a potted scientific analysis of the problem. (...) ... if they are successful, listeners will recognise that the BBC is departing at one point from its general policy of passionless exposition of logical positions. This should, I believe, help listeners to regard broadcasting as more human than they usually are prepared to allow' (Wilson to Maconachie, 14 December 1936). It was decided that a regular team should be used, consisting of John Gloag and Sinclair Wood, both advertising agents, and James Whittaker, an unemployed working man and author, but in the end only Gloag was retained as a regular. He soon adopted the role of chairman and much was made of his 'nice sense of public relations'. Even when the subjects discussed were 'safe' ones, like 'Football' or 'Manners', '. . . it is very difficult for people talking naturally to avoid references to dictatorships, Hitler, Stalin, capitalists, Trade Union demagogues, puritanical spoilsports etc., but our regular participant was always able to carry off such references with a soothing one from the opposite point of view' (Wilson, 1937). The Director of Talks welcomed this series for 'speakers of the "man-in-the-street" type of intelligence'. He had recently attended conferences at Leeds and Birmingham at which the public had offered their comments on broadcasting and was sure that the 'naturalness and vigour' of treatment together with the choice of 'subjects of everyday interest' made them 'of very lively interest to the working-class listener' (Maconachie to Nicolls, 23 April 1937).

In selecting contributors for this series there was an emphasis on personality and style rather than expertise. One speaker was referred to as 'a 50-year-old journeyman bookbinder, who writes admirable short stories of Lancashire life. A robust Lancashire voice, pungent, fundamentally liberal but hard hitting about bogus or academic views of things', another as 'a young lawyer, self-consciously epigrammatic, who will be cynical about anything. A good broadcaster' (Wilson to Maconachie, 22 July 1937).

One consequence of these populist tendencies in presentation was that the programme was not considered a suitable format for the discussion of more serious and sensitive issues. Proposals for dealing with topics such as Isolationism or Russia were turned down by the Director of Talks on the grounds that 'subjects of this importance require a different method of treatment', while a discussion of the Means Test was only acceptable because it had already received 'full dress' treatment in a formal talk (Maconachie to Wilson, 13 February 1937). Another consequence was that expert contributors became wary of taking part in the programme. Cyril Burt, the psychologist, explained to the producer that while he would try to emulate the other speakers in giving replies which were intelligible to the general audience, he would have to consider the reaction of captious colleagues who would be only too ready to criticise loose, popular statements. These reactions set a pattern which was to be repeated in relation to the much more popular and influential *Brains Trust* series during the War. The more the programme exploited the personalities of the panellists and derived its popularity from providing bizarre answers to frivolous questions, the less prepared were the Board of Governors to allow the discussion of serious and controversial issues. On the other hand, the more trivial the questions, the stronger the objections of the academic panellists like Joad and Huxley that their reputations were suffering and that free speech was being stifled. It was a vicious circle. As with the straight talk, so with the discussion, a gulf was established between popular and serious forms not only in terms of style but also in terms of content.

The interviewer

The role of the interviewer as a 'plain man' who mediated between the expert speaker and the lay public was established as early as 1933. A talks assistant who advised the Director of the new Empire Service on the range of techniques then available, recommended this as a purely educational device. 'The idea is to keep the expert on a low level so that he is intelligible to the inexpert listeners and also to add lightness and entertainment to a serious subject by adopting the dialogue form. The ordinary man must be chosen above all for his *ability as a broadcaster*' (Rendall to Empire Programme Director, undated, 1933–35?).

The role of the interviewer in controversial broadcasts was not established until later in the decade. The BBC had generally handled controversial issues in series of straight talks, with a different point of view expressed each week. This system was defended by the Controller of Programmes, Colonel Dawnay, in his evidence to the Ullswater Committee in 1935. 'It resulted of course that each talk in a controversial series, taking it in isolation, was in fact strongly biased and very often highly tendentious. This was because the BBC were seeking to provide the balance through the preceding or the following talk which put the opposite points with equal emphasis and equal freedom' (quoted in Broadcasting Policy, document no. 5, November 1942, p. 43). Dawnay felt that the BBC would always be liable to an enormous volume of criticism from all parties until the public became educated to the point of regarding a controversial series as a whole and not in isolation, speech by speech.

Although the Committee commended the BBC's handling of controversy, discussion about the problem continued within the Corporation. In 1938, the Director of Talks wrote a memorandum justifying the use of the 'Interlocutor Technique'. This was a style of interviewing which involved the interjection of critical questions throughout the talk in order to provide an immediate element of balance. Its use was justified in quite explicit terms.

When I came here I was informed on the highest authority that 'balanced controversy' was regarded as the most important element in serious talks, and one which should be introduced to a greater extent in future. The problem then was to discover the best form in which such 'balanced controversy' could be presented to the public so as—

(a) to allow the speaker the greatest possible freedom of speech

(b) to forestall the tiresome charges of political bias, etc., to which our discussions of controversial subjects had too often given rise in the past.

Both these objects, in my opinion, have been achieved by the free use of the 'interlocutor technique', and cannot be achieved by any other method' (Maconachie to Nicolls, 4 March 1938).

On the same day that he received the memorandum, the Controller of Programmes wrote to the North Region Director to complain that an 'interlocutor' in one of his programmes had not intervened enough. The Director should see to it that 'the interlocutor acts as we expect an interlocutor to act, not merely asking questions but bringing out other points of view on controversial subjects' (Nicolls to North Region Director, 4 March 1938).

The debate

Before 1928 the BBC relayed a number of debates before 'live audiences' from public halls in London. The topics were non-controversial ones, such as 'Are critics taken too seriously', 'Is chivalry dead?' and 'The menace of the leisured woman'. Speakers were professional talkers, actors or well known lecturers such as Shaw, Chesterton and Bertrand Russell. For the usual reasons, the debates were scripted but sounded awkward because the distinguished speakers were unwilling to learn their lines or to rehearse. By early 1928, the difficulties with this format had become so acute that Hilda Matheson wrote to the Director of Programmes, 'The truth is we have about exhausted the supply of people of any standing who are willing to talk on our present terms'. For example, Duff Cooper had refused to take part because he 'does not want to do it, and sees no use in doing it, until we can talk about things in which people are interested' (Matheson to R. Eckersley, 21 February 1928).

After 1928, public debates were dropped in favour of studio discussions which were more in line with the favoured intimate style of broadcasting. But in 1935, a series of unscripted and completely impromptu debates before 'live audiences' on controversial subjects was introduced. The only precautions taken were to limit the non-participating audience by issuing special invitations and to take care with the selection of chairmen, who were all experienced broadcasters and were briefed 'to make good any misunderstanding that may have arisen during the course of the debate, i.e. to protect the BBC's interests if they seem to be at stake' (Adams to Healy, 4 October 1935). There is some evidence that in permitting such unwonted freedom of speech at a time when Talks were entering a cautious phase, the BBC was to some extent conducting a public relations exercise. The Head of Public Relations, Gladstone Murray, wrote: 'Bertrand Russell expressed astonishment that there was really no rehearsal or censorship. He said he had fully expected to be closely examined about what he proposed to say. The fact that he had such a free hand considerably altered his opinion of the BBC' (Gladstone Murray to Controller of Programmes, 19 November 1935). The Programme Committee also stressed the goodwill that had been gained by the absence of censorship and welcomed a new method for dealing with controversial questions. But the BBC cannot have gained the goodwill of Harold Laski who had agreed to take part in a debate on Proportional Representation but was informed that the idea had been dropped because the Director of talks was not sure 'whether the subject is one which is really suitable for the new experimental free debates . . .' (Siepmann to Laski, 30 August 1935). In fact, as Laski realised, there had been other objections to his inclusion. The Controller of Programmes had suggested that he was not qualified to talk on the subject but could be invited to debate on 'Academic Freedom'. But as Laski had often spoken on political subjects in the past, the Director of Talks was forced to adopt an argument in relation to the style of presentation. After a minor row, Reith eventually allowed him to debate the issue of the Second Chamber with Bob Boothby M.P. and when this too was cancelled because a general election had been called, Laski could only congratulate the BBC on a technique so delicate and ingenious that he thought it deserved its victory. Even disregarding this incident, the producer, summing up her experience of the series, wrote, 'Although the absence of censorship was stressed, it was quite clear that speakers considered their obligations seriously and were most restrained in language and ideas. This attitude to broadcasting is, of course, one which is general. Speakers do in fact censor themselves before they begin to write for broadcasting and it is this moral censorship which in fact endangers the freedom of the microphone' (Adams to Maconachie, 13 March 1936).

Live debates only became successful when, with the later emphasis on popular participation, the audience was invited to join in. This was first permitted in the 1939 series, *Public Enquiry*. As might be expected, this was a North Region production and the subjects were confined to local issues. Under the chairmanship of Principal Nicholson of Hull University who, as a member of the Talks Advisory Committee, had often championed the cause of free speech in the BBC, the series became popular and, after the War, was broadcast nationally. The inclusion of ordinary people in a broadcast debate was only one example of a wider movement in the BBC to represent the common man more fully in its programmes.

The promotion of Everyman

The issue of the *Radio Times* for 24 March 1939 carried a supplement on 'The Man In the Street'. One article pointed out that the common man was a veteran broadcaster but that his 'Communal voice has been essentially a background voice'. He had been heard as an incidental sound effect in countless outside broadcasts. At church services, for instance, 'you heard him cough and shuffle his feet as he settled in his pew . . .' and 'you heard his loyal cheers at times of public festivity'. But, the article continued, 'there has gradually developed the notion that the Man-in-the-Street makes an excellent foreground broadcaster'. There had been a procession of London 'characters' in *In Town Tonight*. There had been the more serious representation of working people in the North Region features of D. G. Bridson and Olive Shapley. Finally, the supplement celebrated the fact that, in the 'Standing on the Corner' section of *In Town Tonight*, the interviewer Michael Standing had conducted impromptu *vox pops* with passers-by on a topical question, the Munich Crisis. Until recently the Man-in-the-Street 'was always selected well beforehand and rehearsed. Probably he spoke from a script. Impromptu broadcasts are only the very latest development in his entertainment value' (*Radio Times* 24 March 1939).

It was precisely the question of whether *vox pops* constituted a form of entertainment or a serious projection of public opinion which at that time provoked reactions at the Programme Board. One Head of Department had criticised the recent tendency to include programme items which could not be claimed to be good broadcasting but which, like the *vox populi* in *In Town Tonight*, were supposed to be popular because they presented the undistinguished views of ordinary people'. Shortly afterwards, the Board recommended that there should be 'more emphasis on the personalities of the people interviewed and less on their views upon preselected subjects' (Programme Board, 1939: minutes 174 and 185(b)).

Although the year 1939 was a turning point in radio's portrayal of the common man, his history as a 'foreground broadcaster' was rather longer than the *Radio Times* article suggested. Several ordinary people described their occupations for the 1929 series *My Day's Work*. Some of their talks provide an illustration of the kind of varnish a conscientious talks assistant could apply to the rough surface of a working man's speech. For example, 'Bill', a dock worker, ended his talk as follows. 'Arriving at Higham Bight in the early grey of the morning I have looked at the Hulks and across the Essex shore—where stretches that strange, level country which seemed so much to fascinate Charles Dickens—and fancied in the rising mists the faces of hunted convicts and Joe Gargery and Pip and remembered that it was somewhere in this reach of the river that David Copperfield said adieu to his Mrs Peggoty and Mrs Gummidge, where little Em'ly waved her last farewell ...' (*The Listener*, 1929, vol. 1: 68). Other talks in the series, such as the coalminer's, stuck more closely to descriptions of work and even contained muted protest at pay and conditions; but all were expressed in decorous English, with prosy evocations of local atmosphere and peppered with unlikely allusions. At some stage the ludicrous aspect of these talks must have been brought home to the producers as they ended with a spoof piece from 'a burglar' who retired to bed to read Spinoza after his night's work.

For all its absurdity, this early series was significant in that it combined, in its presentation of ordinary people, two styles which were to develop into distinct traditions. One style owed much to 'human interest' journalism, to the *Punch* tradition of cartoon proletarians and of F. Ansty's comic dialogues, *Voces Populi*. Working people were selected as characters or eccentrics, as simultaneously representative and quirky. The other style owed more to Mayhew, the social researchers of the early twentieth century and the documentary movement of the thirties; typical representatives were chosen to offer evidence of their living and working conditions and of their opinions on contemporary issues.

The 'human interest' approach was best exemplified by the growing number of magazine programmes which, as has been pointed out, prided themselves on the sheer variety and oddity of their contributors. *In Town Tonight* discovered Mrs Wheelabread, the Chocolate Lady of Kensington Gardens, Mrs Nelson, the woman chimney sweeper and the cat's meat man with his peculiar street cry. It was open to the advances of publicity-seekers like Jack Morgan, the Boy with Big Ears, whose earlier exploits included angling an invitation to 10 Downing Street from the Prime Minister's daughter on the grounds that he was 'puzzled about political happenings in the last few years' (Cannell, 1935: 162). North Region's more folksy *Owt About Owt* might offer a bill of fare consisting of 'an aerial flood-shooter, a harmonising boys' club, a well known Northern itinerant bagger of gags, an inveterate drummer, a master of mistletoe and a pantomime star' (*Script*, 7 December 1934). Even the more sober *The World Goes By*, with its emphasis on rural listeners, used 'Gipsy Petulengro' as a regular contributor. The point has already been made that this programme, which began in 1936, was representative of the 'lightening' of talks which took place after the reshuffle of 1935. During the same period, the Talks Department was taking an interest in broadcasting 'Slices of Life'. Paul Bloomfield, a new recruit, was informed by an official that the BBC was looking for someone with journalistic experience to handle these talks. '. . . we want a man—someone upstanding and dignified, a gentleman by all means—but the sort of person who can go into the public bar without the conversation drying up as soon as he goes in'. Bloomfield obliged by discovering a man called Lucock, a saddler who wrote poetry. His talk was successful but Bloomfield felt that he was too much of a local celebrity and that the true 'Slice of Life' should involve 'someone who enjoyed no fame or notoriety or even any particular local reputation. Then what should he have? Simply character, I suppose. Plenitude of life'. He approached a friend, a 'Wodehouse character' and a good conversationalist, who simply offered random observations on life under the heading of *A Good Grouse*. Though this was well received by the Press, the department was clearly concerned about the level at which such items should be pitched. When Bloomfield suggested further broadcasts in this genre, the following exchange took place with Sir Richard Maconachie.

> 'The idea is, sir, to express the common life, without . . . as it were . . . any ulterior motive . . ., the common life, even perhaps low life . . .'.
>
> 'Not *too* low life', said the Director of talks; and that was all he did say.

Bloomfield himself was suspicious of the motives behind such broadcasts. 'I have always felt that realistic broadcasts of the "Slices of Life" nature tend to involve one in making people make an exhibition of themselves more than the results justify' (Bloomfield, 1941: 183–210). It was natural that such exercises in the representation of character and personality which had developed so easily in the Variety Department, should be treated with misgivings by a department with the didactic tradition of Talks.

The serious presentation of 'everyman' can be traced in various early talks on social issues which included working people, often as a democratic twist to the tail end of a series dominated by experts or reporters. By presenting such contributors as typical representatives of their occupation or class, the BBC laid itself open to criticism from government and Parliament. Paddy Scannell has described how evidence from unemployed speakers in the 1934 series *Time To Spare* became a matter of public dispute and provoked governmental pressure on the BBC. In the same year the notorious broadcast of William Ferrie occurred. Ferrie, a representative of the National Union of Vehicle Builders, had been asked to speak in a series on *The National Character* as 'a working man'. In the previous week, Sir Herbert Austin had talked about 'The Effects of Modern Industry on the National Character'. He had stressed recent improvements in working conditions and in the standard of living and foresaw an improvement in the mental life of the nation. 'Mechanisation is relieving the brain of the old tediums and giving it new stimulus. The slaves of metal labour, while the mind of man directs' (*The Listener*, 1934, vol. 11: 410). Ferrie wanted to oppose this argument but the BBC objected to parts of his script in which he referred to the economic exploitation of the working class, rejected calls for equality of sacrifice in the national interest, referred to the rise of Fascism in Europe and Britain and claimed that his work-mates were looking to Russia for a solution. One portion objected to read; 'The dissatisfaction of the workers with their lot is growing. The limitations imposed on us educationally and culturally is making us increasingly determined not to tolerate a social system which denies us the opportunity to develop our material and cultural existence . . .' (*Daily Herald*, 6 March 1934). When the producers asked him to remove the offending passages, Ferrie apparently complied, but on the night of the actual broadcast he abandoned his script and instead delivered a protest at the way in which his talk had been censored. In an era of live broadcasting, this was the realisation of one of the BBCs persistent nightmares. Its critics seized upon the incident as evidence for the censorship they had long suspected, while the BBC itself interpreted Ferrie's action as a breach of trust. In the following week, a 'working woman' offered a pointedly balanced judgement on the national character. 'I believe we're a good deal happier than our mothers were in their day. That doesn't mean to say that things couldn't be better, or that the lot of the British working woman is a bed of roses (. . .). After all we're all human, and I don't believe there's very much difference between us, rich or poor. The thing that matters is not money or education, but character. The great thing is to be independent and capable of looking after your-self. Facing up to things—that's character' (*The Listener*, 1934, vol. 11: 491). Intern-ally, the BBC justified the censorship on the grounds that parts of Ferrie's talk were irrelevant to the subject and were overtly propagandist. There was a place for extreme views in a series in which a variety of speakers were asked to put forward what were clearly labelled as personal opinions. For instance, the *Whither Britain?* series, broadcast in the same year, included at least one Moscow-oriented contribution. But in this case Ferrie had been asked to give a *representative* point of view.

After 1935, although working people, often with radical opinions, were given access to the microphone, they were more likely to be heard in one of the new discussion programmes, like *Men Talking*. These did not raise the same problems as straight talks since the issue discussed tended to be low key and opinions were clearly established as personal and could be balanced by other speakers. The function of reflecting typical working class life was increasingly taken over by documentary features.

One of the first programmes to use ordinary people to voice opinions was *Northern Cockpit*, produced from North Region in 1935. In format, it was a half-way house between the talk and the discussion and was introduced as 'a sort of radio parliament in which social problems are not so much debated as elucidated by means of relevant statements'. Each programme was a symposium of short talks on a subject of regional interest. Topics included 'Back to the Land', 'Cotton', 'Canvassing', 'Problems of Dialect in the North' and 'The Servant Problem'. What is striking about the scripts is the way in which experts and ordinary people contribute on an equal footing. The programme on Canvassing included a housewife, her husband, a canvasser, a sales manager and an economist. Each was given equal weight. The economist was not used to shape the argument or to comment on the other contributions, but simply to supply a wider perspective. Given the limitations of the subjects, fairly extreme views could be expressed. In the programme on 'The Servant Problem', a middle-class housewife advocated the communal organisation of housing estates, with communal creches, common kitchens, no personal servants, but special 'sitters-in' to hold the baby when its parents went to the common cinema. Her aim was to free all those women who wished to do other things from the bondage of household work. This contributor was described internally as 'almost communist in political theory, but fundamentally conventional' (Wilson to Maconachie, June 1937).

The inclusion of working-class speakers in *Men Talking* created certain difficulties. A listening group in Morecambe had complained that, in a discussion on education, all the speakers appeared to belong to the same minority group and evidently did not have children in state schools. The producer admitted that 'this question of working classes is very difficult indeed. We know very few broadcasters who would fulfil the rôle without sounding like *In Town Tonight* or the *Punch* idea of the working man' (Luker to Gibson, 11 October 1937). He reported that the chairman of the discussion 'was astonished when I told him about the storm of protest about the middle class atmosphere of the discussion. At first he was suspicious that this was due to what he calls "the inverted snobbery of left-wing intellectuals", but I (. . .) persuaded him that there was much more to it than this and that we must in the next few talks at any rate, have an unlettered voice' (Luker to Maconachie, 13 October 1937). After the next broadcast it was agreed that 'there appeared to be "the common touch" which was so lamentably lacking in the previous broadcast' (Education Officer, Leeds, 18 October 1937). But the regular contributors now complained that the quality of the conversation had suffered as a result. The producer wondered 'shall we as an experiment one week let all this about the common touch go hang and just have three good talkers in the studio . . .?' (Luker to Quigley, 26 October 1937). In the end it was agreed that, while it was absurd to have 'men with "thousand-a-year voices" discussing the details of a family budget', there were few working-class speakers who could live up to the standard of conversation set by the middle-class regulars. One exception was an unemployed miner and county councillor who was, according to the chairman 'a splendid character' who provided for listeners a 'valuable illustration of the way people can live their lives in economic adversity' (Gloag, notes on series, October/December 1937).

Northern Cockpit was specifically for Northern listeners and *Men Talking* was originally intended for the unemployed. With the emphasis on public participation in broadcasting in the late 1930s there was an increase in programmes directed at specific constituencies, such as women (e.g. *For You Madam*) and youth (*The Under Twenty Club* and *To Start You Talking*). The programmes for youth made a feature of inviting representative young people to participate both as presenters and in discussions with guest experts. But the experts were soon dropped on the advice of the listeners. As one of them put it, 'we like the Under Twenty people best because with them we seem to have a common feeling; they seem to express more or less what we feel about things, not what we're told by the experts' (quoted in Madge *et al.*, 1945). Charles Madge, one of the founders of Mass Observation, took an interest in the programmes and in 1945 contributed to a book about them. He argued that the usual radio discussion between experts 'befogs as much or much more than it clarifies (. . .). The best way of escaping from it is to provide, in the discussion, for the exchange of concrete social experience. Such an exchange fosters an outlook that is practical, empirical, objective' (Madge *et al.*, 1945). This notion that social experience could be used as the basis for exploring political or philosophical topics gained some influence in Talks in the late thirties and the War. It can be associated, in particular, with the work of the producer Christopher Salmon.

Salmon was a philosopher by training and had been involved in adult education. As early as 1936 he had suggested a series in which 'the higher reaches of philosophical experience could be made relevant to the common experience' (Salmon to Maconachie, 12 October 1936). Later, he attempted to use broadcasts of the common experience to elucidate what he saw as the unarticulated values of the community '. . . we still know lamentably little about the ideals of working class experience with the splendid amount of life and humanity which has been poured into it . . .'. He thought of broadcasting 'as a means by which the community's experience, lived as it is at different levels, can be brought to expression and given a useful currency in society' (Salmon to Barnes, 18 July 1941).

One of his first exercises in this vein was a series of talks called *Everyman And The Crisis* which were put out in the weeks following the Munich Crisis of 1938. These were intended to show the impact of the crisis upon the individual conscience by using people whom recent events had placed in some sort of moral dilemma; examples of what was required included 'A young man who didn't know whether he ought to honour the Peace Pledge. . . . An unemployed man to whom war would mean full employment . . .' and even 'A lady with ample pets who didn't know whether to destroy them or not' (note of conversation between Salmon and Last, 11 October 1938). As a result of these not altogether promising proposals, a remarkable set of documents were produced. The talks were delivered anonymously in groups of three, with five second intervals between them and a minimal announcement. According to Salmon, with this austere method of presentation the talks sounded unusually sincere and spontaneous. Certainly the printed scripts reveal an interesting range of reactions and one particularly moving and dignified contribution from a German woman married to an Englishman. But with the coming of war, this kind of talk became routinised into a stock formula for offering moral parables to the public. In 1940, Salmon produced a similar series, *Everyman And The War*. While the crisis broadcasts were open-ended and discursive, a genuine attempt to reflect public opinion, this series was strictly propagandist. The aim was expressed in the following terms. 'It matters now, and is going to matter, what the common man and common woman thinks. I think we could help the people at home enormously by letting them hear what some of the best common men and women do think.' Possible contributions included 'A man and a woman now working overtime in munitions or aircraft work . . . a coalminer responding to Bevin's appeal . . . A woman with a baby in arms whose country it is one day going to be . . . a blind man who knows what makes a free world even though he can't see it with his eyes'. The proposal for the series was anotated, 'This is first rate and dead in line with Ministry of Information policy. Let's go ahead' (Salmon to Maconachie, 28 May 1940). The 'People's War' produced a dramatic increase in the representation of the common man in all forms of radio, but the use that was made of him was often manipulative rather than reflective or enquiring.

Conclusion

At one level, this paper has simply attempted to trace the origins of a number of techniques which have now become standard practice in British broadcasting and to place their development in a historical context. At the same time, an argument runs through the paper about the relationship between serious and popular forms of communication. A number of generalisations could be made about this relationship.

First, popular styles of presentation, originally intended to attract and inform a wide and differentiated audience, in practice came to be regarded as unsuitable vehicles for serious and controversial subjects. In part this reflected a diffidence in the broadcasters; a sense of the integrity both of the subject matter and of the speakers who delivered it, which was to be expected in people of their class and educational background. But the practice was also consonant with the BBC's policy on the broadcasting of controversial matter. The net effect of the differentiation of styles was not simply that serious, controversial talks were delivered in a dispassionate and 'neutral' manner, but that they remained inaccessible to a large proportion of the audience. One can discern a 'not in front of the children' attitude underlying the refusal to allow more accessible programmes like *Men Talking* to cover contentious issues. There was a departure from the public service ideal in the notion that the unintelligent and uniformed section of the community were 'well served' by a programme like *In Town Tonight*.

Second, in programmes which were 'popular' in the sense that they were representative of the people, a similar dichotomy arose. Serious attempts to reflect the experience and opinions of members of the working class tended to provoke strong critical reactions, especially when these representations conflicted with dominant definitions of the condition of the people. These difficulties could be avoided by exploiting the 'human interest' value of working people, emphasising character at the expense of experience, or by decontextualising the opinions of the man-in-the-street by the use of trivial *vox pops*. The taxi-driver and playwright Herbert Hodge, one of the few regular working-class broadcasters of the late thirties offered a perceptive, though by no means radical, criticism of these practices, in a letter to his producer. 'And have you ever considered a series treating working class life as *natural*—instead of quaint? (. . .) Battersea Bridge Road is being repaired and as I write, everybody's dashing out with baths and boxes and perambulators to get wood blocks for their winter fires. There's nothing extraordinary about it. It's the thing to do. But the middle-class commentator either denounces it as a crime; or weeps over the wrongs of the noble proletariat compelled to get their living in this way; or treats it as a quaint custom of the Battersea aborigines' (Hodge to Salmon, 28 September 1937).

Third, devices which were intended to control the presentation of controversy, such as the discussion and debate and the use of 'interlocutors' and chairmen, tended to break the thread of rational discourse. During and immediately after the War, the discussion almost displaced the straight talk as the means for handling controversy. Critics at that time were well aware that this technique tended to obfuscate the issues and that broadcasters appeared to be valuing the form of the clash of ideas over its content (see, for instance, Woodruff, 1946). It has recently been suggested by Kumar (1977) that these tendencies are of much more recent origin. It is true that a new style of aggressive interviewing developed in the late fifties but the tradition was much older. It is interesting that Kumar relates these developments to the break up of a political consensus in the same period. The late thirties were also a period of intense ideological conflict in Britain and the BBC, aware of pressure from the Government, introduced these techniques precisely so that the control and balance of opinions could be seen to operate within its programmes.

One should be cautious in making comparisons between the BBC's output of talks in the 1930s and contemporary coverage, in radio and television, of social and political issues. Talks programmes were listened to by a small minority, they were only loosely topical and significant 'actors' in the political sphere, such as government ministers, members of Parliament and trades union officials rarely, if ever, took part in them. Broadcasting had scarcely begun to usurp the dominant rôle of the press in shaping public opinion. Nevertheless, there are significant parallels between the forms of presentation adopted for talks programmes during the populist phase of the late 1930s and forms of presentation which have been of concern to critics of contemporary broadcasting. Both Kumar (1977) and Elliott (1972) have claimed that broadcasters have become preoccupied with the form at the expense of the content of communication. Others have pointed to a conflict between 'human interest' values in presentation and the need to provide a coherent account of social and political issues. There has been a tendency among British media sociologists to claim that the trivialisation and decontextualisation of these issues is the outcome of the influence of market forces on programming in a period of competitive broadcasting. It is thus argued that a connection can be established between the economic control of broadcasting and the ideological form of its output. In the 1930s competition with commercial radio stations was a marginal influence on the process of popularisation described in this paper. It was only on Sundays that Radio Luxembourg drew significantly from the BBC's audience. The stylistic innovation in talks reflected the problems faced by broadcasters who were committed to an ideal of public service but were becoming increasingly aware of the differentiated structure of their public. If the more populist programmes failed to give adequate coverage to the most important issues of the day, it was not because producers felt that the public would not be interested in these issues. It was because the popular treatment of serious, controversial issues came into conflict with the BBC's policy on the broadcasting of controversial matter. The differentiation of the serious and the popular described in this paper had as much to do with the relationship between broadcasting and the state as with the relationship between broadcasting and the public.

Bibliography

BLOOMFIELD, P. (1941). *BBC*, Eyre and Spottiswoode, London

BRIGGS, A. (1965). *The Golden Age of Wireless*, Oxford University Press, London

BRIGGS, A. (1979). *Governing the BBC*, BBC

BBC Handbooks, 1929 and 1940, BBC

CANNELL, J. C. (1935). *In Town Tonight*, George G. Harrap and Co., London

ELLIOTT, P. (1972). *The Making of a Television Series: a Case Study in the Sociology of Culture*, Constable, London

KUMAR, K. (1977). Holding the middle ground: the BBC, the public and the professional broadcaster, in *Mass Communication and Society* (Curran, J. *et al.*, eds), Edward Arnold, London

MATHESON, H. (1933). *Broadcasting*, Thornton Butterworth, London

MADGE, C. *et al.* (1945). *To Start You Talking*, The Pilot Press, London

WOODRUFF, D. (1946). Debates and discussions: a criticism, in *BBC Quarterly*, October issue, BBC

A symbolic mirror of ourselves: civic ritual in mass society

DAVID CHANEY*

Introduction

In this paper I shall be concerned with the significance for ritual of its being performed in a mass culture. I take the interaction between the actual events in the
ritual forms of ceremonial festivals and their presentation in the mass media to be
an opportunity to study the terms in which the public, at least in part, are able to
participate in the collective life of their nation. The bulk of the paper will be taken
up, therefore, with planning decisions in the BBC about how to cover (represent)
three major festivals between 1946 and 1953—the Victory Parade of 1946, the
Festival of Britain in 1951 and the Coronation of 1953.[1] They are arguably the
major events in the years following the Second World War which brought together
the Monarchy, religious leaders, other members of the traditional British Establishment and political leaders. In a *Times* editorial the Victory Parade was described as
an occasion when the British: 'were enabled to see in a symbolic mirror the image
of themselves' (10 June 1946: 5).

The period of these State occasions is particularly interesting because the ending
of the War, which had itself forced the State into many new kinds of political
mobilization, was followed by the first social democratic government with a large
and unimpeachable mandate for radical social change. As a contribution to social
change one might assume that the imagery and symbolism of the State and Nation
would be altered in ways that were consistent with new structural arrangements.
The radical government lasted six years, in a sense culminating in the Festival of
Britain, to be followed by the first of a series of consumer-oriented new prosperity
conservative governments. It was felt at the time that much of the style of this new
conservatism was expressed by euphoria generated at the Coronation of a young
Queen two years after the change of government. The three State occasions then
span a period of marked differences in social and political climate in which the
symbolism of the nation as community should be a barometer of expectations
about the political community.

Ritual and the Nation State

The difficulties that arise with the use of a concept of ritual are that the term has
been used so often in so many different contexts that it would not be difficult to

* Department of Sociology and Social Policy, University of Durham

become bogged down in justification and explanation. I shall therefore describe some reasons for my use of ritual fairly arbitrarily and not attempt to consider all the implications. The first point is that ritual collects a class of occasions which are felt to be peculiarly significant for the collectivity. The process of imbuing the occasion with formal significance is frequently accomplished through the use of distinctive forms of dress, ceremonial settings and a formal, often archaic, form of speech. As these marking devices, dress, settings and speech are among the most important ways of marking drama from reality it is unsurprising that ritual ceremonies are frequently described in very theatrical terms. Ritual occasions therefore seem to be highly self-conscious, in the way that we say that actors are necessarily conscious of playing with rôle and identity, but they are stagings which purport to be natural in that they are not put on for commercial benefit or political advantage.

The dramatic core to ritual alerts our attention to a second important feature. This is that drama works through structural categories. The idiosyncracies of a particular narrative are dependent upon shared categories of relationship, identity, time and orderliness for comprehensibility and meaning. In a ritual ceremony which is not usually organized about the telling of particular narrative the forms of presentation are more clearly about themselves. The meanings being enacted are those of a necessity of structure and what is being celebrated is the ability to impose order: 'collective ritual can be seen as an especially dramatic attempt to bring some particular part of life firmly and definitely into orderly control' (Moore and Myerhoff, 1977: 3).

Part of the meaning of a ritual is that collectivity is shown to be possible and that doubts and tensions are formally proscribed. The essence of a ritual is that a collectivity is postulated or affirmed which might otherwise only have an ambiguous social existence. This does not mean that all participants in the ritual will be equally convinced of its truth nor that when there is an unequal division of power within a collectivity the more powerful will not use their access to staging rituals as ways of legitimating their authority and precluding alternative political arrangements. Thus, for example, traditional celebrations within an institution such as a school will, at least in part, work to affirm the unbridgeable status divisions between teachers and pupils. The political character of ritual is therefore always present, particularly in civic rituals, but these political aspects are usually expressed paradoxically through being denied in favour of an integrated community.

Bocock has suggested four types of ritual in industrial society which vary by the nature of the sponsoring authority. These are religious, civic, life-cycle and aesthetic rituals although Bocock recognizes that these are analytic distinctions and any particular ritual may contain elements from more than one type. Civic rituals, for example, have a tendency to spread and take over other types of ritual such as secular marriages and funerals, and there is an increasing subordination of religious concerns to State pomp on the occasions of life-cycle rituals of members of the Royal Family. The flowering of civic ritual has been closely interdependent upon the development of national, secular publics and means of communication between such publics. Public life is interrelated with civic ritual in two ways: first, an increasing proportion of media space is devoted to both the rituals and the activities front and backstage of ritual performers to the extent that, as I shall argue, civic ritual has become a distinctive genre of mass communication; second, the spectacular character of civic ritual in mass society has come increasingly to consist of the degree of media attention so that ever larger audiences can be ever more intimately present although their participation remains vicarious.

A nation is an abstract collectivity because it is too big a social entity to be experienced by any individual. Therefore the 'we-feeling' of the community has to be continually engendered by opportunities for identification as the nation is being manufactured: 'A nation becomes 'one and indivisible' through a continual process of communalization. . . . The most effective symbols of implementing the process are those of common historical fate, of common triumphs of the past: national history bespeaking of grandeur; a national mission; assurance of the nation's worth for mankind' (Gerth and Mills, 1954: 296-297). The use of manufacture in relation to communalization is not meant to imply that it is done cynically, but rather that specific people have to be employed in the management, staging and publicity which is part of ceremonial festivals. The interdependence of mass media and civic ritual only extends the army of presenters. The stock of national images and the rhetoric of their presentation have continually to be reconsidered, developed and extended in terms of what presenters perceive the public mood and expectations to be. The mystical significance of master symbols of the nation does not preclude the inclusion of elements of mundane experience. As Kingsley Martin (1962: 116) has pointed out of the Queen's father: 'the importance of his reign is that he restored the ideal conception of the domestically correct and conventional monarch. . . . In so doing he laid the foundation on which the new TV Monarch was built.' The marriage of the mass media and the most traditional institutional symbol of the nation was actively being consummated during the years 1945-1953, which span these festivals.

Media and civic rituals

I have stressed the interdependence of civic ritual with mass media of communication in the urban industrial state, to the point of claiming that such rituals are a distinctive genre of media programming. There seem to be several reasons for this interdependence and they can be organized into those relating to civic ritual and those relating to features of mass communication. The first point is that if such rituals are dramatizations of the nation as a symbolic community then the infinite reproducibility of media performance makes audiences possible on a scale previously unimaginable. Indeed it is the number and complexity of the publics which the audience constitutes that ensures they are essentially abstract for ritual sponsors. Thus, it is not just that ritual makes the abstract nation tangible. Media organizations supposedly acting as the voice of public opinion necessarily usurp the public on whose behalf they speak. It must be so because the pressures of performance production preclude any adequate process of consultation; public opinion is those attitudes available to producers. The sponsors of civic ritual in seeking to democratize the appeal of that which they are staging are forced to adapt to the expectations and presuppositions of the communications forms which make their audience accessible. In doing so the dramatic impact of the ritual is transformed. Of course, for those present at the procession, service or whatever, the primary emotional impact is still present; but they must be aware that for the vicariously listening or viewing mass audience they as onlookers are as essential for the success of the spectacle as more starring performers. There can be no single response then but for performers through onlookers and spectators a series of more or less self-conscious involvement with ritual as programme material. The initial aura of the occasion cannot be retrieved only the potential of the new level of performance can be pursued.

For media producers the attractiveness of civic ritual as a programming resource closely parallels the points made above. The concept of a dramatic spectacle is of a highly formalized parade of social types in an elaborate setting organized by a narrative in which moral certitudes are affirmed in ways which often combine inducing awe in the audience with sentimental involvement. As such civic rituals are spectacular displays for which the framework of audience interest can be presumed. There is an easy combination of news as happening with dramatic sequencing so that the twin criteria of immediacy and significance are self-evidently satisfied. It is relevant in this respect to note that programme producers are likely to feel themselves faced mainly with technical problems of ensuring access, continuity and exhaustiveness rather than more complex issues such as the point of view of whose side should be represented. Technical problems can be solved with ingenuity and enthusiasm leading to the sort of uncritical praise found in contemporary newspaper reports; a process that is doubly reassuring for producers who lack any deep familiarity with the public on whose behalf they are staging the presentation. Finally, it is because civic ritual is about the nation as symbolic community that a nation-wide appeal can be presumed. There is none of the competitiveness between genres associated with conventional programming, the ritual speaks for itself and indeed seems to offer a distillation of what national broadcasting should do best.

The further implication of this argument is that the dramatic dimension to collective experience will not just be retained in mass society but will be importantly extended and transformed in the cultural forms of mass communication. It may well be that there are laws or institutional forms to public drama which help to determine structural change (cf. Klapp, 1964, chap. 9). If this is so it takes us some way towards explaining a paradox in the politics of mass society—that the majority of men and women are able to endorse the commonsense, middle-of-the-road rhetoric of institutionalized normality while at the same time being intermittently willing to pursue sectional interests. The political constituencies of mass society are not consistently based on lines of economic cleavage such as class but are an imprecise mixture of quasi-ritualized rhetoric of concensualism and shifting more localised concerns based on occupation, leisure interests, generation, race and sex etc.

The studies of media content that have been published in recent years have unfortunately in general been inspired by a desire to display bias and partiality in media representations of topics such as industrial disputes or patterns of criminality. Unfortunate because such studies impute an objectivity to the 'real news' which is impossible and because the charge of bias is bitterly resented by individual media producers. In quarrels over accuracy the ritualistic character of the cast list and motivating dialogue in political drama is too often ignored. An example of the sort of study that might be done more often is Phillip Elliott's (1980) work on newspaper coverage of a bombing campaign in England by Irish Republicans.

Elliott is in this study describing what he calls an affirmatory ritual—a ritual in two senses. First, that it is a standardized way of describing a class of political events, and, second, that the very patterning of the representation ritualizes the normal political processes which are being implicitly contrasted with these abnormal events. The organizational structure of British broadcasting should mean that the homogeneity of perspective implicit in ritual will be emphasized particularly when broadcasting in Britain was all produced by the BBC. It has been suggested that the austere legacy of public service associated with the name of John Reith is perhaps a mythology (and certainly did not exist in the simple form by which it is usually characterized), Reith did, however, inspire and sustain an institutional ethos or a corporation spirit. This has continued to guide individual producers as to appropriate attitudes. Such a corporate ethos which, particularly internally, is often praised as professionalism in the public service, is especially significant in the forms of cultural production which Raymond Williams (1981: 55) has recently described as intermediate institutions. Here the institution depends upon public revenue in some form or another but is allowed a significant degree of autonomy in determining day-to-day production policies. The importance of corporate spirit is that it will inform and structure the terms through which affirmatory rituals are articulated. The conceptions of the public and public interest integrating different forms of programming will both set the agenda for a certain level of political participation and help to determine expectations for the ritual performances of public life (in this respect see the study by Blumler *et al.*, 1971).

The Victory Parade 1946

The Victory Parade had. to be more hurriedly prepared for than the other two festivals for although the Corporation had been planning for Victory in Europe for two years, the decision to hold a celebratory procession on 8 June 1946 was only formally announced by Attlee in the House of Commons in February.

At the first meeting to discuss how the BBC should cover it the Director General decided that programmes for that day 'should be generally gay and cheerful' (BBC Written Archives Centre, subsequently referred to as WAC, R34/920, 1 February 1946). Another early choice determining the character of the occasion turned on style of reporting. In the run-up to VE night the decision had been made to present the celebration through the responses of common people as far as possible. This had led to an emphasis upon 'vox pop' broadcasting which had been extensively and favourably commented upon at the time.[2] But the plans for coverage of the Victory Parade suggest a Corporate attitude of sympathetic observation rather than popular identification. Of the five commentary positions selected to cover the event only one was provided with a hand-grip microphone with extension suitable for crowd interviews. There were in addition commentators in the procession itself and in an aircraft circling above, but while these may be said to have added to the breadth of coverage they did not speak from the viewpoint of the man in the street. Similarly the coverage of the evening celebrations had a mix of fixed commentary positions with mobile transmitters in a launch and an aircraft, only the commentary position in Piccadilly Circus had a possibility of direct crowd participation.

An uncertainty in the Corporation's attitude stemmed from more widespread doubts over the purpose and form of this particular ritual. The Conservative press was generally hostile to the idea of a Victory Parade—despite its normal enthusiasm for militarism and chauvinistic self-congratulation. Perhaps because of the conviction that the conflict just ended had been a 'people's war' it had led to the first majority government pledged to massive social change and the Parade celebrating the successful accomplishments in that war was to be held under the aegis of that government. It was therefore only to be expected that there would be some crucial differences between this Parade as a celebration of military valour and the normal military procession. One difference, for example, is that the ceremonial route around certain predictable streets in the West End of London was significantly extended by sending one of the constituent elements in the Parade—the motorized column—on a tour of the proletarian East End. The rationale was that it was the working class districts which had borne at least the initial brunt of the urban bombing campaign, but to celebrate their part in the national resistance was to broaden the concept of the fighting forces and marked a significant shift in the appropriate audience for rituals of national celebration.

Another difference was the emphasis given to the supplementary services. There were of course a flotilla of cars carrying victorious allied leaders and commanders of the naval, army and air services to head the procession, but behind them came a further thirty units of vehicles covering civil defence services, agriculture, transport services, public utilities and general services including mobile canteens from the YMCA and the Church Army and Salvation Army, and National Savings vans. Such a proportion of civilian service vehicles is I think interesting and particularly that a national focus was stressed, so that, for example, as well as two buses from London Transport, two buses from Halifax and Manchester Corporation Passenger Transport Services took part in the mechanized column. The concept of those engaged in the war effort was being significantly extended.

A similar theme of the breadth of the effort that had been necessary to win the war was emphasized in the composition of the marching column. In addition to the massed ranks of troops, who themselves had a strong international flavour, there were two civilian contingents. The first comprised representatives of the Police, National Fire Service, Civil Defence, Nursing Services and Agriculture. The second contingent was even more broadly based and included representatives of transport services including docks, more Civil Defence services such as fire guard and raid spotters, representatives of utility services such as post, gas, electricity and water. This contingent culminated in representatives of what the supplementary notes prepared within the BBC for commentators summarized as: 'workers from every part of the country and from every conceivable trade which helped us along the road to victory. Men from the factories, the mines, the shipyards will march with women who will represent the millions of women who, in addition to running their own homes, worked in every side of the industrial effort' (WAC, T14/1291/ 1, n.d.).

This shift in tone from a parade of a purely military type to one of a more embracing democratic character was well captured in a long editorial in *The Times* the day before the event itself:

There can be few indeed among the spectators who do not feel that they are also qualified by service for some place in the parade, were there room for all who shared in the achievement. That, indeed, is what separates it from the victory celebrations of earlier years. Once the civilian part of the nation saluted the fighting men as sole victors; now the whole people does honour to the whole. It is an act of corporate communion between all sections of the people; and acknowledgement of interdependence by each and all; a renewal of that essential unity of spirit which the war revealed and intensified, and in which it must trust no less implicitly in the strenuous and perhaps dangerous years that lie ahead (7 June 1946: 7).

For the BBC the challenge of representing this 'act of corporate communion' presented peculiar difficulties.

Obviously for the majority of people in the country living outside London their main mode of access would be through radio, but this could be either a vicarious listening-in or an active participation in a democratic celebration. By and large, the Corporation ducked the latter option. Instead the spectacle as a thing external to the audience was emphasized and the formal elements of anthems, displays etc. were rigidly adhered to. In effect this meant that rather than take up the challenge of what victory this parade might have been celebrating, there was an unnecessary emphasis upon military ritual.

The supplementary notes provided for commentators had little to say about those representatives of millions of workers, particularly women, who were included in the second civilian contingent, other than the brief passage quoted above. It seems that the lack of military qualities made them virtually invisible—even to the point that the only remarkable feature of industrial workers as the different coloured overalls or boiler suits they would wear. There was a rich supply of details for the military personnel—decorations, awards for distinguished service and other medals. Likewise military features were produced wherever possible for non-military participants. For the engineers and service corps stress was laid on how often REME recovery teams had been forced to go into the midst of battle, in order to carry out their service and support rôles. The supplementary note on the Women's Voluntary Services contingent could only offer this information to assist the commentator: 'Miss K. M. Halpin, O.B.E., Regional Administrator i/c. The detachment includes personnel with decorations as follows—5 O.B.E., 3 M.B.E., 1 B.E.M.' (WAC, T14/1291/1, n.d.) while the most notable feature of the Home Office contingent was that it was led by two rescue dogs who had been decorated with the Dicken Medal awarded by the People's Dispensary for Sick Animals.

The issues raised by a study of the representation of a civic ritual such as the Victory Parade in 1946 concern ritual in social democratic societies. There is some evidence that the victory being celebrated was conceived by those who planned it in interestingly unusual ways and that public broadcasting had an opportunity to act as a medium for popular participation in ways that were correspondingly challenging. The opportunity was not taken up and there was instead a repetitive stress on predictable features such as military function, bravery, technical complexity and occasional colourful features such as the severally repeated note that the Commander of the West African Contingent in the Parade was an exceptional 'Big Game Hunter'. The character of the occasion was in general presented as uncomplicated national integration, formality and celebration of military virtues. This is not to imply a lack of popularity. The contemporary press was united in praising Corporation coverage and listeners' appreciation indices were consistently high. This should be unsurprising as, of course, the public at large had no more idea of what ritual in a changing society might be like than did Corporation executives—the familiar might therefore be especially welcome.

Festival of Britain

The Festival of Britain posed the nature of collective celebration in a social democracy even more forcefully. The suggestion was resented in certain quarters because it was closely identified with a Labour Government and 'the idea it expressed most, that of the post-war Welfare State' (Strong, 1976: 9); and as Asa Briggs (1979: 19) has commented: 'for the more conservative (with a small c) its predominant styles; ''anti-commercial'' in tone, already grated.' It was a Festival that celebrated social change, without being particularly partisan, from the viewpoint of the common, anonymous, man and woman. In this respect one paradoxical aspect gradually became apparent—for a Festival so identified with post-war Labourism it seemed to celebrate a mood of change which 'marked the climax of the age of austerity and the shift to a new era of affluence' (Briggs, 1979: 392), an era soon to be identified with Conservative governments.

This meant that the Festival was intrinsically political in that it was about what British society could and should be like even if this was to be articulated through versions of previous achievements: 'The Festival tried to regain the national identity of Britain which people had felt during the war: in the South Bank Exhibition, and various local events throughout the country the nation's achievements and goals for the future were to be displayed. The ideal motives about influencing civilisation filled the air again' (Brown, 1978: 245). The political basis to the Festival did not mean, however, that the rituals which constituted the opening of the Festival were significantly different—there were the conventional elements of monarchy, processions, religious services and formalized rhetoric of endorsement. It was rather that these elements were set in a significantly changed political context and the BBC's rôle in articulating the meaning of ritual for this context became particularly problematic.

This Festival differed from the other two under consideration as it was spread over several months rather than concentrated on a single day and even at its inauguration there was not a single procession but a number of ceremonies. On the morning of 3 May there was a royal procession from Buckingham Palace to St Paul's where there was a service of dedication followed by a royal broadcast and the return procession. That afternoon the Festival Gardens at Battersea were opened by Princess Margaret and that evening the Royal Festival Hall was ceremonially opened by the King, an occasion which included another religious service and a special concert. Finally, although the South Bank site was not formally opened in its own right there was a ceremonial visit by the Royal Family the following morning of 4 May.

Although the Festival embodied interesting innovations in national consciousness the opening was set very firmly within traditional forms for ceremonial occasions. The BBC recognized its responsibilities and kept very much to a predictable style. For example the commentary positions for the Royal Procession were at Buckingham Palace, Victoria Memorial, The Citadel, Bush House, Temple Bar, Ludgate Hill and St Paul's, both outlining a traditional route and symbolizing the ceremonial rôle of the commentary. A similar solemnity is shown by the Procession, Service of Dedication and Opening Ceremony being carried simultaneously on both Home and Light Programmes. It is true that on the evening of 3 May the opening was marked on the Home Service by an outside broadcast round various provincial towns including a visit to the Festival ship, and that the King's visit to the South Bank site the next day was followed by a microphone tour co-ordinated by Wynford Vaughan Thomas, but these were hardly exercises in participation. The main innovation was a further advance in the acceptance of broadcasting as a key element in the ceremonial structure. First, television cameras were allowed inside St Paul's to transmit the Dedication Service; and, second, the Speech of

Opening by the King was integrally linked to the Service but was designed to be broadcast. And so, for the first time secular ceremony, religious dedication and national broadcasting were combined as equally important elements in constituting a public occasion.

In their initial attitudes when planning for the Festival there were significant differences between the radio and television services. For the staff of the radio services the Festival was seen at first as primarily a source of news items, although it was recognized that the BBC might complement this material with Festival-type programmes of its own. This was despite the fact that by early 1950 it was clear that Festival organizers had a considerably greater rôle as publicist in mind for the Corporation. It was decided that actual publicity: 'will be judged on its news value' (WAC, R34/363, 19 April 1950), and while recognizing that there was a responsibility to make people festival-minded, 'quality was the aim rather than quantity and any plans were to be subject to ''listeners'' and ''viewers'' ' capacity for sustaining that interest' (WAC, R34/363, 25 April 1950). In part this reluctance to become too directly involved stemmed from unwillingness to be seen as an arm of Government, partly from unwillingness to become involved in any extra expenditure, and partly from an uncertainty within the Corporation over the extent to which it should identify with the Festival's essential purpose: 'to publicise British life and British achievements both to our own people and to the rest of the world' (Festival Council, 1952: 15).

Compared with this foot-dragging response in radio, television programmers were not only quicker off the mark in planning for the Festival (WAC, T14/441/1, 3 February 1948), but were also committed to the idea that television was part of the Festival, for British achievements and technical accomplishments in the field of television were an element in the story the Festival was trying to tell. This enthusiasm also stemmed from the rapid growth in the popularity of television. In June 1946 around one thousand three hundred licences were held but this number had grown to over six hundred thousand by May 1951. Of course the mass audience was still to be reached but such rapid growth made reasonable the producers' suggestion that they were part of the rapid social change they celebrated. The initial ambitious plans for there to be a working television studio on the South Bank site where the public could both see programmes being made and perhaps participate in transmitted items had to be shelved under the recurrent budget restrictions that constrained the Festival. The architect, Wells Coates, did however, design both a television pavilion and the Tele Kinema—which subsequently became the present National Film Theatre. Television was therefore part of the Festival as part of the spectacle, but the television service also tried hard to make the Festival a central element in its programme service throughout the summer. Two new television outside broadcast units were assigned to the South Bank and Battersea Gardens sites for the duration of the Festival and other outside television broadcast facilities were brought in to cover national and regional events as necessary. Based on these facilities *Festival Close-up* was broadcast weekly with further regular programmes in both alternate weeks and monthly. These plus other broadcasts produced 46 television outside broadcasts from Festival sites over the summer and there were in addition frequent visits for material by programmes such as Children's Hour.

The programmes produced to express the spirit of the Festival were of two kinds: prestige programmes and programmes about Britain. Through the former the BBC sought to 'make its own particular contribution, in the spirit of the Festival, by special programmes of an outstanding character during the summer months' (from the Introduction to the BBC's contribution to the Festival of Britain published by the BBC in December 1951). The latter were programmes that particularly addressed the Britishness of the society that was being celebrated.

Prestige programmes devised to accompany the Festival were a heterogeneous set. In part prestige was interpreted as the best and so budgets were agreed for expensive items such as a special season of plays by Shaw and Congreve together with broadcasts of specially commissioned plays from Rattigan and Priestly. At least this collection of playwrights were all British and so related loosely to the Festival. Whereas an equally prestigious outside broadcast of *Cosi Fan Tutte* from Glyndebourne could make sense in relation to cultural standards only ambiguously relevant to a Festival of Britain. Documentaries were prepared on the Metropolitan Police and a London hospital but it is unclear whether these were taken to be paradigmatically British or were symbols of excellence. It was only in the area of lighter entertainment that the historical dimension to the Festival was exploited. For example Light Entertainment built a musical comedy around the 1851 Festival and also staged five hour-long programmes on the five decades of changing styles of entertainment since 1901. Finally, four films were specially made for television, these were two reel specials with themes that seem to me to be very festival-minded —'the sea', 'the land', 'industry' and 'the future'.

As for the Britishness of Britain this was largely conveyed through outside broadcasts whose numbers increased by 50 per cent during the Festival. An earlier suggestion, by Norman Collins then Controller Television, was that the Festival provided an opportunity to capture: 'the face and pageant of London', via a conducted television tour taking in: 'the Pool, the Tower, St. Pauls, Westminster Abbey, St. James' Park, Hyde Park Corner, Marble Arch, the Zoo etc.' (WAC, T14/441/2, 25 April 1950). In a more lyrical vein Cecil McGivern, Collins' successor, proposed that outside broadcasts should try to express: 'The changing scene, the cities and hamlets, the store of treasures in our museums and art galleries, the sports and pastimes, the traditions and ceremonies, the ritual which a long history has bestowed upon us' (WAC, T14/441/2, n.d.). Participating in the Festival from this perspective meant documenting the nation visually, as a rich repository of historic tradition and a way of life, a considerably more innovative approach than broadcasting *Cosi Fan Tutte*. There is also, it should be noted, a fascinating correspondence between this approach to British cultural distinctiveness and the assurance that: 'as outside broadcasts *are television, real* television' (ibid., emphasis in original), such programmes were appropriate to a Festival of Britain.

Although the radio services were initially less enthusiastic than television the Festival was not ignored by radio. By the time it opened broadcasting on all channels and services was dominated by Festival-related material. In May 1951, the first month of the Festival there were 285 radio programmes broadcast which related to or were based upon the Festival of Britain. Less than half the national broadcasts were carried on the Light Programme, these were a mixture of variety shows, popular entertainments magazine programmes and talks. 77 programmes were carried on the Home Service, after the programme concerned with the opening ceremonies and other formal occasions, these including a number of concerts, serious broadcasts (such as a visit to the Science Exhibition which was clearly more educational than entertaining), and a large number of talks, discussions and commentaries on themes raised by aspects of the Festival. The Third Programme was more austere and restrained. It relayed nine concerts from the Festival site and had four talks about it.

An important strand in the inspiration for the Festival was that it should not be confined to London, nor should it be content with ephemeral celebrations: 'an excuse merely to reiterate the nation's past glories, but that permanent improvements and amenities . . . were as much a part of the Festival idea as exhibitions, concerts and pageants' (Festival Council 1952: 4). If the Festival was to succeed there had to be some form of local participation in the Festival; something more than the Festival travelling ship, the *Campania*, or by the Travelling Land Exhibition although these were important. If the BBC as a public institution were to adequately engage with this broader sense of the Festival then regional radio broadcasting became particularly important.

If local broadcasting was to be successful it had to be more than retrospective— the temptation to see the provinces as an endless archive of quaint folkisms runs very deep in British culture. It also had to avoid being either vicarious—as in 'local man visits metropolitan wonders' or as in 'London orchestra gives concert in our town tonight', or merely officious—as in reports of the squirearchy and local governments treating each other at a civic banquet. While there were elements of all these types of programmes in local schedules, there are interesting and consistent differences between regions. If one can generalize, however, it is that programmes on what was happening in the region as part of the Festival, such as outside broadcast visits and feature programmes, for example the West Region broadcast on Fawly Oil Refinery on 9 May 1951, or the extended series of programmes that Midland Region produced about the County of the Week, Northamptonshire in mid-May, all combined to spread the occasion nationwide in interestingly unusual ways.

In conclusion, it should be noted that the confusion over the rôles of publicist as opposed to reporter which was characteristic of home broadcasting, was swiftly precluded for the Overseas Services. As early as February 1949 the BBC's Internal Festival of Britain Committee decided that their task 'would be to give advance publicity, and when the time came to carry concerts etc., and to "report" the Festival in all possible ways' (WAC, R34/363, 22 February 1949). The notion of report has been marked in this minute because, as a later minute makes clear, the Overseas Services had to have regard: 'to their special obligations towards Overseas Listeners' (WAC, R34/363, 25 April 1950). Special obligations which seem to have been less duties owed to those overseas than duties owed to the British Government. A letter from the Private Secretary to the Privy Council Office to the Chairman of the Governors asking about Corporation plans for Festival publicity overseas reminds him 'This is a matter in which the Lord President is personally interested, and I am wondering would you kindly let me know the current position for his information' (WAC, R34/363, 2 February 1951). Within three days the Controller European Services had produced a memorandum describing in detail the planned range of programmes related to the Festival planned, and reassured him that 'since first January we have noticeably stepped up publicity on the Festival of Britain to all territories this side of the Iron Curtain' (WAC, R34/363, 6 February 1951). Governmental nervousness about BBC commitment to publicity may have been related to one potential justification for the Festival. It is all very well for the official 'Story of the Festival' to complain, 'On no aspect of the Festival of Britain was there more widespread misunderstanding than on its rôle in attracting tourists' (Festival Council, 1952: 30). On its own admission it was 'one of the main objectives' and the figures cited in the report do not confirm that it was an aim that was 'fully achieved', indeed for reasons beyond the Government's control such as the Korean War this area was a comparative failure.

Coronation

The third festival, the Coronation, was the most traditional in many ways but coming early in a period of social stability and affluence, it also presaged the ideology of post-war Conservatism. To the extent that the BBC saw itself as looking and commentating on behalf of the nation conservatively (with a small c) then the Coronation should have posed fewer problems in terms of attitude and stance etc., than the previous festivals. In practice new problems were raised by the previous successes of the Corporation. In that it had become generally accepted that civic rituals were public occasions staged and accessible to the media, and thereby mass audiences, it was hard to devise criteria for restricting public access. It was because previously mysterious parts of traditional ritual became literally visible that this Coronation, more than any other royal ceremonial, marked a turning point between symbolism articulating constitutional relationships and ritual as dramatic spectacle. This was realized at the time and was controversial, although the spectacular implications of monarchy as superstar were not fully appreciated. What is particularly interesting is that debates over media participation in civic ritual were not so much raised for the BBC by the wider political society but were initiated by the Corporation in pursuit of what they felt to be the public's rights.

In considering this point we have to recognize a shift in the relative status of radio and television as national broadcasting media. It is one of the established truths of British media history that television came of age with the Coronation. What is less often appreciated is that this shift in relative importance had been tacitly accepted within the Corporation for at least the year spent in preparation for the Coronation. This meant that policy issues centred on television's coverage of the event, while radio was treated largely as a matter for administration and organizational routines. The central reason for this was given in a memorandum from Head of Outside Broadcasts (Sound) summarizing their experience of the Coronation, when he remarked almost complacently that a television monitor 'gave everyone in the sound control point added confidence. On several occasions it enabled me to advise commentators about things that were taking place which they were missing' (WAC, R34/321, 13 August 1953).

Although state ceremonial occasions were public events this had not meant that they were accessible to every member of the public. Television made such accessibility possible and in doing so made it clear that 'public' had in practice previously been used to refer to a social elite, in particular through two innovations.

The first overrode the prejudice that there should be an implicit hierarchy in line-of-sight so that more important people had a better view than less important. Through their television receivers anonymous viewers would have a better view than, for example, Churchill. For some this was self-evidently inappropriate. The second innovation was that television meant that every part of the Service could be broadcast live. There did not seem to be a problem with the Procession but it was very strongly held in some quarters that live broadcasting should not follow the

Queen past the Screen in the Abbey. It is important to realize that it was the live factor that was crucial as newsreel cameras would be present throughout but their coverage required processing and could be edited. The main objection was that if there was a fluff by anyone it would be picked up and might undercut the solemnity of the occasion, but this in itself seems to point a deeper conviction that public ceremonies are primarily dramatic forms requiring careful staging and management. Both innovations therefore violated previous conventions of dramatic distance particularly in respect of unprivileged members of the public.

It is relevant to ask why the Corporation chose to fight for live telecasting, how they countered oppositional doubts, and how they managed the business of a suitable tone and style. A key figure in the Corporation's fight was the Head of Religious Broadcasting, Revd F. H. House. In an early letter he sent to the Dean of Westminster he set out the main points of the Corporation's case (WAC, T16/169, 17 July 1952). These were that the intrusiveness of broadcasting could be met through technical sophistication—for example careful planning of which shots to use at different moments in the ceremony, through the use of wide-angle lens, and through good production techniques such as shifting 'in a fraction of a second' to something less controversial. Problems of taste could be met through a monitor who would sit beside the producer to advise him. He concluded that as the principle of televising religious services had previously been conceded, 'There are very strong religious and national reasons for letting as many people as possible share in the service through television' (ibid). The case against television was doubts over whether mechanical intrusion could be minimized allied with a strong repugnance for theatricality and distaste for highly symbolic moments becoming secularized through public accessibility.

The debate over the form of television coverage was therefore in effect a debate over forms of public drama. It was generally agreed that the symbolism of the Coronation Service culminated in a dramatic transformation of identity, which appropriately took place in a part of the Abbey called the Theatre; what was not agreed was the right of the public at large (and particularly the implications of the exercise of that right) to be present. It would be wrong to characterize the debate as a simple conflict between populism and elitism. While the popular press, such as the *Herald,* the *Mirror* and the *Express*, were all in favour of televisual participation the opposition came not just from conservative journals. For example, the *Sunday People* argued that television was an inappropriate onlooker, almost a peeping tom, at such a sacred ritual. Corporation executives were motivated by a desire to establish television as an integral element in all public occasions and 'as part of the national life'. The meaning of this phrase is the crux of the relationship between broadcasting and public drama, and some light is thrown on its use in this context in a confidential memorandum from the Director of Television Broadcasting to Huw Wheldon, summarizing the implications of the Coronation telecast: 'The effect of the broadcast both in this country and abroad of direct participation in the ceremony and as the ceremony is a service of the Church the religious effect has been profound. . . . The acceptance of television as part of the life of this country comes latest, as with radio, to the governing classes, because they have the least leisure and know how to use what they have' (WAC, T16/169, n.d.).

The importance of television getting full access to the Coronation Service was so self-evident within the Corporation that nobody seems to have queried the internal decision to ignore for as long as possible the Earl Marshal's initial decision to exclude cameras East of the Screen. While planning for how the rest of the Service could be filmed continued, effective lobbying and political pressurizing of all sorts to have this decision reversed continued unabated. It soon became apparent that the traditionalists could not really sustain their case for an exclusive ritual and a quietly smug memorandum dated 25 November 1952 from the Head of Outside Broadcasting Television leaked the news to colleagues that the decision was to be reversed, although there was a delay of some days before the decision was publicly announced. Although the battle had been over a small part of the whole day's happenings the symbolic significance was recognized to have been considerable.

Among the general principles which were laid down to govern the televising of the ceremony in the Abbey were 'There will be no close-ups of any person. There will be no picture of any person during (i) the Anointing, (ii) the Communion prayers, (iii) there will be no picture of any individual kneeling in worship' (WAC, T16/169, n.d.). In addition the same document formulated a distinction, originally made by the Head of Outside Broadcasts for Television, between ordinary shots and symbolic shots. The latter would focus on inanimate features of the Abbey such as 'the altar cross, the Coronation Plate or some Abbey stone work' (ibid.). As there were to be no close-ups the Service would be filmed in a mixture of midshot, longshot and symbolic shot, the latter planned to amount to at least a third of the total footage of the Service. Given this reverential approach, almost pretending not to look, it is perhaps less surprising that the transmission of the pictures on American networks intermingled with advertisements caused such consternation (Briggs, 1979: 457–473).

A concentration upon the Abbey Service was justified by its significance in transforming the meaning of ritual but it was not the only element in television coverage of the Coronation. The attitude was that the importance of the whole occasion justified unheard of expense: 'We must not let it down in any way' (McGivern, Controller, Television Programmes, WAC, T16/169, 22 September 1952). Such a matching of the scale of the occasion would have other beneficial consequences: 'Our programmes around this period should be so interesting and exciting that they will merit considerable advance publicity. They should increase our reputation. They should sell sets' (ibid.). An attitude of a commitment to extravagance set new standards of expectation: 'On the previous Saturday, May 30th, I should like a Gala Coronation Music Hall—two hours long, if (a) It must be the best Music Hall ever or it is just no good. . . . This should be the most exciting and gayest Theatre OB we have ever done or will do for a long time' (ibid.). In practice the programme ideas for the Coronation were the same old styles in the Corporation's representation of national festivals. For example, the Documentary Department was asked to generate documentaries on the East End and Edinburgh to coincide with Royal visits to those places. The Talks Department was asked to prepare programmes on the achievements of British Science over the past 25 years and 'Leading up to the Coronation, a series of programmes on the changes in the once called British Empire over the past 25 years, designed to bring out the breadth of vision of the British as a ruling and civilising force' (ibid.). Possibly most predictably of all there were the usual plans to commission a play (from someone like Rattigan) to be a major drama offering suitably bedecked with stars: 'The above should be 'grand' or tender in atmosphere. If it is, could H. Tel. commission a second play, a comedy under some title like 'oop for t'Coronation', from another playwright, a good comedy or farce writer. J. B. Priestley?' (ibid.). In this framework the complexities of relationship between a new monarch and the post-war political public were not even beginning to be addressed.

This was not an omission that worried the other institutionalized voice of 'British public opinion', the newspapers. They were as usual overly concerned with the scale and complexity of BBC operations so that the international diffusion of commentary was thought more important than any consideration of the purpose of civic rituals. A major theme in press commentary on BBC preparations for the Coronation was a personalization of the commentary team, in particular the female members. Following the great day the press was unified in praise of the sensibility displayed by the Corporation, the dramatic access television produced for the public at large leading to an emphasis upon the human interest possibilities of television for British public life. This post-broadcast euphoria with what had been accomplished was shared within the Corporation—particularly when the Listener Research figures became available. It was reported that 88 per cent of the adult population was estimated to have caught at least part of the Service at the time of transmission and for the first time the television audience (56 per cent) exceeded that for radio (32 per cent). In fact all the programmes that day got good audiences; for example, the Queen's speech that evening was heard by 63 per cent of the adult population. Not only was the public interested in what the BBC made available they were also pleased with what they were offered—98 per cent of the television audience claimed complete satisfaction with what they saw. It was therefore a dramatic triumph to complete the years of the Corporation's monopoly. Some members of the Corporation might have hoped that their success would stave off the threat of commercial competition but the momentum behind the bandwagon was quite independent of the BBC's track record.

Conclusion

I have been concerned with the extent to which programming can be said to have run counter to the social content of each particular festival. In relation to the Victory Parade, the political character of the war which was explicitly addressed in the organization of the Parade was acknowledged by the BBC but was not effectively met by the broadcasts which represented the occasion. Instead the Corporation's coverage was circumspect and there was excessive reliance upon the form of the ritual at the expense of its social democratic aspirations to envisage a new type of collectivity. In relation to the Festival of Britain a judgement as to whether the coverage of ceremonies surrounding its opening ran counter to the social purposes of the Festival has to be mixed. There are several reasons for this. The first is that the ceremonial opening of the Festival was itself a little anomalous in the context of the vision of Britain that was being promoted. Second, the organization of the Festival was ambivalent over the terms and essential features of the Britain that was being celebrated. The Festival was organized by those who were in Michael Frayn's telling phrase 'liberal herbivores'—kindly, paternalistic members of the established intelligentsia. They offered a very distinctive and selective, version of British culture and offered it as something educational rather than celebratory—a style of presentation that was reflected in the narrative themes which were supposed to hold the exhibits and the pavilions together. Although the narrative idea was essentially sound as it was worked out it too often had the moral earnestness and complacency of a school text. To the extent that working class life and experience was noticed it was as something to be preached to rather than explored as a point of view. Against this background it is unsurprising that BBC programming played safe and did not respond in any depth to the promise of a festival of the common man's experiences and achievements.

I have tried to emphasize that there were marked differences within the Corporation over programming for the Festival of Britain; attitudes were more inconsistent than in relation to either of the other Festivals being discussed. The several reasons for this inconsistency can be summarized as a fundamental ambivalence over whether the picture of Britain being created was an account of intellectual accomplishments or institutionalized achievements. To have left the safety of reference points based upon established cultural achievements would have taken Festival producers and sympathetic elements in the BBC, into attempting a completely new conceptualization of British culture and community. Despite the popular mandate for the Labour Government, and perhaps partly because of the way that mandate had been used, the intellectual climate was insufficiently radical to motivate and sustain a deep re-think of contemporary cultural history. But if the Festival of Britain did not inaugurate an era of confidence and prosperity resembling the precedent set by the Great Exhibition a 100 years before, it was, in fact, followed by what has recently been described as a 'particular moment in British cultural history' when in a number of fields there were attempts 'to discover and legitimate a tradition of culture that could authentically be termed "working class"' (Dyer, 1981: 2). I do not think it misplaced to make some connections between this moment and the re-examination of Britain from the perspective of the common man involved in the Festival of 1951.

In relation to the third festival, the Coronation, it is clearer that there was no radical disjuncture between the form of representation developed within the Corporation and the social content of the ritual. And yet there were more important assumptions in the BBC's approach to the Coronation which involved significant developments in the relationship between the public and monarchical rituals —in essence it was established that the television camera acting on behalf of the public had an untrammelled right to be present at the most intimate moments of symbolic ritual. This quasi-democracy of intimate access is characteristic of politics in mass society and therefore the innovations in the coverage of the Coronation were in effect a radical transformation of the ritual form to be more consistent with its social content rather than the latter being subordinated to the former. Subsequent developments in the iconography of the Monarch towards an increasing integration of ceremonial formality with domestic normality are consistent with new modes of civic ritual in which national festivals have become effectively media occasions rather than occasions to which the media has access.

Notes

1. The substantive research reported in this paper was undertaken at the BBC Written Archives Centre, Caversham, Reading. The staff there were consistently helpful and co-operative and the author gratefully acknowledges their generous assistance.
2. The report of the Listener Research Department on the Victory Broadcasts of May 1945 stressed how much the naturalness and social and geographical breadth, had been appreciated: 'If there was a criticism, it was that there had been too much commentary' (WAC, LR/3470/24.5.45).

Bibliography

BANHAM, M. and HILLIER, B. (eds) (1976). *A Tonic to the Nation: The Festival of Britain 1951*, London, Thames and Hudson

BLUMLER, J. G., BROWN, J. K., NEWBANK, A. J. and NOSSITER, T. J. (1971). Attitudes to the Monarchy: Their Structure and Development During a Ceremonial Occasion, *Political Studies*, vol. 19, no. 2

BOCOCK, R. (1974). *Ritual in Industrial Society*, London, George Allen and Unwin

BIRNBAUM, N. (1955). Monarchs and Sociologists, *Sociological Review* vol. 3, no. 1

BRIGGS, A. (1979). *The History of Broadcasting*, vol. IV, London, Oxford University Press

BBC (1951). *The BBC's Contribution to the Festival*, London, BBC Publications

BROWN, G. (1978). Which Way to the Way Ahead? Britain's Years of Reconstruction, *Sight and Sound*, vol. 47, no. 4

DYER, R., GERAGHTY, C., JORDAN, M., LOVELL, T., PATERSON, R. and STEWART, J. (1981). *Coronation Street*, BFI Television Monograph 13, London, British Film Institute

ELLIOTT, P. (1980). Press Performance and Political Ritual, in Christian H. (ed.), *The Sociology of Journalism and the Press*, Sociological Review Monograph 29, Keele, University of Keele

FESTIVAL COUNCIL (1952). *The Story of the Festival of Britain 1951*, London, HMSO

GERTH, H. and WRIGHT MILLS, C. (1954). *Character and Social Structure*, London, Routledge and Kegan Paul

KLAPP, O. (1964). *Symbolic Leaders: Public Drama and Public Men*, Chicago, Aldine

MARTIN, K. (1962). *The Crown and the Establishment*, London, Hutchinson

MOORE, S. G. and MYERHOFF, B. G. (eds) (1977). *Secular Ritual*, Amsterdam, Van Gorcum

SHILS, E. and YOUNG, M. (1953). The Meaning of the Coronation, *Sociological Review*, vol. 1, no. 2

STRONG, R. (1976). Prologue: Utopia Limited in BANHAM, M. and HILLIER. B. (eds), *A Tonic to the Nation: The Festival of Britain 1951*, London, Thames and Hudson

WILLIAMS, R. (1981). *Culture*, London, Fontana

'Terrorism' and the state: a case study of the discourses of television

PHILIP ELLIOTT*, GRAHAM MURDOCK* AND PHILIP
SCHLESINGER†

Introduction

The legitimacy of the liberal-democratic state is no settled question. At the best of times, when peace and prosperity might appear to be the natural order of things, the state seems unshakeable, and the mobilization of popular consent through the medium of representative institutions to be an adequate expression of its solid foundations in civil society. This smooth functioning, however, is sustained by a considerable and continuous process of ideological labour—one which is thrown into relief as we enter a period of crisis. In the present period of profound economic dislocation dating from the early 1970s, Western capitalist democracies are undergoing complex and manifold processes of recomposition of the state and civil society. The question of how ideological processes work to sustain the legitimacy of the social order is now of especial interest.

Within liberal-democratic political thought, the state is usually understood to derive its legitimacy from its constitutionality, from fair and free elections, its foundations in rational-legal norms respecting individual rights, and an adherence to the rule of law. Much less emphasised is the place of force, or of 'legitimate violence', in the preservation of the social order. Thus, for instance, in the sophisticated liberal apologetics of Poggi (1978), or even in the radical democratic theorizing of MacPherson (1977), the state's repressive face is largely ignored.

But as Gramsci has noted, drawing upon the tradition which stems from Machiavelli, the political domain must be understood as combining both coercion and consent. This point was also clearly understood by Max Weber who conceived of the state as a 'compulsory association with a territorial basis' in which the use of force is regarded as legitimate only in so far as it is either permitted by the state or prescribed by it: 'The claim of the modern state to monopolise the use of force is as essential to it as its character of compulsory jurisdiction and of continuous association' (Weber, 1947: 156).

Of course, this general characterization extends well beyond the liberal-democratic state form itself. But Weber's comment that the state lays claim to the *'monopoly* of the *legitimate* use of physical force in the enforcement of its order'* (ibid.: 154) is entirely consonant with a perspective which recognises the combination of coercion and consent in the practice of the liberal-democratic state. Such a

* Centre for Mass Communication Research, University of Leicester.
† School of Social Sciences, Thames Polytechnic.

perspective, as Sol Picciotto rightly notes, is but the starting-point for further investigation since 'the mere combination of the contradictory ideas of consent and coercion does not help to explain what form of coercion is involved, nor *how* the consent is obtained' (Picciotto, 1979: 165).

Nevertheless, those contradictory moments of force and fraud, of repression and ideological hegemony, while needing precise definition in any given set of circumstances, pose inherent problems for the system of ideological representations in a liberal democracy. For if the state swims in the seas of its own legality and legitimacy and emphasizes the moment of consent, how then should politicians, intellectuals and the mass media represent the moment of coercion when the state has recourse to force? Moreover, how should violence which comes up against, or even transgresses the bounds of legality be handled? It is precisely this problem we seek to address in this paper, in which we focus upon how British television variously represents the question of 'terrorism'.

Discourses upon terror: official, alternative and oppositional

As Luigi Bonanate has observed, 'deciding whether an action is terrorist . . . is more the result of a verdict than the establishing of a fact; the formulating of a social judgement rather than the description of a set of phenomena' (Bonanate, 1979*a*: 197). As an essential starting point we have to consider questions of definitional power, how what Chomsky and Herman (1979) call the 'semantics of "terror"' are discursively organized. We will begin by suggesting that it is useful to analyze discourses about terrorism in terms of three ideal types, which we will label the *Official, Alternative* and *Oppositional*.

The *Official discourse* emanates from within the state and is further elaborated by intellectuals engaged in the propaganda war against 'terrorism'. Of particular importance in Britain has been the persistent effort to deny any political character to the armed struggle of Irish republicanism and the insistence upon its criminality. Mrs Thatcher, the British Prime Minister, made this point forcibly in a speech delivered in May 1981. Speaking of the killing of some British soldiers in Northern Ireland (she used the term 'murder'), Mrs Thatcher said:

I hope that when their murderers have been tried and convicted, no one will claim that they are entitled to special privileges—which is what political status means—when they serve their prison sentences.

Of especial interest for our purposes is the way in which she linked her general characterization of terrorism to a view of what a responsible press and broadcasting will do:

They must, of course, report the facts. Nothing would be more damaging than misinformation and lack of balance. Yet the line is hard to draw for terrorism needs publicity. Newspaper and television coverage can provoke the very reaction the terrorist seeks. It can give the convicted criminals on hunger strike the myth of martyrdom they crave, *but the true martyrs are the victims of terrorism* (51st Annual Conservative Women's Conference, our emphasis).

Mrs Thatcher defined a desirable focus *away* from the false martyrs to the true. It is surely no coincidence that shortly after her speech both television organizations (and in particular the BBC) began to present a more victimological view of the Northern Ireland situation, emphasizing in particular the funerals of soldiers and of innocent civilians. Nor is it coincidental that in the fortnight after Mrs

Thatcher's speech a Granada television programme, *Lying in State*, which examined both the Provisional IRA's and the Government's propaganda campaign, was withdrawn after a radical change was demanded by the Independent Broadcasting Authority.[1] This instance illustrates how a given definition injected into public debate at the same time as state pressure, indirectly shapes what television is able to show. But because of the mechanisms employed, the state itself is not open to accusations of overt censorship.[2] It is by repeated interventions of this kind, at different points in the system, that the Official view is sustained.

Aside from the persistent effort to portray politically motivated violence as criminal and lacking in rationality, a further dimension of the Official discourse involves the association of terrorism with communist subversion. The use of communism as a cultural category in the West may be analysed in terms of four major themes which are closely akin to those which predominate in wartime propaganda against an enemy. Those identified as *different*, as not proper members of society, are always a potential enemy. The more *threatening* the behaviour of these outsiders seems, the more clearly is the internal enemy identified. But the continuing presence and support of such outsiders has to be accounted for. Within the society's terms, such support as they may find is *irrational*. On some occasions the *similarity* of outsiders to ourselves may be stressed as a way of countering the positive claims of enemy ideology.[3] The first three of these structures of interpretations are broadly homologous with those used against terrorism.

A particularly clear illustration of the claimed fusion between communism and terrorism was given by the Reagan administration, inaugurating its new tough-sounding antisovietism at the beginning of 1981. According to the US Secretary of State, Mr Alexander Haig, 'International terrorism will take the place of human rights in our concern because it is the ultimate abuse of human rights.[4] The mobilization of 'international terrorism' as part of the foreign policy rhetoric of the major Western power indicates a serious effort to market a new ideological tool—one which is monistic, ubiquitous, and conveniently off-the-shelf. Quite diverse manifestations of political violence around the globe, from El Salvador to Namibia, are interpreted as instances of a global Soviet design for world domination.

The terrorist is the polar example of the extremist, a fanatic and psychopath who lies beyond the pale of the comprehensible, rational politics of a liberal democracy. A particular sign of this exclusion from the humane tradition is the terrorist's disregard for the value of individual human life, and his supposed necessary indiscriminacy in taking it.[5] This perception plays itself out against the view of the state as the embodiment of constitutional practice. It is precisely at this point, however, that the problems of legitimation arise: for the picture of the benign state versus evil terror can be challenged by introducing the concept of state repression or even state terror.

It is here that *Alternatives* appear to challenge the Official discourse. These alternatives derive from civil libertarians, critical academics, foreign policy experts and opposition politicians. All accept the ideal of a nonviolent, liberal-democratic state and reject the use of violence to pursue political ends. This means the alternatives do not offer a fundamental challenge to the claims to legitimacy found in the official discourse. Instead they develop piecemeal challenges at two points. First they question whether the state lives up to its democratic and nonviolent ideals. The more the state adopts repressive measures against its citizens the more do these ideals become tarnished. Second, alternative spokespeople question the official strategy of repressing and exorcising terrorism, advocating instead strategies of political and social engineering designed to defuse the violence and tackle its causes. Arguments posed within the alternative perspective tend to question the human costs of war as against the technicized language of international strategy. This may lead to a far-reaching realignment of the concept of international terrorism, away from pure cold war connotations à la Reagan and Haig. Luigi Bonanate, for instance, places at the centre of analysis the 'balance of terror' (Bonanate, 1979*b*: 60):

It is the sharpest and most overall form of terror, the so-called *balance of terror*, whose relationship to the structure of the international system is so tight that this peculiar form of balance has been considered the fundamental condition for the survival of humanity in a thermonuclear war.

In this optic, it is the strategic relations between the superpowers, and the possibility of mass destruction which is the yardstick against which internal terrorism is judged, significantly diminishing its importance on the international level, and also questioning its efficacy at that of the nation-state.

Finally, we need to consider the ways in which these latter aspects of the alternative perspective are extended and developed into an *Oppositional* viewpoint which justifies the use of violence in the pursuit of political ends. Basically, there are two cases which have been argued by terrorists and their spokespeople or which they have attempted to demonstrate through their actions by 'the propaganda of the deed' or by exposing the hypocrisy of the state's claims to legitimacy. The first justification for political violence is that politically and/or economically the state is a repressive organization practising state terror, and in these circumstances any other form of political action is impossible or ineffective. The second justification is national or sectional liberation in cases where the state can be said to have adopted a colonial rôle towards another people or towards a section of its own population. The subjugation of other peoples may take the form of economic imperialism rather than colonial administration and so be carried out through intermediaries such as client states and dependent governments. In this second case warfare becomes a realistic metaphor for the insurgents to adopt although it is continually rejected by the authorities. It is a metaphor which confers legitimacy upon the insurgents by making their struggle one for territorial self-determination. The terrorist thus claims the rôle of an enemy with defined but limited war objectives. In the first case, however, the aim is the complete overthrow of the state and its political and economic system. Such distinctions are important in considering the cases made by different opposition groups but they are distinctions which are not drawn within the official discourse. Indeed the official discourse specifically rejects them, focusing instead on the violent quality of the acts involved and the loss of life or material and psychic damage which these entail.

'Open' and 'closed' presentations

The official discourse and the alternative and oppositional replies furnish the images, arguments and points of reference around which television's presentations of terrorism and the state's responses are organized. But they do not pass through the television system like a stone through water. The raw ideological material they provide has to be actively worked on and turned into watchable television. This production process is subject to a variety of constraints, ranging from political and market pressures, through restrictions of time and resources, to the limits set by the rules and conventions which define 'good' practice within particular programme forms. Since these constraints operate in different ways and with varying degrees of intensity in different parts of the programme system, presentations of terrorism turn out to be a good deal more diverse and complex than the simpler assumptions about television's relation to the state and to a dominant ideology would predict.

Some types of programming (such as news bulletins and action-adventure series) are relatively *closed* and operate mainly or wholly within the terms of reference set by the official discourse. But other forms (such as 'authored' documentaries and single plays) are relatively *open* in the sense that they provide spaces in which the core assumptions of the official discourse can be interrogated and contested, and alternative and even oppositional themes presented and examined. Before we look at the mechanisms through which these openings and closures operate, however, we need to itemize the major forms of programming dealt with in this study, and to outline the conditions under which they operate.

Forms of actuality television

From the initial distinction between news and current affairs output, almost universal among broadcasting organizations, a variety of different forms have developed within actuality television, the main ones of which are set out in Table 1.

Table 1. *The major forms of actuality television*

	Programme form			
	news bulletin	news magazine	current affairs	documentary
Examples	*News at Ten* (ITV) *BBC News*	*Nationwide* (BBC1) *Newsnight* (BBC2)	*Panorama* (BBC1) *TV Eye* (ITV)	*Heroes* (John Pilger)
Frequency	daily	daily	weekly	irregular
Item length	short (news story)	short (programme item)	long (programme theme)	long (programme subject)
Presentation techniques	visual clips brief interviews	short film report/studio interview	film report studio discussion	film report
Presenter's rôle	reader	reporter/ interviewer	reporter/ chairperson/ interviewer	storyteller
Programme identified with	the broadcasting organization	the production team	the production team	an individual presenter/producer
Presentation structure	relatively closed	⟶		relatively open

Because of the mass audience it attracts and the potential influence on public opinion that this confers, broadcast news has, from the beginning, been hedged around with a powerful set of formal requirements. In Britain both the BBC and the commercial television companies are obliged to present all their news with due accuracy and impartiality and to preserve impartiality in all programmes dealing with matters of political controversy. Since it is news output that attracts the most attention and scrutiny from politicians it is here that the authority and credibility of the broadcasting organizations is most exposed. Consequently, adherence to the rubrics of objectivity and impartiality is as much a matter of institutional survival as of external pressure. By cementing an image of the broadcasters as politically responsible these help to strengthen claims to autonomy and to forestall attempts to impose more stringent controls on their operations. This framework of constraints, however, produces a form of news which appears as a factual report of events happening in the world, rendered in a style that conceals the processes of selection and decision involved in the reports and allows the least room for comment and argumentation. The opinions of selected 'others' outside the broadcasting organizations are presented, but they are almost always confined to the holders of power in the major institutional domains: government ministers and politicians from the major parties; senior members of the police force and the judiciary; trade union leaders; the heads of employers' organizations; and the spokespeople of 'accredited' pressure and interest groups such as churches and professional organizations. As a result, news is one of the more 'closed' forms of presentation and operates almost exclusively within the terms of the official discourse.[6]

News magazine and current affairs programmes have developed as a complement to the news bulletins and are designed to provide space for longer, more reflective treatment of the day-to-day issues of social management. Nevertheless, they remain closely tied to news and are subject to many of the same constraints. They generally take their topics from some recent or forthcoming news event, and they tend to draw on the same cast of spokespeople. Although the rubric of balance and the easing of time constraints ensures that a wider spread of opinions is presented, the range generally remains confined to the positions taken up within the main political parties and 'accredited' interest groups and comparatively little attention is paid to views falling outside this range. Occasionally, these bounds are broken as in the instance (discussed below) when a spokesman for the Irish National Liberation Army was interviewed on the BBC daily news magazine *Tonight*. But these cases are the exception rather than the rule and they invariably provoke heated debate on the legitimacy of giving air-time to enemies of the state.

Within the 'normal' confines of the standard news magazine and current affairs formats, however, there are still important variations of emphasis. These can be seen in the different ways in which presenters perform their rôles of chairperson and interviewer. They may, for example, present themselves as populist spokespeople, articulating what they take to be the prevailing fears and preoccupations of 'ordinary viewers', and basing their questions on some supposed commonsense consensus on the issue (which places the discussion firmly within the parameters of the official discourse). Or, they may choose the rôle of devil's advocate, quizzing their Establishment witnesses from a perspective which incorporates alternative or even oppositional elements. Though here again, there are significant variations in the way this rôle is performed. Presenters may be deferential and apologetic, prefacing their remarks with phrases like 'Some people would argue . . .', or they may be more direct and obtrusive as in 'But surely you do not mean to tell me that . . .'. The aggressive style is most apparent when the witness is putting an alternative or oppositional view as in the interview with the Sinn Fein spokesman on *Newsnight* discussed below.

In choosing between these various rôles presenters are constrained in important ways by the programme's place in the schedules and by the kind of audience it is aimed at. The BBC's early evening news magazine, *Nationwide*, for example, goes out on the Corporation's main channel (BBC1) directly after the early evening national news bulletin and regional news round-ups, and plays a key rôle in building and holding a mass audience for the rest of the prime-time output. This strategic position in the ratings battle pushes the programme towards populist forms of presentation and discourse which work with the most widely held images and assumptions in the interests of mobilising the largest possible audience.[7] *Newsnight* in contrast, is transmitted on the minority channel (BBC2) in a slot (10.55–11.40 pm) which is out of prime-time. This location gives it an audience concentrated among those with post-school education and professional and managerial jobs. And since the presenters can assume that they are addressing people much as they would like to see themselves—well informed, open-minded, and sceptical—they feel freer to present issues in a more complex way which allows greater scope for the consideration of alternative views and positions.

Nevertheless, this flexibility remains subject to the constraints which stem from the BBC's 'special relationship' with the state and with notions of nationhood. In Britain there is an important sense in which the BBC, in spite of its independence, is the national broadcasting organization in a way in which the programme companies making up the ITV network are not. This means that the BBC's general current affairs and documentary output is more closely identified with the organization, the organization is more exposed to political and other criticism, and its regular current affairs output is more closely tied to the political agenda of the day. The weekly *Panorama*, for example, is regarded as the BBC's 'flagship' in current affairs. Its topics and techniques are particularly exposed to political scrutiny and censure. It is expected to act as a national forum and deal with the important issues of the day. The regular current affairs output on ITV on the other hand has more freedom to select its own agenda.

At this point, however, we need to introduce a further distinction, between '*tight*' and '*loose*' programme formats. A '*tight*' format is one in which the evidence and argument is organized to converge upon a single preferred interpretation and to close off other possible readings. A '*loose*' format, in contrast, is one where the ambiguities, contradictions and loose ends are not fully resolved within the programme, leaving the audience with a choice of available interpretations.

This distinction cuts across our earlier dichotomy between 'open' and 'closed' presentations. A programme may be 'open' in the sense that it provides space for anti-official elements, but 'tight' in the way the material is mobilized on behalf of a particular reading. Usually, but not always, tightness confirms the official discourse. Actuality presentations are generally at their most 'closed' and 'tight' when dealing with contemporary terrorism within the boundaries of the British state. Where the imperatives of national security recede (and with them the concomitant threats of censorship or other state intervention) the possibilities of openness expand. This brings us to the operation of another important factor which we can call *proximity*. This operates along several dimensions, the first of which is time. Thus, it is possible to cast a dispassionate, even acerbic eye over British activities in Ireland in an historical documentary series such as *The Troubles*, or a drama-documentary such as *The Crime of Captain Colthurst*. Historical distance allows for the portrayal of economic exploitation and military brutality, and for the admission of past mistakes and excesses on the part of the British state. In depicting the contemporary situation, however, programme-makers bump up against the operation of proximity in its other main dimensions—the geographical and ideological. Other states' problems with terrorism attract an altogether more critical gaze. However, this geographical factor is heavily overlaid by ideological criteria. Hence, television presentations are likely to be at their most 'open' where insurgency takes place within nondemocratic states in which legitimate channels of dissent are either restricted or closed and in which state repression is a prominent feature of the system of rule. In such cases, where violence against the state may be seen as justified as a tactic of last resort, the label 'terrorist' is likely to be replaced by that of 'guerrilla', 'freedom fighter' or member of the 'Resistance'. In other words, attitudes towards insurgencies are inextricably tied to attitudes towards the regimes in which they take place. Feature films, documentaries and popular television series (such as *Secret Army*), for example, constantly celebrate violent acts of resistance against the Nazi occupation of democratic Europe, which would be unambiguously condemned as terroristic in other contexts. Though documentaries are often grouped in a series or occupy a regular time slot, they are less constrained than the regular current affairs output to follow the political issues of the day. They draw their agenda more widely across the full range of social, political and economic questions and often take the form of enquiries into the workings of particular organizations and social institutions. They rely less on studio presentation of the spokespeople for various legitimated views and opinions, more on sequential reports of the material that the producer has managed to put together on a subject. The rubric of balance requires the producer to take note of the major currents of opinion within the field he is investigating. This requirement has relaxed, however, as the notion of 'balanced output' has taken precedence over 'balanced programme', implying that balance need not be achieved within the single programme but in the output taken as a whole. The space opened up by this relaxation is at its maximum in the 'authored' documentary.

Whereas the news and most of the regular current affairs output are so closely identified with the broadcasting organizations as to be seen as 'their' products, for which they bear collective responsibility, 'authored' documentaries are ascribed to an individual reporter or producer and presented as their particular view of the subject. Accordingly, the commissioning organization is usually at pains to distance itself from the programme, by, for example, announcing at the beginning and end that it represents the personal opinions of the makers. This disavowal in turn licences the presenters to ignore the normal constraints of balance, and to offer their individual views backed by whatever material they can command. In the process, they move out of the normal rôles of observer and reporter and into the rôle of 'author', a rôle they share with the creators of television fiction, and more particularly with the writers of single plays.

Forms of television fiction

We decided to include the main forms of television fiction in the present study because taken together, they provide the largest single category of programme output and the bulk of the most widely viewed shows. Consequently, any analysis that fails to incorporate them can only ever produce a partial and limited evaluation of television's presentations of terrorism and of their potential impact on popular consciousness and action. But the inclusion of fiction has benefits for analysis beyond greater *comprehensiveness*. It also allows us to *compare* actuality and fictional forms and to begin exploring the continuities and breaks between them. As Bazalgette and Paterson (1980/1981) have shown, certain narrative codes and ideological reference points cut across forms as varied as comic strips, news bulletins and realist drama. However, as we shall see, fictional forms also allow for a range of representations which are largely excluded from actuality programming.

In the first place, television drama is not subject to the strict requirements of objectivity, balance and impartiality and is therefore able to be more partisan. In addition it is able to depict two key groups of political actors who almost never appear in current affairs and documentary programmes—the terrorists themselves and the members of the military and intelligence service with special responsibilities for counter-insurgency operations. Indeed, the battle between the agents of terror and subversion and the forces of national security has been a stock theme of popular fiction since the turn of the century and still provides plots for television.[8] Moreover, as we shall see, certain fictional forms provide a good deal of space for probing the political motivations and rationales of terrorism and raising questions about the legitimacy and legality of the state's repressive responses. Unlike current affairs producers and documentary makers, writers of fiction can circumvent problems of access to clandestine state operations and high security institutions. And they can therefore explore the workings of the 'secret state' from the 'inside'.

Yet fictional presentations are still subject to a number of pressures and constraints stemming from the forms and genres they employ and from their position within the domestic and international market. For several reasons, these factors exert their strongest pressures towards ideological closure on popular *series* that feature a stable set of characters over different, self-contained episodes. Along with sports programmes, old movies, comedy and variety shows, series are at the centre of the battle for mass audiences which means that they are required to work with images and ideological themes that are most familiar and endorsed by the widest range of potential viewers. Consequently, they tend to draw heavily on elements from the official discourse, since these are the most pervasive and best publicized. In the case of programmes like *The Professionals* which are aimed at international as well as domestic markets, this tendency to closure is reinforced. The producers have to find themes that will be intelligible across cultures and especially so in the United States, since it is American sales which are the major factor in profitability. The result is often a kind of 'mid-Atlantic' style which draws heavily on the themes and formats of the action-adventure series (cf. Murdock and Halloran, 1979). This has two obvious advantages in terms of saleability. It ensures a product that is readily intelligible in any culture familiar with American shows, and because it centres on action (chases, fights, escapes) rather than dialogue, it saves the buyer the cost of extensive dubbing or subtitling. But it also has pertinent effects on the way that representations are organized within the programme itself.

The ratings success of a series largely depends on the extent to which the audience identifies with the core characters (and the stars who play them) since it is this that keeps them watching from week to week. This invitation to identify is inscribed in the titles of the programmes—*The Saint, The Avengers, The Professionals*—and provides the organizing principle around which the narratives are constructed.

The plots revolve around the adventures of the core characters. They are the heroes. The villain's function is to disturb the social and moral order and to present the heroes with puzzles to solve and tasks to be accomplished so that normality can be restored. But the villains do not need to be rounded characters to fulfil this rôle. They simply have to personify threats to order in a readily recognizable form (cf. Palmer, 1978). Consequently, in the action-adventure series, the upholders of order and the agents of disruption are always unequally represented. We know a good deal about the heroes, their private lives, their personalties, past experiences, and existential doubts since each new story can trade off the knowledge presented in past episodes. But we usually know next to nothing about the villains. They appear abruptly at the beginning of the episode and they are purged from the body politic at the end. But they remain drastically undercharacterized, and the action is presented almost exclusively from the heroes' point of view.

In terms of our previous distinctions then, the standard action-adventure series is both relatively 'closed' and relatively 'tight'. It tends to reproduce the emphases of the official discourse and to offer few spaces for alternative and oppositional viewpoints. And it tends to organize the narrative around a struggle between good and evil where the two sides are portrayed with little or no ambiguity or contradiction and where good always triumphs at the end of each episode. But within the general field of popular series and indeed within television drama *as a whole* there are significant variations of form and genre. An intermediate category is the popular *serial* where the plot develops over a number of weeks rather than in series where the action has to be resolved in the space of a single episode. The more relaxed narrative pace of the serial provides opportunities to develop more complex characterizations of terrorists and their motivations, and space to interrogate the nature and operations of the 'secret state'. Indeed, as we shall see with *Blood Money*, the military response to terrorism and the limits of its legitimacy can provide the central theme for popular television series.

This interrogation of the state's democratic credentials is most fully developed however, outside of popular forms, in the single play. Unlike series and serials, television plays are not in the front line of the battle for audiences or programme exports and so they are not under the same pressure to work with the most prevalent ideological themes or to deliver predictable pleasures to the largest possible number of viewers. On the contrary, the producers of single plays are expected to fulfil the rôle of 'authors' and to express their own particular viewpoints and commitments in their own distinctive voice and style. This notion of 'authorship' gives them a licence to raise awkward political questions and to do so in forms that may disturb or even overturn the audience's expectations (Murdock, 1980). This potential for provocation is not always fully realized of course. Plays on sensitive issues (such as the situation in Northern Ireland) are subject to political pressures from inside and outside the broadcasting organizations, and cuts and cancellations are therefore a permanent possibility.[9] Moreover, by no means all television playwrights take advantage of the potential flexibility of presentational forms, to make space for diverse points of view. Nevertheless, a good deal of politically contentious material does get transmitted, and as we shall see in the case of *Psy Warriors*, it is possible to mobilize alternative and oppositional perspectives in a single play in a more complete and sustained way than is generally possible in popular series and serials. They are therefore the most potentially 'open' and 'loose' form of television fiction.

Terrorism in actuality television

Two conclusions stand out from our survey of the treatment of terrorism in the recent current affairs and documentary output of British television. First, the term 'terrorism' and the meanings associated with it are openly contested in most of these programmes. In terms of the distinctions outlined above most programmes are open rather than closed. A variety of meanings and definitions are usually included even if the broadcasters, as interviewers, reporters or presenters, are working for closure in the terms of the official discourse. Second, the repertoire of meanings and definitions which is contested is remarkably narrow, mainly involving defining the violence as terrorism or not terrorism and weighing the reasons for violence against its consequences.

In the official discourse this balance is weighted heavily in favour of the consequences. The consequences in terms of human suffering are horrendous so that nothing can justify the resort to violence and terror. Those who engage in such behaviour do not have 'reasons' in the normal sense of the word. Their behaviour is senseless, irrational and inhuman (Elliott, 1980). No reasons can be given for killing and maiming. The terrorists even more than the other criminals and murderers with whom they are bracketed have put themselves outside civilized society.

An extreme example of this view that terrorists are not human shows one technique broadcasters use to re-establish the official discourse. After a filmed interview with a spokesman holding oppositional views, a spokesman for the Irish National Liberation Army, the organization which killed the Conservative MP and Northern Ireland spokesman Airey Neave, the *Tonight* programme (BBC1, 7 July 1981) reverted to the studio so that a presenter and two Northern Irish politicians could put the interview into perspective. In the interview the INLA spokesman had denied that INLA had 'murdered' Airey Neave, saying instead that he had been 'assassinated' or 'executed'. Following the interview the studio presenter, Robin Day, re-established the point that it was murder before inviting the two MPs to comment.[10] The immediate response of Robert Bradford, the Official Unionist spokesman, was that he had almost refused to take part in a programme which permitted an interview with such a 'subhuman creature'. Jerry Fitt, representing the SDLP, felt that it was unwise of the BBC to air such an interview which could only serve to inflame protestant and loyalist opinion in Northern Ireland. This same interview was cited two years later in a discussion programme on television's reporting of Northern Ireland, as a prime example of the 'irresponsible and reckless use of the medium', in the words of Dr (ex-Major General) Richard Clutterbuck (BBC1, *The Editors*, 28 June 1981). In the same programme two journalists, one from the press the other from television, defended the case for interviewing 'terrorists'. Though the BBC presenter, John Morgan, pursued the official view that such people were 'mere murderers or thugs', this was refused by both journalists who argued that the root of the conflict in Northern Ireland was political, that terrorism was politically motivated, and that the media had a duty to convey this to the British public by interviewing alleged terrorists. A further instance of the refusal of the official definition of terrorism occurred in a *Newsnight* interview with Danny Morrison, a Provisional Sinn Fein spokesman, in the aftermath of the death of the hunger striker Bobby Sands. Morrison attacked the 'two sets of laws' that operated in Northern Ireland which legitimated the violence of British troops (as on Bloody Sunday), while delegitimizing Republican violence as murder. He persistently refused the definition of the hunger strikers as criminals, redefining them as political activists 'in the war going on in Northern Ireland' (BBC2, *Newsnight*, 6 May 1981).

Another inflection of the official discourse on Northern Ireland is to emphasize the continuing human consequences of terrorism on the innocent civilian population of the province. This approach is to be found in all types of actuality coverage, but in its most frequent and popular forms it occurs in the news bulletins and daily current affairs programmes. The 'who, what, where?' format has become standard for reporting incidents in which someone is killed, as have the follow-up filmed reports which concentrate on the bravery and good character of the victim and the sorrow and endurance of their families and kin.

But state bullets inflict death and injury in just the same way as terrorist bullets, and this poses ideological problems for the dominant perspective. The weight of the argument against terrorism is that it causes suffering. If it can be shown that the state and its agents cause suffering there is some explaining to do. One answer given is that state violence is legitimate. But this is relatively rare because it admits that suffering caused by state violence was an isolated mistake, that under provocation some retaliation may be necessary, more general attempts to deny that the incident took place, or that state forces were responsible are more common. A from the initial and ubiquitous euphemism of defence. By comparison arguments that suffering caused by state violence was an isolated mistake, that under provocation some retaliation may be necessary or more general attempts to deny that the incident took place or that state forces were responsible are more common. A favourite British device which has been used in cases like Bloody Sunday when British troops shot dead 13 demonstrators, or following allegations of torture in Northern Ireland, is to resort to Widgery, to set up legal inquiries which, over a period, redefine the problems into acceptable terms. These the media can then report. In the case of Bloody Sunday, Lord Widgery found that there had been 'shooting by the army which bordered on the reckless'. Sir Edmund Compton redefined torture as physical ill-treatment.[11]

In a *Panorama* programme on the North (BBC1 21 September 1981) the latest problem of civilian deaths from plastic bullets, supposedly used as a method of riot control, was set out as an understandable consequence of mistakes and retaliation.

From a street riot/petrol bomb sequence (Peter Taylor, reporter, BBC1, *Panorama* 21 September 1981): . . . Almost inexorably the violence from these mobs has provoked violence in return. Under a hail of petrol bombs, the security forces were bound to retaliate. In an attempt to control the riots they fired plastic bullets. These are meant only to deter but they can be lethal. The IRA has never been slow to exploit mistakes. Plastic bullets have killed seven people since Bobby Sands died. This has only deepened the alienation the Catholic community already feels.

The programme went on to illustrate this point by interviewing the mother of a young girl killed while innocently bringing home some shopping. But in less proximate locations, however, the sufferings of the victims of state force are allowed to carry more weight. In contrast to the presentation of the IRA and INLA, characterizations of the PLO are generally more ambiguous. The Organization is defined simultaneously as both 'terroristic' and as a quasi-state engaged in diplomacy, and this more flexible characterization allows the legitimacy of the Israeli state to be contested and its use of violence to be likened to that of the Palestinians—an equation of state terror and insurgent terror which is impermissible nearer home. South Africa, with its clear-cut racism and rejection of formal equality before the law, is a regime which can make no claim whatever to liberal-democratic legitimacy (although it can claim to be struggling against international communism). Here the ideological space for accepting the legitimacy of state violence against state repression is at its maximum and contestation over definitions hardly figures at all. An instructive comparison may be drawn from the television coverage of the funeral of Bobby Sands in Northern Ireland contrasted with that of Pallas Mallungu, a black striker in South Africa:

Kate Adey, reporter (BBC1, *The 9 o'clock News*, 7 May 1981): To the tens of thousands who watched his coffin to the grave this was the burial of Bobby Sands, martyr . . . . An army helicopter grinding relentlessly overhead all but drowned the tones of the Irish pipes and there were shouts by the stewards as they tried to supervise the coverage by the world's press. Tens of thousands of people from all over Northern Ireland and from the South, a grim-faced demonstration of support for the political aims of the hunger strikers, overtaking the private grief of the Sands family . . .

Outside a shopping centre in Andersons town came the symbolic moment for the Republicans. Three masked men stepped forward and obeyed orders in Irish to fire a three volley salute. Illegal uniforms. Illegal shooting. All grist to the mill for the convictions of republican and loyalist.

The Sands funeral is admitted to be a tragic symbol for his supporters but, according to the reporter it is a symbol arranged for the media which has no more than propaganda value for a cause which we, the reporter and her audience, cannot support. The Mallungu funeral on the other hand is a 'political demonstration'. In that case the reporter (*Panorama*, BBC1, 15 June 1981) develops the story to show how workers and guerrillas are united in the same movement, pursuing the same cause, the 'liberation of the black man'.

Peter Taylor, reporter, against background of chanting mourners at funeral procession (BBC1, *Panorama*, 15 June 1981): Many black workers see themselves as comrades, fighting the same war as the guerrillas. Pallas Mallungu's funeral became a political demonstration. To the crowds who followed his coffin Pallas Mallungu was not just a martyr to the workers' cause. He was a martyr to the cause of black liberation. It's the political message of scenes like this. A mixture of anger and grief which makes the government ever more anxious about the power of the black trade unions. Many black workers see themselves as comrades, fighting the same war as the guerrillas. They share the same enemy, they share the same end. Only the means are different.

Liberation is the oppositional justification which may be allowable in less proximate contexts, so that 'terrorists' become 'guerrillas'. In Northern Ireland however the claims for political status for the IRA by, for instance, Danny Morrison in the interview cited above, were vigorously denied by the interviewer.

The official discourse only uses war as a metaphor, denying the terrorist even the limited legitimacy of being a conventional enemy. It does allow the possibility though that they may be agents of a foreign power whose aim is to subvert our way of life. Thus the *Panorama* programme could rehearse, albeit not too seriously, the South African government's case against the 'red threat' posed by the guerrillas, but in a more proximate case—the attempt on the Pope's life—the red threat was treated much more at its face value. The claim that the KGB was behind the attempt, based on circumstantial evidence and the suppositions of the Italian right, was developed in a format that was both close and tight. With an agency so ideologically distant as the KGB all pretence was dropped that there were alternative views or an oppositional case (ITV, *TV Eye*, 3 September 1981).

But in 'authored' documentaries, which are clearly signalled as the personal viewpoint of their writer/presenter, dominant definitions of terrorism may be both contested and subverted, particularly if they bear on violence that has either passed, even if only recently, or which happened in areas remote from the immediate sphere of British interests. In a *Pilger Report* on the current plight of Vietnam veterans in the United States, the journalist John Pilger drew out the implications of their conditions for current American policy in El Salvador (ITV, *Heroes*, 6 May 1981). In the course of this tight programme Pilger dealt with the same repertoire of meanings and definitions as are to be found in the other coverage of terrorism which we have discussed. But he systematically inverted the official meanings and definitions and provided a clear statement of an equation which is the precise opposite of the dominant view of terrorism. In official discourse insurgent terrorism leads to unacceptable human misery. In Pilger's alternative statement it is state terror which produces unacceptable human costs:

Missing from this film are the other witnesses to the Vietnam period, the Vietnamese. We hear very little about them these days and the American veterans speak little about them perhaps because what was done over there was so terrible that only the victims can afford to speak about it. Such has been the politics of vengeance that the people of Vietnam are now almost completely isolated with only the waiting arms of the Russians to turn to, whom they rightly distrust as much as they distrusted the Americans, the French, the Japanese and Chinese who came to their country selling noble causes.

So here is the news from Vietnam. In the wake of the war's devastation there is now famine. Rations are less than even during the war years, about half the food needed for a healthy survival. There is no milk any more for children over the age of one and unexploded bombs and mines kill children every day.

Like its refusal to help its own victims of the war the American Government has denied all help to the people of Vietnam and so too has the British government.

On the other hand both governments are building the greatest military machine in preparation for a war that may well end all wars and for that our heroes need not apply.

Throughout the programme the sanitized double-speak of the official discourse on war is systematically inverted. In drawing a parallel between Vietnam and El Salvador Pilger used US Ambassador White to redefine terrorism from insurgent terrorism to state terrorism. He then, in an El Salvador sequence, underlined the point by comparing the tragedy of the El Salvadorians and the Vietnamese, both victims of the state's military machine.

This book is a collection of *New York Times* front pages which trace the American involvement in Vietnam and reading it now is an eerie experience. The same headlines are appearing today. The same jargon such as escalation, and light at the end of the tunnel. The same delusions. Delete Vietnam and write in El Salvador and the stories seem almost identical. Like the politicians then—Kennedy, Johnson and Nixon—the politicians now, Haig and Reagan, see the world in the same arrogant, simplistic terms, speaking of dominoes as if nations were blocks of wood. Not societies riven with their own differences and animosities. Today as before, honest men pay with their careers. The American Ambassador in El Salvador, Robert White, has said that the war in that country is caused by social injustice and that the real terrorists are the regime backed by Mr Reagan and Mr Haig and supported of course by the British government . . . .

For speaking the truth the ambassador was sacked. Here is an announcement of US advisers going to Vietnam and US troops going to protect them. The advisers have already arrived in El Salvador. As in Vietnam the people who are dying in the streets and jungles of El Salvador are nameless stick figures on a television news or between the commercials in a re-run Hollywood movie. The American veterans of Vietnam have much in common with them for they too have been declared expendable.

Terrorism in television fiction

The *Pilger Report* is a rare statement in actuality television of the thesis that there is a problem of state terrorism. In contrast, the nature and legitimacy of the state's use of violence is a central theme in television fiction dealing with terrorism, although the way it is handled varies considerably. To illustrate this range we have chosen three programmes which represent the major types of television drama we outlined earlier. They are: an episode from a top-rating action-adventure series, *The Professionals*; a thriller serial written especially for television, *Blood Money*; and a television play, *Psy-Warriors*.[12] As with the actuality programmes just discussed, these instances can be arranged on a continuum running from relatively 'open' to relatively 'closed', as shown in Table 2.

Table 2

	Intended audience		
	maximum ⟶		restricted
Actuality programmes	news magazines e.g. *Nationwide*	current affairs e.g. *Panorama*	'authored' docu- mentaries e.g. *Heroes*
Fiction programmes	action-adventure series, e.g. *The Professionals*	serials, e.g. *Blood Money, A Spy at Evening*	single plays, e.g. *Psy-Warriors*
Programme structure	relatively 'closed' ⟶		relatively 'open'

The Professionals is one of the most successful action-adventure series produced in Britain in recent years. Almost all of the episodes have featured in the top ten most popular programmes and the series has been sold in most of the major overseas markets. The action centres around Bodie and Doyle, the two top agents of CI5, a crack Criminal Intelligence unit which bears more than a passing resemblance to the SAS. According to the publicity blurb for the series:

Anarchy, acts of terror, crimes of violence—its all grist to the mill of the formidable force who make up CI5 (*TV Times Extra*, 1979: 11).

CI5 breaks all the rules: no uniforms, no ranks and no conscience—just results. Formed to combat the vicious tide of violence that threatens law and order, its brief is to counter-attack. And when there's a hijack, a bomb threat, a kidnap or a sniper, men from CI5 storm into action (Blake, 1978).

This brief underscores two key themes in the official discourse. Firstly, it places terrorism firmly within a criminal rather than a political frame and defines it exclusively in terms of the violence it entails. And, secondly, it legitimates the state's use of violent countermeasures by arguing that exceptional threats to the social order require exceptional responses in which consideration of civil liberties, democratic accountability, and due process, are held in abeyance in the interests of efficiency. Within this perspective the end of re-establishing order justifies the use of dubious and even illegal means, and licences the men of CI5 to use the same dirty tricks as their adversaries. We are told that Bodie and Doyle:

believe in fighting violence with violence. They are cold and ruthless. They would think nothing of kidnapping a kidnapper, or chaining a bomber to his own bomb and leaving him to defuse it (*TV Times Extra*, 1979).

But, the fact that they are agents of the state means that popular support for these strong-arm tactics cannot be entirely taken for granted, so the unit's commander, Cowley, tells his men:

Oh, there'll be squeals, and once in a while you'll turn a law-abiding citizen into an authority-hating anarchist. There'll be squeals, and letters to MP's; but that is the price they, and we, have to pay to keep this island clean and smelling, even if ever so faintly of roses and lavender (Blake, 1978: 19).

Hence, while it operates firmly within the terms of the official discourse, the programme must also work *actively* to head off dissent and enlist the audience's support for powerful countermeasures by underlining the exceptional nature of the terrorist threat and pointing up the irrelevance of alternative and oppositional perspectives on state violence. This process of ideological mobilization is well illustrated in the episode entitled *Close Quarters*.

The episode opens with the assassination of a British politician, Sir Denny Forbes, at a check-in desk at London airport, killed by the leader of the Meyer-Helmut terrorist group with a syringe of poison. This precipitating incident introduces four central themes; the essential criminality of terrorism; its identification with the Left; its characterization as an alien incursion originating outside Britain and the absolute contrast between the legitimate pursuit of interests through parliamentary representation and the illegitimacy of direct action. The assassination is a direct attack on the 'body politic' and on the 'British way of life'.

Having detonated these themes in the opening pre-credit sequence, the narrative immediately begins to elaborate them. The audience have already been invited to see Meyer's act as essentially criminal rather than political by the very fact that it is going to be tackled by CI5, a *criminal* intelligence unit. But to reinforce the point the scene immediately after the credits shows Cowley briefing his men in a style familiar from countless crime movies where the chief of police talks his officers through the 'most wanted' list. Although Bodie attends the briefing he is excused active duty because of an injured gun hand, and he decides to take his girlfriend Julie for a picnic on the River Thames at Henley. While on the water he recognizes Meyer standing on the bank. He follows him to the cottage he is using as a 'safe house' and arrests him. But the other members of the group arrive and give chase. Bodie eludes them and makes his getaway in a stolen car. The group pursue him and he barricades himself in a country vicarage which the group, heavily armed, surround.

The group's utter ruthlessness is confirmed when they shoot the vicar in cold blood as he is climbing out of a window in an effort to reason with them. This incident clinches the central ideological theme of the narrative; that you cannot bargain with terrorists and that faced with their arbitrary violence, the state is justified in using similar tactics. Popular support for this position is mobilized through the commonsense response of the housekeeper and Bodie's girlfriend. The audience is invited to see its real-life position as analogous to the women's situation within the narrative; innocent bystanders who are caught up in events they do not fully understand but who can recognize the state's moral right to combat terrorism with all the weapons at its command.

MEYER	How does this concern you? You have no conception of what this fight is
(*addressing the girlfriend and the housekeeper*	about. It's not your fight.

HOUSEKEEPER	I don't understand your politics, but I understand good and evil. You kill without cause. You kill people who cannot possibly stand between you and your ideas. You don't even know who they are.

JULIE	You're right. I have no idea what you're fighting about. I just know it means
(*addressing Meyer*)	violence and killing and someone's got to stop you.

Despite these protestations Julie still has reservations about the legitimacy of Bodie's use of violence (after he has shot two members of the group as they attempted to enter the vicarage). But at the climax of the plot, when the chips are down, Julie overcomes her qualms. As the last member of the gang storms the room where they are hiding, Bodie is disarmed by Meyer and it is Julie who picks up his gun and shoots. The ideological circle is finally closed, around the official discourse.

By no means all popular television fiction is as 'closed' or as 'tight' as this however. Serials in particular, may provide spaces for a more critical appraisal of state violence and point to contradictions which may not be entirely resolved within the scope of the text. This was the case with a six-part serial, *Blood Money*.

The narrative opens with a scene set in an exclusive private boarding school for the sons of the rich. The boys are out on a cross-country run through the sunlit landscape. One of them, Rupert Fitzcharles, is the son of the Administrator General of the United Nations and because of his father's political status he is guarded by a plain clothes policeman working undercover as a school sports master. Suddenly, figures wearing gas masks spring out from behind the hedges, spray the boys with CS gas, abduct the diplomat's son and drive him to their 'safe' house in London. They intend to release him when the authorities agree to meet their demands, but if they refuse the group intend to kill him.

As in the initial scenes of *Close Quarters*, this opening sequence calls into play two of the central themes in the official discourse; the essential ruthlessness of terrorists and their disregard for human life; and their characterization as an alien incursion. And as in *The Professionals*, this opposition between terrorism and the 'British way of life' is represented by idealised images of rural and upper class England on the one hand, and by making the terrorist leader a German (although in this case she is a blonde woman rather than a dark haired man, the model being Ulrike Meinhoff rather than Andreas Bader). As the narrative progresses, the framework established by this opening is made increasingly problematic.

The fact that the narrative is less compressed than in a standard series episode provides space for a fuller characterization of the terrorists and for some discussion of their motivations, and in the process tensions and contradictions begin to emerge. On the one hand, the characterization of the group's leader, Irene Kohl, reinforces the terms of the official discourse. She is consistently depicted as fanatical and ruthless. She shows no sympathy whatever for the kidnapped boy and the fear he feels. She sees him simply as a bargaining counter, necessary for the achievements of the group's political aims, but dispensable if things go wrong. And the fact that she is a woman is constantly used to underscore the official view that terrorism is 'unnatural' and dehumanizing. On the other hand, the characterization of the Irish member of the group, Danny Connors, leads in the opposite direction. He shows considerable sympathy for the boy's distress and eventually establishes a friendly relationship with him. He is portrayed as an essentially decent man who has been led astray by political idealism, but his choice is presented as entirely intelligible given the history of the British ruling class's treatment of the Irish people. This contrast between the depiction of terrorists as fanatical and inhuman on the one hand and as human but politically motivated on the other is never resolved and remains a permanent tension within the text. But the larger and more significant fissures open up around the presentation of the forces of law and order.

Since the kidnap is classified as a crime the investigation is the responsibility of the relevant section of the regular police force commanded by Chief Superintendent Meadows. But because of the political status of the boy's father, Captain Percival of the Secret Intelligence Service is also assigned to the case. Meadows represents the rule of law and due process. His overriding concern is to return the boy safely to his parents and bring the kidnappers to justice. Percival on the other hand, is primarily concerned with eradicating terrorism and he is quite prepared to go behind the back of the law to achieve this. In the ensuing conflict between the two men, the normal connections between law and order are prised apart and the effective maintenance of order is presented as potentially *at odds* with adherence to legal processes.

The series as a whole encapsulates the essential dilemma that democracies face in balancing force against consent, order against law. Either the state can play by its own rules and bring the terrorists to trial thereby giving them a platform for their views and an opportunity to mobilize public opinion. Or it can violate its principles, dispense with due process and eradicate the terrorists without a trial, thereby undermining the popular consent on which its legitimacy rests. The solution to this dilemma is to kill the terrorists clandestinely, away from the glare of publicity. However, as Percival recognizes, the logic of this resort to force is exactly opposite to the logic of justice and the rule of law. To retain popular consent the law must operate in public and justice must be seen to be done, whereas force is best exercised in secret so that the repressive fist within the democratic glove remains concealed. But, as Percival has hinted earlier, there is an alternative—licenced murder by agents of the state—and that is the solution he opts for.

The terrorists have been tricked into thinking that their demands have been met, by a fake news broadcast by Meadows, who aims to arrest them as they leave the 'safe' house. But unknown to him, Percival has surrounded the house with a crack paramilitary unit. As the group step into the street, he gives the order to shoot them in cold blood. The boy is unhurt, but Meadows is outraged:

MEADOWS (*to Percival*)   You bastard!

PERCIVAL   Why? The woman was armed, she was going to kill the child.

Technically, Percival is correct, but since he has made it clear from the beginning that saving the boy's life is secondary to eliminating the terrorists, the audience is invited to read his remarks as a somewhat flimsy and inadequate justification for judicial murder and the abandonment of the rule of law. This is the last exchange of dialogue, and the narrative ends on an ambiguous note with Meadows turning his back on Percival and walking away. Although the tension between order and law is resolved, the nature of that resolution is presented as highly problematic and open to question.

The same issues of state-instigated violence, the rôle and nature of the intelligence services, the use of terror as a normal and *systematic* feature of the democratic state's operation in periods of crisis are opened up in *Psy-Warriors*.

The play is set in a high-security installation whose existence is known only to selected members of military intelligence and senior Ministry of Defence personnel. The action opens with two men and a woman being brought in for questioning. They are suspected of having left a bomb in an Aldershot public house, popular with soldiers from the nearby army camp (a scenario based on an actual incident). Within the unit normal legal rights are suspended. The suspects do not have the right to call a lawyer or to inform their family or friends of their whereabouts and they can be detained without being charged or brought to trial.

The play's opening scenes display the full range of disorientation techniques employed in modern interrogation. The group's leader is stripped naked and made to stand against a wall with his legs apart and a black bag over his head for hours on end. Later, he is led away blindfolded and taken up in an army helicopter and pushed out of the open door. In fact he is only a few feet from the ground but he is told he is over the Thames estuary. The second man is kept in a cage in a white-tiled room under constant glaring light and his regular patterns of sleep are interrupted by bouts of intensive interrogation. The woman's head is covered by a black bag smelling of vomit. She is forced to eat repulsive food, and when she asks to go to the toilet she is forcibly marched there. These techniques of sensory deprivation and psychological warfare are all drawn from official reports of the British army's operations in Ulster and elsewhere, but by displaying them in a particularly graphic way, the play forcefully raises the question of how far the state is justified in suspending basic human rights in the interests of securing confessions or information from suspected terrorists.

Thus the audience is invited to believe that they are watching a play about the way in which the state deals with possible terrorists, but the author then proceeds to overturn this assumption in order to raise less obvious questions about the legality and legitimacy of the state's operations in relation to terrorism.

After the initial interrogation scenes, the action cuts to a meeting between the directors of the unit and a visitor from the Ministry of Defence. It is revealed that the 'suspects' are not in fact terrorists at all, but army volunteers who are being tested for possible recruitment to an elite antiterrorist unit. The training exercise the play presents, requires them to assume the identity of terrorists in order to understand their situation and motivations from the inside so that they will be able to combat them more effectively. This phase of the training programme has culminated in them leaving a live bomb in the pub. But since the exercise is top secret, the police bomb squad were not informed, a fact which once again points up the tension within the state apparatuses between the *forces of law* on the one hand, represented by the regular police force whose actions are open to a certain measure of political and public scrutiny, and the *forces of order and security* on the other, who operate in secret and beyond the purview of parliament.

As well as raising questions about the legality of the 'secret state's' operations, the play's structure provides considerable space for the presentation of oppositional justifications for terrorism. The aim of the exercise presented in the play is to get the volunteers to understand the experience and motivations of terrorists from the inside. The narrative depicts two devices for achieving this. The first is to make them take on the persona of terrorists, act out these assumed identities, and experience the possible consequences. The other is to licence the interrogators to act as devil's advocates, putting the strongest possible oppositional case in order to deepen the recruits' insights into the terrorist's motivations and to toughen up their resistance to counterpropaganda.

The oppositional case for terrorism is particularly powerfully put in the scenes between the chief interrogator and the woman. She has begun to crack under the strain and he needs to push her to the limit ideologically in order to find out where her breaking point is. At the climax of the final interrogation session, the interrogator presents the situation in Northern Ireland in terms derived from the rhetoric of militant Republicanism. This depicts it as Britain's last colonial war and presents the IRA's terrorist campaign as a guerrilla offensive against an army of occupation which consistently violates human rights in the defence of an exploitative colonial power:

Mau Mau, EOKA, the NLF, the IRA. I've spent the greater part of my working life watching British troops being pulled out of places they were never going to leave. A long hard line of colonial campaigns, and on every campaign the British used internment, concentration camps, and intensive interrogation, torture: sticks up bums, bums on blocks of ice, licking the lav bowl clean, nudity, humiliation, running round in circles and pissing in the wind. You name it, we've inflicted it, I've inflicted it, the Empire, your heritage . . . . What you see in Ulster is the rear end of the cruelty and exploitation of over thirty colonial wars. The last colonial battlefield. A dog devouring its own tail. When it reaches its arse it will be in England.

Conclusion

In this analysis of different presentations of terrorism on television we have tried to demonstrate some of the continuities and discontinuities to be found right across the output of the medium, embracing both 'actuality' and 'fiction' and the more popular as against the more exclusive forms. This we have done by looking at the ideological problems that political violence raises for the state and the contest over legitimation that is involved. Our approach, perforce, must challenge and extend the present orthodoxy in media sociology and cultural studies. This orthodoxy— one which we ourselves have helped to establish and develop—has concentrated almost exclusively on news. Factual programmes have come to be seen as virtual paradigms of how the national culture is represented. Consequently, news and current affairs programmes have had a heavy burden to bear. They have been taken by their critics to be a virtually self-contained area which provides the most crucial social map made available by the mass media to the wider public, and therefore as the most important targets. As is plain from our analysis, the frameworks of interpretation which we have delineated play a structuring rôle in forms as varied as news, documentary, the drama series and the single play. Moreover, the precise ways in which a given form may be structured is illuminated by comparison with others. This enables us to be made much more aware of the possibilities and limitations available within each form when it comes to representing an issue such as that of 'terrorism', and the wider relationships of political violence to the state.

Much recent work has reproduced the structure of attention of the media themselves by an excessive concern with the representation of formalized conflicts in the parliamentary arena, industrial relations or processes of law enforcement.[13] In these cases the system of representations to be found in broadcasting is heavily grounded in social institutions of conflict resolution and management, and reproduces the concerns of these institutions and their leaders. Nevertheless in the last two cases particularly much of the conflict in terms, for example, of unofficial strikes, demonstrative picketing, factory occupations, street demonstrations, and riots occur outside the frameworks consecrated by the established institutions of the state and civil society. Where conflict escapes the institutions it is characteristically handled as 'violence' which poses a fundamental threat to the stability of society. We recommend taking violence as the central focus because it is precisely at this point that the legitimacy of the state comes under most pressure. Even if spokespeople for the 'violent' are denied routine access to the centre of the stage (though, as we have seen, their views do not go entirely unrepresented) those who exercise control in this area have to work hard to justify and legitimate repressive action and to maintain their indiscriminate condemnation of the violent, the criminal and the terroristic.

Instead of concentrating on those processes which affirm the stability of the state and civil society it seems fruitful to consider those which are deemed to pose a threat to their very existence. For one thing it brings another range of institutions into view, the apparatuses of the secret state. These are largely invisible in actuality programming but provide much of the substance of drama. An exclusive concern with factual representations is simply too narrow. What is needed is an awareness of the interrelatedness of the components of the national culture.

It would be inaccurate to imply that a radical conception of television as an interrelated culture is absent from the literature. A good case in point, one which follows much of our basic line of argument, is the study of Bazalgette and Paterson (1980/1981). Amongst other recent writings, Silverstone (1981) has attempted to analyse television as a fabricator of myths thus showing some recognition of the broader unity of television's output. George Gerbner has conducted a programme of research taking television output as the cultural indicator, the repository of the contemporary *Weltanschauung* and the functional equivalent of the medieval church (cf. Gerbner and Gross, 1976). Whereas this kind of approach tends to assimilate different forms and homogenize them, our interest has been in discriminating between forms at the same time as bringing out their interrelations. Consequently as we have argued above, a typology of forms can be worked out in terms of a variety of dimensions which gives primacy to the process of production and its constraints. Thus, factors which come into play are periodicity, style, market and organizational considerations, presentational rôles and the assimilation and translation of cultural artefacts and traditions from other media into televisual forms (cf. Tables 1 and 2).

Thus we are arguing for a highly discriminating and situated analysis of television's discourse. Although *Psy-Warriors* was the most 'open' programme we looked at, as we have shown, it was not an altogether isolated instance. Rather, it lies at one end of a continuum which runs from ideological 'closure' to relative 'openness', which operates in complex ways within the major forms of programming, and which provides space for rather more conflict and contestation than the prevailing wisdom of critical media research might predict. That this should be so came as something of a surprise to us, but it was also exhilarating, since it has opened up a whole range of issues for investigation and analysis which have barely been touched on by the work done so far.

Acknowledgements

This is an abridged version of 'The State and "Terrorism" on British Television', originally published in *L'Immagine dell' Uomo* (Florence), no. 1, January–April 1982. The complete version has also been published in Italian translation in the two-volume study *Terrorismo e TV* (ERI, Torino), 1982.

Notes

1. Cf. the reports in *The Guardian*, 'Thatcher warns on danger of media aiding Ulster terror' (21 May 1981) and 'Granada stops films on Ulster' (2 June 1981); also cf. Peter Fiddick's article in the same paper, 'The Irish facts that are not fit to be shown' (9 June 1981).
2. For a synoptic account of the British model of censorship on Northern Ireland and policing, and for a more general discussion, cf. Schlesinger (1981).
3. This is argued out in Elliott and Schlesinger (1979: 195–210). The paragraph draws directly from p. 196.
4. Cf. 'Close watch on Russian conduct' and 'Washington chilled by cold war winds', *The Guardian*, 30 and 31 January 1981.
5. Matters are not so simple. Some 'terrorism studies experts', such as Wilkinson (1981) see terrorism of the non-state variety as necessarily being indiscriminate. However, it is plain that discrimination or indiscriminacy varies with the political strategy of the group in question. The Provisional IRA, for instance, has latterly pursued an almost exclusive policy of 'selective' killing against 'strategic targets'. In Italy, it is *fascist* terrorism which is indiscriminate, whereas 'red' terrorism has been much more selective on the whole (cf. Marletti, 1979).
6. News has become the most studied of all televisual forms. For evidence on these points see for instance Golding and Elliott (1979) and on the cast of accredited spokespeople, Hall *et al.*, (1978).
7. For a fuller analysis of *Nationwide's* populism, see Brunsdon and Morley (1978).
8. On the origins of fiction dealing with terrorism and with the intelligence services, see Laqueur (1977: especially 15–32), Melman and Stafford (1981).
9. On the political sensitivity to television dramas dealing with Northern Ireland, see Hoggart (1980: 261–262) and Madden (1979: 17–21).
10. We are particularly grateful to Mairede Thomas and Paul Kerr of the British Film Institute for helpful suggestions which started us on a number of fruitful lines of enquiry.
11. The relevant texts are, on Bloody Sunday, *The Report of the Widgery Tribunal*, HC 220, HMSO, London (1972) and, on torture, *The Compton Report: Allegations against the Security Forces of Physical Brutality in Northern Ireland*, Cmnd 4823, HMSO, London (1971). The interrogation techniques portrayed in the play *Psy-Warriors* which we discuss below are based on those whose use was confirmed by Compton. For an account of reporting in Northern Ireland in this period see Winchester (1974).
12. *The Professionals* episode *Close Quarters* was written by Brian Clemens, directed by William Brayne and produced by Sidney Hayters. It was broadcast on ITV at 9.00 pm on Friday 5 June 1981. *Blood Money*, a serial in six episodes, was written by Arden Winch, directed by Michael E. Briant and produced by Gerard Glaister. Broadcast on BBC1 from 9.35 to 10.05 pm on Sunday evenings from 6 September to 11 October 1981. *Psy-Warriors* was written by David Leland, directed by Alan Clarke and produced by June Roberts. It was broadcast on BBC1 as a 'Play for Today' from 10.15—11.30 pm on 12 May 1981.
13. For politics see Hall *et al.* (1976); on industrial relations the Glasgow University Media Group (1976) and (1980); on law enforcement within the paradigm of news, Hall *et al.* (1978), and within the paradigm of election broadcasting, Clarke *et al.* (1981).

Bibliography

BAZALGETTE, C. and PATERSON, R. (1980/1981). Real Entertainment: The Iranian Embassy Siege, *Screen Education*, Winter, No. 37

BLAKE, K. (1978). *The Professionals: Where the Jungle Ends*, London, Sphere Books

BONANATE, L. (1979a). Some unanticipated consequences of Terrorism, *Journal of Peace Research*, No. 3, vol XVI

BONANATE, L. (1979b). Terrorism and International Political Analysis, *Terrorism: An International Journal*, vol. 3, nos 1-2

BRUNSDON, C. and MORLEY, D. (1978). *Everyday Television: 'Nationwide'*, London, The British Film Institute

CHOMSKY, N. and HERMAN, E. H. (1979). *The Political Economy of Human Rights*, 2 vols, Nottingham, Spokesman Books

CLARKE, A., TAYLOR, I. and WREN-LEWIS, J. (1981). Inequality of access to political television: the case of the General Election of 1979; paper presented to the Annual Conference of the British Sociological Association, Aberystwyth, Wales

ELLIOTT, P. (1980). Press Performance as Political Ritual, in H. Christian (ed.), *The Sociology of Journalism and the Press*, Sociological Review Monograph no. 29, Keele, University of Keele

ELLIOTT, P. and SCHLESINGER, P. (1979). Some Aspects of Communism as a Cultural Category, *Media, Culture and Society*, vol. 1, part 2

GERBNER, G. and GROSS, L. (1976). Living with Television: the Violence Profile, *Journal of Communication*, vol. 26, no. 2, Spring

GLASGOW MEDIA GROUP, (1976: 1980). *Bad News; More Bad News*, London, Routledge and Kegan Paul

GOLDING, P. and ELLIOTT, P. (1979). *Making the News*, London, Longman

HALL, S., CONNELL, I. and CURTI, L. (1976). The 'unity' of Current Affairs television, Working Papers in Cultural Studies, no. 9

HALL, S., CRITCHER, C., JEFFERSON, T., CLARKE, J. and ROBERTS, B. (1978). *Policing the Crisis*, London, Macmillan

HOGGART, R. (1980). Ulster: a 'switch-off' TV Subject?, *The Listener*, vol. 103, no. 2651, 28 February

LAQUEUR, W. (1979). Interpretations of terrorism: Fact, fiction and political science, *Journal of Contemporary History*, vol. 12, no. 1, January

MACPHERSON, C. B. (1977). *The Life and Times of Liberal Democracy*, Oxford University Press

MADDEN, P. (1979). Banned, Censored and Delayed in *Truth the First Casualty: The British Media and Ireland*, London, The Campaign for Free Speech on Ireland

MARLETTI, C. (1979). Immagini pubbliche e ideologia del terrorismo in L. Bonanate (ed.), *Dimensione del Terrorismo Politico*, Milan

MELMAN, B. (1980). The terrorist in fiction, *Journal of Contemporary History*, vol. 15, no. 3, July

MURDOCK, G. and HALLORAN, J. (1979). Contexts of Creativity in television drama: an exploratory study in Britain, in H.-D. Fischer and S. Melnik (eds), *Entertainment: A Cross-Cultural Examination*, New York, Hastings House

MURDOCK, G. (1980). Authorship and Organisation, *Screen Education*, no. 35, Summer

PALMER, J. (1978). *Thrillers: Genesis and Structure of a Popular Genre*, London, Edward Arnold

PICCIOTTO, S. (1979). The theory of the state, class struggle and the rule of law, in B. Fine *et al.* (eds), *Capitalism and the Rule of Law*, London, Hutchinson

POGGI, G. (1978). *The Development of the Modern State*, London, Hutchinson

SCHLESINGER, P. (1981). 'Terrorism', the media and the liberal-democratic state: a critique of the orthodoxy, *Social Research*, vol. 48, no. 1, Spring

SILVERSTONE, R. (1981). *The Message of Television*, London, Heinemann

STAFFORD, D. (1981). Spies and Gentlemen: The Birth of the British Spy Novel, 1893-1914, *Victorian Studies*, vol. 24, no. 4, Summer

TV TIMES EXTRA, (1979). *Who's Who Among the TV Super Sleuths*, London, Independent Television Publications

WEBER, M. (1947). *The Theory of Social and Economic Organisation*, New York, The Free Press

WILKINSON, P. (1981). Can a state be 'terrorist'?, *International Affairs*, vol. 57, no. 3, Summer

WINCHESTER, S. (1974). *In Holy Terror*, London, Faber and Faber

Broadband Black Death cuts queues. The Information Society and the UK

RICHARD COLLINS*

The Government are on record to scuttle—a betrayal and a surrender; that is what is so shocking and serious; so unnecessary and wrong. Somebody introduced dog-racing into England, we know who, for he is proud of it, and proclaims it *urbi et orbi* in the columns of Who's Who. And somebody introduced Christianity and printing and the uses of electricity. And somebody introduced smallpox, bubonic plague and the Black Death. Somebody is minded now to introduce sponsored broadcasting into this country (Lord Reith, House of Lords Hansard, 22 May 1952).

Another concern that has been voiced has drawn attention to the extent to which the new information technology will encourage the individual to withdraw into his home. There will be no need to go shopping in person, to cash a cheque at the bank, to place a bet at the bookmakers, or, that most sacred of British passions, standing in queues to buy theatre tickets, train tickets, etc. The possible social effects of information technology have hardly begun to be counted (Lord Thompson, Chairman of the IBA at Bath University, 3 March 1983).

Fifty million television sets in America; and now the coaxial cable! (Tom Ewell [in extremis], The Seven Year Itch, 1955).

The messiah has foretold the coming of the post-industrial society and his disciples in Canada, Britain, France and Germany are locked in competition to induce the earliest birth of a viable infant. The spectacle of governments of diverse political colours across the world throwing money up in the air or into holes in the ground should give pause to those sceptical of the power of ideas.

The Information Society

Bell's (1976) thesis of the information society has been embraced as a doctrine that will lead industrial societies currently locked into a cycle of beggar my neighbour protectionism, declining rates of profit and mass unemployment into a new promised land. In the UK, 1982 was designated Information Technology Year (1983 is World Communication Year), in which Government promulgated a number of initiatives to advance the labour of the old industrial society: the telecommunications monopoly of the state-owned British Telecom was terminated with the licensing of a competitive privately-owned network, Mercury, the supply of terminal equipment was opened to competition, Direct Broadcasting by satellite commencing in 1986 was authorized (hardware by Unisat, a consortium owned equally by British Aerospace, British Telecom and General Electric Company–Marconi, software in two TV channels by the BBC), and the 'wired society'—a broadband cable network delivering entertainment television and a

* Polytechnic of Central London.

cornucopia of other services, including interactive security systems, remote banking, shopping and polling encouraged in the report commissioned by the Cabinet Office (the Prime Minister's department), 'The Cabling of Britain'. Nowhere in this sustained performance of prestidigitation by the government and its allies in the 'information society' industries has there been any acknowledgement of the trail of aborted foetuses that have attended previous initiatives, the effects on the existing 'information society' industries, and the possibility of providing most of the notional benefits and services that will flow promiscuously from the IT society's horn of plenty through modest development of existing facilities (e.g., all the interactive cable services can be carried by the existing narrow band telephone system—including, using slow scan TV, security and, using a new GEC gizmo, video telephony).

The Information Society thesis (or 'forecast' as Bell calls it) distinguishes post-industrial societies thus:

The first and simplest characteristic of a post industrial society is that the majority of the labour force is no longer engaged in agriculture or manufacturing but in services, which are defined residually, as trade, finance, transport, health, recreation, research, education and government (Bell, 1976: 15).

Bell offers a triadic division of the labour force into agricultural, industrial and service sectors and cites OECD figures of 1969 for Britain (presumably meaning the UK) showing the percentage of workforce in each sector:

agriculture	3.1%
industry	47.2%
services	49.7%

Figures derived by Wall (1977) are based on—for Bell's thesis better—a quadri-partite division and come from the decennial general censuses taken in the UK for the years 1961 and 1971:

	1961, %	1971, %
agriculture	3.9	3.0
industry	36.2	33.7
services	26.9	26.7
information	33.0	36.6

Crude though Bell and Wall's categorization is (as they recognize) and open to obvious objections such as only counting paid work (doing one's own washing does not count as work, buying a washing machine boosts the industry statistics, taking washing to a laundry boosts the service sector, and presumably the displacement of electro-mechanical controls for washing machines by micro-processor controls boosts the information sector) and constituting definitions of information work extremely widely—including occupations such as typewriter mechanic, bookbinder and clergyman as information workers—there seems no reason to doubt that some kind of shift is going on. Whether it is to a post-industrial society or merely a development in the international division of labour or perhaps a reversion to pre-industrial forms of organization (one could, if clergy are to be counted as information workers count the whole monastic and ecclesiastical structures of the European middle ages as a burgeoning information sector) is another question. But the seduction of Bell's thesis does not inhere alone in its 'explanation' of shifts between employment sectors and the hope he offers of jam for all tomorrow, he also explains—as have a variety of other social theories of twentieth century (e.g. the general shift in Marxist theory whether Hegelian or anti-Hegelian, in the Frankfurt School or in Gramsci or Althusser to emphasizing the importance of ideology rather than repression as the crucial agency in reproducing capitalist society)—the non-realization of the supercession of bourgeois hegemony by proletarian hegemony anticipated by Marx by referring to the crucial agency of the information sector. For Bell the shift is not towards proletarian hegemony but to the hegemony of the 'Angestellten', to an emergent white-collar salariat charged with complex, technocratic control and information functions in a society in which knowledge is power—or where, as the graffiti reproduced on the cover of the British edition of 'The Coming of the Post Industrial Society' has it, 'Knowledge rules O.K.'.

Every modern society now lives by innovation and the social control of change and tries to anticipate the future in order to plan ahead. This commitment to social control introduces the need for planning and forecasting into society (Bell, 1976: 20).

For Bell the information society is distinguished by its reliance on planning and control functions and thus the social groups charged with these functions dispossess the industrial proleteriat of the power vested in them by Marx. The development of novel procedures and technologies for information processing enhance the efficiency of the traditional economy (notably manufacturing but also primary production and services) and call into existence new forms of production—the information industries—and constitute information itself as a commodity. Other commentators though are sceptical:

When I am weary or nasty, I sometimes remark that the post industrial society was a period of 2 or 3 years in the mid 60s when GNP, social policy programmes and social research and universities were flourishing. Things have certainly changed (S. Michael quoted in Kumar, 1978: 185).

Kumar points out that there is no empirical evidence to support Bell's thesis that prosperity attends the infant information society. Bell is careful to buttress his arguments with prudent knee dips to the diseconomies of scale of the large organizations that modern information transmission techniques make possible and acknowledgements of the false dawns of earlier communication revolutions but overall his message is bullish and the 'coming of the Post Industrial Society' is larded with references to the productivity and wealth gains that have followed the application of knowledge to the problems of pre-post industrial societies. But Kumar's *Prophecy and Progress* argues against the central elements of the Bell thesis and in particular its positive correlation of expenditure on knowledge (e.g. industrial research and development) and economic growth or as Bell says, 'the inexorable influence of science on productive methods' (Bell, 1976: 378). Rather Kumar states:

It appears that, as in the past, market forces and political goals (need pull) are far more important in determining the nature and rate of technological innovation than the ideas and inventions springing from pure research (idea push). Post war Japan demonstrates this conclusively with one of the lowest levels of research and development expenditures of all industrialized nations, it has had the highest economic growth rate in the post war period (Kumar, 1978: 226).

One can in turn challenge the conclusiveness of Kumar's demonstration for more recent statistics suggest that Japanese research and development expenditure is not out of line with that of other advanced countries:

R&D expenditure as a percentage of GNP, 1980 (Japan, 1979)

Italy	Japan	FRG	UK	USA
0.84	2.04	3.39	2.20	2.41

(source: Conselio Nazionale delle Richerche, Italy and OECD; quoted in the *Financial Times*, London, 28 March 1983, p. XI).

But neither do these statistics support Bell's propositions that 'The roots of the post-industrial society lie in the inexorable influence of science on productive methods' (Bell, 1976: 378).

And whilst there is clearly not a perfect fit between the information/service sector and invisibles or the manufacturing/agricultural sector and visibles the trade balances between the UK and Japan in visibles and invisibles are hard to reconcile with Bell's overall thrust and suggest that knowledge does not necessarily rule OK and that there is no necessary correspondence between wealth and a post industrial society:

Trade balance UK/Japan, $US Millions + / −
expressed in terms of UK economy

Year	Visible	Invisible
1966	− 58	+ 241
1971	− 102	+ 490
1976	− 616	+ 1498
1981	− 2398	+ 4398

(source: Bank of Japan, 'Balance of payments monthly', cited in J. Bartlett letter, *Financial Times*, London, 13 April 1983).

Kumar's argument that need pull is more important than idea push can be supported by examination of Videotex (a lynch pin of the Information Society and selected by Nora and Minc (1980) in their report 'The Computerisation of Society' as one of five crucial foci for French national information society policy). Videotex has been developed as an 'idea push' technology by state organizations in Canada (Telidon fostered by the Department of Communications), France (Télétel/Antiope by the PTT), and the UK (Prestel by British Telecom). Nowhere has it achieved significant market penetration still less profitability. Prestel for example has received *circa* £50 million in development funds and has achieved a penetration of *circa* 23,000 terminals in early 1983. Contrast the market pulled penetration of videotape recorders in the UK (manufacture of which has recently commenced on a small-scale in the UK under Japanese licence). In 1982, 2,351,000 machines were imported at a cost of £519.2 million (*Broadcast* London, 18 April 1983). To some extent of course the distinction between 'idea push' and 'need pull' is theological—every product or service combines 'idea push' and 'need pull' and the policy question is not of choosing between 'idea push' and 'need pull' but of correctly assessing and articulating the two forces. In the UK though government policy oscillates contradictorily between commitment to need pull and the market (e.g. introducing competition in the provision of telecommunication services) and idea push and the central rôle of the government (e.g. the insistence on establishing a broadband cable infrastructure—an election manifesto commitment of Mrs Thatcher and the funding of 'fifth generation' computer research under the Alvey £200 million program). But a constant element in Conservative government policy is commitment to advancing the birth of the post-industrial society in the UK and force feeding the infant UK information economy. Elsewhere the information society thesis has been embraced and consciously promulgated as state policy but nowhere has national policy considered and successfully articulated the hardware and software elements of the information industries.

The international lemming race

The case of Canada is well known and exemplifies the contradictions of national policy directed to securing an advantageous position in the international communications hardware business (Spar Aerospace, Mitel, Northern Telecom are among the major winners) but which in using the domestic information economy as a base for hardware manufacturers from which international markets may be colonized open the domestic software market to very serious international competition. To be sure the penetration of foreign software into the Canadian market is by no means wholly a consequence of Canadian hardware policy but the Canadian government's hardware policies have done nothing to inhibit the penetration of foreign software.

Canada embraced the Information Society thesis early—the historical importance of communications in establishing and holding together the Canadian nation, the continuing importance of the political as an agency for engineering Canadian national solidarity in a country held together by few cultural, geographical or economic ties perhaps disposed Canada to its early involvement in the development of 'leading edge' communication industries, e.g. communication satellites and Telidon. But the cost has been high—Melody (1979) has described satellites as 'well on their way to becoming 20th century pyramids'. And cultural and information sovereignty has not been protected by legislation, whether by requiring broadcasters to use 'predominantly Canadian creative and other resources' (Section 3d, Broadcasting Act, 1968), or the Bank Act (1980 amended) requiring that client information be stored in Canada. Defensive action on the software front is also extremely costly and attended by no great success; support for Canadian public service broadcasting from federal and provincial budgets is currently in excess of $500 million per annum. Hoskins and McFadyen (1982) state that Canadian television broadcasters obtained in 1975 an average margin per half hour of $21,000 from foreign (i.e. largely US) programs compared with $55 (fifty-five) from Canadian programs. The disincentives to using Canadian software are evident.

Four paragraphs in the 1983 Canadian government publication 'Towards a New National Broadcasting Policy' well exemplify three central themes of the race towards the information society. First that there is a race on—whether or not domestic needs lead government to support information industries international considerations make it imperative. If the French, British and German lemmings are running a Canadian lemming should be in the race too. Second, wealth and employment will accrue to the national hardware industries of the competitors. Third, the double think, software industries will benefit too but in order to benefit they will need financial support from government.

In France, 27 major cities are soon to be cabled, while West Germany will shortly commence large-scale cabling projects in 11 major cities. Australia too is about to begin wiring all its major population centres. Meanwhile, Belguim is rapidly moving ahead of Canada as the world's most heavily cabled country on a per capita basis, while in the United Kingdom the recently released report of the Hunt inquiry advocates a concerted move to cable.

Canadian high technology industries should benefit directly as cable operators retool their plants to carry these new programming and non-programming services. Cable companies will require significant amounts of new capital equipment—such as earth stations, scrambling and descrambling equipment and a variety of other types of cable hardware. Canadian high technology industries manufacture much of this equipment, and jobs should be created as a result.

The new technological environment can be shaped to create opportunities from which the entire program production industry can benefit. The Government of Canada will establish a special Canadian Broadcast Program Development Fund to assist private production companies and independent producers. The fund will be administered by the Canadian Film Development Corporation and will rise from a total of $35 million in the first full year of operation to $60 million in the fifth year.

The need for such funding arises from the continuing metamorphosis of the environment in which programs are produced. The new technology is bringing about a proliferation of programming services, not just in Canada but around the world. This transformation of the global broadcasting environment will result in a continually growing and voracious demand for new programming to fill the multiplicity of channels soon to be available. This hunger for new content represents an enormous opportunity for Canadian program producers.

But, in order to compete effectively in these new markets and in our own domestic market, Canadian program producers must have the resources to produce attractive, high-quality Canadian programming in both official languages and of international calibre—Canadian programming that people will choose to watch (Government of Canada, 1983).

Canada perhaps best exemplifies an enduring contradiction in government policies for an information society. Investment in national communications infra-structure, that is a distribution system, simply creates demand for information products which can be met much more cheaply by importing product from large producers and the controllers of archives. For many information goods are imperishable ('I Love Lucy', 'The Munster's' and 'Sergeant Bilko' are currently scheduled in the UK) and once first copy costs have been amortized then costs of further copies are low and sale is very profitable. The size of the US market is such that US producers are able to amortize very high program budgets by domestic market exploitation. A well-funded product exhibiting high production values is therefore available for sale in other markets at low cost. The UK Government Cable White Paper (HMSO: 1983 51) gives representative figures:

An hour of original material can range from around £20,000 for a current affairs programme to £200,000 for drama (or even more in the case of prestige projects). Bought in material from the USA, where the production costs have already been largely if not wholly recovered on the domestic market, can be obtained by the broadcasters for as little as £2,000 an hour.

Quota restricting import of foreign product can provide some protection for the domestic industries of small nations but once distribution capacity is expanded beyond a certain level then the system can no longer be fed from domestic resources. Foreign product is purchased and consumed, audiences for domestic material decline (not as a consequence of superior quality of the foreign programming but necessarily as the audience is fragmented), revenues for domestic production decline and a spiral develops in which the system as it expands sucks in more and depends more on foreign material. As Melody (1982) points out the effective national policy of Canada has been to 'rather sell satellite hardware in international markets than produce programming content for domestic consumption'. The good intentions of the 1968 Broadcasting Act, the CRTC, Uncle John Meisel and all notwithstanding.

In France the government commissioned two senior officials Simon Nora and Alain Minc to report (Nora and Minc, 1980) on the information society and to recommend policy. Nora and Minc's report is simply one manifestation of a very comprehensive information strategy mounted by the government of France in the last decade. Its dirigisme has been attended with some successes—notably the revitalization of telecommunications and telecommunication manufacturing in France but in other, largely software oriented sectors, success has been less evident. In European Data Base services—the computerized delivery of information to subscribers usually through a Videotex system—Britain leads with an annual market of $235M, France, third to the UK and West Germany, has a market size of $150M and the leading suppliers are loss makers (Frost and Sullivan, 1983; quoted in the *Financial Times*, London, 13 April 1983, p. 16). The leading British supplier, Reuter, announced profits of £35M in 1983—a 100% increase on the previous year. Comparative advantage resting here with British software producers in the European financial information market as it rests with US producers in the world entertainment market.

The strategy of the government of France has been largely formulated in the shadow of 'le défi American' personified by Nora and Minc in the corporate personality of IBM:

IBM is following a strategy that will enable it to set up a communications network and to control it. When it does it will encroach upon a traditional sphere of government power: communications. In the absence of a suitable policy alliances will develop that involve the administrator of the network and the American data banks to which it will facilitate access (Nora and Minc, 1980: 6).

In Britain the seduction of government by the post-industrial society thesis has come relatively late, and is not distinguished by the virulent anti-Americanism of the French. For Nora and Minc the massed ranks of the European PTTs are the last line of defence possible against IBM; 'the only cartel capable of establishing a dialogue with IBM is one that could be formed from an alliance of telecommunications agencies' (Nora and Minc, 1980: 7), in consequence the British government's resolve to privatize its PTT—British Telecom—the choice of a US rather than a European standard for cellular radio (rewarded perhaps by Comsat's licensing of the British MAC satellite transmission system) and the reliance of the leading British manufacturers on US technology, e.g. for large PABXs all products are ultimately of foreign, largely US origin (though Plessey claims its IDX is home grown Rolm is currently suing Plessey in the US for breach of copyright) has provoked the French government to its familiar cry of 'perfide Albion', e.g. in the 'great disappointment' of M. J.-P. Braunet, chairman of the state owned CIT—Alcatel at the harm to 'European collaboration' caused by the British cellular radio decision (*Financial Times*, 21 April 1983; p. 7).

Late and perfidious though British government's enthusiasm for the information society is its commitment is as comprehensive as that of the French though the

Conservative administration of Mrs Thatcher manoeuvres uneasily between the desire to take a leading rôle and its hostility to state dirigism. Unfortunately though the Thatcher embrace of the information society has not been attended by the realization of one of Bell's more enticing predictions: British government discourse remains as untheorized as ever and one looks in vain to Mr Baker, the Minister charged with responsibility for information technology, for the cosmic utterances of Nora and Minc and their French epigones that better exemplify Bell's analysis:

What is distinctive about the post industrial society is the change in the character of knowledge itself. What has become decisive for the organization of decisions and the direction of change is the centrality of theoretical knowledge—the primacy of theory over empiricism and the codification of knowledge into abstract systems used to illuminate many different and varied areas of experience (Bell, 1976: 20).

Production/distribution balance—film and television

In this article I do not propose to consider the matters of telecommunications policy, but rather the consequences of the information society initiatives for broadcasting in the UK. Both because of the place of public service broadcasting in UK cultural life and because of the success of British television software sales to foreign markets. To some extent this is an arbitrary separation, although in the UK broadcasting and telecommunications have remained largely distinct technologies and institutions, the convergence that we are currently experiencing is replete with precedents. The telephone system that has developed in the UK principally as a 'contentless' system in which the numbers of transmitting and receiving stations existed in symmetrical relationships has 'broadcast' elements—the speaking clock, cricket scores and financial statistics services, 'Dial a Disc' and 'Bedtime Stories'. And in the early 1920s the Electrophone Company offered London subscribers the possibility of auditing one of a number of London theatres or on Sundays a chosen church service relayed from a range of places of worship. The Electrophone was killed by radio though radio in turn provided a stimulus to the development of wired systems offering subscribers relays of broadcast radio services. And cable television in the UK is largely the child of the introduction of commercial television in 1955 when for a considerable time markets existed for the relay of a good broadcast television signal to areas shielded by the local topography (e.g. Sheffield, and the area of southeast London served currently by Greenwich Cablevision) from the transmitter or which was at the edge of a number of stations transmission areas (e.g. Swindon).

In the UK, as in most European countries, the broadcasting order has developed constrained by shortage of spectrum capacity relative to that outside Europe, e.g. in the USA. The geographical proximity of European countries has permitted fewer channels for terrestrial broadcast services in a single country than elsewhere. It is customarily argued that this shortage of spectrum capacity has both necessitated and legitimized regulation by the state and that in a number of European countries a fortuitous 'fit' developed between the resources available for national program (software) *production* and the (limited by spectrum availability) capacity of the *distribution* system. This 'fit' resulted in a stable broadcasting system ecology in which national broadcasting systems distributing substantially indigenous product developed, offering a model instance of the planned evolution of a viable and popular national cultural industry. France, West Germany and the UK exemplified the 'fit' and the health of their broadcasting systems compared favourably with the crises of small countries such as Denmark, the Netherlands, or Belgium in which the revenues generated (whether from the sale of broadcasting receiving licences, levies on the sale of receiving apparatus or components, from advertising or directly from the state budget), were insufficient to fund the quantity and quality of program material required for the capacity of the terrestrial broadcast distribution system.

The introduction of new distribution technologies whether cable or direct broadcast satellites separately or in conjunction will upset this comfortable symbiosis by expanding distribution channels, creating a demand for software that cannot be met by the national production industry. The consequential importation of software from overseas will attract audiences away from existing services and reduce the revenues accruing to existing services (whether by having smaller audiences to sell to advertisers or by reducing the political acceptability of expenditure from the state budget or the levying of broadcast receiving licence fees), thus reducing the quality of indigenously produced software and initiating a spiral of decline. The history of the film industry in the UK is the classic example used to support this melancholy prognosis. The PEP report of 1952 defined the problem thus:

The British film industry could not pay its way without a substantial export market. The home market could not compare with the home market of the American industry which was already several times as large. As soon as American production expanded and with its expansion introduced a new and more expensive type of film, there was no longer the same demand in the United States for British films which were of a cheaper and less polished kind. Without an overseas market British producers could not afford to increase the quality and consequently the expense of their films and without that extra quality they could not hope to compete with the Americans . . . . Even in these days of sound the film trade is an international one and the American industry with its enormous home market has most of the advantages. Although in the history of film production many millions of pounds have been wasted, the fact remains that in all but exceptional circumstances the making of films which are both commercially and technically good costs a great deal of money; because of the extent of their home market the American producers are in the best position to meet financial necessities (PEP, 1952: 29).

Though these remarks were made in respect of the period before the First World War the structural problem defined here was enduring and, I suggest, will endure:

In 1926 the proportion of British films shown over the country as a whole appears to have been not more than 5%. The actual proportion of exhibitions of British films on the screen at that time was probably well below 5% owing to the larger percentage of exhibition dates secured by American films through the system of blind and block booking (Moyne Committee Report, para 5, quoted in PEP, 1952: 41).

In 1927 the first of the legal measures enacted by the British government to protect national film production was enacted following the Moyne Committee Report: the Cinematograph Films Act checking the practices of blind and block bookings imposed on exhibitors by the strength of the US major producers and introducing quotas of British films for exhibitors and distributors. The quotas began in 1928 at 7½% for distribution and 5% for exhibitions and rose to 20% in 1935. US interests remained dominant within the industry—particularly important was their commanding position in the distribution sector but government action—particularly quota requirements—had lifted British feature film production to 228 films in 1938 from 96 in 1930 (PEP, 1952: 60, 68). The stimulus offered by quota applied only to the home market and to import substitution: it did not enable producers to successfully exploit world markets. But important substitution and the amortization of production costs by exhibition solely in the British market did not permit 'quality' film production and comparative advantage remained with the US production industry:

Quality films were expensive; the British market alone was not large enough to recover their costs of production; therefore quality films must have a world market (PEP, 1952: 69).

But:

British films could not capture a big enough share of the world market, more particularly of the American market, and the confidence which led to the expansion of the industry and the concomitant loans was unjustified (PEP, 1952: 70).

And:

An assessment of the comparative markets available to British and American producers in 1936 showed that in terms of seating capacity the American home market was two and a half times as large as the British domestic market and that the annual net box-office receipts were four times as large; that 'owing . . . to the common language, nearly every American film is available for and is sent to, all other English speaking countries, giving a much larger market still to the American product and a correspondingly reduced one to British films' (PEP, 1952: 74).

The Cinematograph Films Act of 1938 revised quota requirements to extend protection to short films (pressure had come from John Grierson and documentary film-makers) by establishing a separate short film quota and, (to raise the quality of British productions), establishing a minimum cost of £7500 labour costs per film. and of £1 per foot of film for quota eligibility. Films with higher labour costs of £3 per foot counted for double quota and £5 per foot treble quota.

In 1944 a further Committee of Enquiry into the film industry, the Palache Committee, was appointed and whilst not all of the committee's recommendations were implemented some of its arguments are worth recording for their recognition of the cultural significance of the cinematograph film commodity:

A cinematograph film represents something more than a mere commodity to be bartered against others. Already the screen has great influence both politically and culturally over the minds of the people. Its potentialities are vast, as a vehicle for expression of national life, ideals and tradition, as a dramatic and artistic medium and as an instrument for propaganda . . . . The British public are vitally concerned that the British cinematograph industry should not be allowed to become either a mere reflection of a foreign atmosphere or a channel for disseminating the ideas and aspirations, no matter how worthy in themselves, of one or two dominating personalities in the country (PEP, 1952: 90).

In 1947 Customs Duty of 75% was imposed on all imported films—this 'Dalton Duty' was imposed 'because the country cannot afford to allocate the dollars necessary to pay for the exhibition of American films in this country at the present time' (*Hansard*, 3 November 1947; quoted in PEP 1952: 99) and constituted the most effective protection enjoyed to date by the British film production industry. The 'ad valorem' duty was removed in 1948 after pressure from British exhibitors and American producers in exchange for agreement from the US producers for a phased remission to the US of revenues earned in the UK and measures to promote circulation of British films in the US and US investment in the British industry. In 1948 the recommendations of the Moyne (1927) and Palache (1944) Committees that financial support for British film production should be available was implemented with the establishment of the National Film Finance Corporation. However, the 1948 Cinematograph Films Act removed quota for distributors (retaining it at 45% for first feature exhibition and 25% for supporting programs) and reduced the labour cost per foot requirement for quota elibility by 50%.

In 1949 the reports of the Plant and Gater Committees (on distribution and exhibition of cinematographic films and on film production costs, respectively) were published: their consensual view was that receipts from the share of the domestic market remaining to British producers were still insufficient to sustain film production in Britain, and that the structure of the distribution (dominated by US companies) and exhibition sectors (dominated by two companies with agreements with the US majors resulting in a predominance of US product exhibited) militated against a successful British production sector. *Plus ça change plus c'est la même chose.*

'It is abundantly clear', said Lord Lucas (the government spokesman in the House of Lords), 'that a reorganization is necessary upon the distributive side of this industry and in the arrangements for marketing' (PEP, 1952: 124).

The problems of distribution and exhibition were never satisfactorily tackled but in 1950 the British Film Production Fund (usually known as the Eady Levy after the Civil Servant Sir William Eady) was set up. The fund levies a percentage of exhibitors revenues on admission tickets, and channels the revenues to British producers of British films. Producers benefit (as do a number of other bodies such as the British Film Institute and the Children's Film Foundation), in proportion to the distributors' gross revenues earned by his or her film. Thus Eady taxes the exhibitor's revenue for all (including non-British) films shown and distributes the revenue to the producers of British films. Eady was given the force of statute in 1957 and has reduced the gap between the capacity of the distribution/exhibition sector and the production sector by directing revenues from distribution/ exhibition to support production.

The regime established by the early 1950s of quota, the National Film Finance Corporation and the Eady Levy has persisted for thirty years. During those thirty years the fortunes of the British film industry ebbed and flowed; a pool of skills for film production was maintained (though as the Interim Action Committee on the Film Industry observed in 1979 these skills 'can be used in other sectors of industry, for example in the building trade'), revenues circulated between sectors of the industry and between government and industry (Coulson-Thomas argues persuasively that the financial effect of government intervention in the film industry has been to transfer funds from industry to government; revenues gained from e.g. entertainments tax and corporation tax outweigh revenues lost through the NFFC or the 100% first-year capital allowances against tax given to British film productions), Ealing comedies came and went, the British social realist films of the late 1950s and early 1960s came and went, *Star Wars, Alien* and *Superman* (all British films for the purposes of the Eady Levy and the British government), came and went. In the late 1970s success was such that 'earnings by British film producers from performances overseas have been greater than the money paid out by British exhibitors for screening Hollywood films' (Porter, 1979: 221). But the forces identified by Porter in 1979 as central forces behind the British production industry's success—the 'vertically integrated multinational corporations' of ACC and EMI have rapidly faded from the scene. The recent success of British cinema—*Chariots of Fire* and *Gandhi* are independent productions. British success in the international marketplace, history shows is short-lived and insecure. The long-term movement of the industry has been one of decline—by the early 1980s the British film production industry was making too few films for exhibitions to fulfil quota requirements and in 1982 the quota requirements were reduced to 0%.

Some contra-indications to this melancholy prognosis are clearly visible. *Chariots of Fire*'s success has been followed this year by the perhaps even more emphatic success of *Gandhi*, an Anglo-Indian production with, as in the old days of the Raj, British predominance (60% of the £11 million came from Goldcrest Films a backer of *Chariots of Fire*, and part of the Pearson Longman conglomerate which includes among its extensive media holdings *The Financial Times*, Longmans Publishing and Penguin Books). However although Goldcrest have clearly picked two winners the success of their films is neither unprecedented nor does it compensate for the inactivity of the traditional big indigenous fish in the British pool—Thorn–EMI, Rank and Associated Communication. *The Financial Times* itself headlined its report (13 April 1983) of *Gandhi*'s scoop: '8 Oscars do not a thriving film industry make'. In three years of the late 1940s a similar euphoria about the British industry was talked up on the basis of Oscar successes. In 1946 *The Seventh Veil* got an Oscar for its script and Laurence Olivier an honorary award for *Henry V*. In 1947 *Great Expectations* and *Black Narcissus* divided the Cinematography and Art Direction Academy Awards. In 1948 *Hamlet* and *The Red Shoes* divided a music award and *Hamlet* received the best picture and Laurence Olivier the best actor awards. Also in 1948 the Rank group produced more than 50% of British features and lost £3,350,000 even after massaging the annual accounts with £1,296,466 of non-recurring credits (PEP, 1952: 109) on film production. The PEP Report comments:

The statement of the Rank production losses was the epitaph of another era in British film history. But by the time the announcement was made, in September 1949, the continuance of film-making in this country had already become dependent on loans from public funds (PEP, 1952: 109).

Though state intervention kept an industry in place and permitted sporadic successes, from *The Red Shoes* to *Chariots of Fire*, and *Gandhi*, the structural problems of US predominance in the distribution sector, the exhibition duopoly with its agreements with the US majors 'crowding out' British productions and the small size of the British market compared with that of the US market have in the long-run supervened.

Broadcast television has developed in Britain as a vertically integrated production/distribution/exhibition entity in which state policy has denied entry in all three sectors to competitors of the BBC and the ITCA companies (the companies exclusively franchised by the IBA to sell broadcast advertising in a particular geographical area and which produce the bulk of television programming for the first commercial television channel and a growing proportion of the programming for Channel 4) until the establishment in 1982 of Channel 4 which has little in-house production capacity. Competing producers are further restricted by an 86%

quota for British productions prescribed by the IBA and 'informally' practised by the BBC, though Chapman reckons non-British material at nearer 20% of broadcasts (Chapman, 1981). TV production in the UK has thus been protected by import quotas and control of distribution capacity in a way that the UK film industry never was.

The secure home base of the British television contractors and the potential it offers for secure profits is tempered by the financial regime contrived by the Treasury and the IBA in which an excess profits tax is levied on the profits generated in the UK. That is on the surplus of advertising revenue that remains after costs of programming, the IBA transmitter rentals etc. have been paid for. Profits accruing from sales of programming overseas do not attract excess profits levy. In the year to 31 March 1983 60% of Thames Television's (the major program company franchised by the IBA) profits came from overseas program sales. the licensing and fiscal régime is therefore one that encourages high expenditure on programming (with possible disadvantages to the British public of transfer pricing shifting profit to associated companies , costs of programming inflated by high wage and salary costs and programming oriented to foreign sales not domestic tastes) and foreign sales. On balance though the system serves the public well and has harnessed the revenues generated in the British exhibition and distribution sector to support an internationally competitive production sector consistently producing for domestic and foreign consumption, quality product.

Competition, in the sections of distribution and exhibition has been restricted by the limitations of terrestrial broadcast technology (the propagation characteristics of Herzian waves at the frequencies available for television broadcasts have meant that no offshore television stations serving UK audiences could be established, there is not and has not been a television equivalent to offshore radio stations such as Radio Luxembourg and Radio Caroline or to the spill over of US transmissions into Canada that debilitated Canadian TV production, and by the government declining to allocate all of the spectrum capacity at its disposal for terrestrial TV broadcasting. It is often assumed that there has been a shortage of spectrum capacity for European countries, an objective block to the creation of a plurality of television broadcasters, but whilst spectrum capacity is finite the limits of capacity have, in Britain (and in most other countries including the USA), not yet been reached. The Home Office report on Direct Broadcasting by Satellite (1981) observed that capacity exists for a further terrestrial broadcast television channel. (This would be achieved by re-engineering the VHF 405 line services. These are to be closed in 1984 and the frequencies allocated not to broadcasting but to land mobile radio services. If transmission quality comparable to that of United States television were accepted other TV channels would be available for terrestrial broadcasting.) The report also observed that introduction of the four operating terrestrial broadcast television channels has been phased in order, *inter alia*, to ensure that the productive capacity of the domestic hardware and software industry, the capabilities of the human skills and talent pool etc. are not exhausted thus opening the door to import penetration. BBC Television was re-introduced after World War II in 1946, a commercial television channel was first introduced in 1955, the second BBC channel began in 1964 and Channel 4 in 1982 (the introduction of which was preceded by strenuous attempts, some successful, to foster new British program producers and was attended by considerable scepticism from the ITCA companies as to Channel 4's abilities to fill its schedules).

There is evidence to suggest that expansion of distribution capacity to four channels has overstretched resources. Thames Television's chairman Hugh Dundas regards Thames' contribution of £20 million to Channel 4 as 'intolerable'. Subscriptions to Channel 4 of £100 million from the ITCA companies, 14% of their revenue, for which they are enabled to sell Channel 4 advertising is matched by derisory advertising revenues. Circumstances are still very exceptional and no firm judgement can be reached for revenues from advertising on Channel 4 are depressed because of an enduring dispute between Equity (the performers union) and the Institute of Practitioners in Advertising. However, audiences for Channel 4 peak at about 10% of the peak audiences for ITV and generally remain low. Indeed at Christmas 1982 the Channel 4 audience was only 3.5% of TV viewers.

S4C (Sianel Pedwar Cymru) the largely Welsh language fourth channel for Wales has been extremely successful in attracting audiences and is clearly much valued in Wales, but its costs of £48 million per year (Wordley, 1983) can never hope to be matched by advertising revenues.

Breakfast TV, another recent initiative has the commercial station TV-am achieving audiences of 200,000 (15% of the audiences for the BBC's competing breakfast program) and losing between £500,000 and £1 million per month. Perhaps the point has been reached where capacity of the British television distribution system has outgrown the capacity of the production sector and its revenue base.

The history of the broadcasting industry in the United States offers interesting material for consideration. The US experience is customarily involved by advocates of additional services and a market based broadcasting order. The US system offers consumers in major markets more signals than does UK TV, but here too the system has reached limits, set not by the state but by the market. In most US markets UHF frequencies are available for additional terrestrial broadcast television. The limit to system expansion is reached at the point where the cost per 1000 viewers incurred by the broadcaster in reaching an audience exceeds the revenue that accrues to the broadcaster from the sale of that increment of the audience to advertisers, and at the point where the costs to a cable operator of extending a cable relay system that distributes the signals of distant stations to subscribers exceed the revenues generated from the subscribers. These are limits established in *consumption*. However, there are limits to the US system imposed by *production* factors by the need to concentrate revenues generated in the distribution sector for production. Though US broadcasting is performed by a great plurality of independent stations [nearly 1300 TV stations is the figure given by Head (1976: 169) the broadcasting order is dominated by three entities; the networks. Head glosses his history of television—embedded in his general account 'Broadcasting in America' in which the same tendencies towards concentration of production and networking are recounted in US radio's history—thus:

The economics of the medium drove it inexorably toward syndication. This was true at the local as well as at the network level. Local live production eventually dwindled to news, sports and children's programming, plus a sprinkling of religious, public affairs, homemaking and agricultural features. And even these few so-called local live programs draw much of their content from syndicated material: news agency stories, kiddie cartoons, Department of Agriculture films and canned religious features. A good deal of the newsfilm seen on the local programs of network affiliates consists either of news stories syndicated by the networks to their affiliates 'down the line', at times when the relay facilities lie idle, or of taped repeats of network news stories (Head, 1976:).

The concentration of resources necessary to produce programming of acceptable quality produced in US radio four networks (though it could be argued that market conditions permitted only three, the compulsory divestiture in 1943—prompted by the FCC—by NBC of one of its networks created an unstable situation with the fourth network, Mutual, always financially vulnerable) the greater resources necessary for television production permitted in the US—the largest and richest of world TV markets—only three major production entities.

The tendency for concentration within a national market observed by Head is now taking place on an international scale. Broadcasting, then has not been constrained by a shortage of spectrum capacity in the UK for the limit of spectrum capacity has not yet been reached but rather by a consistent and remarkably enduring series of political and cultural judgements that the national interest is best served by restricting supply of programming to that amount that can be financed and produced indigenously. There has been a tendency towards the same régime in the USA as a consequence of market pressures.

Unlike the experience of the film production industry in Britain the television production industry has been able to benefit from a secure home base from which to colonize foreign software markets. The limitation of distribution capacity (and the imposition of an 86% British quota) enabled production to amortize its costs at home and compete on the world market on the same basis as US producers. The film industry never enjoyed this situation, the distribution and exhibition sector of the film trade in the UK had capacity to fill beyond that capable of being filled by the British production industry. The expansion of television's distribution capacity by DBS and cable currently advocated by Mrs Thatcher's government is likely to reduce the British TV production industry, even protected by quota (and the Cable White Paper, 1983, prefers rather to take into account the proportion of British material intended by franchisees for transmission in judging competing applications for franchises than to continue with an explicit quota. There are, I think, good grounds for scepticism as to whether such 'intentions' are likely to prove enduring), to the condition of the film production industry. But to a government orientated to the market as a better guarantee of the public interest than regulation 'intentions' are likely to prove more than sufficient.

The market and the rôle of the state

British government policy for the information society has been governed by two contradictory principles, that of promoting the rôle of the market and that of foregrounding the rôle of the state in an attempt to create the concentration of resources necessary for innovation and development. But though the rôle of government remains an active one (e.g. in funding the Alvey program of computer development with £200 million), it is the ideology of the market that reigns supreme—the ideology of public service manifested through public sector institutions such as the BBC and British Telecom, with their commitment to universal service and constant pricing through cross-subsidy and through the regulation of commercial broadcasting has been rejected (see Garnham, 1983). The assumption is overwhelmingly that the public interest is, *necessarily*, best served by the market: 'Government policy is one of introducing and promoting competition so that both industry and the consumer can benefit' (HMSO, 1983: 69). British Telecom's network monopoly has been ended with the licensing of the Mercury telecommunications system, competition in supply of terminals, radiotelephony, value added services has been introduced and the government currently has a bill for the privatization of British Telecom before parliament. But of the range of measures and projects that are currently being promoted it is cable to which the government is most firmly committed and which has caught the imagination of the public. The entire stock, 2000 copies, of the Stationary Office's holding of the cable White Paper, *The Development of Cable Systems and Services*, was sold out by 10:00 a.m. on the day following the announcement of the publication to Parliament. Whilst the White Paper (HMSO, 1983) on cable development was jointly produced by the Home Office (generally thought to favour paternalism, control and public service) and the Department of Industry (the market, de-regulation and competition), and contains ritual obeisances to the sanctified principles of protecting the public interest through administrative measures the dominant motif is that of the market:

In the Government's view cable has the potential for increasing the range of good quality services available to the public, and this will best be encouraged by giving the consumer the opportunity to determine what he is willing to buy (HMSO, 1983: 56).

The week of the cable White Paper also saw the publication in *The Times* (26 April 1983, p. 12) of an article by Howard Davies, a recently retired Treasury Civil Servant, advocating 'dismemberment or even abolition of the BBC', the allocation of radio frequencies by auction and predicting that, should the Thatcher govern-ment be returned to power following the 1983 election, a 'radical reappraisal of public service broadcasting' will ensue. It is clear that the dominant (though by no means the only) thread in government thinking is the assumption that market-determined allocations are necessarily superior to other forms of allocation in directing resources and in achieving an equitable distribution of benefits. Other commentators do not share this optimism. Melody (1980) points out that 'transaction and enforcement costs as well as loss of spectrum use would far exceed any claimed allocation efficiency benefits flowing from the introduction of market principles into spectrum allocation' and whilst there is undoubtedly an attractive note struck in Davies' contention, of British broadcasting, that 'the principal beneficiaries . . . are as with any monopoly its employees', he does not consider the introduction into the BBC of an elected control structure accountable to the public as an alternative to the beneficient hand of the market in checking the luxuries enjoyed at viewers and listeners expense (whether the BBC staffs' realization of pet artistic projects or in more material sources of gratification). Nor, perhaps it is needless to say, are the benefits enjoyed by the holders of power in non-monopoly private enterprises considered by Mr Davies. And the 'creaking expensive and out of touch with its taxpayer-viewers' system deplored by Davies succeeds in delivering product to consumers at a cost of 1.5 to 2 pence per viewing hour per viewer (Ehrenberg and Barwise, 1982). Admittedly this calculation is performed on the basis that spectrum resources are costed at zero, but even at the level of costs of £6.50 to £9.95 per month charged by the Pay TV operators operating *existing* cable systems, ten to fifteen viewer hours per day are required for each cable subscription to deliver comparable cost/benefits to those of broadcast television. Many more viewer hours per day will be required for cable systems requiring new infrastructure and entailing consequentially higher subscription fees from consumers to deliver the cost/benefit relationship of existing broadcast TV.

Winners and losers: hardware and software

The Cable White Paper (HMSO, 1983) though makes clear, as have previous government statements and reports, that the unquantifiable benefits of taming the BBC and introducing the market principle aside, the major rôle of pay television delivered by broadband cable is to act as a locomotive for the information society. The proposed cable Authority is, for example, charged with 'responsibility to promote interactive services' (p. 24), 'wideband cable systems', it is argued, 'offer the opportunity for non-entertainment services to be made available to subscribers at marginal price levels since the basic system and infrastructure costs will have been absorbed by the entertainment services' (p. 15). There is, I believe, considerable reason to be sceptical of this scenario, there is no firm evidence that a market for cable television exists that is sufficiently large to amortize the capital costs of the infrastructure. Costs of cabling could be reduced under a number of scenarios that range from using British Telecom ducts and ceding it a *de facto* monopoly in hardware provision to exploiting (as Rothschild's bank did with its acquisition of the assets, holes in the ground, of the London Hydraulic Company) the sewers, disused tramway ducts or any of the underused or discarded existing holes in the ground. Given a cable system in place then the problem becomes one of securing subscriptions. The experience of the thirteen areas experimentally licensed for Pay TV has been very varied but not overall encouraging. Of 300,000 homes passed by cable only 19,000 subscribed to the pay services. The successful penetration of cable in Belgium (64.1%), Canada (57%), and the Netherlands (55%) (Shaw, 1981), has been due to the low quality of broadcast television in those countries *relative* to that available in neighbouring countries broadcasting in a comprehensible language. Thus cable has enabled Dutch subscribers to consume West German television funded by a domestic market more than four times as large as the Netherlands as has Canadian cable enabled Canadians to consume US television funded by the US domestic market larger by a factor of ten than the Canadian market. (Why one wonders given an extensive cable infrastructure in these countries all at least as technically advanced as the UK and all more prosperous has not the cornucopia of interactive services and the transition to the post-industrial society eventuated there?). The Pay cable experience in the USA is most pertinent to the situation in the UK. And here there is disagreement about the benefits in TV programming quality brought by cable. Davies asserts that:

cable has already revolutionized television in large areas of the US. And as the IEA authors (C. G. Veljanovski and W. D. Bishop in 'Choice by Cable', Institute of Economic Affairs, London RC) point out, the choice available to viewers in Manhattan in quality and variety makes a nonsense of the traditional 'quality' argument for the BBC (Davies, *ibid*).

Winston argues the reverse—his argument is not such as to be represented in a single quotation though the title of his article 'Unusual rubbish' encapsulates his view of Manhattan cable programming. Quality is a problematic—though vital— criterion, but Winston establishes a case to answer; a challenge yet to be taken up by cable advocates. He states:

There are for all intents and purposes only four broadcast television networks in the United States. . . . Within any one of them, I regarded it as an achievement to be able to distinguish commercials from programmes, so dense and complex in the presentational style. Final programme credits are regularly augmented by voice over promotions for coming shows . . . so fast and furious is the pace of this electronic juggernaut that programme junctions simply get overridden and lost in the rush. This accepted and amazing cacophony is a base element in creating the false notion of the possibility of a television of abundance (Winston, 1982: 156).

and

In any given month those services (i.e. Manhattan movie channel pay-cable RC) offer around fifty-one per cent identical product—over six months they played 'Rocky II' 44 times, 'The Muppet Movie' 37 times . . . 'And Justice for All' 30 times, 'Close Encounters' 41 times and 'Superman' 53 times (Winston, 1982: 157).

Melvin Goldberg (a Vice-President of the broadcaster ABC and therefore perhaps a partisan witness) states that 12·6 million households in the US (i.e. approx. 17%) subscribe to pay cable, and that of homes receiving 20 or more channels only 8·1 channels were viewed (a view is registered if a channel is viewed for a minimum of 10 minutes per month) (Goldberg, 1982). Cable in the USA has experienced at least one false dawn in which Teleprompter (one of the two franchises for Manhattan) suffered severe financial setbacks in the early nineteen seventies and to survive surrendered expensive franchises granted elsewhere than Manhattan.

The Financial Times of 6 July 1982 reports losses of between $10 million and $15 million for Getty Oils' sports network (ESPN), the news service of Ted Turner is in financial trouble losing in 1981 $13.4 million on sales of $95 million. CBS has closed its arts/cultural channel. The sole major success in the programmers serving US pay cable is that of Home Box Office which reaching 8 million subscribers (i.e. about 12% of US households) generated $75 million profit on a $315 million turnover (*Financial Times* 6 July 1982, p. 20). But HBO was charging a premium of $9 per month for its service in addition to a basic cable charge of say $10 per month (Cohen, 1981). The UK equivalent would be perhaps £12 per month—higher by perhaps 20%–40% than the fee charged in the experimental British pay TV operations which have themselves had an indifferent success. Given the differences in the broadcasting orders of the UK, the USA and the extensively cabled countries there seems room for substantial doubt as to the likely success of cable TV in the UK.

The uptake in the USA for interactive services delivered by broadband cable is put by Winston (Winston, 1982) at 0·.001% of cable homes. All the services currently canvassed by cable advocates can, with the exception of high speed bulk data transfer, be performed over the narrowband telephone system, on which there is (at the level of the local loop which is the level at which cable is being promoted) growing (with digitalization, improvements in switching, etc.) surplus capacity. Even in the wildest fantasies of Daniel Bell and Kenneth Baker there can surely be limited demand by domestic consumers for high speed bulk data transfer and one needs look no further than the experience of AT&T with Picturephone to develop some scepticism about demand for picture telephony. The evidence is that the 64 kilobit/second infrastructure of the British Telecommunication system is adequate for all foreseeable 'need pulled' services—where demand develops for increased transmission capacity it is at the level of trunk routes where concentration may be performed, *ad hoc* increases in capacity delivered whether by cable, terrestrial microwave or satellite. In any case with the establishment of the Mercury network a massive increase in trunk capacity in Britain is about to be implemented. It seems likely that cabling of Britain, if undertaken, and there are signs that few investors will be found (see *The Sunday Times*, 1 May 1983, p. 63, and *The Financial Times*, 28 April 1983, p. 20), will be an investment in an unnecessary duplicated, unplanned communication infrastructure replete with diseconomies of scale as was the excess railway capacity constructed in the railway mania of the nineteenth century. There seems no reason to dissent from the conclusions of the West German Commission for the Development of the Telecommunications System (KtK, 1976: 194) that:

There was no urgent and acute additional demand for an increased number of television programmes. The demand for picture telephony is also low; the costs to meet this demand would be high. On the other hand, the (narrowband) telecommunications network, that is the telephone network in particular, provides an infrastructure whose qualitative possibilities are by far not as yet exploited to the maximum.

There is growing evidence that cable in the UK is an unattractive investment. DeLoitte, Haskins and Sells (one of the consultants and analysts most favourably inclined towards cable) predict fairly modest returns for cable operations and stress that financial success hangs on two factors: The availability of existing ducts and the reduction of rental fees for feature films by the MPEA (Motion Picture Exporters Association of America). For Luton and Dunstable (a prosperous concentrated settlement north of London with excellent road, rail and air communications) a post tax rate return of 6–7% for the first franchise period is predicted with a pre-tax rate of return (i.e. for corporations with losses to set against cable earnings) of 12–14% (*The Financial Times*, 28 February 1983, p. 4). Pre-tax redemption yields on British government stocks in excess of 11% can currently be achieved; with that return available on very low risk readily marketable investments cable, offering a 3% maximum additional return, looks very speculative.

Even assuming that the half of the UK that generous estimates calculate might be cabled is cabled benefits to the national economy look very marginal. The Greater London Council Economic Policy Group (GLC, 1982) calculate (in an extensive report covering other impacts than employment) an employment gain in the UK by 1990 of 23,000 jobs but a loss of 25,000 jobs in other sectors notably in software production. The consultants CSP, in a report for British Telecom (CSP, 1982), an employment gain of 13,750 jobs by 1990 assuming no job loss in software production and an employment growth of 9,000 jobs in the telecommunications/information technology industry by 1990 given a 'high growth investment scenario: accompanied by a growing negative UK balance of trade in this sector of £318 million in 1990'.

Pessimism about technological change and cultural decline are, of course, enduring British tropes. Lord Reith's, in retrospect, hysterical Jeremiad against the introduction of commercial television, only continued the long and mistaken tradition of inveighing against 'illth' and innovations in cultural forms tracked, *inter alia*, by Ruskin, Arnold, Eliot and Leavis. But the banality of the prose of Reith's epigone Lord Thompson (Chairman of the IBA), and the retrospective knowledge that Matthew Arnold disparaged the novel and exalted poetry as the

Crown of Literature, when Dickens, George Eliot and Mrs Gaskell were writing and that commercial television in spite of Reith's predictions has given us 'Strangers', 'Sweeney', 'Out', 'Harry's Game', 'Bill Brand' does not necessarily mean that cultural pessimism is misplaced in the current instance. Or that concern for the nature of programming is the prerogative only of the middle class, who, pace Davies (1983), consume at the expense of the poor 'the unconstrained artistic endeavours of BBC drama producers which largely benefit the middle classes'.

The experience of Canada (see Collins, 1982) has demonstrated the problems for cultural sovereignty, for the quality of mass culture, and for the domestic software production industry of expansion of distribution capacity to a level beyond that which a flow of programming from domestic producers can fill. More does not necessarily mean worse—the fortuitously contrived régime for ITV in the UK shows that—but it may. When one considers that cable has been successful only in those markets where superior television is available in a comprehensible language from a neighbouring country, or where the quality (of transmission, interruption by advertisements and of programming) of television is such as to dispose audiences to subscribe to cable to get a decent signal, ad free programs and a greater variety of rubbish, than one has to see a certain Machiavellian logic to the scenario hinted at by Davies. If cable needs bad broadcast television to be successful then broadcast television in Britain will have to be worsened.

Whether Mrs Thatcher and Mr Baker have 'The Prince' for bedside reading is not known but they, as ruling princes in the UK, have amply demonstrated their ability to rule by fear. The possibility of a cable demarche, however risky a new enterprise for the prince and princess to introduce, should not be ignored, particularly since the CDU government in West Germany is following the same line of march. The government's commitment to cable and satellite television and its communication policies generally draws on two of its most potent ideological reflexes; to technology and to the market. When technology offers the possibility of the introduction of a market rather than an administered public service régime than its seductions are too powerful to resist. But given the costs of entry to the new information technologies, the problematic risk/reward relationships and increasing resistance to an economic and political rationale that seeks to eliminate the category public good from policy discourse paradoxically government will have to dangle larger and larger carrots in front of the donkeys in order to get them to market. The downside risks of impact on the software industries, overinvestment in infrastructure capacity, and high level of public satisfaction with existing services may yet mean that there are too few donkeys drawn by the carrots to make a market. The whip has been applied to British Telecom; it may be that other public sector institutions animated in however traduced and ossified a fashion by public service goals will next feel it across their backs.

Davies is probably right; the BBC and IBA are next. But application of whip or carrot will not resolve the central contradiction in the government's position—its commitment to a market régime, and competition within the boundaries of the UK for industries to which economies of scale apply and which operate in an environment of fierce international competition. Deregulation may have been good for the United States; it is too soon to judge the life expectancy of the Baby Bells (each of which is about the size of British Telecom, itself enormous in the UK industrial landscape), but what was good in the United States for the United States may turn out in Britain to be similarly good for the United States.

There will be 'winners' as well as 'losers' in the UK, but government's legitimacy rests on its ability to represent general and collective interest not sectional and particular interests. The government of Mrs Thatcher judges that the general interest (or public interest though that term is anathema to it) is best served by a rapid move to a market system of allocations with government action directed towards the removal of regulation and selective state support for elite companies that may be trained and hardened for international competition. In the long-term the market system may be a superior system for allocating and generating resources and many spots on the British industrial landscape evidence the debilitating effects of protection from competition. (The telecommunications equipment manufacturing industry is perhaps the prime example.)

But competitors do not enter the marketplace equally well fitted for competition nor are the benefits of market allocations distributed either equally or equitably. It is one thing for a government elected by and disposing of its power within a nation-state to engineer a reconstruction of market forces. Winners and losers remain within those national boundaries. In international competition, even granting the proposition of market theorists that the market is the least worst system of allocation, the winners may be outside the boundaries of the nation-state and the losers within it.

Nor is it necessarily the case that the 'winners' in the international marketplace are those made lean and fit by exposure to competition at home. L. M. Ericsson has used the base of its cosy relationship with the Swedish PTT to become a major force in the world telecommunications equipment market; Plessey favoured similarly in British Telecom's procurement, is being sued by Rolm for theft of intellectual property. Competition among manufacturers of Prestel terminals has had the effect of raising the unit cost of a terminal above that that would have obtained with a monopoly supplier and has slowed the penetration of interactive videotex in the UK and reduced potential revenues for the information providers and British Telecom.

UK Government policy then is directed towards hastening the birth of the Information Society in the UK. But its analysis that pay television delivered through the establishment of a broad band cable network (though even the most optimistic advocates of cable concede that 50% of the UK will remain uncabled), will act as a locomotive drawing prosperity and a raft of information services in its wake seems extremely unlikely. However, expansion of UK television distribution capacity, a policy aimed at stimulating hardware industries important sections of which are of questionable international competitiveness, (The head of British Telecom's research laboratories at Martlesham—the modest but capable UK equivalent of Bell Labs—Mr May, recently observed that after a working life attempting successful collaboration with the British Telecommunication equipment manufacturing industry he welcomed the aspect of Conservative government telecoms policy that would permit British Telecom to buy reliable foreign manufactured equipment in the future), is likely to adversely impact on the British software industry. Is there any reason to doubt that the consistent success of the British television programme production industry has been conditional on its protection by quota and restriction of distribution capacity from the dumping of US programming? The British film production industry has been reduced to a marginal viability in circumstances similar to those that current government policy will reproduce for the television production industry.

In 1958 Ealing Film Studios closed for film production and has since been used for production by the BBC. The commemorative plaque marking the demise of Ealing Films reads: 'Here during a quarter of a century were made many films projecting Britain and the British character.' Current government policy will leave the BBC few options but to erect a similar memorial.

The fruits of the UK government's policies, questions of quality, cultural sovereignty and public good aside, are likely to be those of import penetration, job losses, weakening of the software industries in spite of the large sums of public money devoted to inducing the birth of the information society in the UK. The British competitor in the international lemming race towards the information society may yet best serve the public interest by falling at the first fence.

Bibliography

BELL, D. (1976). *The Coming of the Post Industrial Society*, Harmondsworth, Peregrine

CHAPMAN, G. (1981). *International Television Flow in West Europe*, InterNational Institute of Communication Conference Report

COHEN, F. (1981). The US cable explosion. Home Box Office and Others, *InterMedia*, November

COLLINS, R. (1982). *Lessons for the Old Countries. Broadcasting and National Culture in Canada*, Canada House Lecture, London, Canadian High Commission

CSP (1982). *Telecommunications and the Economy*, London

COULSON-THOMAS C. (1981). *The British Film Production Industry and Government Support*. MA thesis, Polytechnic of Central London

EHRENBERG, A. and BARWISE, T. (1982). *How much does U.K. Television Cost?*, London Business School

GARNHAM, N. (1983). Public service versus the Market, *Screen* vol. 24, no. 1, January–February

GLC (1982). *Cabling in London*, Report of Economic Policy Group, London

GOLDBERG, M. (1982). Will the US networks survive the 1980s?, *InterMedia*, November

GOVERNMENT OF CANADA (1983). *Towards a New National Broadcasting Policy*, Department of Communications, Government of Canada

HEAD, S. (1976). *Broadcasting in America*, Boston, Houghton Mifflin

HMSO (1983), *The Development of Cable Systems and Services*, London, Cmnd 8866

HOSKINS, C. and MCFADYEN, S. (1982). *Market Structure and Television Programming Performance in Canada and the UK. A Comparative Study*. Canadian Public Policy, Summer

ITAP (1982). *Cable Systems*. A report by the Information Technology Advisory Panel, London, HMSO

KtK (1976). Commission for the Development of the Telecommunications System, *Telecommunications Report*, Bonn, Federal Ministry of Posts and Telecommunications

KUMAR, K. (1978). *Prophecy and Progress*, Harmondsworth, Penguin

MELODY, W. (1979). Are satellites the pyramids of the 20th Century?, *In Search*, vol. VI, no. 2, Ottawa

MELODY, W. (1980). Radio spectrum allocation: role of the market, *American Economic Review*, vol. 70, no. 2, March

MELODY, W. (1982). *Direct Broadcast Satellites. The Canadian Experience*. Paper at symposium 'Satellite Communication: National Media Systems and International Communications Policies', Hans Bredow Institute, University of Hamburg, December

NORA, S. and MINC, A. (1980). *The Computerization of Society*, Cambridge, MIT Press

PEP (1952), *The British Film Industry. Political and Economic Planning*, London

PORTER, V. (1979). Film policy for the 80s, *Sight and Sound*, Autumn

SHAW, J. (1981). ITV must respond to satellite opportunities, *InterMedia*, July

WALL, S. (1977). The U.K.: an information economy?, British Telecom mimeo

WINSTON, B. (1982). Unusual rubbish, *Sight and Sound*, Summer

WORDLEY, R. (1983). Letter to *The Times*, 22 March 1983

The impact of advertising on the British mass media

JAMES CURRAN[*]

Introduction

Senior officials at the Independent Broadcasting Authority are adamant that advertising has no effect on commercial television. 'If the suggestion is' writes Ian Haldane, the head of the IBA research department, 'that advertising has some "impact" or influence on ITV programmes, this is not so: the two are absolutely separate as laid down in the IBA Act under which we broadcast, and neither has any influence on the other.'[1] Even the suggestion that the policy of commercial broadcasting companies is influenced, in some way, by advertisers' requirements, provokes sharp denials. 'The programme controllers (of the ITV companies) are more Reithian than the BBC,' declares Stephen Murphy, a TV officer at the IBA with a distinguished record as a BBC producer, '. . . Advertising pressure is simply not transferred through.'[2]

Royal Commissions on the Press are almost equally dismissive about the effect of advertising on the Press. The first Commission concluded that attempts by advertisers to influence editorial policy 'appear to be infrequent and unsuccessful' (RCP, 1949: 143). Similar conclusions were reached by its two successors, neither of which found substantiated evidence that advertisers had ever significantly influenced editorial policy (RCP, 1962: 86–87; 1977: 104–105).

Indeed, the whole question of advertising influence on the media is authoritatively judged to be closed since such marginal influence, as may exist, cannot be adequately measured. 'No Royal Commission can expect to learn,' argued the last Commission, 'what happens from those directly concerned, for it would not be in their interest to speak about the success of advertisers in exerting pressures . . .' (RCP, 1977: 105). 'In its nature', opined its predecessor, 'the subject is one in which one has to rely largely on impression' (RCP, 1962: 86). The head of the IBA research department was even more forthright: this research study, he warned, was likely to be 'sadly lacking in substantial material, even were such material available'.[3]

Such intimidating scepticism, combined with consistent denials of significant advertising influence, would seem to suggest that further enquiry is pointless. Nevertheless, there are grounds for wondering whether the verdict of successive Royal Commissions on the Press and of experienced officials at the IBA is

* School of Communication, Polytechnic of Central London.
[1] Letter to the author, 30 August 1980.
[2] Interview with Stephen Murphy, 22 September 1980.
[3] Letter to the author, 30 August 1980.

correct.[4] Their conclusions are largely based on a rather narrow definition of advertising influence in terms of overt attempts by advertisers to influence media content to their advantage by withholding or giving advertising favours.[5] This reflects the way in which the influence of advertising is often presented by critics from the Left. Thus, Sheridan and Gardiner (1979: 121–122) have recently argued, for instance, that the editorial policy of the press is shaped and moulded by a combination of 'subtle and crude financial pressure' from advertisers, exemplified by some advertisers' boycott of *The Guardian* during the Suez Crisis. In a similar vein, the Glasgow University Media Group (1976: 71) alleged, to the fury and outrage of many in the IBA and elsewhere, that Independent Television News not infrequently suppresses news stories in response to, or in anticipation of, pressure from advertisers.[6]

It is worth investigating, however, alternative ways in which advertisers may influence the mass media other than by overt attempts to influence its content. In particular, attention needs to be given to ways in which advertising as a concealed subsidy system has shaped the mass media; and to ways in which the media have adapted to the marketing needs of advertisers in order to compete for these subsidies.

The nature of these influences has been obscured by the conventional representation of advertisers as having interests identical with those of audiences (e.g. Advertising Association, 1975). Since advertisers want to reach the public in order to sell their products, it is argued, they naturally support the media which are popular with the public. Advertisers are thus portrayed as neutral and passive intermediaries who allocate their media budgets according to the likes and dislikes of media consumers and who consequently *exercise no independent influence of their own*. As John Whale puts it, 'advertising doubles the price on each reader's head . . . but there is not much a newspaperman can do to differentiate a double from a single dose of zeal to attract new readers' (Whale, 1979: 93).

This portrayal of advertisers is based on a misleading representation of media planning and marketing practice. Advertisers rarely think of the media exclusively as a distribution system for advertisements: they also generally make judgements about the effectiveness of different media as agencies of persuasion. They are not 'neutral' in their desire to reach all members of the public: they usually wish to reach—and will pay more to reach—particular segments of the market rather than others. They are not 'passive' and unchanging in the criteria they adopt for media buying: on the contrary, changes in marketing perspectives, research procedures and data inputs have produced changes in how advertisers have spent this money with important long-term consequences for the development of the media. Finally, advertisers are not a uniform group with a common approach and shared objectives: indeed, changes within the economy have resulted in a significant shift in the pattern of advertising expenditure, reflecting the emergence of new advertisers and the decline of others, which have had major repercussions on the media system as a whole.

---

[4] Not least because not all IBA officials I spoke to were of the same mind: some of the younger executives, in particular, were more inclined to perceive advertising as an influence on broadcasting output.

[5] This was not true of the considered comments of S. Murphy of the IBA nor of the last Royal Commission on the Press, although the Commission only seriously addressed itself in its report to a conspiracy model of advertising influence.

[6] The page numbering in the reference refers to the proof copy of *Bad News*. Allegations of direct advertising influence (which were almost certainly untrue) were withdrawn following the threat of a libel action.

What this exploratory study will seek to do, therefore, is to examine ways in which the allocation of advertising, and media competition for this allocation, has influenced the character of the British mass media, and consider how this allocation has been influenced, in turn, by economic and social structures external to the media. To see the impact of advertising only in terms of overt attempts by individual advertisers to influence media content is, it will be argued, to misconceive both the true nature and the significance of advertising influence: advertising patronage is essentially an impersonal means by which Britain's mass media are fashioned according to the marketing needs of the economic system and the class inequalities of power, influence and consumption within British society.

Advertising allocation between media

Advertisers make a larger contribution to the finances of the British mass media than audiences. Commercial broadcasting derives nearly all of its revenue from advertising while newspapers and magazines both derive over half their revenue from advertisements (see Table 1).

Table 1. *Proportion of press revenue derived from advertising in 1979* [*]

National dailies	National Sundays	Regional daily and Sunday papers	Local weeklies	Total newspapers	Trade, technical and professional journals	Other periodicals	Total periodicals
44%	44%	66%	85%	59%	64%	47%	54%

[*] Derived from Department of Industry (1979).

Advertising does not constitute a straight media subsidy. Receipts from advertisers must be set against the costs involved in securing and producing advertisements, and these sometimes represent, as we shall see, a very large proportion of advertising revenue. Generally speaking, though, advertising generates a surplus after relevant costs have been deducted, so that advertising allocations crucially affect the financial resources available to competing media sectors as well as to competing companies within each media sector.

Advertising allocations between media are not closely tied to the pattern of media consumption. Newspapers and magazines absorb much less time, on average, than commercial TV and radio. Yet the press obtains almost three times as much advertising as commercial broadcasting (see Table 2). The continuing ascendancy of the press as an advertising medium (largely due to government restrictions on the development of commercial broadcasting) has helped it to fend off the challenge of TV. During the period of rapid growth of TV ownership during the 50s and early 60s, the press was able to charge very low cover prices and spend very much more heavily on editorial outlay as a result of the rising advertising income it obtained. This contributed, in turn, to its remarkable resilience. The proportion of the adult population reading newspapers and magazines remained stable during the period of TV's rise, while newspaper consumption (when measured adequately) actually increased (Curran, 1970).[7] There is also no close correspondence between the pattern of demand and the amount of advertising expenditure on different sectors of the press. Although the circulation of the regional press was only about two-thirds that of the national press,[8] the regional papers still obtained £246 million more advertising than national papers in 1979. The success of the regional press in attracting advertising has helped to make it more profitable than Fleet Street.

Table 2. *Media advertising expenditure (£m) in 1979* [*]

National newspapers	Regional newspapers	Magazines and periodicals	Trade and technical	Total press	TV	Cinema	Radio
347	593	180	203	1496	471	17	52

[*] Source: Advertising Association (1980: 45).

The trade, technical and professional press also has a very much smaller circulation than that of the rest of the magazine press,[9] but nonetheless still attracts more advertising (see Table 2). This high level of support has helped to sustain a large number of specialist titles many of which have only small sales.

Changes in advertising allocations

Important shifts in the pattern of media advertising expenditure have taken place during the last 40 years, which have altered the character of the media. Before considering these, it is necessary to refer, however, to government economic controls which temporarily distorted advertising trends. Newsprint rationing was maintained on a statutory basis between 1940 and 1956, and on a voluntary basis until 1959. During the height of its severity, newsprint rationing caused national newspapers to shrink to less than a quarter of their pre-war size, and severely curtailed advertising in national newspapers, (Gerald, 1956). Imposed with less severity on the regional press, rationing caused advertising to be redistributed to the provinces (Henry, 1979). And because magazines were exempted from economic controls before newspapers, there was a temporary boom in magazine advertising in the early 1950s (Silverman, 1954). These distortions need to be distinguished from long-term changes.

The most important of these long-term changes have been the decline of traditional mass market advertising media and the linked rise of television; the shift of

[7] Adjusting to declining advertising profits during the 70s, national newspapers sharply increased retail prices appreciably more than the rate of inflation, thereby losing the large price differential they had compared with papers in many Western countries (documented, for instance, by the Royal Commission on the Press (1962) Appendix 9). It is perhaps no coincidence that the audience for newspapers began to decline as a proportion of the adult population during the 1970s.

[8] In 1976, its aggregate circulation was 65% of that of the national press (calculated from RCP, 1977, Annex 3, TI).

[9] The aggregate circulation of the trade, technical and professional press is unknown, but for an indication of its smallness by comparison with the rest of the periodical press, see Coopers and Lybrand (1975: TI. 7).

advertising to the provinces; and the redistribution of advertising within the magazine sector in favour of specialist magazines (see Table 3).

Table 3. *Distribution of advertising expenditure between media* *

	1938 %	1948 %	1954 %	1960 %	1965 %	1970 %	1975 %	1979 %
National newspapers	25	14	17	20	20	20	17	16
Regional newspapers †	27	31	31	21	24	26	29	28
Magazines and periodicals	15	13	19	12	11	9	8	9
Trade and technical journals	12	16	13	10	9	10	9	10
Other publications ‡	2	1	1	1	1	2	2	3
Press production costs §	5	8	6	5	4	6	5	6
Total press	85	83	88	71	70	72	70	70
Television	—	—	—	22	24	23	24	22
Poster and transport	8	14	9	5	4	4	4	4
Cinema	3	4	3	2	1	1	1	1
Radio	3	—	1	—	1	—	1	2

* Sources: Kaldor and Silverman (1948), Silverman (1951), Advertising Association (1951, 1962, 1972, 1980), Critchley (n.d.). All forms of non-media promotional expenditure are excluded. All percentage figures have been rounded off to the nearest whole number.

† Including London evening newspapers.

‡ Directories, guide books, yellow pages, etc.

§ According to the Advertising Association's definition which does not include all relevant costs.

(a) *The contraction of the popular national press*

Commercial TV was established partly in response to political pressure by leading manufacturers, who wanted a new promotional weapon to add to their arsenal (Wilson, 1961). After a brief period, commercial TV became accepted in leading agency circles as the best promotional medium for cheap mass market commodities. Its combination of sound and movement ensured, according to the leading advertising textbook of the late 50s, that 'the selling message came over with a force never before experienced' (Hobson, 1959: 123). Its selling reputation was further enhanced by the introduction of colour transmission which in the words of a more recent textbook, makes TV 'the present day ultimate in communication-effectiveness' (Adams, 1979: 86).

The conviction that commercial TV is superior to the press in selling cheap, mass products, over the long term, has little adequate empirical evidence to support it.[10] The belief nevertheless became so prevalent that even many press representatives, who made their living from selling advertising space, came to accept it unquestioningly. As a Newspaper Proprietors' Association Working Party noted disconsolately

[10] For a critical review of the evidence see MacDonald (1974). There is, indeed, surprisingly little satisfactory evidence about the long-term effectiveness of advertising (Tunstall, 1964; Corkindale and Kennedy, 1975; Broadbent, 1979; among others). In any case, inter-media choices are often based upon intuitive judgements only justified afterwards with arguments about cost effectiveness (Fletcher, 1973: 55; Adams, 1977: 37). As Broadbent caustically observes, 'Many (agency) plans resemble the dinosaur: a pea-sized brain, followed by yard upon yard of analysis, fake justification and arithmetic' (Broadbent, 1979; 187).

in the mid-1960s: 'Press representatives interviewed openly admitted their acceptance of TV superiority, and stated that in many cases they did not think of selling against other media. They seem to view without hope, what they called a "TV product"' (NPA, 1966: 25).

Their pessimism was a response to the steady transfer of major accounts from the press to television. A large number of leading agencies told the second Press Commission that they had shifted business from newspapers and magazines to TV (Thompson, 1962: 127; London Press Exchange, 1962: 78; Masius and Ferguson, 1962: 95; Young and Rubicam, 1962: 137; among others). These reports were borne out by statistical evidence showing that commercial TV gained a dominant position in certain advertising markets, such as household cleaning products, toothpaste, food and drink, where the press had formerly enjoyed unchallenged supremacy (Benson, 1962: 11; London Press Exchange, 1962: 79; NPA, 1966: 47–48) and with evidence showing that many of the leading, often American-controlled agencies, had switched the bulk of the advertising they handled to commercial television by the mid-1960s (NPA, 1966: 12).

The popular press was only partly displaced, of course, by TV. Newspapers continued to be regarded by many advertisers as a superior medium to television for advertisements with a high information content. But the national newspaper press nonetheless failed to regain fully the market share of media advertising expenditure that it had enjoyed before the introduction of newsprint rationing. Its share in 1979, for instance, was down to 16% compared with 25% in 1938. This failure to recover fully from the imposition of government economic controls was due mainly to the rise of TV which acquired a 22% share of media advertising by 1979.

Notwithstanding this evidence, Harry Henry has argued in an influential essay[11] that TV did not divert advertising away from the press. By increasing 'the efficiency of the national distributive system', according to Henry, commercial TV created 'new resources from which to pay for it'. Indeed, 'an overwhelming part of the current level of expenditure on television', he claims, 'can be accounted for by the increase since 1954 in the proportion of the GNP which is directed to advertising' (Henry, 1971: 181).

The evidence cited by Professor Henry is misleading. The most relevant set of figures to consider is not total advertising expenditure but display advertising expenditure since commercial TV is a display medium which does not compete for classified advertising and financial notices.[12] While display advertising expenditure statistics are not available for 1954, they are for 1956, when commercial TV was still in its infancy and accounted for only 7% of total display advertising spending. The total increase of display advertising expenditure as a proportion of GNP between 1956 and 1979 accounted for less than *half* the amount spent on TV advertising in 1979.[13] The data thus scarcely support Henry's contention that commercial TV has been mainly self-financing from the additional advertising it generated.

---

[11] Such was the compelling force of Professor Henry's arguments that the last Press Commission felt unable to decide whether the press had lost advertising to television (RCP, 1977: 38).

[12] Nor does it compete, in the main, for trade and technical journal advertising. The inclusion of trade and technical journal advertising with display advertising does not materially alter, however, the argument that is being advanced.

[13] This was also true in 1968 when Henry first advanced his argument, and in 1971, when his essay was republished.

In any case, Henry's assumption that non-TV advertising should represent a constant proportion of some economic aggregate, like GNP, makes no allowance for changes in marketing and retail practices or for changes in relative prices. Indeed, the lifting of economic controls almost certainly increased the amount of media advertising by enabling advertisers to advertise freely in the press and rely less on 'below-the-line' promotion. This is strongly corroborated by the marked downturn in both press and media advertising as a proportion of GNP during the period of newsprint rationing, and its subsequent rise after economic controls had been lifted.[14]

While the emergence of TV may also have contributed to an increase in advertising expenditure as a proportion of GNP in the short term, it is by no means clear that this effect has been maintained. There has been, in fact, a small downward trend in display advertising as a percentage of GNP since the early 1960s, after allowance is made for cyclical variation (Advertising Association, 1980: T1). Indeed, there has also been a downward trend of manufacturers' consumer advertising (which constitutes the large part of TV advertising) as a percentage of consumer expenditure since the late sixties which suggests that there has been a relative decline of promotional expenditure or a positive shift towards non-media techniques of promotion by manufacturers (Advertising Association, 1980: T3).

The rise of commercial TV not only resulted in the press losing some advertising. Perhaps more important, it seriously depleted the value of the advertising that the press did obtain. Popular newspaper publishers responded to the growing threat posed by commercial TV as an advertising medium by keeping their advertising rates low. Their failure to increase rates in line with inflation resulted in a progressive erosion of advertising profit margins. The real surplus generated by advertising in the popular press declined from an estimated 30–40% in 1965 to zero or even a deficit in 1975[15] (see Table 4).

The rise of TV as a competitor for advertising did not have a uniformly injurious impact on the press. Quality newspapers within the national newspaper press were less seriously affected because their readers tended to be light ITV viewers. Less threatened by commercial TV, quality newspapers suffered a less serious erosion of advertising profit margins. They also benefited from a large increase in classified advertising.

However, the popular newspaper press slipped into a deepening economic crisis by the late 50s. The causes of this crisis are complex, and competition from TV was only one contributory factor.[16] The papers most vulnerable to this competition were those which neither offered better coverage of the mass market than TV nor offered coverage of differentiated markets that TV failed to provide. All the five popular papers that died in the wake of the introduction of commercial TV[17] fall into this

[14] Media advertising expenditure as a proportion of GNP fell from 1.18% in 1938 to below 1.0% between 1940 and 1954 and only exceeded the 1938 proportion in 1958.

[15] It is probably that some newspapers managements were not aware of the extent to which they had allowed advertising profit margins to be eroded since their pricing was generally geared to elasticity of demand rather than to costs. Intense competition between papers also depressed advertising rates. See Cleverley (1976).

[16] Circulations declined mainly due to falling readership duplication, which had been artificially inflated by government economic controls; advertising became more unequally distributed with the lifting of controls; and costs soared largely as a consequence of the non-price competitive strategies adopted by the market leaders. This led to a marked deterioration in the cost and revenue structure of the press, causing the weakest papers to close down. See, in particular RCP (1962) and Economist Intelligence Unit (1966).

[17] *Sunday Graphic* (1960), *Empire News* (1960), *News Chronicle* (1960), *Sunday Dispatch* (1961) and *Daily Herald* (1964).

category. They were all at the bottom of the popular circulation league table, yet did not have a particular appeal amongst young people or the middle class (National Readership Surveys, 1959, 1960, 1963–64).

Table 4. *Costs as a proportion of advertising revenue* [*]

	1960 %	1973 %	1975 %
National popular daily	60	85	100
National quality daily	40	55	65
National popular Sunday	65–70	95	115
National quality Sunday	40–45	60	70

[*] Derived from *Royal Commission on the Press Report* (1962: 66), and *Royal Commission on the Press Final Report* (1977: 39). All percentages are to the nearest 5% and are based upon the costs of newspaper advertisement departments, 10% of managerial expenditure and a proportion of production, depreciation, paper and ink, circulation and distribution costs, apportioned according to the average percentage of space which had been used for advertisements.

The subsequent erosion of advertising profit margins contributed to a further deterioration in the revenue position of the national press. Spending by national papers had been geared to a high level of advertising subsidy. The attrition of this subsidy contributed to a cumulative economic crisis, in which two national papers (the *Daily Sketch* and *Reynolds News*) closed down and a large part of the national press sustained heavy losses during downturns of the advertising cycle (National Board for Prices and Incomes, 1967, 1970; RCP, 1976, 1977). The depressed advertising market due to the deepening economic recession further compounded the difficulties of the national press. Manufacturers' consumer advertising at constant prices was lower in 1979 than it had been in 1969 (Advertising Association, 1980: T3).

(b) *Decline of the general magazine press*

The general magazine press's share of media advertising in 1979 was less than half that of 1954, and significantly below that of the pre-war years. Losing the artificial gains it had acquired during the early 50s, the magazine press suffered a further loss of revenue as a result of TV competition. The real surplus on magazine advertising has probably also declined. Magazine advertising rates increased even more slowly than newspaper rates during the period when national newspaper advertising profit margins were being seriously eroded (Advertising Association, 1980: T15).

However, the impact of TV on the magazine press was uneven. The publications that suffered most were general magazines which provided a broad, undifferentiated coverage of the market, comparable to that of commercial TV, yet lacked the specialized editorial content of the sort that generated linked advertising. Some of these publications—notably *Picture Post, Illustrated,* and *Everybody's,* which all closed in the late 50s—also lost readers to TV, though in some cases the rise of TV merely reinforced a downward spiral that had set in before the rapid growth of TV ownership.[18] Competition from TV probably also contributed to a loss of both sales and advertising by the general women's magazine press.[19]. This resulted in a marked contraction so that there were only four women's weeklies with a circulation of over half a million each in 1967 compared with seven in 1958.

Magazines that offered a differentiated segmentation of the market were much less affected by competition with TV for advertising. They provided an advertising service that TV could not match. They also benefited, as we shall see, from changes in advertising methods.

(c) *Decline of the cinema*

The cinema was a victim of television primarily in the sense that it lost its mass audience to the new medium. Cinema admissions fell from 1585 million in 1945 to 501 million in 1960, and 193 million in 1970 (Curran and Tunstall, 1973: 203). Its declining share of advertising was a direct consequence of its diminishing audience.

The decline of cinema advertising, even during the worst period, was nonetheless relatively modest.[20] Severe restrictions on cinema advertising had discouraged its use by advertisers during the period when it had a mass audience (Eley, 1932; Hobson, 1961). Paradoxically, the contraction of the cinema renewed its advertising utility by redefining its audience. The cinema now appeals primarily to the unmarried young—a group that cannot be readily picked out in isolation from other age groups through TV (Broadbent, 1979: Adams, 1979).

(d) *The shift to the regions*

Unlike the national press, the regional press has increased its share of media advertising during the last 40 years (see Table 2). This is largely because of the rapid gains made by the regional press during the 60s and 70s.

This reflects a change in the structure of advertising expenditure. The growth of home ownership, car ownership and job mobility helped to create a boom in classified advertising.[21] Consequently classified advertising almost doubled as a proportion of total media advertising between 1960 and 1979, rising from only 13 to 22% (Advertising Association, 1980: T5). This generated a large increase in the revenue of the regional press. Whereas classified advertising had accounted for only 22% of local weekly advertising revenue in 1935, it contributed 55% of advertising revenue by 1979 (Kaldor and Silverman, 1948: 35; Department of Industry 1980: Tl). The regional press also benefited from a rapid growth of retail advertising, generated largely as a consequence of the growth of chain ownership of stores and the growth of large retail outlets.

---

[18] The circulation of these magazines had been artificially boosted by the severe newsprint restrictions on newspapers. The easing of these controls contributed to a decline in their readership. The readership of *Picture Post* and *Everybody's* fell by 31 and 46% respectively between 1947 and 1954 (Hulton, 1947: T13; Hulton, 1954: T23). In contrast, the circulation of *Illustrated* only collapsed with the rapid extension of TV ownership. Between 1955 and 1958, its circulation fell by no less than 55% (Belson, 1959: 16).

[19] The causes of this contraction are nonetheless complex and are only partly to do with TV. See, in particular, White (1970, 1977).

[20] There was a 15% reduction in cinema advertising expenditure between 1956 and 1959 (Advertising Association, 1962: T30).

[21] In 1979, recruitment, property and job advertisements accounted for no less than 77% of classified advertising (Advertising Association, 1980: T13).

Regional papers were not unaffected by TV competition. Despite the improvement of their advertising promotion service, they probably lost some display advertising to commercial TV and more recently to commercial radio.[22] But this was more than offset by their gains in the classified market. While these were not sufficient to offset the strong pressures that have reduced competition and increased chain ownership of the regional press (Hartley, Gudgeon and Crafts, 1977), they have nonetheless contributed to its buoyancy. The local daily press is the only sector of the newspaper press not to have experienced a net contraction of titles between 1961 and 1976 (Curran, 1979: T5), largely because of the launch of new evening papers in expanding urban markets.

The established regional press is now seriously threatened, however, by the growth of free distribution sheets, whose total advertising in 1979 even exceeded that of local commercial radio (Advertising Association, 1979: T4 and T12). Advertising expenditure on free sheets has been so sustained, rising from an estimated £1 million to £53 million between 1968 and 1979, as to indicate a significant shift in the orientation of some advertisers to local media. Free distribution sheets generally have a higher penetration of local markets than their cover price rivals; the markets they cover are carefully tailored to the needs of local advertisers; and, due to their low (sometimes non-existent) editorial costs, they generally charge much lower advertising rates than conventional newspapers. The widespread belief that conventional papers command more authority and attention because they contain editorial matter and charge a price to consumers is the somewhat fragile bedrock on which the local weekly press (which derived 85% of its revenue from advertising in 1979) rests. If this belief continues to wane, the character of the local press will be radically altered.

(e) Growth of specialized media

Although trade and technical journals obtained less advertising than magazines and periodicals before the war, they obtained more advertising by the 1970s (see Table 3). Within the broad category of 'magazines and periodicals' there has almost certainly been a shift of advertising away from mass-market magazines to publications with more differentiated audiences.

These shifts partly reflect changes in public demand. They also reflect changes in advertisers' perspectives that encouraged increased use of more differentiated and specialized media. The post-war growth of market research and the growing marketing sophistication that accompanied its development gave rise to more precise definitions of the intended audiences for advertising campaigns. The new approach was based, as a leading pioneer succinctly put it, on 'thinking about the market rather than simply about the product'.[23] This tended to reduce the size of the audiences actively sought in advertising campaigns: vague generalizations like 'the mass market' were superseded by more narrowly defined 'target markets'.[24]

[22] Their share of *display* advertising expenditure declined from 14% in 1961 to 11% in 1979—a significant reduction on their 17% share in 1938. Among other things, the regional press probably lost some test market advertising to TV companies.

[23] Interview with David Wheeler, director of the Institute of Practitioners in Advertising, on 11 September 1980.

[24] The development of Guinness advertising during the last 40 years provides a particularly graphic illustration of this change. During the late 1930s, Guinness advertising was aimed in an indiscriminate, 'buckshot' fashion at the mass market with a remarkably broad and unselective spread of the major national newspapers, general and women's magazines, as well as leading local papers and a large number of poster sites (see the evidence of Arthur Guinness and Son Ltd., *Royal Commission on the Press 1947–1949*, vol. 5 (DE)). It was not until 1952 that

The development of multiple brand marketing by leading manufacturers, notably during the 1960s and 1970s, also produced a further fragmentation of the mass market, thereby encouraging the direction of advertising messages towards more differentiated groups.

The provision of systematic data about media audiences enabled the stress on target marketing to be translated into media schedules using fewer and sometimes more differentiated media. Readership research classifying audiences in terms primarily of demographic characteristics became available on a regular, syndicated basis from 1947 onwards, and eclipsed the use of crude 'popularity ratings' in the form of circulation data.[25] These data were supplemented by increasingly detailed information about the consumer behaviour of media audiences, particularly from the late 1960s onwards.[26] Information thus became available that enabled media planners to spend money more selectively on media that picked out the more narrowly defined target groups they sought to reach.

This pressure towards the use of more specialized media has been restrained by a number of countervailing influences. Mass advertising media, notably TV, are often judged to have more impact: they sometimes have a higher penetration of specialized markets than specialized media; some target groups are sufficiently large to constitute a very large proportion of even mass audiences; mass media can often charge relatively low advertising rates owing to their substantial economies of scale; and, above all, media audiences do not always conveniently fragment into the market groupings that advertisers want.

But these countervailing pressures have merely limited rather than prevented a transfer of resources to minority media. The development of target marketing at a time of growing advertising patronage has provided a positive inducement to publishers to launch new periodicals that pick out specialized or differentiated markets that advertisers want to reach. The very rapid growth of classified advertising has also encouraged new launches in sectors of the specialized press that attract substantial classified advertising.[27] And the rise of TV has encouraged publishers to think of new publishing ventures that can compete with TV as an advertising medium by delivering more differentiated markets to advertisers.

Publishers have consciously sought to diagnose and respond to advertisers' requirements before launching new publications. Audrey Slaughter, for example,

---

Guinness commissioned its first proper market research survey which established basic facts about the Guinness market (such as that more men than women drank Guinness, contrary to the belief of some Guinness executives), leading to a more selective use of advertising media (Wrigglesworth, 1980). By 1980, the principal target groups for Guinness advertising had been honed down to regular pub users (with the object of generating consumer pressure on public houses owned by rival brewers to stock Guinness) and home drinkers of Guinness (with the object of increasing frequency of purchase). Information about the current Guinness advertising strategy kindly provided by Terry Prue, account planner for the Guinness account at J. Walter Thompson.

[25] Hulton Readership Surveys (1947–56); National Readership Surveys (NRS) (1956–67); JICNARS (1968–80).

[26] Product media research was pioneered by Odhams during the 1930s. This pioneering trail was further developed by Odhams in the 1940s and 1950s with a series of special interest surveys, the National Attwood Consumer Panel from 1949, the extension of the Brand Barometer surveys in the early 1950s, a small but expanding 'special group' section in the Hulton, NRS and JICNARS surveys, the BMRB Consumer Survey from 1960, the extended Television Consumer Audit from 1968, and the AMPS surveys (1966–67). But it was not until the launch of a cheap syndicated service, the Target Group Index, in 1968, which cross-analyzed media exposure by consumption of a large range of products, services and even brands, that product media analysis became firmly established.

[27] Between 1960 and 1979, classified advertising increased from 13% to 27% of advertising expenditure on the trade and technical press (Advertising Association, 1980: T11).

interviewed senior advertising agency executives to find out what markets they would like to reach more efficiently, before launching her very successful *Over 21*. IPC undertook detailed research into what advertisers ought to want by examining market trends and produced the unsuccessful *Petticoat*, aimed at 15–19-year old girls with '£250 million a year of uncommitted spending money'. More recently, IPC examined the pattern of advertising spending on different publications and came up with *Women's World*, a publication oriented towards young ABC1's and designed to exploit the large advertising market for cosmetics, fragrances and youngish fashion successfully harvested by *Cosmopolitan* amongst other publications.

The change in advertisers' requirements has provided not only an incentive to launch, but also support for the maintenance of, more differentiated publications. Partly as a consequence of this, a significant change has taken place in the market structure of the periodical press. Between 1965 and 1975, only seven new consumer magazines were launched in the general women's market, compared with 34 new consumer magazines aimed at the women's home interest, women's fashion/beauty/cosmetics, young women and teenager markets (RCP Secretariat, 1977: 32). Within the general consumer field, there has also been a shift from mass market launches to publications aimed at specialized groups of consumers.

The trade and technical press has also grown at a much faster rate than the general consumer press. The second Royal Commission on the Press reported, for instance, that there was a 56% increase in the number of trade and technical publications between 1951 and 1962, compared with a 6% reduction in the number of general magazines and periodicals during the same period.[28] The secretariat of the Third Commission, adopting a narrower definition of trade and technical publications, reported an increase of 283 trade, technical and professional publications between 1966 and 1974, compared with a much smaller increase of 121 consumer publications during the same period (RCP Secretariat 1977: 31).[29]

Advertising allocation within media sectors: some consequences

The last Royal Commission on the Press recoiled from the thought of redistributing advertising according to public service criteria partly on the grounds that it would introduce political judgements in the free processes of the market (RCP, 1977: 117). It did not pause to consider whether free market processes also have political and cultural consequences. It merely assumed that free market allocation of advertising was neutral and consequently that it did not warrant careful investigation.[30] Whether the Commission's assumption is justified remains to be seen.

The Conservative bias of advertising: a reappraisal

The national newspaper press is predominantly conservative—very much more so than its readers, to judge from a comparison of newspapers' and readers' political

[28] Estimated from Table 6, Appendix 3 of the Royal Commission on the Press Report (1962). In absolute numbers this amounted to an increase of 675 trade and technical journals, although trade and technical publications would seem to have been broadly defined by the Commission to include professional publications, some of which received relatively little advertising.

[29] According to another narrower definition, there has been an 86% growth in the number of trade and technical journals between 1956 and 1976 (Lind, 1978: 196). An alternative source gives an estimated 72% growth between 1956 and 1979 (Anon, 1980: 21).

[30] In so far as the Commission was interested in the advertising process, it was largely in order to forecast future trends (see RCP, 1977: Appendix E).

affiliations (Seymour-Ure, 1977).[31] It also derives a substantial proportion of its revenue from advertisers. This has prompted some commentators to assume that the two things are connected: advertisers, it is reasoned, use their financial power to fashion the press according to their political prejudices (Steed, 1938; Labour Research Department, 1946; Orwell, 1970; Hoch, 1974).

It is undoubtedly the case that political bias on the part of advertisers helped to stifle the development of the radical press during the late nineteenth and early twentieth century when the national press evolved in its modern form (Curran, 1977). The subsequent growth of advertising also helped to perpetuate this historical legacy by forcing up press costs and making the launch and establishment of new papers more costly and difficult[32] (Curran and Seaton, 1981).

Nevertheless, the political bias of advertisers was only one factor contributing to the conservative domination of the press in the early twentieth century. In any case, important changes have taken place in the procedures adopted by advertisers in selecting advertising media, which has significantly reduced the influence of political bias on media appropriations (Curran, 1980).

Disparities still persist however in the advertising revenue per copy obtained by Conservative and Labour papers. For example, the net advertisement revenue of the generally Conservative *Sunday Times* was almost four times that of the Labour *Sunday Mirror* in 1975, despite the fact that it had less than half the *Sunday Mirror's* circulation (Curran, 1978: T7). These disparities do not arise from political prejudice but from the fact that, generally speaking, Conservative papers reach readers who have more money to spend, more influence over corporate spending, and watch less ITV than readers of Labour papers.[33]

The pattern of advertising expenditure has consequently enabled some Conservative papers to be economically viable with audiences much smaller than those of Labour papers.[34] The four quality dailies constitute half the national daily titles in Britain, yet they accounted for only 15% of national daily circulation in 1980.[35] Although they charged high cover prices, they still derived over half their revenue from advertising. Mostly Conservative in their politics, they have continued in publication largely because of the high advertising receipts they have obtained as a result of being read by a socially select readership. A similar pattern has developed in the national Sunday press, where three out of seven papers, heavily endowed with advertising, accounted for only 18% of national Sunday circulation in 1980. They have survived and grown only with the aid of advertising bounty.[36] The obverse to this is that Labour papers have died with circulations far larger than those of some Conservative papers. In 1964, for instance, the Labour *Daily Herald*

[31] Seymour-Ure's valuable analysis is confined to the national daily press. The political imbalance is less marked in the case of national Sunday papers.

[32] Since 1918, only three new national papers have been successfully established and only one of these (currently accounting for at most 0.2% of national daily circulation) is on the left. Such adaptation as there has been to the increased strength of the left in the country, has been through changes of ownership and editorial staffing rather than through the launch of new papers.

[33] There are, of course, exceptions such as the Conservative *Sun* which has a below-average (among national dailies) advertising revenue per copy. But it is not a typical Conservative paper since more of its readers voted Labour than Conservative in the last three General Elections.

[34] This remains true despite the erosion of advertising profit margins because Conservative papers generally have suffered less from this erosion than Labour papers.

[35] The *Morning Star* has been excluded since it does not have an audited circulation.

[36] The papers concerned are the *Times, Financial Times, Guardian, Sunday Times, Sunday Telegraph* and *Observer.* Four of these six papers are generally aligned with the Conservative Party. In addition to a high level of advertising support, some of them have also obtained large subsidies from multinational conglomerates.

was forced to close with a readership well over that of *The Times and The Financial Times* combined (National Readership Survey, 1964: T1A).

The political imbalance of the press thus partly reflects class inequalities within society which have generated unequal advertising subsidies between Labour and Conservative papers. This has helped to reinforce Conservative domination of the national press by making it easier for Conservative papers to survive and flourish.

Inequalities of cultural provision

Women's magazines tend to be oriented towards the middle class. This is a consequence of the much higher advertising subsidies that middle-class women readers generate by comparison with working-class readers. Bird (1978) found, for instance, that the correlation between the advertisement revenue of the five big women's weeklies and the size of their ABC1 (i.e. upper middle, middle and lower middle class) readerships was 0.997, very much higher than that between circulation and advertising revenue which was only 0.782. A comparison between individual titles futher underlines the enormous difference in the advertising value of different readers. The predominantly working-class *Women's Weekly* obtained in 1976 only 5p per copy in advertising revenue, compared with the 92p per copy obtained by the up-market *Harpers and Queen*. Within the 'home interest' sector, *House and Garden*, with a mainly middle-class readership, gained in 1976 eight times as much advertising revenue per copy as the mainly working-class magazine *Sewing and Knitting,* and three times as much advertising revenue per copy as the middle-market *Homemaker*. There are also striking differences in the advertising support for middle-market 'young' magazines such as *19* and *Honey*, and their equivalents with a mainly working-class appeal such as *Loving* and *True*.

In some cases, the differences are so great that they cannot be attributed simply to class differences in terms of disposable income. Magazines with a strong appeal to the middle class often have other attributes for advertisers—such as specialized editorial content, coated paper, high readership-per-copy, an editorial style that harmonizes with glossy advertisements, and audiences with low exposure to commercial TV—that reinforce their advertising advantage.

This pattern of advertising expenditure has profoundly affected the development of the women's magazine press. The majority of women's magazines sell at prices (after discounts to distributors) that do not cover costs (Coopers and Lybrand, 1975). Whether they make a profit depends upon whether they attract adequate advertising. Only in the children's and young teenage market are magazines largely dependent on sales. In other sectors of the women's magazine market, the average magazine has relied upon advertising for the majority of its revenue.[37]

Consequently, the majority of adult women's magazine titles are oriented towards the middle class, even though it constitutes little more than one-third of the population.[38] Even some mass market publications pay disproportionate

[37] Advertising accounted for, on average, 60% of young women's magazines and of women's monthlies, and 55% of women's weekly revenue in 1973—74 (RCP Secretariat, 1977: T24).

[38] Significantly, this targetting towards the middle class is much less marked in the case of juvenile and young teen publications. Children's periodicals derived, on average, 90% of their revenue from sales, while teenage magazines obtained, on average, 70% of their revenue from sales, in 1973—74.

attention to the middle class because of its importance to advertisers. As Michael Bird (then marketing director of the National Magazine Company) stressed in an influential paper, magazines are forced to seek not the largest but the 'optimum circulation' defined in relation to advertisers' priorities. 'Pushing circulations to ruinous heights' can be counterproductive if 'the audience profile is diluted' (Bird, 1978: 150; cf. Bird, 1979).

Publications that have not conformed to advertisers' requirements have simply disappeared. For example, *Everywoman* folded in 1967 with the fourth highest sale out of 21 women's magazines sold through newsagents, but with a majority of its readers being drawn from the working class (National Readership Survey, 1966: T19A). This gravitational pull towards the middle class, exerted by advertising, has contributed to the remarkable conservatism of much women's journalism. It has also resulted in a broad range of cultural provision being geared disproportionately to one section of the community.

The class bias of much magazine publishing is matched by an age bias. As early as the 1950s, market researchers were stressing the importance of the age cycle and family structure on the demand pattern for products (e.g. Wheeler, 1954). The relative affluence of the 15–24 age group, at a time of sharply rising consumption, encouraged advertisers to pay increasing attention to youth markets. This orientation was further reinforced by the 'accessibility' of youth markets due to the greater willingness of young people to try out new consumer products. This encouraged publishers to cater for this much-prized advertising market by launching a succession of publications aimed at young people.[39] In marked contrast, few publications have been directed towards elderly people because their disposable income—and consequently advertising utility—is much less than that of young people. Inequalities between age groups are thus reproduced in the market structure of the magazine press through the mediational rôle of advertisers.

Inequalities of age and class have coalesced to produce a further distortion in the women's magazine press. Many of the new women's magazines aimed at the late teen and twenties market have been oriented towards the middle class. Consequently many more magazines now cater primarily for the young (under 35) middle class than for the older (over 35) working class, although the former number about five and a half million and the latter 16 million (Bird, 1979).

The bias of advertisers' priorities

Which sections of the public are serviced with a multiplicity of publications depends, in part, upon their importance to advertisers. Two groups—distribution agents and those influencing corporate spending decisions—are so important that they have over a thousand publications catering for their needs. For example, there were 161 medical publications in 1974, many of which were heavily subsidized by advertising designed to influence spending within the National Health Service.[40]

Another distorting effect of advertising has been to encourage the growth of what may be broadly defined as 'consumer' magazines, but not a whole range of publications that fail to conform to the marketing requirements of advertisers. A

---

[39] Social changes, inducing a change in the pattern of reader demand, also encouraged this shift. See White (1970, 1977).

[40] For an interesting examination of the wider implications of having a medical press heavily subsidized by drug companies in an American context, see Gandy (1980).

good example of this latter group are political periodicals that, generally speaking, are found wanting on three counts. They do not provide an editorial environment conducive to buying particular products or services; they do not 'cover' a consumer market; and they do not reach specialized groups of corporate spenders or distribution agents. Consequently whereas advertising subsidies have assisted the growth of consumer and specialist publications by lowering their cover prices and funding their editorial costs, the lack of large-scale advertising has retarded a comparable development of the political periodical press in Britain.

There are exceptions. Some political periodicals have attracted corporate advertising aimed at opinion leaders as well as advertisements aimed at the business elite. (The growth of this advertising was crucially important, for instance, in the rise of the *Economist* during the 60s and 70s as an influential right-wing political periodical.)[41] Such exceptions as there have been have not included left-wing political publications with a predominantly working-class readership. Even a mainstream publication like *Labour Weekly,* for instance, obtained in 1978 only 4p per copy in advertising (much of it from non-commercial advertisers.)[42] This compares with £2.46 advertising per copy obtained by *Vogue* in 1979 and 57p advertising per copy of *Investors' Chronicle* in 1976.[43]

The mixed economy of broadcasting

The growth of TV advertising revenue more than kept up with inflation during the 1970s largely due to the ability of TV contractors to increase their rates sharply (Advertising Association, 1980: T15). During the same period, successive governments proved much more reluctant to increase the licence fee, from which the BBC derives its revenue, because large increases were thought to be unpopular with the public and inconsistent with maintaining a prices and incomes policy with which most administrations during the 1970s were associated. The rapid growth of colour TV licences and the extension of the BBC's borrowing limit helped to cushion the Corporation to a limited extent from the consequences of this policy. There nonetheless developed a growing disparity in the revenue of the public and private sectors of broadcasting.

Precise comparision between the two sectors is extremely difficult because their mode of operation is different and their true revenue and expenditure position is less than clear.[44] The best available estimate indicates that by 1978, 'each (TV) system spends about the same in total on programmes and transmission' (Broadbent, 1979: 50). In other words, the BBC spends about as much filling two channels as the commercial sector spends filling only one channel. While the BBC's transmission hours are shorter and the BBC is saved the additional expenditure incurred by the more devolved structure of ITV, the BBC is now at a severe competitive disadvantage compared with its private sector rivals.

[41] The dominant position of the quality newspaper press has made this advertising difficult to tap, however. Furthermore, political periodicals need to reach not only an elite, but to provide the right editorial environment. *Private Eye*, for example, has failed to attract a large amount of corporate advertising despite its success, revealed in independent readership research, in reaching a substantial number of businessmen. However, the semi-political weekly, *New Society*, has harvested specialized advertising aimed at social workers and other 'welfare' groups.

[42] Information derived from *Labour Weekly*.

[43] Derived from Mansefield (1980) and Bird (1978).

[44] For an illustration of the difficulties involved in analysing the finances of the ITV companies, see Hindley (1977).

The BBC has less money to spend on its programmes. It pays its skilled technical staff less well.[45] It has lost light entertainment stars (such as Morecambe and Wise and Bruce Forsyth) to ITV. The BBC was forced to impose severe redundancies in 1980, and increase programme repeats. It is now under very strong pressure to shift towards cheaper forms of light entertainment programme and to undertake major series only in collaboration with outside partners.

These cumulative pressures have reinforced the long-term influence of the introduction of commercial TV, to which we shall refer later, in changing the character of the BBC. The growing disparity of revenue between the two sectors of broadcasting has also increased the vulnerability of the BBC to political pressure. It needs the goodwill of government more than ever before to maintain its position within the market.

Dictates of the mass market

TV companies make their money from selling audiences rather than programmes. TV companies therefore seek to make and transmit programmes that *produce* the audiences advertisers want to reach. As Simon Broadbent, the vice-chairman of a leading agency, put it, 'the spot therefore is the packaging, the product inside the package is an audience'.

Contrary to popular belief, advertisers generally do not want to reach a mass audience in an indiscriminate way. As the standard advertising textbook puts it, 'It is wasteful and often futile to aim advertising at everybody' (Broadbent, 1979: 149). Many advertisers would like ideally commercial TV to produce large but variegated and selected audiences.

There have been various ways in which advertisers have classified TV audiences in an attempt to discover whether TV delivers different categories of viewer or different markets. One way, pioneered in the late 1950s, was to describe viewers of different TV programmes and time bands in terms of attitudinal and psychological characteristics in order to discover whether particular programmes or particular times delivered particular types of consumer—such as the experimental consumer who is disposed to try out new products—receptive to particular types of product or message. The failure of psychographic research—as it is often called—to show any significant clustering of viewer around particular programmes has caused this type of approach to be largely abandoned. Had it emerged that certain sorts of programmes produced large numbers of attitudinally homogeneous groups of viewers in a commercially exploitable form, there would have been a strong pressure on TV companies to produce more of these programmes.

Instead, advertisers have been content to rely on classifications of TV audiences in terms of demographic characteristics and, increasingly since the late 1960s, also in terms of consumer behaviour. These regular analyses have produced very disappointing results from the point of view of advertisers anxious to target their advertising to clearly defined prospect groups. As Adams (1979: 121) puts it:

Selectivity of different target groups within the total audience is possible to a small extent, in terms of time of day and day of week, but hardly at all by type of programme. More importantly for the planner, the degree of selectivity which exists is very largely swamped when the cost factors are applied.

[45] Information on pay rates kindly provided by Roy Lockett (Association of Cinematograph, Television and Allied Technicians) and Tony Banks (Association of Broadcasting Staff).

Adam's generalization needs to be qualified. A small number of programmes do 'select' particular groups and, no less important for the media planner, also deter particular groups of consumer.[46] But generally speaking, the pattern of commercial TV programme viewing is very unselective and would seem to be influenced more by the availability of the viewer to watch TV than by what is being shown. As Goodhardt *et al.* (1975) have shown, specialized programmes do not tend to generate specialized audiences; light viewers do not tend to be especially discriminating but tend to watch the most popular programmes; even many regular series have a minority of viewers who saw the previous episode.

The desire of most advertisers to use TV as a medium for reaching selected groups is thus partly frustrated by the relative lack of selectivity of TV viewing. Thus would-be selective, targeting pressure has been converted into a powerful impetus for TV companies to deliver the largest possible audience since this produces the largest possible number of people within the prospect groups that advertisers want to reach. This, in turn, enables TV companies to charge high rates.

Advertisers also exert a strong pressure for commercial TV companies to produce stable, reliable and predictable audiences. Advertisers pay money for spots in anticipation that these will deliver certain quantities of viewers. Most sophisticated agencies also run retrospective checks to see what value for money they obtained from their schedules. If the TV companies do not deliver what is expected of them, there is generally a loud chorus of complaint from their clients.

Advertisers also seek quantity rather than quality. Although the IBA conscientiously analyses audience appreciation of programmes each week, these analyses are not generally available in agencies and, when they are, they are generally ignored. One of the problems, as far as the agencies are concerned, is that they are not sure how to interpret audience appreciation data. Some executives believe that intense appreciation of programmes may divert attention away from advertising. Others believe that audience appreciation provides a general index of attention and therefore enhances responses to advertisements. Such empirical evidence as there is, is rather inconclusive, suggesting that audience appreciation of TV programmes is positively correlated with recall of advertisements, but negatively correlated with positive assessment of advertisements (Isley and Chick, 1978). Most media planners resolve such seemingly contradictory findings by ignoring them.

The effect of this pressure for large audiences is for priority to be given to programmes that are of universal appeal—notably soap operas, situation comedies, the main news bulletin and variety programmes. In 1978–79 for instance, what may be broadly defined as drama, light entertainment, news and news magazine programmes, accounted for 61% of ITV's total output, and the overwhelming proportion of its peak time transmission (IBA, 1979). Programmes that are not of universal appeal such as documentary and current affairs programmes tend to be transmitted outside peak time hours.

Commercial TV companies have also developed scheduling strategies designed to maintain a stable and predictable audience. This generally involves transmitting light entertainment programmes early in the evening, followed by a sequence of programmes that expand and consolidate the mass audience throughout the evening. If ITV contractors are forced as a consequence of IBA pressure, direct or indirect, to transmit a programme of low audience appeal during peak viewing

---

[46] For example, Sunday afternoon football on TV has a particular appeal among lager drinkers.

hours, they often take steps to minimize audience fall-out either by matching it with an equally unpopular programme on BBC1 or by 'hammocking' the programme between two 'bankers' (i.e. programmes with proven audience appeal). The scheduling philosophy of the ITV system is thus essentially cautious and conservative: it is wary of programme innovation during peak time viewing of a sort that might lose viewers to another channel for the rest of the evening.

The pursuit of viewers in crude terms of quantity rather than in terms of their quality of appreciation also provides a built-in bias within the ITV system against current affairs programmes. As Barwise, Ehrenburg and Goodhardt (1979) have shown, 'information' programmes generally gain higher appreciation scores than 'entertainment' programmes, even though they generally attract smaller audiences. Whether reliance on ratings results in advertisers undervaluing the 'pull' of minority programmes is less than clear. Barwise, Ehrenburg and Goodhardt (1979) found that, within the two broad categories of information and entertainment programmes, there was a positive correlation between size of audience and appreciation.[47]

The development of mass audience programming and scheduling strategies within the private sector of broadcasting has compelled a fundamental change of policy within the BBC. When in 1958 its audience share slipped to below 30%, senior BBC executives became convinced that the BBC had to imitate, to some extent, the programme and scheduling policy of ITV. Increasingly, the output and schedules of BBC1 have come to resemble those of its principal rival. The change has produced an increasing uniformity in the content of broadcasting and an increasing reluctance to experiment. As Weldon, then managing director of the BBC, euphemistically put it, 'once you are locked in competition, you cannot afford losers' (Weldon, 1971: 9).

Commercial radio has also responded to mass marketing pressures. Between 6 am and 6 pm, commercial local radio stations are largely geared to satisfying the largest possible audience. This has given rise to styles of radio production very different from those pioneered by the BBC: to programming as distinct from separate programmes, that is to say a miscellany of short items that will include something of interest for almost everyone in the local community, organized in a flexible way and set on 'a music bed'. Within this format, priority is given to those sections of the audience available to listen. It is only in the evening that more conventional programmes are transmitted, including some aimed at minority audiences. These include programmes directed at specialist markets that will attract specialized advertising such as 'Race Track' (Radio Victory) which generates car accessory advertising, and 'Hullaballoo' (Capital Radio) which generated advertisements aimed at teenagers. The shift reflects an attempt to deliver a differentiated audience (which, again, is partly frustrated by unselective radio listening behaviour) of value to advertisers, at a time when the mass audience has been surrendered to TV.

The fluid, fast-moving programming formula of local commercial radio has been highly successful in attracting substantial local audiences to local commercial radio during peak listening times. Its overall share of radio listening in ILR areas in 1980 was 34%, significantly higher than that of any national or local BBC radio channel

---

[47] Whether this would have remained true if very heavy viewers—'lumpers' who will watch most programmes that are being screened—had been eliminated, remains to be investigated. For rather different findings from those of Barwise, Ehrenburg and Goodhardt (1979), see Prue (1979).

(JICRAR, 1980). This share is still substantially lower, however, than the BBC service as a whole, and has not compelled an adjustment on the part of the BBC comparable to the radio reorganization and change in broadcasting philosophy that followed the incursion of illegal commercial radio stations into the mass audience during the 1960s.

A striking feature of local commercial radio output is its inclusion of a substantial local news content. This is a reflection of the pattern of consumer demand. IBA surveys reveal, for example, that 'local news coverage' was rated more favourably than any other aspect of commercial local radio output.[48] The provision of local news is thus consistent with maintaining large audiences in order to maximize advertising, just as the provision of news bulletins is consistent with maximizing TV audiences.

The same is not true of national newspapers. Research undertaken by publishers over a 40-year period shows that most categories of news about public affairs have obtained below-average attention in national papers both before and after the arrival of TV. In particular, public affairs items have generally appealed less to women and to the young than to men and the older age-groups. In contrast, human interest stories and certain entertainment features have been found to have a universal appeal, transcending differences of sex, age and class. As economic pressures have built up for popular newspapers to maximize their sales and advertising revenue by winning bigger audiences, so the proportion of space devoted to public affairs has declined, while common-denominator material has steadily increased. The only departure from this trend over a 50-year period has been the period of strict economic controls when popular newspapers were temporarily insulated from the economic pressures for audience maximization (Curran, Douglas and Whannel, 1980).

There has not been a comparable trend towards depoliticization of the quality press. This is not because there is a wide chasm between reading preferences of mass and elite audiences: the pattern of quality and popular reader interest is in fact rather similar, with certain categories of human interest story being the most read items in both quality and popular papers (Curran, Douglas and Whannel, 1980: 304 *et passim*). Publishers of quality newspapers have merely been restrained from providing more common-denominator material for fear of diluting the social quality of their audiences, and consequently undermining their utility to advertisers as selective media reaching small elite groups.

Defining media audiences

The growing polarization between quality and popular journalism is only one illustration of the way in which advertisers influence media content by helping to define the audiences which media seek to reach. The nature of this indirect advertising influence is clearly illuminated by case studies of media which have been relaunched or markedly changed editorial direction.

Three brief examples—those of the *Sun*, *The Times* and *Homemaker*—must suffice. The *Daily Herald*, with an ageing working-class readership and low

---

[48] 'Local news coverage' scored + 86%, the highest score out of 19 aspects of commercial local radio output based on subtracting 'likes' and 'dislikes' from the question 'which of these aspects do you like, which do you dislike, and which makes no difference to you?' asked in each one of 19 local surveys in the various ILR areas over a period of five years (IBA, unpublished material).

advertising receipts, was relaunched as the *Sun* in 1964 with the objective of attracting young middle-class readers that advertisers would pay more to reach. 'The new paper', confided an internal office memorandum, 'is to have the more representative make-up essential to advertisers' (IPC, 1964). The new product, processed for a coalition of readers with very different interests and outlooks, proved to be both an editorial and commercial failure.[49]

During the 1960s, *The Times* was also compelled to rethink its editorial strategy in relation to advertisers' requirements. Between 1967 and 1969, *The Times* increased its circulation from 270,000 to 450,000 by adopting a more popular mix of news and features and by initiating an aggressive promotion campaign. But as Michael Mander, Deputy Chief Executive of Times Newspapers subsequently recalled, 'its higher sale made it no more attractive as an advertising medium . . . adding to the readership just watered down the essential target group, and increased the cost of reaching it' (Mander, 1978: 75). So the paper deliberately set about shedding its new socially inferior readers with, as Mander notes, 'a consequent dramatic increase in profitability'.[50]

A more recent example is provided by the relaunch of *Homemaker* as *New Homemaker* in March 1980. A major objective of the relaunch was to redefine the magazine's audience in a way that would generate additional advertising. There had been a significant shift from media advertising to point-of-sale promotion in the do-it-yourself market to which *Homemaker* was directed. The *Homemaker's* predominantly male readership also made it an unsuitable advertising medium for a wide range of products. The *Homemaker* was consequently relaunched in 1980 towards a more youthful and less male-oriented audience, with particular attention being given to young couples doing up their home. In keeping with this redirection, editorial features moved away from do-it-yourself tips towards interior decoration features. The shift has been rewarded with new furnishing and paint advertisements, and an overall growth of advertising revenue.[51]

More generally, advertisers have also influenced Britain's mass media by helping to define geographically the audiences they cater for. The shape of the ITV regions, for example, is defined partly in terms of what constitutes a viable advertising base. This has produced regions like Harlech TV which caters for a mixed Welsh and English audience, and Tyne Tees TV which contains such dissonant elements as Teesside and Tyneside. The regional programme production of some of these companies is consequently geared to serving areas that are viable marketing units, rather than genuine cultural entities.

The commercial local radio stations are also generally geared to servicing areas that are much larger than the local communities with which people identify. The IBA has received repeated requests for more localized radio stations. This is consistent with the very parochial definitions of community which the great majority of people felt they belonged to in the survey research undertaken for the Royal Commission on Local Government (RCLG, 1969: vol. 3). Yet more restricted areas are not thought to provide a viable base for local radio, given the existing level of radio advertising expenditure. Even local papers, with generally smaller catchment areas than local radio stations, are often criticized for containing 'too much news that is not local enough' (e.g. Eastern Counties Newspapers, 1977).

[49] For further details of the *Sun*'s launch, and the circumstances that led up to it, see Curran (1978).
[50] For further information on the erratic development of *The Times*, see Hirsch and Gordon (1975).
[51] Information provided by Frank Farmer, Advertising Director of IPC Magazines.

Local newspaper chains have only partially responded to these complaints, because of the need to service the needs of advertisers and secure economies of scale.[52]

More importantly, the national character and metropolitan domination of the British media arises partly out of the marketing needs of advertisers. The national daily press only acquired a larger circulation than the regional press during the inter-war period (Kaldor and Silverman, 1948). Its rapid growth was partly a consequence of its usefulness to the manufacturers who were seeking a national market for factory-produced cheap products; the reputation that national papers acquired among London agencies for having greater impact and 'urgency' than regional papers, as well as greater influence on the retail trade (Russell, 1925; Eley, 1932); and the much cheaper rates it charged compared with the regional press due to its greater economies of scale (Harrison and Mitchell, 1936). Gaining a much larger share of increased advertising expenditure, national dailies were able to finance lavish promotional campaigns and the establishment of new regional production centres, thereby attracting more readers (Political and Economic Planning, 1938).

The ascendancy of five regional TV companies (which produced between them 49.5% of all programmes transmitted by ITV companies in 1978–79) is due to their strategic position in commanding the wealthiest regional advertising markets. They have the largest resources to draw upon. It is also in the interests of all the TV companies to limit competition and spread production costs by conceding a dominant position to the wealthy regional companies through a central networking arrangement. Thus a TV system that was intended to be pluralistic and devolved has developed into a system that is highly centralized.

Creating the right environment

Subjective judgements about whether a medium provides a favourable environment for advertisements has always played a part in some advertisers' choice of media. This has generated pressure on media to create a suitable environment for advertising in order to maximize revenue.

Subjective judgements of media 'communication value' have been based on a number of considerations: whether specific editorial or programme content will attract the attention of particular groups of consumers to adjacent advertising; whether such advertising will gain their attention when they are in the right mood to respond; whether media content will induce a frame of mind that will be responsive to the advertised message; whether the authority or prestige of the medium or particular programme/column will rub off on the client's product; whether the style and tone of the media content harmonizes with the advertisement in a way that reinforces its effectiveness; and whether, in crude terms, the editorial content supports the product that is being advertised.

Such subjective considerations have become much less important in media selection than they were 50 years ago. They are now generally outweighed by calculations of cost of exposure to the target audience and 'experience' based on previous advertising campaigns. There has been, however, a significant shift towards a more intuitive approach to media selection during the last 12 years and this has increased pressures on the media to provide an environment conducive to advertising.

[52] Adaptation usually takes the form of slip editions in which a small part of a local paper is highly localized and the rest contains material syndicated over a larger area.

Commercial television is the mass medium least affected by pressure of this kind. The prohibition of advertising sponsorship within commercial TV has insulated programme controllers from direct influence on programme content. Advertisers do have foreknowledge of programme schedules and consequently are able to select space beside specific programmes. Programmes are sometimes selected because their content is thought to complement a particular advertising campaign. In theory, at least, this could give rise to pressure for more programmes complementing advertising commercials. But in practice, the selection of spots in terms of programmes is unusual.[53] Advertisers generally buy viewers rather than programme environments. The fact that the connection between programmes and audience types or profiles is so elusive, as mentioned earlier, further reduces pressure on TV companies to deliver a suitable programme ambience. Moreover, a belief has developed within agencies that commercials create 'their own environment' unaided by programme content.

When there is a conflict between a commercial and a programme—such as the announcement of an airline crash with an airline advertisement scheduled to follow—the conflict is sometimes eliminated by the withdrawal of the advertisement. But programmes or programme items are not suppressed to protect the commercial interests of advertisers. Commercial TV companies have a monopoly as the sellers of TV airtime and are in a powerful position to resist illicit advertising pressure. Indeed, it is very much in their economic interests not to submit to advertisers' censorship since this would put their franchises at risk.

Commercial radio stations are also insulated, to some extent, from overt advertising pressures. Subject to surveillance by the IBA, local radio companies have a vested interest in maintaining their autonomy from advertisers. The fact that the majority of local radio advertising is bought in packages rather than in spots, with the times of transmission being rotated by radio contractors, further contributes to radio's independence from crude advertising influence.

Newspapers have been more influenced by advertisers, and in some ways less resistant to advertising pressure. Service features on investment, travel, property, motoring and fashion have grown as a proportion of editorial space in national newspapers during the postwar period (Curran, Douglas and Whannel, 1980). Their expansion has been geared, to a large extent, to the advertising they have generated. They represent an efficient means of selling selected subgroups within a mass audience, packaged in a suitable editorial environment. Yet their narrow orientation to readers as consumers has distorted their content (Curran, 1978). Their advertising orientation has encouraged the specialist journalists working on these pages to develop a dependent and generally uncritical relationship with advertisers (Tunstall, 1971). The result has been the development of a subservient genre of journalism in which, as Ian Breach, the former motoring correspondent of *The Guardian*, puts it, 'there is a pervading fear that valuable advertising will drain away in the face of persistent criticism that names and condemns specific products' (Breach, 1978).

This crude form of influence is largely restricted to the advertising-oriented sections of national papers. It is extremely rare for news items to be suppressed or

[53] Instances of commercials skilfully harmonizing with programmes, that were mentioned to me, included an advertisment for 'Black Magic' with a romantic drama, a James Bond commercial alongside 'The Professionals' (a security police drama), a Kattomeat commercial alongside a programme about the conservation of tigers, and so on. They were remarked upon *because* they were unusual.

rewritten in order to placate potential advertisers. Attempts by advertisers to influence general news reporting and comment by withholding advertising is also much less frequent than is generally supposed. The *Sunday Times* continued to receive advertising from Distillers, for example, even when it was campaigning against the company for its 'heartless treatment' of Thalidomide drug victims.

Advertisers are a much more pervasive influence on women's magazines than they are on national newspapers. There is generally less commitment to non-revenue goals within consumer magazine organizations than there is within national news organizations, and consequently less suspicion of advertisers. Consumer magazines are also subject to more advertising pressure because advertisers attach more weight to the editorial environment of magazines than to the content of any other medium.[54]

Pressure from advertisers has crucially influenced the balance of contents of the magazine press. A growing proportion of women's magazines during the 50s and 60s, for instance, were devoted to material consumption partly in order to provide a conducive environment for advertisements. This expansion tended to squeeze out more general articles on social and even political issues (White, 1970).

Much of this consumer journalism has been sychophantic and uncritical. Consumer protection, even straight monitoring and evaluation of rival products, has tended to be avoided because it is liable to give offence to advertising clients (White, 1977). In some cases, relations with advertisers are so close that advertisers are even invited to share the costs of editorial features. *Honey,* for instance, invited advertising clients on a number of occasions in 1973 to pay part of the cost of fashion features it was planning: the client's products were subsequently displayed or favourably mentioned in the editorial features they helped to finance (Insight, 1975).

'Aditorials' are only the most extreme expression of the supportive and subordinate rôle assumed by many women's magazines in relation to advertisers. As the leading advertisers' manual notes approvingly, they have 'a style which can be borrowed and used' (Broadbent, 1979: 318). Not merely specific articles, but the entire content of such magazines is designed to induce a responsive frame of mind to consumer advertising. When the *Woman's Journal* was relaunched in 1977, for example, it was deliberately imbued with 'a tone of voice, a style' that would endear it to advertisers by creating a more glamourizing, flattering ambience for their products.[55] Such conscious artifice in the editorial packaging of advertisements produces publications that express in their totality—often beguilingly and entertainingly—the propaganda of capitalism.

Conclusion

Advertisers have thus played a central rôle in shaping Britain's media system. Firstly, recent changes in advertising allocation *between* media sectors have tended to undermine traditional mass media, promote the growth of specialized media, and favour the development of the regional press.

Second, advertising appropriations *within* each media sector have profoundly

---

[54] This is partly because agencies are encouraged to evaluate the editorial content of magazines in terms of advertising effectiveness by the way in which many magazines sell advertising space. This is very much less true of other media.

[55] Interview with Frank Farmer, IPC Magazines Director, on 3 October 1980.

influenced the character and development of each medium. In particular, they have reinforced the conservative domination of the national press, caused the women's magazine press to be heavily oriented towards the young middle class, and contributed to a growing financial imbalance between the public and private sectors of broadcasting.

Third, the media have adapted to the requirements of advertisers in the ways they have sought to maximize revenue. This has resulted in a growing polarization between popular and quality newspaper journalism, the adoption of limiting programme strategies for producing large and predictable audiences on television, and the increasing subordination of the consumer magazine press to creating a conducive editorial environment for advertisements.

Bibliography

ADAMS, J. (1979). *Media Planning* (2nd edition), Business Books, London

ADVERTISING ASSOCIATION (1962). *Advertising Expenditure 1960*, Advertising Association, London

ADVERTISING ASSOCIATION (1972). Advertising expenditure 1960–71, *Advertising Quarterly*, vol. 32 and 33

ADVERTISING ASSOCIATION (1975). *Evidence to Royal Commission on the Press 1974–77*, HMSO, London

ADVERTISING ASSOCIATION (1980). Advertising expenditure tables, 1960–1979, *Advertising Magazine*, vol. 64

ANON. (1980). The trade and technical scene—a media world viewpoint, *Media World*, August

BARWISE, T. P., EHRENBURG, A. S. C. and GOODHARDT, G. J. (1979). Audience appreciation and audience size, *Journal of the Market Research Society* vol. 21, 4

BELSON, W. (1959). *The British Press*, London Press Exchange, London

BENSON, S. H. (1962). *Evidence to Royal Commission on the Press 1961–1962, vol. 5 Documentary Evidence*, HMSO, London

BIRD, M. (1978). Magazines, markets and money, in Henry, H. (ed.) *Behind the Headlines—the Business of the British Press*, Associated Business Press, London

BIRD, M. (1979). Women's magazines—a survey of the 70s, *Options*, Spring

BREACH, I. (1978). The gentlemen of the road, *Sunday Times Colour Magazine*

BROADBENT, S. (1979). *Spending Advertising Money* (3rd edition), Business Books, London

CLEVERLEY, G. (1976). *The Fleet Street Disaster*, Constable, London

COOPERS and LYBRAND (1975). The periodical publishing industry, unpub., Royal Commission on the Press 1974–77

CORKINDALE, D. R. and KENNEDY, S. H. (1976). *Measuring the Effect of Advertising*, Saxon House, Westmead

CRITCHLEY, R. A. (n.d.) *U.K. Advertising Statistics*, Advertising Association, London

CURRAN, J. (1970). The impact of TV on the audience for national newspapers 1945–68, in Tunstall, J. (ed.), *Media Sociology*, Constable, London

CURRAN, J. (1977). Capitalism and control of the press, 1800–1975, in Curran, J., Gurevitch, M. and Woollacott, J. (eds) *Mass Communication and Society*, Arnold, London

CURRAN, J. (1978). Advertising and the press, in Curran, J. (ed.) *The British Press: A Manifesto*, Macmillan, London

CURRAN, J. (1979). Press freedom as a property right: the crisis of press legitimacy, *Media, Culture and Society*, vol. 1

CURRAN, J. (1980). Advertising as a patronage system, *Sociological Review Monograph*, 29

CURRAN, J., DOUGLAS, A. and WHANNEL, G. (1980). The political economy of the human-interest story, in Smith, A. (ed.) *Newspapers and Democracy*, Massachusetts Institute of Technology Press, Cambridge, Mass.

CURRAN, J. and SEATON, J. (1981). *Power Without Responsibility: Press and Broadcasting in Britain*, Fontana, London

CURRAN, J. and TUNSTALL, J. (1973). Mass media and leisure, in Smith, M., Parker, S. and Smith, C. (eds) *Leisure and Society in Britain*, Allen Lane, London

DEPARTMENT OF INDUSTRY (1979). Newspapers and periodicals, *Business Monitor* (PQ485), Fourth Quarter, HMSO, London

EASTERN COUNTIES NEWSPAPERS (1977). Preliminary research report (mimeo), Conrad Jameson Associates

ECONOMIST INTELLIGENCE UNIT (1966). *The National Newspaper Industry: A Survey*, EIU, London

ELEY, H. W. (1931). *Advertising Media*, Butterworth, London

GANDY, O., Jr. (1980). Information in health: subsidised news, *Media, Culture and Society*, vol. 2

GERALD, J. E. (1956). *The British Press under Government Economic Controls*, University of Minnesota Press, Minneapolis

GLASGOW UNIVERSITY MEDIA GROUP (1976). *Bad News*, Routledge, Kegan and Paul, London

GOODHARDT, G. J., EHRENBURG, A. S. C. and COLLINS, M. A. (1975). *The Television Audience: Patterns of Viewing*, Saxon House, Westmead

GUINNESS, ARTHUR & SON LTD. (1949). *Royal Commission on the Press 1947–1949 Memoranda of Evidence vol. 5*, HMSO, London

HARRISON, G. and MITCHELL, F. G. (1936). *The Home Market: A Handbook of Statistics*, Allen and Unwin, London

HARTLEY, N. (1976). Advertising trends and the press, memorandum ad 6, Royal Commission on the Press 1974–77, unpublished papers

HARTLEY, N., GUDGEON, P., and CRAFTS, R. (1977). *Concentration of ownership in the Provincal Press*, Royal Commission on the Press Research Series 5, HMSO, London

HENRY, H. (1971). The media of mass communication over the next fifteen years, in *Perspectives in Management, Marketing and Research*, Crosby and Lockwood, London

HENRY, H. (1977). Some observations on the effects of newsprint rationing (1939–1959) on the advertising media, *Journal of Advertising History*, vol. 1

HINDLEY, B. V. (1977). The profits of advertising—financed television broadcasting, *Report of the Committee on the Future of Broadcasting* Appendix G, HMSO, London

HIRSCH, F. and GORDON, D. (1975). *Newspaper Money*, Hutchinson, London

HOBSON, J. W. (1961). *The Selection of Advertising Media* 4th edition, Business Publications, London

HOCH, P. (1974). *The Newspaper Game*, Calder and Boyars, London

HULTON, (1947–56). *Readership Surveys*, Hulton, London

INDEPENDENT BROADCASTING AUTHORITY (1980). The audience for ILR, (mimeo), IBA Radio Division

INDEPENDENT BROADCASTING AUTHORITY (1979). *Annual Report 1978–9*, IBA, London

INSIGHT (1975). A taste of honey—or how to buy an aditorial, *Sunday Times*, 6 July

INTERNATIONAL PUBLISHING CORPORATION (1964). Attitudes to newspapers and newspaper reading, Research Services Department records, January

ISLEY, C. and CHICK, M. (1978). The effect of the medium, *Admap*, September

JICNARS (1968–80). *National Readership Surveys*, Joint Industry Committee for National Readership Surveys, London

JICRAR (1980). Independent local radio network surveys, Spring / Autumn

KALDOR, N. and SILVERMAN, R. (1948). *A Statistical Analysis of Advertising Expenditure and of the Press*, Cambridge University Press, Cambridge

LABOUR RESEARCH DEPARTMENT (1946). *The Millionaire Press*, L.R.D., London

LIND, H. (1978). The economics of the trade and technical press, in Henry, H. (ed.), *Behind the Headlines—the Business of the British Press*, Associated Business Press, London

LONDON PRESS EXCHANGE (1962). *Evidence to Royal Commission on the Press 1961–1962, vol. 5 Documentary Evidence*, HMSO, London

MACDONALD, T. (1974). The measurement of the relative effectiveness of press and television as advertising media, unpublished M.Phil. thesis, University of Warwick

MANDER, M. (1971). The integration of advertising and circulation sales policies, in Henry, H. (ed.), *Behind the Headlines—the Business of the British Press*, Associated Business Press, London

MANSEFIELD, T. (1980). The up-market world of classy magazines, *Media World*, June

MASIUS and FERGUSON (1962). *Evidence to Royal Commission on the Press 1961–2, vol. 5 Documentary Evidence*, HMSO, London

NATIONAL BOARD FOR PRICES AND INCOMES (1967). *Costs and Revenue of National Daily Newspapers*, HMSO, London

NATIONAL BOARD FOR PRICES AND INCOMES (1970). *Costs and Revenue of National Newspapers*, HMSO, London

NEWSPAPER PUBLISHERS ASSOCIATION WORKING PARTY (1966). Proposals to promote the business interests of newspapers against television (mimeo)

NATIONAL READERSHIP SURVEYS (1956–67). Institute of the Practioners in Advertising, London

ORWELL, G. (1970). London letter to partisan review, in Orwell, S. and Angus, I. (eds), *The Collected Essays, Journalism and Letters of George Orwell*, vol. 2, Penguin, Harmondsworth

POLITICAL AND ECONOMIC PLANNING (PEP) (1938). *Report on the British Press*, PEP, London

PRUE, T. (1979). The rate for the job, *Options*, vol. 3

Royal Commission on the Press 1947–1949 (1949). HMSO, London

Royal Commission on the Press 1961–1962 (1962). HMSO, London

Royal Commission on the Press Interim Report (1976). HMSO, London

Royal Commission on the Press 1974–1977 Final Report (1977). HMSO, London

ROYAL COMMISSION ON THE PRESS SECRETARIAT (1977). Periodicals and the alternative press, *Royal Commission on the Press Research Series 6*, HMSO, London

Royal Commission on Local Government in England 1966–1969 (1969). Representation and local community: an appraisal of three surveys, vol. 3, Research Appendix 7, HMSO, London

RUSSELL, T. (1925). *A Working Textbook of Advertising*, Russell-Hart, London

SEYMOUR-URE, C. (1977). National daily newspapers and the party system, in *Studies on the Press*, Royal Commission on the Press Working Paper No. 3, HMSO, London

SILVERMAN, R. (1951). *Advertising Expenditure in 1948*, Advertising Association, London

SILVERMAN, R. (1954). *Advertising Expenditure 1952*, Advertising Association, London

STEED, H. WICKHAM (1938). *The Press*, Penguin, Harmondsworth

TUNSTALL, J. (1971). *Journalists at Work*, Constable, London

TUNSTALL, J. (1974). *The Advertising Man in London Advertising Agencies*, Chapman and Hall, London

THOMPSON, J. WALTER (1962). *Evidence to Royal Commission on the Press 1961–1962, Vol. 5 Documentary Evidence*, HMSO, London

WELDON, H. (1971). *Competition in Television*, BBC, London

WHALE, J. (1979). *The Politics of the Media* (rev. edition), Fontana, London

WHEELER, D. (1955). *A New Classification of Households*, British Market Research Bureau, June

WHITE, C. (1970). *Women's Magazines 1963–1968*, Michael Joseph, London

WHITE, C. (1977). *The Women's Periodical Press in Britain 1946–1976*, Royal Commission on the Press Working Paper No. 4, HMSO, London

WRIGGLESWORTH, F. G. (1980). The evolution of Guinness advertising, *Journal of Advertising History*, vol. 3

YOUNG AND RUBICAM (1962). *Evidence to Royal Commission on The Press 1961–1962, vol. 5 Documentary Evidence*, HMSO, London

Corrections

Wrigglesworth should read Wigglesworth in footnote 24 and in the bibliography.

The penultimate sentence of paragraph 4 on page 326 should read ... audience appreciation of TV programmes is correlated negatively with recall of advertisements, but positively correlated with favourable reaction to them (Isley and Chick, 1978).

Index

Notes on contributors

Pierre Bourdieu, born in 1930, is a Professor at the College of France and Director of Studies at L'Ecole des Hautes Etudes. He is the author of numerous books including *La Distinction, Le Sens Pratique, Ce que Parler veut Dire* and *Homo Academicus*.

David Cardiff is a Principal Lecturer in Media Studies at the Polytechnic of Central London. He has written a number of essays on the historical development of broadcasting, and is writing a book on the social history of the BBC with Paddy Scannell.

David Chaney is a Senior Lecturer in Sociology at the University of Durham. His principal publications are *Processes of Mass Communication* (1972) and *Fictions and Ceremonies* (1979). He has also written numerous articles in the fields of mass communication and popular culture and he is currently working on forms of spectacular drama and collective ceremonies in contemporary culture.

Richard Collins is a Senior Lecturer in Film and Media Studies at the Polytechnic of Central London and is an editor of *Media, Culture and Society*. He is the author of *Television News* (1976) and (with Vincent Porter) *WDR and the Arbeiterfilm* (1982). His current research centres on the relations of the state, television and national culture in Canada.

John Corner is a Lecturer in Communication Studies at the University of Liverpool. With Jeremy Hawthorn he edited *Communication Studies* (1980, second edition 1985) and he has written a number of articles on media analysis for books and journals. He is currently editing a book on the documentary and researching into broadcasting policy and TV audiences.

James Curran is The Head of the Department of Communications at Goldsmiths' College, University of London. He wrote with Jean Seaton *Power Without Responsibility: The Press and Broadcasting in Britain* (1981, second edition 1985). He also edited *Mass Communication and Society* (1977), *The British Press: A Manifesto* (1978), *Newspaper History* (1978), *Culture, Society and the Media* (1982), *British Cinema History* (1984) and *The Future of the Left* (1985). He is a former political columnist of *The Times* and founding editor of *New Socialist*, and he is now an editor of *Media, Culture and Society*. He is currently writing a book on the impact of the mass media, based on historical case studies.

Paul DiMaggio is an Associate Professor in the Institute for Social and Policy Studies, Sociology Department, and School of Organization and Management at Yale University. He is currently preparing a book on the social organization of American high culture, to be published by Basic Books.

Philip Elliott was a Research Fellow at the Centre for Mass Communication Research, Leicester University, until his death in 1983. He was a member of the editorial board of *Media, Culture and Society*. He was author or co-author of many books and articles in the field of mass communication. His best-known works are *Demonstrations and Communication* (with J. Halloran and G. Murdock), *The Sociology of the Professions, The Making of a Television Series, Reporting Northern Ireland, Making the News* (with P. Golding) and *Televising 'Terrorism'* (with P. Schlesinger and G. Murdock).

Nicholas Garnham is a Professor at the School of Media Studies at the Polytechnic of Central London and an editor of *Media, Culture and Society*. He is the co-author of *The New Priesthood* and the author of *The Structures of Television*. His recent articles include 'Toward a Theory of Cultural Materialism' in the *Journal of Communication* and 'Telecommunications Policy' in the *Oxford International Encyclopedia of Communication*. He is currently researching telecommunications policy and the economics of culture.

Stuart Hall is the Professor of Sociology at the Open University and was formerly Director of the Centre for Contemporary Cultural Studies at the University of Birmingham. He is the co-author of *Policing the Crisis* and joint editor of *Culture, Media and Language, State and Society in Contemporary Britain*, and *The Politics of Thatcherism*. He is currently researching on the theory of ideology and the emergence of the 'new right'.

Michèle Mattelart was born in France but began research and writing in Latin America, mostly in Chile. She now lives in Paris where she is a researcher. Her principal publications are *La Cultura de la Opresion Femenina* (1974), *De l'Usage des Médias en Temps de Crise* (with Armand Mattelart, 1979), *International Image Markets* (with A. Mattelart and X. Delcourt, 1984), and 'Television, Education and Mass Culture' in a British Film Institute Reader. She is now working on epistemological disjunctures in the analysis of communications and is continuing her research on feminine subjectivity and the processes of communication.

Graham Murdock is a Research Fellow at the University of Leicester, Centre for Mass Communication Research, and has been Visiting Professor at the Free University of Brussels and the University of California, San Diego. His current research is concerned with the political economy of the communications industries and with the social and cultural impact of new media. He is the co-author of *Demonstrations and Communication* (1979), *Mass Media and the Secondary School* (1973) and *Televising 'Terrorism'* (1983). He is co-editor of *Communicating Politics* and has written over sixty articles on aspects of communications and culture.

Paddy Scannell is a Senior Lecturer in Media Studies at the Polytechnic of Central London and an editor of *Media, Culture and Society*. He has published widely on broadcasting history and is writing with David Cardiff a social history of broadcasting.

Philip Schlesinger is currently Head of Sociology at the Thames Polytechnic, London. He is an editor of *Media, Culture and Society* and has been a Social Science Fellow of the Nuffield Foundation and a Jean Monnet Fellow of the European University Institute. He is the author of *Putting 'Reality' Together*, co-author of *Televising 'Terrorism'* (with G.

Murdock and P. Elliott) and co-editor of *Communicating Politics* (with P. Golding and G. Murdock). He is currently researching the intellectuals, nationalism and the public sphere.

Colin Sparks is a Senior Lecturer in Media Studies at the Polytechnic of Central London and an editor of *Media, Culture and Society*. He is also a former editor of *Socialist Review*, the monthly magazine of the Socialist Workers' Party of which he is a member. He has published a number of essays on the mass media and political issues and is the author of *Never Again* (1980).

Raymond Williams was, until recently, Professor of Drama at the University of Cambridge. His published books include *Culture and Society*, *The Long Revolution*, *The Country and the City*, *Drama in Performance*, *Drama from Ibsen to Brecht*, *Modern Tragedy*, *Communications*, *Marxism and Literature*, *The English Novel from Dickens to Lawrence*, *Politics and Letters*, *Keywords* and *Culture*.